Why do you need this new edition?

6 good reasons why you should buy this new edition of
Sociology: A Down-to-Earth Approach, Core Concepts

1. Personalized Learning—The new MySocLab delivers proven results in helping you
    succeed, provides engaging experiences that personalize learning, and comes from
    a trusted partner with educational expertise and a deep commitment to helping
    students and instructors achieve their goals.

2. New Media Activities—MySocLab now features video, reading, and interactive map
    activities for each chapter that bring the content to life.

3. Improve Critical Thinking—Learning objectives have been added to every chapter,
    which help readers build critical thinking and study skills.

4. New Design—*Sociology: A Down-to-Earth Approach, Core Concepts* has been
    redesigned for a new generation of learners to help you see sociology come alive!

5. Living Data—New Living Data activities in MySocLab allows you to interact with
    charts and graphs from the text to explore data on a deeper level.

6. Pearson Choices—We know you want greater value, innovation, and flexibility in
    products. You can choose from a variety of text and media formats to match your
    learning style and your budget.

For specific details on the many changes in this edition, see page xxiv.

PEARSON

FIFTH EDITION

Sociology

A Down-to-Earth Approach
Core Concepts

James M. Henslin
Southern Illinois University, Edwardsville

PEARSON

Boston   Columbus   Indianapolis   New York   San Francisco   Upper Saddle River
Amsterdam   Cape Town   Dubai   London   Madrid   Milan   Munich   Paris   Montreal   Toronto
Delhi   Mexico City   São Paulo   Sydney   Hong Kong   Seoul   Singapore   Taipei   Tokyo

iv

Editorial Director: Craig Campanella
Editor in Chief: Dickson Musslewhite
Senior Acquisitions Editor: Brita Mess
Editorial Assistant: Zoe Lubitz
Director of Marketing: Brandy Dawson
Executive Marketing Manager: Kelly May
Marketing Assistant: Janeli Bitor
Development Editor: Jennifer Auvil
Managing Editor: Maureen Richardson
Project Manager: Marianne Peters-Riordan
Senior Operations Specialist: Sherry Lewis
Creative Director: John Christiana

Art Director/Interior Design: Laura Gardner
Cover Art: Shutterstock
Cover Design: David Drummond
Director, Digital Media: Brian Hyland
Digital Media Editor: Thomas Scalzo
Supplements Editor: Seanna Breen
Full-Service Project Management: Barbara Lipson,
    Cenveo Publisher Services/Nesbitt Graphics, Inc.
Composition: Cenveo Publisher Services/Nesbitt Graphics, Inc.
Printer/Binder and Cover Printer: Courier Companies, Inc.
Text Font: ITC Galliard Std

Credits and acknowledgments borrowed from other sources and reproduced, with permission, in this textbook appear on appropriate page within text (or on page CR1).

Many of the designations by manufacturers and seller to distinguish their products are claimed as trademarks. Where those designations appear in this book, and the publisher was aware of a trademark claim, the designations have been printed in initial caps or all caps.

10 9 8 7 6 5 4 3 2 1

Student Version:
ISBN 10: 1-256-19541-3
ISBN 13: 978-1-256-19541-2

Á la carte Version:
ISBN 10: 0-205-11701-5
ISBN 13: 978-0-205-11701-7

PEARSON

www.pearsonhighered.com

To my fellow sociologists, who do such creative research on social life and who communicate the sociological imagination to generations of students. With my sincere admiration and appreciation,

Jim Henslin

Brief Contents

Contents

Chapter 2   Culture   39

Chapter 3   Socialization   67

Chapter 4   Social Structure and Social Interaction   101

THROUGH THE AUTHOR'S LENS

Vienna: Social Structure and Social
Interaction in a Vibrant City

One of the most difficult sociological concepts to grasp is
social structure. The concreteness of the photos helps capture
this concept, changing it from abstract to part of everyday life.
Students have no problem understanding *social interaction,* of
course, and in this photo essay they can see how social structure
provides the contours for social interaction. (pages 116–117)

THROUGH THE AUTHOR'S LENS

When a Tornado Strikes: Social
Organization Following a Natural Disaster

As I was watching television on March 20, 2003, I heard a
report that a tornado had hit Camilla, Georgia. "Like a big
lawn mower," the report said, it had cut a path of destruction through this little town. In its fury, the tornado had
left behind six dead and about 200 injured. (pages 128–129)

Part II   Social Groups and Social Control

Part III   Social Inequality

Chapter 7   Social Stratification   197

THROUGH THE AUTHOR'S LENS

The Dump People: Working and Living and Playing in the City Dump of Phnom Penh, Cambodia

I went to Phnom Penh, the capital of Cambodia, to inspect orphanages, to see how well the children were being cared for. While there, I was told about people who live in the city dump. *Live* there? I could hardly believe my ears. I knew that people made their living by picking scraps from the city dump, but I didn't know they actually lived among the garbage. This I had to see for myself. (pages 210–211)

Chapter 8   Sex and Gender   243

THROUGH THE AUTHOR'S LENS

Work and Gender:
Women at Work in India

Traveling through India was both a pleasure and an eye-opening experience.
The country is incredibly diverse, the people friendly, and the land culturally
rich. For this photo essay, wherever I went—whether city, village, or countryside—
I took photos of women at work. (pages 256–257)

Part IV   Social Institutions

Special Features

THINKING CRITICALLY

Guide to Social Maps

WELCOME TO SOCIOLOGY! I've loved sociology since I was in my teens, and I hope you enjoy it, too. Sociology is fascinating because it is about human behavior, and many of us find that it holds the key to understanding social life.

If you like to watch people and try to figure out why they do what they do, you will like sociology. Sociology pries open the doors of society so you can see what goes on behind them. *Sociology: A Down-to-Earth Approach, Core Concepts* stresses how profoundly our society and the groups to which we belong influence us. Social class, for example, sets us on a particular path in life. For some, the path leads to more education, more interesting jobs, higher income, and better health, but for others it leads to dropping out of school, dead-end jobs, poverty, and even a higher risk of illness and disease. These paths are so significant that they affect our chances of making it to our first birthday, as well as of getting in trouble with the police. They even influence our satisfaction in marriage, the number of children we will have—and whether or not we will read this book in the first place.

When I took my first course in sociology, I was "hooked." Seeing how marvelously my life had been affected by these larger social influences opened my eyes to a new world, one that has been fascinating to explore. I hope that you will have this experience, too.

From how people become homeless to how they become presidents, from why people commit suicide to why women are discriminated against in every society around the world—all are part of sociology. This breadth, in fact, is what makes sociology so intriguing. We can place the sociological lens on broad features of society, such as social class, gender, and race–ethnicity, and then immediately turn our focus on the smaller, more intimate level. If we look at two people interacting—whether quarreling or kissing—we see how these broad features of society are being played out in their lives.

We aren't born with instincts. Nor do we come into this world with preconceived notions of what life should be like. At birth, we have no concepts of race–ethnicity, gender, age, or social class. We have no idea, for example, that people "ought" to act in certain ways because they are male or female. Yet we all learn such things as we grow up in our society. Uncovering the "hows" and the "whys" of this process is also part of what makes sociology so fascinating.

One of sociology's many pleasures is that as we study life in groups (which can be taken as a definition of sociology), whether those groups are in some far-off part of the world or in some nearby corner of our own society, we gain new insights into who we are and how we got that way. As we see how *their* customs affect *them,* the effects of our own society on us become more visible.

This book, then, can be part of an intellectual adventure, for it can lead you to a new way of looking at your social world—and in the process, help you to better understand both society and yourself.

I wish you the very best in college—and in your career afterward. It is my sincere desire that *Sociology: A Down-to-Earth Approach, Core Concepts* will contribute to that success.

James M. Henslin
Department of Sociology
Southern Illinois University, Edwardsville

P.S. I enjoy communicating with students, so feel free to comment on your experiences with this text. You can reach me by e-mail: henslin@aol.com

REMEMBER WHEN YOU FIRST GOT "HOOKED" on sociology, how the windows of perception opened as you began to see life-in-society through the sociological perspective? For most of us, this was an eye-opening experience. This text is designed to open those windows onto social life, so students can see clearly the vital effects of group membership on their lives. Although few students will get into what Peter Berger calls "the passion of sociology," we at least can provide them the opportunity.

To study sociology is to embark on a fascinating process of discovery. We can compare sociology to a huge jigsaw puzzle. Only gradually do we see how the intricate pieces fit together. As we begin to see these interconnections, our perspective changes as we shift our eyes from the many small, disjointed pieces to the whole that is being formed. Of all the endeavors we c ould have entered, we chose sociology because of the ways in which it joins the "pieces" of society together and the challenges it poses to "ordinary" thinking. To share with students this process of awareness and discovery called the sociological perspective is our privilege.

As instructors of sociology, we have set ambitious goals for ourselves: to teach both social structure and social interaction and to introduce students to the sociological literature—both the classic theorists and contemporary research. As we accomplish this, we would also like to enliven the classroom, encourage critical thinking, and stimulate our students' sociological imagination. Although formidable, these goals are attainable, and this book is designed to help you reach them. Based on many years of frontline (classroom) experience, its subtitle, *A Down-to-Earth Approach, Core Concepts*, was not proposed lightly. My goal is to share the fascination of sociology with students and in doing so to make your teaching more rewarding.

Over the years, I have found the introductory course especially enjoyable. It is singularly satisfying to see students' faces light up as they begin to see how separate pieces of their world fit together. It is a pleasure to watch them gain insight into how their social experiences give shape to even their innermost desires. This is precisely what this text is designed to do—to stimulate your students' sociological imagination so they can better perceive how the "pieces" of society fit together—and what this means for their own lives.

Filled with examples from around the world as well as from our own society, this text helps to make today's multicultural, global society come alive for students. From learning how the international elite carve up global markets to studying the intimacy of friendship and marriage, students can see how sociology is the key to explaining contemporary life—and their own place in it.

In short, this text is designed to make your teaching easier. There simply is no justification for students to have to wade through cumbersome approaches to sociology. I am firmly convinced that the introduction to sociology should be enjoyable and that the introductory textbook can be an essential tool in sharing the discovery of sociology with students.

The Organization of This Text

The text is laid out in four parts. Part I focuses on the sociological perspective, which is introduced in the first chapter. We then look at how culture influences us (Chapter 2), examine socialization (Chapter 3), and compare macrosociology and microsociology (Chapter 4).

Part II, which focuses on groups and social control, adds to the students' understanding of how far-reaching society's influence is—how group membership penetrates even our thinking, attitudes, and orientations to life. We first examine the different types of groups that have such profound influences on us and then take a broad-ranging perspective—from major historical changes in societies to our own small social networks (Chapter 5). After this, we focus on how groups "keep us in line" and sanction those who violate their norms (Chapter 6).

In Part III, we turn our focus on social inequality, examining how it pervades society and how it has an impact on our own lives. We first take a global focus, overviewing the types and principles of social stratification and then examining social class in the United States (Chapter 7). After establishing this context of social stratification, we examine gender, the most global of the inequalities (Chapter 8). Then we focus on inequalities of race and ethnicity (Chapter 9).

In Part IV, we look at a single social institution, one that we all know so intimately. The emphasis is how marriage and family are changing and how their changes, in turn, have an impact on our own lives (Chapter 10).

Themes and Features

Six central themes run throughout this text: down-to-earth sociology, globalization, cultural diversity, critical thinking, the new technology, and the influence of the mass media on our lives. For each of these themes, except globalization, which is incorporated throughout the text, I have written a series of boxes. These boxed features are one of my favorite components of the book. They are especially useful for introducing the controversial topics that make sociology such a lively activity.

Let's look at these six themes.

Down-to-Earth Sociology

As many years of teaching have shown me, all too often textbooks are written to appeal to the adopters of texts rather than to the students who must learn from them. Therefore, a central concern in writing this book has been to present sociology in a way that not only facilitates understanding but also shares its excitement. During the course of writing other texts, I often have been told that my explanations and writing style are "down-to-earth," or accessible and inviting to students—so much so that I chose this phrase as the book's subtitle. The term is also featured in my introductory reader, *Down-to-Earth Sociology: Introductory Readings,* now in its 15th edition (New York: The Free Press, 2012).

This first theme is highlighted by a series of boxed features that explore sociological processes that underlie everyday life. The topics that we review in these *Down-to-Earth Sociology* boxes are highly diverse. Here are some of them.

- the experiences of W. E. B. Du Bois in studying U.S. race relations (Chapter 1)
- 2-D: a new subculture and a different kind of love (Chapter 2)
- the relationship between heredity and environment (Chapter 3)
- how football can help us understand social structure (Chapter 4)
- beauty and success (Chapter 4)

- the naked pumpkin runners and the naked bike riders: deviance or freedom of self-expression? (Chapter 6)
- serial killers living next door (Chapter 6)
- the lifestyles of the super-rich (Chapter 7)
- cold-hearted surgeons and their women victims (Chapter 8)
- affirmative action for men (Chapter 8)

- living in the dorm: contact theory (Chapter 9)
- how cohabitation means different things to people—and how this
- affects their chances of marriage (Chapter 10)
- un-divorce: the paths to perpetual separation (Chapter 10)

This first theme is actually a hallmark of the text, as my goal is to make sociology "down to earth." To help students grasp the fascination of sociology, I continuously stress sociology's relevance to their lives. To reinforce this theme, I avoid unnecessary jargon and use concise explanations and clear and simple (but not reductive) language. I also use student-relevant examples to illustrate key concepts, and I base several of the chapters' opening vignettes on my own experiences in exploring social life. That this goal of sharing sociology's fascination is being reached is evident from the many comments I receive from instructors and students alike that the text helps make sociology "come alive."

Globalization

In the second theme, globalization, we explore the impact of global issues on our lives and on the lives of people around the world. All of us are feeling the effects of an increasingly powerful and encompassing global economy, one that ensnares us as it intertwines the fates of nations. The globalization of capitalism influences the kinds of skills and knowledge we need, the types of work available to us—and whether work is available at all. Globalization also underlies the costs of the goods and services we consume and whether our country is at war or peace—or in some uncharted middle ground between the two, some sort of perpetual war against unseen, sinister, and ever-threatening enemies lurking throughout the world. In addition to the strong emphasis on global issues that runs throughout this text, I have written a separate chapter on global stratification (Chapter 7).

What occurs in Russia, Germany, and China, as well as in much smaller nations such as Afghanistan and Iraq, has far-reaching consequences on our own lives. Consequently, in addition to the global focus that runs throughout the text, the next theme, cultural diversity, also has a strong global emphasis.

Cultural Diversity around the World and in the United States

The third theme, cultural diversity, has two primary emphases. The first is cultural diversity around the world. Gaining an understanding of how social life is "done" in other parts of the world often challenges our taken-for-granted assumptions about social life. At times, when we learn about other cultures, we gain an appreciation for the life of other peoples; at other times, we may be shocked or even disgusted at some aspect of another group's way of life (such as female circumcision) and come away with a renewed appreciation of our own customs.

To highlight this first subtheme, I have written a series of boxes called **Cultural Diversity around the World.** Among the topics with this subtheme are

- food customs that shock people from different cultures (Chapter 2)
- where women become men (Chapter 3)
- human sexuality in Mexico and Kenya (Chapter 6)
- "dogging" in England (Chapter 6)
- female circumcision (Chapter 8)
- love and arranged marriage in India (Chapter 10)

In the second subtheme, **Cultural Diversity in the United States,** we examine groups that make up the fascinating array of people who form the U.S. population. The boxes I have written with this subtheme review such topics as

- racism and job discrimination (Chapter 1)
- the Hmong's culture shock when they arrived in the United States (Chapter 2)
- the controversy over the use of Spanish or English (Chapter 2)
- how the Amish resist social change (Chapter 4)

- do your social networks produce social inequality? (Chapter 5)
- the upward social mobility of African Americans (Chapter 7)
- how Tiger Woods represents a changing racial–ethnic identity (Chapter 9)
- the author's travels with a Mexican who transports undocumented workers to the U.S. border (Chapter 9)

Seeing that there are so many ways of "doing" social life can remove some of our cultural smugness, making us more aware of how arbitrary our own customs are—and how our taken-for-granted ways of thinking are rooted in culture. The stimulating contexts of these contrasts can help students develop their sociological imagination. They encourage students to see connections among key sociological concepts such as culture, socialization, norms, race–ethnicity, gender, and social class. As your students' sociological imagination grows, they can attain a new perspective on their experiences in their own corners of life—and a better understanding of the social structure of U.S. society.

Critical Thinking

In our fourth theme, critical thinking, we focus on controversial social issues, inviting students to examine various sides of those issues. In these sections, titled **Thinking Critically,** I present objective, fair portrayals of positions and do not take a side—although occasionally I do play the "devil's advocate" in the questions that close each of the topics. Like the boxed features, these sections can enliven your classroom with a vibrant exchange of ideas. Among the issues addressed are

- biology versus culture (Chapter 2)
- our tendency to conform to evil authority, as uncovered by the Milgram experiments (Chapter 5)
- cloning (Chapter 5)
- the three-strikes-and-you're-out laws (Chapter 6)

- bounties paid to kill homeless children in Brazil (Chapter 7)
- inequalities in health care (Chapter 7)
- emerging masculinities and femininities (Chapter 8)

These *Thinking Critically* sections are based on controversial social issues that either affect the student's own life or focus on topics that have intrinsic interest for students. Because of their controversial nature, these sections stimulate both critical thinking and lively class discussions. These sections also provide provocative topics for in-class debates and small discussion groups, effective ways to enliven a class and present sociological ideas. In the Instructor's Manual, I describe the nuts and bolts of using small groups in the classroom, a highly effective way of engaging students in sociological topics.

Sociology and the New Technology

The fifth theme, sociology and the new technology, explores an aspect of social life that has come to be central in our lives. We welcome these new technological tools, for they help us to be more efficient at performing our daily tasks, from making a living to communicating with others—whether those people are nearby or on the other side of the globe. The significance of our new technology, however, extends far beyond the tools and the ease and efficiency they bring to our lives. The new technology is better envisioned as a social revolution that will leave few aspects of our lives untouched. Its effects are so profound that it even changes the ways we view life.

This theme is introduced in Chapter 2, where technology is defined and presented as a major aspect of culture. The impact of technology is then discussed throughout the text. Examples include how technology is related to cultural change (Chapter 2), social inequality in early human history (Chapter 7), and its impact on dating (Chapter 10).

To highlight this theme, I have written a series of boxes called **Sociology and the New Technology.** In these boxes, we explore how technology affects our lives as it changes society. We examine how technology

- in the form of avatars, is blurring the distinction between reality and fantasy (Chapter 5)
- through cloning might affect the future of society (Chapter 5)
- is changing the way people find mates (Chapter 10)
- is leading to designer babies (Chapter 10)

The Mass Media and Social Life

In the sixth theme, we stress how the mass media affect our behavior and permeate our thinking. We consider how the media penetrate our consciousness to such a degree that they even influence how we perceive our own bodies. As your students consider this theme, they may begin to grasp how the mass media shape their own attitudes. If so, they will come to view the mass media in a different light, which should further stimulate their sociological imagination.

To make this theme more prominent for students, I have written a series of boxed features called **Mass Media in Social Life.** Among these are

- the presentation of gender in computer games (Chapter 3)
- the worship of thinness—and how this affects our own body images (Chapter 4)
- the issue of censoring high-tech pornography (Chapter 8)
- the arrival of a women's movement in Iran (Chapter 8)

What's New in This Edition?

Because sociology is about social life and we live in a changing global society, an introductory sociology text must reflect the national and global changes that engulf us, as well as represent the new sociological research. I have written eight new boxes for this revision of *Sociology: A Down-to-Earth Approach, Core Concepts.* It also has over 140 new instructional photos and over 150 new references. I have either selected or taken each of the photos, which are tied directly into the content of the text. They are part of the students' learning experience.

I have updated topics and events and used 2011 research sources whenever available. These changes are so numerous and what adopters have come to expect of this text that I won't bother listing these numerous changes that run throughout the text. Instead, on the next page I have listed just the new topics, boxed features, and tables and figures that I have added to this edition. This gives you a good idea of how extensively this edition is revised.

Visual Presentations of Sociology

Showing Changes over Time   In presenting social data, many of the figures and tables show how data change over time. This feature allows students to see trends in

WHAT'S NEW IN THIS EDITION?

CHAPTER 2

Down-to-Earth Sociology box: 2-D: A New Subculture and a Different Kind of Love
Topic: Genetics-informed sociology
Topic: Killing Bin Laden

CHAPTER 3

Topic: Research on babies indicates an inborn morality
Topic: The lack of an abstract, universal morality, unexpected from Kohlberg's theory
Topic: The effects of day care follow children (NICHD research; latest testing at age 15)
Topic: Facial expressions of people blind since birth, upon learning they had won or lost at the Paralympics, were the same as those of sighted people

CHAPTER 4

Through the Author's Lens Vienna: Social Structure and Social Interaction in a Vibrant City

CHAPTER 5

Topic: To receive prizes on a fake game show, 80 percent of contestants gave victims what they thought were near lethal 450 volt shocks
Topic: Perhaps coming soon: Snap-together BioBricks to produce your own life forms
Cultural Diversity box: How Your Social Networks Perpetuate Social Inequality

CHAPTER 6

Topic: How genetic explanations are being used to explain crime
Down-to-Earth Sociology box: The Naked Pumpkin Runners and the Naked Bike Riders: Deviance or Freedom of Self-Expression?

Topic: A corporate decision leads to the deaths of 600 miners in West Virginia
Topic: Courts fine Northrop Grumman $325 million for a white collar crime—and the federal government then awards the company $325 million
Cultural Diversity around the World box: "Dogging" in England
Topic: Anthony Sowell of Cleveland added to the list of serial killers
Topic: Lower crime rate continues even though unemployment increases

CHAPTER 7

Illustration: Table 7.3 Views of Stratification: The Distribution of Society's Resources
Topic: The *suburbanization of poverty*: With the collapse of the housing market, most of the nation's poor now live in the suburbs
Topic: Over a 4-year period, *one-third* (32 percent) of Americans experience poverty for at least two months.
Topic: Upper middle-class parents pay $1,000 to train their 4-year olds in test-taking skills so they can get into public kindergartens for gifted students

CHAPTER 8

Thinking Critically section: Making the Social Explicit: Emerging Masculinities and Femininities
Topic: Disagreement among feminists regarding "erotic capital"
Topic: Male rape

CHAPTER 9

Topic: Rivalry and violence between Latino and African American prisoners

Topic: Arizona proof of citizenship or immigrant status law
Topic: Construction of the fence along the Mexican border cancelled
Topic: Arabs added to Figure 9.5, U.S. Racial–Ethnic Groups
Topic: Michael Kimmel's research on Neo-Nazi skinheads in Sweden
Topic: Susana Martinez elected as the first Latina governor (New Mexico)
Down-to-Earth Sociology box: Living in the Dorm: Contact Theory

CHAPTER 10

New opening vignette
Topic: Adoption by gay and lesbian couples
Topic: *Date Check,* an iPhone app that offers a "sleaze detector" to investigate potential dates
Topic: Feelings of romantic love light up the same area of the brain as does craving for cocaine
Topic: Marital happiness decreases with the birth of a child, increases when the child starts school, and decreases again when the child reaches adolescence
Illustration: Table 10.4 Fathers' Contact with Their Children After Divorce
Sociology and the New Technology box: Online Dating: Risks and Rewards
Sociology and the New Technology box: What Color Eyes? How Tall? Designer Babies on the Way
Down-to-Earth Sociology box: Un-Divorce: The Paths to Perpetual Separation

social life and to make predictions on how these trends might continue—and even affect their own lives. Examples include

- Figure 1.4, *U.S. Marriage, U.S. Divorce* (Chapter 1);
- Figure 3.2, *Transitional Adulthood: A New Stage in Life* (Chapter 3);
- Figure 6.2, *How Much Is Enough? The Explosion in the Number of Prisoners* (Chapter 6);
- Figure 7.6, *The More Things Change, the More They Stay the Same: Dividing the Nation's Income* (Chapter 7);

- Figure 10.2, *In Two-Paycheck Marriages, How Do Husbands and Wives Divide Their Responsibilities?* (Chapter 10);
- Figure 10.4, *The Number of Children Americans Think Are Ideal* (Chapter 10);
- Figure 10.12, *Cohabitation in the United States* (Chapter 10);

This hallmark feature of the text is reinforced with **By the Numbers,** a feature that appears at the end of most chapters: By the Numbers pulls key data and statistics on changing aspects of social life from the tables, figures, and text references in the chapter, and presents the data in paired comparisons. These comparisons represent some of the key changes occurring in our society and around the world.

Through the Author's Lens   Using this format, students are able to look over my shoulder as I experience other cultures or explore aspects of this one. These eight photo essays should expand your students' sociological imagination and open their minds to other ways of doing social life, as well as stimulate thought-provoking class discussion.

Vienna: Social Structure and Social Interaction in a Vibrant City, which appears in Chapter 4, is new to this edition. The photos I took in this city illustrate how social structure surrounds us, setting the scene for our interactions, limiting and directing them.

When a Tornado Strikes: Social Organization Following a Natural Disaster When a tornado hit a small town just hours from where I lived, I photographed the aftermath of the disaster. The police let me in to view the neighborhood where the tornado had struck, destroying homes and killing several people. I was impressed by how quickly people were putting their lives back together, the topic of this photo essay (Chapter 4).

The Dump People of Phnom Penh, Cambodia Among the culture shocks I experienced in Cambodia was not to discover that people scavenge at city dumps, but that people live, work, and play in Phnom Penh's huge city dump. With the aid of an interpreter, I was able to interview these people, as well as photograph them as they went about their everyday lives. An entire community lives in the city dump, complete with restaurants amidst the smoke and piles of garbage. This photo essay reveals not just these people's activities but also their social organization (Chapter 7).

Work and Gender: Women at Work in India As I traveled in India, I took photos of women at work in public places. The more I traveled in this country and the more photos I took, the more insight I gained into gender relations. Despite the general dominance of men in India, women's worlds are far from limited to family and home. Women are found at work throughout the society. What is even more remarkable is how vastly different "women's work" is in India than it is in the United States. This, too, is an intellectually provocative photo essay (Chapter 8).

Other Photo Essays   I am very pleased with the new photo essay on ethnic work in Chapter 9, as it helps students see that ethnicity doesn't "just happen." To help students better understand subcultures, I have retained the photo essay in Chapter 2. Because these photo essays consist of photos taken by others, they are not a part of the series, *Through the Author's Lens.* I think you will appreciate the understanding they can give your students.

Photo Collages   Because sociology lends itself so well to photographic illustrations, this text also includes photo collages. In Chapter 1, the photo collage, in the shape of a wheel, features some of the many women who became sociologists in earlier generations, women who have largely gone unacknowledged as sociologists. In Chapter 2, students can catch a glimpse of the fascinating variety that goes into the cultural relativity of beauty. The collage in Chapter 5 illustrates categories, aggregates, and primary and secondary groups, concepts that students sometimes wrestle to distinguish. The photo collage in Chapter 8 lets students see how differently gender is portrayed in different cultures.

Other Photos by the Author   Sprinkled throughout the text are photos that I took in Austria, Cambodia, India, Latvia, Spain, and the United States. These photos illustrate sociological principles and topics better than photos available from commercial sources. As an example, while in the United States, I received a report about a feral child who had been discovered living with monkeys and who had been taken to an orphanage in Cambodia. The possibility of photographing and interviewing that child was one of the reasons that I went to Cambodia. That particular photo is on page 66. Another of my favorites is on page 150.

Other Special Pedagogical Features

In addition to chapter summaries and reviews, key terms, and a comprehensive glossary, I have included several special features to aid students in learning sociology. **In Sum** sections help students review important points within the chapter before going on to new materials. I have also developed a series of original **Social Maps,** which illustrate how social conditions vary by geography.

Chapter-Opening Vignettes   These accounts feature down-to-earth illustrations of a major aspect of each chapter's content. Several of these are based on my research with the homeless, the time I spent with them on the streets and slept in their shelters (Chapters 1 and 7). Others recount my travels in Africa (Chapters 2 and 8) and Mexico (Chapter 10). I also share my experiences when I spent a night with street people at DuPont Circle in Washington, D.C. (Chapter 4). For other vignettes, I use current and historical events (Chapters 5 and 9) and classical studies in the social sciences (Chapters 3 and 6). Many students have told their instructors that they find these vignettes compelling, that they stimulate interest in the chapter.

Thinking Critically about the Chapters   I close each chapter with critical thinking questions. Each question focuses on a major feature of the chapter, asking students to reflect on and consider some issue. Many of the questions ask the students to apply sociological findings and principles to their own lives.

On Sources   Sociological data are found in a wide variety of sources, and this text reflects that variety. Cited throughout this text are standard journals such as the *American Journal of Sociology, Social Problems, American Sociological Review,* and *Journal of Marriage and Family,* as well as more esoteric journals such as the *Bulletin of the History of Medicine, Chronobiology International,* and *Western Journal of Black Studies.* I have also drawn heavily from standard news sources, especially the *New York Times* and the *Wall Street Journal,* as well as more unusual sources such as *El País.* In addition, I cite unpublished research and theoretical papers by sociologists.

Acknowledgments

The gratifying response to earlier editions indicates that my efforts at making sociology down to earth have succeeded. The years that have gone into writing this text are a culmination of the many more years that preceded its writing—from graduate school to that equally demanding endeavor known as classroom teaching. No text, of course, comes solely from its author. Although I am responsible for the final words on the printed page, I have received excellent feedback from instructors who have taught from the first four editions. I am especially grateful to

Reviewers of the First through Fourth Editions

Francis O. Adeola, *University of New Orleans*

Brian W. Agnitsch, *Marshalltown Community College*

Sandra L. Albrecht, *The University of Kansas*

Christina Alexander, *Linfield College*

Richard Alman, *Sierra College*

Gabriel C. Alvarez, *Duquesne University*

Kenneth Ambrose, *Marshall University*

Alberto Arroyo, *Baldwin–Wallace College*

Karren Baird-Olsen, *Kansas State University*

Rafael Balderrama, *University of Texas—Pan American*

Linda Barbera-Stein, *The University of Illinois*

Brenda Blackburn, *California State University—Fullerton*

Ronnie J. Booxbaum, *Greenfield Community College*

Cecil D. Bradfield, *James Madison University*

Karen Bradley, *Central Missouri State University*

Francis Broouer, *Worcester State College*

Valerie S. Brown, *Cuyahoga Community College*

Sandi Brunette-Hill, *Carrol College*

Richard Brunk, *Francis Marion University*

Karen Bullock, *Salem State College*

Allison R. Camelot, *California State University—Fullerton*

Paul Ciccantell, *Kansas State University*

John K. Cochran, *The University of Oklahoma*

James M. Cook, *Duke University*

Joan Cook-Zimmern, *College of Saint Mary*

Larry Curiel, *Cypress College*

Russell L. Curtis, *University of Houston*

John Darling, *University of Pittsburgh—Johnstown*

Ray Darville, *Stephen F. Austin State University*

Jim David, *Butler County Community College*

Nanette J. Davis, *Portland State University*

Vincent Davis, *Mt. Hood Community College*

Lynda Dodgen, *North Harris Community College*

Terry Dougherty, *Portland State University*

Marlese Durr, *Wright State University*

Helen R. Ebaugh, *University of Houston*

Obi N. Ebbe, *State University of New York—Brockport*

Cy Edwards, Chair, *Cypress Community College*

John Ehle, *Northern Virginia Community College*

Morten Ender, *U.S. Military Academy*

Rebecca Susan Fahrlander, *Bellevue University*

Louis J. Finkle, *Horry-Georgetown Technical College*

Nicole T. Flynn, *University of South Alabama*

Lorna E. Forster, *Clinton Community College*

David O. Friedrichs, *University of Scranton*

Bruce Friesen, *Kent State University—Stark*

Lada Gibson-Shreve, *Stark State College*

Norman Goodman, *State University of New York—Stony Brook*

Rosalind Gottfried, *San Joaquin Delta College*

G. Kathleen Grant, *The University of Findlay*

Bill Grisby, *University of Northern Colorado*

Ramon Guerra, *University of Texas—Pan American*

Remi Hajjar, *U.S. Military Academy*

Donald W. Hastings, *The University of Tennessee—Knoxville*

Lillian O. Holloman, *Prince George's Community College*

Michael Hoover, *Missouri Western State College*

Howard R. Housen, *Broward Community College*

James H. Huber, *Bloomsburg University*

Erwin Hummel, *Portland State University*

Charles E. Hurst, *The College of Wooster*

Nita Jackson, *Butler County Community College*

Jennifer A. Johnson, *Germanna Community College*

Kathleen R. Johnson, *Keene State College*

Tammy Jolley, *University of Arkansas Community College at Batesville*

David Jones, *Plymouth State College*

Arunas Juska, *East Carolina University*

Ali Kamali, *Missouri Western State College*

Irwin Kantor, *Middlesex County College*

Mark Kassop, *Bergen Community College*

Myles Kelleher, *Bucks County Community College*

Mary E. Kelly, *Central Missouri State University*

Alice Abel Kemp, *University of New Orleans*

Diana Kendall, *Austin Community College*

Gary Kiger, *Utah State University*

Gene W. Kilpatrick, *University of Maine—Presque Isle*

Jerome R. Koch, *Texas Tech University*

Joseph A. Kotarba, *University of Houston*

Michele Lee Kozimor-King, *Pennsylvania State University*

Darina Lepadatu, *Kennesaw State University*

Abraham Levine, *El Camino Community College*

Diane Levy, *The University of North Carolina—Wilmington*

Stephen Mabry, *Cedar Valley College*

David Maines, *Oakland University*

Ron Matson, *Wichita State University*

Armaund L. Mauss, *Washington State University*

Evelyn Mercer, *Southwest Baptist University*

Robert Meyer, *Arkansas State University*

Michael V. Miller, *University of Texas—San Antonio*

John Mitrano, *Central Connecticut State University*

W. Lawrence Neuman, *University of Wisconsin— Whitewater*

Charles Norman, *Indiana State University*

Patricia H. O'Brien, *Elgin Community College*

Robert Ostrow, *Wayne State*

Laura O'Toole, *University of Delaware*

Mike K. Pate, *Western Oklahoma State College*

Lawrence Peck, *Erie Community College*

Ruth Pigott, *University of Nebraska—Kearney*

Phil Piket, *Joliet Junior College*

Trevor Pinch, *Cornell University*

Daniel Polak, *Hudson Valley Community College*

James Pond, *Butler Community College*

Deedy Ramo, *Del Mar College*

Adrian Rapp, *North Harris Community College*

Ray Rich, *Community College of Southern Nevada*

Barbara Richardson, *Eastern Michigan University*

Salvador Rivera, *State University of New York—Cobleskill*

Howard Robboy, *Trenton State College*

Paulina X. Ruf, *University of Tampa*

Michael Samano, *Portland Community College*

Michael L. Sanow, *Community College of Baltimore County*

Mary C. Sengstock, *Wayne State University*

Walt Shirley, *Sinclair Community College*

Marc Silver, *Hofstra University*

Roberto E. Socas, *Essex County College*

Susan Sprecher, *Illinois State University*

Mariella Rose Squire, *University of Maine at Fort Kent*

Rachel Stehle, *Cuyahoga Community College*

Marios Stephanides, *University of Tampa*

Randolph G. Ston, *Oakland Community College*

Vickie Holland Taylor, *Danville Community College*

Maria Jose Tenuto, *College of Lake County*

Gary Tiederman, *Oregon State University*

Kathleen Tiemann, *University of North Dakota*

Judy Turchetta, *Johnson & Wales University*

Stephen L. Vassar, *Minnesota State University—Mankato*

William J. Wattendorf, *Adirondack Community College*

Jay Weinstein, *Eastern Michigan University*

Larry Weiss, *University of Alaska*

Douglas White, *Henry Ford Community College*

Stephen R. Wilson, *Temple University*

Anthony T. Woart, *Middlesex Community College*

Stuart Wright, *Lamar University*

Mary Lou Wylie, *James Madison University*

Diane Kholos Wysocki, *University of Nebraska—Kearney*

Stacey G. H. Yap, *Plymouth State College*

William Yoels, *University of Alabama Birmingham*

I couldn't ask for a more outstanding team than the one that I have the pleasure to work with at Allyn and Bacon. I want to thank Brita Mess, whose counsel has been excellent; Jennifer Auvil for coordinating production and attending to the many details; and Karla Walsh, whose copy editing I appreciate; Kate Cebik, for her creativity in photo research—and for her willingness to "keep on looking."

I do appreciate this team. It is difficult to heap too much praise on such fine, capable, and creative people. Their efforts coalesced with mine to produce this text. Students, whom we constantly kept in mind as we prepared this edition, are the beneficiaries of this intricate teamwork.

Since this text is based on the contributions of many, I would count it a privilege if you would share with me your teaching experiences with this book, including suggestions for improving the text. Both positive and negative comments are welcome. It is in this way that I continue to learn.

I wish you the very best in your teaching. It is my sincere desire that *Sociology, A Down-to-Earth Approach, Core Concepts*, contributes to your classroom success.

James M. Henslin
Professor Emeritus
Department of Sociology
Southern Illinois University, Edwardsville

I welcome your correspondence. E-mail is the best way to reach me: henslin@aol.com

Instructor Supplements

Unless otherwise noted, instructor supplements are available at no charge to adopters—in printed or electronic formats through the Instructor's Resource Center (www.pearsonhighered.com/irc).

Instructor's Manual and Test bank

For each chapter in the text, the Instructor's Manual provides a list of key changes to the new edition, chapter summaries and outlines, learning objectives, key terms and people, discussion topics, classroom activities, recommended films and Web sites, and additional references. The Instructor's Manual also includes a section by Jim Henslin on using small, in-class discussion groups and sample syllabi. The Test Bank contains approximately 125 questions per chapter in multiple-choice, true/false, short answer, essay, open-book, and matching formats. There is also a set of questions based on the text's figures, tables, and maps. All questions are scaled to Bloom's Taxonomy and to in-text learning objectives. ISBN: 0-205-11642-6

MyTest Computerized Test Bank

The printed Test Bank is also available online through Pearson's computerized testing system, MyTest. The user-friendly interface allows you to view, edit, and add questions, transfer questions to tests, and print tests in a variety of fonts. Search and sort features allow you to locate questions quickly and to arrange them in whatever order you prefer. The Test Bank can be accessed anywhere with a free MyTest user account. There is no need to download a program or file to your computer. ISBN: 0-205-09660-3

PowerPoint Presentation Slides

Lecture PowerPoint Presentations are available for this edition. The lecture slides outline each chapter of the text, while the line art slides provide the charts, graphs, and maps found in the text. PowerPoint software is not required as PowerPoint viewer is included. ISBN: 0-205-11652-3

Online Course Management

MySocLab

MySocLab is a learning and assessment tool that enables instructors to assess student performance and adapt course content—without investing additional time or resources. MySocLab is designed with instructor flexibility in mind—you decide the extent of integration into your course—from independent self-assessment to total course management. The lab is accompanied with an instructor's manual featuring easy-to-read media grids, activities, sample syllabi, and tips for integrating technology into your course.

New features in MySocLab include:

- Social Explorer—the premier interactive demographics Web site.
- MySocLibrary—with over 100 classic and contemporary primary source readings.
- The Core Concepts in Sociology videos—streaming videos presented in documentary style on core sociological concepts.
- The Social Lens—a sociology blog updated weekly with topics ranging from politics to pop culture.
- Chapter Audio—streaming audio of the entire text.
- MyClassPrep—New from Pearson, **MyClassPrep** makes lecture preparation simpler and less time consuming. It collects the very best class presentation resources—art and figures from our leading texts, videos, lecture activities, classroom activities, demonstrations, and much more—in one convenient online destination. You may search through **MyClassPrep**'s extensive database of tools by content topic (arranged by standard topics within the sociology curriculum) or by content type (video, audio, simulation, Word documents, etc.). You can select resources appropriate for your lecture, many of which can be downloaded directly. Or you may build your own folder of resources and present from within **MyClassPrep**.

About the Author

JIM HENSLIN was born in Minnesota, graduated from high school and junior college in California and from college in Indiana. Awarded scholarships, he earned his master's and doctorate degrees in sociology at Washington University in St. Louis, Missouri. After this, he won a postdoctoral fellowship from the National Institute of Mental Health and spent a year studying how people adjust to the suicide of a family member. His primary interests in sociology are the sociology of everyday life, deviance, and international relations. Among his many books are *Down-to-Earth Sociology: Introductory Readings* (Free Press), now in its 15th edition, and *Social Problems* (Allyn and Bacon), now in its 10th edition. He has also published widely in sociology journals, including *Social Problems* and *American Journal of Sociology*.

While a graduate student, Jim taught at the University of Missouri at St. Louis. After completing his doctorate, he joined the faculty at Southern Illinois University, Edwardsville, where he is Professor Emeritus of Sociology. He says, "I've always found the introductory course enjoyable to teach. I love to see students' faces light up when they first glimpse the sociological perspective and begin to see how society has become an essential part of how they view the world."

Jim enjoys reading and fishing, and he also does a bit of kayaking and weight lifting. His two favorite activities are writing and traveling. He especially enjoys visiting and living in other cultures, for this brings him face to face with behaviors and ways of thinking that challenge his perspectives and "make sociological principles come alive." A special pleasure has been the preparation of the photo essays that appear in this text.

Jim moved to Latvia, an Eastern European country formerly dominated by the Soviet Union, where he had the experience of becoming an immigrant. There he observed firsthand how people struggle to adjust from socialism to capitalism. While there, he also interviewed aged political prisoners who had survived the Soviet gulag. He then moved to Spain, where he was able to observe how people adjust to an economic crisis and the immigration of people from contrasting cultures. (Of course, for this he didn't need to leave the United States.) To better round out his cultural experiences, Jim is making plans for extended stays in India and South America, where he expects to do more photo essays to reflect their fascinating cultures. He is grateful to be able to live in such exciting social, technological, and geopolitical times—and to have access to portable broadband Internet while he pursues his sociological imagination.

The author at work—sometimes getting a little too close to "the action." He is shown here doing research on a religious festival in Spain.

Anita Henslin

1

The Sociological Perspective

From Chapter 1 of *Sociology. A Down-to-Earth Approach, Core Concepts*, Fifth Edition. James M. Henslin.

Even from the glow of the faded red-and-white exit sign, its faint light barely illuminating the upper bunk, I could see that the sheet was filthy. Resigned to another night of fitful sleep, I reluctantly crawled into bed.

I kept my clothes on.

The next morning, I joined the long line of disheveled men leaning against the chain-link fence. Their faces were as downcast as their clothes were dirty. Not a glimmer of hope among them.

No one spoke as the line slowly inched forward.

When my turn came, I was handed a cup of coffee, a white plastic spoon, and a bowl of semi-liquid that I couldn't identify. It didn't look like any food I had seen before. Nor did it taste like anything I had ever eaten.

My stomach fought the foul taste, every spoonful a battle. But I was determined. "I will experience what they experience," I kept telling myself. My stomach reluctantly gave in and accepted its morning nourishment.

The room was strangely silent. Hundreds of men were eating, each one immersed in his own private hell, his mind awash with disappointment, remorse, bitterness.

> I was determined. "I will experience what they experience," I kept telling myself.

As I stared at the Styrofoam cup that held my coffee, grateful for at least this small pleasure, I noticed what looked like teeth marks. I shrugged off the thought, telling myself that my long weeks as a sociological observer of the homeless were finally getting to me. "It must be some sort of crease from handling," I concluded.

I joined the silent ranks of men turning in their bowls and cups. When I saw the man behind the counter swishing out Styrofoam cups in a washtub of murky water, I began to feel sick to my stomach. I knew then that the jagged marks on my cup really had come from another person's mouth.

How much longer did this research have to last? I felt a deep longing to return to my family—to a welcome world of clean sheets, healthy food, and "normal" conversations.

Australia

The Sociological Perspective

Why were these men so silent? Why did they receive such despicable treatment? What was I doing in that homeless shelter? After all, I hold a respectable, professional position, and I have a home and family.

You are in for an exciting and eye-opening experience. Sociology offers a fascinating view of social life. The *sociological perspective* (or imagination) opens a window onto unfamiliar worlds—and offers a fresh look at familiar ones. In this text, you will find yourself in the midst of Nazis in Germany and warriors in South America. Sociology is broad, and your journey will even take you to a group that lives in a city dump. You will also find yourself looking at your own world in a different light. As you view other worlds—or your own—the sociological perspective enables you to gain a new perception of social life. In fact, this is what many find appealing about sociology.

The sociological perspective has been a motivating force in my own life. Ever since I took my introductory course in sociology as a freshman in college, I have been enchanted by the perspective that sociology offers. I have enjoyed both observing other groups and questioning my own assumptions about life. I sincerely hope the same happens to you.

Seeing the Broader Social Context

The **sociological perspective** stresses the social contexts in which people live. It examines how these contexts influence people's lives. At the center of the sociological perspective is the question of how groups influence people, especially how people are influenced by their **society**—a group of people who share a culture and a territory.

To find out why people do what they do, sociologists look at **social location,** the corners in life that people occupy because of their place in a society. Sociologists look at how jobs, income, education, gender, race–ethnicity, and age affect people's ideas and behavior. Consider, for example, how being identified with a group called *females* or with a group called *males* when you were growing up has shaped *your* ideas of who you are. Growing up as a female or a male has influenced not only how you feel about yourself but also your ideas of what you should attain in life and how you relate to others.

Sociologist C. Wright Mills (1959) put it this way: "The sociological imagination [perspective] enables us to grasp the connection between history and biography." By *history,* Mills meant that each society is located in a broad stream of events. This gives each society specific characteristics—such as its ideas about what roles are proper for men and women. By *biography,* Mills referred to our experiences within these historical settings, which give us our orientations to life. In short, people don't do what they do because they inherited some internal mechanism, such as instincts. Rather, *external* influences—our experiences—become part of our thinking and motivation. In short, the society in which we grow up, and our particular location in that society, lie at the center of what we do and how we think.

Consider a newborn baby. As you know, if we were to take the baby away from its U.S. parents and place it with the Yanomamö Indians in the jungles of South America, his or her first words would not be in English. You also know that the child would not think like an American. The child would not grow up wanting credit cards, for example, or designer clothes, a car, a cell phone, an iPod, and the latest video game. He or she would take his or her place in Yanomamö society—perhaps as a food gatherer, a hunter, or a warrior—and would not even know about the world left behind at birth. And, whether male or female, the child would grow up assuming that it is natural to want many children, not debating whether to have one, two, or three children.

If you have been thinking along with me—and I hope you have—you should be thinking about how *your* social groups have shaped *your* ideas and desires. Over and over in this text, you will see that the way you look at the world is the result of your exposure to specific human groups. I think you will enjoy the process of self-discovery that sociology offers.

Read
Invitation to Sociology
by Peter Berger
on **mysoclab.com**

sociological perspective understanding human behavior by placing it within its broader social context

society people who share a culture and a territory

social location the group memberships that people have because of their location in history and society

Why are history and biography both essential elements of the sociological perspective?

The Global Context—and the Local

As is evident to all of us—from the labels on our clothing that say Hong Kong, Brunei, or Macau, to the many other imported products that have become part of our daily lives—our world has become a global village. How life has changed! Our predecessors lived on isolated farms and in small towns. They grew their own food and made their own clothing, buying only sugar, coffee, and a few other items that they couldn't produce. Beyond the borders of their communities lay a world they perceived only dimly.

And how slow communications used to be! In December 1814, the United States and Great Britain signed a peace treaty to end the War of 1812. Yet two weeks *later* their armies fought a major battle at New Orleans. Neither the American nor the British forces there had heard that the war was over (Volti 1995).

Now we can pick up a telephone or use the Internet to communicate instantly with people anywhere on the planet. Yet we also continue to occupy our own little corners of life. Like those of our predecessors, our worlds, too, are marked by differences in family background, religion, job, gender, race–ethnicity, and social class. In these corners, we continue to learn distinctive ways of viewing the world.

One of the beautiful—and fascinating—aspects of sociology is that it enables us to analyze both parts of our current reality: that we are part of a global network *and* that we have unique experiences in our smaller corners of life. In this text, we shall examine both of these vital aspects of our lives.

Origins of Sociology

Tradition versus Science

Just how did sociology begin? Even ancient peoples tried to figure out social life. They, too, asked questions about why war exists, why some people become more powerful than others, and why some are rich, but others are poor. However, they often based their answers on superstition, myth, or even the position of the stars and did not *test* their assumptions.

Science, in contrast, requires theories that can be tested by research. Measured by this standard, sociology emerged about the middle of the 1800s, when social observers began to use scientific methods to test their ideas.

Sociology was born in social upheaval. The Industrial Revolution had just begun, and masses of people were moving to cities in search of work. This broke their ties to the land—and to a culture that had provided ready answers to the difficult questions of life. The city's greeting was harsh: miserable pay, long hours, and dangerous work. Families lived on the edge of starvation, so children had to work alongside the adults. With their ties to the land broken and their world turned upside down, no longer could people count on tradition to provide the answers to the difficult questions of life.

Tradition suffered further blows. With the success of the American and French revolutions, new ideas swept out the old. As the idea that individuals possess inalienable rights caught fire, many traditional Western monarchies gave way to more democratic forms of government. This stimulated even new perspectives.

About this time, the **scientific method**—using objective, systematic observations to test theories—was being tried out in chemistry and physics. This revealed many secrets that had been concealed in nature. With traditional answers falling, the next step was to apply the scientific method to questions about social life. The result was the birth of sociology.

Let's take a quick overview of some of the main figures in this development.

Auguste Comte and Positivism

Auguste Comte (1798–1857) suggested that we apply the scientific method to the social world, a process known as **positivism.** Reflecting on the upheavals of the French Revolution and on the changes he experienced when he moved

scientific method the use of objective, systematic observations to test theories

positivism the application of the scientific approach to the social world

Upsetting the entire social order, the French Revolution removed the past as a sure guide to the present. This stimulated Auguste Comte to analyze how societies change. Shown here is the 1793 Battle of Cholet.

Paul Emile Boutigny/The Bridgeman Art Library/
Getty Images

What is the origin of sociology?

Auguste Comte (1798–1857), who is credited as the founder of sociology, began to analyze the bases of the social order. Although he stressed that the scientific method should be applied to the study of society, he did not apply it himself.

© Roger-Viollet/The Image Works

to Paris from the small town in which he had grown up, Comte wondered what holds society together. He began to ask what creates social order, instead of anarchy or chaos, and why, once society becomes set on a particular course, what causes it to change.

Comte decided that the scientific method held the key to answering such questions. Just as the scientific method had revealed the law of gravity, so, too, it would uncover the laws that underlie society. Comte called this new science **sociology**— "the study of society" (from the Greek *logos*, "study of," and the Latin *socius*, "companion," or "being with others"). The purpose of this new science, he said, would be not only to discover social principles but also to apply them to social reform. Comte developed a grandiose view: Sociologists would reform the entire society, making it a better place to live.

Comte did not do what we today call research, and his conclusions have been abandoned. But because he proposed that we observe and classify human activities to uncover society's fundamental laws and coined the term *sociology* to describe this process, Comte often is credited with being the founder of sociology.

Herbert Spencer and Social Darwinism

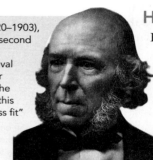

Herbert Spencer (1820–1903), sometimes called the second founder of sociology, coined the term "survival of the fittest." Spencer thought that helping the poor was wrong, that this merely helped the "less fit" survive.

© Huton-Deutsch Collection/Corbis

Herbert Spencer (1820–1903), who grew up in England, is sometimes called the second founder of sociology. Spencer's views were quite different. He said that sociology should *not* guide social reform. Societies are evolving, going from lower ("barbarian") to higher ("civilized") forms. As generations pass, a society's most capable and intelligent ("the fittest") members survive, while the less capable die out. These fittest members produce a more advanced society—unless misguided do-gooders get in the way and help the less fit (the lower classes) survive.

Spencer called this principle the *survival of the fittest*. Although Spencer coined this phrase, it usually is attributed to his contemporary, Charles Darwin, who proposed that organisms evolve over time as they adapt to their environment. Where Spencer referred to the evolution of societies, Darwin referred to the evolution of organisms. Because Darwin is better known, Spencer's idea is called *social Darwinism*. History is fickle, and if fame had gone the other way, we might be speaking of "biological Spencerism."

Like Comte, Spencer did armchair philosophy instead of conducting scientific studies, and his ideas, too, were discarded.

Karl Marx and Class Conflict

Karl Marx (1818–1883) believed that the roots of human misery lay in class conflict, the exploitation of workers by those who own the means of production. Social change, in the form of the workers overthrowing the capitalists, was inevitable from Marx's perspective. Although Marx did not consider himself a sociologist, his ideas have influenced many sociologists, particularly conflict theorists.

© Bettmann/Corbis

Karl Marx (1818–1883) influenced not only sociology but also world history. Marx's influence has been so great that even the *Wall Street Journal*, that staunch advocate of capitalism, has called him one of the three greatest modern thinkers (the other two being Sigmund Freud and Albert Einstein).

Like Comte, Marx thought that people should try to change society. His proposal for change was radical: revolution. This got him thrown out of Germany, and he settled in England. Marx believed that the engine of human history is **class conflict.** Society is made up of two social classes, he said, and they are natural enemies: the **bourgeoisie** (boo-shwa-ZEE) (the *capitalists,* those who own the capital, land, factories, and machines) and the **proletariat** (the exploited workers). Eventually, the workers will unite and break their chains of bondage. The revolution will be bloody, but it will usher in a classless society, one free of exploitation. People will work according to their abilities and receive goods and services according to their needs (Marx and Engels 1848/1967).

Marxism is not the same as communism. Although Marx proposed revolution as the way for workers to gain control of society, he did not develop the political system called *communism.* This is a later application of his ideas. Marx himself was disgusted when

sociology the scientific study of society and human behavior

class conflict Marx's term for the struggle between capitalists and workers

bourgeoisie Marx's term for capitalists, those who own the means of production

proletariat Marx's term for the exploited class, the mass of workers who do not own the means of production

Why is Comte called the founder of sociology? What is social Darwinism? Why is Marx known as a sociologist?

he heard debates about his analysis of social life. After listening to some of the positions attributed to him, he shook his head and said, "I am not a Marxist" (Dobriner 1969b:222; Gitlin 1997:89).

Emile Durkheim and Social Integration

The primary professional goal of Emile Durkheim (1858–1917), who grew up in France, was to get sociology recognized as a separate academic discipline (Coser 1977). Until Durkheim's time, sociology was viewed as part of history and economics. Durkheim achieved his goal in 1887 when the University of Bordeaux awarded him the world's first academic appointment in sociology.

Durkheim's second goal was to show how social forces affect people's behavior. To accomplish this, he conducted rigorous research. Comparing the suicide rates of several European countries, Durkheim (1897/1966) found that each country has a different suicide rate—and that these rates remain about the same year after year. He also found that different groups within a country have different suicide rates and that these, too, remain stable from year to year: Males are more likely than females to kill themselves, Protestants more likely than Catholics or Jews, and the unmarried more likely than the married. From these observations, Durkheim concluded that suicide is not what it appears—individuals here and there deciding to take their lives for personal reasons. Instead, *social factors underlie suicide,* which is why a group's rate remains fairly constant year after year.

Durkheim identified **social integration,** the degree to which people are tied to their social groups, as a key social factor in suicide. He concluded that people who have weaker social ties are more likely to commit suicide. This, he said, explains why Protestants, males, and the unmarried have higher suicide rates. This is how it works: Protestantism encourages greater freedom of thought and action; males are more independent than females; and the unmarried lack the ties that come with marriage. In other words, members of these groups have fewer of the social bonds that keep people from committing suicide. In Durkheim's term, they have less social integration.

Despite the many years that have passed since Durkheim did his research, the principle he uncovered still applies: People who are less socially integrated have higher rates of suicide. Even today, those same groups that Durkheim identified—Protestants, males, and the unmarried—are more likely to kill themselves.

It is important for you to understand the principle that was central in Durkheim's research: Human behavior cannot be understood only in terms of the individual; we need to examine the social forces that affect people's lives. Suicide, for example, appears to be such an intensely individual act that psychologists should study it, not sociologists. As Durkheim stressed, however, if we look at human behavior only in reference to the individual, we miss its social basis.

To better understand what Durkheim meant, look at Figure 1, which shows the methods by which African Americans and whites commit suicide. I'm sure you'll be struck by how similar their methods are.

The French sociologist **Emile Durkheim** (1858–1917) contributed many important concepts to sociology. His comparison of the suicide rates of several countries revealed an underlying social factor: People are more likely to commit suicide if their ties to others in their communities are weak. Durkheim's identification of the key role of *social integration* in social life remains central to sociology today.

© Bettmann/Corbis

social integration the degree to which members of a group or a society feel united by shared values and other social bonds; also known as *social cohesion*

© Joanne Ciccarello/Christian Science Monitor/ The Image Works

© Jamie Carstairs/Impact/HIP/The Image Works

Durkheim believed that modern societies produce feelings of isolation, much of which comes from the division of labor. In contrast, members of traditional societies, who work alongside family and neighbors and participate in similar activities, experience a high degree of *social integration.* The photo on the left shows women preparing millet in Mali.

Why is suicide a topic for sociologists to study? How do the patterns of suicide reveal its *social* nature?

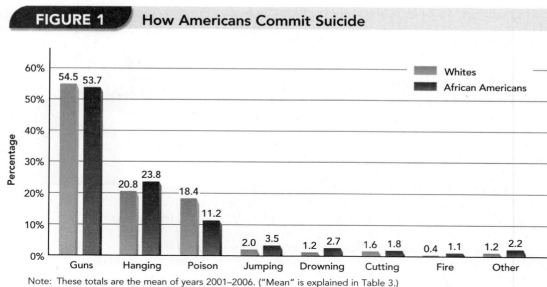

FIGURE 1 How Americans Commit Suicide

Note: These totals are the mean of years 2001–2006. ("Mean" is explained in Table 3.)
Source: By the author. Based on Centers for Disease Control and Prevention data.

It might surprise you that the patterns are so consistent that we can predict, with high accuracy, that 29,000 whites and 2,000 African Americans will commit suicide this year. The patterns are so repetitive and precise that we can also predict that of the 29,000 whites about 15,500 will use guns to kill themselves, and that of the 2,000 African Americans 60 to 70 will jump to their deaths. Since these patterns of the number of people who commit suicide and the ways they do so recur year after year, they indicate something far beyond the individuals who kill themselves. They reflect conditions in society, such as the popularity and accessibility of guns. They also reflect conditions that we don't understand. I'm hoping that one day this text will pique a student's interest enough to investigate these patterns.

Max Weber and the Protestant Ethic

Max Weber (Mahx VAY-ber) (1864–1920), a German sociologist and a contemporary of Durkheim, also became a professor in the new academic discipline of sociology. With Durkheim and Marx, Weber is one of the three most influential sociologists, and you will come across his writings and theories in later chapters. For now, let's consider an issue Weber raised that remains controversial today.

Religion and the Origin of Capitalism.   Weber disagreed with Marx's claim that economics is the central force in social change. That role, he said, belongs to religion. Here's how it works. Roman Catholics were taught that because they were church members they were on the road to heaven. This encouraged them to hold on to traditional ways of life. Protestants, in contrast, those of the Calvinist tradition, were told that they wouldn't know if they were saved until Judgment Day. Understandably, this teaching made them a little uncomfortable. Looking for "signs" that they were in God's will, the Calvinists concluded that financial success was a blessing, indicating that God was on their side. This motivated them to bring about this "sign" and receive spiritual comfort. They began to live frugal lives, saving their money, and investing it in order to make even more. A surprising result of religious teaching, then, was the birth of capitalism, which transformed society.

Weber (1904/1958) called this self-denying approach to life the *Protestant ethic*. He termed the readiness to invest capital in order to make more money the *spirit of capitalism*. To test his theory, Weber compared

Max Weber (1864–1920) was another early sociologist who left a profound impression on sociology. He used cross-cultural and historical materials to trace the causes of social change and to determine how social groups affect people's orientations to life.

The Granger Collection, New York

According to Weber, how did religion produce capitalism?

the extent of capitalism in Roman Catholic and Protestant countries. In line with his theory, he found that capitalism was more likely to flourish in Protestant countries. Weber's conclusion that religion was the key factor in the rise of capitalism was controversial when he made it, and it continues to be debated today (Cantoni 2009).

Sociology in North America

Now let's turn to the development of sociology on this side of the Atlantic Ocean.

Sexism at the Time: Women in Early Sociology

As you may have noticed, all the sociologists we have discussed are men. In the 1800s, sex roles were rigid, with women assigned the roles of wife and mother. In the classic German phrase, women were expected to devote themselves to the four K's: *Kirche, Küchen, Kinder, und Kleider* (the four C's in English: church, cooking, children, and clothes). To try to break out of this mold meant risking severe disapproval.

Few people, male or female, attained any education beyond basic reading and writing and a little math. Higher education, for the rare few who received it, was reserved primarily for men. Of the handful of women who did pursue higher education, some became prominent in early sociology. Marion Talbot, for example, was an associate editor of the *American Journal of Sociology* for thirty years, from its founding in 1895 to 1925. The influence of some early female sociologists went far beyond sociology. Grace Abbott became the first chief of the U.S. government's Children's Bureau, and Frances Perkins was the first woman to hold a cabinet position, serving twelve years as Secretary of Labor under President Franklin Roosevelt. The photo wheel on the next page portrays some of these early sociologists.

The writings of early female sociologists—and their matching social activism—were directed almost exclusively at social reform. They worked to find ways to improve working conditions, relieve poverty, stop lynching, and help integrate immigrants into society. As sociology developed in North America, a debate arose about the proper purpose of sociology: Should it be social reform or objective analysis? At that time, the debate was won by those who held the university positions. These men then wrote the history of sociology. Distancing themselves from the social reformers, they ignored the early female sociologists (Lengermann and Niebrugge 2007). Now that women have again become a voice in sociology—and have begun to rewrite its history—early female sociologists are again, as here, being acknowledged.

Harriet Martineau (1802–1876) provides a classic example of how the contributions of early female sociologists were ignored. Although Martineau was from England, she is included here because she did extensive analyses of U.S. social customs. Sexism was so pervasive that when Martineau first began to analyze social life, she would hide her writing beneath her sewing when visitors arrived, for writing was "masculine" and sewing "feminine" (Gilman 1911:88). Martineau persisted in her interests, however, and eventually she studied social life in both Great Britain and the United States. In 1837, two or three decades before Durkheim and Weber were born, Martineau published *Society in America,* a book that is still worth reading today. Despite her insightful analysis of this new nation's customs—family, race, gender, politics, and religion—Martineau met the same fate as the other early female sociologists and her research was ignored. Until recently, she was known primarily for translating Comte's ideas into English.

Racism at the Time: W. E. B. Du Bois

Not only was sexism assumed to be normal during this early period of sociology, but so was racism, which made life difficult for African American professionals such as W. E. B. Du Bois (1868–1963). Du Bois, who became the first African American to earn a doctorate at Harvard, also studied at the University of Berlin, where he attended lectures by Max Weber. In 1897,

W(illiam) **E**(dward) **B**(urghardt) **Du Bois** (1868–1963) spent his lifetime studying relations between African Americans and whites. Like many early North American sociologists, Du Bois combined the role of academic sociologist with that of social reformer.

© The New York Public Library/Art Resource, NY

What role did women play in early sociology?

FIGURE 2   The Forgotten Sociologists

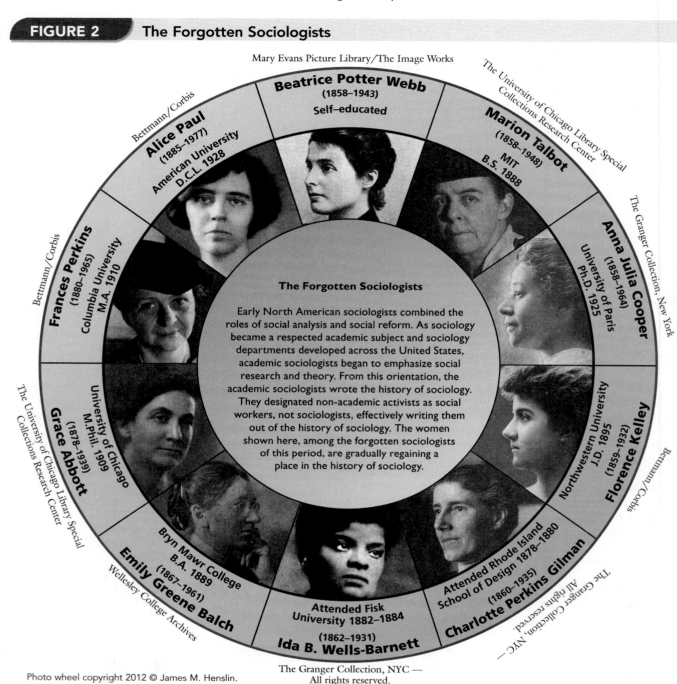

Mary Evans Picture Library/The Image Works

Beatrice Potter Webb
(1858–1943)
Self–educated

The University of Chicago Library Special
Collections Research Center

Marion Talbot
(1858–1948)
MIT
B.S. 1888

Bettmann/Corbis

Alice Paul
(1885–1977)
American University
D.C.L. 1928

The Granger Collection, New York

Anna Julia Cooper
(1858–1964)
University of Paris
Ph.D. 1925

Bettmann/Corbis

Frances Perkins
(1880–1965)
Columbia University
M.A. 1910

Northwestern University
J.D. 1895
Florence Kelley
(1859–1932)

Bettmann/Corbis

The University of Chicago Library Special
Collections Research Center

Grace Abbott
(1878–1939)
University of Chicago
M.Phil. 1909

Wellesley College Archives

Emily Greene Balch
(1867–1961)
Bryn Mawr College
B.A. 1889

Ida B. Wells-Barnett
(1862–1931)
Attended Fisk
University 1882–1884

Attended Rhode Island
School of Design 1878–1880
Charlotte Perkins Gilman
(1860–1935)

The Granger Collection, NYC —

The Forgotten Sociologists

Early North American sociologists combined the roles of social analysis and social reform. As sociology became a respected academic subject and sociology departments developed across the United States, academic sociologists began to emphasize social research and theory. From this orientation, the academic sociologists wrote the history of sociology. They designated non-academic activists as social workers, not sociologists, effectively writing them out of the history of sociology. The women shown here, among the forgotten sociologists of this period, are gradually regaining a place in the history of sociology.

Photo wheel copyright 2012 © James M. Henslin.

The Granger Collection, NYC —

Du Bois went to Atlanta University, where he remained for most of his career. You can get a flavor of this period from the Down-to-Earth Sociology box on the next page.

It is difficult to grasp how racist society was at this time. As Du Bois passed a butcher shop in Georgia one day, he saw the fingers of a lynching victim displayed in the window (Aptheker 1990). When Du Bois went to national meetings of the American Sociological Society, restaurants and hotels would not allow him to eat or room with the white sociologists. How times have changed. Today, sociologists would not only boycott such establishments, but also refuse to hold meetings in that state. At that time,

What was the role of women in early sociology?

Down-to-Earth Sociology

W. E. B. Du Bois: The Souls of Black Folk

Du Bois wrote more like an accomplished novelist than a sociologist. The following excerpt is from pages 66–68 of *The Souls of Black Folk* (1903). In this book, Du Bois analyzes changes that occurred in the social and economic conditions of African Americans during the thirty years following the Civil War.

For two summers, while he was a student at Fisk University, Du Bois taught in a segregated school housed in a log hut "way back in the hills" of rural Tennessee. The following excerpts help us understand conditions at that time.

It was a hot morning late in July when the school opened. I trembled when I heard the patter of little feet down the dusty road, and saw the growing row of dark solemn faces and bright eager eyes facing me. . . . There they sat, nearly thirty of them, on the rough benches, their faces shading from a pale cream to deep brown, the little feet bare and swinging, the eyes full of expectation, with here and there a twinkle of mischief, and the hands grasping Webster's blue-black spelling-book. I loved my school, and the fine faith the children had in the wisdom of their teacher was truly marvelous. We read and spelled together, wrote a little, picked flowers, sang, and listened to stories of the world beyond the hill. . . .

On Friday nights I often went home with some of the children—sometimes to Doc Burke's farm. He was a great, loud, thin Black, ever working, and trying to buy these seventy-five acres of hill and dale where he lived; but people said that he would surely fail and the "white folks would get it all." His wife was a magnificent Amazon, with saffron face and shiny hair, uncorseted and barefooted, and the children were strong and barefooted. They lived in a one-and-a-half-room cabin in the hollow of the farm near the spring. . . .

Often, to keep the peace, I must go where life was less lovely; for instance, 'Tildy's mother was incorrigibly

In the 1800s, most people, no matter their race–ethnicity—were poor, and formal education beyond the first several grades was a luxury. This photo depicts the conditions of the people Du Bois worked with.
© Everett Collection/SuperStock

dirty, Reuben's larder was limited seriously, and herds of untamed insects wandered over the Eddinges' beds. Best of all I loved to go to Josie's, and sit on the porch, eating peaches, while the mother bustled and talked: how Josie had bought the sewing-machine; how Josie worked at service in winter, but that four dollars a month was "mighty little" wages; how Josie longed to go away to school, but that it "looked liked" they never could get far enough ahead to let her; how the crops failed and the well was yet unfinished; and, finally, how mean some of the white folks were.

For two summers I lived in this little world. . . . I have called my tiny community a world, and so its isolation made it; and yet there was among us but a half-awakened common consciousness, sprung from common joy and grief, at burial, birth, or wedding; from common hardship in poverty, poor land, and low wages, and, above all, from the sight of the Veil* that hung between us and Opportunity. All this caused us to think some thoughts together; but these, when ripe for speech, were spoken in various languages. Those whose eyes twenty-five and more years had seen "the glory of the coming of the Lord," saw in every present hindrance or help a dark fatalism bound to bring all things right in His own good time. The mass of those to whom slavery was a dim recollection of childhood found the world a puzzling thing: it asked little of them, and they answered with little, and yet it ridiculed their offering. Such a paradox they could not understand, and therefore sank into listless indifference, or shiftlessness, or reckless bravado.

*"The Veil" is shorthand for the Veil of Race, referring to how race colors all human relations. Du Bois' hope, as he put it, was that "sometime, somewhere, men will judge men by their souls and not by their skins" (p. 261).

For Your Consideration

→ What findings would you expect if women had been included in this study?

however, racism, like sexism, prevailed throughout society, rendering it mostly invisible to white sociologists.

Du Bois did extensive research, for about twenty or so years publishing a book a year on black–white relations. He was also a social activist. Along with Jane Addams and others from Hull-House, Du Bois founded the National Association for the Advancement of Colored People (NAACP). Continuing to battle racism both as a sociologist and as a journalist, Du Bois eventually embraced revolutionary Marxism. He

Under what historical conditions did Du Bois do his research?

became such an outspoken critic of racism that for years the U.S. State Department, fearing he would criticize the United States, refused to issue him a passport (Du Bois 1968). At age 93, dismayed that so little improvement had been made in race relations, he moved to Ghana, where he died and is buried (Stark 1989).

Jane Addams: Sociologist and Social Reformer

Jane Addams (1860–1935) a recipient of the Nobel Prize for Peace, worked on behalf of poor immigrants. With Ellen G. Starr, she founded Hull-House, a center to help immigrants in Chicago. She was also a leader in women's rights (women's suffrage), as well as the peace movement of World War I.

The Granger Collection, New York

Of the many early sociologists who combined the role of sociologist with that of social reformer, none was as successful as Jane Addams (1860–1935), who was a member of the American Sociological Society from its founding in 1905. Like Harriet Martineau, Addams, too, came from a background of wealth and privilege. She attended the Women's Medical College of Philadelphia, but dropped out because of illness (Addams 1910/1981). On a trip to Europe, Addams saw the work being done to help London's poor. The memory wouldn't leave her, she said, and she decided to work for social justice.

In 1889, Addams co-founded Hull-House with Ellen Gates Starr. Located in Chicago's notorious slums, Hull-House was open to people who needed refuge—to immigrants, the sick, the aged, the poor. Sociologists from the nearby University of Chicago were frequent visitors at Hull-House. With her piercing insights into the exploitation of workers and the adjustment of rural immigrants to city life, Addams strove to bridge the gap between the powerful and the powerless. She co-founded the American Civil Liberties Union and campaigned for the eight-hour workday and for laws against child labor. She wrote books on poverty, democracy, and peace. Adams' writings and efforts at social reform were so outstanding that in 1931, she was a co-winner of the Nobel Prize for Peace. She and Emily Greene Balch are the only sociologists to have won this coveted award.

Talcott Parsons and C. Wright Mills: Theory versus Reform

C. Wright Mills was a controversial figure in sociology because of his analysis of the role of the power elite in U.S. society. Today, his analysis is taken for granted by many sociologists and members of the public.

Photo by Yaroslava Mills

Like Du Bois and Addams, many early North American sociologists worked toward the reform of society, but by the 1940s the emphasis had shifted to social theory. Talcott Parsons (1902–1979), for example, a major sociologist of this period, developed abstract models of society that influenced a generation of sociologists. Deploring Parsons' theoretical abstractions and the general dry analyses of this period, C. Wright Mills (1916–1962) urged sociologists to get back to social reform. He said that sociologists were missing the point, that our freedom was threatened by the coalescing interests of a group he called the *power elite*—the top leaders of business, politics, and the military. Shortly after Mills' death came the turbulent 1960s and 1970s. This precedent-shaking era sparked interest in social activism, making Mills' ideas popular among a new generation of sociologists.

The Continuing Tension and Applied Sociology

Basic Sociology.   As we have seen, two contradictory aims—analyzing society versus working toward its reform—have run through North American sociology since its founding. This tension is still with us. Some sociologists see their proper role as doing **basic (or pure) sociology,** analyzing some aspect of society and publishing their findings in books and sociology journals. Others reply, "Knowledge for what?" They argue that sociologists have an obligation to use their expertise to try to help reform society, especially to help bring justice to the poor and oppressed.

basic or pure sociology sociological research for the purpose of making discoveries about life in human groups, not for making changes in those groups

applied sociology the use of sociology to solve problems—from the micro level of classroom interaction and family relationships to the macro level of crime and pollution

Applied Sociology.   As Figure 3 shows, somewhere between these extremes lies **applied sociology,** using sociology to solve problems. Applied sociology is not new, for as we've seen, sociologists founded the NAACP. Although today's applied sociologists lack the early sociologists' broad vision of social reform, their application of sociology is

What is Addams place in early sociology? What does "theory versus reform" mean?

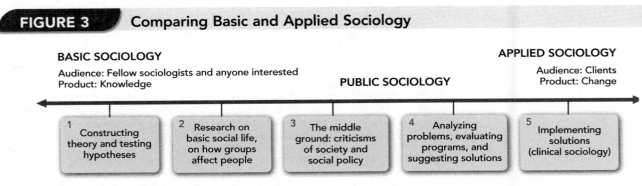

FIGURE 3 Comparing Basic and Applied Sociology

BASIC SOCIOLOGY
Audience: Fellow sociologists and anyone interested
Product: Knowledge

PUBLIC SOCIOLOGY

APPLIED SOCIOLOGY
Audience: Clients
Product: Change

1 Constructing theory and testing hypotheses

2 Research on basic social life, on how groups affect people

3 The middle ground: criticisms of society and social policy

4 Analyzing problems, evaluating programs, and suggesting solutions

5 Implementing solutions (clinical sociology)

Source: By the author. Based on DeMartini 1982, plus events since then.

wide-ranging. Some work for business firms to solve problems in the workplace, while others investigate social problems such as pornography, rape, pollution, or the spread of AIDS. A new application of sociology is determining ways to disrupt terrorist groups (Sageman 2008a).

Public Sociology. To get sociologists to apply sociology in a broader way, the American Sociological Association (ASA) is promoting a middle ground between research and reform called **public sociology.** By this term, the ASA refers to harnessing the sociological perspective for the benefit of the public. Of special interest to the ASA is getting politicians and policy makers to apply the sociological understanding of how society works as they develop social policy (American Sociological Association 2004). Public sociology would incorporate both items 3 and 4 of Figure 3.

With roots that go back a century or more, this debate about the purpose and use of sociology is likely to continue for another generation. At this point, let's consider how theory fits into sociology.

Theoretical Perspectives in Sociology

Facts never interpret themselves. To make sense out of life, we use our common sense. That is, to understand our experiences (our "facts"), we place them into what we "know" about social life, a framework of more-or-less related ideas. Sociologists do this, too, but they place their observations into a conceptual framework called a theory. A **theory** is a general statement about how some parts of the world fit together and how they work. It is an explanation of how two or more "facts" are related to one another.

Sociologists use three major theories: symbolic interactionism, functional analysis, and conflict theory. As we look at each theory, we will first examine its main elements and then apply it to the U.S. divorce rate, to see why it is so high. As we do this, you will see how each theory, or perspective, provides a distinct interpretation of social life.

Symbolic Interactionism

The central idea of **symbolic interactionism** is that *symbols*—things to which we attach meaning—are the key to understanding how we view the world and communicate with one another. Charles Horton Cooley (1864–1929) and George Herbert Mead (1863–1931) developed this perspective in sociology. Let's look at the main elements of this theory.

Symbols in Everyday Life. Without symbols, our social life would be no more sophisticated than that of animals. For example, without symbols we would have no aunts or uncles, employers or teachers—or even brothers and sisters. I know that this sounds strange, but it is symbols that define our relationships. There would still be reproduction, of course, but no symbols to tell us how we are related to whom. We would not know

public sociology applying sociology for the public good; especially the use of the sociological perspective (how things are related to one another) to guide politicians and policy makers

theory a general statement about how some parts of the world fit together and how they work; an explanation of how two or more facts are related to one another

symbolic interactionism a theoretical perspective in which society is viewed as composed of symbols that people use to establish meaning, develop their views of the world, and communicate with one another

George Herbert Mead (1863–1931) is one of the founders of symbolic interactionism, a major theoretical perspective in sociology. He taught at the University of Chicago, where his lectures were popular. Although he wrote little, after his death students compiled his lectures into an influential book, *Mind, Self, and Society.*

University of Chicago

Can you compare basic and applied sociology? What is public sociology?

to whom we owe respect and obligations, or from whom we can expect privileges—the essence of human relationships.

I know it is vague to say that symbols tell you how you are related to others and how you should act toward them, so let's make this less abstract:

Suppose that you have fallen head over heels in love. Finally, after what seems forever, it is the night before your wedding. As you are contemplating tomorrow's bliss, your mother comes to you in tears. Sobbing, she tells you that she had a child before she married your father, a child that she gave up for adoption. Breaking down, she says that she has just discovered that the person you are going to marry is this child.

You can see how the symbol will change overnight—and your behavior, too!

The symbols of boyfriend and brother—or girlfriend and sister—are certainly different, and, as you know, each symbol requires rather different behavior.

Not only do relationships depend on symbols, but so does society itself. Without symbols, we could not coordinate our actions with those of others. We could not make plans for a future day, time, and place. Unable to specify times, materials, sizes, or goals, we could not build bridges and highways. Without symbols, we would have no movies or musical instruments, no hospitals, no government, no religion. The class you are taking could not exist—nor could this book. On the positive side, there would be no war.

In Sum: Symbolic interactionists analyze how social life depends on the ways we define ourselves and others. They study face-to-face interaction, examining how people make sense out of life, how they determine their relationships.

Applying Symbolic Interactionism.   Look at Figure 4, which shows U.S. marriages and divorces over time. Let's see how symbolic interactionists would use changing symbols to explain this figure. For background, you should understand that marriage used to be a *lifelong commitment*. A hundred years ago (and less) getting divorced was viewed as immoral, a flagrant disregard for public opinion, and the abandonment of adult responsibilities. Let's see what changed.

The meaning of marriage: In the 1930s and 1940s, sociologists reported that views of marriage were changing. In 1933, William Ogburn observed that young people were

FIGURE 4   **U.S. Marriage, U.S. Divorce**

Source: By the author. Based on *Statistical Abstract of the United States* 1998:Table 92 and 2011:Tables 78, 129; earlier editions for earlier years. The broken lines indicate the author's estimates.

How do symbols (meaning) underlie our behavior? How do symbols affect the divorce rate?

placing more emphasis on the personality of their potential mates. Then in 1945, Ernest Burgess and Harvey Locke noted that couples were expecting more affection, understanding, and compatibility in marriage. As young people of this time began to view marriage as an arrangement based on attraction and feelings of intimacy—instead of a lifelong commitment based on duty and obligation—marriage became a relationship that could be broken when feelings changed.

The meaning of divorce: As divorce became more common, its meaning also changed. Rather than being a symbol of failure, divorce came to indicate freedom and new beginnings. Removing the stigma from divorce shattered a strong barrier that had prevented husbands and wives from breaking up.

The meaning of parenthood: Parents used to have little responsibility for their children beyond providing food, clothing, shelter, and moral guidance. And they needed to do this for only a short time, because children began to contribute to the support of the family early in life. Among many people, parenthood is still like this. In Colombia, for example, children of the poor often are expected to support themselves by the age of 8 or 10. In industrial societies, however, we assume that children are vulnerable beings who must depend on their parents for financial and emotional support for many years—often until they are well into their 20s. The greater responsibilities that we assign to parenthood place heavy burdens on today's couples and, with them, more strain on marriage.

The meaning of love: And we can't overlook the love symbol. As surprising as it may sound, to have love as the main reason for marriage weakens marriage. In some depth of our being, we expect "true love" to deliver constant feelings of intimacy accompanied by emotional highs. This expectation sets people up for crushed hopes, as dissatisfactions in marriage are inevitable. When they come, spouses tend to blame one another for failing to deliver the expected satisfaction.

In Sum: Symbolic interactionists look at how changing ideas (or symbols) of love, marriage, parenthood, and divorce put pressure on married couples. No single change is *the* cause of our divorce rate, but, taken together, these changes provide a strong push toward divorce.

Functional Analysis

The central idea of **functional analysis** is that society is a whole unit, made up of interrelated parts that work together. Functional analysis (also known as *functionalism* and *structural functionalism*) is rooted in the origins of sociology. Auguste Comte and Herbert Spencer viewed society as a kind of living organism. Just as a person or animal has organs that function together, they wrote, so does society. And like an organism, if society is to function smoothly, its parts must work together in harmony.

Emile Durkheim also viewed society as being composed of many parts, each with its own function. When all the parts of society fulfill their functions, society is in a "normal" state. If they do not fulfill their functions, society is in an "abnormal" or "pathological" state. To understand society, then, functionalists say that we need to look at both *structure* (how the parts of a society fit together to make the whole) and *function* (what each part does, how it contributes to society).

Robert Merton and Functionalism. Robert Merton (1910–2003) dismissed the organic analogy, but he did maintain the essence of functionalism—the image of society as a whole composed of parts that work together. Merton used the term *functions* to refer to the beneficial consequences of people's actions: Functions help keep a group (society, social system) in balance. In contrast, *dysfunctions* are consequences that harm a society: They undermine a system's equilibrium.

Functions can be either manifest or latent. If an action is *intended* to help some part of a system, it is a *manifest function*. For example, suppose that government officials become concerned about our low rate of childbirth. Congress offers a $10,000 bonus for every child born to a married couple. The intention, or manifest

functional analysis a theoretical framework in which society is viewed as composed of various parts, each with a function that, when fulfilled, contributes to society's equilibrium; also known as *functionalism* and *structural functionalism*

Pictorial Parade/Getty Images

Robert K. Merton (1910–2003), who spent most of his academic career at Columbia University, was a major proponent of functionalism, one of the main theoretical perspectives in sociology.

How do functional analysts explain the divorce rate?

function, of the bonus is to increase childbearing within the family unit. Merton pointed out that people's actions can also have *latent functions;* that is, they can have *unintended* consequences that help a system adjust. Let's suppose that the bonus works. As the birth rate jumps, so does the sale of diapers and baby furniture. Because the benefits to these businesses were not the intended consequences, they are latent functions of the bonus.

Of course, human actions can also hurt a system. Because such consequences usually are unintended, Merton called them *latent dysfunctions.* Let's assume that the government has failed to specify a "stopping point" with regard to its bonus system. To collect more bonuses, some people keep on having children. The more children they have, however, the more they need the next bonus to survive. Large families become common, and poverty increases. Welfare is reinstated, taxes jump, and the nation erupts in protest. Because these results were not intended and because they harmed the social system, they would be latent dysfunctions of the bonus program.

In Sum: From the perspective of functional analysis, society is a functioning unit, with each part related to the whole. Whenever we examine a smaller part, we need to look for its functions and dysfunctions to see how it is related to the larger unit. This basic approach can be applied to any social group, whether an entire society, a college, or even a group as small as a family.

Applying Functional Analysis.   Now let's apply functional analysis to the U.S. divorce rate. Functionalists stress that industrialization and urbanization undermined the traditional functions of the family. For example, before industrialization, the family formed an economic team. On the farm where most people lived, each family member had jobs

Sociologists who use the *functionalist perspective* stress how industrialization and urbanization undermined the traditional *functions* of the family. Before industrialization, members of the family worked together as an economic unit, as in this photo of a farm family in Nebraska in the 1890s. As production moved away from the home, it took with it first the father and, more recently, the mother. One consequence is a major dysfunction, the weakening of family ties.

Bettmann/CORBIS

What would functionalists say that industrialization has to do with the divorce rate?

or "chores" to do. The wife was in charge not only of household tasks but also of raising small animals, such as chickens. Milking cows, collecting eggs, and churning butter were also her responsibility—as were cooking, baking, canning, sewing, darning, washing, and cleaning. The daughters helped her. The husband was responsible for caring for large animals, such as horses and cattle, for planting and harvesting, and for maintaining buildings and tools. The sons helped him.

This certainly doesn't sound like life today! But what does it have to do with divorce? Simply put, the husband and wife depended on each other for survival—and there weren't many alternatives.

Other functions also bound family members to one another: educating the children, teaching them religion, providing home-based recreation, and caring for the sick and elderly. To see how sharply family functions have changed, look at this example from the 1800s:

When Phil became sick, Ann, his wife, cooked for him, fed him, changed the bed linens, bathed him, read to him from the Bible, and gave him his medicine. (She did this in addition to doing the housework and taking care of their six children.) Phil was also surrounded by the children, who shouldered some of his chores while he was sick. When Phil died, the male relatives made the casket while Ann, her sisters, and mother washed and dressed the body. Phil was "laid out" in the front parlor (the formal living room), where friends, neighbors, and relatives paid their last respects. From there, friends moved his body to the church for the final message and then to the grave they themselves had dug.

In Sum: When the family loses functions, it becomes more fragile, and the divorce rate increases. Economic production is an excellent example of how the family has lost functions. No longer is making a living a cooperative, home-based effort, where husband and wife depend on one another for their interlocking contributions to a mutual endeavor. In contrast, husbands and wives today earn individual paychecks and increasingly function as separate components in an impersonal, multinational, and even global system. The fewer functions that family members share, the fewer are their "ties that bind"—and these ties are what help husbands and wives get through the problems they inevitably experience.

Conflict Theory

Conflict theory provides a third perspective on social life. Unlike the functionalists, who view society as a harmonious whole, with its parts working together, conflict theorists stress that the groups that make up society are competing with one another for scarce resources. Although the surface may show alliances or cooperation, scratch that surface and you will find a struggle for power.

Karl Marx and Conflict Theory. Karl Marx, the founder of conflict theory, witnessed the Industrial Revolution that transformed Europe. He saw that the peasants who had left the land to find work in cities had to work for wages that barely provided enough to eat. Things were so bad that the average worker died at age 30, the average wealthy person at age 50 (Edgerton 1992:87). Shocked by this suffering and exploitation, Marx began to analyze society and history. As he did so, he developed **conflict theory.** He concluded that the key to human history is *class conflict.* In each society, some small group controls the means of production and exploits those who are not in control. In industrialized societies, the struggle is between the *bourgeoisie,* the small group of capitalists who own the means to produce wealth, and the *proletariat,* the mass of workers who are exploited by the bourgeoisie. The capitalists also control the legal and political system: If the workers rebel, the capitalists call on the power of the state to subdue them.

When Marx made his observations, capitalism was in its infancy and workers were at the mercy of their employers. Workers had none of what we take for granted today—minimum wages, eight-hour days, coffee breaks, five-day work weeks, paid vacations and

conflict theory a theoretical framework in which society is viewed as composed of groups that are competing for scarce resources

Can you explain how the loss of functions increases divorce?

17

holidays, medical benefits, sick leave, unemployment compensation, Social Security, and, for union workers, the right to strike. Marx's analysis reminds us that these benefits came not from generous hearts, but by workers forcing concessions from their employers.

Conflict Theory Today. Many sociologists extend conflict theory beyond the relationship of capitalists and workers. They examine how opposing interests permeate every layer of society—whether in a small group, an organization, a community, or the entire society. For example, when police, teachers, and parents try to enforce conformity, this creates resentment and resistance. It is the same when a teenager tries to "change the rules" to gain more independence. Throughout society, then, there is a constant struggle to determine who has authority or influence and how far that dominance goes (Turner 1978; Leeson 2006; Piven 2008).

Sociologist Lewis Coser (1913–2003) pointed out that conflict is most likely to develop among people who are in close relationships. These people have worked out ways to distribute power and privilege, responsibilities and rewards. Any change in this arrangement can lead to hurt feelings, resentment, and conflict. Even in intimate relationships, then, people are in a constant balancing act, with conflict lying uneasily just beneath the surface.

Feminists and Conflict Theory. Just as Marx examined conflict between capitalists and workers, many feminists analyze conflict between men and women. A primary focus is the historical, contemporary, and global inequalities of men and women—and how the traditional dominance by men can be overcome to bring about equality of the sexes. Feminists are not united by the conflict perspective, however. They tackle a variety of topics and use whatever theory applies.

Applying Conflict Theory. To explain why the U.S. divorce rate is high, conflict theorists focus on how men's and women's relationships have changed. For millennia, men dominated women. Women had few alternatives other than to accept that dominance. Then industrialization ushered in a new world, one in which women could meet their basic survival needs outside of marriage. Industrialization also fostered a culture in which females participate in social worlds beyond the home. With this new ability to refuse to bear burdens that earlier generations accepted as inevitable, today's women are likely to dissolve a marriage that becomes intolerable—or even unsatisfactory.

In Sum: The dominance of men over women was once considered natural and right. As women gained education and earnings, they first questioned and then rejected this assumption. As wives strove for more power and grew less inclined to put up with relationships that they felt were unfair, the divorce rate increased. From the conflict perspective, then, our high divorce rate does not mean that marriage has weakened, but, rather, that women are making headway in their historical struggle with men.

Putting the Theoretical Perspectives Together

Which of these theoretical perspectives is *the* right one? You have seen how each produces a contrasting picture of divorce and how the pictures that emerge are quite different from the commonsense understanding that two people are simply "incompatible." *Because each theory focuses on different features of social life, each provides a distinctive interpretation. Consequently, we need to use all three theoretical lenses to analyze human behavior. By combining the contributions of each, we gain a more comprehensive picture of social life.*

Levels of Analysis: Macro and Micro

A major difference among these three theoretical perspectives is their level of analysis. Functionalists and conflict theorists focus on the **macro level;** that is, they examine large-scale patterns of society. In contrast, symbolic interactionists usually focus on the **micro level,** on **social interaction**—what people do when they are in one another's presence. These levels are summarized in Table 1 on the next page.

macro-level analysis an examination of large-scale patterns of society

micro-level analysis an examination of small-scale patterns of society, such as how the members of a group interact

social interaction what people do when they are in one another's presence, but includes communications at a distance

Can you use conflict theory to explain why the U.S. divorce rate increased?

| TABLE 1 | Three Theoretical Perspectives in Sociology |

Theoretical Perspective	Usual Level of Analysis	Focus of Analysis	Key Terms	Applying the Perspective to the U.S. Divorce Rate
Symbolic Interactionism	Microsociological: examines small-scale patterns of social interaction	Face-to-face interaction, how people use symbols to create social life	Symbols Interaction Meanings Definitions	Industrialization and urbanization changed marital roles and led to a redefinition of love, marriage, children, and divorce.
Functional Analysis (also called functionalism and structural functionalism)	Macrosociological: examines large-scale patterns of society	Relationships among the parts of society; how these parts are functional (have beneficial consequences) or dysfunctional (have negative consequences)	Structure Functions (manifest and latent) Dysfunctions Equilibrium	As social change erodes the traditional functions of the family, family ties weaken, and the divorce rate increases.
Conflict Theory	Macrosociological: examines large-scale patterns of society	The struggle for scarce resources by groups in a society; how the elites use their power to control the weaker groups	Inequality Power Conflict Competition Exploitation	When men control economic life, the divorce rate is low because women find few alternatives to a bad marriage. The high divorce rate reflects a shift in the balance of power between men and women.

To make this distinction between micro and macro levels clearer, let's return to the example of the homeless, with which we opened this chapter. To study homeless people, symbolic interactionists would focus on the micro level. They would analyze what homeless people do when they are in shelters and on the streets. They would also analyze their communications, both their talk and their **nonverbal interaction** (gestures, use of space, and so on). The observations I made at the beginning of this chapter about the silence in the homeless shelter, for example, would be of interest to symbolic interactionists.

This micro level, however, would not interest functionalists and conflict theorists. They would focus instead on the macro level, how changes in society increase homelessness. Functionalists might focus on changes in the family—how because of divorce and small families many people who can't find work don't have others to fall back on. For their part, conflict theorists would stress the struggle between social classes. They would be interested in how decisions by international elites on global production and trade affect the local job market, and along with it unemployment and homelessness.

How Theory and Research Work Together

Theory cannot stand alone. As sociologist C. Wright Mills (1959) so forcefully argued, if theory isn't connected to research, it will be abstract and empty. It won't represent the way life really is. It is the same for research. Without theory, Mills said, research is also of little value; it is simply a collection of meaningless "facts."

Theory and research, then, go together like a hand and glove. Every theory must be tested, which requires research. And as sociologists do research, they often come up with surprising findings. Those findings must be explained, and for that, we need theory. As sociologists study social life, then, they combine research and theory.

And how do sociologists do research? Let's find out.

✳ Explore
Living Data
on **mysoclab.com**

nonverbal interaction communication without words through gestures, use of space, silence, and so on

Can you compare micro and macro sociology?

hypothesis a statement of how variables are expected to be related to one another, often according to predictions from a theory

variable a factor thought to be significant for human behavior, which can vary (or change) from one case to another

operational definition the way in which a researcher measures a variable

research method (or research design) one of seven procedures that sociologists use to collect data: surveys, participant observation, case studies, secondary analysis, documents, experiments, and unobtrusive measures

validity the extent to which an operational definition measures what it is intended to measure

reliability the extent to which research produces consistent or dependable results

Doing Sociological Research

Around the globe, people make assumptions about the way the world "is." Common sense, the things that "everyone knows are true," may or may not be true, however. It takes research to find out. Are you ready to test your own common sense? Take the little quiz on the next page.

To understand social life, we need to move beyond "common sense" and learn what is really going on. Let's look at how sociologists do their research.

A Research Model

As shown in Figure 5, scientific research follows eight basic steps. This is an ideal model, however, and in the real world of research some of these steps may run together. Some may even be omitted.

1. *Selecting a topic.* First, what do you want to know more about? Let's choose spouse abuse as our topic.
2. *Defining the problem.* The next step is to narrow the topic. Spouse abuse is too broad; we need to focus on a specific area. For example, you may want to know why men are more likely than women to be the abusers. Or perhaps you want to know what can be done to reduce domestic violence.
3. *Reviewing the literature.* You must review the literature to find out what has been published on the problem. You don't want to waste your time rediscovering what is already known.
4. *Formulating a hypothesis.* The fourth step is to formulate a **hypothesis,** a statement of what you expect to find according to predictions based on a theory. A hypothesis predicts a relationship between or among **variables,** factors that vary, or change, from one person or situation to another. For example, the statement "Men who are more socially isolated are likelier to abuse their wives than men who are more socially integrated" is a hypothesis.

Your hypothesis will need **operational definitions,** that is, precise ways to measure the variables. In this example, you would need operational definitions for three variables: social isolation, social integration, and spouse abuse.

5. *Choosing a research method.* The way you collect your data is called a **research method** or *research design.* Sociologists use seven basic research methods, which are outlined in the next section. You should choose the method that will best answer your particular questions.
6. *Collecting the data.* When you gather your data, you have to take care to ensure their **validity;** that is, your operational definitions must measure what they are intended to measure. In this case, you must be certain that you really are measuring social isolation, social integration, and spouse abuse—and not something else. Spouse abuse, for example, seems to be obvious. Yet what some people consider abusive is not regarded as abuse by others. Which definition will you choose? In other words, your operational definitions must be so precise that no one has any question about what you are measuring.

You must also be sure that your data are reliable. **Reliability** means that if other researchers use your operational definitions, their findings will be consistent with yours. If your operational definitions

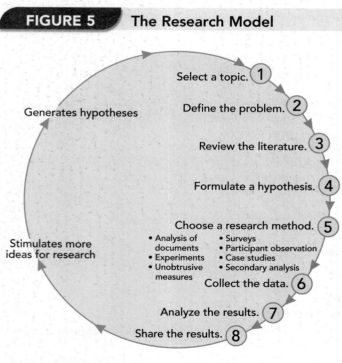

FIGURE 5 **The Research Model**

Select a topic. ①
Define the problem. ②
Review the literature. ③
Formulate a hypothesis. ④
Choose a research method. ⑤
- Analysis of documents
- Experiments
- Unobtrusive measures
- Surveys
- Participant observation
- Case studies
- Secondary analysis
Collect the data. ⑥
Analyze the results. ⑦
Share the results. ⑧

Generates hypotheses

Stimulates more ideas for research

Source: Adapted from Figure 2.2 of Schaefer 1989.

What is the basic research model that sociologists follow?

Down-to-Earth Sociology

Enjoying a Sociology Quiz—Sociological Findings versus Common Sense

Some findings of sociology support commonsense understandings of social life, and others contradict them. Can you tell the difference? To enjoy this quiz, complete *all* the questions before turning the page to check your answers.

1. **True/False** More U.S. students are killed in school shootings now than ten or fifteen years ago.
2. **True/False** The earnings of U.S. women have just about caught up with those of U.S. men.
3. **True/False** With life so rushed and more women working for wages, today's parents spend less time with their children than previous generations did.
4. **True/False** It is more dangerous to walk near topless bars than fast-food restaurants.
5. **True/False** Most rapists are mentally ill.
6. **True/False** A large percentage of terrorists are mentally ill.
7. **True/False** Most people on welfare are lazy and looking for a handout. They could work if they wanted to.
8. **True/False** Compared with women, men make more eye contact in face-to-face conversations.
9. **True/False** Couples who lived together before marriage are usually more satisfied with their marriage than couples who did not live together before marriage.
10. **True/False** Because bicyclists are more likely to wear helmets now than a few years ago, their rate of head injuries has dropped.

(Please answer all ten questions before turning the page.)

are sloppy, husbands who have committed the same act of violence might be included in some research but excluded in other studies. You would end up with erratic results. You might show a 5 percent rate of spouse abuse, but another researcher may conclude that it is 30 percent. This would make your research unreliable.

Because sociologists find all human behavior to be valid research topics, their research ranges from the macro level of the globalization of capitalism to the micro level of social interaction. Shown here is Tomatina, a tomato-throwing festival held each year at Buñon, Spain. Sociologists would study the leadership of the organization, relationship of visitors to townspeople, and the activities and interaction of the participants.

Biel Alino/epa/Corbis

Why do we need sociological research when we have common sense?

Down-to-Earth Sociology

Sociological Findings versus Common Sense—Answers to the Sociology Quiz

1. **False.** More students were shot to death at U.S. schools in the early 1990s than now (National School Safety Center 2010).
2. **False.** Over the years, the wage gap has narrowed, but only slightly. On average, full-time working women earn about 72 percent of what full-time working men earn. This low figure is actually an improvement over earlier years.
3. **False.** Today's parents actually spend *more* time with their children (Bianchi et al. 2006).
4. **False.** The crime rate outside fast-food restaurants is considerably higher. The likely reason for this is that top-less bars hire private security and parking lot attendants (Linz et al. 2004).
5. **False.** Sociologists compared the psychological profiles of prisoners convicted of rape and prisoners convicted of other crimes. Their profiles were similar. Like robbery, rape is a learned behavior (Scully and Marolla 1984).

6. **False.** Extensive testing of Islamic terrorists shows that they actually tend to score more "normal" on psychological tests than most "normal" people. As a group, they are in better mental health than the rest of the population (Sageman 2008b:64).
7. **False.** Most people on welfare are elderly, sick, mentally or physically handicapped, or are children or young mothers with few skills. Less than 2 percent fit the stereotype of an able-bodied man.
8. **False.** Women make considerably more eye contact (Henley et al. 1985).
9. **False.** The opposite is true. Among other reasons, couples who cohabit before marriage are usually less committed to one another—and a key to marital success is strong commitment (Dush et al. 2003; Osborne et al. 2007).
10. **False.** Bicyclists today are more likely to wear helmets, but their rate of head injuries is higher. Apparently, they take more risks because the helmets make them feel safer (Barnes 2001).

✳ Explore
Living Data
on **mysoclab.com**

7. *Analyzing the results.* You will have been trained in a variety of techniques to analyze your data—from those that apply to observations of people in small settings to the analysis of large-scale surveys. If a hypothesis has been part of your research, now is when you will test it. (Some research, especially case studies and participant observation, has no hypothesis. You may know so little about the setting you are going to research that you cannot even specify the variables in advance.)

8. *Sharing the results.* To wrap up your research, you will write a report to share your findings with the scientific community. You will review how you did your research, including your operational definitions. You will also compare your findings with published reports on the topic and how they support or disagree with the theories that others have applied. As Table 2 on the next page illustrates, sociologists often summarize their findings in tables.

Let's look in greater detail at the fifth step to see what research methods sociologists use.

Research Methods

As we review the seven research methods (or *research designs*) that sociologists use, we will continue our example of spouse abuse. As you will see, the method you choose will depend on the questions you want to answer. So that you can have a yardstick for comparing the results of your research, you will want to know what "average" is in your study. Table 3 discusses the three ways ways sociologists measure average.

What does "research method" mean?

TABLE 2   How to Read a Table

Tables summarize information. Because sociological findings are often presented in tables, it is important to understand how to read them. Tables contain six elements: title, headnote, headings, columns, rows, and source. When you understand how these elements fit together, you know how to read a table.

1. The *title* states the topic. It is located at the top of the table. What is the title of this table? Please determine your answer before looking at the correct answer at the bottom of this page.

2. The *headnote* is not always included in a table. When it is present, it is located just below the title. Its purpose is to give more detailed information about how the data were collected or how data are presented in the table. What are the first eight words of the headnote for this table?

3. The *headings* tell what kind of information is contained in the table. There are three headings in this table. What are they? In the second heading, what does *n* = 25 mean?

Comparing Violent and Nonviolent Husbands

Based on interviews with 150 husbands and wives in a Midwestern city who were getting a divorce.

Husband's Achievement and Job Satisfaction	Violent Husbands (*n* = 25)	Nonviolent Husbands (*n* = 125)
He started but failed to complete high school or college.	44%	27%
He is very dissatisfied with his job.	44%	18%
His income is a source of constant conflict.	84%	24%
He has less education than his wife.	56%	14%
His job has less prestige than his father-in-law's.	37%	28%

Source: Modification of Table 1 in O'Brien 1975.

4. The *columns* present information arranged vertically. What is the fourth number in the second column and the second number in the third column?

5. The *rows* present information arranged horizontally. In the fourth row, which husbands are more likely to have less education than their wives?

6. The *source* of a table, usually listed at the bottom, provides information on where the data in the table originated. Often, as in this instance, the information is specific enough for you to consult the original source. What is the source for this table?

Some tables are much more complicated than this one, but all follow the same basic pattern. To apply these concepts to a table with more information.

ANSWERS
1. Comparing Violent and Nonviolent Husbands
2. Based on interviews with 150 husbands and wives
3. Husband's Achievement and Job Satisfaction, Violent Husbands, Nonviolent Husbands. The *n* is an abbreviation for number, and *n* = 25 means that 25 violent husbands were in the sample.
4. 56%, 18%
5. Violent Husbands
6. A 1975 article by O'Brien (listed in the References section of this text).

Do you know how to read a table?

TABLE 3	Three Ways to Measure "Average"	
The Mean	**The Median**	**The Mode**
The term *average* seems clear enough. As you learned in grade school, to find the average you add a group of numbers and then divide the total by the number of cases that you added. Assume that the following numbers represent men convicted of battering their wives	To compute the second average, the *median*, first arrange the cases in order—either from the highest to the lowest or the lowest to the highest. That arrangement will produce the following distribution.	The third measure of average, the *mode*, is simply the cases that occur the most often. In this instance the mode is 57, which is way off the mark.

EXAMPLE

The Mean	The Median		The Mode
321	57	1,795	57
229	57	321	57
57	136	289	136
289	229 or 229		229
136	289	136	289
57	321	57	321
1,795	1,795	57	1,795

The total is 2,884. Divided by 7 (the number of cases), the average is 412. Sociologists call this form of average the *mean*. The mean can be deceptive because it is strongly influenced by extreme scores, either low or high. Note that six of the seven cases are less than the mean. Two other ways to compute averages are the median and the mode.	Then look for the middle case, the one that falls halfway between the top and the bottom. That number is 229, for three numbers are lower and three numbers are higher. When there is an even numbers of cases, the median is the halfway mark between the two middle cases.	Because the mode is often deceptive, and only by chance comes close to either of the other two averages, sociologists seldom use it. In addition, not every distribution of cases has a mode. And if two or more numbers appear with the same frequency, you can have more than one mode.

◉ Watch

Multiracial Identity
on **mysoclab.com**

survey the collection of data by having people answer a series of questions

population a target group to be studied

sample the individuals intended to represent the population to be studied

random sample a sample in which everyone in the target population has the same chance of being included in the study

stratified random sample a sample from selected subgroups of the target population in which everyone in those subgroups has an equal chance of being included in the research

Surveys

Let's suppose that you want to know how many wives are abused each year. Some husbands also are abused, of course, but let's assume that you are going to focus on wives. An appropriate method for this purpose would be the **survey,** in which you ask individuals a series of questions. Before you begin your research, however, you must deal with practical matters that face all researchers. Let's look at these issues.

Selecting a Sample. Ideally, you might want to learn about all wives in the world, but obviously you don't have enough resources to do this. You will have to narrow your **population,** the target group that you are going to study.

Let's assume that your resources (money, assistants, time) allow you to investigate spouse abuse only on your campus. Let's also assume that your college enrollment is large, so you won't be able to survey all the married women who are enrolled. Now you must select a **sample,** individuals from among your target population. How you choose a sample is crucial, for your choice will affect the results of your research. For example, married women enrolled in introductory sociology and engineering courses might have quite different experiences. If so, surveying just one or the other would produce skewed results.

Remember that your goal is to get findings that apply to your entire school. For this, you need a sample that represents the students. How can you get a representative sample?

The best way is to use a **random sample.** This does not mean that you would stand on some campus corner and ask questions of any woman who happens to walk by. *In a random sample, everyone in your population (the target group) has the same chance of being included in the study.* In this case, because your population is every married woman enrolled in your college, all married women—whether first-year or graduate students, full- or part-time—must have the same chance of being included in your sample.

Do you know the three ways to measure average?

How can you get a random sample? First, you need a list of all the married women enrolled in your college. Then you assign a number to each name on the list. Using a table of random numbers, you then determine which of these women will become part of your sample. (Tables of random numbers are available in statistics books and online, or they can be generated by a computer.)

A random sample will represent your study's population fairly—in this case, married women enrolled at your college. This means that you will be able to generalize your findings to *all* the married women students on your campus, even if they were not included in your sample.

What if you want to know only about certain subgroups, such as freshman and seniors? For this, you would need a list of the freshman and senior married women. Then, using random numbers, you would select a sample from each group. This would produce a **stratified random sample,** which would allow you to generalize to all the freshmen and senior married women at your college. You would not be able to draw any conclusions about the sophomores or juniors.

Asking Neutral Questions. After deciding on your population and sample, your next task is to make certain that your questions are neutral. The questions must allow **respondents,** the people who answer your questions, to express their own opinions. Otherwise, you will end up with biased answers—which are worthless. For example, if you were to ask, "Don't you think that men who beat their wives should go to prison?" you would be tilting the answer toward agreement with a prison sentence. For examples of flawed research, see the Down-to-Earth Sociology box on the next page.

Types of Questions. You must also decide whether to use closed- or open-ended questions. **Closed-ended questions** are followed by a list of possible answers. This format would work for questions about someone's age (possible ages would be listed), but not for many other items. For example, how could you list all the opinions that people hold about what should be done to spouse abusers? The answers provided for closed-ended questions can miss the respondent's opinions.

As Table 4 illustrates, you can use **open-ended questions,** which allow people to answer in their own words. Although open-ended questions allow you to tap the full range of people's opinions, they make it difficult to compare answers. For example, how would you compare these answers to the question, Why do you think men abuse their wives?

> "They're sick."

> "I think they must have had problems with their mother."

> "We ought to string them up!"

Establishing Rapport. Will women who have been abused really give honest answers to strangers? If you were to walk up to women on the street and ask if their husbands have ever beaten them, there would be little reason to take your findings seriously. If, however, you establish **rapport** ("ruh-POUR"), a feeling of trust, with your respondents, you will find that people will talk about sensitive matters. A good example is rape. Each year, researchers interview a random sample of 100,000 Americans. They ask them whether they have been victims of burglary, robbery, and other crimes. After establishing rapport, the researchers ask about rape. This National Crime

Gaetan Bally/Keystone/Corbis

If sociologists were to study stone throwing, participants and observers, they could use a variety of methods. Based on what you have learned in this chapter, how do you think this activity should be studied? This photo is from Switzerland.

respondents people who respond to a survey, either in interviews or by self-administered questionnaires

closed-ended questions questions that are followed by a list of possible answers to be selected by the respondent

open-ended questions questions that respondents answer in their own words

rapport (ruh-POUR) a feeling of trust between researchers and the people they are studying

TABLE 4	Closed- and Open-Ended Questions
A. Closed-Ended Question	**B. Open-Ended Question**
Which of the following best fits your idea of what should be done to someone who has been convicted of spouse abuse?	What do you think should be done to someone who has been convicted of spouse abuse?
1. Probation 2. Jail time 3. Community service 4. Counseling 5. Divorce 6. Nothing—It's a family matter	

How can a researcher get a random sample? Why do we need neutral questions? What good is rapport in research?

Down-to-Earth Sociology

Loading the Dice: How *Not* to Do Research

The methods of science lend themselves to distortion, misrepresentation, and downright fraud. Consider these findings from surveys:

Americans overwhelmingly prefer Toyotas to Chryslers.
Americans overwhelmingly prefer Chryslers to Toyotas.

Obviously, these opposite conclusions cannot both be true. In fact, both sets of findings are misrepresentations, even though the responses came from surveys conducted by so-called independent researchers. It turns out that some consumer researchers load the dice. Hired by firms that have a vested interest in the outcome of the research, they deliver the results their clients are looking for (Armstrong 2007). Here are six ways to load the dice.

1. **Choose a biased sample.** If you want to "prove" that Americans prefer Chryslers over Toyotas, interview unemployed union workers who trace their job loss to Japanese imports. You'll get what you're looking for.
2. **Ask biased questions.** Even if you choose an unbiased sample, you can phrase questions in such a way that you direct people to the answer you're looking for. Suppose that you ask this question:

   We are losing millions of jobs to workers overseas who work for just a few dollars a day. After losing their jobs, some Americans are even homeless and hungry. Do you prefer a car that gives jobs to Americans, or one that forces our workers to lose their homes?

   This question is obviously designed to channel people's thinking toward a predetermined answer—quite contrary to the standards of scientific research.
3. **List biased choices.** Another way to load the dice is to use closed-ended questions that push people into the answers you want. Consider this finding:

   U.S. college students overwhelmingly prefer Levis 501 to the jeans of any competitor.

   Sound good? Before you rush out to buy Levis, note what these researchers did: In asking students which jeans would be the most popular in the coming year, their list of choices included no other jeans but Levis 501!

CM Holmgren/Lightbox

4. **Discard undesirable results.** Researchers can keep silent about results they find embarrassing, or they can continue to survey samples until they find one that matches what they are looking for.
5. **Misunderstand the subjects' world.** Even researchers who use an adequate sample and word their questions properly can end up with skewed results. They may, for example, fail to anticipate that people may be embarrassed to express an opinion that isn't "politically correct." For example, surveys show that 80 percent of Americans are environmentalists. Is this an accurate figure? Most Americans are probably embarrassed to tell a stranger otherwise. Today, that would be like going against the flag, motherhood, and apple pie.
6. **Analyze the data incorrectly.** Even when researchers strive for objectivity, the sample is good, the wording is neutral, and the respondents answer the questions honestly, the results can still be skewed. The researchers may make a mistake in their calculations, such as entering incorrect data into computers. This, too, of course, is inexcusable in research.

Of these six sources of bias, the first four demonstrate fraud. The final two reflect sloppiness, which is also not acceptable in science.

As has been stressed in this chapter, research must be objective if it is to be scientific. The underlying problem with the research cited here—and with so many surveys bandied about in the media as fact—is that survey research has become big business. Simply put, the money offered by corporations has corrupted some researchers.

The beginning of the corruption is subtle. Paul Light, dean at the University of Minnesota, put it this way: "A funder will never come to an academic and say, 'I want you to produce finding X, and here's a million dollars to do it.' Rather, the subtext is that if the researchers produce the right finding, more work—and funding—will come their way."

Sources: Based on Crossen 1991; Goleman 1993; Barnes 1995; Resnik 2000; Augoustinos et al. 2009.

Can you use the contents of this box to explain how to do *good* sociological research?

Victimization Survey shows that rape victims will talk about their experiences (Weiss 2009; *Statistical Abstract* 2011:Tables 311, 312).

To gather data on sensitive areas, some researchers use Computer-Assisted Self-Interviewing, which overcomes lingering problems of distrust. In this technique, the interviewer gives the individual a laptop computer, then moves aside while he or she answers questions on the computer. In some versions of this method, the individual listens to the questions on headphones and provides answers on the computer screen. When he or she clicks the "Submit" button, the interviewer has no idea how any question was answered. Although many people like the privacy that this technique provides, some prefer a live questioner even for sensitive areas of their lives. They say that they want positive feedback from interviewers (Estes et al. 2010).

Participant Observation (Fieldwork)

In **participant observation,** or **fieldwork,** the researcher *participates* in a research setting while *observing* what is happening in that setting. But how is it possible to study spouse abuse by participant observation? Obviously, you would not sit around and watch someone being abused.

Let's suppose that you want to know how abuse has changed women's relationships with their husbands. Or maybe how it has changed their hopes and dreams? Or their ideas about men? By observing the women as they live their everyday lives, participant observation could provide insight into such questions.

If your campus has a crisis intervention center, you might be able to observe victims of spouse abuse from the time they report the attack through their participation in counseling. With good rapport, you might even be able to spend time with them at their homes or with friends. What they say and how they interact with others might help you to understand how the abuse has affected them. This, in turn, could give you insight into how to improve college counseling services.

If you were doing participant observation, you would face this dilemma: How involved should you get in the lives of the people you are observing? Consider this as you read the Down-to-Earth Sociology box on the next page.

Case Studies

To do a **case study,** the researcher focuses on a single event, situation, or individual. The purpose is to understand the dynamics of relationships, power, or even the thought processes that motivate people. Sociologist Ken Levi (2009), for example, wanted to study hit men. He would have loved having many hit men to interview, but he had access to only one. He interviewed this man over and over, giving us an understanding of how someone can kill others for money. On another level entirely, sociologist Kai Erikson (1978) investigated the bursting of a dam in West Virginia that killed several hundred people. He focused on the events that led up to this disaster and how people tried to put their lives together afterwards. For spouse abuse, a case study would focus on a single wife and husband, exploring the couple's history and relationship.

As you can see, case studies reveal a lot of detail about some particular situation, but the question always remains: How much of this detail applies to other situations? This problem of *generalizability*, which plagues case studies, is the primary reason that few sociologists use this method.

Secondary Analysis

If you were to analyze data that someone else has already collected, you would be doing **secondary analysis.** For example, examining the original data from a study of women who had been abused by their husbands is secondary analysis.

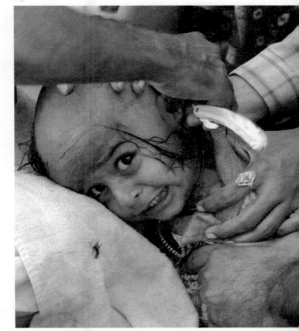
© Dinodia/The Image Works

Participant observation, participating and observing in a research setting, is usually supplemented by interviewing, asking questions to better understand why people do what they do. In this instance, the sociologist would want to know what this hair removal ceremony in Gujarat, India, means to the child's family and to the community.

participant observation or fieldwork research in which the researcher participates in a research setting while observing what is happening in that setting

case study an intensive analysis of a single event, situation, or individual

secondary analysis the analysis of data that have been collected by other researchers

What is participant observation? What are case studies? What is secondary analysis?

Down-to-Earth Sociology

Gang Leader for a Day: Adventures of a Rogue Sociologist

Next to the University of Chicago is an area of poverty so dangerous that the professors warn students to avoid it. One graduate student in sociology, Sudhir Venkatesh, the son of immigrants from India, who was working on a research project with William Julius Wilson, ignored the warning.

With clipboard in hand, Sudhir entered "the projects." Ignoring the glares of the young men standing around, he went into the lobby of a high-rise. Seeing a gaping hole where the elevator was supposed to be, he decided to climb the stairs, where he was almost overpowered by the smell of urine. After climbing five flights, Sudhir came upon some young men shooting craps in a dark hallway. One of them jumped up, grabbed Sudhir's clipboard, and demanded to know what he was doing there.

Sudhir blurted, "I'm a student at the university, doing a survey, and I'm looking for some families to interview."

One man took out a knife and began to twirl it. Another pulled out a gun, pointed it at Sudhir's head, and said, "I'll take him."

Then came a series of rapid-fire questions that Sudhir couldn't answer. He had no idea what they meant: "You flip right or left? Five or six? You run with the Kings, right?"

Grabbing Sudhir's bag, two of the men searched it. They could find only questionnaires, pen and paper, and a few sociology books. The man with the gun then told Sudhir to go ahead and ask him a question.

Sweating despite the cold, Sudhir read the first question on his survey, "How does it feel to be black and poor?" Then he read the multiple-choice answers: "Very bad, somewhat bad, neither bad nor good, somewhat good, very good."

As you might surmise, the man's answer was too obscenity laden to be printed here.

As the men deliberated Sudhir's fate ("If he's here and he don't get back, you know they're going to come looking for him"), a powerfully built man with a few glittery gold teeth and a sizable diamond earring appeared. The man, known as J. T., who, it turned out, directed the drug trade in the building, asked what was going on. When the younger men

mentioned the questionnaire, J. T. said to ask *him* a question.

Amidst an eerie silence, Sudhir asked, "How does it feel to be black and poor?"

"I'm not black," came the reply.

"Well, then, how does it feel to be African American and poor?"

"I'm not African American either. I'm a nigger."

Sudhir was left speechless. Despite his naïveté, he knew better than to ask, "How does it feel to be a nigger and poor?"

As Sudhir stood with his mouth agape, J.T. added, "Niggers are the ones who live in this building. African Americans live in the suburbs. African Americans wear ties to work. Niggers can't find no work."

Not exactly the best start to a research project.

But this weird and frightening beginning turned into several years of fascinating research. Over time, J. T. guided Sudhir into a world that few outsiders ever see. Not only did Sudhir get to know drug dealers, crackheads, squatters, prostitutes, and pimps, but he also was present at beatings by drug crews, drive-by shootings done by rival gangs, and armed robberies by the police.

Sudhir Venkatesh, who now teaches at Columbia University, New York City.

Stephen Lovekin/WireImage/Getty Images

How Sudhir got out of his predicament in the stairwell, his immersion into a threatening underworld—the daily life for many people in "the projects"—and his moral dilemma at witnessing so many crimes are part of his fascinating experience in doing participant observation of the Black Kings.

Sudhir, who was reared in a middle-class suburb in California, even took over this Chicago gang for a day. This is one reason that he calls himself a rogue sociologist—the decisions he made that day were serious violations of law, felonies that could bring years in prison. There are other reasons, too: During the research, he kicked a man in the stomach, and he was present as the gang planned drive-by shootings.

Sudhir survived, completed his Ph.D., and now teaches at Columbia University.

Source: Based on Venkatesh 2008.

---

documents in its narrow sense, written sources that provide data; in its extended sense, archival material of any sort, including photographs, movies, CDs, DVDs, and so on

Analysis of Documents

Documents, or written sources, include books, newspapers, bank records, immigration files, and so on. To study spouse abuse, you might examine police reports to find out how many men in your community have been arrested for abuse. You might also use court records to find out what proportion of those men were charged, convicted,

---

Why do participant observers face the dilemma of getting involved in their subjects' lives? Why is this a dilemma?

or put on probation. If you wanted to learn about the social and emotional adjustment of the victims, however, these documents would tell you nothing. Other documents, though, might provide those answers. For example, a crisis intervention center might have records that contain key information—but gaining access to them is almost impossible. Perhaps an unusually cooperative center might ask victims to keep diaries for you to study.

The *research methods* that sociologists choose depend partially on the questions they want to answer. They might want to learn, for example, which forms of publicity are more effective in increasing awareness of spouse abuse as a social problem.

Experiments

Do you think abusers need therapy? This sounds like common sense, but no one knows whether therapy would make any difference. Here is where **experiments** are useful, as they allow us to determine cause and effect. To see the basic requirements of cause and effect, look at Table 5 on the next page. Let's suppose that you propose an experiment to a judge and she gives you access to men who have been arrested for spouse abuse. As in Figure 6 you would divide the men randomly into two groups. This would help ensure that their individual characteristics (attitudes, number of arrests, severity of crimes, education, race–ethnicity, age, and so on) are distributed between the groups. You then would arrange for the men in the **experimental group** to receive some form of therapy that the men in the **control group** would not get.

The therapy would be your **independent variable,** something that causes a change in another variable. Your **dependent variable,** the variable that might change, would be the men's behavior, whether they abuse women after they get out of jail. Unfortunately, your operational definition of the men's behavior will be sloppy: either reports from the wives or records indicating who has been rearrested for abuse. This is sloppy because some of the women will not report the abuse, and some of the men who abuse their wives will not be arrested. Yet it might be the best you can do.

Let's assume that you choose rearrest as your operational definition. If fewer of the men who received therapy are rearrested for abuse, you can conclude that the therapy worked. If you find *no difference* in rearrest rates, you can conclude that the therapy was ineffective. And if you find that the men who received the therapy have a higher rearrest rate, you can conclude that the therapy backfired.

© Syracuse Newspapers/M Gabel/The Image Works

experiment the use of control and experimental groups and dependent and independent variables to test causation

experimental group the group of subjects in an experiment who are exposed to the independent variable

control group the group of subjects in an experiment who are *not* exposed to the independent variable

independent variable a factor that causes a change in another variable, called the *dependent variable*

dependent variable a factor in an experiment that is changed by an independent variable

FIGURE 6 The Experiment

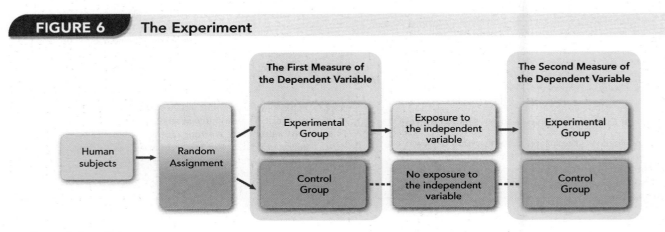

Source: By the author.

Can you explain how an experiment works? Can you use the basic terms in doing so?

TABLE 5   Cause, Effect, and Spurious Correlations

Causation means that a change in one variable is caused by another variable. Three conditions are necessary for causation: correlation, temporal priority, and no spurious correlation. Let's apply each of these conditions to spouse abuse and alcohol abuse.

1 The first necessary condition is *correlation*

If two variables exist together, they are said to be correlated. If batterers get drunk, battering and alcohol abuse are correlated.

Spouse Abuse + Alcohol Abuse

People sometimes assume that correlation is causation. In this instance, they conclude that alcohol abuse causes spouse abuse.

Alcohol Abuse ⟶ Spouse Abuse

But *correlation never proves causation. Either* variable could be the cause of the other. Perhaps battering upsets men and they then get drunk.

Spouse Abuse ⟶ Alcohol Abuse

2 The second necessary condition is *temporal priority.*

Temporal priority means that one thing happens before something else does. For a variable to be a cause (*the independent variable*), it must *precede* that which changed (*the dependent variable*).

Alcohol Abuse — precedes ⟶ Spouse Abuse

If the men had not drunk alcohol until after they beat their wives, obviously alcohol abuse could not be the cause of the spouse abuse. Although the necessity of temporal priority is obvious, in many studies this is not easy to determine.

3 The third necessary condition is *no spurious correlation.*

This is the necessary condition that really makes things difficult. Even if we identify the correlation of getting drunk and spouse abuse and can determine temporal priority, we still don't know that alcohol abuse is the cause. We could have a *spurious correlation*; that is, the cause may be some underlying third variable. These are usually not easy to identify. Some sociologists think that male culture is that underlying third variable.

Male Culture ⟶ Spouse Abuse

Socialized into dominance, some men learn to view women as objects on which to take out their frustration. In fact, this underlying third variable could be a cause of both spouse abuse and alcohol abuse.

Male Culture ⟶ Spouse Abuse / Alcohol Abuse

But since only some men beat their wives, while all males are exposed to male culture, other variables must also be involved. Perhaps specific subcultures that promote violence and denigrate women lead to both spouse abuse and alcohol abuse.

Male Subculture ⟶ Spouse Abuse / Alcohol Abuse

If so, this does *not* mean that it is the only causal variable, for spouse abuse probably has many causes. Unlike the movement of amoebas or the action of heat on some object, human behavior is infinitely complicated. Especially important are people's *definitions of the situation*, including their views of right and wrong. To explain spouse abuse, then, we need to add such variables as the ways that men view violence and their ideas about the relative rights of women and men. It is precisely to help unravel such complicating factors in human behavior that we need the experiment method.

MORE ON CORRELATIONS

Correlation simply means that two or more variables are present together. The more often that these variables are found together, the stronger their relationship. To indicate their strength, sociologists use a number called a *correlation coefficient*. If two variables are always related, that is, they are always present together, they have what is called a *perfect positive correlation*. The number 1.0 represents this correlation coefficient. Nature has some 1.0's such as the lack of water and the death of trees. 1.0's also apply to the human physical state, such as the absence of nutrients and the absence of life. But social life is much more complicated than physical conditions, and there are no 1.0's in human behavior.

Two variables can also have a *perfect negative correlation*. This means that when one variable is present, the other is always absent. The number -1.0 represents this correlation coefficient.

Positive correlations of 0.1, 0.2, and 0.3 mean that one variable is associated with another only 1 time out of 10, 2 times out of 10, and 3 times out of 10. In other words, in most instances the first variable is *not* associated with the second, indicating a weak relationship. A strong relationship may indicate causation, but not necessarily. Testing the relationship between variables is the goal of some sociological research. .

What is necessary to prove causation? What is a correlation? What is a spurious correlation?

Unobtrusive Measures

Some researchers use **unobtrusive measures,** observing the behavior of people who are not aware that they are being studied. To determine whiskey consumption in a town that was legally "dry," researchers counted the empty bottles in trashcans (Lee 2000). Researchers have also gone high-tech. When you shop, cameras can follow you from the second you enter a store to the minute you hit the checkout counter, recording each item you touch, as well as every time you pick your nose (Rosenbloom 2010; Singer 2010). Some billboards read information embedded on a chip in your car key. As you drive by, the billboard displays *your* name with a personal message. The same device can *collect* information as you pass by (Feder 2007). Some Web coupons are embedded with bar codes that record your name and Facebook information. The cameras, billboards, and coupons, which raise ethical issues of invasion of privacy, are part of marketing, not sociological research.

To study spouse abuse, it would be considered unethical to use most unobtrusive measures. You could, however, analyze 911 calls. Also, if abused or abusing spouses held a public forum on the Internet, you could record and analyze the online conversations. Ethics in unobtrusive research are still a matter of dispute: To secretly record the behavior of people in public settings, such as a crowd, is generally considered acceptable, but to do so in private settings is not.

© ilian casino/Alamy

To prevent cheating by customers and personnel, casinos use *unobtrusive measures.* In the ceiling above this blackjack table's and roulette wheels are video cameras that record every action. Observers are also posted there.

Gender in Sociological Research

You know how significant gender is in your own life, how it affects your orientations and your attitudes. Because gender is also influential in social research, researchers take steps to prevent it from biasing their findings (Davis et al. 2009). For example, sociologists Diana Scully and Joseph Marolla (1984, 2012) interviewed convicted rapists in prison. They were concerned that their gender might lead to *interviewer bias*—that the prisoners might shift their answers, sharing certain experiences or opinions with Marolla, but saying something else to Scully. To prevent gender bias, each researcher interviewed half the sample.

In our imagined research on spouse abuse, could a man even do participant observation of women who have been beaten by their husbands? Technically, the answer is yes. But because the women have been victimized by men, they might be less likely to share their experiences and feelings with men. If so, women would be better suited for this research, more likely to achieve valid results. The supposition that these victims will be more open with women than with men, however, is just that—a supposition. Research alone will verify or refute this assumption.

Gender issues can pop up in unexpected ways in sociological research. I vividly recall an incident in San Francisco.

> *The streets were getting dark, and I was still looking for homeless people. When I saw someone lying down, curled up in a doorway, I approached the individual. As I got close, I began my opening research line, "Hi, I'm Dr. Henslin from. . . ." The individual began to scream and started to thrash wildly. Startled by this sudden, high-pitched scream and by the rapid movements, I quickly backed away. When I later analyzed what had happened, I concluded that I had intruded into a woman's bedroom.*

This incident also holds another lesson. Researchers do their best, but they make mistakes. Sometimes these mistakes are minor, and even humorous. The woman sleeping in the doorway wasn't frightened. It was only just getting dark, and there were many people on the street. She was just assertively marking her territory and letting me know in no uncertain terms that I was an intruder. If we make a mistake in research, we pick up and go on. As we do so, we take ethical considerations into account, which is the topic of our next section.

Read
The Promise and Pitfalls of Going Into the Field by Patricia Adler and Peter Adler on **mysoclab.com**

unobtrusive measures ways of observing people so they do not know they are being studied

How is gender a factor in sociological research?

Ethics in Sociological Research

In addition to choosing an appropriate research method, we must also follow the ethics of sociology (American Sociological Association 1999). Research ethics require honesty, truth, and openness (sharing findings with the scientific community). Ethics obviously forbid the falsification of results. They also condemn plagiarism—that is, stealing someone else's work. Another ethical guideline states that, generally, people should be informed that they are being studied and that they never should be harmed by the research. Sociologists are also required to protect the anonymity of those who provide information. Sometimes people reveal things that are intimate, potentially embarrassing, or otherwise harmful to themselves or others. Finally, although not all sociologists agree, it generally is considered unethical for researchers to misrepresent themselves.

Sociologists take their ethical standards seriously. To illustrate the extent to which they go to protect their respondents, consider the research conducted by Mario Brajuha.

Zoriah/EyePress/Newscom

Ethics in social research are of vital concern to sociologists. As discussed in the text, sociologists may disagree on some of the issue's finer points, but none would approve of slipping LSD to unsuspecting subjects like this Marine. This was done to U.S. soldiers in the 1960s under the guise of legitimate testing—just "to see what would happen."

Protecting the Subjects: The Brajuha Research

Mario Brajuha, a graduate student at the State University of New York at Stony Brook, was doing participant observation of restaurant workers. He lost his job as a waiter when the restaurant where he was working burned down—a fire of "suspicious origin," as the police said. When detectives learned that Brajuha had taken field notes, they asked to see them (Brajuha and Hallowell 1986). Because he had promised to keep the information confidential, Brajuha refused to hand them over. When the district attorney subpoenaed the notes, Brajuha still refused. The district attorney then threatened to put Brajuha in jail. By this time, Brajuha's notes had become rather famous, and unsavory characters—perhaps those who had set the fire—also wanted to know what was in them. They, too, demanded to see them, accompanying their demands with threats of a different nature. Brajuha found himself between a rock and a hard place.

For two years, Brajuha refused to hand over his notes, even though he grew anxious and had to appear at several court hearings. Finally, the district attorney dropped the subpoena. When the two men under investigation for setting the fire died, the threats to Brajuha, his wife, and their children ended.

Sociologists applaud the way Brajuha protected his respondents and the professional manner in which he handled himself, but our next example is a little different.

Misleading the Subjects: The Humphreys Research

What should sociologists tell participants about their research? Can a sociologist be deceitful in order to get data? Let's look at the case of Laud Humphreys, whose research forced sociologists to rethink and refine their ethical stance.

Laud Humphreys, a classmate of mine at Washington University in St. Louis, was an Episcopal priest who decided to become a sociologist. For his Ph.D. dissertation, Humphreys (1971, 1975) studied social interaction in "tearooms," public restrooms where some men go for quick, anonymous oral sex with other men.

Why is protecting subjects essential to sociological research?

Humphreys found that some restrooms in Forest Park, just across from our campus, were tearooms. He began a participant observation study by hanging around these restrooms. He found that in addition to the two men having sex, a third man—called a "watch queen"—served as a lookout for police and other unwelcome strangers. Humphreys took on the role of watch queen, not only watching for strangers but also observing what the men did. He wrote field notes after the encounters.

Humphreys then decided that he wanted to learn about the regular lives of these men. For example, what about the wedding rings that many of the men wore? He came up with an ingenious technique: Many of the men parked their cars near the tearooms, and Humphreys recorded their license plate numbers. A friend in the St. Louis police department gave Humphreys each man's address. About a year later, Humphreys arranged for these men to be included in a medical survey conducted by some of the sociologists on our faculty.

Disguising himself with a different hairstyle and clothing, Humphreys visited the men at home, supposedly to interview them for the medical study. He found that they led conventional lives. They voted, mowed their lawns, and took their kids to Little League games. Many reported that their wives were not aroused sexually or were afraid of getting pregnant because their religion did not allow birth control. Humphreys concluded that heterosexual men were also using the tearooms for a form of quick sex.

This study stirred controversy among sociologists and nonsociologists alike. Many sociologists criticized Humphreys, and a national columnist wrote a scathing denunciation of "sociological snoopers" (Von Hoffman 1970). One of our professors even tried to get Humphreys' Ph.D. revoked. As the controversy heated up and a court case loomed, Humphreys feared that his list of respondents might be subpoenaed. He gave me the list to take from Missouri to Illinois, where I had begun teaching. When he called and asked me to destroy it, I burned the list in my backyard.

Was this research ethical? This question is not decided easily. Although many sociologists sided with Humphreys—and his book reporting the research won a highly acclaimed award—the criticisms continued. At first, Humphreys defended his position vigorously, but five years later, in a second edition of his book (1975), he stated that he should have identified himself as a researcher.

Before we close this chapter, I would like to give you a glimpse of two trends that are shaping sociology.

Trends Shaping the Future of Sociology

Sociology is never static. It is always changing as sociologists analyze society, responding to its many currents of social change. As we review changing directions in sociology, let's look first at an early issue that is still being argued—social reform, and then at a more recent trend—globalization.

Sociology's Continuing Tension: Research versus Reform

Three Stages in Sociology. As you have seen, a tension between social reform and social analysis runs through the history of sociology. To better understand this tension, we can divide sociology into three time periods (Lazarsfeld and Reitz 1989). At first, until the 1920s, the primary purpose of research was to improve society. During the second phase, from the 1920s until World War II, the concern switched to developing abstract knowledge. We are now in a third phase, which began around the end of World War II, in which sociologists increasingly seek ways to apply their research findings. Many sociology departments now offer courses in applied sociology, with some providing internships at both the graduate and undergraduate levels. From the Cultural Diversity box on the next page, you can see that applied sociology and the "abstract knowledge" of basic sociology are not necessarily separate endeavors.

Why did the Humphreys research create such controversy?

Cultural Diversity in the United States

Unanticipated Public Sociology: Studying Job Discrimination

Basic sociology—research aimed at learning more about some behavior—can turn into public sociology. Here is what happened to Devah Pager, a graduate student at the University of Wisconsin in Madison. When she was doing volunteer work in a homeless shelter, some of the men told her how hard it was to find work if they had had been in prison. Were the men exaggerating she wondered? To find out what difference a prison record makes in getting a job, she sent pairs of college men to apply for 350 entry-level jobs in Milwaukee. One team was African American, and one

was white. Pager prepared identical résumés for the teams, but with one difference: On each team, one of the men said he had served eighteen months in prison for possession of cocaine.

Figure 7 shows the difference that the prison record made. Men without a prison record were two or three times as likely to be called back.

But Pager came up with another significant finding. Look at the difference that race–ethnicity made. White men with a prison record were more likely to be offered a job than African American men who had a clean record!

Sociological research often remains in obscure journals, read by only a few specialists. But Pager's findings got around, turning into public sociology. Someone told President George W. Bush about the research, and he announced in his State of the Union speech that he wanted Congress to fund a $300 million program to provide mentoring and other support to help former prisoners get jobs (Kroeger 2004).

Pager repeated her research in New York City and found similar results (Pager et al. 2009).

As you can see, sometimes only a thin line separates basic and public sociology.

For Your Consideration

➤ What findings would you expect if women had been included in this research?

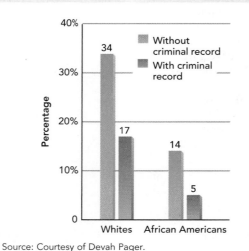

FIGURE 7 Call-Back Rates by Race–Ethnicity and Criminal Record

Source: Courtesy of Devah Pager.

Figure from "The Mark of a Criminal Record" by Devah Pager, from AMERICAN JOURNAL OF SOCIOLOGY, March 2003. Volume 108(5). Copyright © 2003 by Devah Pager. Reprinted with permission by University of Chicago Press.

Diversity of Orientations. I want to stress that sociology is filled with diverse opinions. (From my observations, I would say that when two sociologists meet, they will express three firmly held, contradictory opinions.) In any event, a division into three separate phases overlooks as much as it reveals. During the first phase, for example, some leading sociologists campaigned against helping the poor, saying that their deaths were good for the progress of society (Stokes 2009). Similarly, during the second phase, those who wanted to reform society chafed at the focus on understanding. And today, many in the field want the emphasis to remain on basic research. Some say that applied sociology is not "real" sociology; it is social work or psychology in masquerade. As you can see, sociologists do not move in lockstep toward a single goal.

Can you contrast basic and public sociology? What does "unanticipated public sociology" mean?

Each particular period, however, does have basic emphases, and this division of sociology into three phases pinpoints major trends. The tension that has run through sociology—between gaining knowledge and applying knowledge—will continue. During this current phase, the pendulum is swinging toward applying sociological knowledge.

globalization the extensive interconnections among nations

globalization of capitalism capitalism becoming the globe's dominant economic system

Globalization

A second major trend, globalization, is also leaving its mark on sociology. **Globalization** is the breaking down of national borders because of advances in communications, trade, and travel. Because the United States dominates sociology and we U.S. sociologists tend to concentrate on events and relationships that occur in our own country, most of our findings are based on U.S. samples. Globalization is destined to broaden our horizons, directing us to a greater consideration of global issues. This, in turn, is likely to motivate us to try more vigorously to identify universal principles.

Globalization in This Text.   You are personally experiencing globalization, one of the most significant events in all of world history. This process is shaping your life, hopes, and future—sometimes even twisting them. As globalization shrinks the globe, that is, as people around the world become more interconnected within the same global village, your welfare is increasingly tied to that of people in other nations. From time to time in the following pages, you will also explore how the **globalization of capitalism**—that is, capitalism becoming the world's dominant economic system—is having profound effects on your life. You will also confront the developing *new world order*, which, if it can shave off its rough edges, also appears destined to play a significant role in your future.

To help broaden your horizons, in the following chapters you will visit many cultures around the world, looking at what life is like for the people of those cultures. Seeing how *their* society affects their behavior and orientations to life should help you better understand how *your* society influences what you do and how you feel about life. This, of course, takes us to one of the main goals of this book.

I wish you a happy sociological journey, one with new insights around every corner.

Summary and Review

The Sociological Perspective

What is the sociological perspective?

The **sociological perspective** stresses that people's social experiences—the groups to which they belong and their experiences within these groups—underlie their behavior. C. Wright Mills referred to this as the intersection of biography (the individual) and history (social factors that influence the individual).

Origins of Sociology

When did sociology first appear as a separate discipline?

Sociology emerged in the mid-1800s in western Europe, during the onset of the Industrial Revolution. Industrialization affected all aspects of human existence—where people lived, the nature of their work, their relationships, and how they viewed life. Early sociologists who focused on these social changes include Auguste Comte, Herbert Spencer, Karl Marx, Emile Durkheim, Max Weber, Harriet Martineau, and W. E. B. Du Bois.

Sociology in North America

What was the position of women and minorities in early sociology?

The few women who received the education required to become sociologists, such as Jane Addams, tended to focus on social reform. W. E. B. Du Bois was a well-known African American reformer who faced deep racism in his sociological career. The debate between social reform and social analysis was won by male university professors who ignored the contributions of the women.

Why are the positions of Parsons and Mills important?

C. Wright Mills took the position that Parsons' abstract analysis of the components of society does nothing for social reform, which should be the goal of sociologists. This fundamental debate about the purpose and use of sociology continues today.

Theoretical Perspectives in Sociology

What is a theory?

A **theory** is a statement about how facts are related to one another. A theory provides a conceptual framework for interpreting facts.

What are sociology's major theoretical perspectives?

Sociologists have three primary theoretical frameworks to interpret social life. **Symbolic interactionists** examine how people use symbols (meanings) to develop and share their views of the world. Symbolic interactionists usually focus on the **micro level**—on small-scale, face-to-face interaction. **Functional analysts,** in contrast, focus on the **macro level**—on large-scale patterns of society. Functional theorists stress that a social system is made up of interrelated parts. When working properly, each part contributes to the stability of the whole, fulfilling a function that contributes to the system's equilibrium. **Conflict theorists** also focus on large-scale patterns of society. They stress that society is composed of competing groups that struggle for scarce resources.

What is the value of understanding all three perspectives?

With each perspective focusing on select features of social life, and each providing a unique interpretation, no single perspective is adequate. The combined insights of all three yield a more comprehensive picture of social life.

What is the relationship between theory and research?

Theory and research depend on one another. Sociologists use theory to interpret the data they gather. Theory also generates questions that need to be answered by research, while research, in turn, helps to generate theory. Theory without research is not likely to represent real life, while research without theory is merely a collection of empty facts.

Doing Sociological Research

Why do we need sociological research when we have common sense?

Common sense is unreliable. Research often shows that commonsense ideas are limited or false.

What are the eight basic steps in sociological research?

(1) Selecting a topic, (2) Defining the problem, (3) Reviewing the literature, (4) Formulating a **hypothesis,** (5) Choosing a research method, (6) Collecting the data, (7) Analyzing the results, and (8) Sharing the results.

Research Methods

How do sociologists gather data?

To gather data, sociologists use seven **research methods** (or **research designs**): **surveys, participant observation, case studies, secondary analysis, analysis of documents, experiments,** and **unobtrusive measures.**

Gender in Sociological Research

How can gender affect research?

Gender can lead to *interviewer bias*, with participants shaping their responses based on the gender of the researcher.

Ethics in Sociological Research

How important are ethics in sociological research?

Ethics are of fundamental concern to sociologists, who are committed to openness, honesty, truth, and protecting their subjects from harm. The Brajuha research on restaurant workers and the Humphreys research on "tearooms" illustrate ethical issues of concern to sociologists.

Trends Shaping the Future of Sociology

What trends are likely to have an impact on sociology?

Sociology has gone through three phases: In the first, the emphasis was on reforming society; in the second, the focus was on basic sociology; the third, today's phase, with its **applied sociology** and **public sociology,** is taking us closer to our roots of applying sociology to social change. Today's **globalization** is likely to broaden sociological horizons, refocusing research and theory away from its concentration on U.S. society.

Thinking Critically about this Chapter

1. Do you think that sociologists should try to reform society or just study it to gain knowledge?

2. Of the three theoretical perspectives, which one would you prefer to use if you were a sociologist? Why?

3. Considering the macro- and micro-level approaches in sociology, which one do you think better explains social life? Why?

4. What are the differences between good and bad sociological research? How can biases be avoided?

5. What ethics govern sociological research?

6. Do you think it is OK for sociologists to not identity themselves when they do research? To misrepresent themselves?

References

Addams, Jane. *Twenty Years at Hull-House.* New York: Signet, 1981. Originally published 1910.

American Sociological Association. "Code of Ethics and Policies and Procedures of the ASA Committee on Professional Ethics." Washington, D.C.: American Sociological Association, 1999.

American Sociological Association. "An Invitation to Public Sociology." 2004.

Aptheker, Herbert. "W. E. B. Du Bois: Struggle Not Despair." *Clinical Sociology Review, 8,* 1990:58–68.

Armstrong, David. "Hard Case: When Academics Double as Expert Witnesses." *Wall Street Journal,* June 22, 2007.

Augoustinos, Martha, Ameilia Russin, and Amanda LeCouteur. "Representations of the Stem-Cell Cloning Fraud: From Scientific Breakthrough to Managing the Stake and Interest of Science." *Public Understanding of Science, 18,* 6, 2009:687–703.

Barnes, Fred. "How to Rig a Poll." *Wall Street Journal,* June 14, 1995:A14.

Barnes, Helen. "A Comment on Stroud and Pritchard: Child Homicide, Psychiatric Disorder and Dangerousness." *British Journal of Social Work, 31,* 3, June 2001.

Berger, Peter. "Invitation to Sociology." In *Down to Earth Sociology: Introductory Readings,* 15th ed., James M. Henslin, ed. New York: Free Press, 2012. Originally published 1963.

Bianchi, Suzanne M., John P. Robinson, and Melissa A. Milkie. *Changing Rhythms of American Family Life.* New York: Russell Sage Foundation, 2006.

Brajuha, Mario, and Lyle Hallowell. "Legal Intrusion and the Politics of Fieldwork: The Impact of the Brajuha Case." *Urban Life, 14,* 4, January 1986:454–478.

Burgess, Ernest W., and Harvey J. Locke. *The Family: From Institution to Companionship.* New York: American Book, 1945.

Cantoni, Davide. "The Economic Effects of the Protestant Reformation: Testing the Weber Hypothesis in the German Lands." Harvard University Job Market Paper, November 10, 2009.

Coser, Lewis A. *Masters of Sociological Thought: Ideas in Historical and Social Context,* 2nd ed. New York: Harcourt Brace Jovanovich, 1977.

Crossen, Cynthia. "Margin of Error: Studies Galore Support Products and Positions, but Are They Reliable?" *Wall Street Journal,* November 14, 1991:A1.

Davis, R. E., M. P. Couper, N. K. Janz, C. H. Caldwell, and K. Resnicow. "Interviewer Effects in Public Health Surveys." *Health Education Research,* September 17, 2009:13–20.

DeMartini, Joseph R. "Basic and Applied Sociological Work: Divergence, Convergence, or Peaceful Co-existence?" *The Journal of Applied Behavioral Science, 18,* 2, 1982:203–215.

Dobriner, William M. *Social Structures and Systems.* Pacific Palisades, California: Goodyear, 1969b.

Du Bois, W. E. B. *The Souls of Black Folk: Essays and Sketches.* Chicago: McClurg, 1903.

Du Bois, W. E. B. *The Autobiography of W. E. B. Du Bois: A Soliloquy on Viewing My Life from the Last Decade of Its First Century.* New York: International, 1968.

Durkheim, Emile. *Suicide: A Study in Sociology,* John A. Spaulding and George Simpson, trans. New York: Free Press, 1966. Originally published 1897.

Dush, Claire M. Kamp, Catherine L. Cohan, and Paul R. Amato. "The Relationship between Cohabitation and Marital Quality and Stability: Change across Cohorts?" *Journal of Marriage and Family, 65,* 3, August 2003:539–549.

Edgerton, Robert B. *Sick Societies: Challenging the Myth of Primitive Harmony.* New York: Free Press, 1992.

Erikson, Kai T. *Everything in Its Path: Destruction of Community in the Buffalo Creek Flood.* New York: Simon and Schuster, 1978.

Estes, Larissa J., Linda E. Lloyd, Michelle Teti, et al. "Perceptions of Audio Computer-Assisted Self-Interviewing (ACASI) among Women in an HIV-Positive Prevention Program." *PLoS ONE, 5,* 2, February 10, 2010:e9149.

Feder, Barnaby. "Billboards That Know You by Name." *New York Times,* January 29, 2007.

Gilman, Charlotte Perkins. *The Man-Made World or, Our Androcentric Culture.* New York: 1971. Originally published 1911.

Gitlin, Todd. *The Twilight of Common Dreams: Why America Is Wracked by Culture Wars.* New York: Metropolitan Books, 1997.

Goleman, Daniel. "Pollsters Enlist Psychologists in Quest for Unbiased Results." *New York Times,* September 7, 1993:C1, C11.

Henley, Nancy, Mykol Hamilton, and Barrie Thorne. "Womanspeak and Manspeak." In *Beyond Sex Roles,* Alice G. Sargent, ed. St Paul, MN: West, 1985.

Humphreys, Laud. *Tearoom Trade: Impersonal Sex in Public Places,* enlarged ed. Chicago: Aldine, 1975. Originally published 1970.

Humphreys, Laud. "Impersonal Sex and Perceived Satisfaction." In *Studies in the Sociology of Sex,* James M. Henslin, ed. New York: Appleton-Century-Crofts, 1971:351–374.

Kroeger, Brooke. "When a Dissertation Makes a Difference." *New York Times,* March 20, 2004.

Lazarsfeld, Paul F., and Jeffrey G. Reitz. "History of Applied Sociology." *Sociological Practice, 7,* 1989:43–52.

Lee, Raymond M. *Unobtrusive Methods in Social Research.* Philadelphia: Open University Press, 2000.

Leeson, Peter T. "Cooperation and Conflict: Evidence on Self-Enforcing Arrangements and Heterogeneous Groups." *American Journal of Economics and Sociology,* October 2006.

Lengermann, Madoo, and Gillian Niebrugge. *The Women Founders: Sociology and Social Theory, 1830–1930.* Prospect Heights, Ill.: Waveland Press, 2007.

Levi, Ken. "Becoming a Hit Man." In *Exploring Social Life: Readings to Accompany Essentials of Sociology: A Down-to-Earth Approach,* 4th ed., James M. Henslin, ed. Boston: Allyn and Bacon, 2009. Originally published 1981.

Linz, Daniel, Paul Bryant, et al. "An Examination of the Assumption That Adult Businesses Are Associated with Crime in Surrounding Areas: A Secondary Effects Study in Charlotte, North Carolina." *Law & Society, 38,* 1, March 2004:69–104.

Marx, Karl, and Friedrich Engels. *Communist Manifesto.* New York: Pantheon, 1967. Originally published 1848.

Mills, C. Wright. *The Sociological Imagination.* New York: Oxford University Press, 1959.

National School Safety Center. "School Associated Violent Deaths." Westlake Village, Calif., 2011.

O'Brien, John E. "Violence in Divorce-Prone Families." In *Violence in the Family,* Suzanne K. Steinmetz and Murray A. Straus, eds. New York: Dodd, Mead, 1975:65–75.

Osborne, Cynthia, Wendy D. Manning, and Pamela J. Smock. "Married and Cohabiting Parents' Relationship Stability: A Focus on Race and Ethnicity." *Marriage and Family, 69,* December 2007:1345–1366.

Pager, Devah. "The Mark of a Criminal Record." *American Journal of Sociology, 108,* 5, March 2003:937–975.

Pager, Devah, Bruce Western, and Bart Bonikowski. "Discrimination in a Low-Wage Labor Market: A Field Experiment." *American Sociological Review, 74,* 5, October 2009:777–799.

Piven, Frances Fox. "Can Power from Below Change the World?" *American Sociological Review, 73,* 1, February 2008:1–14.

Resnik, David B. "Financial Interests and Research Bias." *Perspectives on Science, 8,* 3, Fall 2000:255–283.

Rosenbloom, Stephanie. "In Bid to Sway Sales, Cameras Track Shoppers." *New York Times,* March 19, 2010.

Sageman, Marc. "Explaining Terror Networks in the 21st Century." *Footnotes,* May–June 2008a:7.

Sageman, Marc. *Leaderless Jihad: Terror Networks in the Twenty-First Century.* Philadelphia: University of Pennsylvania Press, 2008b.

Schaefer, Richard T. *Sociology,* 3rd ed. New York: McGraw-Hill, 1989.

Scully, Diana, and Joseph Marolla. "Convicted Rapists' Vocabulary of Motive: Excuses and Justifications." *Social Problems, 31,* 5, June 1984:530–544.

Scully, Diana, and Joseph Marolla. "'Riding the Bull at Gilley's': Convicted Rapists Describe the Rewards of Rape." In *Down to Earth Sociology: Introductory Readings,* 15th ed., James M. Henslin, ed. New York: Free Press, 2012.

Singer, Natasha. "Shoppers Who Can't Have Secrets." *New York Times,* April 30, 2010.

Stark, Rodney. *Sociology,* 3rd ed. Belmont, Calif.: Wadsworth, 1989.

Statistical Abstract of the United States. Washington D.C.: U.S. Census Bureau, published annually.

Stokes, Randall. "Over 60 Years of Sociology at UMass–Amherst." *ASA Footnotes,* May–June 2009:6.

Turner, Jonathan H. *The Structure of Sociological Theory.* Homewood, Ill.: Dorsey, 1978.

Venkatesh, Sudhir. *Gang Leader for a Day: A Rogue Sociologist Takes to the Streets.* New York: Penguin, 2008.

Volti, Rudi. *Society and Technological Change,* 3rd ed. New York: St. Martin's Press, 1995.

Von Hoffman, Nicholas. "Sociological Snoopers." *Transaction 7,* May 1970:4, 6.

Weber, Max. *The Protestant Ethic and the Spirit of Capitalism.* New York: Scribner's, 1958. Originally published 1904–1905.

Weiss, Karen G. "'Boys Will Be Boys' and Other Gendered Accounts: An Exploration of Victims' Excuses and Justifications for Unwanted Sexual Contact and Coercion." *Violence against Women, 15,* 2009:810–834.

Culture

From Chapter 2 of *Sociology: A Down-to-Earth Approach, Core Concepts*, Fifth Edition. James M. Henslin.
Copyright © 2012 by Pearson Education, Inc. All rights reserved.

When I first arrived in Morocco, I found the sights that greeted me exotic—not unlike the scenes in *Casablanca* or *Raiders of the Lost Ark.* The men, women, and even the children really did wear those white robes that reached down to their feet. What was especially striking was that the women were almost totally covered. Despite the heat, they wore not only full-length gowns but also head coverings that reached down over their foreheads with veils that covered their faces from the nose down. You could see nothing but their eyes—and every eye seemed the same shade of brown.

And how short everyone was! The Arab women looked to be, on average, 5 feet, and the men only about three or four inches taller. As the only blue-eyed, blond, 6-foot-plus person around, and the only one who was wearing jeans and a pullover shirt, in a world of white-robed short people I stood out like a creature from another planet. Everyone stared. No matter where I went, they stared. Wherever I looked, I saw people watching me intently. Even staring back had no effect. It was so different from home, where, if you caught someone staring at you, that person would look embarrassed and immediately glance away.

> **"Everyone stared. No matter where I went, they stared."**

And lines? The concept apparently didn't even exist. Buying a ticket for a bus or train meant pushing and shoving toward the ticket man (always a man—no women were visible in any public position), who took the money from whichever outstretched hand he decided on.

And germs? That notion didn't seem to exist here either. Flies swarmed over the food in the restaurants and the unwrapped loaves of bread in the stores. Shopkeepers would considerately shoo off the flies before handing me a loaf. They also offered home delivery. I watched a bread vendor deliver a loaf to a woman who was standing on a second-floor balcony. She first threw her money to the bread vendor, and he then threw the unwrapped bread up to her. Unfortunately, his throw was off. The bread bounced off the wrought-iron balcony railing and landed in the street, which was filled with people, wandering dogs, and the ever-present urinating and defecating donkeys. The vendor simply picked up the unwrapped loaf and threw it again. This certainly wasn't his day, for he missed again. But he made it on his third attempt. The woman smiled as she turned back into her apartment, apparently to prepare the noon meal for her family.

Dia de los Muertos (Day of the Dead) California

What Is Culture?

Watch
The Storytelling Class
on mysoclab.com

What is culture? The concept is sometimes easier to grasp by description than by definition. For example, suppose you meet a young woman from India who has just arrived in the United States. That her culture is different from yours is immediately evident. You first see it in her clothing, jewelry, makeup, and hairstyle. Next you hear it in her speech. It then becomes apparent by her gestures. Later, you might hear her express unfamiliar beliefs about relationships or what is valuable in life. All of these characteristics are indicative of **culture**—the language, beliefs, values, norms, behaviors, and even material objects that are passed from one generation to the next.

In northern Africa, I was surrounded by a culture quite different from mine. It was evident in everything I saw and heard. The **material culture**—such things as jewelry, art, buildings, weapons, machines, and even eating utensils, hairstyles, and clothing—provided a sharp contrast to what I was used to seeing. There is nothing inherently "natural" about material culture. That is, it is no more natural (or unnatural) to wear gowns on the street than it is to wear jeans.

I also found myself immersed in an unfamiliar **nonmaterial culture,** that is, a group's ways of thinking (its beliefs, values, and other assumptions about the world) and doing (its common *patterns of behavior*, including language, gestures, and other forms of interaction). North African assumptions that it is acceptable to stare at others in public and to push people aside to buy tickets are examples of nonmaterial culture. So are U.S. assumptions that it is wrong to do either of these things. Like material culture, neither custom is "right." People simply become comfortable with the customs they learn during childhood, and—as happened when I visited northern Africa—uncomfortable when their basic assumptions about life are challenged.

Culture and Taken-for-Granted Orientations to Life

To develop a sociological imagination, it is essential to understand how culture affects people's lives. If we meet someone from a different culture, the encounter may make us aware of culture's pervasive influence on all aspects of a person's life. Attaining the same level of awareness regarding our own culture, however, is quite another matter. We usually take *our* speech, *our* gestures, *our* beliefs, and *our* customs for granted. We assume that they are "normal" or "natural," and we almost always follow them without question. As anthropologist Ralph Linton (1936) said, "The last thing a fish would ever notice would be water." So also with people: Except in unusual circumstances, most characteristics of our own culture remain imperceptible to us.

Yet culture's significance is profound; it touches almost every aspect of who and what we are. We came into this life without a language; without values and morality; with no ideas about religion, war, money, love, use of space, and so on. We possessed none of these fundamental orientations that are so essential in determining the type of people we become. Yet by this point in our lives, we all have acquired them—and take them for granted. Sociologists call this *culture within us.* These learned and shared ways of believing and of doing (another definition of culture) penetrate our beings at an early age and quickly become part of our taken-for-granted assumptions about what normal behavior is. *Culture becomes the lens through which we perceive and evaluate what is going on around us.* Seldom do we question these assumptions, for, like water to a fish, the lens through which we view life remains largely beyond our perception.

The rare instances in which these assumptions are challenged, however, can be upsetting. Although as a sociologist I should be able to look at my own culture "from the outside," my trip to Africa quickly revealed how fully I had internalized my own culture. My upbringing in Western culture had given me assumptions about aspects of social life that had become rooted deeply in my being—appropriate eye contact, proper hygiene, and the use of space. But in this part of Africa these assumptions

culture the language, beliefs, values, norms, behaviors, and even material objects that characterize a group and are passed from one generation to the next

material culture the material objects that distinguish a group of people, such as their art, buildings, weapons, utensils, machines, hairstyles, clothing, and jewelry

nonmaterial culture a group's ways of thinking (including its beliefs, values, and other assumptions about the world) and doing (its common patterns of behavior, including language and other forms of interaction); also called *symbolic culture*

What is culture? How does it provide our basic orientations to life?

AFP PHOTO/KARIM SAHIB/Newscom

were useless in helping me navigate everyday life. No longer could I count on people to stare only surreptitiously, to take precautions against invisible microbes, or to stand in line in an orderly fashion, one behind the other.

As you can tell from the opening vignette, I found these unfamiliar behaviors unsettling, for they violated my basic expectations of "the way people *ought* to be"—and I did not even realize how firmly I held these expectations until they were challenged so abruptly. When my nonmaterial culture failed me—when it no longer enabled me to make sense out of the world—I experienced a disorientation known as **culture shock.** In the case of buying tickets, the fact that I was several inches taller than most Moroccans and thus able to outreach others helped me to adjust partially to their different ways of doing things. But I never did get used to the idea that pushing ahead of others was "right," and I always felt guilty when I used my size to receive preferential treatment.

Culture shock is a two-way street, of course. You can imagine what culture shock people from a tribal society would experience if they were thrust into the United States. This actually happened, as the Cultural Diversity box on the next page describes.

An important consequence of culture within us is **ethnocentrism,** a tendency to use our own group's ways of doing things as a yardstick for judging others. All of us learn that the ways of our own group are good, right, and even superior to other ways of life. As sociologist William Sumner (1906), who developed this concept, said, "One's own group is the center of everything, and all others are scaled and rated with reference to it." Ethnocentrism has both positive and negative consequences. On the positive side, it creates in-group loyalties. On the negative side, ethnocentrism can lead to discrimination against people whose ways differ from ours.

The many ways in which culture affects our lives fascinate sociologists. In this chapter, we'll examine how profoundly culture influences everything we are and whatever we do. This will serve as a basis from which you can start to analyze your own assumptions of reality. I should give you a warning at this point: You might develop a changed perspective on social life and your role in it. If so, life will never look the same.

In Sum: To avoid losing track of the ideas under discussion, let's pause for a moment to summarize and, in some instances, clarify the principles we have covered.

1. There is nothing "natural" about material culture. Arabs wear gowns on the street and feel that it is natural to do so. Americans do the same with jeans.
2. There is nothing "natural" about nonmaterial culture. It is just as arbitrary to stand in line as to push and shove.
3. Culture penetrates deeply into our thinking, becoming a taken-for-granted lens through which we see the world and obtain our perception of reality.
4. Culture provides implicit instructions that tell us what we ought to do and how we ought to think. It establishes a fundamental basis for our decision making.
5. Culture also provides a "moral imperative"; that is, the culture that we internalize becomes the "right" way of doing things. (I, for example, believed deeply that it was wrong to push and shove to get ahead of others.)
6. Coming into contact with a radically different culture challenges our basic assumptions of life. (I experienced culture shock when I discovered that my deeply ingrained cultural ideas about hygiene and the use of personal space no longer applied.)
7. Although the particulars of culture differ from one group of people to another, culture itself is universal. That is, all people have culture, for a society cannot exist without developing shared, learned ways of dealing with the challenges of life.
8. All people are ethnocentric, which has both positive and negative consequences.

What a tremendous photo for sociologists! Seldom are we treated to such cultural contrasts. Can you see how the cultures of these women have given them not only different orientations concerning the presentation of their bodies but also of gender relations, how they expect to relate to men?

culture shock the disorientation that people experience when they come in contact with a fundamentally different culture and can no longer depend on their taken-for-granted assumptions about life

ethnocentrism the use of one's own culture as a yardstick for judging the ways of other individuals or societies, generally leading to a negative evaluation of their values, norms, and behaviors

What is culture shock? Ethnocentrism? How are they related to our assumptions about life?

Cultural Diversity in the United States

Culture Shock: The Arrival of the Hmong

Imagine that you were a member of a small tribal group in the mountains of Laos. Village life and the clan were all you knew. There were no schools, and you learned everything you needed to know from your relatives. U.S. agents recruited the men of your village to fight communists, and they gained a reputation as fierce fighters. When the U.S. forces were defeated in Vietnam, your people were moved to the United States so they wouldn't be killed in reprisal.

U.S.A.

Here is what happened. Keep in mind that you had never seen a television or a newspaper and that you had never gone to school. Your entire world had been the village.

They put you in a big house with wings. It flew.

They gave you strange food on a tray. The Sani-Wipes were hard to chew.

After the trip, you were placed in a house. This was an adventure. You had never seen locks before, as no one locked up anything in the village. Most of the village homes didn't even have doors, much less locks.

You found the bathroom perplexing. At first, you tried to wash rice in the bowl of water, which seemed to be provided for this purpose. But when you pressed the handle, the water and rice disappeared. After you learned what the toilet was for, you found it difficult not to slip off the little white round thing when you stood on it. In the village, you didn't need a toilet seat when you squatted in a field to defecate.

When you threw water on the electric stove to put out the burner, it sparked and smoked. You became afraid to use the stove because it might explode.

And no one liked it when you tried to plant a vegetable garden in the park.

Your new world was so different that, to help you adjust, the settlement agency told you (Fadiman 1997):

1. To send mail, you must use stamps.
2. The door of the refrigerator must be shut.

GARY PORTER/KRT/Newscom

Children make a fast adjustment to a new culture, although, as with this Hmong child and her grandmother in Minneapolis, they are caught between the old and the new.

3. Do not stand or squat on the toilet since it may break.
4. Always ask before picking your neighbor's flowers, fruit, or vegetables.
5. In colder areas you must wear shoes, socks, and appropriate outerwear. Otherwise, you may become ill.
6. Always use a handkerchief or a tissue to blow your nose in public places or inside a public building.
7. Picking your nose or ears in public is frowned upon in the United States.
8. Never urinate in the street. This creates a smell that is offensive to Americans. They also believe that it causes disease.

To help the Hmong assimilate, U.S. officials dispersed them across the nation. This, they felt, would help them to adjust to the dominant culture and prevent a Hmong subculture from developing. The dispersal brought feelings of isolation to the clan- and village-based Hmong. As soon as they had a chance, the Hmong moved from these towns scattered across the country to live in areas with other Hmong, the major one being in California's Central Valley. Here they renewed village relationships and helped one another adjust to the society they had never desired to join.

For Your Consideration

→ Do you think you would have reacted differently if you had been a displaced Hmong? Why did the Hmong need one another more than their U.S. neighbors to adjust to their new life? What cultural shock do you think a U.S.-born 19-year-old Hmong would experience if his or her parents decided to return to Laos?

Practicing Cultural Relativism

To counter our tendency to use our own culture as the standard by which we judge other cultures, we can practice **cultural relativism;** that is, we can try to understand a culture on its own terms. This means looking at how the elements of a culture fit together, without judging those elements as superior or inferior to our own way of life.

cultural relativism not judging a culture but trying to understand it on its own terms

Why did the Hmong need their fellow villagers to help them adjust to American life? What is cultural relativism?

With our own culture embedded so deeply within us, however, practicing cultural relativism can challenge our orientations to life. For example, most U.S. citizens appear to have strong feelings against raising bulls for the purpose of stabbing them to death in front of crowds that shout "Olé!" According to cultural relativism, however, bullfighting must be viewed from the perspective of the culture in which it takes place—*its* history, *its* folklore, *its* ideas of bravery, and *its* ideas of sex roles.

You may still regard bullfighting as wrong, of course, particularly if your culture, which is deeply ingrained in you, has no history of bullfighting. We all possess culturally specific ideas about cruelty to animals, ideas that have evolved slowly and match other elements of our culture. In some areas of the United States, cock fighting, dog fighting, and bear–dog fighting were once common. Only as the culture changed were they gradually eliminated.

None of us can be entirely successful at practicing cultural relativism. I think you will enjoy the Cultural Diversity box on the next page, but my best guess is that you will evaluate these "strange" foods through the lens of your own culture. Applying cultural relativism, however, is an attempt to refocus that lens so we can appreciate other ways of life rather than simply asserting "Our way is right." Look at the photos a few pages ahead. As you view them, try to appreciate the cultural differences they illustrate about standards of beauty.

Although cultural relativism helps us to avoid cultural smugness, this view has come under attack. In a provocative book, *Sick Societies* (1992), anthropologist Robert Edgerton suggests that we develop a scale for evaluating cultures on their "quality of life," much as we do for U.S. cities. He also asks why we should consider cultures that practice female circumcision, gang rape, or wife beating, or cultures that sell little girls into prostitution, as morally equivalent to those that do not. Cultural values that result in exploitation, he says, are inferior to those that enhance people's lives.

Edgerton's sharp questions and incisive examples bring us to a topic that comes up repeatedly in this text: the disagreements that arise among scholars as they confront contrasting views of reality. It is such questioning of assumptions that keeps sociology interesting.

JESUS DIGES/EPA/Landov
Many Americans perceive bullfighting as a cruel activity that should be illegal everywhere. To most Spaniards, bullfighting is a sport that pits matador and bull in a unifying image of power, courage, and glory. *Cultural relativism* requires that we suspend our own perspectives in order to grasp the perspectives of others, something easier described than attained.

Components of Symbolic Culture

Sociologists often refer to nonmaterial culture as **symbolic culture,** because it consists of the symbols that people use. A **symbol** is something to which people attach meaning and that they use to communicate with one another. Symbols include gestures, language, values, norms, sanctions, folkways, and mores. Let's look at each of these components of symbolic culture.

Gestures

Gestures, movements of the body to communicate with others, are shorthand ways to convey messages without using words. Although people in every culture of the world use gestures, a gesture's meaning may change completely from one culture to another. North Americans, for example, communicate a succinct message by raising the middle finger in a short, upward stabbing motion. I wish to stress "North Americans," for this gesture does not convey the same message in most parts of the world.

I was surprised to find that this particular gesture was not universal, having internalized it to such an extent that I thought everyone knew what it meant. When I was comparing gestures with friends in Mexico, however, this gesture drew a blank look from them. After I explained its intended meaning, they laughed and showed me their rudest gesture—placing the hand under the armpit and moving the upper arm up and down. To me, they simply looked as if they were imitating monkeys, but to them the gesture meant "Your mother is a whore"—the worst possible insult in that culture.

symbolic culture another term for nonmaterial culture

symbol something to which people attach meaning and then use to communicate with one another

gestures the ways in which people use their bodies to communicate with one another

What does this statement mean? "Cultural relativism helps us to avoid cultural smugness."

Cultural Diversity around the World

You Are What You Eat? An Exploration in Cultural Relativity

Here is a chance to test your ethnocentrism and ability to practice cultural relativity. You probably know that the French like to eat snails and that in some Asian cultures chubby dogs and cats are considered a delicacy ("Ah, lightly browned with a little doggy sauce!"). But did you know that cod sperm is a delicacy in Japan (Halpern 2011)? That flies, scorpions, crickets, and beetles are on the menu of restaurants in parts of Thailand (Gampbell 2006)?

Marston Bates (1967), a zoologist, noted this ethnocentric reaction to food:

> I remember once, in the llanos of Colombia, sharing a dish of toasted ants at a remote farmhouse. . . . My host and I fell into conversation about the general question of what people eat or do not eat, and I remarked that in my country people eat the legs of frogs.
>
> The very thought of this filled my ant-eating friends with horror; it was as though I had mentioned some repulsive sex habit.

Then there is the experience of a friend, Dusty Friedman, who told me:

> When traveling in Sudan, I ate some interesting things that I wouldn't likely eat now that I'm back in our society. Raw baby camel's liver with chopped herbs was a delicacy. So was camel's milk cheese patties that had been cured in dry camel's dung.

You might be able to see yourself eating frog legs and toasted ants, beetles, even flies. (Or maybe not.) Perhaps you could even stomach cod sperm and raw camel liver, maybe even dogs and cats, but here's another test of your ethnocentrism and cultural relativity. Maxine Kingston (1975),

an English professor whose parents grew up in China, wrote:

> "Do you know what people in [the Nantou region of] China eat when they have the money?" my mother began. "They buy into a monkey feast. The eaters sit around a thick wood table with a hole in the middle. Boys bring in the monkey at the end of a pole. Its neck is in a collar at the end of the pole, and it is screaming. Its hands are tied behind it. They clamp the monkey into the table; the whole table fits like another collar around its neck. Using a surgeon's saw, the cooks cut a clean line in a circle at the top of its head. To loosen the bone, they tap with a tiny hammer and wedge here and there with a silver pick. Then an old woman reaches out her hand to the monkey's face and up to its scalp, where she tufts some hairs and lifts off the lid of the skull. The eaters spoon out the brains."

MARIANA BAZO/Reuters/Landov

What some consider food, even delicacies, can turn the stomachs of others. This ready-to-eat guinea pig was photographed in Lima, Peru.

For Your Consideration

➔ What is your opinion about eating toasted ants? Beetles? Flies? Fried frog legs? Cod sperm? About eating puppies and kittens? About eating brains scooped out of a living monkey?

➔ If you were reared in U.S. society, more than likely you think that eating frog legs is okay; eating ants or beetles is disgusting; and eating flies, cod sperm, dogs, cats, and monkey brains is downright repugnant. How would you apply the concepts of ethnocentrism and cultural relativism to your perceptions of these customs?

Gestures not only facilitate communication but also, because they differ around the world, can lead to misunderstanding, embarrassment, or worse. One time in Mexico, for example, I raised my hand to a certain height to indicate how tall a child was. My hosts began to laugh. It turned out that Mexicans use three hand gestures to indicate height: one for people, a second for animals, and yet another for plants. They were amused because I had used the plant gesture to indicate the child's height. (See Figure 1.)

To get along in another culture, then, it is important to learn the gestures of that culture. If you don't, you will fail to achieve the simplicity of communication that gestures allow and you may overlook or misunderstand much of what is happening, run the risk of appearing foolish, and possibly offend people. In some cultures, for example,

Bates, Marston. Gluttons and Libertines: *Human Problems of Being Natural.* New York: Vintage Books, 1967. Quoted in Crapo, Richley H. *Cultural Anthropology: Understanding Ourselves and Others,* 5th ed. Boston: McGraw Hill, 2002.

Kingston, Maxine Hong. *The Woman Warrior.* New York: Vintage Books, 1975:108. Quoted in Frank J. Zulke and Jacqueline P. Kirley. *Through the Eyes of Social Science,* 6th ed. Prospect Heights, Ill.: Waveland Press, 2002.

How does cultural relativism apply to food customs?

Figure 1	Gestures to Indicate Height, Southern Mexico

C.M. Holmgren/Lightbox

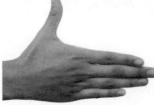

© Steve Hamblin/Alamy Royalty Free

By the author.

C.M. Holmgren/Lightbox

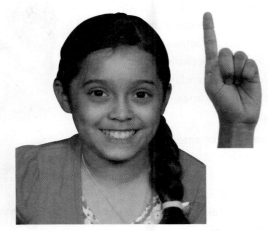

Lena Leal-Floyd/Lightbox

you would provoke deep offense if you were to offer food or a gift with your left hand, because the left hand is reserved for dirty tasks, such as wiping after going to the toilet. Left-handed Americans visiting Arabs, please note!

Suppose for a moment that you are visiting southern Italy. After eating one of the best meals in your life, you are so pleased that when you catch the waiter's eye, you smile broadly and use the standard U.S. "A-OK" gesture of putting your thumb and forefinger together and making a large "O." The waiter looks horrified, and you are struck speechless when the manager asks you to leave. What have you done? Nothing on purpose, of course, but in that culture this gesture refers to a lower part of the human body that is not mentioned in polite company (Ekman et al. 1984).

Is it really true that there are no universal gestures? There is some disagreement on this point. Some anthropologists claim that no gesture is universal. They point out that even nodding the head up and down to indicate "yes" is not universal, because in some parts of the world, such as areas of Turkey, nodding the head up and down means "no" (Ekman et al. 1984). However, ethologists, researchers who study biological bases of behavior, claim that expressions of anger, pouting, fear, and sadness are built into our biological makeup and are universal (Eibl-Eibesfeldt 1970:404; Horwitz and Wakefield 2007). They point out that even infants who are born blind and deaf, who have had no chance to learn these gestures, express themselves in the same way.

Although this matter is not yet settled, we can note that gestures tend to vary remarkably around the world. It is also significant that certain gestures can elicit emotions; some gestures are so closely associated with emotional messages that the gestures themselves summon up emotions. For example, my introduction to Mexican gestures of insult mentioned earlier took place at a dinner table. It was evident that my husband-and-wife hosts were trying to hide their embarrassment at using their culture's obscene gesture at their dinner table. And I felt the same way—not about *their* gesture, of course, which meant nothing to me—but about the one I was teaching them.

James M. Henslin

Although most *gestures* are learned, and therefore vary from culture to culture, some gestures that represent fundamental emotions such as sadness, anger, and fear appear to be inborn. This crying child whom I photographed in India differs little from a crying child in China—or the United States or anywhere else on the globe. In a few years, however, this child will demonstrate a variety of gestures highly specific to his Hindu culture.

How are gestures an essential part of symbolic culture?

Standards of Beauty

Standards of beauty vary so greatly from one culture to another that what one group finds attractive, another may not. Yet, in its *ethnocentrism*, each group thinks that its standards are the best—that the appearance reflects what beauty "really" is.

As indicated by these photos, around the world men and women aspire to their group's norms of physical attractiveness. To make themselves appealing to others, they try to make their appearance reflect those standards.

© Prisma/SuperStock

Jordan Siemens/Photodisc/Getty Images Royalty Free

Ecuador

United States

Jean-Pierre Lescourret/Corbis

Thailand

Panorama/The Image Works

China

© Piers Cavendish/Impact/HIP/The Image Works

Kenya

Cameroon

© ilse schrama/Alamy

Tibet

Picture Finders Ltd./eStock Photo

New Guinea

© Pacific Stock/SuperStock

How is beauty an essential part of symbolic culture?

Language

The primary way in which people communicate with one another is through **language**—symbols that can be combined in an infinite number of ways for the purpose of communicating abstract thought. Each word is actually a symbol, a sound to which we have attached some particular meaning. Although all human groups have language, there is nothing universal about the meanings given to particular sounds. Like gestures, in different cultures the same sound may mean something entirely different—or may have no meaning at all. In German, for example, *gift* means "poison," so if you give a box of chocolates to a non-English-speaking German and say, "Gift, Eat" . . . .

Because *language allows culture to exist,* its significance for human life is difficult to overstate. Consider the following effects of language.

Language Allows Human Experience to Be Cumulative.   By means of language, we pass ideas, knowledge, and even attitudes on to the next generation. This allows others to build on experiences in which they may never directly participate. As a result, humans are able to modify their behavior in light of what earlier generations have learned. This takes us to the central sociological significance of language: *Language allows culture to develop by freeing people to move beyond their immediate experiences.*

Without language, human culture would be little more advanced than that of the lower primates. If we communicated by grunts and gestures, we would be limited to a short time span—to events now taking place, those that have just taken place, or those that will take place immediately—a sort of slightly extended present. You can grunt and gesture, for example, that you want a drink of water, but in the absence of language how could you share ideas concerning past or future events? There would be little or no way to communicate to others what event you had in mind, much less the greater complexities that humans communicate—ideas and feelings about events.

Language Provides a Social or Shared Past.   Without language, we would have few memories, for we associate experiences with words and then use those words to recall the experience. In the absence of language, how would we communicate the few memories we had to others? By attaching words to an event, however, and then using those words to recall it, we are able to discuss the event. This is highly significant for what we are as humans, for our talking is far from "just talk." As we talk about past events, we develop shared understandings about what those events mean. In short, through talk, people develop a shared past.

Language Provides a Social or Shared Future.   Language also extends our time horizons forward. Because language enables us to agree on times, dates, and places, it allows us to plan activities with one another. Think about it for a moment. Without language, how could you ever plan future events? How could you possibly communicate goals, times, and plans? Whatever planning could exist would be limited to rudimentary communications, perhaps to an agreement to meet at a certain place when the sun is in a certain position. But think of the difficulty, perhaps the impossibility, of conveying just a slight change in this simple arrangement, such as "I can't make it tomorrow, but my neighbor can take my place, if that's all right with you."

Language Allows Shared Perspectives.   Our ability to speak, then, provides us with a social (or shared) past and future. This is vital for humanity. It is a watershed that distinguishes us from animals. But speech does much more than this. When we talk with one another, we are exchanging ideas about events; that is, we are sharing perspectives. Our words are the embodiment of our experiences, distilled into a readily exchangeable form, one that is mutually understandable to people who have learned that language. *Talking about events allows us to arrive at the shared understandings that form the basis of social life.* Not sharing a language while living alongside one another, however, invites miscommunication and suspicion. This risk, which comes with a diverse society, is discussed in the Cultural Diversity box on the next page.

language a system of symbols that can be combined in an infinite number of ways and can represent not only objects but also abstract thought

How does *language* provide a shared past, present, and future?

Cultural Diversity in the United States

Miami—Continuing Controversy over Language

Immigration from Cuba and other Spanish-speaking countries has been so vast that most residents of Miami are Latinos. Half of Miami's 400,000 residents have trouble speaking English. Only *one-fourth* of Miamians speak English at home. Many English-only speakers are leaving Miami, saying that not being able to speak Spanish is a handicap to getting work. "They should learn Spanish," some reply. As Pedro Falcon, an immigrant from Nicaragua, said, "Miami is the capital of Latin America. The population speaks Spanish."

As the English-speakers see it, this pinpoints the problem: Miami is in the United States, not in Latin America.

Controversy over immigrants and language isn't new. The millions of Germans who moved to the United States in the 1800s brought their language with them. Not only did they hold their religious services in German, but they also opened schools taught in German; published German-language newspapers; and spoke German at home, in the stores, and in the taverns.

Some of their English-speaking neighbors didn't like this a bit. "Why don't those Germans assimilate?" they wondered. "Just whose side would they fight on if we had a war?"

This question was answered, of course, with the participation of German Americans in two world wars. It was even a

Heather Boone/Lightbox

Mural on Calle Ocho in Miami

general descended from German immigrants (Eisenhower) who led the armed forces that defeated Hitler.

But what happened to all this German language? The first generation of immigrants spoke German almost exclusively. The second generation assimilated, speaking English at home, but also speaking German when they visited their parents. For the most part, the third generation knew German only as "that language" that their grandparents spoke.

The same thing is happening with the Latino immigrants. Spanish is being kept alive longer, however, because Mexico borders the United States, and there is constant traffic between the countries. The continuing migration from Mexico and other Spanish-speaking countries also feeds the language.

If Germany bordered the United States, there would still be a lot of German spoken here.

Sources: Based on Sharp 1992; Usdansky 1992; Kent and Lalasz 2007; Salomon 2008.

Language Allows Shared, Goal-Directed Behavior. Common understandings enable us to establish a *purpose* for getting together. Let's suppose you want to go on a picnic. You use speech not only to plan the picnic but also to decide on reasons for having the picnic—which may be anything from "because it's a nice day and it shouldn't be wasted studying" to "because it's my birthday." Language permits you to blend individual activities into an integrated sequence. In other words, through discussion you decide when and where you will go; who will drive; who will bring the hamburgers, the potato chips, the soda; where and when you will meet. Only because of language can you participate in such a common yet complex event as a picnic—or build roads and bridges or attend college classes.

In Sum: The sociological significance of language is that it takes us beyond the world of apes and allows culture to develop. Language frees us from the present, actually giving us a social past and a social future. That is, language gives us the capacity to share understandings about the past and to develop shared perceptions about the future. Language also allows us to establish underlying purposes for our activities. In short, *language is the basis of culture.*

Language and Perception: The Sapir-Whorf Hypothesis

In the 1930s, two anthropologists, Edward Sapir and Benjamin Whorf, became intrigued when they noticed that the Hopi Indians of the southwestern United States

How does language both unite and divide people? How can language be a basis of conflict?

had no words to distinguish the past, the present, and the future. English, in contrast—as well as French, Spanish, Swahili, and other languages—carefully distinguishes these three time frames. From this observation, Sapir and Whorf began to think that words might be more than labels that people attach to things. Eventually, they concluded that *language has embedded within it ways of looking at the world*. In other words, language not only expresses our thoughts and perceptions, but language also shapes the way we think and perceive (Sapir 1949; Whorf 1956).

The **Sapir-Whorf hypothesis** challenges common sense: It indicates that rather than objects and events forcing themselves onto our consciousness, it is our language that determines our consciousness, and hence our perception of objects and events. Sociologist Eviatar Zerubavel (1991) points out that his native language, Hebrew, does not have separate words for jam and jelly. Both go by the same term, and only when Zerubavel learned English could he "see" this difference, which is "obvious" to native English speakers. Similarly, if you learn to classify students as Jocks, Goths, Stoners, Skaters, Band Geeks, and Preps, you will perceive students in entirely different ways from someone who does not know these classifications.

When I lived in Spain, I was struck by the relevance of the Sapir-Whorf hypothesis. As a native English speaker, I had learned that the term *dried fruits* refers to apricots, apples, and so on. In Spain, I found that *frutos secos* refers not only to such objects but also to things like almonds, walnuts, and pecans. My English makes me see fruits and nuts as quite separate types of objects. This seems "natural" to me, while combining them into one unit seems "natural" to Spanish speakers. If I had learned Spanish first, my perception of these objects would be different.

Although Sapir and Whorf's observation that the Hopi do not have tenses was inaccurate (Edgerton 1992:27), they did stumble onto a major truth about social life. Learning a language means not only learning words but also acquiring the perceptions embedded in that language. In other words, language both reflects and shapes our cultural experiences (Boroditsky 2010). The racial–ethnic terms that our culture provides, for example, influence how we see both ourselves and others, a point that is discussed in the Cultural Diversity box on the next page.

Values, Norms, and Sanctions

To learn a culture is to learn people's **values,** their ideas of what is desirable in life. When we uncover people's values, we learn a great deal about them, for values are the standards by which people define what is good and bad, beautiful and ugly. Values underlie our preferences, guide our choices, and indicate what we hold worthwhile in life.

Every group develops expectations concerning the "right" way to reflect its values. Sociologists use the term **norms** to describe those expectations (or rules of behavior) that develop out of a group's values. The term **sanctions** refers to the reactions people receive for following or breaking norms. A **positive sanction** expresses approval for following a norm, and a **negative sanction** reflects disapproval for breaking a norm. Positive sanctions can be material, such as a prize, a trophy, or money, but in everyday life they usually consist of hugs, smiles, a pat on the back, or even handshakes and "high fives." Negative sanctions can also be material—being fined in court is one example—but negative sanctions, too, are more likely to be symbolic: harsh words, or gestures such as frowns, stares, clenched jaws, or raised fists. Getting a raise at work is a positive sanction, indicating that you have followed the norms clustering around work values. Getting fired, in contrast, is a negative sanction, indicating that you have violated these norms. The North American finger gesture discussed earlier is, of course, a negative sanction.

Sapir-Whorf hypothesis Edward Sapir and Benjamin Whorf's hypothesis that language creates ways of thinking and perceiving

values the standards by which people define what is desirable or undesirable, good or bad, beautiful or ugly

norms expectations of "right" behavior

sanctions either expressions of approval given to people for upholding norms or expressions of disapproval for violating them

positive sanction a reward or positive reaction for following norms, ranging from a smile to a material reward

negative sanction an expression of disapproval for breaking a norm, ranging from a mild, informal reaction such as a frown to a formal reaction such as a prison sentence

Many societies relax their *norms* during specified occasions. At these times, known as moral holidays, behavior that is ordinarily not permitted is allowed. Shown here at Mardi Gras in New Orleans is a woman who is about to show her breasts to get beads dropped to her from the balcony. When a moral holiday is over, the usual enforcement of rules follows.

Chris Graythen/Getty Images

According to the Sapir-Whorf hypothesis, how does language influence our perception?

Cultural Diversity in the United States

Race and Language: Searching for Self-Labels

The groups that dominate society often determine the names that are used to refer to racial–ethnic groups. If those names become associated with oppression, they take on negative meanings. For example, the terms *Negro* and *colored people* came to be associated with submissiveness and low status. To overcome these meanings, those referred to by these terms began to identify themselves as *black* or *African American*. They infused these new terms with respect—a basic source of self-esteem that they felt the old terms denied them.

In a twist, African Americans—and to a lesser extent Latinos, Asian Americans, and Native Americans—have changed the rejected term *colored people* to *people of color*. Those who embrace this modified term are imbuing it with meanings that offer an identity of respect. The term also has political meanings. It implies bonds that cross racial–ethnic lines, mutual ties, and a sense of identity rooted in historical oppression.

There is *always* disagreement about racial–ethnic terms, and this one is no exception. Although most rejected the term *colored people*, some found in it a sense of respect and claimed it for themselves. The acronym NAACP, for example, stands for the National Association for the Advancement of Colored People. The new term, *people of color*, arouses similar feelings. Some individuals whom this term would include point out that this new label still makes color the primary identifier of people. They stress that humans transcend race–ethnicity, that what we have in

The ethnic terms we choose—or which are given to us—are major self-identifiers. They indicate both membership in some group and a separation from other groups.
© Owen Franken/CORBIS

common as human beings goes much deeper than what you see on the surface. They stress that we should avoid terms that focus on differences in the pigmentation of our skin.

The language of self-reference in a society that is so conscious of skin color is an ongoing issue. As long as our society continues to emphasize such superficial differences, the search for adequate terms is not likely to ever be "finished." In this quest for terms that strike the right chord, the term *people of color* may become a historical footnote. If it does, it will be replaced by another term that indicates a changing self-identification within a changing culture.

For Your Consideration

➤ What terms do you use to refer to your race–ethnicity? What "bad" terms do you know that others have used to refer to your race–ethnicity? What is the difference in meaning between the terms you use and the "bad" terms? Where does that meaning come from?

Because people can find norms stifling, some cultures relieve the pressure through *moral holidays,* specified times when people are allowed to break norms. Moral holidays such as Mardi Gras often center on getting rowdy. Some activities for which people would otherwise be arrested are permitted—and expected—including public drunkenness and some nudity. The norms are never completely dropped, however—just loosened a bit. Go too far, and the police step in.

Some societies have *moral holiday places,* locations where norms are expected to be broken. Red light districts of our cities are examples. There, prostitutes are allowed to work the streets, bothered only when political pressure builds to "clean up" the area. If these same prostitutes attempt to solicit customers in adjacent areas, however, they are promptly arrested. Each year, the hometown of the team that wins the Super Bowl becomes a moral holiday place—for one night.

One of the more interesting examples is "Party Cove" at Lake of the Ozarks in Missouri, a fairly straightlaced area of the country. During the summer, hundreds of boaters—those operating everything from cabin cruisers to jet skis—moor their vessels together in a highly publicized cove, where many get drunk, take off their clothes, and dance on the boats. In one of the more humorous incidents, boaters complained that a

Read
Body Ritual Among the Nacirema by Horace Miner
on **mysoclab.com**

How are values, norms, and sanctions related to one another? How are moral holidays related to values, norms, and sanctions?

nude woman was riding a jet ski outside of the cove. The water patrol investigated but refused to arrest the woman because she was within the law—she had sprayed shaving cream on certain parts of her body. The Missouri Water Patrol has even given a green light to Party Cove, announcing in the local newspaper that officers will not enter this cove, supposedly because "there is so much traffic that they might not be able to get out in time to handle an emergency elsewhere."

Folkways, Mores, and Taboos

Norms that are not strictly enforced are called **folkways.** We expect people to comply with folkways, but we are likely to shrug our shoulders and not make a big deal about it if they don't. If someone insists on passing you on the right side of the sidewalk, for example, you are unlikely to take corrective action, although if the sidewalk is crowded and you must move out of the way, you might give the person a dirty look.

Other norms, however, are taken much more seriously. We think of them as essential to our core values, and we insist on conformity. These are called **mores** (MORE-rays). A person who steals, rapes, or kills has violated some of society's most important mores. As sociologist Ian Robertson (1987:62) put it,

> *A man who walks down a street wearing nothing on the upper half of his body is violating a folkway; a man who walks down the street wearing nothing on the lower half of his body is violating one of our most important mores, the requirement that people cover their genitals and buttocks in public.*

It should also be noted that one group's folkways may be another group's mores. Although a man walking down the street with the upper half of his body uncovered is deviating from a folkway, a woman doing the same thing is violating the mores. In addition, the folkways and mores of a subculture (discussed in the next section) may be the opposite of mainstream culture. For example, to walk down the sidewalk in a nudist camp with the entire body uncovered would conform to that subculture's folkways.

A **taboo** refers to a norm so strongly ingrained that even the thought of its violation is greeted with revulsion. Eating human flesh and parents having sex with their children are examples of such behaviors. When someone breaks a taboo, the individual is usually judged unfit to live in the same society as others. The sanctions are severe and may include prison, banishment, or death.

The violation of *mores* is a serious matter. In this case, it is serious enough that the security at a football match in Edmonton, Alberta (Canada) have swung into action to protect the public from seeing a "disgraceful" sight, at least one so designated by this group.

REUTERS/Dan Riedlhuber/Landov

Many Cultural Worlds

Subcultures

Groups of people who occupy some small corner in life, such as an occupation, tend to develop specialized ways to communicate with one another. To outsiders, their talk, even if it is in English, can seem like a foreign language. Here is one of my favorite quotes by a politician:

> *There are things we know that we know. There are known unknowns; that is to say, there are things that we now know we don't know. But there are also unknown unknowns; there are things we do not know we don't know. (Donald Rumsfeld, quoted in Dickey and Barry 2006:38)*

Whatever Rumsfeld, the former secretary of defense under George W. Bush, meant by his statement probably will remain a known unknown. (Or would it be an unknown known?)

folkways norms that are not strictly enforced

mores norms that are strictly enforced because they are thought essential to core values or the well-being of the group

taboo a norm so strong that it often brings revulsion if violated

Can you explain the difference between folkways, mores, and taboos?

subculture the values and related behaviors of a group that distinguish its members from the larger culture; a world within a world

counterculture a group whose values, beliefs, norms, and related behaviors place its members in opposition to the broader culture

We have a similar problem in the subculture of sociology. Try to figure out what this means:

Path analysis showed that parental involvement fully mediated the effect of parental acculturation on intergenerational relationship, whereas intergenerational relationship mediated the effect of parental involvement on child outcomes. (Ying and Han 2008)

As much as possible, I will spare you from such "insider" talk.

Sociologists and politicians form a **subculture,** *a world within the larger world of the dominant culture.* Subcultures are not limited to occupations, for they include any corner in life in which people's experiences lead them to have distinctive ways of looking at the world. Even if we cannot understand the quotation from Donald Rumsfeld, it makes us aware that politicians don't view life in quite the same way most of us do.

U.S. society contains *thousands* of subcultures. Some are as broad as the way of life we associate with teenagers, others as narrow as those we associate with body builders—or with politicians. Some U.S. ethnic groups also form subcultures: Their values, norms, and foods set them apart. So might their religion, music, language, and clothing. Even sociologists form a subculture. As you are learning, they also use a unique language in their efforts to understand the world.

For a subculture in another society, one that might test the limits of your sense of cultural relativism, read the Down-to-Earth Sociology box on the next page. For a visual depiction of subcultures, see the photo essay a few pages ahead.

Countercultures

Consider this quote from another subculture:

If everyone applying for welfare had to supply a doctor's certificate of sterilization, if everyone who had committed a felony were sterilized, if anyone who had mental illness to any degree were sterilized—then our economy could easily take care of these people for the rest of their lives, giving them a decent living standard—but getting them out of the way. That way there would be no children abused, no surplus population, and, after a while, no pollution. . . .

When the . . . present world system collapses, it'll be good people like you who will be shooting people in the streets to feed their families. (Zellner 1995:58, 65)

Welcome to the world of the Aryan supremacist survivalists, where the message is much clearer than that of politicians—and much more disturbing.

The values and norms of most subcultures blend in with mainstream society. In some cases, however, as with the survivalists quoted above, some of the group's values and norms place it at odds with the dominant culture. Sociologists use the term **counterculture** to refer to such groups. To better see this distinction, consider motorcycle enthusiasts and motorcycle gangs. Motorcycle enthusiasts—who emphasize personal freedom and speed *and* affirm cultural values of success through work or education—are members of a subculture. In contrast, the Hell's Angels, Pagans, and Bandidos not only stress freedom and speed but also value dirtiness and contempt toward women, work, and education. This makes them a counterculture.

An assault on core values is always met with resistance. To affirm their own values, members of the mainstream culture may ridicule, isolate, or even attack members of the counterculture. The Mormons, for example, were driven out of several states before they finally settled in Utah, which was at that time a wilderness. Even there, the federal government would not let them practice *polygyny* (one man having more than one wife), and Utah's statehood was made conditional on its acceptance of monogamy (Anderson 1942/1966; Williams 2007).

Zellner, William W. *Countercultures: A Sociological Analysis.* New York: St. Martin's, 1995.

AP Images/John Raoux

Why is salsa dancing a *subculture* and not a counterculture?

Can you explain the difference between subcultures and countercultures?

2-D: A New Subculture and a Different Kind of Love

" I 've experienced so many amazing things because of her. She has really changed my life." —Nisan

Nisan, a 37-year old man who lives in Tokyo, has strong feelings for his girlfriend, Nemu, and loves dating her. Nemu is on the shy side, though, and in restaurants she sits quietly on the chair next to Nisan. When they ride in his Toyota, she sits silently in the passenger's seat. Never once has Nemu uttered even a single word.

The silence hasn't stopped Nisan from spending his vacations with Nemu. They have traveled hundreds of miles to Kyoto and Osaka. This has been a little hard on Nisan's modest budget, but Nemu seems to enjoy the travel. To save money while vacationing, they sleep together in the car. Sometimes they crash on friends' couches (Katayama 2009).

That's Nisan in the photo to the right. And that's Nemu that he is holding.

Nisan isn't joking. He is serious about the feelings that he has for Nemu, a video game character.

And so are the other Japanese men who belong to the 2-D (two-dimensional) subculture. Some of these men have never been able to attract real women. Others have been disappointed in real-life love. For them, cartoon and video characters take on a lifelike reality.

To Westerners raised on Freudian imagery, the 2-D subculture stimulates haunting thoughts. But the Japanese seem to see matters differently. A Japanese author who has written widely on the 2-D subculture—and is himself a member of it—stresses that his subculture exists because romance has

Nisan and Nemu
Masato Seto

become a commodity. The mass media glorify good looks and money, he says, which denies romance to many men. Some of these men train their minds to experience romantic love when they look at a cartoon. As one man put it, the pillow covers represent "cute girls who live in my imagination."

Sociologically, we might point out that in Japan the sexes don't mix as easily as they do in the West. About half of Japanese adults, both men and women, have no friends of the opposite sex (Katayama 2009).

The 2-D subculture is growing. Tokyo has shops that feature 2-D products such as body pillows and dolls for men. In some Tokyo restaurants, the waitresses dress up like video-game characters.

There is even an island resort that specializes in honeymoons for men who have fallen in love with their cartoon cuties. The men check into the hotel, pay for a room for two, and immerse themselves in their virtual relationships, controlled through their hand-held devices (Wakabayashi 2010a, 2010b). The local businesses, which sell special meals with heart-shaped dishes and cakes that the lovers give their cartoon characters, are pleased with their new visitors—the flesh-and-blood ones who pay the bills.

For Your Consideration

→ Do you agree with this statement: If a man in the United States were to carry around a body pillow like the one in the photo on this page, he would find less acceptance than do Nisan and the men like him in Japan? If so, why do you think this difference exists? Do you think that 2-D will thrive as a subculture in the United States? Why or why not?

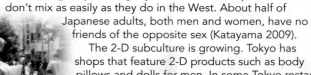

Values in U.S. Society

An Overview of U.S. Values

As you know, the United States is a **pluralistic society,** made up of many different groups. The United States has numerous religious and racial–ethnic groups, as well as countless interest groups that focus on activities as divergent as hunting deer or collecting Barbie dolls. Within this huge diversity, sociologists have tried to identify the country's **core values,** those that are shared by most of the groups that make up U.S. society. Here are ten that sociologist Robin Williams (1965) identified:

1. *Achievement and success.* Americans praise personal achievement, especially outdoing others. This value includes getting ahead at work and school, and attaining wealth, power, and prestige.
2. *Individualism.* Americans cherish the ideal that an individual can rise from the bottom of society to its very top. If someone fails to "get ahead," Americans generally

pluralistic society a society made up of many different groups

core values the values that are central of a group, those around which it builds a common identity

Can you use 2-D to explain the essential elements of a subculture?

Subcultures can form around any interest or activity. Each subculture has its own values and norms that its members share, giving them a common identity. Each also has special terms that pinpoint the group's corner of life and that its members use to communicate with one another. Some of us belong to several subcultures.

As you can see from these photos, most subcultures are compatible with the values and norms of the mainstream culture. They represent specialized interests around which its members have chosen to build tiny worlds. Some subcultures, however, conflict with the mainstream culture. Sociologists give the name *countercultures* to subcultures whose values (such as those of outlaw motorcyclists) or activities and goals (such as those of terrorists) are opposed to the mainstream culture. Countercultures, however, are exceptional, and few of us belong to them.

Each subculture provides its members with values and distinctive ways of viewing the world. What values and perceptions do you think are common among body builders? What other subculture do you see here?

REUTERS/Ali Jarekji/Landov

Membership in this subculture is not easily awarded. Not only must high-steel ironworkers prove that they are able to work at great heights but also that they fit into the group socially. Newcomers are tested by members of the group, and they must demonstrate that they can take joking without offense.

PETER MORGAN/Reuters/Landov

56

James X Nova/Lightbox

Specialized values and interests are two of the characteristics that mark subcultures. What values and interests distinguish the modeling subculture?

The subculture that centers around tattooing previously existed on the fringes of society, with seamen and circus folk its main participants. It now has entered mainstream society, but not to this extreme.

NICKY LOH/Reuters/Landov

© Blend Images/Alamy

Todd Glaser/Aurora Photos

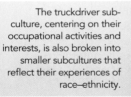

The truckdriver sub-culture, centering on their occupational activities and interests, is also broken into smaller subcultures that reflect their experiences of race–ethnicity.

With their specialized language and activities, surfers are highly recognized as members of a subculture. This surfer is "in the tube."

Why would someone decorate himself like this? Among the many reasons, one is to show solidarity with the football subculture.

REUTERS/Jeff Haynes/Landov

Even subcultures can have subcultures. The rodeo subculture is a subculture of "western" subculture. The values that unite its members are reflected in their speech, clothing, and specialized activities, such as the one shown here.

AFP PHOTO/TIMOTHY A. CLARY/Newscom

find fault with that individual rather than with the social system for placing road-blocks in his or her path.

3. *Hard work*. Americans expect people to work hard to achieve financial success and material comfort.

4. *Efficiency and practicality*. Americans award high marks for getting things done efficiently. Even in everyday life, Americans consider it important to do things fast, and they seek ways to increase efficiency.

5. *Science and technology*. Americans have a passion for applied science, for using science to control nature—to tame rivers and harness winds—and to develop new technology, from iPads to pedal-electric hybrid vehicles.

6. *Material comfort*. Americans expect a high level of material comfort. This includes not only good nutrition, medical care, and housing but also late-model cars and recreational playthings—from iPhones to motor homes.

7. *Freedom*. This core value pervades U.S. life. It underscored the American Revolution, and Americans pride themselves on their personal freedom.

8. *Democracy*. By this term, Americans refer to majority rule, to the right of everyone to express an opinion, and to representative government.

9. *Equality*. It is impossible to understand Americans without being aware of the central role that the value of equality plays in their lives. Equality of opportunity has significantly influenced U.S. history and continues to mark relations between the groups that make up U.S. society.

10. *Group superiority*. Although it contradicts the values of freedom, democracy, and equality, Americans regard some groups more highly than others and have done so throughout their history. The denial of the vote to women, the slaughter of Native Americans, and the enslavement of Africans are a few examples of how the groups considered superior have denied equality and freedom to others.

In an earlier publication, I updated Williams' analysis by adding these three values.

1. *Education*. Americans are expected to go as far in school as their abilities and finances allow. Over the years, the definition of an "adequate" education has changed, and today a college education is considered an appropriate goal for most Americans. Those who have an opportunity for higher education and do not take it are sometimes viewed as doing something "wrong"—not merely as making a bad choice, but as somehow being involved in an immoral act.

2. *Religiosity*. There is a feeling that "every true American ought to be religious." This does not mean that everyone is expected to join a church, synagogue, or mosque, but that everyone ought to acknowledge a belief in a Supreme Being and follow some set of matching precepts. This value is so pervasive that Americans stamp "In God We Trust" on their money and declare in their national pledge of allegiance that they are "one nation under God."

3. *Romantic love*. Americans feel that the only proper basis for marriage is romantic love. Songs, literature, mass media, and "folk beliefs" all stress this value. Americans grow misty-eyed at the theme that "love conquers all."

Value Clusters

As you can see, values are not independent units; some cluster together to form a larger whole. In the **value cluster** that surrounds success, for example, we find hard work, education, material comfort, and individualism bound up together. Americans are expected to go far in school, to work hard afterward, and then to attain a high level of material comfort, which, in turn, demonstrates success. Success is attributed to the individual's efforts; lack of success is blamed on his or her faults.

Value Contradictions

value cluster values that together form a larger whole

You probably were surprised to see group superiority on the list of dominant American values. This is an example of how sociology upsets people

Can you use U.S. values to illustrate the concept of core values?

and creates resistance. Few people want to bring something like this into the open. It violates today's *ideal* culture, a concept we discuss on the next page. But this is what sociologists do—they look beyond the façade to penetrate what is really going on. And when you look at our history, there is no doubt that group superiority has been a dominant value. It still is, but values change, and this one is diminishing.

Value contradictions, then, are part of culture. Not all values are wrapped in neat packages, and you can see how group superiority contradicts freedom, democracy, and equality. There simply cannot be full expression of freedom, democracy, and equality along with racism and sexism. Something has to give. One way in which Americans in the past sidestepped this contradiction was to say that freedom, democracy, and equality applied only to some groups. The contradiction was bound to surface over time, however, and so it did with the Civil War and the women's liberation movement. *It is precisely at the point of value contradictions, then, that one can see a major force for social change in a society.*

An Emerging Value Cluster

A value cluster of four interrelated core values—leisure, self-fulfillment, physical fitness, and youthfulness—is emerging in the United States. So is a fifth core value—concern for the environment.

1. *Leisure.* The emergence of leisure as a value is reflected in a huge recreation industry—from computer games, boats, vacation homes, and spa retreats to sports arenas, home theaters, adventure vacations, and luxury cruises.
2. *Self-fulfillment.* This value is reflected in the "human potential" movement, which emphasizes becoming "all you can be," and in magazine articles, books, and talk shows that focus on "self-help," "relating," and "personal development."
3. *Physical fitness.* Physical fitness is not a new U.S. value, but the greater emphasis on it is moving it into this emerging cluster. You can see this trend in the publicity given to nutrition, organic foods, weight, and diet; the joggers, cyclists, and backpackers; and the countless health clubs and physical fitness centers.
4. *Youthfulness.* Valuing youth and disparaging old age are also not new, but some analysts note a sense of urgency in today's emphasis on youthfulness. They attribute this to the huge number of aging baby boomers, who, aghast at the physical changes that accompany their advancing years, are attempting to deny or at least postpone their biological fate. One physician even claimed that "aging is not a normal life event, but a disease" (Cowley 1996).
5. *Concern for the environment.* During most of U.S. history, the environment was viewed as something to be exploited—a wilderness to be settled, forests to be cleared for farm land and lumber, rivers and lakes to be fished, and animals to be hunted. One result was the near extinction of the bison and the extinction in 1914 of the passenger pigeon, a species of bird previously so numerous that its annual migration would darken the skies for days. Today, Americans have developed a genuine and apparently long-term concern for the environment.

In Sum: Values don't "just happen." They are related to conditions of society. This emerging value cluster is a response to fundamental changes in U.S. culture. Earlier generations of Americans were focused on forging a nation and fighting for economic survival. But today, millions of Americans are freed from long hours of work, and millions retire from work at an age when they anticipate decades of life ahead of them. This value cluster centers on helping people to maintain their health and vigor during their younger years and enabling them to enjoy their years of retirement. You can see how longer lives and retiring from work are related to economic development.

Only when an economy produces adequate surpluses can a society afford these values. Concern for the environment is a remarkable example. People act on environmental concerns only *after* they have met their basic needs. The world's poor nations, for example, have a difficult time "affording" this value at this point in their development (Gokhale 2009).

Explore
Living Data
on **mysoclab.com**

value contradiction values that contradict one another; to follow the one means to come into conflict with the other

Explain the value cluster that is emerging in U.S. culture.

When Values Clash

Challenges in core values are met with strong resistance by the people who hold them dear. They see change as a threat to their way of life, an undermining of both their present and their future. Efforts to change gender roles, for example, arouse intense controversy, as do same-sex marriages. Alarmed at such onslaughts against their values, traditionalists fiercely defend historical family relationships and the gender roles they grew up with. Some use the term *culture wars* to refer to the clash in values between traditionalists and those advocating change, but the term is highly exaggerated. Compared with the violence directed against the Mormons, today's culture clashes are mild.

Values as Distorting Lenses

Values and their supporting beliefs are lenses through which we see the world. The views produced through these lenses are often of what life *ought* to be like, not what it is. For example, Americans value individualism so highly that they tend to see almost everyone as free and equal in pursuing the goal of success. This value blinds them to the significance of the circumstances that keep people from achieving success. The dire consequences of family poverty, parents' low education, and dead-end jobs tend to drop from sight. Instead, Americans see the unsuccessful as not putting out enough effort. And they "know" they are right, for the mass media dangle before their eyes enticing stories of individuals who have succeeded despite the greatest of handicaps.

"Ideal" Versus "Real" Culture

Many of the norms that surround cultural values are followed only partially. Differences always exist between a group's ideals and what its members actually do. Consequently, sociologists use the term **ideal culture** to refer to the values, norms, and goals that a group considers ideal, worth aiming for. Success, for example, is part of ideal culture. Americans glorify academic progress, hard work, and the display of material goods as signs of individual achievement. What people actually do, however, usually falls short of the cultural ideal. Compared with their abilities, for example, most people don't work as

Values, both those held by individuals and those that represent a nation or people, can undergo deep shifts. It is difficult for many of us to grasp the pride with which earlier Americans destroyed trees that took thousands of years to grow, are located only on one tiny speck of the globe, and that we today consider part of the nation's and world's heritage. But this is a value statement, representing current views. The pride expressed on these woodcutters' faces represents another set of values entirely.

Clarke Memorial Museum, Eureka, California

How do values affect our perception? What are ideal and real culture?

hard as they could or go as far as they could in school. Sociologists call the norms and values that people actually follow **real culture.**

Cultural Universals

With the amazing variety of human cultures around the world, are there any **cultural universals**—values, norms, or other cultural traits that are found everywhere?

To answer this question, anthropologist George Murdock (1945) combed through the data that anthropologists had gathered on hundreds of groups around the world. He compared their customs concerning courtship, marriage, funerals, games, laws, music, myths, incest taboos, and even toilet training. He found that these activities are present in all cultures, but *the specific customs differ from one group to another.* There is no universal form of the family, no universal way of toilet training children, nor a universal way of disposing of the dead.

Incest is a remarkable example. Groups even differ on their view of what incest is. The Mundugumors of New Guinea extend the incest taboo so far that for each man, seven of every eight women are ineligible marriage partners (Mead 1935/1950). Other groups go in the opposite direction and allow some men to marry their own daughters (La Barre 1954). Some groups even *require* that brothers and sisters marry one another, although only in certain circumstances (Beals and Hoijer 1965). The Burundi of Africa even insist that a son have sex with his mother—but only to remove a certain curse (Albert 1963). Such sexual relations, so surprising to us, are limited to special people (royalty) or to extraordinary situations (such as when a lion hunter faces a dangerous hunt). No society permits generalized incest for its members.

In Sum: Although there are universal human activities (singing, playing games, storytelling, preparing food, marrying, child rearing, disposing of the dead, and so on), there is no universal way of doing any of them. Humans have no biological imperative that results in one particular form of behavior throughout the world. As indicated in the following Thinking Critically section, although a few sociologists take the position that genes significantly influence human behavior, almost all sociologists reject this view.

THINKING CRITICALLY

Are We Prisoners of Our Genes? Sociobiology and Human Behavior

A controversial view of human behavior, called **sociobiology** (also known as neo-Darwinism and evolutionary psychology), provides a sharp contrast to the perspective of this chapter, that the key to human behavior is culture. Sociobiologists (evolutionary psychologists, evolutionary anthropologists) believe that because of natural selection, biology is a basic cause of human behavior.

Charles Darwin (1859), who adopted Spencer's idea of *natural selection*, pointed out that the genes of a species—the units that contain the individual's traits—are not distributed evenly among the offspring. The characteristics that some members inherit make it easier for them to survive their environment, increasing the likelihood that they will pass their genetic traits

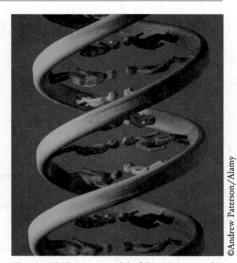

The double helix, a model of the structure of our DNA.

©Andrew Paterson/Alamy

cultural universal a value, norm, or other cultural trait that is found in every group

sociobiology a framework of thought that views human behavior as the result of natural selection and considers biological factors to be a fundamental cause of human behavior

Why are there few, if any, cultural universals?

technology in its narrow sense, tools; its broader sense includes the skills or procedures necessary to make and use those tools

new technology the emerging technologies of an era that have a significant impact on social life

to the next generation. Over thousands of generations, the genetic traits that aid survival become common in a species, while those that do not aid survival become less common or even disappear. Natural selection explains not only the physical characteristics of animals but also their behavior, for over countless generations, instincts emerged.

Edward Wilson (1975), an insect specialist, set off an uproar when he claimed that human behavior, like the behavior of cats, rats, bats, and gnats, has been bred into *Homo sapiens* through evolutionary principles. Wilson went on to claim that competition and cooperation, envy and altruism—even religion, slavery, genocide, and war and peace—can be explained by sociobiology. He provocatively added that because human behavior can be explained in terms of genetic programming, sociobiology will eventually absorb sociology, as well as anthropology and psychology.

Obviously, sociologists disagree with Wilson. It is not that sociologists deny that biology is important in human behavior—at least in the sense that it takes a highly developed brain to develop human culture and abstract thought and that there would be no speech if humans had no tongue or larynx. We also must eat and keep from freezing if we are to stay alive, which motivates some of our behavior. Biology is so significant that it could even underlie the origin of gender inequality.

Some sociologists are developing what they call *genetics-informed sociology,* an emphasis on the influence of genes on human behavior. They are coming up with interesting findings. For example, males who have the "protective" gene (9R/9R) average fewer sexual partners than people without this gene. These individuals are also less likely to binge drink and more likely to wear seat belts (Guo et al. 2008). And the social? The influences of this and other genes are modified by social experiences. For example, student subcultures that encourage or discourage sexual behavior override the 9R/9R gene. To their surprise, researchers have even found that social experiences can change a person's genes (Ledger 2009).

In Sum: To find that genetics has an influence on human behavior is a far cry from saying that genetics determines human behavior, that we act as we do because of genetics. On the contrary, pigs act like pigs and spiders act like spiders because instincts control their behavior. We humans, in contrast, possess a self and engage in abstract thought. We develop purposes and goals and discuss the reasons that people do things. Unlike pigs and spiders, we are immersed in a world of symbols that we use to consider, reflect, and make reasoned choices. Because we humans are not prisoners of our genes, we have developed fascinatingly diverse ways of life around the world—which we will be exploring in this text. ∎

OLIVER BERG/EPA/Landov

Language is the basis of human culture around the world. The past decade has seen major developments in communication—the ease and speed with which we can "speak" to people across the globe. This development is destined to have vital effects on culture.

Technology in the Global Village

The New Technology

The gestures, language, values, folkways, and mores that we have discussed all are part of symbolic (nonmaterial) culture. Culture, as you recall, also has a material aspect: a group's *things,* from its houses to its toys. Central to a group's material culture is its technology. In its simplest sense, **technology** can be equated with tools. In a broader sense, technology also includes the skills or procedures necessary to make and use those tools.

We can use the term **new technology** to refer to an emerging technology that has a significant impact on social life. Although people develop minor technologies all the time, most are only slight modifications of existing technologies. Occasionally, however, they develop a technology that makes a major impact on human life. It is primarily to these innovations that the term *new technology* refers. Five hundred years ago, the new technology was the printing press. For us, the new technology consists of computers, satellites, and the Internet.

Can you contrast sociology and sociobiology? How does human behavior differ from the behavior of cats, bats, rats, and gnats?

The sociological significance of technology goes far beyond the tool itself. *Technology sets the framework for a group's nonmaterial culture.* If a group's technology changes, so do the ways its people think and how they relate to one another. An example is gender relations. Through the centuries and throughout the world, it has been the custom (nonmaterial culture) for men to dominate women. Today's global communications (material culture) make this custom more difficult to maintain. For example, when Arab women watch Western television, they observe an unfamiliar freedom in gender relations. As these women use e-mail and telephones to talk to one another about what they have seen, they both convey and create discontent, as well as feelings of sisterhood. These communications motivate some of them to agitate for social change.

In today's world, the long-accepted idea that it is proper to withhold rights on the basis of someone's sex can no longer be sustained. What usually lies beyond our awareness in this revolutionary change is the role of the new technology, which joins the world's nations into a global communications network.

Cultural Lag and Cultural Change

Three or four generations ago, sociologist William Ogburn (1922/1938) coined the term **cultural lag.** By this, Ogburn meant that not all parts of a culture change at the same pace. When one part of a culture changes, other parts lag behind.

Ogburn pointed out that *a group's material culture usually changes first, with the nonmaterial culture lagging behind.* This leaves the nonmaterial (or symbolic) culture playing a game of catch-up. For example, when we get sick, we can type our symptoms into a computer and get an instant diagnosis and recommended course of treatment. In some tests, computer programs outperform physicians. Yet our customs have not caught up with our technology, and we continue to visit the doctor's office.

Sometimes nonmaterial culture never does catch up. We can rigorously hold onto some outmoded form—one that once was needed, but that long ago was bypassed by technology. Have you ever wondered why our "school year" is nine months long, and why we take summers off? For most of us, this is "just the way it's always been," and we have never questioned it. But there is more to this custom than meets the eye. In the late 1800s, when universal schooling came about, the school year matched the technology of the time. Most parents were farmers, and for survival they needed their children's help at the crucial times of planting and harvesting. Today, generations later, when few people farm and there is no need for the "school year" to be so short, we still live with this cultural lag.

Technology and Cultural Leveling

For most of human history, communication was limited and travel slow. Consequently, in their relative isolation, human groups developed highly distinctive ways of life as they responded to the particular situations they faced. The unique characteristics they developed that distinguished one culture from another tended to change little over time. The Tasmanians, who live on a remote island off the coast of Australia, provide an extreme example. For thousands of years, they had no contact with other people. They were so isolated that they did not even know how to make clothing or fire (Edgerton 1992).

Except in such rare instances as these, humans have always had *some* contact with other groups. During these contacts, people learned from one another, adopting things they found desirable. In this process, called **cultural diffusion,** groups are most open to changes in their technology or material culture. They usually are eager, for example, to adopt superior weapons and tools. In remote jungles in South America one can find metal cooking pots, steel axes, and even bits of clothing spun in mills in South Carolina. Although the direction of cultural diffusion today is primarily from the West to other parts of the world, cultural diffusion is not a one-way street—as bagels, woks, hammocks, and sushi in the United States attest.

LITERATURE

"JUST THINK OF IT AS IF YOU'RE READING A LONG TEXT-MESSAGE."

© Dave Carpenter/www.CartoonStock.com

Technological advances are now so rapid that there can be cultural gaps between generations.

cultural lag Ogburn's term for human behavior lagging behind technological innovations

cultural diffusion the spread of cultural traits from one group to another; includes both material and nonmaterial cultural traits

How does technology lead to change in cultures?

cultural leveling the process by which cultures become similar to one another; refers especially to the process by which Western culture is being exported and diffused into other nations

With today's travel and communications, cultural diffusion is occurring rapidly. Air travel has made it possible to journey around the globe in a matter of hours. In the not-so-distant past, a trip from the United States to Africa was so unusual that only a few adventurous people made it, and newspapers would herald their feat. Today, hundreds of thousands make the trip each year.

The changes in communication are no less vast. Communication used to be limited to face-to-face speech, written messages that were passed from hand to hand, and visual signals such as smoke or light that was reflected from mirrors. Despite newspapers and even the telegraph, people in some parts of the United States did not hear that the Civil War had ended until weeks and even months after it was over. Today's electronic communications transmit messages across the globe in a matter of seconds, and we learn almost instantaneously what is happening on the other side of the world. During the Iraq War, reporters traveled with U.S. soldiers, and for the first time in history, the public was able to view video reports of battles as they took place. When Navy Seals executed Osama bin Laden under President Obama's orders, Obama and Hillary Clinton watched the helicopter land in bin Laden's compound, listened to reports of the killing, and watched the Seals leave (Schmidle 2011).

Travel and communication bridge time and space to such an extent that there is almost no "other side of the world" anymore. One result is **cultural leveling,** a process in which cultures become more and more similar to one another. The globalization of capitalism brings with it both technology and Western culture. Japan, for example, has adopted not only capitalism but also Western forms of dress and music, transforming it into a blend of Western and Eastern cultures.

Cultural leveling is apparent to any international traveler. The golden arches of McDonald's welcome visitors to Tokyo, Paris, London, Madrid, Moscow, Hong Kong, and Beijing. When I visited a jungle village in India—no electricity, no running water, and so remote that the only entrance was by a footpath—I saw a young man sporting a cap with the Nike emblem.

Although the bridging of geography, time, and culture by electronic signals and the exportation of Western icons do not in and of themselves mark the end of traditional cultures, the inevitable result is some degree of *cultural leveling*. We are producing a blander, less distinctive way of life—U.S. culture with French, Japanese, and Brazilian accents, so to speak. Although the "cultural accent" remains, something vital is lost forever.

Cultural leveling is occurring rapidly, with some strange twists. These men from an Amazon tribe, who have just come back from a week hunting in the jungle, are wearing traditional headdress and using traditional weapons, but you can easily spot something else that is jarringly out of place.

What is cultural leveling? How does this photo illustrate it?

Summary and Review

What Is Culture?

How do sociologists understand culture?

All human groups possess **culture**—language, beliefs, values, norms, and material objects that are passed from one generation to the next. **Material culture** consists of objects (art, buildings, clothing, weapons, tools). **Nonmaterial (or symbolic) culture** is a group's ways of thinking and its patterns of behavior. **Ideal culture** is a group's ideal values, norms, and goals. **Real culture** is people's actual behavior, which often falls short of their cultural ideals.

What are cultural relativism and ethnocentrism?

People are **ethnocentric;** that is, they use their own culture as a yardstick for judging the ways of others. In contrast, those who embrace **cultural relativism** try to understand other cultures on those cultures' own terms.

Components of Symbolic Culture

What are the components of nonmaterial culture?

The central component of **nonmaterial culture** is **symbols,** anything to which people attach meaning and that they use to communicate with others. Universally, the symbols of nonmaterial culture are **gestures, language, values, norms, sanctions, folkways,** and **mores.**

Why is language so significant to culture?

Language allows human experience to be goal-directed, cooperative, and cumulative. It also lets humans move beyond the present and share a past, future, and other common perspectives. According to the **Sapir-Whorf hypothesis,** language even shapes our thoughts and perceptions.

How do values, norms, sanctions, folkways, and mores reflect culture?

All groups have **values,** standards by which they define what is desirable or undesirable, and **norms,** rules or expectations about behavior. Groups use **positive sanctions** to show approval of those who follow their norms and **negative sanctions** to show disapproval of those who violate them. Norms that are not strictly enforced are called **folkways,** while **mores** are norms to which groups demand conformity because they reflect core values.

Many Cultural Worlds

How do subcultures and countercultures differ?

A **subculture** is a group whose values and related behaviors distinguish its members from the general culture. A **counterculture** holds some values that stand in opposition to those of the dominant culture.

Values in U.S. Society

What are some core U.S. values?

Although the United States is a **pluralistic society,** made up of many groups, each with its own set of values, certain values dominate. These are called its **core values.** Some values cluster together to form a larger whole called **value clusters. Value contradictions** (such as equality versus sexism and racism) indicate areas of tension, which are likely points of social change. Leisure, self-fulfillment, physical fitness, youthfulness, and concern for the environment form an emerging value cluster. Core values do not change without opposition.

Cultural Universals

Do cultural universals exist?

Cultural universals are values, norms, or other cultural traits that are found in all cultures. Although all human groups have customs concerning cooking, childbirth, funerals, and so on, because these customs differ from one culture to another, there are no cultural universals.

Technology in the Global Village

How is technology changing culture?

William Ogburn coined the term **cultural lag** to describe how a group's nonmaterial culture lags behind its changing technology. With today's technological advances in travel and communications, **cultural diffusion** is occurring rapidly. This leads to **cultural leveling,** groups becoming similar as they adopt items from other cultures. Much of the richness of the world's diverse cultures is being lost in the process.

Thinking Critically about this Chapter

1. Do you favor ethnocentrism or cultural relativism? Explain your position.
2. Do you think that the language change in Miami, Florida, indicates the future of the United States? Why or why not?
3. Are you a member of any subcultures? Which one(s)? Why do you think that your group is a subculture? What is your group's relationship to the mainstream culture?

References

All new references are printed in cyan.

Albert, Ethel M. "Women of Burundi: A Study of Social Values." In *Women of Tropical Africa,* Denise Paulme, ed. Berkeley: University of California Press, 1963:179–215.

Anderson, Nels. *Desert Saints: The Mormon Frontier in Utah.* Chicago: University of Chicago Press, 1966. Originally published 1942.

Bates, Marston. *Gluttons and Libertines: Human Problems of Being Natural.* New York: Vintage Books, 1967. Quoted in Crapo, Richley H. *Cultural Anthropology: Understanding Ourselves and Others,* 5th ed. Boston: McGraw Hill, 2002.

Beals, Ralph L., and Harry Hoijer. *An Introduction to Anthropology,* 3rd ed. New York: Macmillan, 1965.

Boroditsky, Lera. "Lost in Translation." *Wall Street Journal,* July 24, 2010.

Cowley, Geoffrey. "Attention: Aging Men." *Newsweek,* November 16, 1996:66–75.

Darwin, Charles. *The Origin of Species.* Chicago: Conley, 1859.

Dickey, Christopher, and John Barry. "Iran: A Rummy Guide." *Newsweek,* May 8, 2006.

Edgerton, Robert B. *Sick Societies: Challenging the Myth of Primitive Harmony.* New York: Free Press, 1992.

Eibl-Eibesfeldt, Irrenäus. *Ethology: The Biology of Behavior.* New York: Holt, Rinehart, and Winston, 1970.

Ekman, Paul, Wallace V. Friesen, and John Bear. "The International Language of Gestures." *Psychology Today,* May 1984:64.

Fadiman, Anne. *The Spirit Catches You and You Fall Down.* New York: Farrar, Straus and Giroux, 1997.

Gampbell, Jennifer. "In Northeast Thailand, a Cuisine Based on Bugs." *New York Times,* June 22, 2006.

Gokhale, Ketaki. "India Plans Focus on Environment." *Wall Street Journal,* August 14, 2009.

Guo, Guang, Yuying Tong, and Tianji Cai. "Gene by Social Context Interactions for Number of Sexual Partners among White Male Youths: Genetics-Informed Sociology." *American Journal of Sociology, 114,* Supplement, 2008:S36–S66.

Halpern, Jack. "Iceland's Big Thaw." *New York Times,* May 13, 2011.

Horwitz, Allan V., and Jerome C. Wakefield. *The Loss of Sadness: How Psychiatry Transformed Normal Sorrow into Depressive Disorder.* New York: Oxford University Press, 2007.

Katayama, Lisa. "Love in 2-D." *New York Times,* July 21, 2009.

Kent, Mary, and Robert Lalasz. "In the News: Speaking English in the United States." Population Reference Bureau, January 18, 2007.

Kingston, Maxine Hong. *The Woman Warrior.* New York: Vintage Books, 1975:108. Quoted in Frank J. Zulke and Jacqueline P. Kirley. *Through the Eyes of Social Science,* 6th ed. Prospect Heights, Ill.: Waveland Press, 2002.

La Barre, Weston. *The Human Animal.* Chicago: University of Chicago Press, 1954.

Ledger, Kate. "Sociology and the Gene." *Contexts, 8,* 3, 2009:16–20.

Mead, Margaret. *Sex and Temperament in Three Primitive Societies.* New York: New American Library, 1950. Originally published 1935.

Murdock, George Peter. "The Common Denominator of Cultures." In *The Science of Man and the World Crisis,* Ralph Linton, ed. New York: Columbia University Press, 1945.

Ogburn, William F. *Social Change with Respect to Culture and Human Nature.* New York: W. B. Huebsch, 1922. (Other editions by Viking in 1927, 1938, and 1950.)

Robertson, Ian. *Sociology,* 3rd ed. New York: Worth, 1987.

Salomon, Gisela, "In Miami, Spanish Is Becoming the Primary Language." Associated Press, May 29, 2008.

Sapir, Edward. *Selected Writings of Edward Sapir in Language, Culture, and Personality,* David G. Mandelbaum, ed. Berkeley: University of California Press, 1949.

Schmiddle Nicholas. "Getting Bin Laden." *The New Yorker,* August 8, 2011.

Sharp, Deborah. "Miami's Language Gap Widens." *USA Today,* April 3, 1992:A1, A3.

Sumner, William Graham. *Folkways: A Study in the Sociological Importance of Usages, Manners, Customs, Mores, and Morals.* New York: Ginn, 1906.

Usdansky, Margaret L. "English a Problem for Half of Miami." *USA Today,* April 3, 1992:A1, A3, A30.

Wakabayashi, Daisuke. "Atami Welcomes Virtual Girls, Real Boys." *Wall Street Journal,* September 1, 2010a.

Wakabayashi, Daisuke. "Only in Japan, Real Men Go to a Hotel with Virtual Girlfriends." *Wall Street Journal,* August 31, 2010b.

Whorf, Benjamin. *Language, Thought, and Reality,* J. B. Carroll, ed. Cambridge, MA: MIT Press, 1956.

Williams, Jasmin K. "Utah—The Beehive State." *New York Post,* June 12, 2007.

Williams, Robin M., Jr. *American Society: A Sociological Interpretation,* 2nd ed. New York: Knopf, 1965.

Wilson, Edward O. *Sociobiology: The New Synthesis.* Cambridge, Mass.: Harvard University Press, 1975.

Ying, Yu-Wen, and Meekyung Han. "Parental Contributions to Southeast Asian American Adolescents' Well-Being." *Youth and Society, 40,* 2, December 2008:289–306.

Zellner, William W. *Countercultures: A Sociological Analysis.* New York: St. Martin's, 1995.

Zerubavel, Eviatar. *The Fine Line: Making Distinctions in Everyday Life.* New York: Free Press, 1991.

Socialization

From Chapter 3 of *Sociology: A Down-to-Earth Approach, Core Concepts*, Fifth Edition. James M. Henslin.

Socialization

The old man was horrified when he found out. Life never had been good since his daughter lost her hearing when she was just 2 years old. She couldn't even talk—just fluttered her hands around trying to tell him things.

Over the years, he had gotten used to this. But now . . . he shuddered at the thought of her being pregnant. No one would be willing to marry her; he knew that. And the neighbors, their tongues would never stop wagging. Everywhere he went, he could hear people talking behind his back.

If only his wife were still alive, maybe she could come up with something. What should he do? He couldn't just kick his daughter out into the street.

After the baby was born, the old man tried to shake his feelings, but they wouldn't let loose. Isabelle was a pretty name, but every time he looked at the baby he felt sick to his stomach.

> **"Her behavior toward strangers, especially men, was almost that of a wild animal, manifesting much fear and hostility."**

He hated doing it, but there was no way out. His daughter and her baby would have to live in the attic.

Unfortunately, this is a true story. Isabelle was discovered in Ohio in 1938 when she was about 6½ years old, living in a dark room with her deaf-mute mother. Isabelle couldn't talk, but she did use gestures to communicate with her mother. An inadequate diet and lack of sunshine had given Isabelle a disease called rickets.

[Her legs] were so bowed that as she stood erect the soles of her shoes came nearly flat together, and she got about with a skittering gait. Her behavior toward strangers, especially men, was almost that of a wild animal, manifesting much fear and hostility. In lieu of speech she made only a strange croaking sound. (Davis 1940/2007:156–157)

When the newspapers reported this case, sociologist Kingsley Davis decided to find out what had happened to Isabelle after her discovery. We'll come back to that later, but first let's use the case of Isabelle to gain insight into human nature.

Peru

social environment the entire human environment, including interaction with others

feral children children assumed to have been raised by animals, in the wilderness, isolated from humans

Society Makes Us Human

"What do you mean, society makes us human?" is probably what you are asking. "That sounds ridiculous. I was born a human." The meaning of this statement will become more apparent as we get into the chapter. Let's start by considering what is human about human nature. How much of a person's characteristics comes from "nature" (heredity) and how much from "nurture" (the **social environment,** contact with others)? Experts are trying to answer the nature–nurture question by studying identical twins who were separated at birth and reared in different environments, such as those discussed in the Down-to-Earth Sociology box on the next page.

Another way is to examine children who have had little human contact. Let's consider such children.

Feral Children

The naked child was found in the forest, walking on all fours, eating grass and lapping water from the river. When he saw a small animal, he pounced on it. Growling, he ripped at it with his teeth. Tearing chunks from the body, he chewed them ravenously.

This is an apt description of reports that have come in over the centuries. Supposedly, these **feral** (wild) **children** could not speak; they bit, scratched, growled, and walked on all fours. They drank by lapping water, ate grass, tore eagerly at raw meat, and showed insensitivity to pain and cold. Why am I even mentioning stories that sound so exaggerated?

It is because of what happened in 1798. In that year, such a child was found in the forests of Aveyron, France. "The wild boy of Aveyron," as he became known, would have been written off as another folk myth, except that French scientists took the child to a laboratory and studied him. Like the feral children in the earlier informal reports, this child, too, gave no indication of feeling the cold. Most startling, though, the boy would growl when he saw a small animal, pounce on it, and devour it uncooked. Even today, the scientists' detailed reports make fascinating reading (Itard 1962).

Ever since I read Itard's account of this boy, I've been fascinated by the seemingly fantastic possibility that animals could rear human children. In 2002, I received a report from a contact in Cambodia that a feral child had been found in the jungles. When I had the opportunity the following year to visit the child and interview his caregivers, I grabbed it. The boy's photo is to the left.

If we were untouched by society, would we be like feral children? By nature, would our behavior be like that of wild animals? This is the sociological question. Unable to study feral children, sociologists have studied isolated children, like Isabelle in our opening vignette. Let's see what we can learn from them.

Isolated Children

What can isolated children tell us about human nature? We can first conclude that humans have no natural language, for Isabelle and others like her are unable to speak.

But maybe Isabelle was mentally impaired. Perhaps she simply was unable to progress through the usual stages of development. It certainly looked that way—she scored practically zero on her first intelligence test. But after a few months of language training, Isabelle was able to speak in short sentences. In just a year, she could write a few words, do simple addition, and retell stories after hearing them. Seven months later, she had a vocabulary of almost 2,000 words. In just two years, Isabelle reached the intellectual level that is normal for her age. She then went on to school, where she was "bright, cheerful, energetic . . . and participated in all school activities as normally as other children" (Davis 1940/in Henslin 15th ed, 2012).

Read
Final Note on a Case of Extreme Isolation
by Kingsley Davis
on **mysoclab.com**

One of the reasons I went to Cambodia was to interview a feral child—the boy shown here—who supposedly had been raised by monkeys. When I arrived at the remote location where the boy was living, I was disappointed to find that the story was only partially true. When the boy was about two months old, the Khmer Rouge killed his parents and abandoned him. Months later, villagers shot the female monkey who was carrying the baby. Not quite a feral child—but Mathay is the closest I'll ever come to one.

James M. Henslin

What do feral children tell us about "being human"?

Down-to-Earth Sociology

Heredity or Environment?
The Case of Jack and Oskar, Identical Twins

Identical twins are identical in their genetic heritage. They are born when one fertilized egg divides to produce two embryos. If heredity determines personality—or attitudes, temperament, skills, and intelligence—then identical twins should be identical not only in their looks but also in these characteristics.

The fascinating case of Jack and Oskar helps us unravel this mystery. From their experience, we can see the far-reaching effects of the environment—how social experiences override biology.

Jack Yufe and Oskar Stohr are identical twins. Born in 1932 to a Roman Catholic mother and a Jewish father, they were separated as babies after their parents divorced. Jack was reared in Trinidad by his father. There, he learned loyalty to Jews and hatred of Hitler and the Nazis. After the war, Jack and his father moved to Israel. When he was 17, Jack joined a kibbutz and later served in the Israeli army.

Oskar's upbringing was a mirror image of Jack's. Oskar was reared in Czechoslovakia by his mother's mother, who was a strict Catholic. When Oskar was a toddler, Hitler annexed this area of Czechoslovakia, and Oskar learned to love Hitler and to hate Jews. He joined the Hitler Youth (a sort of Boy Scout organization, except that this one was designed to instill the "virtues" of patriotism, loyalty, obedience—and hatred).

In 1954, the two brothers met. It was a short meeting, and Jack had been warned not to tell Oskar that they were Jews. Twenty-five years later, in 1979, when they were 47 years old, social scientists at the University of Minnesota brought them together again. These researchers figured that because Jack and Oskar had the same genes, any differences they showed

The relative influence of heredity and the environment in human behavior has fascinated and plagued researchers. Especially intriguing are cases like these twins who, although separated at birth and not knowing one another, each became a firefighter.

Photo credit: © Thomas Wanstall/The Image Works

would be the result of their environment—their different social experiences.

Not only did Jack and Oskar hold different attitudes toward the war, Hitler, and Jews, but their basic orientations to life were also different. In their politics, Jack was liberal, while Oskar was more conservative. Jack was a workaholic, while Oskar enjoyed leisure. And, as you can predict, Jack was proud of being a Jew. Oskar, who by this time knew that he was a Jew, wouldn't even mention it.

This would seem to settle the matter. But consider these other behaviors. As children, Jack and Oskar had both excelled at sports but had difficulty with math. They also had the same rate of speech, and both liked sweet liqueur and spicy foods. Strangely, each flushed the toilet both before and after using it, and they each enjoyed startling people by sneezing in crowded elevators.

For Your Consideration

→ Heredity or environment? How much influence does each have? The question is not yet settled, but at this point it seems fair to conclude that the *limits* of certain physical and mental abilities are established by heredity (such as ability at sports and aptitude for mathematics), while attitudes are the result of the environment. Basic temperament, though, seems to be inherited. Although the answer is still fuzzy, we can put it this way: For some parts of life, the blueprint is drawn by heredity; but even here the environment can redraw those lines. For other parts, the individual is a blank slate, and it is up to the environment to determine what is written on that slate.

Sources: Based on Begley 1979; Chen 1979; Wright 1995; Segal and Hershberger 2005; Ledger 2009; Johnson et al. 2009.

Language is the key to human development. Without language, people have no mechanism for developing thought and communicating their experiences. Unlike animals, humans have no instincts that take the place of language. If an individual lacks language, he or she lives in a world of internal silence, without shared ideas, lacking connections to others.

Without language, there can be no culture—no shared way of life—and culture is the key to what people become. Each of us possesses a biological heritage, but this heritage does not determine specific behaviors, attitudes, or values. It is our culture that superimposes the specifics of what we become onto our biological heritage.

What do studies of identical twins tell us about "being human"?

Institutionalized Children

Other than language, what else is required for a child to develop into what we consider a healthy, balanced, intelligent human being? We find part of the answer in an intriguing experiment from the 1930s. Back then, orphanages were common because parents were more likely than now to die before their children were grown. Children reared in orphanages tended to have low IQs. "Common sense" made it seem obvious that their low intelligence was because of poor brains ("They're just born that way"). But two psychologists, H. M. Skeels and H. B. Dye (1939), began to suspect a social cause.

Skeels (1966) provides this account of a "good" orphanage in Iowa, one where he and Dye were consultants:

> *Until about six months, they were cared for in the infant nursery. The babies were kept in standard hospital cribs that often had protective sheeting on the sides, thus effectively limiting visual stimulation; no toys or other objects were hung in the infants' line of vision. Human interactions were limited to busy nurses who, with the speed born of practice and necessity, changed diapers or bedding, bathed and medicated the infants, and fed them efficiently with propped bottles.*

Perhaps, thought Skeels and Dye, the problem was the absence of stimulating social interaction, not the children's brains. To test their controversial idea, they selected thirteen infants who were so slow mentally that no one wanted to adopt them. They placed them in an institution for mentally retarded women. They assigned each infant, then about 19 months old, to a separate ward of women ranging in mental age from 5 to 12 and in chronological age from 18 to 50. The women were pleased. They enjoyed taking care of the infants' physical needs—diapering, feeding, and so on. And they also loved to play with the children. They cuddled them and showered them with attention. They even competed to see which ward would have "its baby" walking or talking first. In each ward, one woman became particularly attached to the child and figuratively adopted him or her:

> *As a consequence, an intense one-to-one adult–child relationship developed, which was supplemented by the less intense but frequent interactions with the other adults in the environment. Each child had some one person with whom he [or she] was identified and who was particularly interested in him [or her] and his [or her] achievements. (Skeels 1966)*

The researchers left a control group of twelve infants at the orphanage. These infants received the usual care. They also had low IQs, but they were considered somewhat higher in intelligence than the thirteen in the experimental group. Two and a half years later, Skeels and Dye tested all the children's intelligence. Their findings are startling: Those cared for by the women in the institution gained an average of 28 IQ points while those who remained in the orphanage lost 30 points.

What happened after these children were grown? Did these initial differences matter? Twenty-one years later, Skeels and Dye did a follow-up study. The twelve in the control group, those who had remained in the orphanage, averaged less than a third-grade education. Four still lived in state institutions, and the others held low-level jobs. Only two had married. The thirteen in the experimental group, those cared for by the institutionalized women, had an average education of twelve grades (about normal for that period). Five had completed one or more years of college. One had even gone to graduate school. Eleven had married. All thirteen were self-supporting or were homemakers (Skeels 1966). Apparently, "high intelligence" depends on early, close relations with other humans.

A recent experiment in India confirms this early research. Some of India's orphanages are like those that Skeels and Dye studied—dismal places where unattended children lie in bed all day. When experimenters added stimulating play and interaction to the children's activities, the children's motor skills improved and their IQs increased (Taneja et al. 2002). The longer that children lack stimulating interaction, though, the more difficulty they have intellectually (Meese 2005).

An orphanage in Kaliyampoondi, India. The treatment of these children is likely to affect their ability to reason and to function as adults.

© ELISE JACOB-UNEP/Still Pictures/The Image Works

Excerpt from "A Study of the Effects of Differential Stimulation on Mentally Retarded Children" by H.M. Skeels and H.B. Dye, from PROCEEDINGS AND ADDRESSES OF THE AMERICAN ASSOCIATION ON MENTAL DEFICIENCY, 1939, Volume 44. Copyright © 1939 by AAID. Reprinted with permission.

What does research on institutionalized children tell us about "being human"?

From Chapter 1 of *Sociology: A Down-to-Earth Approach, Core Concepts*, Fifth Edition. James M. Henslin.

Timing and Human Development.   From the case of Genie, you can see how important timing is in the development of "human" characteristics. Genie, who was discovered when she was 13 years old, had been locked in a small room and tied to a chair since she was 20 months old:

> *Apparently Genie's father (70 years old when Genie was discovered in 1970) hated children. He probably had caused the death of two of Genie's siblings. Her 50-year-old mother was partially blind and frightened of her husband. Genie could not speak, did not know how to chew, was unable to stand upright, and could not straighten her hands and legs. On intelligence tests, she scored at the level of a 1-year-old. After intensive training, Genie learned to walk and to say simple sentences (although they were garbled). Genie's language remained primitive as she grew up. She would take anyone's property if it appealed to her, and she went to the bathroom wherever she wanted. At the age of 21, she was sent to a home for adults who cannot live alone. (Pines 1981)*

In Sum: From Genie's pathetic story and from the research on institutionalized children, we can conclude that the basic human traits of intelligence and the ability to establish close bonds with others depend on early interaction with other humans. In addition, there seems to be a period prior to age 13 in which children must learn language and experience human bonding if they are to develop normal intelligence and the ability to be sociable and follow social norms.

Deprived Animals

Finally, let's consider animals that have been deprived of normal interaction. In a series of experiments with rhesus monkeys, psychologists Harry and Margaret Harlow demonstrated the importance of early learning. The Harlows (1962) raised baby monkeys in isolation. They gave each monkey two artificial mothers. One "mother" was only a wire frame with a wooden head, but it did have a nipple from which the baby could nurse. The frame of the other "mother," which had no bottle, was covered with soft terrycloth. To obtain food, the baby monkeys nursed at the wire frame.

When the Harlows (1965) frightened the baby monkeys with a mechanical bear or dog, the babies did not run to the wire frame "mother." Instead, as shown in the photo on this page, they would cling pathetically to their terrycloth "mother." The Harlows concluded that infant–mother bonding is not the result of feeding but, rather, of what they termed "intimate physical contact." To most of us, this phrase means cuddling.

The monkeys raised in isolation could not adjust to monkey life. Placed with other monkeys when they were grown, they didn't know how to participate in "monkey interaction"—to play and to engage in pretend fights—and the other monkeys rejected them. Despite their futile attempts, they didn't even know how to have sexual intercourse. The experimenters designed a special device, which allowed some females to become pregnant. Their isolation, however, made them "ineffective, inadequate, and brutal mothers." They "struck their babies, kicked them, or crushed the babies against the cage floor."

In one of their many experiments, the Harlows isolated baby monkeys for different lengths of time and then put them in with the other monkeys. Monkeys that had been isolated for shorter periods (about three months) were able to adjust to normal monkey life. They learned to play and engage in pretend fights.

Nina Leen/Time Life Pictures/Getty Images

Like humans, monkeys need interaction to thrive. Those raised in isolation are unable to interact with others. In this photograph, we see one of the monkeys described in the text. Purposefully frightened by the experimenter, the monkey has taken refuge in the soft terrycloth draped over an artificial "mother."

What does the case of Genie and research on deprived animals tell us about "being human"?

Those isolated for six months or more, however, couldn't make the adjustment, and the other monkeys rejected them. In other words, the longer the period of isolation, the more difficult its effects are to overcome. In addition, there seems to be a critical learning stage: If this stage is missed, it may be impossible to compensate for what has been lost. This may have been the case with Genie.

Because humans are not monkeys, we must be careful about extrapolating from animal studies to human behavior. The Harlow experiments, however, support what we know about children who are reared in isolation.

In Sum: Babies do not develop "naturally" into social adults. If children are reared in isolation, their bodies grow, but they become little more than big animals. Without the concepts that language provides, they can't grasp relationships between people (the "connections" we call brother, sister, parent, friend, teacher, and so on). And without warm, friendly interactions, they can't bond with others. They don't become "friendly" or cooperate with others. In short, it is through human contact that people learn to be members of the human community. This process by which we learn the ways of society (or of particular groups), called socialization, is what sociologists have in mind when they say "Society makes us human."

To add to our understanding of how society makes us human, let's look at how we develop our self-concept, our ability to "take the role of others," and our ability to reason.

Socialization into the Self and Mind

When you were born, you had no ideas. You didn't know that you were a son or daughter. You didn't even know that you were a he or she. How did you develop a **self,** your image of who you are? And how did you develop your ability to reason? Let's find out.

Cooley and the Looking-Glass Self

About a hundred years ago, Charles Horton Cooley (1864–1929), a symbolic interactionist who taught at the University of Michigan, concluded that the self is part of how *society* makes us human. He said that *our sense of self develops from interaction with others.* To describe the process by which this unique aspect of "humanness" develops, Cooley (1902) coined the term **looking-glass self.** He summarized this idea in the following couplet:

> *Each to each a looking-glass*
> *Reflects the other that doth pass.*

The looking-glass self contains three elements:

1. *We imagine how we appear to those around us.* For example, we may think that others perceive us as witty or dull.
2. *We interpret others' reactions.* We come to conclusions about how others evaluate us. Do they like us for being witty? Do they dislike us for being dull?
3. *We develop a self-concept.* How we interpret others' reactions to us frames our feelings and ideas about ourselves. A favorable reflection in this *social mirror* leads to a positive self-concept; a negative reflection leads to a negative self-concept.

Note that the development of the self does *not* depend on accurate evaluations. Even if we grossly misinterpret how others think about us, those misjudgments become part of our self-concept. Note also that *although the self-concept begins in childhood, its development is an ongoing, lifelong process.* During our everyday lives, we monitor how others react to us. As we do so, we continually modify the self. The self, then, is never a finished product—it is always in process, even into our old age.

Mead and Role Taking

Another symbolic interactionist, George Herbert Mead (1863–1931), who taught at the University of Chicago, pointed out how important play is in developing a self.

self the unique human capacity of being able to see ourselves "from the outside"; the views we internalize of how others see us

looking-glass self a term coined by Charles Horton Cooley to refer to the process by which our self develops through internalizing others' reactions to us

taking the role of the other putting yourself in someone else's shoes; understanding how someone else feels and thinks, so you anticipate how that person will act

significant other an individual who significantly influences someone else

generalized other the norms, values, attitudes, and expectations of people "in general"; the child's ability to take the role of the generalized other is a significant step in the development of a self

What is the looking-glass self? How does it develop?

As we play with others, we learn to **take the role of the other.** That is, we learn to put ourselves in someone else's shoes—to understand how someone else feels and thinks and to anticipate how that person will act.

This doesn't happen overnight. We develop this ability over a period of years (Mead 1934; Denzin 2007). Psychologist John Flavel (1968) asked 8- and 14-year-olds to explain a board game to children who were blindfolded and also to others who were not. The 14-year-olds gave more detailed instructions to those who were blindfolded, but the 8-year-olds gave the same instructions to everyone. The younger children could not yet take the role of the other, while the older children could.

As we develop this ability, at first we can take only the roles of **significant others,** individuals who significantly influence our lives, such as parents or siblings. By assuming their roles during play, such as dressing up in our parents' clothing, we cultivate the ability to put ourselves in the place of significant others.

As our self gradually develops, we internalize the expectations of more and more people. Our ability to take the role of another eventually extends to being able to take the role of "the group as a whole." Mead used the term **generalized other** to refer to our perception of how people in general think of us.

Taking the role of others is essential if we are to become cooperative members of human groups—whether they are family, friends, or co-workers. This ability allows us to modify our behavior by anticipating how others will react—something Genie never learned.

As Figure 1 illustrates, we go through three stages as we learn to take the role of the other:

1. *Imitation.* Under the age of 3, we can only mimic others. We do not yet have a sense of self separate from others, and we can only imitate people's gestures and words. (This stage is actually not role taking, but it prepares us for it.)
2. *Play.* During the second stage, from the ages of about 3 to 6, we pretend to take the roles of specific people. We might pretend that we are a firefighter, a wrestler, a nurse, Supergirl, Spider-Man, a princess, and so on. We also like costumes at this stage and enjoy dressing up in our parents' clothing, or tying a towel around our neck to "become" Superman or Wonder Woman.
3. *Team Games.* This third stage, organized play, or team games, begins roughly when we enter school. The significance for the self is that to play these games we must be able to take multiple roles. One of Mead's favorite examples was that of a baseball game, in which each player must be able to take the role of any other player. To play baseball, it isn't enough that we know our own role; we also must be able to anticipate what everyone else on the field will do when the ball is hit or thrown.

Mead also said the self has two parts, the "I" and the "me." The "I" is *the self as subject,* the active, spontaneous, creative part of the self. In contrast, the "me" is *the self as object.* It is made up of attitudes we internalize from our interactions with others. Mead chose these pronouns because in English "I" is the active agent, as in "I shoved him," while "me" is the object of action, as in "He shoved me." Mead stressed that we are not passive in the socialization process. We are not like robots, with programmed software shoved into us. Rather, our "I" actively evaluates the

FIGURE 1 How We Learn to Take the Role of the Other: Mead's Three Stages

Stage 1: Imitation
Children under age 3
No sense of self
Imitate others

Stage 2: Play
Ages 3 to 6
Play "pretend" others
(princess, Spider-Man, etc.)

Stage 3: Team Games
After about age 6 or 7
Team games
("organized play")
Learn to take multiple roles

Source: By the author.

Ariel Skelley/Corbis

To help his students understand the term *generalized other,* Mead used baseball as an illustration. Why are team sports and organized games excellent examples to use in explaining this concept?

Why is learning to take the role of the other essential for "becoming human"?

Mead analyzed *taking the role of the other* as an essential part of learning to be a full-fledged member of society. At first, we are able to take the role only of *significant others*, as this child is doing. Later we develop the capacity to take the role of the *generalized other*, which is essential not only for cooperation but also for the control of antisocial desires.

© BE&W/SuperStock

reactions of others and organizes them into a unified whole. Mead added that the "I" even monitors the "me," fine-tuning our ideas and attitudes to help us better meet what others expect of us.

In Sum: In studying the details, you don't want to miss the main point, which some find startling: *Both our self and our mind are social products.* Mead stressed that we cannot think without symbols. But where do these symbols come from? Only from society, which gives us our symbols by giving us language. If society did not provide the symbols, we would not be able to think and so would not possess a self-concept or that entity we call the mind. The self and mind, then, like language, are products of society.

Piaget and the Development of Reasoning

The development of the mind—specifically, how we learn to reason—was studied in detail by Jean Piaget (1896–1980). This Swiss psychologist noticed that when young children take intelligence tests, they often give similar wrong answers. This set him to thinking that the children might be using some consistent, but incorrect, reasoning. It might even indicate that children go through some natural process as they learn how to reason.

Stimulated by this intriguing possibility, Piaget set up a laboratory where he could give children of different ages problems to solve (Piaget 1950, 1954; Flavel et al. 2002). After years of testing, Piaget concluded that children go through a natural process as they develop their ability to reason. This process has four stages. (If you mentally substitute "reasoning" or "reasoning skills" for the term *operational* as you review these stages, Piaget's findings will be easier to understand.)

1. **The sensorimotor stage** (from birth to about age 2). During this stage, our understanding is limited to direct contact—sucking, touching, listening, looking. We aren't able to "think." During the first part of this stage, we do not even know that our bodies are separate from the environment. Indeed, we have yet to discover that we have toes. Neither can we recognize cause and effect. That is, we do not know that our actions cause something to happen.

2. **The preoperational stage** (from about age 2 to age 7). During this stage, we *develop the ability to use symbols.* However, we do not yet understand common concepts such as size, speed, or causation. Although we are learning to count, we do not really understand what numbers mean. Nor do we yet have the ability to take the role of the other. Piaget asked preoperational children to describe a clay model of a mountain range. They did just fine. But when he asked them to describe how the mountain range looked from where another child was sitting, they couldn't do it. They could only repeat what they saw from their view.

Bill Anderson/Photo Researchers, Inc.

Shown here is Jean Piaget with one of the children he studied in his analysis of the development of human reasoning.

3. **The concrete operational stage** (from the age of about 7 to 12). Although our reasoning abilities are more developed, they remain *concrete*. We can now understand numbers, size, causation, and speed, and we are able to take the role of the other. We can even play team games. Unless we have concrete examples, however, we are unable to talk about concepts such as truth, honesty, or justice. We can explain why Jane's answer was a lie, but we cannot describe what truth itself is.

4. **The formal operational stage** (after the age of about 12). We now are capable of abstract thinking. We can talk about concepts, come to conclusions based on general principles, and use rules to solve abstract problems. During this stage, we are likely to become young philosophers (Kagan 1984). If we were shown a photo of a slave during our concrete operational stage, we might have said, "That's wrong!" Now at the formal operational stage we are likely to add, "If our county was founded on equality, how could anyone own slaves?"

According to Piaget's theory, how do we develop our ability to reason?

Global Aspects of the Self and Reasoning

Cooley's conclusions about the looking-glass self appear to be true for everyone around the world. So do Mead's conclusions about role taking and the mind and self as social products, although researchers are finding that the self may develop earlier than Mead indicated. The stages of reasoning that Piaget identified probably also occur worldwide, although researchers have found that the stages are not as distinct as Piaget concluded and the ages at which individuals enter the stages differ from one person to another (Flavel et al. 2002). Even during the sensorimotor stage, for example, children show early signs of reasoning, which may indicate an innate ability that is wired into the brain. Although Piaget's theory is being refined, his contribution remains: *A basic structure underlies the way we develop reasoning, and children all over the world begin with the concrete and move to the abstract.*

Interestingly, some people seem to get stuck in the concreteness of the third stage and never reach the fourth stage of abstract thinking (Kohlberg and Gilligan 1971; Suizzo 2000). College, for example, nurtures the fourth stage, and people with this experience apparently have more ability for abstract thought. Social experiences, then, can modify these stages.

Learning Personality, Morality, and Emotions

"Becoming human" also means to develop a personality, morality, and emotions. Let's look at how we learn these essential aspects of our being.

Freud and the Development of Personality

As the mind and the self develop, so does the personality. Sigmund Freud (1856–1939) developed a theory of the origin of personality that has had a major impact on Western thought. Freud, a physician in Vienna in the early 1900s, founded *psychoanalysis,* a technique for treating emotional problems through long-term exploration of the subconscious mind. Let's look at his theory.

Freud believed that personality consists of three elements. Each child is born with the first element, an **id,** Freud's term for inborn drives that cause us to seek self-gratification. The id of the newborn is evident in its cries of hunger or pain. The pleasure-seeking id operates throughout life. It demands the immediate fulfillment of basic needs: food, safety, attention, sex, and so on.

The id's drive for immediate gratification, however, runs into a roadblock: primarily the needs of other people, especially those of the parents. To adapt to these constraints, a second component of the personality emerges, which Freud called the ego. The **ego** is the balancing force between the id and the demands of society that suppress it. The ego also serves to balance the id and the **superego,** the third component of the personality, more commonly called the *conscience.*

The superego represents *culture within us,* the norms and values we have internalized from our social groups. As the *moral* component of the personality, the superego provokes feelings of guilt or shame when we break social rules, or pride and self-satisfaction when we follow them.

According to Freud, when the id gets out of hand, we follow our desires for pleasure and break society's norms. When the superego gets out of hand, we become overly rigid in following those norms and end up wearing a straitjacket of rules that inhibit our lives. The ego, the balancing force, tries to prevent either the superego or the id from dominating. In the emotionally healthy individual, the ego succeeds in balancing these conflicting

id Freud's term for our inborn basic drives

ego Freud's term for a balancing force between the id and the demands of society

superego Freud's term for the conscience; the internalized norms and values of our social groups

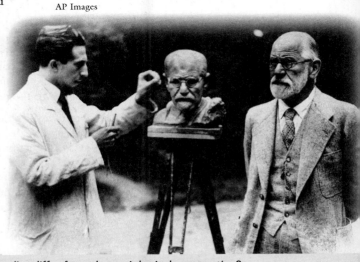

AP Images

Shown here is Sigmund Freud in 1931 as he poses for a sculptor in Vienna, Austria. Although Freud was one of the most influential theorists of the twentieth century, most of his ideas have been discarded.

How does Freud's theory of the development of personality differ from the sociological perspective?

demands of the id and the superego. In the maladjusted individual, the ego fails to control the conflict between the id and the superego. Either the id or the superego dominates this person, leading to internal confusion and problem behaviors.

Sociological Evaluation. Sociologists appreciate Freud's emphasis on socialization—his assertion that the social group into which we are born transmits norms and values that restrain our biological drives. Sociologists, however, object to the view that inborn and subconscious motivations are the primary reasons for human behavior. *This denies the central principle of sociology:* that factors such as social class (income, education, and occupation) and people's roles in groups underlie their behavior (Epstein 1988; Bush and Simmons 1990).

Feminist sociologists have been especially critical of Freud. Although what I just summarized applies to both females and males, Freud assumed that "male" is "normal." He even referred to females as inferior, castrated males (Chodorow 1990; Gerhard 2000). It is obvious that sociologists need to continue to research how we develop personality.

Kohlberg and the Development of Morality

If you have observed young children, you know that they want immediate gratification and show little or no concern for others. ("Mine!" a 2-year-old will shout, as she grabs a toy from another child.) Yet, at a later age this same child will be considerate of others and try to be fair in her play. How does this change happen?

Kohlberg's Theory. Psychologist Lawrence Kohlberg (1975, 1984, 1986; Reed 2008) concluded that we go through a sequence of stages as we develop morality. Building on Piaget's work, he found that children start in the *amoral stage* I just described. For them, there is no right or wrong, just personal needs to be satisfied. From about ages 7 to 10, children are in what Kohlberg called a *preconventional stage.* They have learned rules, and they follow them to stay out of trouble. They view right and wrong as what pleases or displeases their parents, friends, and teachers. Their concern is to get rewards and to avoid punishment. At about age 10, they enter the *conventional stage.* During this period, morality means following the norms and values they have learned. This is followed by a *postconventional stage* in which individuals reflect on abstract principles of right and wrong and judge people's behavior according to these principles.

Criticisms of Kohlberg. Carol Gilligan, another psychologist, was one of the first to criticize Kohlberg. She noticed that Kohlberg had studied only boys. When she interviewed men and women, she concluded that women are more likely to evaluate morality in terms of personal relationships—how an act affects others and the harm it might bring to loved ones. Other researchers followed up, finding that both men and women use personal relationships and abstract principles when they make moral judgments (Wark and Krebs 1996).

To test Kohlberg's theory, researchers checked how it applies in different cultures. They found that the preconventional and conventional stages apply around the world, but that most societies do not have the postconventional stage of universal reasoning. This stage appears to be mostly a Western concept, and not widely practiced even there (Jensen 2009). Apparently, there is no universal, abstract way of figuring what is moral. Instead, different cultures have their own ways to determine morality, and each teaches its members to use its norms in deciding what is moral.

Research with Babies. Researchers have developed ingenious experiments to explore the morality of babies (Bloom 2010). In one experiment, they showed babies a puppet that helps another puppet and one that interferes with the other puppet. They found that babies—even under 1 year of age—prefer the "good" puppet and want the "bad" puppet punished. The conclusion that seems best warranted from these experiments is that we are born with a basic morality upon which society builds its particular moral codes.

As with personality, in this vital area of human development, sociological research is also notably absent.

According to Kohlberg's theory, how do we develop morality?

Socialization into Emotions

As you know so intimately, emotions are also an essential aspect of who you are. Sociologists have found that emotions are not simply the results of our biology. Like the mind, our emotions also depend on socialization (Hochschild 2008). This may sound strange. Don't all people get angry? Doesn't everyone cry? Don't we all feel guilt, shame, sadness, happiness, fear? What has socialization to do with our emotions?

Global Emotions.   At first, it may look as though socialization is not relevant, that we simply express universal feelings. Paul Ekman (1980), a psychologist who studied emotions in several countries, concluded that everyone experiences six basic emotions: anger, disgust, fear, happiness, sadness, and surprise. He also said that we all show the same facial expressions when we feel these emotions. A person from Peru, for example, could tell from just the look on an American's face that she is angry, disgusted, or fearful, and we could tell from the Peruvian's face that he is happy, sad, or surprised. Because we all show the same facial expressions when we experience these six emotions, Ekman concluded that they are hard-wired into our biology.

A study of facial expressions at the Paralympics supports this observation (Matsumoto and Willingham 2009). Upon learning if they had won or lost, those blind from birth had the same facial expressions as those of sighted people, something the blind could not have learned.

Following "Feeling Rules."   If we have universal facial expressions to express certain emotions, then this is biology, something that Darwin noted back in the 1800s (Horwitz and Wakefield 2007:41). What, then, does sociology have to do with expressing emotions? Facial expressions are only one way by which we show our feelings. We also use our bodies, voices, and gestures.

> *Jane and Sushana have been best friends since high school. They were hardly ever apart until Sushana married and moved to another state a year ago. Jane has been waiting eagerly at the arrival gate for Sushana's flight, which has been delayed. When Sushana exits, she and Jane hug one another, making "squeals of glee" and even jumping a bit.*

If you couldn't tell from their names that these were women, you could tell from their behavior. To express delight, U.S. women are allowed to make "squeals of glee" in public places and to jump as they hug. In contrast, in the exact circumstances, U.S. men are expected to shake hands or to give a brief hug. If they gave out "squeals of glee," they would be violating fundamental "gender rules."

Not only do we have "gender rules" for expressing emotions, but we also have "feeling rules" based on culture, social class, relationships, and settings. Consider *culture*. Two close Japanese friends who meet after a long separation don't shake hands or hug—they bow. Two Arab men will kiss. *Social class* is so significant that it, too, cuts across other lines, even gender. Upon seeing a friend after a long

Gary Hershorn/Reuters/Corbis   Lynne Fernandes/The Image Works   AP Images/Matt York   © Tim Graham Picture Library/ Getty Images   UPI Photo/Aaron Kehoe/ Landov

What emotions are these people expressing? Are these emotions global? Is their way of expressing them universal?

How do "feeling rules" guide how we express our emotions? How do "feeling rules" operate in your life?

absence, upper-class women and men are likely to be more reserved in expressing their delight than are lower-class women and men. *Relationships* also make a big difference. We express our feelings more openly if we are with close friends, more guardedly if we are at a staff meeting with the corporate CEO. The *setting*, then, is also important, with each setting having its own "rules" about emotions. As you know, the emotions you can express at a rock concert differ considerably from those you express in a classroom. If you think about your childhood, you will realize that a good part of your early socialization centered on learning your culture's feeling rules.

What We Feel

Joan, a U.S. woman who had been married for seven years, had no children. When she finally gave birth and the doctor handed her a healthy girl, she was almost overcome with joy. Tafadzwa, in Zimbabwe, had been married for seven years and had no children. When the doctor handed her a healthy girl, she was almost overcome with sadness.

You can easily understand why the U.S. woman felt happy, but why did the woman in Zimbabwe feel sad? The effects of socialization on our emotions go much deeper than guiding how, where, and when we express our feelings. Socialization also affects *what* we feel (Clark 1997; Shields 2002). In Zimbabwe culture, to not give birth to a male child lowers a woman's social status and is even considered a good reason for her husband to divorce her (Horwitz and Wakefield 2007:43).

Research Needed. Although Ekman identified only six emotions as universal in facial expression, I suspect that there are more. It is likely that people around the world have similar feelings and facial expressions when they experience helplessness, despair, confusion, and shock. We need cross-cultural research to find out whether these emotions are universal. We also need more research into how culture guides us in what we feel and how we express our feelings.

Society within Us: The Self and Emotions as Social Control

Much of our socialization is intended to turn us into conforming members of society. Socialization into the self and emotions is essential to this process, for *both the self and our emotions mold our behavior*. Although we like to think that we are "free," consider for a moment just some of the factors that influence how you act: the expectations of your friends and parents, of neighbors and teachers; classroom norms and college rules; city, state, and federal laws. For example, if in a moment of intense frustration, or out of a devilish desire to shock people, you wanted to tear off your clothes and run naked down the street, what would stop you?

The answer is your socialization—*society within you*. Your experiences in society have resulted in a self that thinks along certain lines and feels particular emotions. This helps to keep you in line. Thoughts such as "Would I get kicked out of school?" and "What would my friends (parents) think if they found out?" represent an awareness of the self in relationship to others. So does the desire to avoid feelings of shame and embarrassment. Your *social mirror*, then—the result of your being socialized into a self and emotions—sets up effective internal controls over your behavior. In fact, socialization into self and emotions is so effective that some people feel embarrassed just thinking about running naked in public!

In Sum: Socialization is essential for our development as human beings. From our interaction with others, we learn how to think, reason, and feel. The net result is the shaping of our behavior—including our thinking and emotions—according to cultural standards. This is what sociologists mean when they refer to "*society within us.*"

What does the term "society within us" mean? How is it an essential part of social control?

Socialization into Gender

Learning the Gender Map

For a child, society is unexplored territory. A major signpost on society's map is **gender,** the attitudes and behaviors that are expected of us because we are a male or a female. In learning the gender map (called **gender socialization**), we are nudged into different lanes in life—into contrasting attitudes and behaviors. We take direction so well that, as adults, most of us act, think, and even feel according to this gender map, our culture's guidelines to what is appropriate for our sex.

The significance of gender is emphasized throughout this book, but for now, though, let's briefly consider some of the "gender messages" that we get from our family and the mass media.

Gender Messages in the Family

Our parents are the first significant others to show us the gender map. Sometimes they do this consciously, perhaps by bringing into play pink and blue, colors that have no meaning in themselves but that are now associated with gender. Our parents' own gender orientations are embedded so firmly that they do most of their gender teaching without being aware of what they are doing.

This is illustrated in a classic study by psychologists Susan Goldberg and Michael Lewis (1969), whose results have been confirmed by other researchers (Connors 1996; Clearfield and Nelson 2006; Best 2010).

> *Goldberg and Lewis asked mothers to bring their 6-month-old infants into their laboratory, supposedly to observe the infants' development. Covertly, however, they also observed the mothers. They found that the mothers kept their daughters closer to them. They also touched their daughters more and spoke to them more frequently than they did to their sons. By the time the children were 13 months old, the girls stayed closer to their mothers during play, and they returned to their mothers sooner and more often than the boys did.*
> *Then Goldberg and Lewis did a little experiment. They set up a barrier to separate the children from their mothers, who were holding toys. The girls were more likely to cry and motion for help; the boys, to try to climb over the barrier.*

Goldberg and Lewis concluded that the mothers had subconsciously rewarded their daughters for being passive and dependent, and their sons for being active and independent.

Our family's gender lessons are thorough. On the basis of our sex, our parents give us different kinds of toys. Boys are more likely to get guns and "action figures" that destroy enemies. Girls are more likely to get dolls and jewelry. Some parents try to choose "gender neutral" toys, but kids know what is popular, and they feel left out if they don't have what the other kids have. The significance of toys in gender socialization can be summarized this way: Most parents would be upset if someone gave their son Barbie dolls.

Play also teaches gender. In ways we haven't yet studied, parents subtly "signal" to their sons that is is okay for them to participate in more rough-and-tumble play. In general, parents expect their sons to get dirtier and to be more defiant, their daughters to be daintier and more compliant (Gilman 1911/1971; Henslin 2012a; Nordberg 2010). And in large part, parents get what they expect. Such experiences in socialization lie at the heart of the sociological explanation of male–female differences. For a fascinating account of how socialization can trump biology, read the Cultural Diversity box on the next page.

Excerpt from "Play Behavior in the Year-Old Infant: Early Sex Differences" by Susan Goldberg and Michael Lewis, from CHILD DEVELOPMENT, March 1969, Volume 40. Copyright © 1969 by Susan Goldberg and Michael Lewis. Reprinted with permission by John Wiley & Sons Ltd.

gender the behaviors and attitudes that a society considers proper for its males and females; masculinity or femininity

gender socialization learning society's "gender map," the paths in life set out for us because we are male or female

TON KOENE/dpa/Landov

The gender roles that we learn during childhood become part of our basic orientations to life. Although we refine these roles as we grow older, they are built on the framework established during childhood.

How do gender messages in the family nudge us into behavior considered appropriate for our sex?

Cultural Diversity around the World

When Women Become Men: The Sworn Virgins

"I will become a man," said Pashe. "I will do it."

The decision was final. Taking a pair of scissors, she soon had her long, black curls lying at her feet. She took off her dress—never to wear one again in her life—and put on her father's baggy trousers. She armed herself with her father's rifle. She would need it.

Going before the village elders, she swore to never marry, to never have children, and to never have sex.

Pashe had become a sworn virgin—and a man.

There was no turning back. The penalty for violating the oath was death.

In northern Albania, where Pashe Keqi lives, and in parts of Bosnia and Serbia, some women become men. They are neither transsexuals nor lesbians. Nor do they have a sex-change operation, something which is unknown in those parts.

This custom, which goes back centuries, is a practical matter, a way to protect and support the family. In these traditional societies, women stay home and take care of the children and household. They can go hardly anywhere except to the market and mosque. Women depend on men for survival.

And when there is no man? This is the problem.

Pashe's father was killed in a blood feud. In these traditional groups, when the family patriarch (male head) dies and there are no male heirs, how are the women to survive? In the fifteenth century, people in this area hit upon a solution: One of the women gives an oath of lifelong virginity and takes over the man's role. She then becomes a social he—she wears male clothing, carries a gun, owns property, and moves freely throughout the society.

She drinks in the tavern with the men. She sits with the men at weddings. She prays with the men at the mosque.

When a man wants to marry a girl of the family, she is the one who approves or disapproves of the suitor.

In short, the woman really becomes a man. Actually, a social man, sociologists would add. Her biology does not change, but her gender does. Pashe had become the man of the house, a status she occupied her entire life.

Taking this position at the age of 11—Pashe is in her 70s now—also made her responsible for avenging her father's

Ben Speck/Getty Images

Sokol (Zhire) Zmajli, aged 80, changed her name from Zhire to the male name Sokol when she was young. She heads the family household consisting of her nephew, his wife, their sons and their wives.

murder. But when his killer was released from prison, her 15-year-old nephew (she is his uncle) rushed in and did the deed instead.

Sworn virgins walk like men, they talk like men, and they hunt with the men. They also take up manly occupations. They become shepherds, security guards, truck drivers, and political leaders. Those around them know that they are biological women, but in all ways they treat them as men. When a sworn virgin talks to women, the women recoil in shyness.

The sworn virgins of Albania are a fascinating cultural contradiction: In the midst of a highly traditional group, one built around male superiority that severely limits women, we find both the belief and practice that a biological woman can do the work of a man and function in all of a man's social roles. The sole exception is marriage.

Under communist rule until 1985, with travel restricted by law and custom, mountainous northern Albania had been cut off from the rest of the world. Now there is a democratic government, and the region is connected to the world by better roads, telephones, and even television. As modern life trickles into these villages, few women want to become men. "Why should we?" they ask. "Now we have freedom. We can go to the city and work and support our families."

For Your Consideration

➜ How do the sworn virgins of Albania help to explain what gender is? Apply functionalism: How was the custom and practice of sworn virgins functional for this society? Apply symbolic interactionism: How do symbols underlie and maintain a woman's shift to becoming a man in this society? Apply conflict theory: How do power relations between men and women underlie this practice?

Sources: Based on Zumbrun 2007; Bilefsky 2008; Young and Twigg 2009.

How do sworn virgins illustrate the social nature of masculinity and femininity?

Frank and Ernest

SOON WE'LL GIVE UP DOLLS AND HOPSCOTCH---BUT THEY'LL BE INTO FOOTBALL FOREVER.

12-10
THAVES

www.cartoonistgroup.com

The *gender roles* that we learn during childhood become part of our basic orientations to life. Although we refine these roles as we grow older, they remain built around the framework established during childhood.

Gender Messages from Peers

Sociologists stress how this sorting process into gender that begins in the family is reinforced as the child is exposed to other aspects of society. Of those other influences, one of the most powerful is the **peer group,** individuals of roughly the same age who are linked by common interests. Examples of peer groups are friends, classmates, and "the kids in the neighborhood."

As you grew up, you saw girls and boys teach one another what it means to be a female or a male. You might not have recognized what was happening, however, so let's eavesdrop on a conversation between two eighth-grade girls studied by sociologist Donna Eder (2007).

CINDY: The only thing that makes her look anything is all the makeup …
PENNY: She had a picture, and she's standing like this. (Poses with one hand on her hip and one by her head)
CINDY: Her face is probably this skinny, but it looks that big 'cause of all the makeup she has on it.
PENNY: She's ugly, ugly, ugly.

Do you see how these girls were giving gender lessons? They were reinforcing images of appearance and behavior that they thought were appropriate for females.

Boys, too, reinforce cultural expectations of gender. Sociologist Melissa Milkie (1994), who studied junior high school boys, found that much of their talk centered on movies and TV programs. Of the many images they saw, the boys would single out those associated with sex and violence. They would amuse one another by repeating lines, acting out parts, and joking and laughing at what they had seen.

If you know boys in their early teens, you've probably seen a lot of behavior like this. You may have been amused, or even have shaken your head in disapproval. But did you peer beneath the surface? Milkie did. What is really going on? The boys, she concluded, were using media images to develop their identity as males. They had gotten the message: "Real" males are obsessed with sex and violence. Not to joke and laugh about murder and promiscuous sex would have marked a boy as a "weenie," a label to be avoided at all costs.

Gender Messages in the Mass Media

As you can see with the boys Milkie studied, another guide to our gender map is the **mass media,** forms of communication that are directed to large audiences. Let's look further at how media images reinforce **gender,** how they help teach us the behaviors and attitudes considered appropriate for our sex.

Advertising. From an early age, the media bombard us with stereotypical images. If you are average, you are exposed to a blistering 30,000 commercials a year (Larson 2001). In commercials geared toward children, boys are more likely to be shown as

peer group a group of individuals, often of roughly the same age, who are linked by common interests and orientations

mass media forms of communication, such as radio, newspapers, and television that are directed to mass audiences

Eder, Donna. "On Becoming Female: Lessons Learned in School." In *Down to Earth Sociology: Introductory Readings*, 14th ed., James M. Henslin, ed. New York: Free Press, 2007.

How do peers teach gender to one another? How have your peers shaped your images of gender?

competing in outdoor settings, while girls are more likely to be portrayed as cooperating in indoor settings. Action figures are pitched to boys, and dolls to girls (Kahlenberg and Hein 2010).

As adults, we are still peppered with ads. Although their purpose is to sell products—from booze and bras to cigarettes and cell phones—these ads continue our gender lessons. I'm sure you have noticed the ads that portray men as dominant and rugged and women as sexy and submissive. The stereotypical images—from cowboys who roam the wide-open spaces to scantily clad women whose physical assets couldn't possibly be real—become part of our own images of the sexes. So do the stereotype-breaking images. Whether overt and exaggerated or subtle and below our awareness, the mass media continue our gender lessons.

◉—Watch
Play Again
on mysoclab.com

Movies and Television.   Television and movies also teach lessons in gender. With male characters outnumbering female characters, prime-time television continues to point to the greater importance of males in society. But the times are changing, and more dominant, aggressive females are also being portrayed. In cartoons, Kim Possible divides her time between cheerleading practice and saving the world from evil. With tongue in cheek, the Powerpuff Girls are touted as "the most elite kindergarten crime-fighting force ever assembled." This changed gender portrayal is especially evident in the violent females who play lead characters in action movies, from the assassin in *Kill Bill* to Angelina Jolie in *Salt* (Gilpatric 2010).

The gender messages, however, are mixed. While girls are presented as more powerful than they used to be, they have to be skinny and gorgeous and wear the latest fashions. Such messages present a dilemma for girls, for continuously thrust before them is a model that is almost impossible to replicate in real life.

Video Games.   The movement, color, virtual dangers, unexpected dilemmas, and ability to control the action make video games highly appealing. High school and college students find them a seductive way of escaping from the demands of life. The first members of the "Nintendo Generation," now in their 30s, are still playing video games—with babies on their laps.

Sociologists have begun to study how video games portray the sexes, but we still know little about their influence on the players' ideas of gender. Females are even more underrepresented in video games than on television, with 90 percent of the main characters being male (Williams et al. 2009). Because these games are on the cutting edge of society, they sometimes also reflect cutting-edge changes in sex roles, the topic of the Mass Media in Social Life box on the next page.

Harry Briggs/Corbis

The gender messages of *anime*, an increasingly popular art form, are yet to be explored.

Anime.   Because anime, a Japanese cartoon form, crosses boundaries of video games, television, movies, and books (comic), we shall consider it as a separate category. The depiction of gender roles in anime is far from simple. A pornographic form features passive little girls and women who are exploited sexually by older boys and men, sometimes brutally so. Directed largely to children, another form features big-eyed little girls and fighting little boys. As in the illustration to the left, young women are also depicted in violent roles. A sociological question is, What gender lessons are children learning from this form of mass media?

In Sum: In every society, "male" and "female" are powerful symbols. As children learn their society's symbols of gender, they learn that different behaviors and attitudes are expected of boys and girls. First transmitted by the family, these gender messages are reinforced by other social institutions. As these symbols become integrated into our views of the world, we form a picture of "how" males and females "are." Because gender serves as a primary basis for *social inequality*—giving privileges and obligations to one group of people while denying them to another—gender images are especially important in our socialization.

How do the mass media teach gender? How have the mass media shaped your images of gender?

Lara Croft, Tomb Raider: Changing Images of Women in the Mass Media

With digital advances, video games have crossed the line from games to something that more closely resembles interactive movies. Costing several million dollars to produce and millions more to market, video games have intricate subplots. Some use celebrity voices for the characters and introduce new songs by major rock groups (Levine 2008). Sociologically, what is significant is the *content* of video games. They expose gamers not only to action but also to ideas and images. Just as in other forms of the mass media, video images communicate powerful gender messages.

Lara Croft, an adventure-seeking archeologist and star of *Tomb Raider* and its many sequels, is the essence of this new gender image. Lara is smart, strong, and able to utterly vanquish foes. With both guns blazing, Lara breaks stereotypical gender roles and dominates what previously was the domain of men. She was the first female protagonist in a field of muscle-rippling, gun-toting macho caricatures (Taylor 1999).

Yet the old remains powerfully encapsulated in the new. As the photos here make evident, Lara is a fantasy girl for young men of the digital generation. No matter her foe, no matter her predicament, Lara oozes sex. Her form-fitting outfits, which flatter her voluptuous figure, reflect the mental images of the men who created this digital character.

Lara has caught young men's fancy to such an extent that they have bombarded corporate headquarters with questions about her personal life. Lara is the star of two movies and a comic book. There is also a Lara Croft action figure.

MARCUS BRANDT/dpa/Landov

SHNS photo courtesy Eido via Newscom

The mass media not only reflect gender stereotypes but they also play a role in changing them. Sometimes they do both simultaneously. The images of Lara Croft not only reflect women's changing role in society, but also, by exaggerating the change, they mold new stereotypes.

For Your Consideration

→ A sociologist who reviewed this text said, "It seems that for women to be defined as equal, we have to become symbolic males—warriors with breasts." Why is gender change mostly one-way—females adopting traditional male characteristics? These two questions should help: Who is moving into the traditional territory of the other? Do people prefer to imitate power or weakness?

→ Finally, consider just how far stereotypes have actually been left behind. One reward for beating time trials is to be able to see Lara wearing a bikini.

Agents of Socialization

Individuals and groups that influence our orientations to life—our self-concept, emotions, attitudes, and behavior—are called **agents of socialization.** We have already considered how three of these agents—the family, our peers, and the mass media—influence our ideas of gender. Now we'll look more closely at how agents of socialization prepare us in other ways to take our place in society. We shall consider the family, then the neighborhood, religion, day care, school and peers, and the workplace.

The Family

The first group to have a major impact on us is our family. Our experiences in the family are so intense that their influence is lifelong. These experiences establish our initial motivations, values, and beliefs. In the family, we receive our basic sense of self, ideas about who we are and what we deserve out of life. It is here that we begin to think of ourselves

agents of socialization people or groups that affect our self-concept, attitudes, behaviors, or other orientations toward life

How do video games socialize people into gender? Have they been part of your socialization into gender?

as strong or weak, smart or dumb, good-looking or ugly—or more likely, somewhere in between. And as already noted, the lifelong process of defining ourselves as feminine or masculine also begins in the family.

Let's look at the difference that social class makes in how families socialize their children.

Social Class and Type of Work.   Sociologist Melvin Kohn (1959, 1963, 1977, 2006) found that the main concern of working-class parents is that their children stay out of trouble. They tend to use physical punishment. Middle-class parents, in contrast, focus more on developing their children's curiosity, self-expression, and self-control. They are more likely to reason with their children than to use physical punishment.

These differences puzzled Kohn. As a sociologist, he knew that the answer was life experiences of some sort. He found the answer in the world of work. Blue-collar workers are usually told exactly what to do. Since they expect their children's lives to be like theirs, they stress obedience. The work of middle-class parents, in contrast, requires more initiative, and they socialize their children into the qualities they find valuable.

Kohn was still puzzled. Some working-class parents act more like middle-class parents, and vice versa. As Kohn probed this puzzle, the pieces fell into place. The key turned out to be the parents' type of job. Middle-class office workers, for example, are supervised closely, and Kohn found that they follow the working-class pattern of child rearing, emphasizing conformity. And some blue-collar workers, such as those who do home repairs, have a good deal of freedom. These workers follow the middle-class model in rearing their children (Pearlin and Kohn 1966; Kohn and Schooler 1969).

Social Class and Play.   Working-class and middle-class parents also have different ideas of how children develop, ideas that have fascinating consequences for children's play (Lareau 2002; Bodovski and Farkas 2008). For working-class parents children are like wild flowers—they develop naturally. Since the child's development will take care of itself, good parenting primarily means to provide food, shelter, and comfort. These parents set limits on their children's play ("Don't go near the railroad tracks") and let them play as they wish. To middle-class parents, in contrast, children are like tender house plants—they need a lot of guidance to develop correctly. These parents want their children's play to accomplish something. They may want them to play baseball, for example, not for the enjoyment of the sport, but to help them learn how to be team players.

This photo captures an extreme form of family socialization. The father seems to be more emotionally involved in the goal—and in more pain—than his daughter, as he pushes her toward the finish line in the Teen Tours of America Kid's Triathlon.

Lannis Waters/The Palm Beach Post

The Neighborhood

As all parents know, some neighborhoods are better than others for children. Parents try to move to the better neighborhoods—if they can afford them. Their common-sense evaluations are borne out by sociological research. Children from poor neighborhoods are more likely to get in trouble with the law, to become pregnant, to drop out of school, and even to have worse mental health (Levanthal and Brooks-Gunn 2000; Wheaton and Clarke 2003; Chauhan et al. 2009; DeLuca and Dayton 2009).

Sociologists have also found that the residents of more affluent neighborhoods keep a closer eye on the children than do the residents of poor neighborhoods (Sampson et al. 1999). The basic reason is that the more affluent neighborhoods have fewer families in transition, so the adults are more likely to know the local children and their parents. This better equips them to help keep the children safe and out of trouble.

Religion

How important is religion in your life? Most Americans belong to a local congregation, but what if you are among the 16 percent who do not identify with a religion (Newport

How are social class and neighborhoods important agents of socialization?

2010)? We would miss the point if we were to assume that religion influences only people who are "religious." Religion plays a powerful role even for people who wouldn't be caught dead near a church, synagogue, or mosque. How? Religious ideas so pervade U.S. society that they provide the foundation of morality for both the religious and the nonreligious.

For many Americans, the influence of religion is more direct. This is especially true for the two of every five Americans who report that during a typical week they attend a religious service (Gallup Poll 2010). On the obvious level, through their participation in religious services they learn doctrines, values, and morality, but the effects of religion on their lives go far beyond this. As they learn beliefs about the hereafter, for example, they also learn what kinds of clothing, speech, and manners are appropriate for formal occasions. Life in congregations also provides them a sense of identity, a feeling of belonging. Religious participation also helps to integrate immigrants into their new society, offers an avenue of social mobility for the poor, provides social contacts for jobs, and for African Americans, has been a powerful influence in social change.

Day Care

It is rare for social science research to make national news, but occasionally it does. This is what happened when researchers published their findings on 1,200 kindergarten children they had studied since they were a month old. They observed the children multiple times both at home and at day care. They also videotaped and made detailed notes on the children's interaction with their mothers (National Institute of Child Health and Human Development 1999; Guensburg 2001). What caught the media's attention? Children who spend more time in day care have weaker bonds with their mothers and are less affectionate to them. They are also less cooperative with others and more likely to fight and to be "mean." By the time they get to kindergarten, they are more likely to talk back to teachers and to disrupt the classroom. This holds true regardless of the quality of the day care, the family's social class, or whether the child is a girl or a boy (Belsky 2006). On the positive side, the children also scored higher on language tests.

Are we producing a generation of "smart but mean" children? This is not an unreasonable question, since the study was well designed and an even larger study of children in England has come up with similar findings (Belsky 2006). Some point out that the differences between children who spend a lot of time in day care and those who spend less time are slight. Others stress that with 5 million children in day care (*Statistical Abstract* 2010:Table 566), slight differences can be significant for society.

The researchers continued to test these children as they went through school, and the surprise is that the initial effects of day care followed the children. At age 15, the children who had lower quality care and those who spent more time in child care did slightly worse academically and had slightly more behavioral problems than the children who had the higher quality care or who spent less time in child care (Vandell et al. 2010).

The School

Part of the **manifest function,** or *intended* purpose, of formal education is to teach knowledge and skills, such as reading, writing, and arithmetic. The teaching of such skills is certainly part of socialization, but so are the schools' **latent functions,** the *unintended consequences* that help the social system. Let's look at this less obvious aspect of education. At home, children learn attitudes and values that match their family's situation in life. At school, they learn a broader perspective that helps prepare them to take a role in the world beyond the family. At home, a child may have been the almost exclusive focus of doting parents, but in school, the child learns *universality*—that the same rules apply to everyone, regardless of who their parents are or how special they may be at home. The Cultural Diversity box on the next page explores how these new values and ways of looking at the world sometimes even replace those the child learns at home.

manifest functions the intended beneficial consequences of people's actions

latent functions unintended beneficial consequences of people's actions

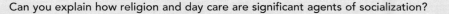

Schools are a primary agent of socialization. One of their functions is to teach children the attitudes and skills they are thought to need as adults. As indicated by this photo, in the United States this process starts early.

Dane Rex/Lightbox

Can you explain how religion and day care are significant agents of socialization?

Cultural Diversity in the United States

Immigrants and Their Children: Caught between Two Worlds

It is a struggle to adapt to a new culture, for its behaviors and ways of thinking may be at odds with the ones already learned. This exposure to two worlds can lead to inner turmoil. One way to handle the conflict is to cut ties with your first culture. Doing so, however, can create a sense of loss, one that is perhaps recognized only later in life.

Richard Rodriguez, a literature professor and essayist, was born to working-class Mexican immigrants. Wanting their son to be successful in their adopted land, his parents named him Richard instead of Ricardo. Although this English–Spanish hybrid name indicates his parents' aspirations for their son, it was also an omen of the conflict that Richard would experience.

Like other children of Mexican immigrants, Richard first spoke Spanish—a rich mother tongue that introduced him to the world. Until the age of 5, when he began school, Richard knew only fifty words in English. He describes what happened when he began school:

> The change came gradually but early. When I was beginning grade school, I noted to myself the fact that the classroom environment was so different in its styles and assumptions from my own family environment that survival would essentially entail a choice between both worlds. When I became a student, I was literally "remade"; neither I nor my teachers considered anything I had known before as relevant. I had to forget most of what my culture had provided, because to remember it was a disadvantage. The past and its cultural values became detachable, like a piece of clothing grown heavy on a warm day and finally put away.

Stockbyte/Getty Images Royalty Free

As happened to millions of immigrants before him, whose parents spoke German, Polish, Italian, and so on, learning English eroded family and class ties and ate away at his ethnic roots. For Rodriguez, language and education were not simply devices that eased the transition to the dominant culture. They also slashed at the roots that had given him life.

To face conflicting cultures is to confront a fork in the road. Some turn one way and withdraw from the new culture—a clue that helps to explain why so many Latinos drop out of U.S. schools. Others go in the opposite direction. Cutting ties with their family and cultural roots, they embrace the new culture.

Rodriguez took the second road. He excelled in his new language—so much, in fact, that he graduated from Stanford University and then became a graduate student in English at the University of California at Berkeley. He was even awarded a Fulbright fellowship to study English Renaissance literature at the University of London.

But the past shadowed Rodriguez. Prospective employers were impressed with his knowledge of Renaissance literature. At job interviews, however, they would skip over the Renaissance training and ask him if he would teach the Mexican novel and be an adviser to Latino students. Rodriguez was also haunted by the image of his grandmother, the warmth of the culture he had left behind, and the language and ways of thinking to which he had become a stranger.

Richard Rodriguez represents millions of immigrants—not just those of Latino origin but those from other cultures, too—who want to integrate into U.S. culture yet not betray their past. Fearing loss of their roots, they are caught between two cultures, each beckoning, each offering rich rewards.

For Your Consideration

➜ I saw this conflict firsthand with my father, who did not learn English until after the seventh grade (his last in school). He left German behind, eventually coming to the point that he could no longer speak it, but broken English and awkward expressions remained for a lifetime. Then, too, there were the lingering emotional connections to old ways, as well as the haughtiness and slights of more assimilated Americans. He longed for security by grasping the past, but at the same time, he wanted to succeed in the everyday reality of the new culture. Have you seen similar conflicts?

Sources: Based on Richard Rodriguez 1975, 1982, 1990, 1991, 1995.

Rodriguez, Richard. *Hunger of Memory: The Education of Richard Rodriguez.* Boston: Godine, 1982.

Why do immigrants experience culture conflict? What alternatives do they face?

Sociologists have also identified a *hidden curriculum* in our schools. This term refers to values that, although not taught explicitly, are part of a school's "cultural message." For example, the stories and examples that are used to teach math and English may bring with them lessons in patriotism, democracy, justice, and honesty. There is also a *corridor curriculum*, what students teach one another outside the classroom. Unfortunately, the corridor curriculum seems to emphasize racism, sexism, illicit ways to make money, and coolness (Hemmings 1999). You can determine for yourself which of these is functional and which is dysfunctional.

Conflict theorists point out that social class separates children into different educational worlds. Children born to wealthy parents go to private schools, where they learn skills and values that match their higher position. Children born to middle-class parents go to public schools where they learn that good jobs, even the professions, beckon, while children from blue-collar families learn that not many of "their kind" will become professionals or leaders. This is one of the many reasons that children from blue-collar families are less likely to take college prep courses or to go to college. In short, our schools reflect and reinforce our social class divisions.

Peer Groups

As a child's experiences with agents of socialization broaden, the influence of the family decreases. Entry into school marks only one of many steps in this transfer of allegiance. One of the most significant aspects of education is that it exposes children to peer groups that help children resist the efforts of parents and schools to socialize them.

When sociologists Patricia and Peter Adler (1998) observed children at two elementary schools in Colorado, they saw how children separate themselves by sex and develop separate gender worlds. The norms that made boys popular were athletic ability, coolness, and toughness. For girls, popularity came from family background, physical appearance (clothing and use of makeup), and the ability to attract popular boys. In this children's subculture, academic achievement pulled in opposite directions: For boys, high grades lowered their popularity, but for girls, good grades increased their standing among peers.

You know from your own experience how compelling peer groups are. It is almost impossible to go against a peer group, whose cardinal rule seems to be "conformity or rejection." Anyone who doesn't do what the others want becomes an "outsider," a "nonmember," an "outcast." For preteens and teens just learning their way around in the world, it is not surprising that the peer group rules.

As a result, the standards of our peer groups tend to dominate our lives. If your peers, for example, listen to rap, Nortec, death metal, rock and roll, country, or gospel, it is almost inevitable that you also prefer that kind of music. In high school, if your friends take math courses, you probably do, too (Crosnoe et al. 2008). It is the same for clothing styles and dating standards. Peer influences also extend to behaviors that violate social norms. If your peers are college-bound and upwardly striving, this is most likely what you will be; but if they use drugs, cheat, and steal, you are likely to do so, too.

The Workplace

Another agent of socialization that comes into play somewhat later in life is the workplace. Those initial jobs that we take in high school and college are much more than just a way to earn a few dollars. From the people we rub shoulders with at work, we learn not only a set of skills but also perspectives on the world.

Most of us eventually become committed to some particular line of work, often after trying out many jobs. This may involve **anticipatory socialization,** learning to play a role before entering

anticipatory socialization the process of learning in advance an anticipated future role or status

Gradeschool boys and girls often separate themselves by gender, as in this lunchroom in Schenectady, New York. The socialization that occurs during self-segregation by gender is a topic of study by sociologists.

© Ellen B. Senisi

In what ways are schools, peer groups, and the workplace important agents of socialization?

it. Anticipatory socialization is a sort of mental rehearsal for some future activity. We may talk to people who work in a particular career, read novels about that type of work, or take a summer internship in that field. Such activities allow us to gradually identify with the role, to become aware of what would be expected of us. Sometimes this helps people avoid committing themselves to an empty career, as with some of my students who tried student teaching, found that they couldn't stand it, and then moved on to other fields more to their liking.

An intriguing aspect of work as a socializing agent is that the more you participate in a line of work, the more this work becomes part of your self-concept. Eventually you come to think of yourself so much in terms of the job that if someone asks you to describe yourself, you are likely to include the job in your self-description. You might say, "I'm a teacher," "I'm a nurse," or "I'm a sociologist."

Resocialization

What does a woman who has just become a nun have in common with a man who has just divorced? The answer is that they both are undergoing **resocialization;** that is, they are learning new norms, values, attitudes, and behaviors to match their new situation in life. In its most common form, resocialization occurs each time we learn something contrary to our previous experiences. A new boss who insists on a different way of doing things is resocializing you. Most resocialization is mild—only a slight modification of things we have already learned.

Resocialization can also be intense. People who join Alcoholics Anonymous (AA), for example, are surrounded by reformed drinkers who affirm the destructive effects of excessive drinking. Some students experience an intense period of resocialization when they leave high school and start college—especially during those initially scary days before they find companions, start to fit in, and feel comfortable. The experiences of people who join a cult or begin psychotherapy are even more profound, for they learn views that conflict with their earlier socialization. If these ideas "take," not only does the individual's behavior change but he or she also learns a fundamentally different way of looking at life.

Total Institutions

Relatively few of us experience the powerful agent of socialization that sociologist Erving Goffman (1961) called the **total institution.** He coined this term to refer to a place in which people are cut off from the rest of society and where they come under almost total control of the officials who are in charge. Boot camp, prisons, concentration camps, convents, some religious cults, and some military schools, such as West Point, are total institutions.

A person entering a total institution is greeted with a **degradation ceremony** (Garfinkel 1956), an attempt to remake the self by stripping away the individual's current identity and stamping a new one in its place. This unwelcome greeting may involve fingerprinting, photographing, or shaving the head. Newcomers may be ordered to strip, undergo an examination (often in a humiliating, semipublic setting), and then put on a uniform that designates their new status. Officials also take away the individual's personal identity kit, items such as jewelry, hairstyles, clothing, and other body decorations used to express individuality.

Total institutions are isolated from the public. The bars, walls, gates, and guards not only keep the inmates in but also keep outsiders out. Staff members supervise the day-to-day lives of the residents. Eating, sleeping, showering, recreation—all are standardized. Inmates learn that their previous statuses—student, worker, spouse, parent—mean nothing. The only thing that counts is their current status.

No one leaves a total institution unscathed, for the experience brands an indelible mark on the individual's self and colors the way he or she sees the world. Boot camp,

resocialization the process of learning new norms, values, attitudes, and behaviors

total institution a place that is almost totally controlled by those who run it, in which people are cut off from the rest of society and the society is mostly cut off from them

degradation ceremony a term coined by Harold Garfinkel to refer to a ritual whose goal is to remake someone's self by stripping away that individual's self-identity and stamping a new identity in its place

What is resocialization? How do total institutions resocialize their members?

as described in the Down-to-Earth Sociology box below, is brutal but swift. Prison, in contrast, is brutal and prolonged. Neither recruit nor prisoner, however, has difficulty in knowing that the institution has had profound effects on attitudes and orientations to life.

life course the stages of our life as we go from birth to death

Socialization through the Life Course

You are at a particular stage in your life now, and college is a good part of it. You know that you have more stages ahead as you go through life. These stages, from birth to death, are called the **life course** (Elder 1975; 1999). The sociological significance of the life course is twofold. First, as you pass through a stage, it affects your behavior and orientations. You simply don't think about life in the same way when you are 30, are

Down-to-Earth **Sociology**

Boot Camp as a Total Institution

The bus arrives at Parris Island, South Carolina, at 3 A.M. The early hour is no accident. The recruits are groggy, confused. Up to a few hours ago, the young men were ordinary civilians. Now, as a sergeant sneeringly calls them "maggots," their heads are buzzed (25 seconds per recruit), and they are quickly thrust into the harsh world of Marine boot camp.

Buzzing the boys' hair is just the first step in stripping away their identity so that the Marines can stamp a new one in its place. The uniform serves the same purpose. There is a ban on using the first person "I." Even a simple request must be made in precise Marine style or it will not be acknowledged. ("Sir, Recruit Jones requests permission to make a head call, Sir.")

Every intense moment of the next eleven weeks reminds the recruits, men and women, that they are joining a subculture of self-discipline. Here pleasure is suspect and sacrifice is good. As they learn the Marine way of talking, walking, and thinking, they are denied the diversions they once took for granted: television, cigarettes, cars, candy, soft drinks, video games, music, alcohol, drugs, and sex.

Lessons are taught with fierce intensity. When Sgt. Carey checks brass belt buckles, Recruit Robert Shelton nervously blurts, "I don't have one." Sgt. Carey's face grows red as his neck cords bulge. "I?" he says, his face just inches from the recruit. With spittle flying from his mouth, he screams, " 'I' is gone!"

"Nobody's an individual" is the lesson that is driven home again and again. "You are a team, a Marine. Not a civilian. Not black or white, not Hispanic or Indian or some hyphenated American—but a Marine. You will live like a Marine, fight like a Marine, and, if necessary, die like a Marine."

Each day begins before dawn with close-order formations. The rest of the day is filled with training in hand-to-hand com-

A recruit with a drill instructor

moodboard/Corbis Royalty Free

bat, marching, running, calisthenics, Marine history, and—always—following orders.

"An M-16 can blow someone's head off at 500 meters," Sgt. Norman says. "That's beautiful, isn't it?"

"Yes, sir!" shout the platoon's fifty-nine voices.

"Pick your nose!" Simultaneously fifty-nine index fingers shoot into nostrils.

The pressure to conform is intense. Those who are sent packing for insubordination or suicidal tendencies are mocked in cadence during drills. ("Hope you like the sights you see/ Parris Island casualty.") As lights go out at 9 P.M., the exhausted recruits perform the day's last task: The entire platoon, in unison, chants the virtues of the Marines.

Recruits are constantly scrutinized. Subpar performance is not accepted, whether a dirty rifle or a loose thread on a uniform. The underperformer is shouted at, derided, humiliated. The group suffers for the individual. If one recruit is slow, the entire platoon is punished.

The system works.

One of the new Marines (until graduation, they are recruits, not Marines) says, "I feel like I've joined a new society or religion."

He has.

For Your Consideration

→ Of what significance is the recruits' degradation ceremony? Why are recruits not allowed video games, cigarettes, or calls home? Why are the Marines so unfair as to punish an entire platoon for the failure of an individual? Use concepts in this chapter to explain why the system works.

Sources: Based on Garfinkel 1956; Goffman 1961; Ricks 1995; Dyer 2007.

Why is Marine boot camp a good example of a total institution? Why does it work?

married, and have a baby and a mortgage, as you do when you are 18 or 20, single, and in college. (Actually, you don't even see life the same way as a freshman and as a senior.) Second, your life course differs by social location. Your social class, race–ethnicity, and gender, for example, map out distinctive worlds of experience.

This means that the typical life course differs for males and females, the rich and the poor, and so on. To emphasize this major sociological point, in the sketch that follows I will stress the *historical* setting of people's lives. Because of your particular social location, your own life course may differ from this sketch, which is a composite of stages that others have suggested (Levinson 1978; Carr et al. 1995; Quadagno 2007).

Childhood (from birth to about age 12)

Consider how different your childhood would have been if you had grown up in another historical era. Historian Philippe Ariès (1965) noticed that in European paintings from about A.D. 1000 to 1800 children were always dressed in adult clothing. If they were not depicted stiffly posed, as in a family portrait, they were shown doing adult activities.

From this, Ariès drew a conclusion that sparked a debate among historians. He said that Europeans of this era did not regard childhood as a special time of life. They viewed children as miniature adults and put them to work at an early age. At the age of 7, for example, a boy might leave home for good to learn to be a jeweler or a stonecutter. A girl, in contrast, stayed home until she married, but by the age of 7 she assumed her share of the household tasks. Historians do not deny that these were the customs of that time, but some say that Ariès' conclusion is ridiculous, that other evidence indicates that these people viewed childhood as a special time of life (Orme 2002).

Having children work like adults did not disappear with the Middle Ages. This practice was still common around the world in the 1800s. Even today, children in the Least Industrialized Nations work in many occupations—from blacksmiths to waiters. As tourists are shocked to discover, children in these nations also work as street peddlers, hawking everything from shoelaces to chewing gum.

Child rearing, too, used to be remarkably different. Three hundred years ago, parents and teachers considered it their *moral* duty to *terrorize* children. To keep children from "going bad," they would frighten them with bedtime stories of death and hellfire, lock them in dark closets, and force them to witness events like this:

From paintings, such as this one of Sir Walter Raleigh from 1602, some historians conclude that Europeans once viewed children as miniature adults who assumed adult roles early in life. From the 1959 photo taken in Harlem, New York, you can see why this conclusion is now being challenged, if not ridiculed.

© Photos 12/Alamy

© Bob Adelman/Corbis

How does childhood depend on social location: historical, geographical, and gender?

A common moral lesson involved taking children to visit the gibbet [an upraised post on which executed bodies were left hanging], where they were forced to inspect the rotting corpses as an example of what happens to bad children when they grow up. Whole classes were taken out of school to witness hangings, and parents would often whip their children afterwards to make them remember what they had seen. (DeMause 1975)

Industrialization transformed the way we perceive children. When children had the leisure to go to school and postponed taking on adult roles, parents and officials came to think of them as tender and innocent, as needing more care, comfort, and protection. Such attitudes of dependency grew, and today we view children as needing gentle guidance if they are to develop emotionally, intellectually, morally, even physically. We take our view for granted—after all, it is only "common sense." Yet, as you can see, our view is not "natural." It is, instead, rooted in society—in geography, history, and economic development.

In Sum: Childhood is more than biology. Everyone's childhood occurs at some point in history and is embedded in specific social locations, especially social class and gender. *These social factors are as vital as our biology, for they determine what our childhood will be like.* Although a child's *biological* characteristics (such as being small and dependent) are universal, the child's *social* experiences (the kind of life the child lives) are not. Because of this, sociologists say that childhood varies from culture to culture.

Adolescence (ages 13–17)

It might seem strange to you, but adolescence is a *social invention,* not a "natural" age division. In earlier centuries, people simply moved from childhood to young adulthood, with no stopover in between. The Industrial Revolution allowed adolescence to be invented. It brought such an abundance of material surpluses that for the first time in history people in their teens were not needed as workers. At the same time, education became more important for achieving success. As these two forces in industrialized societies converged, they created a gap between childhood and adulthood. The term *adolescence* was coined to indicate this new stage in life (Hall 1904), one that has become renowned for uncertainty, rebellion, and inner turmoil.

To mark the passage of children into adulthood, tribal societies hold *initiation rites.* This grounds the self-identity, showing these young people how they fit in the society. In the industrialized world, however, adolescents must "find" themselves. They grapple with the dilemma of "I am neither a child nor an adult. Who am I?" As they attempt to carve out an identity that is distinct from both the "younger" world being left behind and the "older" world that still lingers out of reach, adolescents develop their own subcultures, with distinctive clothing, hairstyles, language, gestures, and music. We usually fail to realize that contemporary society, not biology, created this period of inner turmoil that we call *adolescence.*

Transitional Adulthood (ages 18–29)

If society invented adolescence, can it also invent other periods of life? As Figure 2 on the next page illustrates, this is actually happening now. Postindustrial societies are adding another period of extended youth to the life course, which sociologists call **transitional adulthood** (also known as *adultolescence*).

After high school, millions of young adults postpone adult responsibilities by going to college. They are mostly freed from the control of their parents, yet they don't have to support themselves. After college, many live at home, so they can live cheaply while they establish themselves in a career—and, of course, continue to "find themselves." During this

transitional adulthood a term that refers to a period following high school when young adults have not yet taken on the responsibilities ordinarily associated with adulthood; also called *adultolescence*

In many societies, manhood is not bestowed upon males simply because they reach a certain age. Manhood, rather, signifies a standing in the community that must be achieved. Shown here is a boy of the Dinka tribe in Sudan being initiated into manhood. To show pain when the six horizontal lines are cut around his head would bring dishonor.

Eye Ubiquitous/Glow Images

Can you explain why adolescence is not a natural age division, but a social creation?

FIGURE 2 Transitional Adulthood: A New Stage in the Life Course

Who has completed the transition?

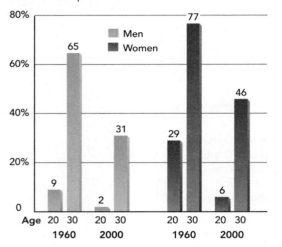

The bars show the percentage who have completed the transition to adulthood, as measured by leaving home, finishing school, getting married, having a child, and being financially independent.

Source: Furstenberg et al. 2004.
"Growing up is Harder to do" by Frank F. Furstenburg, Sheela Kennedy, Vonnie C. McLoyd, Ruben G. Rumbaut and Richard A. Settersten, JR., from CONTEXTS, Volume 3, Number 2, Summer 2004. Copyright © 2004 by SAGE. Reprinted with permission of SAGE publications.

✳ Explore
Living Data
on mysoclab.com

transitional older years an emerging stage of the life course between retirement and when people are considered old; approximately age 65 to 75

time, people are "neither psychological adolescents nor sociological adults" (Keniston 1971). At some point during this period of extended youth, young adults ease into adult responsibilities. They take a full-time job, become serious about a career, engage in courtship rituals, get married—and go into debt.

The Middle Years (ages 30–65)

The Early Middle Years (ages 30–49). During their early middle years, most people are more sure of themselves and of their goals in life. As with any point in the life course, however, the self can receive severe jolts. Common upheavals during this period are divorce and losing jobs. It may take years for the self to stabilize after such ruptures.

The early middle years pose a special challenge for many U.S. women, who have been given the message, especially by the media, that they can "have it all." They can be superworkers, superwives, and supermoms—all rolled into one superwoman. Reality, however, hits them in the face: too little time, too many demands, even too little sleep. Something has to give, and attempts to resolve this dilemma are anything but easy.

The Later Middle Years (ages 50–65). During the later middle years, health issues and mortality begin to loom large as people feel their bodies change, especially if they watch their parents become frail, fall ill, and die. The consequence is a fundamental reorientation in thinking—*from time since birth to time left to live* (Neugarten 1976). With this changed orientation, people attempt to evaluate the past and come to terms with what lies ahead. They compare what they have accomplished with what they had hoped to achieve. Many people also find themselves caring not only for their own children but also for their aging parents. Because of this double burden, which is often crushing, people in the later middle years sometimes are called the "sandwich generation."

In contrast, many people experience few of these stresses and find late middle age to be the most comfortable period of their lives. They enjoy job security or secure marriages and a standard of living higher than ever before. They have a bigger house (one that may even be paid for), drive newer cars, and take longer and more exotic vacations. The children are grown, the self is firmly planted, and fewer upheavals are likely to occur.

As they anticipate the next stage of life, however, most people do not like what they see.

The Older Years (about age 65 on)

The Transitional Older Years. In agricultural societies, when most people died early, old age was thought to begin at around age 40. As industrialization brought improved nutrition, medicine, and public health, allowing more people to live longer, the beginning of "old age" gradually stretched out. Today, people who enjoy good health don't think of their 60s as old age, but as an extension of their middle years. This change is so recent that a *new stage of life* seems to be evolving, the period between retirement (averaging about 63) and old age—which people are increasingly coming to see as beginning around age 75 ("Schwab Study" 2008). We can call this stage the **transitional older years.**

Researchers who are focusing on this transitional stage of life have found that social isolation harms both the body and brain, that people who are more integrated into social networks stay mentally sharper (Ertel et al. 2008). With improved health, two-thirds of the men and two-fifths of the women between their late 60s and age 75 continue to be sexually active (Lindau et al. 2007). Not only are people in this stage of life having more sex, but they also are enjoying it more (Beckman et al. 2008).

What are transitional adulthood and the transitional older years? How do they illustrate the social basis of the life course?

Because we have a self and can reason abstractly, we can contemplate death. In our early years, we regard death as a vague notion, a remote possibility. As people see their parents and friends die and observe their own bodies no longer functioning as before, however, the thought of death becomes less abstract. Increasingly during this stage in the life course, people feel that "time is closing in" on them.

The Later Older Years.   As with the preceding periods of life, except the first one, there is no precise beginning point to this last stage. For some, the 75th birthday may mark entry into this period of life. For others, that marker may be the 80th or even the 85th birthday. For most, this stage is marked by growing frailty and illness. For all who reach this stage, it is ended by death. For some, the physical decline is slow, and a rare few manage to see their 100th birthday mentally alert and in good physical health.

The Sociological Significance of the Life Course

The sociological significance of the life course is that it does not merely represent biology, things that naturally occur to all of us as we add years to our lives. Rather, *social* factors influence our life course. As you just saw, *when* you live makes a huge difference in the course that your life takes. And with today's rapid social change, the difference in historical time does not have to be vast. Being born just ten years earlier or later may mean that you experience war or peace, an expanding economy or a depression—factors that vitally affect what happens to you not just during childhood but throughout your life.

Your *social location*, such as social class, gender, and race–ethnicity, is also highly significant. Your experience of society's events will be similar to that of people who share your social location, but different from that of people who do not. If you are poor, for example, you likely will feel older sooner than most wealthy people for whom life is less demanding. Individual factors—such as your health or marrying early or entering college late—can also throw your life course "out of sequence."

For all these reasons, this sketch of the life course may not reflect your own past, present, and future. As sociologist C. Wright Mills (1959) would say, if employers are beating a path to your door, or failing to do so, you will be more inclined to marry, to buy a house, and to start a family—or to postpone these life course events. In short, changing times change lives, steering the life course into different directions.

Are We Prisoners of Socialization?

From our discussion of socialization, you might conclude that sociologists think of people as robots: The socialization goes in, and the behavior comes out. People cannot help what they do, think, or feel, for everything is a result of their exposure to socializing agents.

Sociologists do *not* think of people in this way. Although socialization is powerful, and affects all of us profoundly, we have a self. Established in childhood and continually modified by later experience, our self is dynamic. Our self is not a sponge that passively absorbs influences from the environment, but, rather, it is a vigorous, essential part of our being that allows us to act on our environment.

Precisely because people are not robots, individual behavior is hard to predict. The countless reactions of others merge in each of us. As the self develops, we each internalize or "put together" these innumerable reactions, which become the basis for how we reason, react to others, and make choices in life. The result is a unique whole called the *individual.*

Rather than being passive sponges in this process, *each of us is actively involved in the construction of the self.* Our experiences in the family and other groups during childhood lay down our basic orientations to life, but we are not doomed to keep these orientations if we do not like them. We can purposely expose ourselves to other groups and ideas. Those experiences, in turn, have their own effects on our self. In short, we influence our socialization as we make choices. We can change even the self within the limitations of the framework laid down by our social locations. And that self—along with the options available within society—is the key to our behavior.

AP Images

This January 1937 photo from Sneedville, Tennessee, shows Eunice Johns, age 9, and her husband, Charlie Johns, age 22. The groom gave his wife a doll as a wedding gift. The new husband and wife planned to build a cabin, and, as Charlie Johns phrased it, "go to housekeepin'." This couple illustrates the cultural relativity of life stages, which we sometimes mistake as fixed. It also is interesting from a symbolic interactionist perspective— that of changing definitions.

The marriage lasted. The couple had 7 children, 5 boys and 2 girls. Charlie died in 1997 at age 83, and Eunice in 2006 at age 78. The two were buried in the Johns Family Cemetery.

What is the sociological significance of the life course? Why aren't we prisoners of socialization?

By the Numbers: Changes Over Time

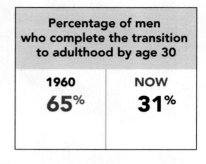

Percentage of men who complete the transition to adulthood by age 30	
1960	NOW
65%	31%

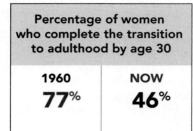

Percentage of women who complete the transition to adulthood by age 30	
1960	NOW
77%	46%

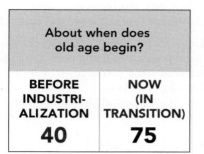

About when does old age begin?	
BEFORE INDUSTRI-ALIZATION	NOW (IN TRANSITION)
40	75

Summary and Review

Society Makes Us Human

How much of our human characteristics come from "nature" (heredity) and how much from "nurture" (the social environment)?

Observations of isolated, institutionalized, and **feral children** help to answer the nature–nurture question, as do experiments with monkeys that were raised in isolation. Language and intimate social interaction—aspects of "nurture"—are essential to the development of what we consider to be human characteristics.

Socialization into the Self and Mind

How do we acquire a self?

Humans are born with the *capacity* to develop a **self,** but the self must be socially constructed; that is, its contents depend on social interaction. According to Charles Horton Cooley's concept of the **looking-glass self,** our self develops as we internalize others' reactions to us. George Herbert Mead identified the ability to **take the role of the other** as essential to the development of the self. Mead concluded that even the mind is a social product.

How do children develop reasoning skills?

Jean Piaget identified four stages that children go through as they develop the ability to reason: (1) *sensorimotor,* in which understanding is limited to sensory stimuli such as touch and sight; (2) *preoperational,* the ability to use symbols; (3) *concrete operational,* in which reasoning ability is more complex but not yet capable of complex abstractions; and (4) *formal operational,* or abstract thinking.

Learning Personality, Morality, and Emotions

How do sociologists evaluate Freud's psychoanalytic theory of personality development?

Sigmund Freud viewed personality development as the result of our **id** (inborn, self-centered desires) clashing with the demands of society. The **ego** develops to balance the id and the **superego,** the conscience. Sociologists, in contrast, do not examine inborn or subconscious motivations, but, instead, consider how *social* factors—social class, gender, religion, education, and so forth—underlie personality.

How do people develop morality?

That even babies exhibit a sense of morality seems to indicate that a basic morality could be inborn. Lawrence Kohlberg identified four stages children go through as they learn morality: amoral, preconventional, conventional, and postconventional. As they make moral decisions, both men and women use personal relationships and abstract principles. The answer to "What is moral?" differs from society to society.

How does socialization influence emotions?

Socialization influences not only *how we express our emotions* but also *what emotions we feel.* Socialization into emotions is one of the means by which society produces conformity.

Socialization into Gender

How does gender socialization affect our sense of self?

Gender socialization—sorting males and females into different roles—is a primary way that groups control human behavior. Children receive messages about **gender** even in infancy. A society's ideals of sex-linked behaviors are reinforced by its social institutions.

Agents of Socialization

What are the main agents of socialization?

The **agents of socialization** include the family, neighborhood, religion, day care, school, **peer groups,** the **mass media,** and the workplace. Each has its particular influences in socializing us into becoming full-fledged members of society.

Resocialization

What is resocialization?

Resocialization is the process of learning new norms, values, attitudes, and behavior. Most resocialization is voluntary, but some, as with residents of some **total institutions,** is involuntary.

Socialization through the Life Course

Does socialization end when we enter adulthood?

Socialization occurs throughout the life course. In industrialized societies, the **life course** can be divided into childhood, adolescence, young adulthood, the middle years, and the older years. The West is adding two new stages, **transitional adulthood** and **transitional older years.** Life course patterns vary by geography, history, gender, race–ethnicity, and social class, as well as by individual experiences such as health and age at marriage.

Are We Prisoners of Socialization?

Although socialization is powerful, we are not merely the sum of our socialization experiences. Just as socialization influences our behavior, so we act on our environment and influence even our self-concept.

Thinking Critically about this Chapter

1. What two agents of socialization have influenced you the most? Can you pinpoint their influence on your attitudes, beliefs, values, or other orientations to life?

2. Summarize your views of the "proper" relationships of women and men. What in your socialization has led you to have these views?

3. Where are you located in the life course? How does the text's summary of this location compare with your experiences? Explain the similarities and differences.

References

All new references are printed in cyan.

Adler, Patricia A., and Peter Adler. *Peer Power: Preadolescent Culture and Identity.* New Brunswick, N.J.: Rutgers University Press, 1998.

Ariès, Philippe. *Centuries of Childhood,* R. Baldick, trans. New York: Vintage Books, 1965.

Beckman, Nils, Magda Waerm, Deborah Gustafson, and Ingmar Skoog. "Secular Trends in Self Reported Sexual Activity and Satisfaction in Swedish 70 Year Olds: Cross Sectional Survey of Four Populations, 1971–2001." *BMJ,* 2008:1–7.

Begley, Sharon. "Twins: Nazi and Jew." *Newsweek, 94,* December 3, 1979:139.

Belsky, Jay. "Early Child Care and Early Child Development: Major Findings of the NICHD Study of Early Child Care." *European Journal of Developmental Psychology, 3,* 1, 2006:95–110.

Best, Deborah L. "The Contribution of the Whitings to the Study of the Socialization of Gender." *Journal of Cross-Cultural Psychology, 41,* 2010:534–545.

Bilefsky, Dan. "Albanian Custom Fades: Woman as Family Man." *New York Times,* June 25, 2008.

Bloom, Paul. "The Moral Life of Babies." *New York Times Magazine,* May 3, 2010.

Bodovski, Katerina, and George Farkas. "'Concerted Cultivation' and Unequal Achievement in Elementary School." *Social Science Research, 37,* 2008:903–919.

Bush, Diane Mitsch, and Robert G. Simmons. "Socialization Processes over the Life Course." In *Social Psychology: Sociological Perspectives,* Morris Rosenberger and Ralph H. Turner, eds. New Brunswick, N.J.:Transaction, 1990:133–164.

Carr, Deborah, Carol D. Ryff, Burton Singer, and William J. Magee. "Bringing the 'Life' Back into Life Course Research: A 'Person-Centered' Approach to Studying the Life Course." Paper presented at the annual meetings of the American Sociological Association, 1995.

Chauhan, Preeti, N. Dickon Reppucci, and Eric N. Turkheimer. "Racial Differences in the Associations of Neighborhood Disadvantage, Exposure to Violence, and Criminal Recidivism among Female Juvenile Offenders." *Behavioral Sciences and the Law, 27,* June 2009:531–552.

Chen, Edwin. "Twins Reared Apart: A Living Lab." *New York Times Magazine.* December 9, 1979:112.

Chodorow, Nancy J. "What Is the Relation between Psychoanalytic Feminism and the Psychoanalytic Psychology of Women?" In *Theoretical Perspectives on Sexual Difference,* Deborah L. Rhode, ed. New Haven, Conn.: Yale University Press, 1990:114–130.

Clark, Candace. *Misery and Company: Sympathy in Everyday Life.* Chicago: University of Chicago Press, 1997.

Clearfield, Melissa W., and Naree M. Nelson. "Sex Differences in Mothers' Speech and Play Behavior with 6-, 9-, and 14-Month-Old Infants." *Sex Roles, 54,* 1–2, January 2006:127–137.

Connors, L. "Gender of Infant Differences in Attachment: Associations with Temperament and Caregiving Experiences." Paper presented at the Annual Conference of the British Psychological Society, Oxford, England, 1996.

Cooley, Charles Horton. *Human Nature and the Social Order.* New York: Scribner's, 1902.

Crosnoe, Robert, Catherine Riegle-Crumb, Sam Field, Kenneth Frank, and Chandra Muller. "Peer Group Contexts of Girls' and Boys' Academic Experiences." *Child Development, 79,* 1, February 2008:139–155.

Davis, Kingsley. "Extreme Isolation." In *Down to Earth Sociology: Introductory Readings,* 15th ed., James M. Henslin, ed. New York: Free Press, 2012. Originally published as "Extreme Social Isolation of a Child." *American Journal of Sociology, 45,* January 4, 1940:554–565.

DeLuca, Stephanie, and Elizabeth Dayton. "Switching Social Contexts: The Effects of Housing Mobility and School Choice Programs on Youth Outcomes." *Annual Review of Sociology, 35,* 2009:457–491.

DeMause, Lloyd. "Our Forebears Made Childhood a Nightmare." *Psychology Today 8,* 11, April 1975:85–88.

Denzin, Norman K. *Symbolic Interactionism and Cultural Studies: The Politics of Interpretation.* Cambridge, Mass.: Blackwell 2007.

Dyer, Gwynne. "Anybody's Son Will Do." In *Down to Earth Sociology: Introductory Readings,* 14th ed., James M. Henslin, ed. New York: Free Press, 2007.

Eder, Donna. "On Becoming Female: Lessons Learned in School." In *Down to Earth Sociology: Introductory Readings,* 14th ed., James M. Henslin, ed. New York: Free Press, 2007.

Ekman, Paul. *Faces of Man: Universal Expression in a New Guinea Village.* New York: Garland Press, 1980.

Elder, Glen H., Jr. "Age Differentiation and Life Course." *Annual Review of Sociology, 1,* 1975:165–190.

Elder, Glen H., Jr. *Children of the Great Depression: Social Change in Life Experience.* Boulder: Westview Press, 1999.

Epstein, Cynthia Fuchs. *Deceptive Distinctions: Sex, Gender, and the Social Order.* New Haven, Conn.: Yale University Press, 1988.

Ertel, Karen A., M. Maria Glymour, and Lisa F. Berkman. "Effects of Social Integration on Preserving Memory Function in a Nationally Representative US Elderly Population." *American Journal of Public Health, 98,* 7, July 2008:1215–1220.

Flavel, John H., et al. *The Development of Role-Taking and Communication Skills in Children.* New York: Wiley, 1968.

Flavel, John, Patricia H. Miller, and Scott A. Miller. *Cognitive Development,* 4th ed. Upper Saddle River, N.J.: Prentice Hall, 2002.

Furstenberg, Frank F., Jr., Sheela Kennedy, Vonnie C. McLoyd, Ruben G. Rumbaut, and Richard A. Settersten, Jr. "Growing Up Is Harder to Do." *Contexts, 3,* 3, Summer 2004:33–41.

Gallup Poll. "Very Religious Americans Lead Healthier Lives." Princeton, N.J.: Gallup Organization, December 23, 2010.

Garfinkel, Harold. "Conditions of Successful Degradation Ceremonies." *American Journal of Sociology, 61,* 2, March 1956:420–424.

Gerhard, Jane. "Revisiting 'The Myth of the Vaginal Orgasm': The Female Orgasm in American Sexual Thought and Second Wave Feminism." *Feminist Studies, 26,* 2, Fall 2000:449–477.

Gilman, Charlotte Perkins. *The Man-Made World or, Our Androcentric Culture.* New York: 1971. Originally published 1911.

Gilpatric, Katy. "Violent Female Action Characters in Contemporary American Cinema." *Sex Roles, 62,* 2010:734–746.

Goffman, Erving. *Asylums: Essays on the Social Situation of Mental Patients and Other Inmates.* Chicago: Aldine, 1961.

Goldberg, Susan, and Michael Lewis. "Play Behavior in the Year-Old Infant: Early Sex Differences." *Child Development, 40,* March 1969:21–31.

Guensburg, Carol. "Bully Factories." *American Journalism Review, 23,* 6, 2001:51–59.

Hall, G. Stanley. *Adolescence: Its Psychology and Its Relations to Physiology, Anthropology, Sociology, Sex, Crime, Religion, and Education.* New York: Appleton, 1904.

Harlow, Harry F., and Margaret K. Harlow. "Social Deprivation in Monkeys." *Scientific American, 207,* 1962:137–147.

Harlow, Harry F., and Margaret K. Harlow. "The Affectional Systems." In *Behavior of Nonhuman Primates: Modern Research Trends,* Vol. 2, Allan M. Schrier, Harry F. Harlow, and Fred Stollnitz, eds. New York: Academic Press, 1965:287–334.

Hemmings, Annette. "The 'Hidden' Corridor Curriculum." *High School Journal, 83,* December 1999:1–12.

Hochschild, Arlie. "Feelings around the World." *Contexts, 7,* 2, Spring 2008:80.

Horwitz, Allan V., and Jerome C. Wakefield. *The Loss of Sadness: How Psychiatry Transformed Normal Sorrow into Depressive Disorder.* New York: Oxford University Press, 2007.

Itard, Jean Marc Gospard. *The Wild Boy of Aveyron,* George and Muriel Humphrey, trans. New York: Appleton-Century-Crofts, 1962.

Jensen, Lene Arnett. "Through Two Lenses: A Cultural-Developmental Approach to Moral Psychology." *Developmental Review, 28,* 2009:289–315.

Johnson, Wendy, Eric Turkheimer, Irving I. Gottesman, and Thomas J. Bouchard, Jr. "Beyond Heritability: Twin Studies in Behavioral Research." *Current Directions in Psychological Science, 18,* 4, 2009:217–220.

Kagan, Jerome. "The Idea of Emotions in Human Development." In *Emotions, Cognition, and Behavior,* Carroll E. Izard, Jerome Kagan, and Robert B. Zajonc, eds. New York: Cambridge University Press, 1984:38–72.

Kahlenberg, Susan G., and Michelle M. Hein. "Progression on Nickelodeon? Gender-Role Stereotypes in Toy Commercials." *Sex Roles, 62,* 2010:830–847.

Keniston, Kenneth. *Youth and Dissent: The Rise of a New Opposition.* New York: Harcourt, Brace, Jovanovich, 1971.

Kohlberg, Lawrence. "Moral Education for a Society in Moral Transition." *Educational Leadership, 33,* 1975:46–54.

Kohlberg, Lawrence. *The Psychology of Moral Development: Moral Stages and the Life Cycle.* San Francisco: Harper and Row, 1984.

Kohlberg, Lawrence. "A Current Statement on Some Theoretical Issues." In *Lawrence Kohlberg: Consensus and Controversy,* Sohan Modgil and Celia Modgil, eds. Philadelphia: Falmer Press, 1986:485–546.

Kohlberg, Lawrence, and Carol Gilligan. "The Adolescent as a Philosopher: The Discovery of the Self in a Postconventional World." *Daedalus, 100,* 1971:1051–1086.

Kohn, Melvin L. "Social Class and Parental Values." *American Journal of Sociology, 64,* 1959:337–351.

Kohn, Melvin L. "Social Class and Parent–Child Relationships: An Interpretation." *American Journal of Sociology, 68,* 1963:471–480.

Kohn, Melvin L. *Class and Conformity: A Study in Values,* 2nd ed. Homewood, Ill.: Dorsey Press, 1977.

Kohn, Melvin L. *Change and Stability: A Cross-National Analysis of Social Structure and Personality.* Boulder, CO.: Paradigm, 2006.

Kohn, Melvin L., and Carmi Schooler. "Class, Occupation, and Orientation." *American Sociological Review, 34,* 1969:659–678.

Lareau, Annette. "Invisible Inequality: Social Class and Childrearing in Black Families and White Families." *American Sociological Review, 67,* October 2002:747–776.

Larson, Mary Strom. "Interactions, Activities and Gender in Children's Television Commercials: A Content Analysis." *Journal of Broadcasting and Electronic Media, 45,* Winter 2001:41–51.

Ledger, Kate. "Sociology and the Gene." *Contexts, 8,* 3, 2009:16–20.

Levanthal, Tama, and Jeanne Brooks-Gunn. "The Neighborhood They Live in: Effects of Neighborhood Residence on Child and Adolescent Outcomes." *Psychological Bulletin, 126,* 2000:309–337.

Levine, Robert. "Planned Guns N' Roses Deal Underscores Power of Video to Sell Songs." *Wall Street Journal,* July 14, 2008.

Levinson, D. J. *The Seasons of a Man's Life.* New York: Knopf, 1978.

Lindau, Stacy Tessler, L. Philip Schumm, Edward O. Laumann, Wendy Levinson, Colm A. O'Muircheartaigh, and Linda J. Waite. "A Study of Sexuality and Health among Older Adults in the United States." *New England Journal of Medicine, 357,* 8, August 23, 2007:762–774.

Matsumoto, D., and B. Willingham. "Spontaneous Facial Expressions of Emotion of Congenitally and Noncongenitally Blind Individuals." *Journal of Personality and Social Psychology, 96,* 2009:1–10.

Mead, George Herbert. *Mind, Self and Society.* Chicago: University of Chicago Press, 1934.

Meese, Ruth Lyn. "A Few New Children: Postinstitutionalized Children of Intercountry Adoption." *Journal of Special Education, 39,* 3, 2005:157–167.

Milkie, Melissa A. "Social World Approach to Cultural Studies." *Journal of Contemporary Ethnography, 23,* 3, October 1994:354–380.

Mills, C. Wright. *The Sociological Imagination.* New York: Oxford University Press, 1959.

National Institute of Child Health and Human Development. "Child Care and Mother–Child Interaction in the First 3 Years of Life." *Developmental Psychology, 35,* 6, November 1999:1399–1413.

Neugarten, Bernice L. "Middle Age and Aging." In *Growing Old in America,* Beth B. Hess, ed. New Brunswick, N.J.: Transaction, 1976:180–197.

Newport, Frank. "In U.S., Increasing Numbers Have No Religious Identity." Gallup Poll, May 21, 2010.

Nordberg, Jenny. "In Afghanistan, Boys Are Prized and Girls Live the Part." *New York Times,* September 20, 2010.

Orme, Nicholas. *Medieval Children.* New Haven: Yale University Press, 2002.

Pearlin, L. I., and Melvin L. Kohn. "Social Class, Occupation, and Parental Values: A Cross-National Study." *American Sociological Review, 31,* 1966:466–479.

Piaget, Jean. *The Psychology of Intelligence.* London: Routledge & Kegan Paul, 1950.

Piaget, Jean. *The Construction of Reality in the Child.* New York: Basic Books, 1954.

Pines, Maya. "The Civilizing of Genie." *Psychology Today, 15,* September 1981:28–34.

Quadagno, Jill. *Aging and the Life Course: An Introduction to Gerontology,* 4th ed. New York: McGraw-Hill, 2007.

Reed, Don Collins. "A Model of Moral Stages." *Journal of Moral Education, 37,* 3, September 2008:357–376.

Ricks, Thomas E. "'New' Marines Illustrate Growing Gap between Military and Society." *Wall Street Journal,* July 27, 1995:A1, A4.

Rodriguez, Richard. "The Education of Richard Rodriguez." *Saturday Review,* February 8, 1975:147–149.

Rodriguez, Richard. *Hunger of Memory: The Education of Richard Rodriguez.* Boston: Godine, 1982.

Rodriguez, Richard. "The Late Victorians: San Francisco, AIDS, and the Homosexual Stereotype." *Harper's Magazine,* October 1990:57–66.

Rodriguez, Richard. "Mixed Blood." *Harper's Magazine, 283,* November 1991:47–56.

Rodriguez, Richard. "Searching for Roots in a Changing Society." In *Down to Earth Sociology: Introductory Readings,* 8th ed., James M. Henslin, ed. New York: Free Press, 1995:486–491.

Sampson, Robert J., Jeffrey D. Morenoff, and Felton Earls. "Beyond Social Capital: Spatial Dynamics of Collective Efficacy for Children." *American Sociological Review, 64,* October 1999:633–660.

"Schwab Study Finds Four Generations of American Adults Fundamentally Rethinking Planning for Retirement." Reuters, July 15, 2008.

Segal, Nancy L., and Scott L. Hershberger. "Virtual Twins and Intelligence." *Personality and Individual Differences, 39,* 6, 2005:1061–1073.

Shields, Stephanie A. *Speaking from the Heart: Gender and the Social Meaning of Emotion.* New York: Cambridge University Press, 2002.

Skeels, H. M. *Adult Status of Children with Contrasting Early Life Experiences: A Follow-up Study.* Monograph of the Society for Research in Child Development, *31,* 3, 1966.

Skeels, H. M., and H. B. Dye. "A Study of the Effects of Differential Stimulation on Mentally Retarded Children." *Proceedings and Addresses of the American Association on Mental Deficiency, 44,* 1939:114–136.

Statistical Abstract of the United States. Washington D.C.: U.S. Census Bureau, published annually.

Suizzo, Marie-Anne. "The Social-Emotional and Cultural Contexts of Cognitive Development: Neo-Piagetian Perspectives." *Child Development, 71,* 4, August 2000:846–849.

Taneja, V., S. Sriram, R. S. Beri, V. Sreenivas, R. Aggarwal, R. Kaur, and J. M. Puliyel. "'Not by Bread Alone': Impact of a Structured 90-Minute Play Session on Development of Children in an Orphanage." *Child Care, Health & Development, 28,* 1, 2002:95–100.

Taylor, Chris. "The Man behind Lara Croft." *Time,* December 6, 1999:78.

Vandell, Deborah Lowe, Jay Belsky, Margaret Burchinal, Laurence Steinberg, and Nathan Vandergrift. "No Effects of Early Child Care Extend to Age 15 Years? Results from the NICHD Study of Early Child Care and Youth Development." *Child Development, 81,* 3, May/June 2010:737–756.

Wark, Gillian R., and Dennis L. Krebs. "Gender and Dilemma Differences in Real-Life Moral Judgment." *Developmental Psychology, 32,* 1996:220–230.

Wheaton, Blair, and Philippa Clarke. "Space Meets Time: Integrating Temporal and Contextual Influences on Mental Health in Early Adulthood." *American Sociological Review, 68,* 2003:680–706.

Williams, Dmitri, Nicole Martins, Mia Consalvo, and James D. Ivory. "The Virtual Census: Representations of Gender, Race, and Age in Video Games." *New Media & Society, 11,* 5, 2009:815–834.

Wright, Lawrence. "Double Mystery." *The New Yorker,* August 7, 1995:45–62.

Young, Antonia, and Larenda Twigg. "'Sworn Virgins' as Enhancers of Albanian Patriarchal Society in Contrast to Emerging Roles for Albanian Women." *Emoloska Tribuna, 39,* 2009:117–134.

Zumbrun, Joshua. "The Sacrifices of Albania's 'Sworn Virgins.'" *Washington Post,* August 11, 2007.

Social Structure and Social Interaction

From Chapter 4 of *Sociology: A Down-to-Earth Approach, Core Concepts*, Fifth Edition. James M. Henslin.

Thailand

My curiosity had gotten the better of me. When the sociology convention was over, I climbed aboard the first city bus that came along. I didn't know where the bus was going, and I didn't know where I would spend the night.

This was my first visit to Washington, D.C., so everything was unfamiliar to me. I had no destination, no plans, not even a map. I carried no billfold, just a driver's license shoved into my jeans for emergency identification, some pocket change, and a $10 bill tucked into my sock. My goal was simple: If I saw something interesting, I would get off the bus and check it out.

As we passed row after row of apartment buildings and stores, I could see myself riding buses the entire night. Then something caught my eye. Nothing spectacular—just groups of people clustered around a large circular area where several streets intersected.

I got off the bus and made my way to what turned out to be Dupont Circle. I took a seat on a sidewalk bench. As the scene came into focus, I noticed several streetcorner men drinking and joking with one another. One of the men broke from his companions and sat down next to me. As we talked, I mostly listened.

> "Suddenly one of the men jumped up, smashed the empty bottle against the sidewalk, and . . ."

As night fell, the men said that they wanted to get another bottle of wine. I contributed. They counted their money and asked if I wanted to go with them. As we left the circle, the three men began to cut through an alley. "Oh, no," I thought. "This isn't what I had in mind."

I had but a split second to make a decision. I held back half a step so that none of the three was behind me. As we walked, they passed around the remnants of their bottle. When my turn came, I didn't know what to do. I shuddered to think about the diseases lurking within that bottle. In the semidarkness I faked it, letting only my thumb and forefinger touch my lips and nothing enter my mouth.

When we returned to Dupont Circle, we sat on the benches, and the men passed around their new bottle of Thunderbird. I couldn't fake it in the light, so I passed, pointing at my stomach to indicate that I was having digestive problems.

Suddenly one of the men jumped up, smashed the emptied bottle against the sidewalk, and thrust the jagged neck outward in a menacing gesture. He glared straight ahead at another bench, where he had spotted someone with whom he had some sort of unfinished business. As the other men told him to cool it, I moved slightly to one side of the group—ready to flee, just in case.

macrosociology analysis of social life that focuses on broad features of society, such as social class and the relationships of groups to one another; usually used by functionalists and conflict theorists

microsociology analysis of social life that focuses on social interaction; typically used by symbolic interactionists

social interaction what people do when they are in one another's presence; includes communications at a distance

AP Images/Doug Mills

Sociologists use both macro and micro levels of analysis to study social life. Those who use macrosociology to analyze the homeless (or any human behavior) focus on broad aspects of society, such as the economy and social classes. Sociologists who use the microsociological approach analyze how people interact with one another. This photo illustrates social structure (the disparities between power and powerlessness are amply evident). It also illustrates the micro level (the isolation of this man).

Levels of Sociological Analysis

On this sociological adventure, I almost got in over my head. Fortunately, it turned out all right. The man's "enemy" didn't look our way, the man put the broken bottle next to the bench "in case he needed it," and my intriguing introduction to a life that up until then I had only read about continued until dawn.

Sociologists Elliot Liebow (1967/1999), Mitchell Duneier (1999), and Elijah Anderson (1978, 1990, 1990/2006) have written fascinating accounts about men like my companions from that evening. Although streetcorner men may appear to be disorganized—simply coming and going as they please and doing whatever feels good at the moment—sociologists have analyzed how, like us, these men are influenced by the norms and beliefs of our society. This will become more apparent as we examine the two levels of analysis that sociologists use.

Macrosociology and Microsociology

The first level, **macrosociology,** focuses on broad features of society. Conflict theorists and functionalists use this approach to analyze such things as social class and how groups are related to one another. If they were to analyze streetcorner men, for example, they would stress that these men are located at the bottom of the U.S. social class system. Their low status means that many opportunities are closed to them: The men have few job skills, little education, hardly anything to offer an employer. As "able-bodied" men, however, they are not eligible for welfare—even for a two-year limit—so they hustle to survive. As a consequence, they spend their lives on the streets.

In the second level, **microsociology,** the focus is on **social interaction,** what people do when they come together. Sociologists who use this approach are likely to analyze the men's rules, or "codes," for getting along; their survival strategies ("hustles"); how they divide up money, wine, or whatever other resources they have; their relationships with girlfriends, family, and friends; where they spend their time and what they do there; their language; their pecking order; and so on. Microsociology is the primary focus of symbolic interactionists.

Because each approach has a different focus, macrosociology and microsociology yield distinctive perspectives; both are needed to gain a fuller understanding of social life. We cannot adequately understand streetcorner men, for example, without using macrosociology. It is essential that we place the men within the broad context of how groups in U.S. society are related to one another—for, as is true for ourselves, the social class of these men helps to shape their attitudes and behavior. Nor can we adequately understand these men without microsociology, for their everyday situations also form a significant part of their lives—as they do for all of us.

Let's look in more detail at how these two approaches in sociology work together to help us understand social life. As we examine them more closely, you may find yourself feeling more comfortable with one approach than the other. This is what happens with sociologists. For reasons that include personal background and professional training, sociologists find themselves more comfortable with one approach and tend to use it in their research. Both approaches, however, are necessary to understand life in society.

The Macrosociological Perspective: Social Structure

Why did the street people in our opening vignette act as they did, staying up all night drinking wine, prepared to use a lethal weapon? Why don't *we* act like this? Social structure helps us answer such questions.

Can you explain the difference between *macrosociology* and *microsociology*? Why do we need both to understand social life?

The Sociological Significance of Social Structure

To better understand human behavior, we need to understand *social structure,* the framework of society that was already laid out before you were born. **Social structure** refers to the typical patterns of a group, such as the usual relationships between men and women or students and teachers. *The sociological significance of social structure is that it guides our behavior.*

Because this term may seem vague, let's consider how you experience social structure in your own life. As I write this, I do not know your race–ethnicity. I do not know your religion. I do not know whether you are young or old, tall or short, male or female. I do not know whether you were reared on a farm, in the suburbs, or in the inner city. I do not know whether you went to a public high school or to an exclusive prep school. But I do know that you are in college. And this, alone, tells me a great deal about you.

From this one piece of information, I can assume that the social structure of your college is now shaping what you do. For example, let's suppose that today you felt euphoric over some great news. I can be fairly certain (not absolutely, mind you, but relatively confident) that when you entered the classroom, social structure overrode your mood. That is, instead of shouting at the top of your lungs and joyously throwing this book into the air, you entered the classroom in a fairly subdued manner and took your seat.

The same social structure influences your instructor, even if he or she, on the one hand, is facing a divorce or has a child dying of cancer or, on the other, has just been awarded a promotion or a million-dollar grant. Your instructor may feel like either retreating into seclusion or celebrating wildly, but most likely he or she will conduct class in the usual manner. In short, social structure tends to override our personal feelings and desires.

Just as social structure influences you and your instructor, so it also establishes limits for street people. They, too, find themselves in a specific location in the U.S. social structure—although it is quite different from yours or your instructor's. Consequently, they are affected in different ways. Nothing about their social location leads them to take notes or to lecture. Their behaviors, however, are as logical an outcome of where they find themselves in the social structure as are your own. In their position in the social structure, it is just as "natural" to drink wine all night as it is for you to stay up studying all night for a crucial examination. It is just as "natural" for you to nod and say, "Excuse me," when you enter a crowded classroom late and have to claim a desk on which someone has already placed books as it is for them to break off the neck of a wine bottle and glare at an enemy. To better understand social structure, read the Down-to-Earth Sociology box on the next page.

In Sum: People learn their behaviors and attitudes because of their location in the social structure (whether they be privileged, deprived, or in between), and they act accordingly. This is as true of street people as it is of us. *The differences in behavior and attitudes are due not to biology (race–ethnicity, sex, or any other supposed genetic factors), but to people's location in the social structure.* Switch places with street people and watch your behaviors and attitudes change!

Because social structure is so vital for us—affecting who we are and what we are like—let's look more closely at its major components: culture, social class, social status, roles, groups, and social institutions.

Culture

At this point, let's simply summarize culture's main impact. Sociologists use the term *culture* to refer to a group's language, beliefs, values, behaviors, and even gestures. Culture also includes the material objects that a group uses. Culture is the broadest framework that determines what kind of people we become. If we are reared in Chinese, Arab, or U.S. culture, we will grow up to be like most Chinese, Arabs, or Americans. On the outside, we will look and act like them; and on the inside, we will think and feel like them.

social structure the framework of society that surrounds us; consists of the ways that people and groups are related to one another; this framework gives direction to and sets limits on our behavior

College Football as Social Structure

To gain a better idea of what *social structure* is, think of college football (Dobriner 1969a). You probably know the various positions on the team: center, guards, tackles, ends, quarterback, running backs, and the like. Each is a *status*; that is, each is a social position. For each of the statuses shown in Figure 1, there is a *role*; that is, each of these positions has certain expectations attached to it. The center is expected to snap the ball, the quarterback to pass it, the guards to block, the tackles to tackle or block, the ends to receive passes, and so on. Those role expectations guide each player's actions; that is, the players try to do what their particular role requires.

Let's suppose that football is your favorite sport and you never miss a home game at your college. Let's also suppose that you graduate, get a great job, and move across the country. Five years later, you return to your campus for a nostalgic visit. The climax of your visit is the biggest football game of the season. When you get to the game, you might be surprised to see a different coach, but you are not surprised that each playing position is occupied by people you don't know, for all the players you knew have graduated, and their places have been filled by others.

This scenario mirrors *social structure*, the framework around which a group exists. In football, this framework consists of the coaching staff and the eleven playing positions. The game does not depend on any particular individual, but, rather, on *social statuses*, the positions that the individuals occupy. When someone leaves a position, the game can go on because someone else takes over that position or status and plays the role. The game will continue even though not a single individual remains from one period of time to the next. Notre Dame's football team endures today even though Knute Rockne, the Gipper, and his teammates are long dead.

Even though you may not play football, you do live your life within a clearly established social structure. The statuses that you occupy and the roles you play were already in place

FIGURE 1 **Team Positions (Statuses) in Football**

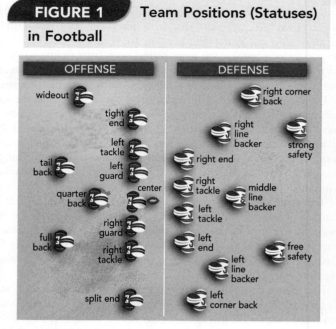

Source: By the author.

before you were born. You take your particular positions in life, others do the same, and society goes about its business. Although the specifics change with time, the game—whether of life or of football—goes on.

For Your Consideration

→ How does social structure influence your life? To answer this question, you can begin by analyzing your social statuses.

Social Class

To understand people, we must examine the social locations that they hold in life. Especially significant is *social class*, which is based on income, education, and occupational prestige. Large numbers of people who have similar amounts of income and education and who work at jobs that are roughly comparable in prestige make up a **social class.** It is hard to overemphasize this aspect of social structure, for our social class influences not only our behaviors but even our ideas and attitudes. We have this in common, then, with the street people described in the opening vignette: We both are influenced by our location in the social class structure. Theirs may be a considerably less privileged position, but it has no less influence on their lives.

social class large numbers of people who have similar amounts of income and education and who work at jobs that are roughly comparable in prestige

Do you understand how football—or some other sport—is an example of social structure? What is social class?

Social Status

When you hear the word *status,* you are likely to think of prestige. These two words are wedded together in people's minds. As you saw in the box on football, however, sociologists use **status** in a different way—to refer to the *position* that someone occupies. That position may carry a great deal of prestige, as in the case of a judge or an astronaut, or it may bring little prestige, as in the case of a convenience store clerk or a waitress at the local truck stop. The status may also be looked down on, as in the case of a streetcorner man, an ex-convict, or a thief.

Like other aspects of social structure, statuses are part of our basic framework of living in society. The example I gave of students and teachers who come to class and do what others expect of them despite their particular circumstances and moods illustrates how statuses affect our actions—and those of the people around us. Our statuses—whether daughter or son, teacher or student—serve as guides for our behavior.

Status Sets.   All of us occupy several positions at the same time. You may simultaneously be a son or daughter, a worker, a date, and a student. Sociologists use the term **status set** to refer to all the statuses or positions that you occupy. Obviously your status set changes as your particular statuses change. For example, if you graduate from college and take a full-time job, get married, buy a home, have children, and so on, your status set changes to include the positions of worker, spouse, homeowner, and parent.

Ascribed and Achieved Statuses.   An **ascribed status** is involuntary. You do not ask for it, nor can you choose it. At birth, you inherit ascribed statuses such as your race–ethnicity, sex, and the social class of your parents, as well as your statuses as female or male, daughter or son, niece or nephew. Others, such as teenager and senior citizen, are related to the life course, and are given to you later in life.

Achieved statuses, in contrast, are voluntary. These you earn or accomplish. As a result of your efforts you become a student, a friend, a spouse, or a lawyer. Or, for lack of effort (or for efforts that others fail to appreciate), you become a school dropout, a former friend, an ex-spouse, or a debarred lawyer. In other words, achieved statuses can be either positive or negative; both college president and bank robber are achieved statuses.

Each status provides guidelines for how we are to act and feel. Like other aspects of social structure, statuses set limits on what we can and cannot do. Because social statuses are an essential part of the social structure, all human groups have them.

Status Symbols.   People who are pleased with their social status often want others to recognize their particular position. To elicit this recognition, they use status symbols, signs that identify a status. For example, people wear wedding rings to announce their marital status; uniforms, guns, and badges to proclaim that they are police officers (and not so subtly, to let you know that their status gives them authority over you); and "backward" collars to declare that they are Lutheran ministers or Roman Catholic or Episcopal priests.

Some social statuses are negative and so, therefore, are their status symbols. The scarlet letter in Nathaniel Hawthorne's book by the same title is one example. Another is the CONVICTED DUI (Driving Under the Influence) bumper sticker that some U.S. courts require convicted drunk drivers to display if they wish to avoid a jail sentence.

All of us use status symbols. We use them to announce our statuses to others and to help smooth our interactions in everyday life. Can you identify your own status symbols and what they communicate? For example, how does your clothing announce your statuses of sex, age, and college student?

Master Statuses.   A **master status** cuts across your other statuses. Some master statuses are ascribed. One example is your sex. Whatever you do, people perceive you as a male or as a female. If you are working your way through college by flipping burgers, people see you not only as a burger flipper and a student but also as a *male* or *female* burger flipper and a *male* or *female* college student. Other ascribed master statuses are race–ethnicity and age.

Social class and social status are significant factors in social life. Fundamental to what we become, they affect our orientations to life. Can you see how this photo illustrates this point?

REUTERS/Arko Datta /Landov

status the position that someone occupies in a social group (also called social status)

status set all the statuses or positions that an individual occupies

ascribed status a position an individual either inherits at birth or receives involuntarily later in life

achieved statuses positions that are earned, accomplished, or involve at least some effort or activity on the individual's part

master status a status that cuts across the other statuses that an individual occupies

What is social status? What kinds are there? How do your social statuses guide your behavior?

Some master statuses are achieved. If you become very, very wealthy (and it doesn't matter whether your wealth comes from a successful invention, a hit song, or from winning the lottery—it is still *achieved* as far as sociologists are concerned), your wealth is likely to become a master status. For example, people might say, "She is a very rich burger flipper"—or, more likely, "She's very rich, and she used to flip burgers!"

Similarly, people who become disfigured find, to their dismay, that their condition becomes a master status. For example, a person whose face is scarred from severe burns will be viewed through this unwelcome master status regardless of occupation or accomplishments. In the same way, people who are confined to wheelchairs can attest to how their wheelchair overrides all their other statuses and influences others' perceptions of everything they do.

Status Inconsistency.   Our statuses usually fit together fairly well, but some people have a mismatch among their statuses. This is known as **status inconsistency** (or discrepancy). A 14-year-old college student is an example. So is a 40-year-old married woman who is dating a 19-year-old college sophomore.

These examples reveal an essential aspect of social statuses: Like other components of social structure, our statuses come with built-in *norms* (that is, expectations) that guide our behavior. When statuses mesh well, as they usually do, we know what to expect of people. This helps social interaction to unfold smoothly. Status inconsistency, however, upsets our expectations. In the preceding examples, how are you supposed to act? Are you supposed to treat the 14-year-old as you would a young teenager, or as you would your college classmate? Do you react to the married woman as you would to the mother of your friend, or as you would to a classmate's date?

Master statuses are those that overshadow our other statuses. Shown here is Stephen Hawking, who is severely disabled by Lou Gehrig's disease. For some, his *master status* is that of a person with disabilities. Because Hawking is one of the greatest physicists who has ever lived, however, his outstanding achievements have given him another *master status*, that of a world-class physicist in the ranking of Einstein.

SHERYL NADLER/Reuters/Landov

Roles

All the world's a stage
And all the men and women merely players.
They have their exits and their entrances;
And one man in his time plays many parts . . .

(William Shakespeare, As You Like It, *Act II, Scene 7)*

Like Shakespeare, sociologists see roles as essential to social life. When you were born, **roles**—the behaviors, obligations, and privileges attached to a status—were already set up for you. Society was waiting with outstretched arms to teach you how it expected you to act as a boy or a girl. And whether you were born poor, rich, or somewhere in between, that, too, attached certain behaviors, obligations, and privileges to your statuses.

The difference between role and status is that you *occupy* a status, but you *play* a role (Linton 1936). For example, being a son or daughter is your status, but your expectations of receiving food and shelter from your parents—as well as their expectations that you show respect to them—are part of your role. Or, again, your status is student, but your role is to attend class, take notes, do homework, and take tests.

Roles are like fences. They allow us a certain amount of freedom, but for most of us that freedom doesn't go very far. Suppose that a woman decides that she is not going to wear dresses—or a man that he will not wear suits and ties—regardless of what anyone

status inconsistency ranking high on some dimensions of social status and low on others; also called *status discrepancy*

role the behaviors, obligations, and privileges attached to a status

What are your master statuses, and how do they influence your life? What is status inconsistency?

Watch
Ways We Live
on mysoclab.com

says. In most situations, they'll stick to their decision. When a formal occasion comes along, however, such as a family wedding or a funeral, they are likely to cave in to norms that they find overwhelming. Almost all of us follow the guidelines for what is "appropriate" for our roles. Few of us are bothered by such constraints, for our socialization is thorough, and we usually *want* to do what our roles indicate is appropriate.

The sociological significance of roles is that they lay out what is expected of people. As individuals throughout society perform their roles, those many roles mesh together to form this thing called *society*. As Shakespeare put it, people's roles provide "their exits and their entrances" on the stage of life. In short, roles are remarkably effective at keeping people in line—telling them when they should "enter" and when they should "exit," as well as what to do in between.

Groups

A **group** consists of people who interact with one another and who feel that the values, interests, and norms they have in common are important. The groups to which we belong—just like social class, statuses, and roles—are powerful forces in our lives. By belonging to a group, we assume an obligation to affirm the group's values, interests, and norms. To remain a member in good standing, we need to show that we share those characteristics. This means that *when we belong to a group we yield to others the right to judge our behavior*—even though we don't like it!

Although this principle holds true for all groups, some groups wield influence over only small segments of our behavior. For example, if you belong to a stamp collectors' club, the group's influence may center on your display of knowledge about stamps and perhaps your fairness in trading them. Other groups, in contrast, such as the family, control many aspects of our behavior. When parents say to their 15-year-old daughter, "As long as you are living under our roof, you had better be home by midnight," they show an expectation that their daughter, as a member of the family, will conform to their ideas about many aspects of life, including their views on curfew. They are saying that as long as the daughter wants to remain a member of the family in good standing, her behavior must conform to their expectations.

Let's look at the next component of social structure, social institutions.

Social Institutions

At first glance, the term *social institution* may seem cold and abstract—with little relevance to your life. In fact, however, **social institutions**—the standard or usual ways that a society meets its basic needs—vitally affect your life. They not only shape your behavior but even color your thoughts. How can this be?

The first step in understanding how this can be is to look at Figure 2 on the next page. Social institutions include the family, religion, education, economics, medicine, politics, law, science, the military, and the mass media. By weaving the fabric of society, social institutions set the context for your behavior and orientations to life. Note that each institution satisfies a basic need and has its own groups, statuses, values, and norms. Social institutions are so significant that an entire part of this book, Part IV, focuses on them.

Social institutions profoundly affect your life, but much of their influence lies beyond your ordinary awareness. For example, because of our economic institution, it is common to work eight hours a day five days a week. There is nothing normal or natural about this pattern, however. This rhythm is only an arbitrary arrangement for dividing work and leisure. Yet this one aspect of a single social institution has far-reaching effects. Not only does it dictate how people divide up their days, but it also lays out a structure for our interaction with family and friends and for how we meet our personal needs.

Each of the other social institutions also has far-reaching effects on our lives. *Social institutions are so significant that if they were different, our orientations to life itself would be different.* Let's consider just the mass media.

group people who have something in common and who believe that what they have in common is significant; also called a *social group*

social institution the organized, usual, or standard ways by which society meets its basic needs

How do your roles and group memberships guide your behavior?

109

FIGURE 2 **Social Institutions in Industrial and Postindustrial Societies**

Social Institution	Basic Needs of Society	Some Groups or Organizations	Some Statuses	Some Values	Some Norms
Family	Regulate reproduction, socialize and protect children	Relatives, kinship groups	Daughter, son, father, mother, brother, sister, aunt, uncle, grandparent	Sexual fidelity, providing for your family, keeping a clean house, respect for parents	Have only as many children as you can afford, be faithful to your spouse
Religion	Concerns about life after death, the meaning of suffering and loss; desire to connect with the Creator	Congregation, synagogue, mosque, denomination, charity, clergy associations	Priest, minister, rabbi, imam, worshipper, teacher, disciple, missionary, prophet, convert	God and the holy texts such as the Torah, the Bible, and the Qur'an should be honored	Go to worship services, follow the teachings, contribute money
Education	Transmit knowledge and skills across generations	School, college, student senate, sports team, PTA, teachers' union	Teacher, student, dean, principal, football player, cheerleader	Academic honesty, good grades, being "cool"	Do homework, prepare lectures, don't snitch on classmates
Economy	Produce and distribute goods and services	Credit unions, banks, credit card companies, buying clubs	Worker, boss, buyer, seller, creditor, debtor, advertiser	Making money, paying bills on time, producing efficiently	Maximize profits, "the customer is always right," work hard
Medicine	Heal the sick and injured, care for the dying	AMA, hospitals, pharmacies, HMOs, insurance companies	Doctor, nurse, patient, pharmacist, medical insurer	Hippocratic oath, staying in good health, following doctor's orders	Don't exploit patients, give best medical care available
Politics	Allocate power, determine authority, prevent chaos	Political party, congress, parliament, monarchy	President, senator, lobbyist, voter, candidate, spin doctor	Majority rule, the right to vote as a privilege and a sacred trust	One vote per person, be informed about candidates
Law	Maintain social order, enforce norms	Police, courts, prisons	Judge, police officer, lawyer, defendant, prison guard	Trial by one's peers, innocence until proven guilty	Give true testimony, follow the rules of evidence
Science	Master the environment	Local, state, regional, national, and international associations	Scientist, researcher, technician, administrator, journal editor	Unbiased research, open dissemination of research findings, originality	Follow scientific method, be objective, disclose findings, don't plagiarize
Military	Protection from enemies, enforce national interests	Army, navy, air force, marines, coast guard, national guard	Soldier, recruit, enlisted person, officer, veteran, prisoner, spy	To die for one's country is an honor, obedience unto death	Follow orders, be ready to go to war, sacrifice for your buddies
Mass Media	Disseminate information, report events, mold public opinion	TV networks, radio stations, publishers, association of bloggers	Journalist, newscaster, author, editor, publisher, blogger	Timeliness, accuracy, freedom of the press	Be accurate, fair, timely, and profitable

Source: By the author.

An Example: The Mass Media. Far beyond serving simply as sources of information, the mass media influence our attitudes toward social issues, the ways we view other people, and even our self-concept. Because the media significantly shape public opinion, all governments attempt to influence them. Totalitarian governments try to control them.

The mass media are relatively new in human history, originating with the invention of the printing press in the 1400s. This single invention had profound consequences

How do social institutions guide your behavior? How do they provide your orientations to life?

on all social institutions. The printing of the Bible altered religion, for instance, while the publication of political broadsides and newspapers altered politics. From these beginnings, a series of inventions—from radio and movies to television and the microchip—has made the media an increasingly powerful force.

One of the most significant questions we can ask about this social institution is, Who controls it? That control, which in totalitarian countries is obvious, is much less visible in democratic nations. Functionalists might conclude that the media in a democratic nation represent the varied interests of the many groups that make up that nation. Conflict theorists, in contrast, see the matter quite differently: The mass media—at least a country's most influential newspapers and television stations—represent the interests of the political elite. They give coverage to mildly dissenting opinions, but they stand solidly behind the government. The most obvious example is the positive treatment that the media give to the inauguration of a president.

Since the mass media are so influential in our lives today, the answer to this question of who controls the media is of more than passing interest. This matter is vital to our understanding of contemporary society.

Comparing Functionalist and Conflict Perspectives

Just as the functionalist and conflict perspectives of the mass media differ, so do their views of the nature of social institutions. Let's compare these views.

The Functionalist Perspective.   Because the first priority is to survive, all societies establish customary ways to meet their basic needs. As a result, no society is without social institutions. In tribal societies, some social institutions are less visible because the group meets its basic social needs in more informal ways. A society may be too small to have people specialize in education, for example, but it will have established ways of teaching skills and ideas to the young. It may be too small to have a military, but it will have some mechanism of self-defense.

What are society's basic needs? Functionalists identify five *functional requisites* (basic needs) that each society must meet if it is to survive (Aberle et al. 1950; Mack and Bradford 1979).

1. *Replacing members.* Obviously, if a society does not replace its members, it cannot continue to exist. With reproduction fundamental to a society's existence, and the need to protect infants and children universal, all groups have developed some version of the family. The family gives the newcomer to society a sense of belonging by providing a *lineage*, an account of how he or she is related to others. The family also functions to control people's sex drive and to maintain orderly reproduction.
2. *Socializing new members.* Each baby must be taught what it means to be a member of the group into which it is born. To accomplish this, each human group develops devices to ensure that its newcomers learn the group's basic expectations. As the primary "bearer of culture," the family is essential to this process, but other social institutions, such as religion and education, also help meet this basic need.
3. *Producing and distributing goods and services.* Every society must produce and distribute basic resources, from food and clothing to shelter and education. Consequently, every society establishes an *economic* institution, a means of producing goods and services along with routine ways of distributing them.
4. *Preserving order.* Societies face two threats of disorder: one internal, the potential for chaos, and the other external, the possibility of attack. To protect themselves from internal threat, they develop ways to police themselves, ranging from informal means such as gossip to formal means such

Mike Maple/Woodfin Camp & Associates

Functionalist theorists have identified *functional requisites* for the survival of society. One, providing a sense of purpose, is often met through religious groups. To most people, snake handling, as in this church service in Sand Mountain, Alabama, is nonsensical. From a functional perspective, however, it makes a great deal of sense. Can you identify its sociological meanings?

What is the functionalist perspective on social institutions?

as armed groups. To defend themselves against external conquest, they develop a means of defense, some form of the military.

5. *Providing a sense of purpose.* Every society must get people to yield self-interest in favor of the needs of the group. To convince people to sacrifice personal gains, societies instill a sense of purpose. Human groups develop many ways to implant such beliefs, but a primary one is religion, which attempts to answer questions about ultimate meaning. Actually, all of a society's institutions are involved in meeting this functional requisite; the family provides one set of answers about the sense of purpose, the school another, and so on.

The Conflict Perspective. Although conflict theorists agree that social institutions were designed originally to meet basic survival needs, they do not view social institutions as working harmoniously for the common good. On the contrary, conflict theorists stress that powerful groups control our society's institutions, manipulating them in order to maintain their own privileged position of wealth and power (Useem 1984; Domhoff 1999a, 1999b, 2006, 2007).

Conflict theorists point out that a fairly small group of people has garnered the lion's share of our nation's wealth. Members of this elite group sit on the boards of our major corporations and our most prestigious universities. They make strategic campaign contributions to influence (or control) our lawmakers, and it is they who are behind the nation's major decisions: to go to war or to refrain from war; to increase or to decrease taxes; to raise or to lower interest rates; and to pass laws that favor or impede moving capital, technology, and jobs out of the country.

Feminist sociologists (both women and men) have used conflict theory to gain a better understanding of how social institutions affect gender relations. Their basic insight is that gender is also an element of social structure, not simply a characteristic of individuals. In other words, throughout the world, social institutions divide males and females into separate groups, each with unequal access to society's resources.

In Sum: Functionalists view social institutions as working together to meet universal human needs, but conflict theorists regard social institutions as having a single primary purpose—to preserve the social order. For them, this means safeguarding the wealthy and powerful in their positions of privilege.

Changes in Social Structure

As you can see, this enveloping system that we call social structure powerfully affects our lives. This means that as social structure changes, so, too, do our orientations to life. Our culture is not static. It is continuously evolving as it responds to changing values, to new technology, and to contact with cultures around the world. As our culture changes, so do we. Similarly, as our economy responds to globalization, it either opens or closes opportunities, changing our lives, sometimes brutally so. New groups such as the Department of Homeland Security come into being, wielding extraordinary power over us. In short, the corner in life that we occupy, though small and seemingly private, is not closed off; rather, it is pushed and pulled and stretched in different directions as our social structure changes.

What Holds Society Together?

Not only does our society have antagonistic groups that would love to get at one another's throats, but we also are in the midst of social change so extensive that it threatens to rip our society apart. How does society manage to hold together? Sociologists have proposed two answers. Let's examine these, starting with a bit of history.

© Topham/The Image Works

Durkheim used the term *mechanical solidarity* to refer to the shared consciousness that develops among people who perform similar tasks. Can you see from this photo why this term applies so well to small farming groups, why they share such similar views about life?

Can you explain how the conflict perspective differs from the functionalist perspective on social institutions?

Mechanical and Organic Solidarity. Sociologist Emile Durkheim (1893/1933) was interested in how societies manage to create **social integration**—their members united by shared values and other social bonds. He found the answer in what he called **mechanical solidarity.** By this term, Durkheim meant that people who perform similar tasks develop a shared consciousness. Think of a farming community in which everyone is involved in growing crops—planting, cultivating, and harvesting. Because they share so much in common, they share similar views about life. Societies with mechanical solidarity tolerate little diversity in behavior, thinking, or attitudes, for their unity depends on sharing similar views.

As societies get larger, they develop different kinds of work, a specialized **division of labor.** Some people mine gold, others turn it into jewelry, and still others sell it. This disperses people into different interest groups where they develop different ideas about life. No longer do they depend on one another to have similar ideas and behaviors. Rather, they depend on one another to do specific work, with each person contributing to the group. Durkheim called this new form of cohesion **organic solidarity.**

To see why Durkheim used the term *organic solidarity,* think about your body. The organs of your body need one another. Your lungs depend on your heart to pump your blood, and your heart depends on your lungs to oxygenate your blood. To move from the physical to the social, think about how you need your teacher to guide you through this course and how your teacher needs students to have a job. You and your teacher are *like two organs in the same body.* (The "body" in this case is the college.) Like the heart and lungs, you perform different tasks, but need one another.

The change to organic solidarity changed the basis for social integration. In centuries past, you would have had views similar to your neighbors because you lived in the same village, did farming together, and had relatives in common. To catch a glimpse of why, look at the photo on the previous page. But no longer does social integration require this. Like organs in a body, our separate activities contribute to the welfare of the group. The change from mechanical to organic solidarity allows our society to tolerate a wide diversity of orientations to life and still manage to work as a whole.

Gemeinschaft and *Gesellschaft.* Ferdinand Tönnies (1887/1988) also analyzed this fundamental shift in relationships. He used the term *Gemeinschaft* (Guh-MINE-shoft), or "intimate community," to describe village life, the type of society in which everyone knows everyone else. He noted that in the society that was emerging, the personal ties, kinship connections, and lifelong friendships that marked village life were being crowded out by short-term relationships, individual accomplishments, and self-interest. Tönnies called this new type of society *Gesellschaft* (Guh-ZELL-shoft), or "impersonal association."

social integration the degree to which members of a group or a society are united by shared values and other social bonds; also known as *social cohesion*

mechanical solidarity Durkheim's term for the unity (a shared consciousness) that people feel as a result of performing the same or similar tasks

division of labor the splitting of a group's or a society's tasks into specialties

organic solidarity Durkheim's term for the interdependence that results from the division of labor; as part of the same unit, we all depend on others to fulfill their jobs

Gemeinschaft a type of society in which life is intimate; a community in which everyone knows everyone else and people share a sense of togetherness

Gesellschaft a type of society that is dominated by impersonal relationships, individual accomplishments, and self-interest

AP Images/Scott Dalton   Piotr Redlinski/Redux

The warm, more intimate relationships of *Gemeinschaft* society are apparent in the photo taken during Oktoberfest in Munich, Germany. The more impersonal relationships of *Gesellschaft* society are evident in this Internet cafe in Brooklyn, where customers are ignoring one another.

How does society hold together despite it having antagonistic groups?

He did not mean that we no longer have intimate ties to family and friends but, rather, that our lives no longer center on them. Few of us take jobs in a family business, for example, and contracts replace handshakes. Much of our time is spent with strangers and short-term acquaintances.

How Relevant Are These Concepts Today?   I know that *Gemeinschaft, Gesellschaft,* and *mechanical* and *organic solidarity* are strange terms and that Durkheim's and Tönnies' observations must seem like a dead issue. The concern these sociologists expressed, however—that their world was changing from a community in which people were united by close ties and shared ideas and feelings to an anonymous association built around impersonal, short-term contacts—is still very real. In large part, this same concern explains the rise of Islamic fundamentalism (Volti 1995). Islamic leaders fear that Western values will uproot their traditional culture, that cold rationality will replace the warm, informal, personal relationships among families and clans. They fear, rightly so, that this will also change their views on life and morality. Although the terms may sound strange, even obscure, you can see that the ideas remain a vital part of today's world.

In Sum: Whether the terms are *Gemeinschaft* and *Gesellschaft* or *mechanical solidarity* and *organic solidarity,* they indicate that as societies change, so do people's orientations to life. *The sociological point is that social structure sets the context for what we do, feel, and think, and ultimately, then, for the kind of people we become.* As you read the Cultural Diversity box on the next page, which describes one of the few remaining *Gemeinschaft* societies in the United States, think of how fundamentally different your life would be if you had been reared in an Amish family.

The Microsociological Perspective: Social Interaction in Everyday Life

As you have seen, macrosociologists examine the broad features of society. Microsociologists, in contrast, examine narrower slices of social life. Their primary focus is *face-to-face interaction*—what people do when they are in one another's presence. Before you study the main features of social interaction, look at the photo essay on the next few pages. See if you can identify both social structure and social interaction in each of the photos.

Symbolic Interaction

Symbolic interactionists are especially interested in the symbols people use. They want to know how people view things and how this, in turn, affects their behavior and orientations to life. Of the many areas of social life symbolic interactionists study, let's look at just a few aspects of social interaction—stereotypes, personal space, eye contact, smiling, and body language.

Stereotypes in Everyday Life.   You are familiar with how first impressions set the tone for interaction. When you first meet someone, you cannot help but notice certain features, especially the person's sex, race–ethnicity, age, and clothing. Despite your best intentions, your assumptions about these characteristics shape your first impressions. They also affect how you act toward that person—and, in turn, how that person acts toward you. These fascinating aspects of our social interaction are discussed in the Down-to-Earth Sociology box.

Personal Space.   We all surround ourselves with a "personal bubble" that we go to great lengths to protect. We open the bubble to intimates—to our friends, children, and parents—but we're careful to keep most people out of this space. In a crowded hallway between classes, we might walk with our books clasped in front of us (a strategy often chosen by females). When we stand in line, we make certain there is enough space so that we don't touch the person in front of us and aren't touched by the person behind us.

Cultural Diversity in the United States

The Amish: *Gemeinschaft* Community in a *Gesellschaft* Society

One of the best examples of a *Gemeinschaft* community in the United States is the Old Order Amish, followers of a group that broke away from the Swiss-German Mennonite church in the 1600s and settled in Pennsylvania around 1727. Most of today's 225,000 Old Order Amish live in just three states—Pennsylvania, Ohio, and Indiana.

Because Amish farmers use horses instead of tractors, most of their farms are one hundred acres or less. To the five million tourists who pass through Lancaster County each year, the rolling green pastures, white farmhouses, simple barns, horse-drawn buggies, and clotheslines hung with somber-colored garments convey a sense of peace and innocence reminiscent of another era. Although just sixty-five miles from Philadelphia, "Amish country" is a world away.

The external differences are obvious— the horses and buggies from so long ago, the language (a dialect of German known as Pennsyl-vania Dutch), and the plain clothing—often black, no belt, whose style has remained unchanged for almost 300 years. Beyond these externals is a value system that binds the Amish together, with religion and discipline the glue that maintains their way of life.

Tim Landis/Sipa Press/0610041641 via Newscom

Amish life is based on separation from the world—an idea taken from Christ's Sermon on the Mount—and obedi-ence to the church's teachings and leaders. This rejection of worldly concerns, writes sociologist Donald Kraybill (2002), "provides the foundation of such Amish values as humility, faithfulness, thrift, tradition, communal goals, joy of work, a slow-paced life, and trust in divine providence." The Amish believe that violence is bad, even personal self-defense, and they register as conscientious objectors during times of war. They pay no Social Security, and they receive no government benefits.

To maintain this separation from the world, Amish children attend schools that are run by the Amish, and they attend only until the age of 13. (In 1972, the Supreme Court ruled that Amish parents have the right to take their children out of school after the eighth grade.) To go to school beyond the eighth grade would expose the children to values that would drive a wedge between the children and their community.

The *Gemeinschaft* of village life that has been largely lost to industrialization remains a vibrant part of Amish life. The Amish make their decisions in weekly meetings, where, by consensus, they follow a set of rules, or *Ordnung*, to guide

their behavior. Brotherly love and the welfare of the com-munity are paramount values. In times of birth, sickness, and death, neighbors pitch in with the chores. The family is also vital for Amish life. Nearly all Amish marry, and divorce is forbidden. The major events of Amish life take place in the home, including weddings, births, funerals, and church services. In these ways, they maintain the bonds of intimate community.

Because they cannot resist all change, the Amish try to adapt in ways that will least disrupt their core values. Urban sprawl poses a special threat as it has driven up the price of farmland. Unable to afford farms, about half of Amish men now work at jobs other than farming. The men go to great lengths to avoid leaving the home. Most work in farm-related businesses or operate woodcraft shops, but some have taken jobs in factories. With intimate, or *Gemeinschaft*, society essential to the Amish way of life, concerns have grown about how the men who work for non-Amish businesses are being exposed to the outside world. Some are using modern technology such as cell phones and computers at work. During the economic crisis, some who were laid off from their jobs even accepted un-employment checks—violating the fundamental principle of taking no help from the government.

Despite the threats posed by a materialistic and secular culture, the Amish are managing to retain their way of life. Perhaps the most poignant illustration of how greatly the Amish differ from the dominant culture is this: When in 2006 a non-Amish man shot several Amish girls and himself at a one-room school, the Amish community established chari-table funds not only for the families of the dead children but also for the family of the killer.

Sources: Aeppel 1996; Kephart and Zellner 2001; Kraybill 2002; Johnson-Weiner 2007; Scolforo 2008; Coyne 2009.

For Your Consideration

➤ Identify some of your *specific* ideas, attitudes, and be-haviors that would be different if you had been reared in an Amish family. What do you like and dislike about Amish life? Why?

How do you think your orientations to life would be different if you had grown up Amish?

THROUGH THE AUTHOR'S LENS

Vienna: Social Structure and Social Interaction

We live our lives within social structure. Just as a road is to a car, providing limits to where it can go, so social structure limits our behavior. Social structure—our culture, social class, statuses, roles, group memberships, and social institutions—points us in particular directions in life. Most of this direction-giving is beyond our awareness. But it is highly effective, giving shape to our social interactions, as well as to what we expect from life.

These photos that I took in Vienna, Austria, make visible some of social structure's limiting, shaping, and direction-giving. Most of the social structure that affects our lives is not physical, as with streets and buildings, but social, as with norms, belief systems, obligations, and the goals held out for us because of our ascribed statuses. In these photos, you should be able to see how social interaction takes form within social structure.

Vienna provides a mixture of the old and the new. Stephan's Dom (Cathedral) dates back to 1230, the carousel to now.

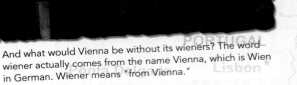

And what would Vienna be without its wieners? The word wiener actually comes from the name Vienna, which is Wien in German. Wiener means "from Vienna."

The main square in Vienna, Stephan Platz, provides a place to have a cup of coffee, read the newspaper, enjoy the architecture, or just watch the hustle and bustle of the city.

Part of the pull of the city is its offering of rich culture. I took this photo at one of the many operas held in Vienna each night.

In the appealing street cafes of Vienna, social structure and social interaction are especially evident. Can you see both in this photo?

The city offers something for everyone, including unusual places for people to rest and to talk and to flirt with one another.

And what would Vienna be without its world-famous beers? The city's entrepreneurs make sure that the beer is within easy reach.

To be able to hang out with friends, not doing much, but doing it in the midst of stimulating sounds and sights—this is the vibrant city.

© James M. Henslin

Beauty May Be Only Skin Deep, But Its Effects Go On Forever: Stereotypes in Everyday Life

Mark Snyder, a psychologist, wondered whether **stereotypes**—our assumptions of what people are like—might be self-fulfilling. He came up with an ingenious way to test this idea. Snyder (1993) gave college men a Polaroid snapshot of a woman (supposedly taken just moments before) and told each man that he would be introduced to her after they talked on the telephone. Actually, the photographs—showing either a pretty or a homely woman—had been prepared before the experiment began. The photo was *not* of the woman the men would talk to.

Stereotypes came into play immediately. As Snyder gave each man the photograph, he asked him what he thought the woman would be like. The men who saw the photograph of the attractive woman said that they expected to meet a poised, humorous, outgoing woman. The men who had been given a photo of the unattractive woman described her as awkward, serious, and unsociable.

The men's stereotypes influenced the way they spoke to the women on the telephone, who did *not* know about the photographs. The men who had seen the photograph of a pretty woman were warm, friendly, and humorous. This, in turn, affected the women they spoke to, for they responded in a warm, friendly, outgoing manner. And the men who had seen the photograph of a homely woman? On the phone, they were cold, reserved, and humorless, and the women they spoke to became cool, reserved, and humorless. Keep in mind that the women did not know that their looks had been evaluated—and that the photographs were not even of them. In short, stereotypes tend to produce behaviors that match the stereotype. This principle is illustrated in Figure 3.

Beauty might be only skin deep, but it has real consequences. Not only do pretty people get a pass in a lot of situations, but they also are likely to make more money (Judge et al. 2009). For example, advertising agencies with better-looking executives have higher revenues (Pfann et al. 2000). Apparently, people are more willing to hire individuals whom they perceive as good-looking.

For Your Consideration

➤ Stereotypes have no single, inevitable effect. People can resist stereotypes and change outcomes. However, these studies do illustrate that stereotypes deeply influence how we react to one another.

➤ Instead of beauty, consider gender and race–ethnicity. How do you think they affect those who do the stereotyping and those who are stereotyped?

Dane Rex

Plush Studios/Digital Vision/Getty Images Royalty Free

Based on the experiments summarized here, how do you think men would modify their interactions if they were to meet these two women? And if women were to meet these two women, would they modify their interactions in the same way?

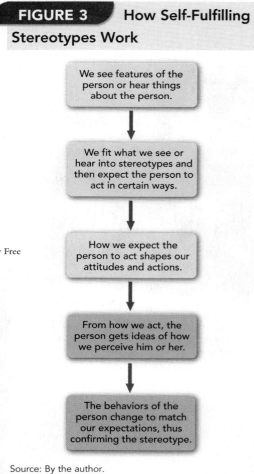

FIGURE 3 How Self-Fulfilling Stereotypes Work

We see features of the person or hear things about the person.

↓

We fit what we see or hear into stereotypes and then expect the person to act in certain ways.

↓

How we expect the person to act shapes our attitudes and actions.

↓

From how we act, the person gets ideas of how we perceive him or her.

↓

The behaviors of the person change to match our expectations, thus confirming the stereotype.

Source: By the author.

How do stereotypes influence people's behavior? How about yours?

How people use space as they interact is studied by sociologists who have a microsociological focus. What do you seen in common in these two photos?

At times, we extend our personal space. In the library, for example, you might place your coat on the chair next to you—claiming that space for yourself even though you aren't using it. If you want to really extend your space, you might even spread books in front of the other chairs, keeping the whole table to yourself by giving the impression that others have just stepped away.

The amount of space that people prefer varies from one culture to another. South Americans, for example, like to be closer when they speak to others than do people reared in the United States. Anthropologist Edward Hall (1959; Hall and Hall 2012) recounts a conversation with a man from South America who had attended one of his lectures.

> *He came to the front of the class at the end of the lecture. . . . We started out facing each other, and as he talked I became dimly aware that he was standing a little too close and that I was beginning to back up. Fortunately I was able to suppress my first impulse and remain stationary because there was nothing to communicate aggression in his behavior except the conversational distance. . . .*
>
> *By experimenting I was able to observe that as I moved away slightly, there was an associated shift in the pattern of interaction. He had more trouble expressing himself. If I shifted to where I felt comfortable (about twenty-one inches), he looked somewhat puzzled and hurt, almost as though he were saying, "Why is he acting that way? Here I am doing everything I can to talk to him in a friendly manner and he suddenly withdraws. Have I done anything wrong? Said something I shouldn't?" Having ascertained that distance had a direct effect on his conversation, I stood my ground, letting him set the distance.*

As you can see, despite Hall's extensive knowledge of other cultures, he still felt uncomfortable in this conversation. He first interpreted the invasion of his personal space as possible aggression, for people get close (and jut out their chins and chests) when they are hostile. But when he realized that this was not the case, Hall resisted his impulse to move.

After Hall (1969; Hall and Hall 2007) analyzed situations like this, he observed that North Americans use four different "distance zones."

1. *Intimate distance.* This is the zone that the South American unwittingly invaded. It extends to about 18 inches from our bodies. We reserve this space for comforting, protecting, hugging, intimate touching, and lovemaking.
2. *Personal distance.* This zone extends from 18 inches to 4 feet. We reserve it for friends and acquaintances and ordinary conversations. This is the zone in which Hall would have preferred speaking with the South American.
3. *Social distance.* This zone, extending out from us about 4 to 12 feet, marks impersonal or formal relationships. We use this zone for such things as job interviews.
4. *Public distance.* This zone, extending beyond 12 feet, marks even more formal relationships. It is used to separate dignitaries and public speakers from the general public.

stereotype assumptions of what people are like, whether true or false

Excerpt from STUDIES IN ETHNOMETHODOLOGY by Harold Garfinkel. Copyright © 1967 by Harold Garfinkel. Reprinted with permission by John Wiley & Sons Ltd.

How do you use personal space in your own interactions?

Eye contact is a fascinating aspect of everyday life. We use fleeting eye contact for most of our interactions, such as those with clerks or people we pass in the hall between classes. Just as we reserve our close personal space for intimates, so, too, we reserve soft, lingering eye contact for them.

Jason Stitt/Shutterstock

body language the ways in which people use their bodies to give messages to others

dramaturgy an approach, pioneered by Erving Goffman, in which social life is analyzed in terms of drama or the stage; also called *dramaturgical analysis*

impression management people's efforts to control the impressions that others receive of them

front stage places where people give performances

© 20thCentFox/Courtesy Everett Collection

In *dramaturgy*, a specialty within sociology, social life is viewed as similar to the theater. In our everyday lives, we all are actors. Like those in the cast of *Family Guy*, we, too, perform roles, use props, and deliver lines to fellow actors—who, in turn, do the same.

Eye Contact. One way that we protect our personal bubble is by controlling eye contact. Letting someone gaze into our eyes—unless the person is an eye doctor—can be taken as a sign that we are attracted to that person, even as an invitation to intimacy. Wanting to become "the friendliest store in town," a chain of supermarkets in Illinois ordered its checkout clerks to make direct eye contact with each customer. Female clerks complained that male customers were taking their eye contact the wrong way, as an invitation to intimacy. Management said they were exaggerating. The clerks' reply was, "We know the kind of looks we're getting back from men," and they refused to continue making direct eye contact with them.

Smiling. In the United States, we take it for granted that clerks will smile as they wait on us. But it isn't this way in all cultures. Apparently, Germans aren't used to smiling clerks, and when Wal-Mart expanded into Germany, it brought its American ways with it. The company ordered its German clerks to smile at their customers. They did—and the customers complained. The German customers interpreted the smiles as flirting (Samor et al. 2006).

Body Language. While we are still little children, we learn to interpret **body language,** the ways people use their bodies to give messages to others. This skill in interpreting facial expressions, posture, and gestures is essential for getting through everyday life. Without it—as is the case for people with Asperger's syndrome—we wouldn't know how to react to others. It would even be difficult to know whether someone were serious or joking.

Applied Body Language. Our common and essential skill of interpreting body language has become one of the government's tools in its fight against terrorism. Because many of our body messages lie beneath our consciousness, airport personnel and interrogators are being trained to look for telltale facial signs—from a quick downturn of the mouth to rapid blinking—that might indicate nervousness or lying (Davis et al. 2002).

This is an interesting twist for an area of sociology that had been entirely theoretical. Let's now turn to dramaturgy, a special area of symbolic interactionism.

Dramaturgy: The Presentation of Self in Everyday Life

It was their big day, two years in the making. Jennifer Mackey wore a white wedding gown adorned with an 11-foot train and 24,000 seed pearls that she and her mother had sewn onto the dress. Next to her at the altar in Lexington, Kentucky, stood her intended, Jeffrey Degler, in black tie. They said their vows, then turned to gaze for a moment at the four hundred guests.

That's when groomsman Daniel Mackey collapsed. As the shocked organist struggled to play Mendelssohn's "Wedding March," Mr. Mackey's unconscious body was dragged away, his feet striking—loudly—every step of the altar stairs.

"I couldn't believe he would die at my wedding," the bride said. (Hughes 1990)

Sociologist Erving Goffman (1922–1982) added a new twist to microsociology when he recast the theatrical term **dramaturgy** into a sociological term. Goffman (1959/1999) used the term to mean that social life is like a drama or a stage play: Birth ushers us onto the stage of everyday life, and our socialization consists of learning to perform on that stage. The self lies at the center of our performances. We have ideas about how we want others to think of us and we use our roles in everyday life to communicate these ideas. Goffman called our efforts to manage the impressions that others receive of us **impression management.**

Stages. Everyday life, said Goffman, involves playing our assigned roles. We have **front stages** on which to perform them, as did Jennifer and Jeffrey. (By the way, Daniel Mackey didn't really die—he had just fainted.) But we don't have to

How do you use your body to give messages to others?

look at weddings to find front stages. Everyday life is filled with them. Where your teacher lectures is a front stage. And if you wait until your parents are in a good mood to tell them some bad news, you are using a front stage. In fact, you spend most of your time on front stages, for a front stage is wherever you deliver your lines. We also have **back stages,** places where we can retreat and let our hair down. When you close the bathroom or bedroom door for privacy, for example, you are entering a back stage.

The same setting can serve as both a back and a front stage. For example, when you get into your car and look over your hair in the mirror or check your makeup, you are using the car as a back stage. But when you wave at friends or if you give that familiar gesture to someone who has just cut in front of you in traffic, you are using your car as a front stage.

Role Performance, Conflict, and Strain.   As discussed earlier, everyday life brings many statuses. We may be a student, a shopper, a worker, and a date, as well as a daughter or a son. Although the roles attached to these statuses lay down the basic outline for our performances, they also allow a great deal of flexibility. The particular interpretation that you give a role, your "style," is known as **role performance.** Consider how you play your role as a son or daughter—which might be as an ideal daughter or son—being respectful, coming home at the hours your parents set, and so forth. Or this description may not even come close to your particular role performance.

Ordinarily, our statuses are separated sufficiently that we find little conflict between our role performances. Occasionally, however, what is expected of us in one status (our role) is incompatible with what is expected of us in another status. This problem, known as **role conflict,** is illustrated in Figure 4, in which family, friendship, student, and work roles come crashing together. Usually, however, we manage to avoid role conflict by segregating our statuses, although doing so can require an intense juggling act.

Sometimes the *same* status contains incompatible roles, a conflict known as **role strain.** Suppose that you are exceptionally well prepared for a particular class assignment. Although the instructor asks an unusually difficult question, you find yourself knowing the answer when no one else does. If you want to raise your hand, yet don't want to make your fellow students look bad, you will experience role strain. As illustrated in

back stages places where people rest from their performances, discuss their presentations, and plan future performances

role performance the ways in which someone performs a role; showing a particular "style" or "personality"

role conflict conflicts that someone feels *between* roles because the expectations are at odds with one another

role strain conflicts that someone feels within a role

Read
The Presentation of Self
by Irving Goffman
on **mysoclab.com**

FIGURE 4   **Role Strain and Role Conflict**

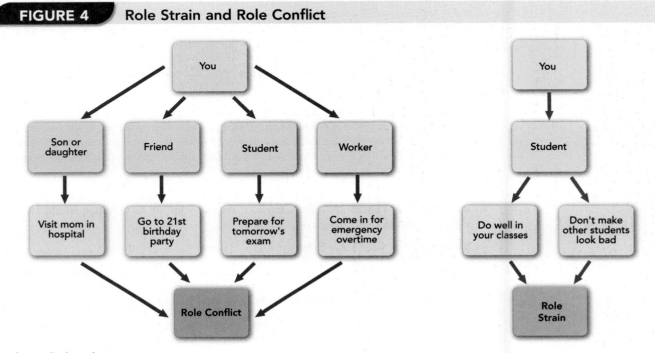

Source: By the author.

What is the difference between role conflict and role strain?

sign-vehicle the term used by Goffman to refer to how people use social setting, appearance, and manner to communicate information about the self

teamwork the collaboration of two or more people to manage impressions jointly

face-saving behavior techniques used to salvage a performance (interaction) that is going sour

✳️—Explore
Living Data
on **mysoclab.com**

Figure 4, the difference between role conflict and role strain is that role conflict is conflict *between* roles, while role strain is conflict *within* a role.

Sign-Vehicles. To communicate information about the self, we use three types of **sign-vehicles:** the social setting, our appearance, and our manner. The *social setting* is the place where the action unfolds. This is where the curtain goes up on your performance, where you find yourself on stage playing parts and delivering lines. A social setting might be an office, dorm, living room, classroom, church, or bar. It is wherever you interact with others. The social setting includes *scenery,* the furnishings you use to communicate messages, such as desks, blackboards, scoreboards, couches, and so on.

The second sign-vehicle is *appearance,* or how you look when you play your roles. On the most obvious level is your choice of hairstyle to communicate messages about yourself. (You might be proclaiming "I'm wild and sexy" or "I'm serious and professional" and quite certainly, "I'm masculine" or "I'm feminine"). Your appearance also includes props, which are like scenery except that they decorate your body rather than the setting. Your most obvious prop is your costume, ordinarily called clothing. You switch costumes as you play your roles, wearing quite different costumes for attending class, swimming, jogging or working out at the gym, and dating.

Your appearance lets others know what to expect from you and how they should react. Think of the messages that props communicate. Some people use clothing to say they are college students, others to say they are older adults. Some use clothing to let you know they are clergy, others to give the message that they are prostitutes. In the same way, people choose models of cars and brands of cigarettes and liquor to convey messages about the self.

The body itself is a sign-vehicle, its shape proclaiming messages about the self. The messages that are attached to various shapes change over time, but, as explored in the Mass Media box on the next page, thinness currently screams desirability.

The third sign-vehicle is *manner,* the attitudes you show as you play your roles. You use manner to communicate information about your feelings and moods. When you show that you are angry or indifferent, sincere or in good humor, you are indicating what others can expect of you as you play your roles.

Teamwork. Being a good role player brings positive recognition from others, something we all covet. To accomplish this, we use **teamwork**—two or more people working together to help a performance come off as planned. If you laugh at your boss's jokes, even though you don't find them funny, you are practicing teamwork to help your boss give a good performance.

If a performance doesn't come off quite right, the team might try to save it by using **face-saving behavior.**

> *Suppose your teacher is about to make an important point. Suppose also that her lecturing has been outstanding and the class is hanging on every word. Just as she pauses for emphasis, her stomach lets out a loud growl. She might then use a face-saving technique by remarking, "I was so busy preparing for class that I didn't get breakfast this morning."*

It is more likely, however, that both the teacher and class will simply ignore the sound, giving the impression that no one heard a thing—a face-saving technique called *studied nonobservance.* This allows the teacher to make the point or, as Goffman would say, it allows the performance to go on.

Becoming the Roles We Play.

> *Have you ever noticed how some clothing simply doesn't "feel" right for certain occasions? Have you ever changed your mind about something you were wearing and decided to change your clothing? Or maybe you just switched shirts or added a necklace?*

What you were doing was fine-tuning the impressions you wanted to make. Ordinarily, we are not this aware that we're working on impressions, but sometimes we are, especially those "first impressions"—the first day in college, a first date, visiting the parents

How do you use sign vehicles to communicate with others?

"Nothing Tastes as Good as Thin Feels": Body Images and the Mass Media

When you stand before a mirror, do you like what you see? Do you watch your weight or work out? Where did you get your ideas about what you should look like?

"Your body isn't good enough!" Daily, you are bombarded with this message. The way to improve your body, of course, is to buy the advertised products: diet programs, hair extensions, "uplifting" bras, and exercise equipment. Muscular hulks show off machines that magically produce "six-pack abs" and incredible biceps—in just a few minutes a day. Female celebrities go through tough workouts without even breaking into a sweat. Members of the opposite sex will flock to you if you purchase that wonder-working workout machine.

We try to shrug off such messages, knowing that they are designed to sell products, but these messages penetrate our thinking and feelings. They help shape the ideal images we hold of how we "ought" to look. Those models so attractively clothed and coiffed as they walk down the runway, could they be any thinner? For women, the message is clear: You can't be thin enough. The men's message is also clear: You can't be muscular enough.

With impossibly shaped models at Victoria's Secret and skinny models showing off the latest fashions in *Vogue* and *Seventeen*, half of U.S. adolescent girls feel fat and count calories (Grabe et al. 2008). Sixty percent of girls think that the secret to popularity is being thin (Zaslow 2009). Some teens even call the plastic surgeon. Anxious lest their child trail behind in her race for popularity, parents foot the bill. Some pay $25,000 just to give their daughters a flatter tummy (Gross 1998).

Cruise the Internet, and you will find "thinspiration" videos on YouTube that feature emaciated girls proudly displaying their skeletal frames. You will also find "pro-ana" (pro-anorexic) sites where eating disorders are promoted as a lifestyle choice (Zaslow 2009). The title of this box, "Nothing Tastes as Good as Thin Feels," is taken from one of these sites.

The thinness craze has moved to the East. Glossy magazines there also feature skinny models. Not limited by our rules, advertisers in Japan and China push a soap that "sucks up fat through the skin's pores" (Marshall 1995). What a dream

product! After all, even though our TV models smile as they go through their paces, those exercise machines do look like a lot of hard work.

And attractiveness does pay off. Economists studied looks and earnings, and people considered attractive earn more (Judge et al. 2009). "Good-looking" men and women earn the most, "average-looking" men and women earn average amounts, and the "plain" and the "ugly" earn the least (Hamermesh and Biddle 1994). In Europe, too, the more attractive workers earn more (Brunello and D'Hombres 2007). Then there is that potent cash "bonus" available to "attractive" women: They attract and marry higher-earning men (Kanazawa and Kovar 2004).

More popularity *and* more money? Maybe you can't be thin enough after all. Maybe those exercise machines are a good investment. If only we could catch up with the Japanese and develop a soap that would suck the fat right out of our pores. You can practically hear the jingle now.

For Your Consideration

→ What images do you have of your body? How do cultural expectations of "ideal" bodies underlie your images? Can you recall any advertisements or television programs that have influenced your body image?

→ To counteract the emphasis on being skinny, some clothing companies are featuring "plus-size" models. What do you think of this?

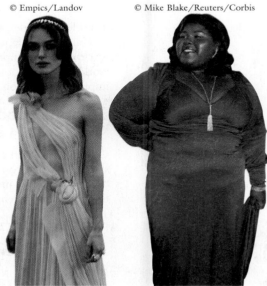

© Empics/Landov   © Mike Blake/Reuters/Corbis

All of us contrast the reality we see when we look in the mirror with our culture's ideal body types. The thinness craze, discussed in this box, encourages some people to extremes, as with Keira Knightley. It also makes it difficult for larger people to have positive self-images. Overcoming this difficulty, Gabourey Sidibe is in the forefront of promoting an alternative image.

How have the media influenced your ideas about your body?

of our loved one for the first time, and so on. Usually we are so used to the roles we play in everyday life that we tend to think we are "just doing" things, not that we are actors on a stage who manage impressions. Yet every time we dress for school, or for any other activity, we are preparing for impression management.

A fascinating characteristic of roles is that *we tend to become the roles we play.* That is, roles become incorporated into our self-concept, especially roles for which we prepare long and hard and that become part of our everyday lives. Helen Ebaugh (1988) experienced this firsthand when she quit being a nun to become a sociologist. With her own heightened awareness of *role exit,* she interviewed people who had left marriages, police work, the military, medicine, and religious vocations. Just as she had experienced, these roles had become so intertwined with the individual's self-concept that leaving it threatened the person's identity. The question these people struggled with was "Who am I, now that I am not a nun (or wife, police officer, colonel, physician, and so on)?"

A statement made by one of my respondents illustrates how roles become part of the person. Notice how a role can linger even after the person is no longer playing that role:

> *After I left the ministry, I felt like a fish out of water. Wearing that backward collar had become a part of me. It was especially strange on Sunday mornings when I'd listen to someone else give the sermon. I knew that I should be up there preaching. I felt as though I had left God.*

Applying Impression Management. I can just hear someone say, "Impression management is interesting, but is it really important?" It certainly is. Impression management is so significant that it can even make a vital difference in your career. To be promoted, you must be perceived as someone who *should* be promoted. You must appear dominant. You certainly cannot go unnoticed. But how you manage this impression is crucial. If a female executive tries to appear dominant by wearing loud clothing, using garish makeup, and cursing, this will get her noticed—but it will not put her on the path to promotion. How, then, can she exhibit dominance in the right way? To help women walk this fine line between femininity and dominance, career counselors advise women on how to do impression management. They recommend clothing that doesn't wrinkle and makeup that doesn't have to be reapplied during the day. During executive sessions, place your hands on the table, not in your lap. And don't carry a purse—stash it inside your briefcase (Needham 2006; Brinkley 2008; Agins 2009).

Male or female, in your own life you will have to walk this fine line, finding the best way to manage impressions in order to further your career. Much success in the work world depends not on what you actually know but, instead, on your ability to give the impression that you know what you should know.

Ethnomethodology: Uncovering Background Assumptions

Certainly one of the strangest words in sociology is *ethnomethodology.* To better understand this term, consider the word's three basic components. *Ethno* means "folk" or "people"; *method* means how people do something; *ology* means "the study of." Putting them together, then, *ethno–method–ology* means "the study of how people do things."

Both individuals and organizations do *impression management,* trying to communicate messages about the self (or organization) that best meets their goals. At times, these efforts fail.

How have roles become part of your self concept?

What things? **Ethnomethodology** is the study of how people use commonsense understandings to make sense of life.

Let's suppose that during a routine office visit, your doctor remarks that your hair is rather long, then takes out a pair of scissors and starts to give you a haircut. You would feel strange about this, for your doctor would be violating **background assumptions**—your ideas about the way life is and the way things ought to work. These assumptions, which lie at the root of everyday life, are so deeply embedded in our consciousness that we are seldom aware of them, and most of us fulfill them unquestioningly. Thus, your doctor does not offer you a hair-cut, even if he or she is good at cutting hair and you need one!

The founder of ethnomethodology, sociologist Harold Garfinkel, conducted exercises to reveal our background assumptions. Garfinkel (1967, 2002) asked his students to act as though they did not understand the basic rules of social life. Some tried to bargain with supermarket clerks; others would inch close to people and stare directly at them. They were met with surprise, bewilderment, even indignation and anger. In one exercise, Garfinkel asked students to act as though they were boarders in their own homes. They addressed their parents as "Mr." and "Mrs.," asked permission to use the bathroom, sat stiffly, were courteous, and spoke only when spoken to. As you can imagine, the other family members didn't know what to make of this (Garfinkel 1967):

All of us have *background assumptions*, deeply ingrained assumptions of how the world operates. What different background assumptions do you think are operating here?

> They vigorously sought to make the strange actions intelligible and to restore the situation to normal appearances. Reports (by the students) were filled with accounts of astonishment, bewilderment, shock, anxiety, embarrassment, and anger, and with charges by various family members that the student was mean, inconsiderate, selfish, nasty, or impolite. Family members demanded explanations: What's the matter? What's gotten into you? . . . Are you sick? . . . Are you out of your mind or are you just stupid?

In another exercise, Garfinkel asked students to take words and phrases literally. When a student asked his girlfriend what she meant when she said that she had a flat tire, she said:

> What do you mean, "What do you mean?" A flat tire is a flat tire. That is what I meant. Nothing special. What a crazy question!

Another conversation went like this:

ACQUAINTANCE: How are you?
STUDENT: How am I in regard to what? My health, my finances, my school-work, my peace of mind, my . . . ?
ACQUAINTANCE: (red in the face): Look! I was just trying to be polite. Frankly, I don't give a damn how you are.

Students can be highly creative when they are asked to break background assumptions. The young children of one of my students were surprised one morning when they came down for breakfast to find a sheet spread on the living room floor. On it were dishes, silverware, lit candles—and bowls of ice cream. They, too, wondered what was going on, but they dug eagerly into the ice cream before their mother could change her mind.

This is a risky assignment to give students, however, for breaking some background assumptions can make people suspicious. When a colleague of mine gave this assignment, a couple of his students began to wash dollar bills in a laundromat. By the time they put the bills in the dryer, the police had arrived.

In Sum: Ethnomethodologists explore *background assumptions*, the taken-for-granted ideas about the world that underlie our behavior. Most of these assumptions, or basic

ethnomethodology the study of how people use background assumptions to make sense out of life

background assumption a deeply embedded, common understanding of how the world operates and of how people ought to act

What background assumptions do you have? How do they help you navigate social life?

Thomas theorem William I. and Dorothy S. Thomas' classic formulation of the definition of the situation: "If people define situations as real, they are real in their consequences"

social construction of reality the use of background assumptions and life experiences to define what is real

rules of social life, are unstated. We learn them as we learn our culture, and we violate them only with risk. Deeply embedded in our minds, they give us basic directions for living everyday life.

The Social Construction of Reality

On a visit to Morocco, in northern Africa, I decided to buy a watermelon. When I indicated to the street vendor that the knife he was going to use to cut the watermelon was dirty (encrusted with filth would be more apt), he was very obliging. He immediately bent down and began to swish the knife in a puddle on the street. I shuddered as I looked at the passing burros that were urinating and defecating as they went by. Quickly, I indicated by gesture that I preferred my melon uncut after all.

"If people define situations as real, they are real in their consequences," said sociologists W. I. and Dorothy S. Thomas in what has become known as *the definition of the situation,* or the **Thomas theorem.** For that vendor of watermelons, germs did not exist. For me, they did. And each of us acted according to our definition of the situation. My perception and behavior did not come from the fact that germs are real but, rather, from *my having grown up in a society that teaches that germs are real.* Microbes, of course, *objectively* exist, and whether or not germs are part of our thought world makes no difference as to whether we are infected by them. Our behavior, however, does not depend on the *objective* existence of something but, rather, on our *subjective interpretation,* on what sociologists call our *definition of reality.* In other words, it is not the reality of microbes that impresses itself on us, but society that impresses the reality of microbes on us.

Let's consider another example. Do you remember the identical twins, Oskar and Jack, who grew up so differently? Jack was reared in Trinidad and learned to hate Hitler, while Oskar was reared in Germany and learned to love Hitler. As you can see, what Hitler meant to Oskar and Jack (and what he means to us) depends not on Hitler's acts, but, rather, on how we view his acts—that is, on our definition of the situation.

Sociologists call this the **social construction of reality.** From the social groups to which we belong (the *social* part of this process), we learn ways of looking at life. We learn ways to view Hitler and Osama bin Laden (they're good, they're evil), germs (they exist, they don't exist), and *just about everything else in life.* In short, through our interaction with others, we *construct reality;* that is, we learn ways of interpreting our experiences in life.

Gynecological Examinations. To better understand the social construction of reality, consider pelvic examinations. When I interviewed a gynecological nurse who had been present at about 14,000 vaginal examinations, I focused on *how doctors construct social reality in order to define the examination as nonsexual* (Henslin and Biggs 1971/2012). It became apparent that the pelvic examination unfolds much as a stage play does. I will use "he" to refer to the physician because only male physicians were part of this study. Perhaps the results would be different with female gynecologists.

Scene 1 (the patient as person) *In this scene, the doctor maintains eye contact with his patient, calls her by name, and discusses her problems in a professional manner. If he decides that a vaginal examination is necessary, he tells a nurse, "Pelvic in room 1." By this statement, he is announcing that a major change will occur in the next scene.*

Scene 2 (from person to pelvic) *This scene is the depersonalizing stage. In line with the doctor's announcement, the patient begins the transition from a "person" to a "pelvic." The doctor leaves the room, and a female nurse enters to help the patient make the transition. The nurse prepares the "props" for the coming examination and answers any questions the woman might have.*

What occurs at this point is essential for the social construction of reality, for *the doctor's absence removes even the suggestion of sexuality.* To undress in front of him could

Do you understand the definition of the situation? How is it an essential part of your social interaction?

suggest either a striptease or intimacy, thus undermining the reality that the team is so carefully defining: that of nonsexuality.

The patient, too, wants to remove any hint of sexuality, and during this scene she may express concern about what to do with her panties. Some mutter to the nurse, "I don't want him to see these." Most women solve the problem by either slipping their panties under their other clothes or placing them in their purse.

> Scene 3 (the person as pelvic) *This scene opens when the doctor enters the room. Before him is a woman lying on a table, her feet in stirrups, her knees tightly together, and her body covered by a drape sheet. The doctor seats himself on a low stool before the woman and says, "Let your knees fall apart" (rather than the sexually loaded "Spread your legs"), and begins the examination.*

The drape sheet is crucial in this process of desexualization, for it *dissociates the pelvic area from the person:* Leaning forward and with the drape sheet above his head, the physician can see only the vagina, not the patient's face. Thus dissociated from the individual, the vagina is transformed dramaturgically into an object of analysis. If the doctor examines the patient's breasts, he also dissociates them from her person by examining them one at a time, with a towel covering the unexamined breast. Like the vagina, each breast becomes an isolated item dissociated from the person.

In this third scene, the patient cooperates in being an object, becoming, for all practical purposes, a pelvis to be examined. She withdraws eye contact from the doctor and usually from the nurse, is likely to stare at a wall or at the ceiling, and avoids initiating conversation.

> Scene 4 (from pelvic to person) *In this scene, the patient becomes "repersonalized." The doctor has left the examining room; the patient dresses and fixes her hair and makeup. Her reemergence as a person is indicated by such statements to the nurse as "My dress isn't too wrinkled, is it?" showing a need for reassurance that the metamorphosis from "pelvic" back to "person" has been completed satisfactorily.*

> Scene 5 (the patient as person) *In this final scene, sometimes with the doctor seated at a desk, the patient is once again treated as a person rather than as an object. The doctor makes eye contact with her and addresses her by name. She, too, makes eye contact with the doctor, and the usual middle-class interaction patterns are followed. She has been fully restored.*

In Sum: For an outsider to our culture, the custom of women going to male strangers for a vaginal examination might seem bizarre. But not to us. We learn that pelvic examinations are nonsexual. To sustain this definition requires teamwork—doctors, nurses, and the patient working together to *socially construct reality.*

It is not just pelvic examinations or our views of microbes that make up our definitions of reality. Rather, *our behavior depends on how we define reality.* Our definitions (our constructions of reality) provide the basis for what we do and how we view life. To understand human behavior, then, we must know how people define reality.

The Need for Both Macrosociology and Microsociology

As noted earlier, both microsociology and macrosociology make vital contributions to our understanding of human behavior. Without one or the other, our understanding of social life would be vastly incomplete. The photo essay on the next two pages should help to make clear why we need *both* perspectives.

To illustrate this point, let's consider two groups of high school boys studied by sociologist William Chambliss (1973/2012). Both groups attended Hanibal High

Why do we need both macrosociology and microsociology?

When a Tornado Strikes: Social Organization Following a Natural Disaster

As I was watching television on March 20, 2003, I heard a report that a tornado had hit Camilla, Georgia. "Like a big lawn mower," the report said, it had cut a path of destruction through this little town. In its fury, the tornado had left behind six dead and about 200 injured.

From sociological studies of natural disasters, I knew that immediately after the initial shock the survivors of natural disasters work together to try to restore order to their disrupted lives. I wanted to see this restructuring process first-hand. The next morning, I took off for Georgia.

These photos, taken the day after the tornado struck, tell the story of people in the midst of trying to put their lives back together. I was impressed at how little time people spent commiserating about their misfortune and how quickly they took practical steps to restore their lives.

As you look at these photos, try to determine why you need both microsociology and macrosociology to understand what occurs after a natural disaster.

For children, family photos are not as important as toys. This girl has managed to salvage a favorite toy, which will help anchor her to her previous life.

Personal relationships are essential in putting lives together. Consequently, reminders of these relationships are one of the main possessions that people attempt to salvage. This young man, having just recovered the family photo album, is eagerly reviewing the photos.

After making sure that their loved ones are safe, one of the next steps people take is to recover their possessions. The cooperation that emerges among people, as documented in the sociological literature on natural disasters, is illustrated here.

© James M. Henslin

In addition to the inquiring sociologist, television teams also were interviewing survivors and photographing the damage. This was the second time in just three years that a tornado had hit this neighborhood.

GEORGIA

Formal organizations also help the survivors of natural disasters recover. In this neighborhood, I saw representatives of insurance companies, the police, the fire department, and an electrical co-op. The Salvation Army brought meals to the neighborhood.

No building or social institution escapes a tornado as it follows its path of destruction. Just the night before, members of this church had held evening worship service. After the tornado, someone mounted a U.S. flag on top of the cross, symbolic of the church members' patriotism and religiosity—and of their enduring hope.

The owners of this house invited me inside to see what the tornado had done to their home. In what had been her dining room, this woman is trying to salvage whatever she can from the rubble. She and her family survive by taking refuge in the bathroom. They had been there only five seconds, she said, when the tornado struck.

Like electricity and gas, communications need to be restored as soon as possible.

School. In one group were eight middle-class boys who came from "good" families and were perceived by the community as "going somewhere." Chambliss calls this group the "Saints." The other group consisted of six lower-class boys who were seen as headed down a dead-end road. Chambliss calls this group the "Roughnecks."

Boys in both groups skipped school, got drunk, got in fights, and vandalized property. The Saints were actually truant more often and involved in more vandalism, but the Saints had a good reputation. It was the Roughnecks who were seen by teachers, the police, and the general community as no good and headed for trouble.

The boys' reputations set them on distinct paths. Seven of the eight Saints went on to graduate from college. Three studied for advanced degrees: One finished law school and became active in state politics, one finished medical school, and one went on to earn a Ph.D. The four other college graduates entered managerial or executive training programs with large firms. After his parents divorced, one Saint failed to graduate from high school on time and had to repeat his senior year. Although this boy tried to go to college by attending night school, he never finished. He was unemployed the last time Chambliss saw him.

In contrast, only four of the Roughnecks finished high school. Two of these boys did exceptionally well in sports and were awarded athletic scholarships to college. They both got degrees and became high school coaches. Of the two others who graduated from high school, one became a small-time gambler and the other disappeared "up north," where he was last reported to be driving a truck. The two who did not complete high school were convicted of separate murders and sent to prison.

To understand what happened to the Saints and the Roughnecks, we need to grasp both social structure and social interaction. Using *macrosociology,* we can place these boys within the larger framework of the U.S. social class system. This reveals how opportunities open or close to people depending on their social class and how people learn different goals as they grow up in different groups. We can then use *microsociology* to follow their everyday lives. We can see how the Saints manipulated their "good" reputations to skip classes and how their access to automobiles allowed them to protect their reputations by spreading their troublemaking around different communities. In contrast, the Roughnecks, who did not have cars, were highly visible. Their lawbreaking, which was limited to a small area, readily came to the attention of the community. Microsociology also reveals how their reputations opened doors of opportunity to the first group of boys while closing them to the other.

It is clear that we need both kinds of sociology.

Summary and Review

Levels of Sociological Analysis

What two levels of analysis do sociologists use?

Sociologists use macrosociological and microsociological levels of analysis. In **macrosociology,** the focus is placed on large-scale features of social life, while in **microsociology,** the focus is on **social interaction.** Functionalists and conflict theorists tend to use a macrosociological approach, while symbolic interactionists are more likely to use a microsociological approach.

The Macrosociological Perspective: Social Structure

How does social structure influence our behavior?

The term **social structure** refers to the social envelope that surrounds us and establishes limits on our behavior. Social structure consists of culture, social class, social statuses, roles, groups, and social institutions. Our location in the social structure underlies our perceptions, attitudes, and behaviors.

Culture lays the broadest framework, while **social class** divides people according to income, education, and occupational prestige. Each of us receives **ascribed statuses** at birth; later we add **achieved statuses.** Our statuses guide our roles, put boundaries around our behavior, and give us orientations to life. These are further influenced by the **groups** to which we belong, and our experiences with social institutions. These components of society work together to help maintain social order.

What are social institutions?

Social institutions are the standard ways that a society develops to meet its basic needs. As summarized in Figure 2, industrial and postindustrial societies have ten social institutions—the family, religion, education, economy, medicine, politics, law, science, the military, and the mass media. From the functionalist perspective, social institutions meet universal group needs, or *functional requisites.* Conflict theorists stress how society's elites use social institutions to maintain their privileged positions.

What holds society together?

According to Emile Durkheim, in agricultural societies people are united by **mechanical solidarity** (having similar views and feelings). With industrialization comes **organic solidarity** (people depend on one another to do their more specialized jobs). Ferdinand Tönnies pointed out that the informal means of control in *Gemeinschaft* (small, intimate) societies are replaced by formal mechanisms in *Gesellschaft* (larger, more impersonal) societies.

The Microsociological Perspective: Social Interaction in Everyday Life

What is the focus of symbolic interactionism?

In contrast to functionalists and conflict theorists, who as macrosociologists focus on the "big picture," symbolic interactionists tend to be microsociologists who focus on face-to-face social interaction. Symbolic interactionists analyze how people define their worlds, and how their definitions, in turn, influence their behavior.

How do stereotypes affect social interaction?

Stereotypes are assumptions of what people are like. When we first meet people, we classify them according to our perceptions of their visible characteristics. Our ideas about these characteristics guide our reactions to them. Our behavior,

in turn, can influence them to behave in ways that reinforce our stereotypes.

Do all human groups share a similar sense of personal space?

In examining how people use physical space, symbolic interactionists stress that we surround ourselves with a "personal bubble" that we carefully protect. People from different cultures use "personal bubbles" of varying sizes, so the answer to the question is no. Americans typically use four different "distance zones": intimate, personal, social, and public.

What is body language?

Body language is using our bodies to give messages. We do this through facial expressions, posture, smiling, and eye contact. Interpreting unintended body language is becoming a tool in the fight against terrorism.

What is dramaturgy?

Erving Goffman developed **dramaturgy** (or dramaturgical analysis), in which everyday life is analyzed in terms of the stage. At the core of this analysis is **impression management,** our attempts to control the impressions we make on others. For this, we use the **sign-vehicles** of setting, appearance, and manner. Our **role performances** on the **front stages** of life often call for **teamwork** and **face-saving behavior.** They sometimes are hampered by **role conflict** or **role strain.**

What is ethnomethodology?

Ethnomethodology is the study of how people make sense of everyday life. Ethnomethodologists try to uncover **background assumptions,** the basic ideas about the way life is that guide our behavior.

What is the social construction of reality?

The phrase **social construction of reality** refers to how we construct our views of the world, which, in turn, underlie our actions.

The Need for Both Macrosociology and Microsociology

Why are both levels of analysis necessary?

Because microsociology and macrosociology focus on different aspects of the human experience, each is necessary for us to understand social life.

Thinking Critically about this Chapter

1. The major components of social structure are culture, social class, social status, roles, groups, and social institutions. Use social structure to explain why Native Americans have such a low rate of college graduation.

2. Dramaturgy is a form of microsociology. Use dramaturgy to analyze a situation with which you are intimately familiar (such as interaction with your family or friends or at work or in one of your college classes).

3. To illustrate why we need both macrosociology and microsociology to understand social life, analyze the situation of a student getting kicked out of college.

References

All new references are printed in cyan.

Aberle, David F., A. K. Cohen, A. K. David, M. J. Leng, Jr., and F. N. Sutton. "The Functional Prerequisites of a Society." *Ethics, 60,* January 1950:100–111.

Aeppel, Timothy. "More Amish Women Are Tending to Business." *Wall Street Journal,* February 8, 1996:B1, B2.

Agins, Teri. "When to Carry a Purse to a Meeting." *Wall Street Journal,* October 1, 2009.

Anderson, Elijah. *A Place on the Corner.* Chicago: University of Chicago Press, 1978.

Anderson, Elijah. *Streetwise: Race, Class, and Change in an Urban Community.* Chicago: University of Chicago Press, 1990.

Anderson, Elijah. "Streetwise." In *Exploring Social Life: Readings to Accompany Essentials of Sociology,* 2nd ed., James M. Henslin, ed. Boston: Allyn and Bacon, 2006:147–156. Originally published 1990.

Brinkley, Christina. "Women in Power: Finding Balance in the Wardrobe." *Wall Street Journal,* January 24, 2008.

Brunello, Giorgio, and Beatrice D'Hombres. "Does Body Weight Affect Wages? Evidence from Europe." *Economics and Human Biology, 5,* 2007:1–19.

Chambliss, William J. "The Saints and the Roughnecks." In *Down to Earth Sociology: Introductory Readings,* 15th ed., James M. Henslin, ed. New York: The Free Press, 2012.

Coyne, Tom. "Money or Tradition: Ind. Amish Face Uneasy Dilemma." Associated Press, May 9, 2009.

Davis, Ann, Joseph Pereira, and William M. Bulkeley. "Security Concerns Bring Focus on Translating Body Language." *Wall Street Journal,* August 15, 2002.

Dobriner, William M. "The Football Team as Social Structure and Social System." In *Social Structures and Systems: A Sociological Overview.* Pacific Palisades, Calif.: Goodyear, 1969a:116–120.

Domhoff, G. William. "The Bohemian Grove and Other Retreats." In *Down to Earth Sociology: Introductory Readings,* 10th ed., James M. Henslin, ed. New York: Free Press, 1999a:391–403.

Domhoff, G. William. "State and Ruling Class in Corporate America (1974): Reflections, Corrections, and New Directions." *Critical Sociology,* 25, 2–3, July 1999b:260–265.

Domhoff, G. William. *Who Rules America? Power, Politics, and Social Change,* 5th ed. New York: McGraw-Hill, 2006.

Domhoff, G. William. "C. Wright Mills, Power Structure Research, and the Failures of Mainstream Political Science." *New Political Science, 29,* 2007:97–114.

Duneier, Mitchell. *Sidewalk.* New York: Farrar, Straus and Giroux, 1999.

Durkheim, Emile. *The Division of Labor in Society,* George Simpson, trans. New York: Free Press, 1933. Originally published 1893.

Ebaugh, Helen Rose Fuchs. *Becoming an Ex: The Process of Role Exit.* Chicago: University of Chicago Press, 1988.

Garfinkel, Harold. *Studies in Ethnomethodology.* Englewood Cliffs, N.J.: Prentice Hall, 1967.

Garfinkel, Harold. *Ethnomethodology's Program: Working Out Durkheim's Aphorism.* Lanham, Md.: Rowman & Littlefield, 2002.

Goffman, Erving. *The Presentation of Self in Everyday Life.* New York: Peter Smith, 1999. Originally published 1959.

Grabe, Shelly, L. Monique Ward, and Janet Shibley Hyde. "The Role of the Media in Body Image Concerns among Women: A Meta-Analysis of Experimental and Correlational Studies." *Psychological Bulletin, 134,* 3:2008:460–476.

Gross, Jane. "In the Quest for the Perfect Look, More Girls Choose the Scalpel." *New York Times,* November 29, 1998.

Hall, Edward T. *The Silent Language.* New York: Doubleday, 1959.

Hall, Edward T. *The Hidden Dimension.* Garden City, N.Y.: Anchor Books, 1969.

Hall, Edward T., and Mildred R. Hall. "The Sounds of Silence." In *Down to Earth Sociology: Introductory Readings,* 15th ed., James M. Henslin, ed. New York: Free Press, 2012.

Hamermesh, Daniel S., and Jeff E. Biddle. "Beauty and the Labor Market." *American Economic Review, 84,* 5, December 1994:1174–1195.

Henslin, James M., and Mae A. Biggs. "Behavior in Pubic Places: The Sociology of the Vaginal Examination." In *Down to Earth Sociology: Introductory Readings,* 15th ed., James M. Henslin, ed. New York: Free Press, 2012. Originally published 1971.

Hughes, Kathleen A. "Even Tiki Torches Don't Guarantee a Perfect Wedding." *Wall Street Journal,* February 20, 1990:A1, A16.

Johnson-Weiner, Karen. *Train Up a Child: Old Order Amish and Mennonite Schools.* Baltimore: Johns Hopkins University Press, 2007.

Judge, Timothy A., Charlice Hurst, and Lauren S. Simon. "Does It Pay to Be Smart, Attractive, or Confident (or All Three)? Relationships among General Mental Ability, Physical Attractiveness, Core Self-Evaluations, and Income." *Journal of Applied Psychology, 94,* 3, 2009:742–755.

Kanazawa, Satoshi, and Jody L. Kovar. "Why Beautiful People Are More Intelligent." *Intelligence, 32,* 2004:227–243.

Kephart, William M., and William W. Zellner. *Extraordinary Groups: An Examination of Unconventional Life-Styles,* 7th ed. New York: Worth Publishing, 2001.

Kraybill, Donald B. *The Riddle of Amish Culture,* rev. ed. Baltimore: Johns Hopkins University Press, 2002.

Liebow, Elliott. *Tally's Corner: A Study of Negro Streetcorner Men* Boston: Little, Brown, 1999. Originally published 1967.

Linton, Ralph. *The Study of Man.* New York: Appleton-Century-Crofts, 1936.

Mack, Raymond W., and Calvin P. Bradford. *Transforming America: Patterns of Social Change,* 2nd ed. New York: Random House, 1979.

Marshall, Samantha. "It's So Simple: Just Lather Up, Watch the Fat Go Down the Drain." *Wall Street Journal,* November 2, 1995:B1.

Needham, Sarah E. "Grooming Women for the Top: Tips from Executive Coaches." *Wall Street Journal,* October 31, 2006.

Pfann, Gerard A., et al. "Business Success and Businesses' Beauty Capital." *Economics Letters, 67,* 2, May 2000:201–207.

Samor, Geraldo, Cecilie Rohwedder, and Ann Zimmerman. "Innocents Abroad?" *Wall Street Journal,* May 5, 2006.

Scolforo, Mark. "Amish Population Nearly Doubles in 16 Years." *Chicago Tribune,* August 20, 2008.

Snyder, Mark. "Self-Fulfilling Stereotypes." In *Down to Earth Sociology: Introductory Readings,* 7th ed., James M. Henslin, ed. New York: Free Press, 1993:153–160.

Tönnies, Ferdinand. *Community and Society (Gemeinschaft und Gesellschaft),* with a new introduction by John Samples. New Brunswick, N.J.: Transaction, 1988. Originally published 1887.

Useem, Michael. *The Inner Circle: Large Corporations and the Rise of Business Political Activity in the U.S. and U.K.* New York: Oxford University Press, 1984.

Volti, Rudi. *Society and Technological Change,* 3rd ed. New York: St. Martin's Press, 1995.

Zaslow, Jeffrey. "Thinness, Women, and School Girls: Body Image." *Wall Street Journal,* September 2, 2009.

Societies to Social Networks

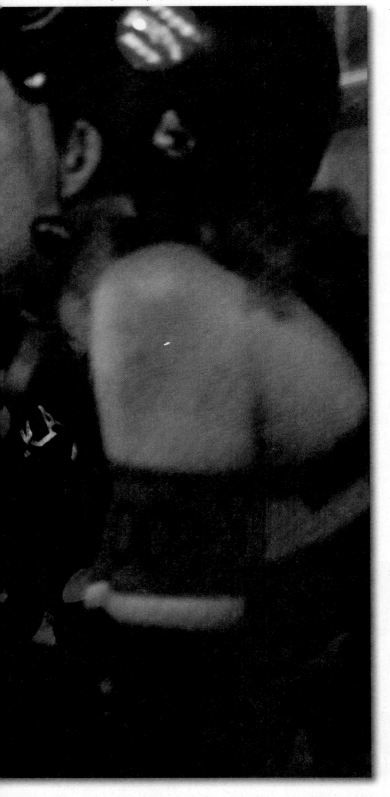

When Kody Scott joined the L.A. Crips, his initiation had two parts. Here's the first:

> *"How old is you now anyway?"*
> *"Eleven, but I'll be twelve in November."*
> *I never saw the blow to my head come from Huck. Bam! And I was on all fours. . . . Kicked in the stomach, I was on my back counting stars in the blackness. A solid blow to my chest exploded pain on the blank screen that had now become my mind. Bam! Blows rained on me from every direction. . . .*
> *Then I just started swinging, with no style or finesse, just anger and the instinct to survive. . . . [This] reflected my ability to represent the set [gang] in hand-to-hand combat. The blows stopped abruptly. . . . My ear was bleeding, and my neck and face were deep red. . . .*

Scott's beating was followed immediately by the second part of his initiation. For this, he received the name *Monster,* which he carried proudly:

> *"Give Kody the pump"* [12-gauge pump action shotgun] . . . *"Tonight we gonna rock they world."* . . . *Hand slaps were passed around the room. . . . "Kody, you got eight shots, you don't come back to the car unless they all are gone."*

> **"Kody, you got eight shots, you don't come back to the car unless they all are gone."**

> *"Righteous," I said, eager to show my worth. . . .*
> *Hanging close to buildings, houses, and bushes, we made our way, one after the other, to within spitting distance of the Bloods. . . . Huck and Fly stepped from the shadows simultaneously. . . . Boom! Boom! Heavy bodies hitting the ground, confusion, yells of dismay, running. . . . By my sixth shot I had advanced past the first fallen bodies and into the street in pursuit of those who had sought refuge behind cars and trees. . . .*
> *Back in the shack we smoked more pot and drank more beer. . . .*
> *Tray Ball said, "You got potential, 'cause you eager to learn. Bangin' [being a gang member] ain't no part-time thang, it's full-time, it's a career. . . . It's gettin' caught and not tellin'. Killin' and not caring, and dyin' without fear. It's love for your set and hate for the enemy. You hear what I'm sayin'?"*

Kody adds this insightful remark:

> *. . . The supreme sacrifice was to "take a bullet for a homie" [fellow gang member]. Nothing held a light to the power of the set. If you died on the trigger you surely were smiled upon by the Crip God.*

Excerpts from Scott 1994:8–13, 103.

British Columbia, Canada

group people who have something in common and who believe that what they have in common is significant; also called a *social group*

society people who share a culture and a territory

hunting and gathering society a human group that depends on hunting and gathering for its survival

shaman the healing specialist of a tribe who attempts to control the spirits thought to cause a disease or injury; commonly called a witch doctor

Could you be like Kody and shoot strangers in cold blood—just because others tell you to pull the trigger? Although none of us want to think that we could, don't bet on it. In this chapter, you are going to read some surprising things about **groups**—people who interact with one another and who think of themselves as belonging together. As we move into this topic, let's first look at the big picture, how societies have changed over time.

Societies and Their Transformation

The largest and most complex group that sociologists study is **society,** which consists of people who share a culture and a territory. Society, which surrounds us, sets the stage for our life experiences. *The sociological principle is that the type of society we live in is the fundamental reason for why we become who we are.* Not only does our society lay the broad framework for our behavior, but it also influences the ways we think and feel. Its effects are so significant that if you had grown up in a different society, you would be a different type of person.

To see how our society developed, look at Figure 1 on the next page. You can see that technology is the key to understanding the sweeping changes that produced our society. Let's review these broad changes. As we do, picture yourself as a member of each society. Consider how your life—even your thoughts and values—would be different as a member of these societies.

Hunting and Gathering Societies

As the name implies, for their survival the members of **hunting and gathering societies** depend on hunting animals and gathering plants. In some groups, the men do the hunting, and the women the gathering. In others, both men and women (and children) gather plants, the men hunt large animals, and both men and women hunt small animals. The groups usually have a **shaman,** an individual thought to be able to influence spiritual forces, but shamans, too, must help obtain food. Although these groups give greater prestige to the men hunters, who supply most of the meat, the women gatherers contribute more food to the group, perhaps even four-fifths of their total food supply (Bernard 1992).

Hunting and gathering societies are small. Groups usually have only twenty-five to forty members. This is because a region cannot support a large number of people who hunt animals and gather plants (group members do not plant—they only gather what is already there). For the same reason, these groups are nomadic. As their food supply dwindles in one area, they move to another location. Because of disease, drought, and pestilence, children have only about a fifty-fifty chance of surviving to adulthood (Lenski and Lenski 1987).

Of all societies, hunters and gatherers are the most egalitarian. Because what they hunt and gather is perishable, the people accumulate few personal possessions. Consequently, no one becomes wealthier than anyone else. There are no rulers, and most decisions are arrived at through discussion. Because their needs are basic and they do not work to store up material possessions, hunters and gatherers have the most leisure of all human groups (Sahlins 1972; Volti 1995).

All human groups were once hunters and gatherers. Until several hundred years ago, these societies were common, but only about 300 remain today (Stiles 2003). Some were wiped out when different groups took over their lands. Others moved to villages and took up a new way of life. The hunting and gathering groups that remain include the pygmies of central Africa, the aborigines of Australia,

Tobias Schwarz/Reuters/Corbis

As society—the largest and most complex type of group—changes, so, too, do the groups, activities, and, ultimately, the type of people who form that society. This photo is of Asa Sandell, Sweden, and Laila Ali, United States, as they fought in Berlin. What social changes can you identify from this photo?

What are the main characteristics of hunting and gathering societies?

and various groups in South America. With today's expanding populations, these groups seem doomed to a similar fate, with their way of life disappearing from the human scene (Lenski and Lenski 1987; Bearak 2010).

Pastoral and Horticultural Societies

About ten thousand years ago, some groups found that they could tame and breed some of the animals they hunted—primarily goats, sheep, cattle, and camels. Others discovered that they could cultivate plants. As a result, hunting and gathering societies branched into two directions, each with different means of acquiring food.

The key to understanding the first branching is the word pasture; **pastoral** (or herding) **societies** are based on the *pasturing of animals*. Pastoral societies developed in regions where low rainfall made it impractical to build life around growing crops. Groups that took this turn remained nomadic, for they follow their animals to fresh pasture. The key to understanding the second branching is the word *horticulture*, or plant cultivation. **Horticultural** (or gardening) **societies** are based on the *cultivation of plants by the use of hand tools*. Because they no longer had to abandon an area as the food supply gave out, these groups developed permanent settlements.

We can call the domestication of animals and plants the *first social revolution*. As shown in Figure 2, the **domestication revolution** changed human history. The changes, which occurred over thousands of years, touched almost every aspect of human life. The more dependable food supply allowed groups to grow larger. With it no longer necessary for everyone to work at providing food, a *division of labor* developed. Some people began to make jewelry, others tools, others weapons, and so on. This led to a surplus of objects, which, in turn, stimulated trade. As groups traded with one another, they began to accumulate objects they prized, such as gold, jewelry, and utensils.

From Figure 2, you can see how these changes led to *social inequality*. Some families (or clans) acquired more goods than others. This led to feuds and war, for groups now possessed animals, pastures, croplands, jewelry, and other material goods to fight about. War, in turn, opened the door to slavery, for people found it convenient to let captives do their drudge work. Social inequality remained limited, however, for the surplus itself was limited. But as individuals passed their possessions on to their descendants, wealth grew more concentrated. So did power, and for the first time, some individuals became chiefs.

Note the pattern that runs through this transformation: the change from *fewer to more possessions and from greater to lesser equality*. As it is now, where people were located *within* the hierarchy of a society became vital for determining what happened to them in life.

Agricultural Societies

The invention of the plow about five or six thousand years ago once again changed social life forever. Compared with hoes and digging sticks, using animals to pull plows is immensely more efficient. As the earth was plowed, more nutrients were returned to the

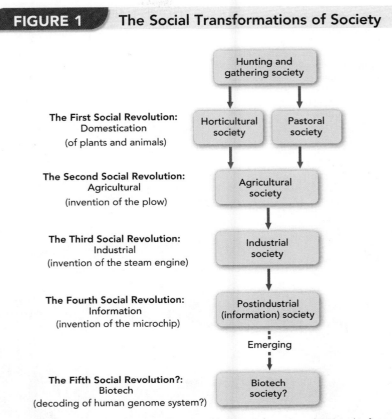

FIGURE 1   **The Social Transformations of Society**

Hunting and gathering society

The First Social Revolution: Domestication (of plants and animals) → Horticultural society | Pastoral society

The Second Social Revolution: Agricultural (invention of the plow) → Agricultural society

The Third Social Revolution: Industrial (invention of the steam engine) → Industrial society

The Fourth Social Revolution: Information (invention of the microchip) → Postindustrial (information) society

Emerging

The Fifth Social Revolution?: Biotech (decoding of human genome system?) → Biotech society?

Note: Not all the world's societies will go through the transformations shown in this figure. Whether any hunting and gathering societies will survive, however, remains to be seen. A few might, perhaps kept on small "reserves" that will be off limits to developers—but open to guided "ethnotours" at a hefty fee.

Source: By the author.

pastoral society a society based on the pasturing of animals

horticultural society a society based on cultivating plants by the use of hand tools

domestication revolution the first social revolution, based on the domestication of plants and animals, which led to pastoral and horticultural societies

agricultural society a society based on large-scale agriculture

agricultural revolution the second social revolution, based on the invention of the plow, which led to agricultural societies

How did social inequality emerge? How is it related to changes in society?

The simplest forms of societies are called hunting and gathering societies. Members of these societies have adapted well to their environments, and they have more leisure than the members of other societies. Not many hunting and gathering groups remain on earth. This Hambukushu woman of Botswana is fishing.

Frans Lanting/Corbis

soil, making the land more productive. The food surplus of the **agricultural revolution** was unlike anything ever seen in human history. It allowed even more people to engage in activities other than farming. In this new **agricultural society,** people developed cities and what is popularly known as "culture," activities such as philosophy, art, music, literature, and architecture. Accompanied by other fundamental inventions, like the wheel, writing, and numbers, the changes were so profound that this period is sometimes referred to as "the dawn of civilization."

The social inequality of pastoral and horticultural societies turned out to be only a hint of what was to come. When some people managed to gain control of the growing surplus of resources in agricultural societies, *inequality became a fundamental feature of life in society.* To protect their expanding privileges and power, this elite surrounded itself with armed men. This small group even levied taxes on others, who now had become their "subjects." As conflict theorists point out, this concentration of resources and power—along with the oppression of people not in power—was the forerunner of the state.

No one knows exactly how it happened, but during this period females also became subject to males. Sociologist Elise Boulding (1976) theorizes that this change occurred because men were in charge of plowing and the cows. She suggests that when metals were developed, men took on the new job of attaching the metal as tips to the wooden plows and doing the plowing. As a result,

> the shift of the status of the woman farmer may have happened quite rapidly, once there were two male specializations relating to agriculture: plowing and the care of cattle. This situation left women with all the subsidiary tasks, including weeding and carrying water to the fields. The new fields were larger, so women had to work just as many hours as they did before, but now they worked at more secondary tasks. . . . This would contribute further to the erosion of the status of women.

This explanation, however, raises more questions than it answers. Why, for example, did men take over metal work and plowing? Why didn't women? It also does not account for why men control societies in which women are in charge of the cattle. In short, we are left in the dark as to why and how men became dominant, a reason likely to remain lost in human history. This leaves us a topic perfect for endless speculation, as we try to tie together different strands of history. What do you think? Was it metal tips or something more fundamental?

Industrial Societies

The *third* social revolution also turned society upside down. The **Industrial Revolution** began in Great Britain in 1765 when the steam engine was first used to run machinery. Before this, a few machines (such as windmills and water wheels) had helped to harness nature, but most machines depended on human and animal power. The resulting **industrial society** is defined by sociologist Herbert Blumer (1990) as one in which goods are produced by machines powered by fuels, instead of by the brute force of humans or animals.

The efficiency of the steam engine, greater than anything that preceded it, was another push toward even more social inequality. The cities had a massive supply of desperate labor, people who had been thrown off the lands that their ancestors had farmed as tenants for centuries. Homeless, they faced the choice of stealing, starving, or being paid the equivalent of a loaf of bread for a day of work. Some of the men who first harnessed the steam engine and employed these desperate workers accumulated such wealth that their riches outran the imagination of royalty.

Workers had few legal rights. They could not unionize, and they didn't even have the right to safe working conditions. If workers protested, they were fired. If they returned to the factory, they were arrested for trespassing on private property. Strikes were illegal, and strikers were arrested—or beaten by the employer's private security force. During the early 1900s, some U.S. strikers were shot by private police and even by the National Guard. Against these odds, workers gradually won their fight to unionize and to improve their working conditions.

Industrialization brought an abundance of goods, and as workers won what we call basic rights, a surprising change occurred—*the pattern of growing inequality was reversed.* Home ownership became common, as did the ownership of automobiles and an incredible variety of consumer goods. Today's typical worker enjoys a high standard of living in terms of health care, food, housing, material possessions, and access to libraries and education. On an even broader scale of growing equality came the abolition of slavery, the shift from monarchies to more representative political systems, greater rights for women and minorities, and the rights to vote, to a jury trial, and to cross-examine witnesses. A recent extension of these equalities is the right to set up your own Internet blog where you can bemoan life in your school or criticize the president.

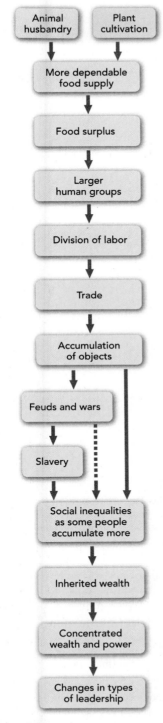

FIGURE 2 Consequences of Animal Domestication and Plant Cultivation

Source: By the author.

Boulding, Elise. *The Underside of History.* Boulder, Colo.: Westview Press, 1976.

How did gender inequality develop? How did social inequality decrease?

Postindustrial (Information) Societies

If you were to choose one word to characterize our society, what would it be? Of the many candidates, the word *change* would have to rank high. The primary source of the sweeping changes that are transforming our lives is the development of technology centering on the microchip. The change is so vast that sociologists say that a new type of society has emerged. They call it the **postindustrial** (or **information**) **society.**

What are the main characteristics of this new society? Unlike industrial society, its hallmark is not turning raw materials into products. Rather, its basic component is *information*. Teachers pass knowledge on to students, while lawyers sell their specialized understanding of law, physicians their expertise on the body, bankers their skills with money, and interior decorators their ideas regarding color schemes. Unlike the factory workers of an industrial society, these individuals don't *produce* anything. Rather, they transmit or apply information to provide services that others are willing to pay for.

The United States was the first country to have more than half of its workers in service industries such as banking, counseling, education, entertainment, government, health, insurance, law, mass media, research, and sales. Australia, Japan, New Zealand, and western Europe soon followed. This trend away from manufacturing and toward selling information and services shows no sign of letting up.

The changes are so profound that they have led to a *fourth social revolution*. The surface changes of this new technology are obvious. Our purchases are scanned and billed in some remote place. While we ride in cars, trucks, boats, and airplanes, we can call home or talk to people on the other side of the globe. We probe remote regions of space and examine the surface of Mars. We pay out billions of dollars on Internet purchases, and millions of children (and adults) spend countless hours battling virtual video villains. Beyond these surface changes, the microchip is transforming relations among people. It is also uprooting our old perspectives and replacing them with new ones. In the Sociology and the New Technology box on the next page, we explore an extreme aspect of virtual reality.

Biotech Societies: Is a New Type of Society Emerging?

- Tobacco that fights cancer. ("Yes, smoke your way to health!")
- Corn that blocks herpes and prevents pregnancy. ("Corn flakes in the morning—and safe sex all day!")
- Goats' milk that contains spider silk to make fishing lines and body armor. ("Got milk? The best bulletproofing.")
- Part-human animals that produce medicines for humans. ("Ah, those liver secretions. Good for what ails you.")
- DNA that you can snap together like Lego blocks. ("Our BioBricks build better life forms.")
- Bacteria that excrete diesel fuel. ("Put our germ droppings in your gas tank.")

I know that such products sound like science fiction, but we *already* have the goats that make spider silk. Human genes have been inserted into animals, and they do produce medicine (Elias 2001; Kristoff 2002; Osborne 2002). The snap-together BioBricks should be available soon (Mooallem 2010). Perhaps one day, you will be able to design your own bacterium—or elephant. We already have the bacteria that produce diesel fuel, but it isn't harvestable yet (Mooallem 2010).

The changes swirling around us are so extensive that we may be stepping into a new type of society. If so, the economy of this new **biotech society** will center on applying and altering genetic structures—both plant and animal—to produce food, medicine, and materials.

If there is a new society—and this is not certain—when did it begin? There are no firm edges to new societies, for each new one overlaps the one it is replacing. The opening to a biotech society could have been 1953, when Francis Crick and James Watson identified the double-helix structure of DNA. Or perhaps historians will trace the date to the decoding of the human genome in 2001.

Industrial Revolution the third social revolution, occurring when machines powered by fuels replaced most animal and human power

industrial society a society based on the harnessing of machines powered by fuels

postindustrial (information) society a society based on information, services, and high technology, rather than on raw materials and manufacturing

biotech society a society whose economy increasingly centers on modifyied genetics to produce food, medicine, and materials

What are the main characteristics of postindustrial and biotech societies?

Sociology and the New Technology

Avatar Fantasy Life: The Blurring Lines of Reality

Dissatisfied with your current life? Would you like to become someone else? Maybe someone rich? You can. Join a world populated with virtual people and live out your fantasy.

Second Life and other Internet sites that offer an alternative virtual reality have exploded in popularity. Of the 8 million "residents" of *Second Life*, 450,000 spend twenty to forty hours a week in their alternative life (Alter 2007).

To start your second life, you select your avatar, a kind of digital hand puppet, to be your persona in this virtual world. Your avatar comes in just a basic form, although you can control its movements just fine. But that bare body certainly won't do. You will want to clothe it. For this, you have your choice of outfits for every occasion. Although you buy them from other avatars in virtual stores, you have to spend real dollars. You might want some hair, too. For that, too, you'll have your choice of designers. And again, you'll spend real dollars. And you might want to have a sex organ. There is even a specialty store for that.

All equipped the way you want to be?

Then it is time to meet other avatars, the virtual personas of real-life people. As you interact with them in this virtual world, you will be able to share stories, talk about your desires in life, and have drinks in virtual bars. You can also buy property and open businesses.

Avatars flirt, too. Some even date and marry.

For most people, this second life is just an interesting game. They come and go, as if playing *Tomb Raider* or *World of Warcraft* now and then. Some people, though, get so caught up in their virtual world that their everyday life shrinks in appeal, and they neglect friends and family. For them, the virtual displaces the real, with the real fading into nonreality.

Ric Hoogestraat in Phoenix, Arizona, operates his avatar, Dutch—a macho motorcycle man, who is also filthy rich—from the time he gets up to the time he goes to bed. Dutch visits his several homes, where he can lounge on specially designed

A scene from Second Life. *Each image is an avatar, a real person's fantasy self.*
LINDEN/SIPA/Newscom

furniture. He pours his favorite drink and from his penthouse watches the sun setting over the ocean (Alter 2007).

Dutch met his wife, Tenaj, on *Second Life*. As courtships go, theirs went well. Their wedding was announced, of course, and about twenty avatar friends attended. They gave the newlyweds real congratulations, in a virtual sort of way.

Dutch and Tenaj have two dogs and pay the mortgage together. They love cuddling and intimate talks. Their love life is quite good, as avatars can have virtual sex.

But Sue is not pleased that Ric spends so much time in his virtual world. Sue feels neglected. She also doesn't appreciate Tenaj. Sue, you see, is also Ric's wife, but in real life.

The whole thing has become more than a little irritating. "I'll try to talk to him or bring him a drink, and he'll be having sex with a cartoon," she says.

The real life counterpart of Tenaj, the avatar, is Janet, who lives in Canada. Ric and Janet have never met—nor do they plan to meet. They haven't even talked on the phone as Ric and Janet—just a lot of sweet talking in their virtual world as Dutch and Tenaj.

For gamers, the virtual always overlaps the real to some extent, but for some the virtual overwhelms the real. A couple from South Korea even let their 3-month old daughter starve to death while they nurtured a virtual daughter online (Frayer 2010).

For Your Consideration

→ How much time do you spend on computer games? Are you involved in any virtual reality? Do you think that Ric is cheating on Sue? (One wife divorced her husband when she caught a glimpse of his avatar having sex with an avatar prostitute ["Second Life Affair . . ." 2008]). Other than the sexual aspect, is having a second life really any different from people's involvement in fantasy football? (Keep in mind the term *football widows*.)

Whether the changes that are engulfing our lives are part of a new type of society or just a continuation of the one before it is not the main point. Keep your eye on the *sociological significance of these changes: As society is transformed, it sweeps us along with it. The transformation we are experiencing is so fundamental that it will change even the ways we think about the self and life.* We might even see changes in the human species, an implication of the Sociology and the New Technology box on the next page.

👁 Watch
Play Again
on mysoclab.com

How does the microchip affect your life? Influence your views of life?

"So, You Want to Be Yourself?" Cloning and the Future of Society

No type of society ends abruptly. The edges are fuzzy, as the old merges into the new. With time speeded up, our information society hasn't even matured, and it looks as though a biotech society is hard on its heels. Let's try to peer over the edge of today's society to glimpse the one that might be pressing on us. If it arrives, what will life be like? We could examine many issues, but since space is limited, let's consider just one: cloning. Since human embryos have been cloned, it seems inevitable that some group somewhere will complete the process. If cloning humans becomes routine—well, consider these two scenarios:

It turns out that you can't have children. You go to your area's cloning clinic, pay the standard fee, and clone either yourself or your spouse. But is that little boy or girl, in effect, either yourself or your spouse—as a child? Or instead of a daughter or son, is this child even your sister or brother?

Or suppose that you love your mother dearly, and she is dying. With her permission, you decide to clone her. Who is the clone? Would you be rearing your own mother?

© Stockbyte/Getty Images Royalty Free

When we have genetic replicates, we will have to wrestle with new questions of human relationships: What is a clone's relationship to its "parents"? Indeed, what are "parents" and "children"?

Sources: Based on Kaebnick 2000; McGee 2000; Bjerklie et al. 2001; Davis 2001; Weiss 2004; Regalado 2005.

For Your Consideration

→ I'm sure you have heard people object that cloning is immoral. But have you heard the opposite, that cloning should be our moral choice? Let's suppose that mass cloning becomes possible. Let's also assume that geneticists trace to specific genes such characteristics as great creative ability, high intelligence, compassion, and a propensity for peace—along with the ability to create beautiful poetry, music, and architecture; to excel in mathematics, science, and other intellectual pursuits; even to be successful in love. Why, then, should we leave human reproduction to people who have inferior traits—genetic diseases, low IQs, perhaps even the propensity to be violent? Should we select people with the finer characteristics to reproduce—and to clone?

In Sum: Each society sets boundaries around its members. By laying a framework of statuses, roles, groups, and social institutions, society establishes the prevailing behaviors and beliefs. It also determines the type and extent of social inequality. These factors, in turn, set the stage for relationships between men and women, racial–ethnic groups, the young and the elderly, the rich and the poor, and so on.

Society is not stagnant, and *you* are affected directly by the sweeping historical changes that transform it. On the obvious level, if you lived in a hunting and gathering society you would not be listening to your favorite music, watching TV, playing video games—or taking this course. On a deeper level, you would not feel the same about life, have the same beliefs, or hold your particular aspirations for the future. Actually, no aspect of your life would be the same. You would be locked into the attitudes and views that come with a hunting and gathering way of life.

Introducing you to these major historical shifts in societies is just the beginning of what we want to do in this chapter. The goal is to help you understand how groups influence your life. So let's continue.

Groups within Society

Our society is huge and dominating, sometimes even threatening and oppressive. This can create a bewildering sense of not belonging. Sociologist Emile Durkheim (1893/1933) called this condition *anomie* (AN-uh-mee). He said that small groups help prevent anomie by standing as a buffer between the individual and the larger society. By providing intimate relationships, small groups give us a sense of belonging, something that we all need. Because smaller groups are essential for our well-being, let's look at them in detail.

How do people's views of life depend on the type of society they live in? How about yours?

But first, let's distinguish two terms that are sometimes confused with "group," *aggregate* and *category*. An **aggregate** consists of individuals who temporarily share the same physical space but who do not see themselves as belonging together. Shoppers standing in a checkout line or drivers waiting at a red light are an aggregate. A **category** is simply a statistic. It consists of people who share similar characteristics, such as all college women who wear glasses or all men over 6 feet tall. Unlike group members, the individuals who make up a category don't think of themselves as belonging together, and they don't interact with one another. These concepts are illustrated in the photos on the next page.

Primary Groups

How important has your family been to you?

Your first group, the family, has given you your basic orientations to life. Later, among friends, you have found more intimacy and an expanded sense of belonging. These groups are what sociologist Charles Cooley called **primary groups.** By providing intimate, face-to-face interaction, they give us an identity, a feeling of who we are. As Cooley (1909) put it,

> By primary groups I mean those characterized by intimate face-to-face association and cooperation. They are primary in several senses, but chiefly in that they are fundamental in forming the social nature and ideals of the individual.

Producing a Mirror Within.   Cooley, who developed the concept *looking glass self,* called primary groups the "springs of life." By this, he meant that primary groups, such as family and friends, are essential to our emotional well-being. As humans, we have an intense need for face-to-face interaction that generates feelings of self-esteem. By offering a sense of belonging and a feeling of being appreciated—and sometimes even loved—primary groups are uniquely equipped to meet this basic need. From our opening vignette, you can see that gangs are also primary groups.

Primary groups are also significant because their values and attitudes become fused into our identity. We internalize their views, which then become the lenses through which we view life. Even when we are adults—no matter how far we move away from our childhood roots—early primary groups remain "inside" us. There, they continue to form part of the perspective from which we look out onto the world. Ultimately, then, it is difficult, if not impossible, for us to separate the self from our primary groups, for inside us the self and these groups merge into a "we."

Secondary Groups

Compared with primary groups, **secondary groups** are larger, more anonymous, and more formal and impersonal. These groups are based on shared interests or activities, and their members are likely to interact on the basis of specific statuses, such as president, manager, worker, or student. Examples include college classes, the American Sociological Association, and the Democratic Party. Contemporary society could not function without secondary groups. They are part of the way we get our education, make our living, spend our money, and use our leisure time.

As necessary as secondary groups are for contemporary life, they often fail to satisfy our deep needs for intimate association. Consequently, *secondary groups tend to break down into primary groups.* At school and work, we form friendships. Our interaction with our friends is so important that we sometimes feel that if it weren't for them, school or work "would drive us crazy." The primary groups that we form within secondary groups, then, serve as a buffer between ourselves and the demands that secondary groups place on us.

aggregate individuals who temporarily share the same physical space but who do not see themselves as belonging together

category people, objects, and events that have similar characteristics and are classified together

primary group a small group characterized by intimate, long-term, face-to-face association and cooperation

secondary group compared with a primary group, a larger, relatively temporary, more anonymous, formal, and impersonal group based on some interest or activity

Why aren't categories and aggregates groups? Can you contrast primary and secondary groups?

Groups have a deep impact on our actions, views, orientations, even what we feel and think about life. Yet, as illustrated by these photos, not everything that appears to be a group is actually a group in the sociological sense.

Brand X Images/Jupiter Royalty Free

The outstanding trait that these three people have in common does not make them a group, but a **category**.

John Birdsall/The Image Works; Konstantin Sutyagin/Shutterstock; © Michael N. Paras/Veer Royalty Free

Primary groups such as the family play a key role in the development of the self. As a small group, the family also serves as a buffer from the often-threatening larger group known as society. The family has been of primary significance in forming the basic orientations of this couple, as it will be for their son.

REUTERS/Miss Universe Organization L.P., LLLP /Landov

Secondary groups are larger and more anonymous, formal, and impersonal than primary groups. Why are these contestants for Miss Universe an example of a secondary group?

Alex Segre/Alamy

Aggregates are people who happen to be in the same place at the same time.

146

In-Groups and Out-Groups

What groups do you identify with? Which groups in our society do you dislike?

We all have **in-groups,** groups toward which we feel loyalty. And we all have **out-groups,** groups toward which we feel antagonism. For Monster Kody in our opening vignette, the Crips were an in-group, while the Bloods were an out-group. That the Crips—and we—make such a fundamental division of the world has far-reaching consequences for our lives.

Implications for a Socially Diverse Society: Shaping Perception and Morality. You know how vital some groups are to you, the sense of belonging they give you. This can bring positive consequences for others, such as our tendency to excuse the faults of people we love and to encourage them to do better. Unfortunately, dividing the world into a "we" and "them" also leads to discrimination, hatred, and, as we saw in our opening vignette, even murder.

From this, you can see that the sociological significance of in-groups is how they shape our perception of the world, our view of right and wrong, and our behavior. Let's look at two examples. The first you see regularly—prejudice and discrimination on the basis of sex. As sociologist Robert Merton (1949/1968) said, our favoritism creates a fascinating double standard. We tend to view the traits of our in-group as virtues, while we perceive those *same* traits as vices in out-groups. Men may perceive an aggressive man as assertive but an aggressive woman as pushy. They may think that a male employee who doesn't speak up "knows when to keep his mouth shut," while they consider a quiet woman as too timid to make it in the business world.

The "we" and "they" division of the world can lead to such twisted perception that harming others comes to be viewed as right. The Nazis provide one of the most startling examples. For them, the Jews were an out-group who symbolized an evil that should be eliminated. Many ordinary, "good" Germans shared this view and defended the Holocaust as "dirty work" that someone had to do (Hughes 1962/2005).

An example from way back then, you might say—and the world has moved on. But our inclination to divide the world into in-groups and out-groups has not moved on—nor has the twisting of perception that accompanies it. After the terrorist attacks of September 11, 2001, top U.S. officials came to view Arabs as sinister, bloodthirsty villains, and inflicting pain on prisoners became "dirty work" that someone had to do. They said that being "cruel, inhuman, and degrading" to prisoners was not torture unless it caused "death, organ failure, or permanent damage" (Gonzales 2002; Johnston and Shane 2008). Caught up in the torture exuberance of the time, Alan Dershowitz, a professor at Harvard Law School who usually takes very liberal views, said that we should make torture legal so judges could issue "torture warrants" (Schulz 2002). Can you see the principle at work—and understand that in-group/out-group thinking can be so severe that even "good people" can support torture? And with a good conscience.

Economic downturns are especially perilous in this regard. The Nazis took power during a depression so severe that it was wiping out the middle classes. In depressions, immigrants are transformed from "nice people who work for low wages at jobs that Americans think are beneath them" to "sneaky people who steal jobs from friends and family." Depressions bring national anti-immigration policies, often accompanied by a resurgence of hate groups such as the neo-Nazis, the Ku Klux Klan, and skinheads.

In short, to divide the world into in-groups and out-groups is a natural part of social life—one that produces both functional and dysfunctional consequences.

Reference Groups

Suppose you have just been offered a good job. It pays double what you hope to make even after you graduate from college. You have only two days to make up your mind. If you accept the job, you will have to drop out of college. As you consider the matter, thoughts like this may go through your mind: "My friends will say I'm a fool if I don't take the job . . .

"So long, Bill. This is my club. You can't come in."

How our participation in social groups shapes our self-concept is a focus of symbolic interactionists. In this process, knowing who we are *not* is as significant as knowing who we are.

in-groups groups toward which one feels loyalty

out-groups groups toward which one feels antagonism

What are in-groups and out-groups? How do your in-groups and out-groups influence your behavior?

All of us have *reference groups*—the groups we use as standards to evaluate ourselves. How do you think the reference groups of these members of the KKK who are demonstrating in Jaspar, Texas, differ from those of the police officer who is protecting their right of free speech? Although the KKK and this police officer use different groups to evaluate their attitudes and behaviors, the process is the same.

AP Images/David J. Phillip

but Dad and Mom will practically go crazy. They've made sacrifices for me, and they'll be crushed if I don't finish college. They've always said I've got to get my education first, that good jobs will always be there. . . . But, then, I'd like to see the look on the faces of those neighbors who said I'd never amount to much!"

Evaluating Ourselves. This is an example of how people use **reference groups,** the groups we refer to when we evaluate ourselves. Your reference groups may include your family, neighbors, teachers, classmates, co-workers, or the members of your church, synagogue, or mosque. If you were like Monster Kody in our opening vignette, the "set" would be your main reference group. For others, it could be the Scouts. Even a group you don't belong to can be a reference group. For example, if you are thinking about going to graduate school, graduate students or members of the profession you want to join may form a reference group. You would consider their standards as you evaluate your grades or writing skills.

Reference groups exert tremendous influence on us. For example, if you want to become a corporate executive, you might start to dress more formally, try to improve your vocabulary, read the *Wall Street Journal,* and change your major to business or law. In contrast, if you want to become a rock musician, you might get elaborate tattoos and body piercings, dress in ways your parents and many of your peers consider extreme, read *Rolling Stone,* drop out of college, and hang around clubs and rock groups.

Exposure to Contradictory Standards in a Socially Diverse Society. From these examples, you can see how you use reference groups to evaluate your life. When you see yourself as measuring up to a reference group's standards, you feel pleased. But you can experience inner turmoil if your behavior—or aspirations—does not match the group's standards. Although for most of us, wanting to become a corporate executive would create no inner turmoil, it would for someone who had grown up in an Amish home. The Amish strongly disapprove of such aspirations for their children. They ban high school and college education, suits and ties, and corporate employment. Similarly, if you want to join the military and your parents are dedicated pacifists, you likely would feel deep conflict, because your parents would have quite different aspirations for you.

Contradictions that lead to internal turmoil are common because of two chief characteristics of our society—social diversity and social mobility. These expose us to standards and orientations that are inconsistent with those we learned during childhood. The "internal recordings" that play contrasting messages from different reference groups, then, are one price we pay for our social mobility.

Social Networks

Although we live in a huge and diverse society, we don't experience social life as a sea of nameless, strange faces. This is because of the groups we have been discussing. Among these is our **social network,** people who are linked to one another. Your social network includes your family, friends, acquaintances, people at work and school, and even "friends of friends." Think of your social network as a spider's web. You are at the center, with lines extending outward, gradually encompassing more and more people.

If you are a member of a large group, you probably associate regularly with a few people within that group. In a sociology class I was teaching at a commuter campus, six women who didn't know one another ended up working together on a project. They got along well, and they began to sit together. Eventually they planned a Christmas party at one of their homes. This type of social network, the clusters within a group, or its internal factions, is called a **clique** (cleek).

The analysis of social networks has become part of applied sociology. One of its surprising applications was the capture of Saddam Hussein.

After U.S.-led forces took over Baghdad, Hussein was nowhere to be found. Rumors placed him all over the map, from neighboring countries to safe houses in Baghdad. To find him, U.S. intelligence officers began to apply network analysis. On a color-coded "people map,"

reference group a group whose standards we refer to as we evaluate ourselves

social network the social ties radiating outward from the self that link people together

clique a cluster of people within a larger group who choose to interact with one another

What are reference groups? Social networks? How do your reference groups and social networks affect your behavior?

We all use *reference groups* to evaluate our accomplishments, failures, values, and attitudes. We compare what we see in ourselves with what we perceive as normative in our reference groups. From these two photos, can you see how the *reference groups* and *social networks* of these youths are not likely to lead them to the same social destination?

they placed Hussein's photo in a yellow circle, like a bull's-eye. They then drew links to people who were connected to Hussein, placing their photos closer to or farther from Hussein's photo on the basis of how close they were to Hussein (Schmitt 2003; Hougham 2005).

The photos closest to Hussein represented an intimate and loyal group. These people were the most likely to know where Hussein was, but because of their close ties to him, they also were the least likely to reveal this information. Those who were pictured slightly farther away knew people in this more intimate group, so it was likely that some of them had information about Hussein's whereabouts. Because these people's social ties to Hussein were not as strong, they represented the weaker links that might be broken.

The approach worked. Using software programs to sift through vast amounts of information gained from informants and electronic intercepts, the analysts drew a "people map" that pictured these social relationships. Identifying the weaker links led to Hussein's capture.

The Small World Phenomenon.   Social scientists have wondered just how extensive the connections are among social networks. If you list everyone you know and each of those individuals lists everyone he or she knows, and you keep doing this, would almost everyone in the United States eventually be included on those lists?

It would be too cumbersome to test this hypothesis by drawing up such lists, but psychologist Stanley Milgram (1933–1984) came up with an interesting idea. In a classic study known as "the small world phenomenon," Milgram (1967) addressed a letter to "targets": the wife of a divinity student in Cambridge and a stockbroker in Boston. He sent the letter to "starters," who did not know these people. He asked them to send the letter to someone they knew on a first-name basis, someone they thought might know the "target." The recipients, in turn, were asked to mail the letter to a friend or acquaintance who might know the "target," and so on. The question was, Would the letters ever reach the "target"? If so, how long would the chain be?

Think of yourself as part of this study. What would you do if you were a "starter," but the "target" lived in a state in which you knew no one? You would send the letter to a contact who might know someone in that state. This, Milgram reported, is just what happened. Although none of the senders knew the targets, the letters reached the designated individual in an average of just six jumps.

Milgram's study caught the public's fancy, leading to the phrase "six degrees of separation." This expression means that, on average, everyone in the United States is separated by just six individuals. Milgram's conclusions have become so popular that a game, "Six Degrees of Kevin Bacon," was built around it.

What is the small group phenomenon? Is it real?

group dynamics the ways in which individuals affect groups and the ways in which groups influence individuals

small group a group small enough for everyone to interact directly with all the other members

dyad the smallest possible group, consisting of two persons

Is the Small World Phenomenon an Academic Myth? Unfortunately, it just isn't true. When psychologist Judith Kleinfeld (2002b) decided to replicate Milgram's study, she went to the archives at Yale University Library to get more details. Going through Milgram's papers, she found that he had stacked the deck in favor of finding a small world. The "starters" came from mailing lists of people who were likely to have higher incomes and therefore were not representative of average people. In addition, one of the "targets" was a stockbroker, and that person's "starters" were investors in blue-chip stocks. Kleinfeld also found another discrepancy: On average, only 30 percent of the letters reached their "target." In one of Milgram's studies, the success rate was just 5 percent.

Since most letters did *not* reach their targets, even with the deck stacked in favor of success, we can draw the *opposite* conclusion: People who don't know one another are dramatically separated by social barriers. How great the barriers are is illustrated by attempts to replicate Milgram's study. Using thousands of e-mail chains, researchers found that only ½ to 1½ percent reached their targets (Dodds et al. 2003; Muhamad 2010).

As Kleinfeld says, "Rather than living in a small world, we may live in a world that looks like a bowl of lumpy oatmeal, with many small worlds loosely connected and perhaps some small worlds not connected at all." Somehow, I don't think that the phrase "lumpy oatmeal phenomenon" will become standard, but the criticism of Milgram's research is valid: We do *not* live in a small world where everyone is connected by six links.

Implications for a Socially Diverse Society. Besides geography, the barriers that separate us into many disjointed small worlds are primarily those of social class, gender, and race–ethnicity. Overcoming these social barriers is difficult because even our own social networks contribute to social inequality, a topic that we explore in the Cultural Diversity box on the next page.

Implications for Science. Kleinfeld's revelations of the flaws in Milgram's research reinforce the need for replication, a topic discussed in the previous chapter. For our knowledge of social life, we cannot depend on single studies—there may be problems of generalizability on the one hand, or those of negligence or even fraud on the other. Replication by objective researchers is essential to build and advance solid social knowledge.

Japanese companies encourage their employees to think of themselves, not as individuals, but as members of a group. Similarity of appearance and activity help to fuse group identity and company loyalty. Why do you think there are two subgroups in this photo?

Group Dynamics

Group dynamics is a fascinating area of sociology. This term refers to how groups influence us and how we influence groups. Most of the ways that groups influence us lies below our sense of awareness, however, so let's see if we can bring some of this to the surface. Let's consider how even the size of a group makes a difference and then examine leadership, conformity, and decision making.

Before doing so, we should define **small group,** which is a group small enough so that each member can interact directly with all the others. Small groups can be either primary or secondary. A wife, husband, and children make up a *primary* small group, as do workers who take their breaks together. Students in a small introductory sociology class and bidders at an auction form *secondary* small groups.

Effects of Group Size on Stability and Intimacy

Writing in the early 1900s, sociologist Georg Simmel (1858–1918) noted the significance of group size. He used the term **dyad** for the smallest possible group, which consists of two people. Dyads, which include marriages, love affairs, and close friendships, show two distinct qualities. First, they are the most intense or intimate of human groups. Because only two people are involved, the

What is the "lumpy oatmeal" phenomenon?

Cultural Diversity in the United States

How Your Social Networks Perpetuate Social Inequality

Suppose that an outstanding job—great pay, interesting work, opportunity for advancement—has just opened up where you work. Who are you going to tell?

Consider some of the principles we have reviewed. We tend to form in-groups, people with whom we identify; we use reference groups to evaluate our attitudes and behavior; and we interact in social networks. Our in-groups, reference groups, and social networks are likely to consist of people whose backgrounds are similar to our own. For most of us, this means that just as social inequality is built into society, so it is built into our relationships. One consequence is that we tend to perpetuate social inequality.

Go back to the extract that opens this box. Who will you tell about the opening for this outstanding job? Most likely it will be someone you know, a friend or someone to whom you owe a favor. And most likely your social network is made up of people who look much like yourself—similar to your age, education, social class, race–ethnicity, and probably also, gender. You can see how *our social networks both reflect the inequality in our society and help to perpetuate it.*

Consider a network of white men in some corporation. As they learn of opportunities (jobs, investments, real estate, and so on), they share this information with their networks. This causes opportunities and good jobs to flow to people whose characteristics are similar to theirs. This perpetuates the "good old boy"' network, bypassing people who have different characteristics—in this example women and minorities. No intentional discrimination need be involved. It is just a reflection of our contacts and how we interact.

When people learn of opportunities, they share this information with their networks. Opportunities then flow to people whose characteristics are similar to theirs.
p77/ZUMA Press/Newscom

To overcome this barrier, women and minorities do networking. They try to meet "someone who knows someone" to help advance their careers (Kanter 2009). Like the "good old boys," they go to parties and join clubs, religious organizations, and political parties. They also use *Facebook* and other online networking sites. The network that African American leaders have cultivated is so tight that one-fifth of the entire national African American leadership knows one another personally. Add some "friends of a friend," and *three-fourths* of the entire leadership belong to the same network (Taylor 1992).

Women also cultivate their own network as they climb the career ladder. The women in this "new girl" network steer business to one another, and like the "good old boys" who preceded them, they have a ready set of reasons to justify their practice of excluding the opposite sex (Jacobs 1997).

For Your Consideration

➤ You can see that the perpetuation of social inequality does not require intentional discrimination. Just as social inequality is built into society, so it is built into our personal relationships. How do you think your social network helps to perpetuate social inequality? How do you think we can break this cycle? How can we create diversity in our social networks?

interaction is focused on them. Second, dyads tend to be unstable. Because dyads require that both members participate, if one member loses interest, the dyad collapses. In larger groups, by contrast, even if one person withdraws, the group can continue, for its existence does not depend on any single member (Simmel 1950).

A **triad** is a group of three people. As Simmel noted, the addition of a third member fundamentally changes the group. With three people, interaction between the first two decreases. This can create strain. For example, with the birth of a child, hardly any aspect of a couple's relationship goes untouched. Attention focuses on the baby, and interaction between the husband and wife diminishes. Despite this, the marriage usually becomes stronger. Although the intensity of interaction is less in triads, they are inherently stronger and give greater stability to a relationship.

Yet, as Simmel noted, triads, too, are unstable. They tend to produce **coalitions**—two group members aligning themselves against one. This common tendency for two people

triad a group of three people

coalition the alignment of some members of a group against others

How does group size affect the stability and intimacy of groups?

to develop stronger bonds and prefer one another leaves the third person feeling hurt and excluded. Another characteristic of triads is that they often produce an arbitrator or mediator, someone who tries to settle disagreements between the other two. In one-child families, you can often observe both of these characteristics of triads—coalitions and arbitration.

The general principle is this: *As a small group grows larger, it becomes more stable, but its intensity, or intimacy, decreases.* To see why, look at Figure 3 on the next page. As each new person comes into a group, the connections among people multiply. In a dyad, there is only 1 relationship; in a triad, there are 3; in a group of four, 6; in a group of five, 10. If we expand the group to six, we have 15 relationships, while a group of seven yields 21 relationships. If we continue adding members, we soon are unable to follow the connections: A group of eight has 28 possible relationships; a group of nine, 36 relationships; a group of ten, 45; and so on.

It is not only the number of relationships that makes larger groups more stable. As groups grow, they also tend to develop a more formal structure. For example, leaders emerge and more specialized roles come into play. This often results in such familiar offices as president, secretary, and treasurer. This structure provides a framework that helps the group survive over time.

Effects of Group Size on Attitudes and Behavior

Imagine that you are taking a team-taught course in social psychology and your professors have asked you to join a few students to discuss your adjustment to college life. When you arrive, they tell you that to make the discussion anonymous they want you to sit unseen in a booth. You will participate in the discussion over an intercom, talking when your microphone comes on. The professors say that they will not listen to the conversation, and they leave.

You find the format somewhat strange, to say the least, but you go along with it. You have not seen the other students in their booths, but when they talk about their experiences, you find yourself becoming wrapped up in the problems they begin to share. One student even mentions how frightening it is to be away from home because of his history of epileptic seizures. Later, you hear this individual breathe heavily into the microphone. Then he stammers and cries for help. A crashing noise follows, and you imagine him lying helpless on the floor.

Nothing but an eerie silence follows. What do you do?

Your professors, John Darley and Bibb Latané (1968), staged the whole thing, but you don't know this. No one had a seizure. In fact, no one was even in the other booths. Everything, except your comments, was on tape.

Some participants were told that they would be discussing the topic with just one other student, others with two, and still others with three, four, or five. Darley and Latané found that all students who thought they were part of a dyad rushed out to help. If they thought they were in a triad, only 80 percent went to help—and they were slower in leaving the booth. In six-person groups, only 60 percent went to see what was wrong—and they were even slower.

Group size has a significant influence on how people interact. When a group changes from a dyad (two people) to a triad (three people), the relationships among the participants undergo a shift. How do you think the birth of this child affected the relationship between the mother and father?

C.A. SWINSON/Lightbox

This experiment demonstrates how deeply group size influences our attitudes and behavior: It even affects our willingness to help one another. Students in the dyad knew that no one else could help the student in trouble. The professor was gone, and it was up to them. In the larger groups, including the triad, students felt a *diffusion of responsibility:* Giving help was no more their responsibility than anyone else's.

You probably have observed the second consequence of group size firsthand. When a group is small, its members act informally, but as the group grows, the members lose their sense of intimacy and become more formal with one another. No longer can the members assume that the others are "insiders" in sympathy with what they say. Now they must take a "larger audience" into consideration, and instead of merely "talking," they begin to "address" the group. As their speech becomes more formal, their body language stiffens.

You probably have observed a third aspect of group dynamics, too. In the early stages of a party, when only a few people are present, almost everyone talks with everyone else. But as others arrive, the guests break into smaller groups. Some hosts, who want their guests to mix together, make a nuisance of themselves trying to achieve *their* idea of what a group should be like. The division into small groups is inevitable, however, for it follows the basic sociological principles that we have just reviewed. Because the addition of each person rapidly increases connections (in this case, "talk lines"), conversation becomes more difficult. The guests break into smaller groups in which they can look at each other directly and interact comfortably with one another.

Leadership

All of us are influenced by leaders, so it is important to understand leadership. Let's look at types of leaders, how people become leaders, and different styles of leadership. Before we do this, though, it is important to clarify that leaders don't necessarily hold formal positions in a group. **Leaders** are people who influence the behaviors, opinions, or attitudes of others. Even a group of friends has leaders.

Types of Leaders. Groups have two types of leaders (Bales 1950, 1953; Cartwright and Zander 1968). The first is easy to recognize. The **instrumental leader** (or *task-oriented leader*) is someone who tries to keep the group moving toward its goals. They try to keep group members from getting sidetracked, reminding them of what they are supposed to accomplish. The **expressive leader** (or *socioemotional leader*), in contrast, usually is not recognized as a leader, but he or she certainly is one. This person is likely to do things that lift the group's morale, to crack jokes or to offer sympathy. Both types of leaders are essential: the one keeps the group on track, while the other increases harmony and minimizes conflicts.

It is difficult for the same person to be both an instrumental and an expressive leader, for these roles tend to contradict one another. Instrumental leaders are task oriented, so they sometimes create friction as they prod the group to get on with the job. Their actions often cost them popularity. Expressive leaders, in contrast, who stimulate personal bonds and reduce friction, are usually more popular (Olmsted and Hare 1978).

Who Becomes a Leader? Are leaders born with characteristics that propel them to the forefront of a group? No sociologist would agree with such an idea. In general, people who become leaders are perceived by group members as strongly representing their values, as able to lead a group out of a crisis (Trice and Beyer 1991), or as having a talent for economic success. Leaders tend to be more talkative, outgoing, determined, and self-confident (Ward et al. 2010).

These findings may not be surprising, since such traits are related to what we expect of leaders. Researchers, however, have also discovered traits that seem to have no bearing on the ability to lead. For example, taller people and those judged better looking are more likely to become leaders (Stodgill 1974; Judge and Cable 2004). Some of the factors that go into our choice of leaders are quite subtle, as social psychologists Lloyd Howells and Selwyn Becker (1962) found in a simple experiment. They had groups of five people who did not know one another sit at a rectangular table. Three, of course, sat on one side, and

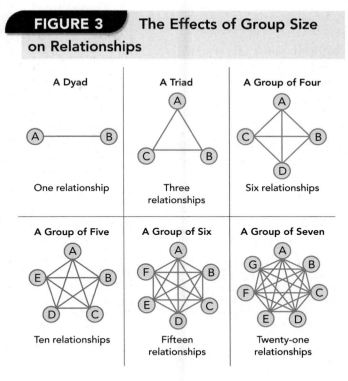

FIGURE 3 The Effects of Group Size on Relationships

A Dyad
One relationship

A Triad
Three relationships

A Group of Four
Six relationships

A Group of Five
Ten relationships

A Group of Six
Fifteen relationships

A Group of Seven
Twenty-one relationships

leader someone who influences other people

instrumental leader an individual who tries to keep the group moving toward its goals; also known as a *task-oriented leader*

expressive leader an individual who increases harmony and minimizes conflict in a group; also known as a *socioemotional leader*

What types of leaders are there? Who becomes a leader?

leadership styles ways in which people express their leadership

authoritarian leader an individual who leads by giving orders

democratic leader an individual who leads by trying to reach a consensus

laissez-faire leader an individual who leads by being highly permissive

two on the other. After discussing a topic for a set period of time, each group chose a leader. The findings are startling: Although only 40 percent of the people sat on the two-person side, 70 percent of the leaders emerged from there. The explanation is that we tend to interact more with people facing us than with people to our side.

Leadership Styles. Let's suppose that the president of your college has asked you to head a task force to determine how to improve race relations on campus. You can adopt a number of **leadership styles,** or ways of expressing yourself as a leader. Of the three basic styles, you could be an **authoritarian leader,** one who gives orders; a **democratic leader,** one who tries to gain a consensus; or a **laissez-faire leader,** one who is highly permissive. Which style should you choose?

Social psychologists Ronald Lippitt and Ralph White (1958) carried out a classic study of these leadership styles. They matched boys for IQ, popularity, physical energy, and leadership and assigned them to "craft clubs" made up of five boys each. They trained men in the three leadership styles, and then peered through peepholes, took notes, and made movies as the men rotated among the clubs. To control possible influences of the men's personalities, each man played all three styles.

The *authoritarian* leaders assigned tasks to the boys and told them what to do. They also praised or condemned the boys' work arbitrarily, giving no explanation for why they judged it good or bad. The *democratic* leaders discussed the project with the boys, outlining the steps that would help them reach their goals. When they evaluated the boys' work, they gave "facts" as the bases for their decisions. The *laissez-faire* leaders, who gave the boys almost total freedom to do as they wished, offered help when asked, but made few suggestions. They did not evaluate the boys' projects, either positively or negatively.

Adolf Hitler, shown here in Nuremberg in 1938, was one of the most influential—and evil—persons of the twentieth century. Why did so many people follow Hitler? This question stimulated the research by Stanley Milgram.

Pictorial Press Ltd/Alamy

What kinds of leadership styles are there?

The results? The boys under authoritarian leadership grew dependent on their leader. They also became either apathetic or aggressive, with the aggressive boys growing hostile toward their leader. In contrast, the boys in the democratic clubs were friendlier and looked to one another for approval. When the leader left the room, they continued to work at a steady pace. The boys with laissez-faire management goofed off a lot and were notable for their lack of achievement. The researchers concluded that the democratic style of leadership works best. This conclusion, however, may be biased, as the researchers favored a democratic style of leadership in the first place (Olmsted and Hare 1978). Apparently, this same bias in studies of leadership continues (Cassel 1999).

You may have noticed that only boys and men were involved in this experiment. It is interesting to speculate how the results might differ if we were to repeat the experiment with all-girl groups, with groups of girls and boys, or with boys and girls from different social classes—and if we used both women and men as leaders. Perhaps you will become the sociologist to study such variations of this classic experiment.

Leadership Styles in Changing Situations. Different situations require different styles of leadership. Suppose that you are leading a dozen backpackers in the mountains, and it is time to make dinner. A laissez-faire style would be appropriate if the backpackers had brought their own food, or perhaps a democratic style if everyone is expected to pitch in. Authoritarian leadership—telling the hikers how to prepare their meals—would create resentment. This, in turn, would likely interfere with meeting the primary goal of the group, which in this case is to have a good time while enjoying nature.

Now assume the same group but a different situation: One of your party is lost, and a blizzard is on its way. This situation calls for you to exercise authority. To simply shrug your shoulders and say "You figure it out" would invite disaster—and probably a lawsuit.

The Power of Peer Pressure: The Asch Experiment

From the analysis so far, you can see that groups are highly influential in our lives. But how influential? To answer this, let's look first at *conformity* in the sense of going along with our peers. They have no authority over us, only the influence that we allow.

Imagine again that you are taking a course in social psychology, this time with Dr. Solomon Asch. You have agreed to participate in an experiment. As you enter his laboratory, you see seven chairs, five of them already filled by other students. You are given the sixth. Soon the seventh person arrives. Dr. Asch stands at the front of the room next to a covered easel. He explains that he will first show a large card with a vertical line on it, then another card with three vertical lines. Each of you is to tell him which of the three lines matches the line on the first card (see Figure 4).

Dr. Asch then uncovers the first card with the single line and the comparison card with the three lines. The correct answer is easy, for two of the lines are obviously wrong, and one is exactly right. Each person, in order, states his or her answer aloud. You all answer correctly. The second trial is just as easy, and you begin to wonder why you are there.

Then on the third trial, something unexpected happens. Just as before, it is easy to tell which lines match. The first student, however, gives a wrong answer. The second gives the same incorrect answer. So do the third and the fourth. By now, you are wondering what is wrong. How will the person next to you answer? You can hardly believe it when he, too, gives the same wrong answer. Then it is your turn, and you give what you know is the right answer. The seventh person also gives the same wrong answer.

On the next trial, the same thing happens. You know that the choice of the other six is wrong. They are giving what to you are obviously wrong answers. You don't know what to think. Why aren't they seeing things the same way you are? Sometimes they do, but in twelve trials they don't. Something is seriously wrong, and you are no longer sure what to do.

Figure from "Opinions and Social Pressure" by Solomon E. Asch, from SCIENTIFIC AMERICAN, November 1955, Volume 193(5). Copyright © 1955 by Scientific American, Inc. All rights reserved. Reprinted with permission.

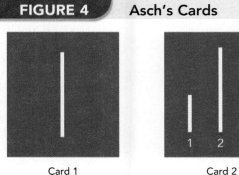

FIGURE 4 **Asch's Cards**

Card 1   Card 2

The cards used by Solomon Asch in his classic experiment on group conformity

Source: Asch 1952:452–453.

Explore
Living Data
on **mysoclab.com**

Describe the Asch experiment. What are its implications for society?

When the eighteenth trial is finished, you heave a sigh of relief. The experiment is finally over, and you are ready to bolt for the door. Dr. Asch walks over to you with a big smile on his face and thanks you for participating in the experiment. He explains that you were the only real subject in the experiment! "The other six were stooges. I paid them to give those answers," he says. Now you feel real relief. Your eyes weren't playing tricks on you after all.

What were the results? Asch (1952) tested fifty people. One-third (33 percent) gave in to the group half the time, providing what they knew to be wrong answers. Another two out of five (40 percent) gave wrong answers, but not as often. One-quarter (25 percent) stuck to their guns and always gave the right answer. I don't know how I would do on this test (if I knew nothing about it in advance), but I like to think that I would be part of the 25 percent. You probably feel the same way about yourself. But why should we feel that we wouldn't be like *most* people?

The results are disturbing, and researchers are still replicating Asch's experiment (Bond 2005). In our "land of individualism," the group is so powerful that most people are willing to say things that they know are not true. And this was a group of strangers! How much more conformity can we expect when our group consists of friends, people we value highly and depend on for getting along in life? Again, maybe you will become the sociologist to run that variation of Asch's experiment, perhaps using female subjects.

The Power of Authority: The Milgram Experiment

Let's look at the results of another experiment in the following Thinking Critically section.

THINKING CRITICALLY

If Hitler Asked You to Execute a Stranger, Would You? The Milgram Experiment

Imagine that Dr. Stanley Milgram (1963, 1965), a former student of Dr. Asch's, has asked you to participate in a study on punishment and learning. Assume that you do not know about the Asch experiment and have no reason to be wary. When you arrive at the laboratory, you and a second student draw lots for the roles of "teacher" and "learner." You are to be the teacher. When you see that the learner's chair has protruding electrodes, you are glad that you are the teacher. Dr. Milgram shows you the machine you will run. You see that one side of the control panel is marked "Mild Shock, 15 volts," while the center says "Intense Shock, 350 Volts," and the far right side reads "DANGER: SEVERE SHOCK."

"As the teacher, you will read aloud a pair of words," explains Dr. Milgram. "Then you will repeat the first word, and the learner will reply with the second word. If the learner can't remember the word, you press this lever on the shock generator. The shock will serve as punishment, and we can then determine if punishment improves memory." You nod, now very relieved that you haven't been designated the learner.

In the 1960s, social psychologists did highly creative but controversial experiments. This photo, taken during Stanley Milgram's experiment, should give you an idea of how convincing the experiment was to the "teacher."

Courtesy of Alexandra Milgram. Copyright 1968 by Stanley Milgram. Copyright renewed 1993 by Alexandra Milgram. From the film OBEDIENCE, distributed by Penn State Media Sales.

"Every time the learner makes an error, increase the punishment by 15 volts," instructs Dr. Milgram. Then, seeing the look on your face, he adds, "The shocks can be very painful, but they won't cause any permanent tissue damage." He pauses, and then says, "I

Describe the Milgram experiment. What are its implications for society?

want you to see." You then follow him to the "electric chair," and Dr. Milgram gives you a shock of 45 volts. "There. That wasn't too bad, was it?" "No," you mumble.

The experiment begins. You hope for the learner's sake that he is bright, but unfortunately he turns out to be rather dull. He gets some answers right, but you have to keep turning up the dial. Each turn makes you more and more uncomfortable. You find yourself hoping that the learner won't miss another answer. But he does. When he received the first shocks, he let out some moans and groans, but now he is screaming in agony. He even protests that he suffers from a heart condition.

How far do you turn that dial?

By now, you probably have guessed that there was no electricity attached to the electrodes and that the "learner" was a stooge who only pretended to feel pain. The purpose of the experiment was to find out at what point people refuse to participate. Does anyone actually turn the lever all the way to "DANGER: SEVERE SHOCK"?

Milgram wanted the answer because millions of ordinary people did nothing to stop the Nazi slaughter of Jews, gypsies, Slavs, homosexuals, people with disabilities, and others whom the Nazis designated as "inferior." The cooperation of so many ordinary people in the face of all this killing seemed bizarre, and Milgram wanted to see how Americans might react to orders from an authority (Russell 2010).

What he found upset Milgram. Some "teachers" broke into a sweat and protested that the experiment was inhuman and should be stopped. But when the experimenter calmly replied that the experiment must go on, this assurance from an "authority" ("scientist, white coat, university laboratory") was enough for most "teachers" to continue, even though the "learner" screamed in agony. Even "teachers" who were "reduced to twitching, stuttering wrecks" continued to follow orders.

Milgram varied the experiments. He used both men and women. In some experiments, he put the "teachers" and "learners" in the same room, so the "teacher" could see the suffering. In others, he put the "learners" in an adjacent room, and had them pound and kick the wall during the first shocks and then go silent. The results varied. When there was no verbal feedback from the "learner," 65 percent of the "teachers" pushed the lever all the way to 450 volts. Of those who could see the "learner," 40 percent turned the lever all the way. When Milgram added a second "teacher," a stooge who refused to go along with the experiment, only 5 percent of the "teachers" turned the lever all the way.

Milgram's research set off a stormy discussion about research ethics. Researchers agreed that to reduce subjects to "twitching, stuttering wrecks" was unethical, and almost all deception was banned. Universities began to require that subjects be informed of the nature and purpose of social research.

Although researchers were itching to replicate Milgram's experiment, it took almost fifty years before they found a way to satisfy the committees that approve research. The findings: People today obey the experimenter at about the same rate that people did in the 1960s (Burger 2009). The results were even higher on *The Game of Death,* a fake game show in France, where the contestants were prodded by the show's host and a shouting audience to administer shocks and win prizes. The contestants kept turning up the dial, with 80 percent of them giving victims what they thought were near lethal 450-volt shocks (Crumley 2010).

For Your Consideration

Taking into account the significance of Milgram's findings, do you think that the scientific community overreacted to these experiments? Should we allow such research? Consider both the Asch and Milgram experiments, and use symbolic interactionism, functionalism, and conflict theory to explain why groups have such influence over us. ∎

Global Consequences of Group Dynamics: Groupthink

Suppose you are a member of the U.S. president's inner circle. It is midnight, and the president has called an emergency meeting. There has just been a terrorist attack, and you must decide how to respond to it. You and the others suggest several options. Eventually,

Describe the Milgram experiment. What are its implications for society?

these are narrowed to only a couple of choices, and at some point, everyone seems to agree on what now appears to be "the only possible course of action." To criticize the proposed solution at this point will bring you in conflict with all the other important people in the room, and mark you as "not a team player." So you keep your mouth shut. As a result, each step commits you—and them—more and more to the "only" course of action.

groupthink a narrowing of thought by a group of people, leading to the perception that there is only one correct answer and that to even suggest alternatives is a sign of disloyalty

Under some circumstances, as in this example, the influence of authority and peers can lead to **groupthink.** Sociologist Irving Janis (1972, 1982) used this term to refer to the collective tunnel vision that group members sometimes develop. As they begin to think alike, they become convinced that there is only one "right" viewpoint and a single course of action to follow. They take any suggestion of alternatives as a sign of disloyalty. With their perspective narrowed and fully convinced that they are right, they may even put aside moral judgments and disregard risk (Hart 1991; Flippen 1999).

Groupthink can bring catastrophe. Consider the *Columbia* space shuttle disaster of 2003.

Foam broke loose during launch, raising concerns that this might have damaged tiles on the nose cone, making reentry dangerous. Engineers sent e-mails to NASA officials, warning them about the risk. One suggested that the crew do a "space walk" to examine the tiles (Vartabedian and Gold 2003). The team in charge of the Columbia *shuttle, however, disregarded the warnings. Convinced that a piece of foam weighing less than two pounds could not seriously harm the shuttle, they refused to even consider the possibility (Wald and Schwartz 2003). The fiery results of their closed minds were transmitted around the globe.*

Groupthink can lead to consequences even greater than this. In 1941, President Franklin D. Roosevelt and his chiefs of staff had evidence that the Japanese were preparing to attack Pearl Harbor. Refusing to believe it, they decided to continue naval operations as usual. The destruction of the U.S. naval fleet ushered the United States into World War II. During the Vietnam war, U.S. officials had evidence of the strength and determination of the North Vietnamese military. These officials arrogantly threw the evidence aside, refusing to believe that "little, uneducated, barefoot people in pajamas" could defeat the mighty U.S. military.

In each of these cases, options closed as officials committed themselves to a single course of action. Questioning the decisions would have indicated disloyalty and disregard for "team play." No longer did those in power try to weigh events objectively. Interpreting ongoing events as supporting their one "correct" decision, they plunged ahead, blind to disconfirming evidence and alternative perspectives.

Groupthink can lead "good" people to do "bad" things. Consider what I mentioned earlier, when in the aftermath of 9/11 government officials defended torture as moral, "the lesser of two evils." Thought narrowed so greatly that the U.S. Justice Department ruled that the United States was not bound by the Geneva Convention that prohibits torture (Lewis 2005). Medical professionals even advised the CIA interrogators, telling them when to adjust or stop the waterboarding, slamming prisoners' heads into walls, or shackling a prisoner's arms to the ceiling (Shane 2009). Shades of the Nazis right here in our homeland!

Do you see the power of groups and groupthink?

Preventing Groupthink. The leaders of a government tend to surround themselves with an inner circle that closely reflects their own views. In "briefings," written summaries, and "talking points," this inner circle spoon-feeds the leaders information it has selected. As a result, the top leaders, such as the president, are largely cut off from information that does not support their own opinions. You can see how the mental captivity and intellectual paralysis known as groupthink is built into this arrangement.

Perhaps the key to preventing groupthink is the widest possible circulation—especially among a nation's top government officials—of research by social scientists independent of the government and information that media reporters have gathered freely. If this conclusion comes across as an unabashed plug for sociological research and the free exchange of ideas, it is. Giving free rein to diverse opinions can curb groupthink, which—if not prevented—can lead to the destruction of a society and, in today's world of nuclear, chemical, and biological weapons, the obliteration of Earth's inhabitants.

What is groupthink? How can we prevent being captive to it?

Summary and Review

Societies and Their Transformation

What is a group?

Sociologists use many definitions of groups, but, in general, a **group** consists of people who interact with one another and who think of themselves as belonging together. **Societies** are the largest and most complex group that sociologists study.

How is technology linked to the change from one type of society to another?

On their way to postindustrial society, humans passed through four types of societies. Each emerged from a social revolution that was linked to new technology. The **domestication revolution,** which brought the pasturing of animals and the cultivation of plants, transformed **hunting and gathering societies** into **pastoral** and **horticultural societies.** Then the invention of the plow ushered in the **agricultural society,** while the **Industrial Revolution,** brought about by machines powered by fuels, led to **industrial society.** The computer chip ushered in a new type of society called **postindustrial (or information) society.** Another new type of society, the **biotech society,** may be emerging.

How is social inequality linked to the transformation of societies?

Hunting and gathering societies had little social inequality, but as societies changed social inequality grew. The root of the transition to social inequality was the accumulation of a food surplus, made possible through the domestication revolution. This surplus stimulated the division of labor, trade, the accumulation of material goods, the subordination of females by males, the emergence of leaders, and the development of the state. Social inequality increased with each type of new society. A reversal of this trend occurred in the latter part of the industrial society.

Groups within Society

How do sociologists classify groups?

Sociologists divide groups into primary groups, secondary groups, in-groups, out-groups, reference groups, and networks. The cooperative, intimate, long-term, face-to-face relationships provided by **primary groups** are fundamental to our sense of self. **Secondary groups** are larger, relatively temporary, and more anonymous, formal, and impersonal than primary groups. **In-groups** provide members with a strong sense of identity and belonging. **Out-groups** also foster identity by showing in-group members what they are *not.* **Reference groups** are groups whose standards we refer to as we evaluate ourselves. **Social networks** consist of social ties that link people together.

Group Dynamics

How does a group's size affect its dynamics?

The term **group dynamics** refers to how individuals affect groups and how groups influence individuals. In a **small group,** everyone can interact directly with everyone else. As a group grows larger, intimacy decreases but the group's stability increases. A **dyad,** consisting of two people, is the most unstable of human groups, but it provides the most intimate relationships. The addition of a third person, forming a **triad,** fundamentally alters relationships. Triads are unstable, as **coalitions** (the alignment of some members of a group against others) tend to form.

What characterizes a leader?

A **leader** is someone who influences others. **Instrumental leaders** try to keep a group moving toward its goals, even though this causes friction and they lose popularity. **Expressive leaders** focus on creating harmony and raising group morale. Both types are essential to the functioning of groups.

What are three leadership styles?

Authoritarian leaders give orders, **democratic leaders** try to lead by consensus, and **laissez-faire leaders** are highly permissive. An authoritarian style appears to be more effective in emergency situations, a democratic style works best for most situations, and a laissez-faire style is usually ineffective.

How do groups encourage conformity?

The Asch experiment was cited to illustrate the influence of peer pressure, the Milgram experiment to show the power of authority. Both experiments demonstrate how easily we can succumb to **groupthink,** a kind of collective tunnel vision. Preventing groupthink requires the free circulation of diverse and opposing ideas.

Thinking Critically about this Chapter

1. How would your orientations to life (your ideas, attitudes, values, goals) be different if you had been reared in a hunting and gathering society? In an agricultural society?

2. Identify your in-groups and your out-groups. How have your in-groups influenced the way you see the world? How have out-groups affected your views?

3. Asch's experiments illustrate the power of peer pressure. How has peer pressure operated in your life? Think about something that you did, despite not wanting to, because of peer pressure.

References

All new references are printed in cyan.

Alter, Alexandra. "Is This Man Cheating on His Wife?" *Wall Street Journal,* August 10, 2007.

Asch, Solomon. "Effects of Group Pressure upon the Modification and Distortion of Judgments." In *Readings in Social Psychology,* Guy Swanson, Theodore M. Newcomb, and Eugene L. Hartley, eds. New York: Holt, Rinehart and Winston, 1952.

Bales, Robert F. *Interaction Process Analysis.* Reading, Mass.: Addison-Wesley, 1950.

Bales, Robert F. "The Equilibrium Problem in Small Groups." In *Working Papers in the Theory of Action,* Talcott Parsons et al., eds. New York: Free Press, 1953:111–115.

Bearak, Barry. "For Some Bushmen, a Homeland Worth a Fight." *New York Times,* November 5, 2010.

Bernard, Jessie. "The Good-Provider Role." In *Marriage and Family in a Changing Society,* 4th ed., James M. Henslin, ed. New York: Free Press, 1992:275–285.

Bjerklie, David, Andrea Dorfman, Wendy Cole, et al. "Baby, It's You: And You, and You . . . " *Time,* February 19, 2001:47–57.

Blumer, Herbert George. *Industrialization as an Agent of Social Change: A Critical Analysis,* David R. Maines and Thomas J. Morrione, eds. Hawthorne, N.Y.: Aldine de Gruyter, 1990.

Bond, Rod. "Group Size and Conformity." *Group Processes and Intergroup Relations, 8,* 4, 2005:331–354.

Boulding, Elise. *The Underside of History.* Boulder, Colo.: Westview Press, 1976.

Burger, Jerry M. "Replicating Milgram: Would People Still Obey Today?" *American Psychologist, 64,* 1, January 2009:1–11.

Cartwright, Dorwin, and Alvin Zander, eds. *Group Dynamics,* 3rd ed. Evanston, Ill.: Peterson, 1968.

Cassel, Russell N. "Examining the Basic Principles for Effective Leadership." *College Student Journal, 33,* 2, June 1999:288–301.

Cooley, Charles Horton. *Social Organization.* New York: Schocken Books, 1962. Originally published by Scribner's, 1909.

Crumley, Bruce. "The Game of Death: France's Shocking TV Experiment." *Time,* March 17, 2010.

Darley, John M., and Bibb Latané. "Bystander Intervention in Emergencies: Diffusion of Responsibility." *Journal of Personality and Social Psychology, 8,* 4, 1968:377–383.

Davis, Stan. *Lessons From the Future: Making Sense of a Blurred World.* New York: Capstone Publishers, 2001.

Dodds, Peter Sheridan, Roby Muhamad, and Duncan J. Watts. "An Experimental Study of Search in Global Social Networks." *Science, 301,* August 8, 2003:827–830.

Durkheim, Emile. *The Division of Labor in Society,* George Simpson, trans. New York: Free Press, 1933. Originally published 1893.

Elias, Paul. "'Molecular Pharmers' Hope to Raise Human Proteins in Crop Plants." *St. Louis Post-Dispatch,* October 28, 2001:F7.

Flippen, Annette R. "Understanding Groupthink from a Self-Regulatory Perspective." *Small Group Research, 30,* 2, April 1999:139–165.

Frayer, Lauren. "Police: Baby Starved as Couple Nurtured Virtual Kid." AOL News, March 5, 2010.

Gonzales, Alberto R. "Memorandum for Albert R. Gonzales, Counsel to the President: Re: Standards of Conduct for Interrogation under *18 U.S.C. 2340–2340A.*" August 2, 2002.

Hart, Paul. "Groupthink, Risk-Taking and Recklessness: Quality of Process and Outcome in Policy Decision Making." *Politics and the Individual, 1,* 1, 1991:67–90.

Hougham, Victoria. "Sociological Skills Used in the Capture of Saddam Hussein." *Footnotes,* July–August 2005.

Howells, Lloyd T., and Selwyn W. Becker. "Seating Arrangement and Leadership Emergence." *Journal of Abnormal and Social Psychology, 64,* February 1962:148–150.

Hughes, Everett C. "Good People and Dirty Work." In *Life in Society: Readings to Accompany Sociology: A Down-to-Earth Approach,* 7th ed. James M. Henslin, ed. Boston: Allyn and Bacon, 2005: 125–134. Article originally published 1962.

Jacobs, Margaret A. "'New Girl' Network Is Boon for Women Lawyers." *Wall Street Journal,* March 4, 1997:B1, B7.

Janis, Irving L. *Victims of Groupthink.* Boston: Houghton Mifflin, 1972.

Janis, Irving. L. *Groupthink: Psychological Studies of Policy Decisions and Fiascoes.* Boston: Houghton Mifflin, 1982.

Johnston, David, and Scott Shane. "Memo Sheds New Light on Torture Issue." *New York Times,* April 3, 2008.

Judge, Timothy A., and Daniel M. Cable. "The Effect of Physical Height on Workplace Success and Income: Preliminary Test of a Theoretical Model." *Journal of Applied Psychology, 89,* 3, 2004:428–441.

Kaebnick, Gregory E. "On the Sanctity of Nature." *Hastings Center Report, 30,* 5, September–October 2000:16–23.

Kantor, Jodi. "In First Family, a Nation's Many Faces." *New York Times,* January 16, 2009.

Kleinfeld, Judith S. "The Small World Problem." *Society,* January–February, 2002b:61–66.

Kristoff, Nicholas D. "Interview with a Humanoid." *New York Times,* July 23, 2002.

Lenski, Gerhard, and Jean Lenski. *Human Societies: An Introduction to Macrosociology,* 5th ed. New York: McGraw-Hill, 1987.

Lewis, Neil A. "Justice Dept. Toughens Rules on Torture." *New York Times,* January 1, 2005.

Lippitt, Ronald, and Ralph K. White. "An Experimental Study of Leadership and Group Life." In *Readings in Social Psychology,* 3rd ed., Eleanor E. Maccoby, Theodore M. Newcomb, and Eugene L. Hartley, eds. New York: Holt, Rinehart and Winston, 1958:340–365. (As summarized in Olmsted and Hare 1978:28–31.)

McGee, Glenn. "Cloning, Sex, and New Kinds of Families." *Journal of Sex Research, 37,* 3, August 2000:266–272.

Merton, Robert K. *Social Theory and Social Structure.* Glencoe, Ill.: Free Press, 1949. Enlarged ed., 1968.

Milgram, Stanley. "Behavioral Study of Obedience." *Journal of Abnormal and Social Psychology, 67,* 4, 1963:371–378.

Milgram, Stanley. "Some Conditions of Obedience and Disobedience to Authority." *Human Relations, 18,* February 1965:57–76.

Milgram, Stanley. "The Small World Problem." *Psychology Today, 1,* 1967:61–67.

Mooallem, Jon. "Do-It-Yourself Genetic Engineering." *New York Times,* February 14, 2010.

Muhamad, Roby. *Search in Social Networks.* Ph.D. dissertation, Columbia University, 2010.

Olmsted, Michael S., and A. Paul Hare. *The Small Group,* 2nd ed. New York: Random House, 1978.

Osborne, Lawrence. "Got Silk." *New York Times Magazine,* June 15, 2002.

Regalado, Antonio. "Seoul Team Creates Custom Stem Cells from Cloned Embryos." *Wall Street Journal,* May 20, 2005.

Russell, Nestar John Charles. "Milgram's Obedience to Authority Experiments: Origins and Early Evolution." *British Journal of Social Psychology,* 2010:1–23.

Sahlins, Marshall D. *Stone Age Economics.* Chicago: Aldine, 1972.

Schulz, William F. "The Torturer's Apprentice: Civil Liberties in a Turbulent Age." *The Nation,* May 13, 2002.

Scott, Monster Cody. *Monster: The Autobiography of an L.A. Gang Member.* New York: Penguin Books, 1994.

"Second Life Affair Ends in Divorce." www.cnn.com, November 15, 2008.

Shane, Scott. "Report Outlines Medical Workers' Role in Torture." *New York Times,* April 6, 2009.

Simmel, Georg. *The Sociology of Georg Simmel,* Kurt H. Wolff, ed. and trans. Glencoe, Ill.: Free Press, 1950. Originally published between 1902 and 1917.

Stiles, Daniel. "The Hunters Are the Hunted." *Geographical, 75,* June 2003:28–32.

Stodgill, Ralph M. *Handbook of Leadership: A Survey of Theory and Research.* New York: Free Press, 1974.

Taylor, Howard F. "The Structure of a National Black Leadership Network: Preliminary Findings." Unpublished manuscript, 1992. (As cited in Margaret L. Andersen and Howard F. Taylor, *Sociology: Understanding a Diverse Society.* Belmont, Calif.: Wadsworth, 2000.)

Trice, Harrison M., and Janice M. Beyer. "Cultural Leadership in Organization." *Organization Science, 2,* 2, May 1991:149–169.

Vartabedian, Ralph, and Scott Gold. "New Questions on Shuttle Tile Safety Raised." *Los Angeles Times,* February 27, 2003.

Volti, Rudi. *Society and Technological Change,* 3rd ed. New York: St. Martin's Press, 1995.

Wald, Matthew L., and John Schwartz. "Alerts Were Lacking, NASA Shuttle Manager Says." *New York Times,* July 23, 2003.

Ward, Rose Marie, Halle C. Popson, and Donald G. DiPaolo. "Defining the Alpha Female: A Female Leadership Measure." *Journal of Leadership and Organizational Studies 17,* 3, 2010:309–320.

Weiss, Rick. "Mature Human Embryos Cloned." *Washington Post,* February 12, 2004:A1.

Deviance and Social Control

Deviance and Social Control

In just a few moments I was to meet my first Yanomamö, my first primitive man. What would it be like? . . . I looked up [from my canoe] and gasped when I saw a dozen burly, naked, filthy, hideous men staring at us down the shafts of their drawn arrows. Immense wads of green tobacco were stuck between their lower teeth and lips, making them look even more hideous, and strands of dark-green slime dripped or hung from their noses. We arrived at the village while the men were blowing a hallucinogenic drug up their noses. One of the side effects of the drug is a runny nose. The mucus is always saturated with the green powder, and the Indians usually let it run freely from their nostrils. . . . I just sat there holding my notebook, helpless and pathetic. . . .

The whole situation was depressing, and I wondered why I ever decided to switch from civil engineering to anthropology in the first place. . . . [Soon] I was covered with red pigment, the result of a dozen or so complete examinations. . . . These examinations capped an otherwise grim day. The Indians would blow their noses into their hands, flick as much of the mucus off that would separate in a snap of the wrist, wipe the residue into their hair, and then care-

> "They would "clean" their hands by spitting slimy tobacco juice into them."

fully examine my face, arms, legs, hair, and the contents of my pockets. I said [in their language], "Your hands are dirty"; my comments were met by the Indians in the following way: they would "clean" their hands by spitting a quantity of slimy tobacco juice into them, rub them together, and then proceed with the examination.

This is how Napoleon Chagnon describes the culture shock he felt when he met the Yanomamö tribe of the rain forests of Brazil. His ensuing months of fieldwork continued to bring surprise after surprise, and often Chagnon (1977) could hardly believe his eyes—or his nose.

Arizona

If you were to list the deviant behaviors of the Yanomamö, what would you include? The way they appear naked in public? Use hallucinogenic drugs? Let mucus hang from their noses? Or the way they rub hands filled with mucus, spittle, and tobacco juice over a frightened stranger who doesn't dare to protest? Perhaps. But it isn't this simple, for as we shall see, deviance is relative.

What Is Deviance?

Sociologists use the term **deviance** to refer to any violation of norms, whether the infraction is as minor as driving over the speed limit, as serious as murder, or as humorous as Chagnon's encounter with the Yanomamö. This deceptively simple definition takes us to the heart of the sociological perspective on deviance, which sociologist Howard S. Becker (1966) described this way: *It is not the act itself, but the reactions to the act, that make something deviant.* What Chagnon saw disturbed him, but to the Yanomamö those same behaviors represented normal, everyday life. What was deviant to Chagnon was *conformist* to the Yanomamö. From their viewpoint, you *should* check out strangers the way they did—and nakedness is good, as are hallucinogenic drugs. And it is natural to let mucus flow.

The Relativity of Deviance. Chagnon's abrupt introduction to the Yanomamö allows us to see the *relativity of deviance,* a major point made by symbolic interactionists. Because different groups have different norms, *what is deviant to some is not deviant to others.* This principle applies not just to cultures but also to groups within the same society. Look at the photo on this page and the one a few pages ahead. We explore this idea further in the Cultural Diversity box on the next page.

This principle also applies to a specific form of deviance known as **crime,** the violation of rules that have been written into law. In the extreme, an act that is applauded by one group may be so despised by another group that it is punishable by death. Making a huge profit on business deals is one example. Americans who do this are admired. Like Donald Trump and Warren Buffet, they may even write books about their exploits. In China, however, until recently this same act was considered a crime called *profiteering.* Those found guilty were hanged in a public square as a lesson to all.

A Neutral Term. Unlike the general public, sociologists use the term *deviance* nonjudgmentally, to refer to any act to which people respond negatively. When sociologists use this term, it does *not* mean that they agree that an act is bad, just that people judge it negatively. To sociologists, then, *all* of us are deviants of one sort or another, for we all violate norms from time to time.

Stigma. To be considered deviant, a person does not even have to *do* anything. Sociologist Erving Goffman (1963) used the term **stigma** to refer to characteristics that discredit people. These include violations of norms of appearance (a facial birthmark, a huge nose or ears) and norms of ability (blindness, deafness, mental handicaps). Also included are involuntary memberships, such as being a victim of AIDS or the brother of a rapist. The stigma can become a person's master status, defining him or her as deviant. A master status cuts across all other statuses that a person occupies.

How Norms Make Social Life Possible

No human group can exist without norms, for *norms make social life possible by making behavior predictable*. What would life be like if you could not predict what others would do? Imagine for a moment that you have gone to a store to purchase milk:

I took this photo on the outskirts of Hyderabad, India. Is this man deviant? If this were a U.S. street, he would be. But here? No houses have running water in his neighborhood, and the men, women, and children bathe at the neighborhood water pump. This man, then, would not be deviant in this culture. And yet, he is actually mugging for my camera, making the three bystanders laugh. Does this additional factor make this a scene of deviance?

James M. Henslin

deviance the violation of norms (or rules or expectations)

crime the violation of norms written into law

stigma "blemishes" that discredit a person's claim to a "normal" identity

What is deviance? Why is deviance relative? How do norms make social life possible?

Cultural Diversity around the World

Human Sexuality in Cross-Cultural Perspective

Human sexuality illustrates how a group's *definition* of an act, not the act itself, determines whether it will be considered deviant. Let's look at some examples reported by anthropologist Robert Edgerton (1976).

Norms of sexual behavior vary so widely around the world that what is considered normal in one society may be considered deviant in another. In Kenya, a group called the Pokot place high emphasis on sexual pleasure, and they expect that both a husband and wife will reach orgasm. If a husband does not satisfy his wife, he is in trouble—especially if she thinks that his failure is because of adultery. If this is so, the wife and her female friends will sneak up on her husband when he is asleep. The women will tie him up, shout obscenities at him, beat him, and then urinate on him. Before releasing him, as a final gesture of their contempt they will slaughter and eat his favorite ox. The husband's hours of painful humiliation are intended to make him more dutiful concerning his wife's conjugal rights.

People can also become deviants for following their group's ideal norms instead of its real norms. As with many groups, the Zapotec Indians of Mexico profess that sexual relations should take place exclusively between husband and wife. Sexual affairs among the Zapotec are common, however, as the Zapotec also have a covert norm, an unspoken understanding, that married people will have affairs, but that they should be discreet about them. In one Zapotec community, the *only* person who did not have an extramarital affair was condemned by everyone in the village. The reason was not that she did not have an affair but that she told the other wives the names of the women their husbands were

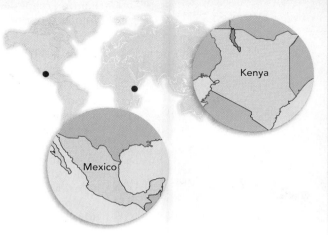

sleeping with. It is an interesting case, for if this virtuous woman had had an affair—and kept her mouth shut—she would not have become a deviant. Clearly, real norms can conflict with ideal norms—another illustration of the gap between ideal and real culture.

For Your Consideration

→ How do the behaviors of the Pokot wives and husbands mentioned here look from the perspective of U.S. norms? What are those U.S. norms? Did the Zapotec woman break norms of sexual behavior or of gossip and privacy? How does cultural relativity apply to the Pokot and Zapotec?

A Pokot married woman, Kenya
John Warburton-Lee Photography/Alamy

Suppose the clerk says, "I won't sell you any milk. We're overstocked with soda, and I'm not going to sell anyone milk until our soda inventory is reduced."

You don't like it, but you decide to buy a case of soda. At the checkout, the clerk says, "I hope you don't mind, but there's a $5 service charge on every fifteenth customer." You, of course, are the fifteenth.

Just as you start to leave, another clerk stops you and says, "We're not working anymore. We decided to have a party." Suddenly a CD player begins to blast, and everyone in the store begins to dance. "Oh, good, you've brought the soda," says a different clerk, who takes your package and passes sodas all around.

Life is not like this, of course. You can depend on grocery clerks to sell you milk. You can also depend on paying the same price as everyone else and not being forced to attend a party in the store. Why can you depend on this? Because we are socialized to follow norms, to play the basic roles that society assigns to us.

How do ideal and real norms work together in determining what is deviant?

Violating background assumptions is a common form of deviance. Although we have no explicit rule that says, "Do not put snakes through your nose," we all know that it exists (perhaps as a subcategory of "Don't do strange things in public"). Is this act also deviant for this man in Chennai, India?
REUTERS/Babu/Landov

social order a group's usual and customary social arrangements, on which its members depend and on which they base their lives

social control a group's formal and informal means of enforcing its norms

negative sanction an expression of disapproval for breaking a norm, ranging from a mild, informal reaction such as a frown to a formal reaction such as a prize or a prison sentence

positive sanction a reward or positive reaction for following norms, ranging from a smile to a material reward

genetic predisposition inborn tendencies (for example, a tendency to commit deviant acts)

street crime crimes such as mugging, rape, and burglary

Without norms, we would have social chaos. Norms lay out the basic guidelines for how we should play our roles and interact with others. In short, norms bring about **social order,** a group's customary social arrangements. Our lives are based on these arrangements, which is why deviance often is perceived as threatening: *Deviance undermines predictability, the foundation of social life.* Consequently, human groups develop a system of **social control**—formal and informal means of enforcing norms.

Sanctions

People do not enforce folkways strictly, but they become upset when people break mores (MO-rays). Expressions of disapproval for deviance, called **negative sanctions,** range from frowns and gossip for breaking folkways to imprisonment and capital punishment for violating mores. In general, the more seriously the group takes a norm, the harsher the penalty for violating it. In contrast, **positive sanctions**—from smiles to formal awards—are used to reward people for conforming to norms. Getting a raise is a positive sanction; being fired is a negative sanction. Getting an A in intro to sociology is a positive sanction; getting an F is a negative one.

Most negative sanctions are informal. You might stare if you observe someone dressed in what you consider to be inappropriate clothing, or you might gossip if a married person you know spends the night with someone other than his or her spouse. Whether you consider the breaking of a norm merely an amusing matter that warrants no sanction or a serious infraction that does, however, depends on your perspective. Let's suppose that a woman appears at your college graduation in a bikini. You might stare, laugh, and nudge the person next to you, but if this is *your* mother, you are likely to feel that different sanctions are appropriate. Similarly, if it is *your* father who spends the night with an 18-year-old college freshman, you are likely to do more than gossip.

In Sum: In sociology, the term deviance refers to all violations of social rules, regardless of their seriousness. The term is neutral, not a judgment about the behavior. Deviance is relative, for what is deviant in one group may be conformist in another. Consequently, we must consider deviance from within a group's own framework, for it is their meanings that underlie their behavior.

Competing Explanations of Deviance: Sociobiology, Psychology, and Sociology

If social life is to exist, norms are essential. So why do people violate them? To better understand the reasons, it is useful to know how sociological explanations differ from biological and psychological ones.

Biosocial Explanations. *Sociobiologists* explain deviance by looking for answers within individuals. They assume that **genetic predispositions** lead people to such behaviors as juvenile delinquency and crime (Lombroso 1911; Wilson and Herrnstein 1985; Goozen et al. 2007). An early explanation was that men with an extra Y chromosome (the "XYY" theory) were more likely to become criminals. Another was that people with "squarish, muscular" bodies were more likely to commit **street crime**—acts such as mugging, rape, and burglary. These theories were abandoned when research did not support them.

With advances in the study of genetics, biosocial explanations are being proposed to explain differences in crime by age (juvenile delinquency), sex, race, and social class (Walsh and Beaver 2009). The basic explanation is that over the millennia people with certain characteristics were more likely to survive than were people with different characteristics. As a result, different groups today inherit different propensities (tendencies) for empathy, self-control, and risk-taking.

How are norms and sanctions essential for maintaining the social order?

A universal finding is that in all known societies men commit more violent crimes than women do. There are no exceptions. Here is how sociobiologists explain this. It took only a few pelvic thrusts for men to pass on their genes. After that, they could leave if they wanted to. The women, in contrast, had to carry, birth, and nurture the children. Women who were more empathetic (inclined to nurture their children) engaged in less dangerous behavior. These women passed genes for more empathy, greater self-control, and less risk-taking to their female children. As a result, all over the world, men engage in more violent behavior, which comes from their lesser empathy, lower self-control, and greater tendency for taking risks.

Biosocial theorists stress that deviant behavior does not depend on genes alone. Our inherited propensities (the *bio* part) are modified and stimulated by our environment (the *social* part). Biosocial research is promising and holds the potential of opening a new understanding of deviance.

Psychological Explanations. Psychologists focus on abnormalities *within* the individual. Instead of genes, they examine what are called **personality disorders.** Their supposition is that deviating individuals have deviating personalities (Barnes 2001; Mayer 2007) and that sub-conscious motives drive people to deviance.

Researchers have never found a specific childhood experience to be invariably linked with deviance. For example, some children who had "bad toilet training," "suffocating mothers," or "emotionally aloof fathers" do become embezzling bookkeepers—but others become good accountants. Just as college students and police officers represent a variety of bad—and good—childhood experiences, so do deviants. Similarly, people with "suppressed anger" can become freeway snipers or military heroes—or anything else. In short, there is no inevitable outcome of any childhood experience. Deviance is not associated with any particular personality.

Sociological Explanations. Sociologists, in contrast with both sociobiologists and psychologists, search for factors *outside* the individual. They look for social influences that "recruit" people to break norms. To account for why people commit crimes, for example, sociologists examine such external influences as socialization, membership in subcultures, and social class. *Social class* refers to people's relative standing in terms of education, occupation, and especially income and wealth.

To explain deviance, sociologists apply the three sociological perspectives—symbolic interactionism, functionalism, and conflict theory. Let's compare these three explanations.

Rick Madonik/Toronto Star/ZUMA Press/Corbis

Every society has boundaries that divide what is considered socially acceptable from what is not acceptable. Lady Gaga has made her claim to fame by challenging those boundaries.

The Symbolic Interactionist Perspective

As we examine symbolic interactionism, it will become more evident why sociologists are not satisfied with explanations that are rooted in sociobiology or psychology. A basic principle of symbolic interactionism is that we are thinking beings who act according to our interpretations of situations. Let's consider how our membership in groups influences how we view life and, from there, our behavior.

Differential Association Theory

The Theory. Going directly against the idea that biology or personality is the source of deviance, sociologists stress our experiences in groups (Deflem 2006; Chambliss 1973/2012). Consider an extreme: boys and girls who join street gangs and those who join the Scouts. Obviously, each will learn different attitudes and behaviors concerning deviance and conformity. Edwin Sutherland coined the term **differential association** to indicate this: From the *different* groups we *associate* with, we learn to deviate from or conform to society's norms (Sutherland 1924, 1947; McCarthy 2011).

personality disorders the view that a personality disturbance of some sort causes an individual to violate social norms

differential association Edwin Sutherland's term to indicate that people who associate with some groups learn an "excess of definitions" of deviance, increasing the likelihood that they will become deviant

Can you contrast biosocial, psychological, and sociological explanations of deviance?

Sutherland's theory is more complicated than this, but he basically said that the different groups with which we associate (our "*differential* association") give us messages about conformity and deviance. We may receive mixed messages, but we end up with more of one than the other (an "excess of definitions," as Sutherland put it). The end result is an imbalance—attitudes that tilt us in one direction or another. Consequently, we learn to either conform or to deviate.

Watch
Motherhood Manifesto
on **mysoclab.com**

Families. Since our family is so important for teaching us attitudes, it probably is obvious to you that the family makes a big difference in whether we learn deviance or conformity. Researchers have confirmed this informal observation. Of the many confirming studies, this one stands out: Of all prison inmates across the United States, about half have a father, mother, brother, sister, or spouse who has served time in prison (*Sourcebook of Criminal Justice Statistics* 2003:Table 6.0011; Glaze and Maruschak 2008:Table 11). In short, families that are involved in crime tend to set their children on a lawbreaking path.

Friends, Neighborhoods, and Subcultures. Most people don't know the term *differential association*, but they do know how it works. Most parents want to move out of "bad" neighborhoods because they know that if their kids have delinquent friends, they are likely to become delinquent, too. Sociological research also supports this common observation (Miller 1958; Chung and Steinberg 2006; Church et al. 2009).

In some neighborhoods, violence is so woven into the subculture that even a wrong glance can mean your death ("Why you lookin' at me?") (Gardiner and Fox 2010). If the neighbors feel that a victim deserved to be killed, they refuse to testify because "he got what was coming to him" (Kubrin and Weitzer 2003). Killing can even be viewed as honorable:

Sociologist Ruth Horowitz (1983, 2005), who did participant observation in a lower-class Chicano neighborhood in Chicago, discovered how the concept of "honor" propels young men to deviance. The formula is simple. "A real man has honor. An insult is a threat to one's honor. Therefore, not to stand up to someone is to be less than a real man."

Now suppose you are a young man growing up in this neighborhood. You likely would do a fair amount of fighting, for you would interpret many things as attacks on your honor. You might even carry a knife or a gun, for words and fists wouldn't always be sufficient. Along with members of your group, you would define fighting, knifing, and shooting quite differently from the way most people do.

SuperStock

Members of the Mafia also intertwine ideas of manliness with killing. For them, *to kill is a measure of their manhood.* If a Mafia member were to seduce the *capo*'s wife or girlfriend, for example, the seduction would slash at the *capo*'s manliness and honor. The only course open would be direct retaliation. The offender's body would be found with his penis stuffed in his mouth. However, not all killings are accorded the same respect, for "the more awesome and potent the victim, the more worthy and meritorious the killer" (Arlacchi 1980).

From this example, you can see how relative deviance is. Although killing is deviant to mainstream society, for members of the Mafia, *not* to kill after certain rules are broken is the deviant act.

To experience a sense of belonging is a basic human need. Membership in groups is a primary way that people meet this need. Regardless of the orientation of the group—whether to conformity, as with the Girl Scouts, or to deviance, as with the Mafia—the process is the same.

Prison or Freedom? An issue that comes up over and over again in sociology is whether we are prisoners of socialization. Symbolic interactionists stress that we are not mere pawns in the hands of others. We are not destined to think and act as our groups dictate. Rather, we *help to produce our own orientations to life.* By joining one group rather than another (differential association), for example, we help to shape the self. For instance, one college student may join a

What is differential association theory? How do family and friends fit into this theory?

feminist group that is trying to change the treatment of women in college, while another associates with women who shoplift on weekends. Their choices point them in different directions. The one who joins the feminist group may develop an even greater interest in producing social change, while the one who associates with shoplifters may become even more oriented toward criminal activities.

Control Theory

Do you ever feel the urge to do something that you know you shouldn't, even something that would get you in trouble? Most of us fight temptations to break society's norms. We find that we have to stifle things inside us—urges, hostilities, raunchy desires of various sorts. And most of the time, we manage to keep ourselves out of trouble. The basic question that **control theory** tries to answer is, With the desire to deviate so common, why don't we all just "bust loose"?

The Theory. Sociologist Walter Reckless (1973), who developed control theory, stressed that two control systems work against our motivations to deviate. Our *inner controls* include our internalized morality—conscience, religious principles, ideas of right and wrong. Inner controls also include fears of punishment, feelings of integrity, and the desire to be a "good" person (Hirschi 1969; McShane and Williams 2007). Our *outer controls* consist of people—such as family, friends, and the police—who influence us not to deviate.

The stronger our bonds are with society, the more effective our inner controls are (Hirschi 1969). Bonds are based on *attachments* (our affection and respect for people who conform to mainstream norms), *commitments* (having a stake in society that you don't want to risk, such as a respected place in your family, a good standing at college, a desirable job), *involvements* (participating in approved activities), and *beliefs* (convictions that certain actions are morally wrong).

This theory can be summarized as *self*-control, says sociologist Travis Hirschi. The key to learning strong self-control is socialization, especially in childhood. Parents help their children to develop self-control by supervising them and punishing their deviant acts (Gottfredson and Hirschi 1990; Church et al. 2009). They sometimes use shame to keep their children in line. You probably had that forefinger shaken at you. I certainly recall it aimed at me. Do you think that more use of shaming, discussed in the Down-to-Earth Sociology box on the next page, could help increase people's internal controls?

Applying Control Theory.

Suppose that some friends invite you to go to a nightclub with them. When you get there, you notice that everyone seems unusually happy—almost giddy. They seem to be euphoric in their animated conversations and dancing. Your friends tell you that almost everyone here has taken the drug Ecstasy, and they invite you to take some with them.
What do you do?

Let's not explore the question of whether taking Ecstasy in this setting is a deviant or a conforming act. This is a separate issue. Instead, concentrate on the pushes and pulls you would feel. The pushes toward taking the drug: your friends, the setting, and your curiosity. Then there are your inner controls—those inner voices of your conscience and your parents, perhaps of your teachers, as well as your fears of arrest and the dangers you've heard about illegal drugs. There are also the outer controls—perhaps the uniformed security guard looking in your direction.

So, what *did* you decide? Which was stronger: your inner and outer controls or the pushes and pulls toward taking the drug? It is you who can best weigh these forces, for they differ with each of us. This little example puts us at the center of what control theory is all about.

The social control of deviance takes many forms, including the actions of the police. Being arrested here is a Florida woman accused of prostitution. Chris Matula via Newscom

control theory the idea that two control systems—inner controls and outer controls—work against our tendencies to deviate

What is control theory? How do internal and external controls work in your life?

171

Down-to-Earth Sociology

Shaming: Making a Comeback?

Shaming can be effective, especially when members of a primary group use it. In some communities, where the individual's reputation was at stake, shaming was the centerpiece of the enforcement of norms. Violators were marked as deviant and held up for all the world to see. In Nathaniel Hawthorne's *The Scarlet Letter*, town officials forced Hester Prynne to wear a scarlet A sewn on her dress. The A stood for *adulteress*. Wherever she went, Prynne had to wear this badge of shame, and the community expected her to wear it every day for the rest of her life.

As our society grew large and urban, the sense of community diminished, and shaming lost its effectiveness. Now shaming is starting to make a comeback (Appiah 2010). One Arizona sheriff makes the men in his jail wear striped prison uniforms—and pink underwear (Billeaud 2008). They also wear pink while they work in chain gangs. Women prisoners, too, are put in chain gangs and forced to pick up street trash. Online shaming sites have also appeared. Captured on cell phone cameras are bad drivers, older men who leer at teenaged girls, and dog walkers who don't pick up their dog's poop (Saranow 2007). Some sites post photos of the offenders, as well as their addresses and phone numbers. In Spain, where one's reputation with neighbors still matters, debt collectors, dressed in tuxedo and top hat, walk slowly to the front door. The sight shames debtors into paying (Catan 2008).

Sociologist Harold Garfinkel (1956) gave the name **degradation ceremony** to an extreme form of shaming. The individual is called to account before the group, witnesses denounce him or her, the offender is pronounced guilty, and steps are taken to strip the individual of his or her identity as a group member. In some courts martial, officers who are found guilty stand at attention before their peers while others rip the insignia of rank from their uniforms. This procedure screams that the individual is no longer a member of the group. Although Hester Prynne was not

To avoid jail time, this woman in Pennsylvania chose the judge's option of public shaming.
Photo Provided Courtesy of Bedford County District Attorney Bill Higgins

banished from the group physically, she was banished morally; her degradation ceremony proclaimed her a *moral* outcast from the community. The scarlet A marked her as not "one of them."

Although we don't use scarlet A's today, informal degradation ceremonies still occur. Consider what happened to this New York City police officer (Chivers 2001):

Joseph Gray had been a police officer in New York City for fifteen years. As with some of his fellow officers, alcohol and sex helped relieve the pressures of police work. After spending one afternoon drinking in a topless bar, bleary-eyed, Gray plowed his car into a vehicle carrying a pregnant woman, her son, and her sister. All three died. Gray was accused of manslaughter and drunk driving.

The New York Times and New York television stations kept hammering this story to the public. Three weeks later, Gray resigned from the police force. As he left police headquarters after resigning, an angry crowd surrounded him. Gray hung his head in public disgrace as Victor Manuel Herrera, whose wife and son were killed in the crash, followed him, shouting, "You're a murderer!" (Gray was later convicted of drunk driving and manslaughter.)

For Your Consideration

→ 1. How do you think law enforcement officials might use shaming to reduce law breaking?

2. How do you think school officials could use shaming?

3. Suppose that you were caught shoplifting at a store near where you live. Would you rather spend a week in jail with no one but your family knowing it (and no permanent record) or a week walking in front of the store you stole from wearing a placard that proclaims in bold red capital letters: I AM A THIEF! and in smaller letters says: "I am sorry for stealing from this store and making you pay higher prices"? Why?

What conditions do you think would be necessary for shaming to be effective?

Labeling Theory

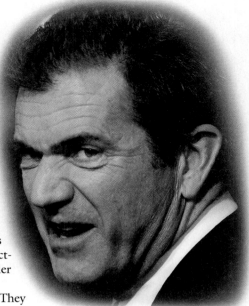

Suppose for one undesirable moment that people around you thought of you as a "whore," a "pervert," or a "cheat." (Pick one.) What power such a reputation would have—both on how others would see you and on how you would see yourself. How about if you became known as "very intelligent," "truthful in everything," or "honest to the core"? (Choose one.) You can see that such a reputation would give people different expectations of your character and behavior.

This is what **labeling theory** focuses on, the significance of reputations, how they help set us on paths that propel us into deviance or divert us away from it.

Rejecting Labels: How People Neutralize Deviance.   Not many of us want to be called "whore," "pervert," or "cheat." We resist negative labels, even lesser ones than these that others might try to pin on us. Some people are so successful at rejecting labels that even though they beat people up and vandalize property they consider themselves to be conforming members of society. How do they do it?

Sociologists Gresham Sykes and David Matza (1957/1988) studied boys like this. They found that the boys used five **techniques of neutralization** to deflect society's norms.

Denial of responsibility. Some boys said, "I'm not responsible for what happened because . . ." and then they were quite creative about the "becauses." Some said that what happened was an "accident." Other boys saw themselves as "victims" of society. What else could you expect? They were like billiard balls shot around the pool table of life.

Denial of injury. Another favorite explanation was "What I did wasn't wrong because no one got hurt." The boys would define vandalism as "mischief," gang fights as a "private quarrel," and stealing cars as "borrowing." They might acknowledge that what they did was illegal, but claim that they were "just having a little fun."

Denial of a victim. Some boys thought of themselves as avengers. Vandalizing a teacher's car was done to get revenge for an unfair grade, while shoplifting was a way to even the score with "crooked" store owners. In short, even if the boys did accept responsibility and admit that someone had gotten hurt, they protected their self-concept by claiming that the people "deserved what they got."

Condemnation of the condemners. Another technique the boys used was to deny that others had the right to judge them. They might accuse people who pointed their fingers at them of being "a bunch of hypocrites": The police were "on the take," teachers had "pets," and parents cheated on their taxes. In short, they said, "Who are *they* to accuse *me* of something?"

Appeal to higher loyalties. A final technique the boys used to justify their activities was to consider loyalty to the gang more important than the norms of society. They might say, "I had to help my friends. That's why I got in the fight." Not incidentally, the boy may have shot two members of a rival group, as well as a bystander!

In Sum: These techniques of neutralization have implications far beyond this group of boys, for it is not only delinquents who try to neutralize the norms of mainstream society. Look again at these techniques—don't they sound familiar? (1) "I couldn't help myself"; (2) "Who really got hurt?"; (3) "Don't you think she deserved that, after what she did?"; (4) "Who are you to talk?"; and (5) "I had to help my friends—wouldn't you have done the same thing?" All of us attempt to neutralize the moral demands of society, for neutralization helps us to sleep at night.

Embracing Labels: The Example of Outlaw Bikers.   Although most of us resist attempts to label us as deviant, some people revel in a deviant identity. Some teenagers, for example, make certain by their clothing, music, hairstyles, and body art that no one

How powerful are labels? Consider Mel Gibson. Previously, he had a sterling reputation (a label) as actor and film maker. After anti-Semitic rants when stopped for drunk driving and, later, threats to a pregnant girlfriend, Gibson's reputation changed abruptly. How do you think his new label will affect his life? Do you think Gibson can rescue his reputation?

LUCY NICHOLSON/AFP/Getty Images/Newscom

degradation ceremony a term coined by Harold Garfinkel to refer to a ritual whose goal is to remake someone's self by stripping away that individual's self-identity and stamping a new identity in its place

labeling theory the view that the labels people are given affect their own and others' perceptions of them, thus channeling their behavior into either deviance or conformity

techniques of neutralization ways of thinking or rationalizing that help people deflect (or neutralize) society's norms

How do juvenile delinquents neutralize their deviance? How do you?

While most people resist labels of deviance, some embrace them. In what different ways does this photo illustrate the embracement of deviance?

REUTERS/Wolfgang Rattay/Landov

▣ Read
The Saints and the Roughnecks
by William Chambliss
on **mysoclab.com**

misses their rejection of adult norms. Their status among fellow members of a subculture—within which they are almost obsessive conformists—is vastly more important than any status outside it.

One of the best examples of a group that embraces deviance is a motorcycle gang. Sociologist Mark Watson (1980/2006) did participant observation with outlaw bikers. He rebuilt Harleys with them, hung around their bars and homes, and went on "runs" (trips) with them. He concluded that outlaw bikers see the world as "hostile, weak, and effeminate." Holding this conventional world in contempt, gang members pride themselves on breaking its norms and getting in trouble, laughing at death, and treating women as lesser beings whose primary value is to provide them with services—especially sex. They pride themselves in looking "dirty, mean, and generally undesirable," taking pleasure in shocking people by their appearance and behavior. Outlaw bikers also regard themselves as losers, a view that becomes woven into their unusual embrace of deviance.

The Power of Labels: The Saints and the Roughnecks. Labels are powerful. When courts label teenagers as delinquents, it often triggers a process that leads to greater involvement in deviant groups (Bernburg et al. 2006). We can see how powerful labeling is by referring back to the "Saints" and the "Roughnecks," research. As you recall, both groups of high school boys were "constantly occupied with truancy, drinking, wild parties, petty theft, and vandalism." Yet their teachers looked on one group, the Saints, as "headed for success" and the other group, the Roughnecks, as "headed for trouble." By the time they finished high school, not one Saint had been arrested, while the Roughnecks had been in constant trouble with the police.

Why did the members of the community perceive these boys so differently? Chambliss (1973/2012) concluded that this split vision was due to *social class.* As symbolic interactionists emphasize, social class is like a lens that focuses our perceptions. The Saints came from respectable, middle-class families, while the Roughnecks were from less respectable, working-class families. These backgrounds led teachers and the authorities to expect good behavior from the Saints but trouble from the Roughnecks. And, like the rest of us, teachers and police saw what they expected to see.

The boys' social class also affected their visibility. The Saints had automobiles, and they did their drinking and vandalism outside of town. Without cars, the Roughnecks hung around their own street corners, where their drinking and boisterous behavior drew the attention of police, confirming the negative impressions that the community already had of them.

The boys' social class also equipped them with distinct *styles of interaction.* When police or teachers questioned them, the Saints were apologetic. Their show of respect for authority elicited a positive reaction from teachers and police, allowing the Saints to escape school and legal problems. The Roughnecks, said Chambliss, were "almost the polar opposite." When questioned, they were hostile. Even when they tried to assume a respectful attitude, everyone could see through it. Consequently, while teachers and police let the Saints off with warnings, they came down hard on the Roughnecks.

Certainly, what happens in life is not determined by labels alone, but the Saints and the Roughnecks did live up to the labels that the community gave them. As you may recall, all but one of the Saints went on to college. One earned a Ph.D., one became a lawyer, one a doctor, and the others business managers. In contrast, only two of the Roughnecks went to college. They earned athletic scholarships and became coaches. The other Roughnecks did not fare so well. Two of them dropped out of high school, later became involved in separate killings, and were sent to prison. Of the final two, one became a local bookie, and no one knows the whereabouts of the other.

Can you explain why labels are powerful? How does reputation influence your behavior?

How do labels work? Although the matter is complex, because it involves the self-concept and reactions that vary from one individual to another, we can note that labels open and close doors of opportunity. Unlike its meaning in sociology, the term *deviant* in everyday usage is emotionally charged with a judgment of some sort. This label can lock people out of conforming groups and push them into almost exclusive contact with people who have been similarly labeled.

In Sum: Symbolic interactionists examine how people's definitions of the situation underlie their deviating from or conforming to social norms. They focus on group membership (differential association), how people balance pressures to conform and to deviate (control theory), and the significance of people's reputations (labeling theory).

The Functionalist Perspective

When we think of deviance, its dysfunctions are likely to come to mind. Functionalists point out that deviance also has functions.

Can Deviance Really Be Functional for Society?

Most of us are upset by deviance, especially crime, and assume that society would be better off without it. The classic functionalist theorist Emile Durkheim (1893/1933, 1895/1964), however, came to a surprising conclusion. Deviance, he said—including crime—is functional for society, for it contributes to the social order in these three ways:

1. *Deviance clarifies moral boundaries and affirms norms.* A group's ideas about how people should think and act mark its *moral boundaries.* Deviant acts challenge those boundaries. To call a member into account is to say, in effect, "You broke an important rule, and we cannot tolerate that." Punishing deviants affirms the group's norms and clarifies what it means to be a member of the group.
2. *Deviance encourages social unity.* To affirm the group's moral boundaries by punishing deviants fosters a "we" feeling among the group's members. In saying, "You can't get away with that," the group affirms the rightness of its own ways.
3. *Deviance promotes social change.* Groups do not always agree on what to do with people who push beyond their accepted ways of doing things. Some group members may even approve of the rule-breaking behavior. Boundary violations that gain enough support become new, acceptable behaviors. Deviance, then, may force a group to rethink and redefine its moral boundaries, helping groups—and whole societies—to adapt to changing circumstances.

In the Down-to-Earth Sociology box on the next page, you can see these three functions of deviance, as well as the central point of symbolic interactionism, that *deviance* involves a clash of competing definitions.

Strain Theory: How Mainstream Values Produce Deviance

Functionalists argue that crime is a *natural* part of society, not an aberration or some alien element in our midst. Mainstream values can even generate crime. Consider what sociologists Richard Cloward and Lloyd Ohlin (1960) identified as the crucial problem of the industrialized world: the need to locate and train its talented people—whether they were born into wealth or into poverty—so that they can take over the key technical jobs of society. When children are born, no one knows which ones will have the ability to become dentists, nuclear physicists, or engineers. To get the most talented people to compete with one another, society tries to motivate *everyone* to strive for success. It does this by arousing discontent—making people feel dissatisfied with what they have so they will try to "better" themselves.

We are quite successful in getting almost everyone to want **cultural goals,** success of some sort, such as wealth or prestige. But we aren't even close to successful in equalizing access to the **institutionalized means,** the legitimate ways to reach these goals. Sociologist Robert Merton (1956, 1949/1968) developed **strain theory** to explain

cultural goals the objectives held out as legitimate or desirable for the members of a society to achieve

institutionalized means approved ways of reaching cultural goals

strain theory Robert Merton's term for the strain engendered when a society socializes large numbers of people to desire a cultural goal (such as success), but withholds from some the approved means of reaching that goal; one adaptation to the strain is crime, the choice of an innovative means (one outside the approved system) to attain the cultural goal

How is deviance functional for society? How do mainstream values produce deviance?

Down-to-Earth Sociology

The Naked Pumpkin Runners and the Naked Bike Riders: Deviance or Freedom of Self-Expression?

They can hardly sleep the night before Halloween, thinking about how they will carve their pumpkins and all the fun to come. When night falls, they put sneakers on their feet, the pumpkins on their heads, and run into the street. There is nothing between the pumpkins and the sneakers—except whatever nature endowed them with (Simon 2009).

They join one another for their annual chilly, late-night run. Do the gawkers bother them? Maybe a little, but it's all in good fun. The crowd is waiting, hooting and hollering and waving them on.

"Not so fast," reply the police in Boulder, Colorado, where the naked pumpkin run is held on the last day of each October. "You are breaking the law."

If the naked pumpkin run isn't enough, the Boulder police also have to deal with the annual World Naked Bike Ride, which has become so popular that it is held in 70 cities around the world (Vigil 2009). The naked bike rides seem to be a celebration of youth and freedom—and as older people join in, just freedom and maybe the joy of being alive.

Though the Boulder police have prided themselves on tolerance, they don't see the run and ride in quite the same way as the participants do. "The law," they say, "clearly states that no one can show genitalia in public."

"Are women's breasts genitalia?" they've been asked. "No, those are okay," replied the police. "But watch the

rest of it—uh, that is, don't watch . . . uh, that is, don't show anything else. You know what we mean. If you do, we will arrest you, and you'll end up on the sexual offenders list."

"Bad sports," reply the naked pumpkin runners and the naked bike riders, pouting just a bit. "You're trying to ruin our fun."

"We didn't make the laws," the police reply, not pleased about the many who have become angry at their lack of understanding. "We just enforce them."

Trying to recover their tolerance, the police add, "Just wear a thong or a jock strap, and run and ride to your hearts' content."

The annual Naked Pumpkin Run, Boulder, Colorado
RICK WILKING/Reuters/Landov

The American Civil Liberties Union has stepped into the fray, too, saying that nakedness is a form of free speech. Participants should be able to express their, well, whatever it is they are expressing.

For Your Consideration
→ Here is a basic principle of deviance: As people break rules, sometimes deliberately to test the boundaries of acceptable behavior, the group enforces its norms, or bends them to accommodate the deviants. How do the naked pumpkin runners and the naked bike riders illustrate this principle? What do you think the result will be in Boulder, Colorado?

how people react when their access to success is blocked. *Strain* refers to the frustrations they feel. It is easy to identify with mainstream norms (such as working hard or pursuing higher education) when they help you get ahead, but when they don't seem to be getting you anywhere, you feel frustrated. You might even feel wronged by the system. If mainstream rules seem illegitimate, you experience a gap that Merton called *anomie*, a sense of normlessness.

Table 1 compares the ways that people react to these goals and means. The first reaction, which Merton said is the most common, is *conformity*, using socially acceptable means to try to reach cultural goals. In industrialized societies most people try to get good jobs, a quality education, and so on. If well-paid jobs are unavailable, they take less desirable jobs. If they are denied access to Harvard or Stanford, they go to a state university. Others take night classes and go to vocational schools. In short, most people take the socially acceptable path.

What do you think the social functions of group public nudity are?

TABLE 1	How People Match Their Goals to Their Means		
Do They Feel the Strain That Leads to Anomie?	Mode of Adaptation	Cultural Goals	Institutionalized Means
No	Conformity	Accept	Accept
	Deviant Paths:		
Yes	1. Innovation	Accept	Reject
	2. Ritualism	Reject	Accept
	3. Retreatism	Reject	Reject
	4. Rebellion	Reject/Replace	Reject/Replace

Source: Based on Merton 1968.

Four Deviant Paths.   The remaining four responses, which are deviant, represent reactions to the strain that people feel between the goals they want and their access to the institutionalized means to reach them. Let's look at each. *Innovators* are people who accept the goals of society but use illegitimate means to try to reach them. Crack dealers, for instance, accept the goal of achieving wealth, but they reject the legitimate avenues for doing so. Other examples are embezzlers, robbers, and con artists.

The second deviant path is taken by people who become discouraged and give up on achieving cultural goals. Yet they still cling to conventional rules of conduct. Merton called this response *ritualism*. Although ritualists have given up on getting ahead at work, they survive by rigorously following the rules of their job. Teachers whose idealism is shattered (who are said to suffer from "burnout"), for example, remain in the classroom, where they teach without enthusiasm. Their response is considered deviant because they cling to the job even though they have abandoned the goal, which may have been to stimulate young minds or to make the world a better place.

People who choose the third deviant path, *retreatism*, reject both the cultural goals and the institutionalized means of achieving them. Some people stop pursuing success and retreat into alcohol or drugs. Although their path to withdrawal is considerably different, women who enter a convent or men a monastery are also retreatists.

The final deviant response is *rebellion*. Convinced that their society is corrupt, rebels, like retreatists, reject both society's goals and its institutionalized means. Unlike retreatists, however, rebels seek to give society new goals, as well as new means for reaching them. Revolutionaries are the most committed type of rebels.

In Sum: Strain theory underscores the sociological principle that deviants are the product of society. Mainstream social values (cultural goals and institutionalized means to reach those goals) can produce strain (frustration, dissatisfaction). People who feel this strain are more likely than others to take the deviant (nonconforming) paths summarized in Table 1.

Illegitimate Opportunity Structures: Social Class and Crime

Let's look at how social class produces distinct styles of crime.

Street Crime.   In applying strain theory, functionalists point out that industrialized societies have no trouble socializing the poor into wanting to own things. Like others, the poor are bombarded with messages urging them to buy everything from Xboxes and iPods to designer jeans and new cars. Television and movies are filled with images of middle-class people enjoying luxurious lives. The poor get the message—all full-fledged Americans can afford society's many goods and services.

Can you explain the four deviant paths outlined in strain theory?

illegitimate opportunity structure opportunities for crimes that are woven into the texture of life

white-collar crime Edwin Sutherland's term for crimes committed by people of respectable and high social status in the course of their occupations; for example, bribery of public officials, securities violations, embezzlement, false advertising, and price fixing

corporate crime crimes committed by executives in order to benefit their corporation

Yet, the most common route to success, education, presents a bewildering world. Run by the middle class, schools are at odds with the background of the poor. In the schools, what the poor take for granted is unacceptable, questioned, and mocked. Their speech, for example, is built around nonstandard grammar. It is also often laced with what the middle class considers obscenities. Their ideas of punctuality and their poor preparation in reading and paper-and-pencil skills also make it difficult to fit in. Facing such barriers, the poor are more likely than their more privileged counterparts to drop out of school. Educational failure, of course, slams the door on many legitimate avenues to financial success.

It is not that the poor are left without opportunities for financial success. Woven into life in urban slums is what Cloward and Ohlin (1960) called an **illegitimate opportunity structure.** An alternative door to success opens: "hustles" such as robbery, burglary, drug dealing, prostitution, pimping, gambling, and other crimes (Anderson 1978, 1990/2006; Duck and Rawls 2011). Pimps and drug dealers, for example, present an image of a glamorous life—people who are in control and have plenty of "easy money." For many of the poor, the "hustler" becomes a role model.

In the Down-to-Earth Sociology box on the next page, let's look at how gangs are part of the illegitimate opportunity structure that beckons disadvantaged youth.

White-Collar Crime. Like the poor, the *forms* of crime of the more privileged classes also match their life situation. And how different their illegitimate opportunities are! Physicians don't hold up cabbies, but they do cheat Medicare. Investment managers like Bernie Madoff run fraudulent schemes that cheat customers around the world. Mugging, pimping, and burgling are not part of this more privileged world, but evading income tax, bribing public officials, and embezzling are. Sociologist Edwin Sutherland (1949) coined the term **white-collar crime** to refer to crimes that people of respectable and high social status commit in the course of their occupations.

A special form of white-collar crime is **corporate crime,** executives violating the law in order to benefit their corporation. For example, to increase corporate profits, Sears executives defrauded $100 million from victims so poor that they had filed for bankruptcy. To avoid a criminal trial, Sears pleaded guilty. This frightened the parent companies of Macy's and Bloomingdales, which were doing similar things, and they settled out of court (McCormick 1999). Citigroup is notorious for stealing from the poor. In 2004, this firm had to pay $70 million for its crimes (O'Brien 2004). But, like a career criminal, it continued its law-breaking ways. The firm "swept" money from its customers' credit cards, even from the cards of people who had died. Caught red-handed once again—even stealing from the dead—in 2008 this company was forced to pay another $18 million (Read 2008). *Not one of the corporate thieves at Sears, Macy's, Bloomingdales, or Citigroup spent a day in jail.*

Pam Francis/Liaison/Getty Images

White collar crime usually involves only the loss of property, but not always. To save money, Ford executives kept faulty Firestone tires on their Explorers. The cost? The lives of over 200 people. Shown here in Houston is one of their victims. She survived a needless accident, but was left a quadriplegic. Not one Ford executive spent even a single day in jail.

Seldom is corporate crime taken seriously, even when it results in death. In the 1930s, workers were hired to blast a tunnel through a mountain in West Virginia. The company knew the silica dust would kill the miners, and in just three months about 600 died (Dunaway 2008). No owner went to jail. In the 1980s, Firestone executives recalled faulty tires in Saudi Arabia and Venezuela but allowed them to remain on U.S. vehicles. When their tires blew out, about 200 Americans died (White et al. 2001). The photo at the left shows another human cost. Not a single Firestone executive went to jail.

Consider this: Under federal law, causing the death of a worker by *willfully* violating safety rules is a misdemeanor punishable by up to six months in prison. Yet to harass a wild burro on federal lands is punishable by a year in prison (Barstow and Bergman 2003).

How do street crime and white-collar crime reflect opportunity structures?

Down-to-Earth **Sociology**

Islands in the Street: Urban Gangs in the United States

For more than ten years, sociologist Martín Sánchez-Jankowski (1991) did participant observation of thirty-seven African American, Chicano, Dominican, Irish, Jamaican, and Puerto Rican gangs in Boston, Los Angeles, and New York City. The gangs earned money through gambling, arson, mugging, armed robbery, and selling moonshine, drugs, guns, stolen car parts, and protection. Sánchez-Jankowski ate, slept, and fought with the gangs, but by mutual agreement he did not participate in drug dealing or other illegal activities. He was seriously injured twice during the study.

Contrary to stereotypes, Sánchez-Jankowski did not find that the motive for joining was to escape a broken home (there were as many members from intact families as from broken homes) or to seek a substitute family (the same number of boys said they were close to their families as those who said they were not). Rather, the boys joined to gain access to money, to have recreation (including sex and drugs), to maintain anonymity in committing crimes, to get protection, and to help the community. This last reason

A. Ramey/PhotoEdit Inc.

may seem surprising, but in some neighborhoods, gangs protect residents from outsiders and spearhead political change (Kontos et al. 2003). The boys also saw the gang as an alternative to the dead-end—and deadening—jobs held by their parents.

Neighborhood residents are ambivalent about gangs. On the one hand, they fear the violence. On the other hand, gang members are the children of people who live in the neighborhood, many of the adults once belonged to gangs, and some gangs provide better protection than the police.

Particular gangs will come and go, but gangs will likely always remain part of the city. As functionalists point out, gangs fulfill needs of poor youth who live on the margins of society.

For Your Consideration

➤ What functions do gangs fulfill (what needs do they meet)? Suppose that you have been hired as an urban planner for the city of Los Angeles. How could you arrange to meet the needs that gangs fulfill in ways that minimize violence and encourage youth to follow mainstream norms?

At several hundred billion dollars a year, the cost of white-collar crime runs at least ten times the cost of street crime (Ramirez 2009). This refers only to dollar costs. No one has yet figured out a way to compare, for example, the suffering experienced by a rape victim with the pain felt by an elderly couple who have lost their life savings to white-collar fraud.

Fear, however, centers on street crime, especially the violent stranger who will change your life forever. As the Social Map (Figure 1) on the next page shows, the chances of such an encounter depend on where you live. You can see that entire regions are safer—or more dangerous–than others. In general, the northern states are safer, and the southern states more dangerous.

Gender and Crime.   Gender is not just something we are or do. It is a feature of society that surrounds us from birth. Gender pushes us, as male or female, into different corners in life, offering and nurturing some behaviors while it withdraws others. The opportunity to commit crime is one of the many consequences of how society sets up a gender order. The social changes that opened business and the professions to women also brought new opportunities for women to commit crime. From car theft to illegal weapons, Table 2 on the next page shows how women have taken advantage of this new opportunity.

In Sum: Functionalists stress that just as the social classes differ in opportunities for income and education, so they differ in opportunities for crime. As a result, street crime is greater among the lower social classes and white-collar crime greater among the higher

What functions do gangs serve? For their members? For society?

FIGURE 1 How Safe Is Your State? Violent Crime in the United States

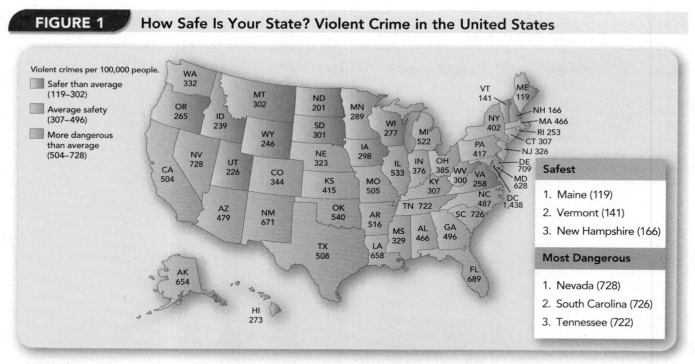

Note: Violent crimes are murder, rape, robbery, and aggravated assault. The chance of becoming a victim of these crimes is six times higher in Nevada, the most dangerous state, than in Maine, the safest state. Washington, D.C., not a state, is in a class by itself. Its rate of 1,438 is *twelve* times higher than Maine's rate.

Source: By the author. Based on *Statistical Abstract of the United States* 2011:Table 304.

social classes. The growing crime rates of women illustrate how changing gender roles have given women more access to what sociologists call "illegitimate opportunities."

The Conflict Perspective

Class, Crime, and the Criminal Justice System

TABLE 2 Women and Crime: What a Difference a Few Years Make

Of all those arrested, what percentage are women?

Crime	1992	2008	Change
Burglary	9.2%	14.6%	+63%
Stolen property	12.5%	20.3%	+62%
Car theft	10.8%	17.2%	+59%
Drunken driving	13.8%	21.4%	+55%
Aggravated assault	14.8%	21.5%	+45%
Robbery	8.5%	11.6%	+36%
Larceny/theft	32.1%	41.2%	+28%
Arson	13.4%	15.7%	+17%
Illegal drugs	16.4%	18.4%	+13%
Forgery and counterfeiting	34.7%	37.8%	+9%
Fraud	42.1%	44.0%	+5%
Illegal weapons	7.5%	7.5%	0%

Source: By the author. Based on *Statistical Abstract of the United States* 2011:Table 330.

TRW sold transistors to the federal government to use in its satellites. The transistors failed, and the government had to shut down its satellite program. TRW said that the failure was a surprise, that it was due to some unknown defect. U.S. officials then paid TRW millions of dollars to investigate the failure.

Then a whistle blower appeared, informing the government that TRW knew the transistors would fail in satellites even before it sold them. The government sued Northrop Grumman Corporation, which had bought TRW, and the corporation was found guilty (Drew 2009).

What was the punishment for a crime this serious? These are military satellites, and they compromised the defense of the

How is gender related to crime?

United States. When the executives of TRW were put on trial, how long were their prison sentences? Actually, these criminals weren't even put on trial, and not one spent even a night in jail. Grumman was fined $325 million. Then—and this is hard to believe, too—on the same day, the government settled a lawsuit that Grumman had brought against it for $325 million. Certainly a rare coincidence.

Contrast this backdoor deal between educated, influential people with poor people who are caught stealing cars. They are sent to prison for years. How can a legal system that proudly boasts "justice for all" be so inconsistent? According to conflict theory, this question is central to the analysis of crime and the **criminal justice system**—the police, courts, and prisons that deal with people who are accused of having committed crimes. Let's see what conflict theorists have to say about this.

The Criminal Justice System as an Instrument of Oppression

Conflict theorists regard power and social inequality as the main characteristics of society. They stress that the power elite uses the criminal justice system to protect its position of power and privilege. The idea that the law operates impartially to bring justice, they say, is a cultural myth promoted by the capitalist class. They point out that the law is really an instrument of oppression, a tool designed by the powerful to maintain their privileged position (Spitzer 1975; Reiman 2004; Chambliss 2000, 1973/2012).

criminal justice system the system of police, courts, and prisons set up to deal with people who are accused of having committed a crime

In early capitalism, children worked alongside adults. At that time, just as today, most street criminals came from the *marginal working class*, as did the boys shown in this 1911 yarn mill in Yazoo City, Mississippi.

Lewis Hine/Underwood Photo Archives/ SuperStock

Why do conflict theorists view the criminal justice system as an instrument of oppression?

Explore
Living Data
on **mysoclab.com**

With their large numbers, the working class and those below them pose a special threat to the power elite. Receiving the least of society's material rewards, they hold the potential to rebel and overthrow the current social order. To prevent this, the law comes down hard on its members who get out of line. The working poor and the underclass are a special problem. They are the least rooted in society. They have few skills and only low-paying, part-time, or seasonal work—if they have jobs at all. Because their street crimes threaten the social order that keeps the elite in power, they are punished severely. From this class come *most* of the prison inmates in the United States.

The criminal justice system, then, does not focus on the executives of corporations and the harm they do through manufacturing unsafe products, creating pollution, and manipulating prices. Yet the violations of the capitalist class cannot be ignored totally, for if they become too outrageous or oppressive they might outrage the working class, encouraging them to rise up and revolt. To prevent this, a flagrant violation by a member of the capitalist class is occasionally prosecuted. The publicity given to the case helps to stabilize the social system by providing evidence of the "fairness" of the criminal justice system.

The powerful, however, are usually able to bypass the courts altogether, appearing instead before an agency that has no power to imprison (such as the Federal Trade Commission). These agencies are directed by people from wealthy backgrounds who sympathize with the intricacies of the corporate world. It is they who oversee most cases of price manipulation of stocks, insider trading, violations of fiduciary duty, and so on. Is it surprising, then, that the typical sanction for corporate crime is a token fine?

In Sum: Conflict theorists stress that the power elite uses the legal system to control workers and to stabilize the social order, all with the goal of keeping itself in power. The poor pose a threat, for if they rebel as a group they can dislodge members of the power elite from their place of privilege. To prevent this, the power elite makes certain that heavy penalties come down on those whose crimes could upset the social order.

Reactions to Deviance

Whether it involves cheating on a sociology quiz or holding up a liquor store, any violation of norms invites reaction. Before we examine reactions in the United States, let's take a little side trip to England. I think you'll enjoy this little excursion in the Cultural Diversity box a few pages ahead.

Street Crime and Prisons

Let's turn back to the United States. Figure 2 shows the surge in the U.S. prison population. Not able to build prisons fast enough to hold all of their incoming prisoners, the state and federal governments have hired private companies to operate additional prisons for them. About 130,000 prisoners are held in these "for-profit" prisons (*Sourcebook of Criminal Justice Statistics* 2010:Table 6.32.2009). Actually, the United States has even more prisoners than shown in Figure 2, since this total does not include jail inmates. If we add them, the total comes to about 2.3 million people—about one out of every 135 citizens. Not only does the United States have more prisoners than any other nation in the world, but it also has a larger percentage of its population in prison as well (Warren et al. 2008).

Who are these prisoners? Let's compare them with the U.S. population. As you look at Table 3, several things may strike you. About half

The cartoonist's hyperbole makes an excellent commentary on the social class disparity of our criminal justice system. Not only are the crimes of the wealthy not as likely to come to the attention of authorities as are the crimes of the poor, but when they do, the wealthy can afford legal expertise that the poor cannot.

"If you want justice, it's two hundred dollars an hour. Obstruction of justice runs a bit more."

Why do conflict theorists view the criminal justice system as an instrument of oppression?

TABLE 3	Inmates in U.S. State and Federal Prisons	
Characteristics	**Percentage of Prisoners with These Characteristics**	**Percentage of U.S. Population with These Characteristics**
Age		
18–24	15.9%	9.8%
25–34	33.6%	13.5%
35–44	29.1%	14.0%
45–54	14.8%	14.6%
55 and older	6.7%	23.9%
Race–Ethnicity		
African American	38.4%	12.8%
White	34.3%	65.6%
Latino	20.3%	15.4%
Other[a]	6.9%	5.5%
Sex		
Male	93.2%	49.2%
Female	6.8%	50.8%
Marital Status		
Never married	59.8%	26.0%
Divorced	15.5%	10.4%
Married	17.3%	57.3%
Widowed	1.1%	6.4%
Education		
Less than high school	39.7%	13.4%
High school graduate	49.0%	31.2%
Some college[b]	9.0%	26.0%
College graduate	2.4%	29.4%

[a]Asian Americans and Native Americans are included in this category.
[b]Includes associate's degrees.

Source: By the author. Based on *Sourcebook of Criminal Justice Statistics* 2003:Tables 6.000b, 6.28; 2006:Tables 6.34, 6.45; 2009:Table 6.33.2008; *Statistical Abstract of the United States* 2011:Tables 8, 10, 56, 227.

(49 percent) of all prisoners are younger than 35, and almost all prisoners are men. Then there is this remarkable statistic: Although African Americans make up just 12.8 percent of the U.S. population, close to two of five prisoners are African Americans. On any given day, *one out of every nine* African American men ages 20 to 34 is in jail or prison. (For Latinos, the rate is one of twenty-six; for whites one of one hundred [Warren et al. 2008].)

Finally, note how marriage and education—two of the major ways that society "anchors" people into mainstream behavior—keeps people out of prison. *Most* prisoners have never married. And look at the power of education, a major component of social class. As I mentioned earlier, social class funnels some people into the criminal justice system and diverts others away from it. You can see how people who drop out of high school have a high chance of ending up in prison—and how unlikely it is for a college graduate to have this unwelcome destination in life.

For about the past twenty years or so, the United States has followed a "get tough" policy. One of the most significant changes was "three-strikes-and-you're-out" laws, which have had unanticipated consequences, as you will see in the following Thinking Critically section.

Why don't the characteristics of prisoners match those of the U.S. population?

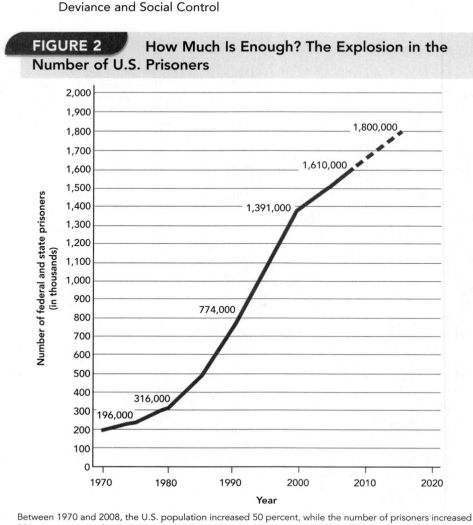

FIGURE 2   How Much Is Enough? The Explosion in the Number of U.S. Prisoners

Between 1970 and 2008, the U.S. population increased 50 percent, while the number of prisoners increased 821 percent, a rate that is *sixteen times greater* than population growth. If the number of prisoners had grown at the same rate as the U.S. population, we would have about 294,000 prisoners, only one-fifth to one-sixth of today's total. Or if the U.S. population had increased at the same rate as that of U.S. prisoners, the U.S. population would be 1,670,000,000—approximately the population of China and all of Europe combined.

Sources: By the author. Based on *Statistical Abstract of the United States* 1995:Table 349; 2011:Tables 1, 6, 344. The broken line is the author's estimate.

THINKING CRITICALLY
"Three Strikes and You're Out!" Unintended Consequences of Well-Intended Laws

As the violent crime rate soared in the 1980s, Americans grew fearful. They demanded that their lawmakers do something. Politicians heard the message, and many responded by passing "three-strikes" laws in their states. Anyone who is convicted of a third felony receives an automatic mandatory sentence. Although some mandatory sentences carry life imprisonment, judges are not allowed to consider the circumstances. While few of us would feel sympathy if a man convicted of a third brutal rape or a third murder were sent to prison for life, in their haste to appease the public the politicians did not limit the three-strike laws to *violent* crimes. And they did not consider that some minor crimes are considered felonies. As the functionalists would say, this has led to unanticipated consequences.

Here are some actual cases:

How are the three-strikes laws part of the reason for the explosion in the number of U.S. prisoners?

- In Los Angeles, a 27-year-old man who stole a pizza was sentenced to 25 years in prison (Cloud 1998).
- In Sacramento, a man passed himself off as Tiger Woods and went on a $17,000 shopping spree. He was sentenced to *200 years* in prison (Reuters 2001).
- Also in California, Michael James passed a bad check for $94. He was sentenced to 25 years to life (Jones 2008).
- In Utah, a 25-year-old sold small bags of marijuana to a police informant. The judge who sentenced the man to 55 years in prison said the sentence was unjust, but he had no choice (Madigan 2004).
- In New York City, a man who was about to be sentenced for selling crack said to the judge, "I'm only 19. This is terrible." He then hurled himself out of a courtroom window, plunging to his death sixteen stories below (Cloud 1998).

For Your Consideration
➤ Apply the symbolic interactionist, functionalist, and conflict perspectives to the three-strikes laws. For *symbolic interactionism*, what do these laws represent to the public? How does your answer differ depending on what part of "the public" you are referring to? For *functionalism*, who benefits from these laws? What are some of their functions? Their dysfunctions? For the *conflict perspective*, which groups are in conflict? Who has the power to enforce their will on others? ■

Cultural Diversity around the World

"Dogging" in England

In some places in England, people like to "dog" it. This is their term for having sex in public so others can watch. The sex often is between strangers who have arranged to meet through the Internet.

"Dogging" is a strange term, and no one knows its origin. The term might come from voyeurs who doggedly follow people who are having sex. Or it might refer to the similarity to female dogs in heat that have sex with any dog around. Or it might even come from the statement "I'm just going to walk the dog," when they are really going out to do something else entirely.

Regardless of the term's origin, frolicking in the fields is popular. Internet sites even lay out basic rules, such as "Only join in if you are asked."

The Internet sites also rate England's dogging locations. The field in Puttenham, a village an hour's drive from London, is ranked Number 2 in England. The field is mostly used by homosexuals during the day, with heterosexuals taking over at night.

One motorist who stopped his car to use the bushes for a bathroom break was startled when a group of eager men surrounded him. He said that he took the quickest pee in his life.

Dogging isn't legal, but the police mostly ignore it. The police have even warned the public, but in a discreet English way. They have designated the field in Puttenham as a "public sex environment."

Some village residents are upset at the litter left behind, from condoms to tea cups. Others are upset that the dogging field is just 400 yards from the village nursery school. A woman who went to the police to complain showed them a pink vibrator she had found in the field. "What should we do with it?" asked the officer. Seeing that she was going to get nowhere, she said they could just put it in Lost and Found.

After listening to citizen complaints, the County Council Cabinet wanted to know if anyone had practical solutions. One suggested that the police patrol the site with dogs. Another said they should fill the field with bad-tempered bulls.

Distressed at such inconsiderate reactions, one empathetic cabinet member said, "If you close this site, they wouldn't have anywhere else to go. There might be an increase in suicides."

The citizens and Council members reached a compromise: They would put up a sign. "Don't have sex here" seemed too direct for the English, so the sign, much more polite and circuitous, says, "Do not engage in activities of an unacceptable nature."

Source: Based on Lyall 2010.

For Your Consideration
➤ What do you think the police would do if there were a "dogging" field in your town? What do you think the public's reaction would be? Why do you think the police are so "heavy handed" in the United States while those in England take such a lighter approach?

Compare the reactions to "dogging" in England with the "three-strikes" laws in the United States.

"It's interesting—with each conviction I learn a little more about myself."

Unfortunately, whatever prisoners do learn about themselves in prison—if anything—fails to keep them from coming back.

recidivism rate the percentage of released convicts who are rearrested

The Decline in Violent Crime

As legislators passed three-strikes laws, and judges put more and more people in prison, the crime rate dropped sharply. This has led to a controversy in sociology. Some sociologists conclude that getting tough on criminals reduced violent crime (Conklin 2003). Others point to higher employment, a drop in drug use, and even abortion (Rosenfeld 2002; Reiman 2004; Blumstein and Wallman 2006). We can rule out employment, for when the unemployment rate shot up with the economic crisis the lower crime rates continued (Oppel 2011). This matter is not yet settled. We'll see what answers future research brings.

Recidivism

If a goal of prisons is to teach their clients to stay away from crime, they are colossal failures. We can measure their failure by the **recidivism rate**—the percentage of former prisoners who are rearrested. For people sent to prison for crimes of violence, within just three years of their release, two out of three (62 percent) are rearrested, and half (52 percent) are back in prison (*Sourcebook of Criminal Justice Statistics* 2003:Table 6.52). Looking at Figure 3, which gives a breakdown of three-year recidivism by type of crime, it is safe to conclude that prisons do not teach people that crime doesn't pay.

The Death Penalty and Bias

As you know, **capital punishment,** the death penalty, is the most extreme measure the state takes. As you also know, the death penalty arouses impassioned opposition and support. Advances in DNA testing have given opponents of the death penalty a strong argument: Innocent people have been sent to death row, and some have been executed. Others are just as passionate about retaining the death penalty. They point to such crimes as those of the serial killers discussed in the Down-to-Earth Sociology box on the next page.

Apart from anyone's personal position on the death penalty, it certainly is clear that the death penalty is not administered evenly. Consider geography: The Social Map shows that where people commit murder greatly affects their chances of being put to death.

The death penalty also shows social class bias. As you know from news reports, it is rare for a rich person to be sentenced to death. Although the government does not collect statistics on social class and the death penalty, this common observation is borne out by the education of the prisoners on death row. *Half* of the prisoners on death row (50 percent) have not finished high school (*Sourcebook of Criminal Justice Statistics* 2009:Table 6.81).

There is also a gender bias in the death penalty. It is so strong that it is almost unheard of for a woman to be sentenced to death, much less executed. Although women commit 9.6 percent of the murders, they make up only 1.8 percent

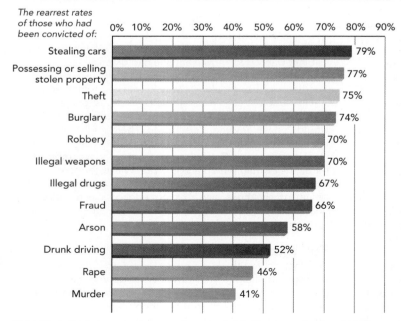

FIGURE 3   Recidivism of U.S. Prisoners

Of 272,000 prisoners released from U.S. prisons, what percentage were rearrested within three years?

The rearrest rates of those who had been convicted of:

- Stealing cars 79%
- Possessing or selling stolen property 77%
- Theft 75%
- Burglary 74%
- Robbery 70%
- Illegal weapons 70%
- Illegal drugs 67%
- Fraud 66%
- Arson 58%
- Drunk driving 52%
- Rape 46%
- Murder 41%

Note: The individuals were not necessarily rearrested for the same crime for which they had originally been imprisoned.
Source: By the author. Based on *Sourcebook of Criminal Justice Statistics* 2003:Table 6.50.

Based on recidivism, how effective are our prisons? Why do you think we have a gender bias in the death penalty?

Down-to-Earth Sociology

The Killer Next Door: Serial Murderers in Our Midst

Here is my experience with serial killers. As I was watching television one night, I was stunned by the images coming from Houston, Texas. Television cameras showed the police digging up dozens of bodies from under a boat storage shed. Fascinated, I waited impatiently for spring break. A few days later, I drove from Illinois to Houston, where 33-year-old Dean Corll had befriended Elmer Wayne Henley and David Brooks, two teenagers from broken homes. Together, they had killed twenty-seven boys. Elmer and David would pick up young hitchhikers and deliver them to Corll to rape and kill. Sometimes they even brought him their own high school classmates.

I talked to one of Elmer's neighbors, as he was painting his front porch. His 15-year-old son had gone to get a haircut one Saturday morning. That was the last time he saw his son alive. The police refused to investigate. They insisted that his son had run away. On a city map, I plotted the locations of the homes of the local murder victims. Many clustered around the homes of the teenage killers.

I decided to spend my coming sabbatical writing a novel on this case. To get into the minds of the killers, I knew that I would have to "become" them day after day for months. Corll kept a piece of plywood in his apartment. In each of its corners, he had cut a hole. He and the boys would spread-eagle their handcuffed victims on this board and torture them for hours. Sometimes, they would even pause to order pizza. I began to wonder about immersing myself in torture and human degradation. Would I be the same person afterwards? I decided not to write the book.

The three killers led double lives so successfully that their friends and family were unaware of their criminal activities. Henley's mother swore to me that her son couldn't possibly be guilty—he was a good boy. Some of Elmer's high school friends told me that that his being involved in homosexual rape and murder was ridiculous—he was interested only in girls. I was interviewing them in Henley's bedroom, and for proof they pointed to a pair of girls' panties that were draped across a lamp shade.

AP Images/Pool

Ted Bundy is shown here with his defense attorney, when he was on trial in Miami for killing two college students. You can get a glimpse of his charm and wit and how, like most serial killers, he blended in with society. Bundy was executed for his murders.

Serial murder is the killing of victims in three or more separate events. The murders may occur over several days, weeks, or years. The elapsed time between murders distinguishes serial killers from *mass murderers*, those who do their killing all at once. Here are some infamous examples:

- During the 1960s and 1970s, Ted Bundy raped and killed dozens of women in four states.
- Between 1974 and 1991, Dennis Rader killed ten people in Wichita, Kansas. Rader had written to the newspapers, proudly calling himself the BTK (Bind, Torture, and Kill) strangler.
- In the late 1980s and early 1990s, Aileen Wuornos hitchhiked along Florida's freeways. She killed seven men after having had sex with them.
- The serial killer with the most victims appears to be Harold Shipman, a physician in Manchester, England. From 1977 to 2000, during house calls Shipman gave lethal injections to 230 to 275 of his elderly female patients.
- In 2009, Anthony Sowell of Cleveland, Ohio, was discovered living with eleven decomposing bodies of women he had raped and strangled (UPI 2009).

Is serial murder more common now than it used to be? Not likely. In the past, police departments had little communication with one another, and seldom did anyone connect killings in different jurisdictions. Today's more efficient communications, investigative techniques, and DNA matching make it easier for the police to know when a serial killer is operating in an area. Part of the perception that there are more serial killers today is also due to ignorance of our history: In our frontier past, for example, serial killers went from ranch to ranch.

For Your Consideration

→ Do you think that serial killers should be given the death penalty? Why or why not? How does your social location influence your opinion?

of death row inmates (*Sourcebook of Criminal Justice Statistics* 2009:Table 6.81). Even on death row, the gender bias continues: Of those condemned to death, the state is more likely to execute a man than a woman. As Figure 5 shows, only 0.9 percent of the 1,137 prisoners executed in the United States since 1977 have been women. This gender bias could reflect the women's previous offenses and the relative brutality of their murders, but we need research to determine if this is so.

capital punishment the death penalty

serial murder the killing of several victims in three or more separate events

What do you think the penalty for serial killers should be? Why?

FIGURE 4   **Executions in the United States**

Executions since 1977, when the death penalty was reinstated.

- States without death penalty
- States with death penalty that have not executed anyone
- States with death penalty

WA 4
OR 2
MT 3
ND 0
MN 0
WI 0
MI 0
VT 0
ME 0
NH 0
MA 0
RI 0
CT 1
NY 0
PA 3
NJ 0
DE 14
MD 5
DC 0
ID 1
WY 1
SD 1
IA 0
IL 12
IN 20
OH 33
WV 0
VA 105
NV 12
UT 6
CO 1
NE 3
KS 0
MO 67
KY 3
NC 43
CA 13
AZ 23
NM 1
OK 91
AR 27
TN 6
SC 42
MS 10
AL 44
GA 46
TX 447
LA 27
FL 68
AK 0
HI 0

Highest Number of Executions

1. Texas (447)
2. Virginia (105)
3. Oklahoma (91)

Source: By the author. Based on *Statistical Abstract of the United States* 2011:Table 350.

Bias was once so flagrant that it put a stop to the death penalty. Donald Partington (1965), a lawyer in Virginia, was shocked by the bias he saw in the courtroom, and he decided to document it. He found that 2,798 men had been convicted for rape and attempted rape in Virginia between 1908 and 1963—56 percent whites and 44 percent blacks. For attempted rape, 13 had been executed. For rape, 41 men had been executed. *All those executed were black.* Not one of the whites was executed.

After listening to evidence like this, in 1972 the Supreme Court ruled in *Furman v. Georgia* that the death penalty, as applied, was unconstitutional. The execution of prisoners stopped—but not for long. The states wrote new laws, and in 1977 they again began to execute prisoners. Since then, 65 percent of those put to death have been white and 35 percent African American (*Statistical Abstract* 2011:Table 349). (Latinos are evidently counted as whites in this statistic.) While living on death row is risky for anyone, the risk is higher for African Americans and Latinos who killed whites. They are more likely to be executed (Jacobs et al. 2007). The most accurate predictor of who will be put to death, though, is somewhat surprising: Those who have the least education are the most likely to be executed (Karamouzis and Harper 2007). Table 4 shows the race–ethnicity of the prisoners on death row.

Legal Change

Did you know that it is a crime in Saudi Arabia for a woman to drive a car (Fattah 2007)? A crime in Florida to sell alcohol before 1 P.M. on Sundays? Or illegal in Wells, Maine, to advertise on tombstones?

hate crime a crime that is punished more severely because it is motivated by hatred (dislike, hostility, animosity) of someone's race–ethnicity, religion, sexual orientation, disability, or national origin

As has been stressed in this chapter, deviance, including the form called *crime,* is so relative that it varies from one society to another, and from one group to another within the same society. Crime also varies from one time period to another, as opinions change or as different groups gain access to power. We discuss one of these changes in the following Thinking Critically section.

What bias in the application of the death penalty led to it being declared unconstitutional?

TABLE 4	The Race–Ethnicity of the 3,316 Prisoners on Death Row	
	Percentage	
	on Death Row	in U.S. Population
Whites	44%	67%
African Americans	41%	13%
Latinos	12%	14%
Asian Americans	1%	4%
Native Americans	1%	1%

Source: By the author. Based on *Sourcebook of Criminal Justice Statistics* 2010:Table 6.80.

THINKING CRITICALLY
Changing Views: Making Hate a Crime

Because crime consists of whatever acts authorities decide to assign that label, new crimes emerge from time to time. A prime example is juvenile delinquency, which Illinois lawmakers designated a separate type of crime in 1899. Juveniles committed crimes before 1899, of course, but youths were not considered to be a separate type of lawbreaker. They were just young people who committed crimes, and they were treated the same as adults who committed the same crime.

Crimes motivated by hate are common around the world. This photo of a vandalized muslim grave was taken in Copenhagen, Denmark.
Francis Dean/Dean Pictures/The Image Works

Sometimes new technology leads to new crimes. Motor vehicle theft, a separate crime in the United States, obviously did not exist before the automobile was invented.

In the 1980s, another new crime was born when state governments developed the classification **hate crime,** crimes motivated by *bias* (dislike, hatred) against someone's race–ethnicity, religion, sexual orientation, disability, or national origin. Before this, people attacked others or destroyed their property out of these same motivations, but when authorities dealt with the crime the motivation was not the issue. If someone injured or killed another person because of that person's race–ethnicity, religion, sexual orientation, national origin, or disability, he or she was charged with assault or murder. Today, motivation has become a central issue, and hate crimes carry more severe sentences than equivalent acts that do not have hatred as their motive. Table 5 on the next page summarizes the victims of hate crimes.

We can be certain that the "evolution" of crime is not yet complete. As society changes and as different groups gain access to power, we can expect the definitions of crime to change accordingly.

For Your Consideration
➔ Why should we have a separate classification called *hate crime*? Why aren't the crimes of assault, robbery, and murder adequate? As one analyst (Sullivan 1999) said, "Was the brutal murder of gay college student Matthew Shepard in Laramie, Wyoming, in 1998 (a hate crime) worse than the abduction, rape, and murder of an eight-year-old Laramie girl by a pedophile (not a hate crime) that same year?"

➔ How do you think your social location (race–ethnicity, gender, social class, sexual orientation, or physical ability) affects your opinion? ■

FIGURE 5	Who Gets Executed? Gender Bias in Capital Punishment

99.1%

0.9%

| 5,004 Men | 43 Women |

Source: By the author. Based on *Statistical Abstract of the United States* 2011:Table 349.

How are the hate crime laws an example of an evolving criminal justice system?

TABLE 5	Hate Crimes
Directed Against	**Number of Victims**
Race–Ethnicity	
African Americans	3,596
Whites	829
Latinos	792
Multiracial	276
Asian Americans	170
Native Americans	63
Religion	
Jews	1,145
Muslims	130
Catholics	89
Protestants	62
Sexual Orientation	
Homosexual	1,706
Male Homosexual	981
Female Homosexual	198
General	466
Heterosexual	34
Bisexual	27
Disabilities	
Mental	57
Physical	28

Note: The number is the cumulative victims from 2000 to 2008, the latest year available.
Source: By the author. Based on *Statistical Abstract of the United States* 2011:Table 318.

The Trouble with Official Statistics

Both the findings of symbolic interactionists (that stereotypes operate when authorities deal with groups such as the Saints and the Roughnecks) and the conclusion of conflict theorists (that the criminal justice system serves the ruling elite) demonstrate the need for caution in interpreting official statistics. Crime statistics do not have an objective, independent existence. They are not like oranges that you pick out in a grocery store. Rather, crime statistics are a human creation. One major element in producing them is the particular laws that exist. Another is how those laws are enforced. Still another is how officials report their statistics. Change these factors, and the statistics also change.

Consider this: According to official statistics, working-class boys are more delinquent than middle-class boys. Yet, as we have seen, who actually gets arrested for what is influenced by social class, a point that has far-reaching implications. As symbolic interactionists point out, the police follow a symbolic system as they enforce the law. Ideas of "typical criminals" and "typical good citizens," for example, permeate their work. The more a suspect matches their stereotypes of a lawbreaker (which they call "criminal profiles"), the more likely that person is to be arrested. **Police discretion,** the decision whether to arrest someone or even to ignore a matter, is a routine part of police work. Consequently, official crime statistics reflect these and many other biases.

In Sum: Reactions to deviants vary from such mild sanctions as frowns and stares to such severe responses as imprisonment and death. Some sanctions are formal—court hearings, for example—but most are informal, as when friends refuse to talk to each other. One sanction is to label someone a deviant, which can have powerful consequences for the person's life, especially if the label closes off conforming activities and opens deviant ones. The degradation ceremony, in which someone is publicly labeled "not one of us," is a powerful sanction. So is imprisonment. Official statistics must be viewed with caution, for they reflect biases.

The Medicalization of Deviance: Mental Illness

Another way in which society deals with deviance is to "medicalize" it. Let's look at what this means.

Neither Mental Nor Illness? To **medicalize** something is to make it a medical matter, to classify it as a form of illness that properly belongs in the care of physicians. For the past hundred years or so, especially since the time of Sigmund Freud (1856–1939), the Viennese physician who founded psychoanalysis, there has been a growing tendency toward the **medicalization of deviance.** In this view, deviance, including crime, is a sign of mental sickness. Rape, murder, stealing, cheating, and so on are external symptoms of internal disorders, consequences of a confused or tortured mind.

This also applies to "unusual" behaviors that disturb people. When they cannot find a satisfying explanation for why someone is "like that," they often say that a "sickness in the head" is causing the unacceptable behavior. Thomas Szasz (1986, 1996, 1998), a renegade in his profession of psychiatry, argues that what are called *mental illnesses are neither mental nor illnesses. They are simply problem behaviors.* Szasz breaks these behaviors for which we don't have a ready explanation into two causes: physical illness and learned deviance.

Some behaviors that are called "mental illnesses" have physical causes. That is, something in an individual's body results in unusual perceptions or behavior. Some depression, for example, is caused by a chemical imbalance in the brain, which can be treated by drugs. The

AP Images

People whose behaviors violate norms often are called mentally ill. "Why else would they do such things?" is a common response to deviant behaviors that we don't understand. Mental illness is a label that contains the assumption that there is something wrong "within" people that "causes" their disapproved behavior. The surprise with this man, who changed his legal name to "Scary Guy," is that he speaks at schools across the country, where he promotes acceptance, awareness, love, and understanding.

Why aren't official crime statistics exact? What is the medicalization of deviance?

behaviors that are associated with depression—crying, long-term sadness, and lack of interest in family, work, school, or grooming—are only symptoms of a physical problem.

Attention-deficit disorder (ADD) is an example of a new "mental illness" that has come out of nowhere. As Szasz says, "No one explains where this disease came from or why it didn't exist 50 years ago. No one is able to diagnose it with objective tests." ADD is diagnosed because a teacher or parent is complaining about a child misbehaving. Misbehaving children have been a problem throughout history, but now, with doctors looking to expand their territory, this problem behavior has become a sign of "mental illness."

All of us have troubles. Some of us face a constant barrage of problems as we go through life. Most of us continue the struggle, perhaps encouraged by friends or motivated by job, family responsibilities, religious faith, and life goals. Even when the odds seem hopeless, we carry on, not perfectly, but as best we can. Some people, however, fail to cope well with life's challenges. Overwhelmed, they become depressed, uncooperative, or hostile. Some strike out at others; and some, in Merton's terms, become retreatists and withdraw into their apartments or homes, refusing to come out. Although these ways of coping create problems, they are *behaviors, not mental illnesses,* stresses Szasz. "Mental illness," Szasz concludes, is a myth foisted on a naïve public. Our medical profession uses pseudo-scientific jargon that people don't understand so it can expand its area of control and force nonconforming people to accept society's definitions of "normal."

Szasz's controversial claim forces us to look anew at the forms of deviance that we usually refer to as mental illness. To explain behavior that people find bizarre, he directs our attention not to causes hidden deep within the "subconscious," but, instead, to how people learn such behaviors. To ask, "What is the origin of someone's inappropriate or bizarre behavior?" then becomes similar to asking, "Why do some women steal?" "Why do some men rape?" "Why do some teenagers cuss their parents and stalk out of the room, slamming the door?" *The answers depend on those people's particular experiences in life, not on an illness in their minds.* In short, some sociologists find Szasz's renegade analysis refreshing because it indicates that *social experiences*, not some illness of the mind, underlie bizarre behaviors—as well as deviance in general.

The Homeless Mentally Ill

Jamie was sitting on a low wall surrounding the landscaped courtyard of an exclusive restaurant. She appeared unaware of the stares elicited by her layers of mismatched clothing, her matted hair and dirty face, and the shopping cart that overflowed with her meager possessions.

After sitting next to Jamie for a few minutes, I saw her point to the street and concentrate, slowly moving her finger horizontally. I asked her what she was doing.

"I'm directing traffic," she replied. "I control where the cars go. Look, that one turned right there," she said, now withdrawing her finger.

"Really?" I said.

After a while she confided that her cart talked to her.

"Really?" I said again.

"Yes," she replied. "You can hear it, too." At that, she pushed the shopping cart a bit. "Did you hear that?" she asked.

When I shook my head, she demonstrated again. Then it hit me. She was referring to the squeaking wheels!

I nodded.

When I left Jamie, she was pointing to the sky, for, as she told me, she also controlled the flight of airplanes.

To most of us, Jamie's behavior and thinking are bizarre. They simply do not match any reality we know. Could you or I become like Jamie?

Suppose for a bitter moment that you are homeless and have to live on the streets. You have no money, no place to sleep, no bathroom. You do not know *if* you are going to eat, much less where. You have no friends or anyone you can trust. You live in constant fear of rape and other violence. Do you think this might be enough to drive you over the edge?

police discretion the practice of the police, in the normal course of their duties, to either arrest or ticket someone for an offense or to overlook the matter

medicalization the transformation of a human condition into a matter to be treated by physicians

medicalization of deviance to make deviance a medical matter, a symptom of some underlying illness that needs to be treated by physicians

Mental illness is common among the homeless. This photo was taken in New York City, but it could have been taken in any large city in the United States.

Dane Rex/Lightbox

What is the argument that mental illnesses are problem behaviors, not mental illnesses?

Consider just the problems involved in not having a place to bathe. (Shelters are often so dangerous that many homeless people prefer to sleep in public settings.) At first, you try to wash in the restrooms of gas stations, bars, the bus station, or a shopping center. But you are dirty, and people stare when you enter and call the management when they see you wash your feet in the sink. You are thrown out and told in no uncertain terms never to come back. So you get dirtier and dirtier. Eventually, you come to think of being dirty as a fact of life. Soon, maybe, you don't even care. The stares no longer bother you—at least not as much.

No one will talk to you, and you withdraw more and more into yourself. You begin to build a fantasy life. You talk openly to yourself. People stare, but so what? They stare anyway. Besides, they are no longer important to you.

Jamie might be mentally ill. Some organic problem, such as a chemical imbalance in her brain, might underlie her behavior. But perhaps not. How long would it take you to exhibit bizarre behaviors if you were homeless—and hopeless? The point is that *living on the streets can cause mental illness*—or whatever we want to label socially inappropriate behaviors that we find difficult to classify. *Homelessness and mental illness are reciprocal:* Just as "mental illness" can cause homelessness, so the trials of being homeless, of living on cold, hostile streets, can lead to unusual thinking and behaviors.

The Need for a More Humane Approach

As Durkheim (1895/1964:68) pointed out, deviance is inevitable—even in a group of saints.

> *Imagine a society of saints, a perfect cloister of exemplary individuals. Crimes, properly so called, will there be unknown; but faults which appear invisible to the layman will create there the same scandal that the ordinary offense does in ordinary society.*

With deviance inevitable, one measure of a society is how it treats its deviants. Our prisons certainly don't say much good about U.S. society. Filled with the poor, uneducated, and unskilled, they are warehouses of the unwanted. White-collar criminals continue to get by with a slap on the wrist while street criminals are punished severely. Some deviants, who fail to meet current standards of admission to either prison or mental hospital, take refuge in shelters, as well as in cardboard boxes tucked away in urban recesses. Although no one has *the* answer, it does not take much reflection to see that there are more humane approaches than these.

Because deviance is inevitable, the larger issues are to find ways to protect people from deviant behaviors that are harmful to themselves or others, to tolerate behaviors that are not harmful, and to develop systems of fairer treatment for deviants. In the absence of fundamental changes that would bring about an equitable social system, most efforts are, unfortunately, like putting a Band-Aid on a gunshot wound. What we need is a more humane social system, one that would prevent social inequalities.

Summary and Review

What Is Deviance?

Deviance (the violation of norms) is relative. What people consider deviant varies from one culture to another and from group to group within the same society. As symbolic inter-actionists stress, it is not the act, but the reactions to the act, that make something deviant. All groups develop systems of **social control** to punish **deviants**—those who violate their norms.

How are homelessness and mental illness reciprocal (each contributing to the other)?

How do sociological and individualistic explanations of deviance differ?

To explain why people deviate, sociobiologists and psychologists look for reasons *within* the individual, such as **genetic predispositions** or **personality disorders.** Sociologists, in contrast, look for explanations *outside* the individual, in social experiences.

The Symbolic Interactionist Perspective

How do symbolic interactionists explain deviance?

Symbolic interactionists have developed several theories to explain deviance such as **crime** (the violation of norms that are written into law). According to **differential association** theory, people learn to deviate by associating with others. According to **control theory,** each of us is propelled toward deviance, but most of us conform because of an effective system of inner and outer controls. People who have less effective controls deviate. They use **labeling theory** to focus on how labels (names, reputations) help to funnel people into or divert them away from deviance. People who commit deviant acts often use **techniques of neutralization** to deflect social norms.

The Functionalist Perspective

How do functionalists explain deviance?

Functionalists point out that deviance, including criminal acts, is functional for society. Functions include affirming norms and promoting social unity and social change. According to **strain theory,** societies socialize their members into desiring **cultural goals.** Many people are unable to achieve these goals in socially acceptable ways—that is, by **institutionalized means.** *Deviants,* then, are people who either give up on the goals or use disapproved means to attain them. Merton identified five types of responses to cultural goals and institutionalized means: conformity, innovation, ritualism, retreatism, and rebellion. Because of **illegitimate opportunity structures,** some people have easier access to illegal means of achieving goals.

The Conflict Perspective

How do conflict theorists explain deviance?

Conflict theorists take the position that the group in power imposes its definitions of deviance on other groups. From this perspective, the law is an instrument of oppression used by the powerful to maintain their position of privilege. The ruling class uses the **criminal justice system** to punish the crimes of the poor while diverting its own criminal activities away from this punitive system.

Reactions to Deviance

What are common reactions to deviance in the United States?

In following a "get-tough" policy, the United States has imprisoned millions of people. African Americans and Latinos make up a disproportionate percentage of U.S. prisoners. The death penalty shows biases by geography, social class, gender, and race–ethnicity. In line with conflict theory, as groups gain political power, their views are reflected in the criminal code. **Hate crime** legislation was considered in this context.

Are official statistics on crime reliable?

The conclusions of both symbolic interactionists (that the police operate with a large measure of discretion) and conflict theorists (that a power elite controls the legal system) indicate that we must be cautious when using crime statistics.

What is the medicalization of deviance?

The medical profession has attempted to **medicalize** many forms of **deviance,** claiming that they represent mental illnesses. Thomas Szasz disagrees, asserting that they are problem behaviors, not mental illnesses. The situation of homeless people indicates that problems in living can lead to bizarre behavior and thinking.

What is a more humane approach?

Deviance is inevitable, so the larger issues are to find ways to protect people from deviance that harms themselves and others, to tolerate deviance that is not harmful, and to develop systems of fairer treatment for deviants.

Thinking Critically about this Chapter

1. Select some deviance with which you are personally familiar. (It does not have to be your own—it can be something that someone you know did.) Choose one of the three theoretical perspectives to explain what happened.

2. As explained in the text, deviance can be mild. Recall some instance in which you broke a social rule in dress, etiquette, or speech. What was the reaction? Why do you think people reacted like that? What was your response to their reactions?

3. What do you think should be done about the U.S. crime problem? What sociological theories support your view?

References

All new references are printed in cyan.

Anderson, Elijah. *A Place on the Corner.* Chicago: University of Chicago Press, 1978.

Anderson, Elijah. "Streetwise." In *Exploring Social Life: Readings to Accompany Essentials of Sociology,* 2nd ed., James M. Henslin, ed. Boston: Allyn and Bacon, 2006:147–156. Originally published 1990.

Appiah, Kwame Anthony. "The Best Weapon against Honor Killers: Shame." *Wall Street Journal,* September 25, 2010.

Arlacchi, P. *Peasants and Great Estates: Society in Traditional Calabria.* Cambridge, England: Cambridge University Press, 1980.

Barnes, Helen. "A Comment on Stroud and Pritchard: Child Homicide, Psychiatric Disorder and Dangerousness." *British Journal of Social Work, 31,* 3, June 2001.

Barstow, David, and Lowell Bergman. "Death on the Job, Slaps on the Wrist." *Wall Street Journal,* January 10, 2003.

Becker, Howard S. *Outsiders: Studies in the Sociology of Deviance.* New York: Free Press, 1966.

Bernburg, Jon Gunnar, Marvin D. Krohn, and Craig J. Rivera. "Official Labeling, Criminal Embeddedness, and Subsequent Delinquency: A Longitudinal Test of Labeling Theory." *Journal of Research in Crime and Delinquency, 43,* 1, February 2006:67–88.

Billeaud, Jacques. "Arizona Sheriff Defends Illegal-Immigrant Sweeps." *Seattle Times,* April 26, 2008.

Blumstein, Alfred, and Joel Wallman. "The Crime Drop and Beyond." *Annual Review of Law and Social Science, 2,* December 2006:125–146.

Catan, Thomas. "Spain's Showy Debt Collectors Wear a Tux, Collect the Bucks." *Wall Street Journal,* October 11, 2008.

Chagnon, Napoleon A. *Yanomamo: The Fierce People,* 2nd ed. New York: Holt, Rinehart and Winston, 1977.

Chambliss, William J. *Power, Politics, and Crime.* Boulder: Westview Press, 2000.

Chambliss, William J. "The Saints and the Roughnecks." In *Down to Earth Sociology: Introductory Readings,* 15th ed., James M. Henslin, ed. New York: The Free Press, 2012.

Chivers, C. J. "Officer Resigns before Hearing in D.W.I. Case." *New York Times,* August 29, 2001.

Chung, He Len, and Laurence Steinberg. "Relations between Neighborhood Factors, Parenting Behaviors, Peer Deviance, and Delinquency among Serious Juvenile Offenders." *Developmental Psychology, 42,* 2, 2006:319–331.

Church, Wesley T., II, Tracy Wharton, and Julie K. Taylor. "An Examination of Differential Association and Social Control Theory: Family Systems and Delinquency." *Youth Violence and Juvenile Justice, 7,* 1, January 2009:3–15.

Cloud, John. "For Better or Worse." *Time,* October 26, 1998:43–44.

Cloward, Richard A., and Lloyd E. Ohlin. *Delinquency and Opportunity: A Theory of Delinquent Gangs.* New York: Free Press, 1960.

Conklin, John E. *Why Crime Rates Fell.* Boston: Allyn and Bacon, 2003.

Deflem, Mathieu, ed. *Sociological Theory and Criminological Research: Views from Europe and the United States.* San Diego: JAI Press, 2006.

Drew, Christopher. "Military Contractor Agrees to Pay $325 Million to Settle Whistle-Blower Lawsuit." *New York Times,* April 2, 2009.

Duck, W. O., and Anne W. Rawls, "Interaction Orders of Drug Dealing Spaces: Local Orders of Sensemaking in a Poor Black American Place." *Crime, Law and Social Change,* 2011.

Dunaway, Wilma A. *Women, Work, and Family in the Antebellum Mountain South.* New York: Cambridge University Press, 2008.

Durkheim, Emile. *The Division of Labor in Society,* George Simpson, trans. New York: Free Press, 1933. Originally published 1893.

Durkheim, Emile. *The Rules of Sociological Method,* Sarah A. Solovay and John H. Mueller, trans. New York: Free Press, 1938, 1958, 1964. Originally published 1895.

Edgerton, Robert B. *Deviance: A Cross-Cultural Perspective.* Menlo Park, Calif.: Benjamin/Cummings, 1976.

Fattah, Hassan M. "After First Steps, Saudi Reformers See Efforts Stall." *New York Times,* April 26, 2007.

Gardiner, Sean, and Alison Fox. "Glance May Have Led to Murder." *New York Times,* December 6, 2010.

Garfinkel, Harold. "Conditions of Successful Degradation Ceremonies." *American Journal of Sociology, 61,* 2, March 1956:420–424.

Glaze, Lauren E., and Laura M. Maruschak. "Parents in Prison and Their Minor Children." Bureau of Justice Statistics Special Report, August 2008:1–25.

Goffman, Erving. *Stigma: Notes on the Management of Spoiled Identity.* Englewood Cliffs, N.J.: Prentice Hall, 1963.

Goozen, Stephanie H. M. van, Graeme Fairchild, Heddeke Snoek, and Gordon T. Harold. "The Evidence for a Neurobiological Model of Childhood Antisocial Behavior." *Psychological Bulletin, 133,* 1, 2007:149–182.

Gottfredson, Michael R., and Travis Hirschi. *A General Theory of Crime.* Stanford, Calif.: Stanford University Press, 1990.

Hirschi, Travis. *Causes of Delinquency.* Berkeley: University of California Press, 1969.

Horowitz, Ruth. *Honor and the American Dream: Culture and Identity in a Chicano Community.* New Brunswick, N.J.: Rutgers University Press, 1983.

Horowitz, Ruth. "Studying Violence among the 'Lions.'" In *Social Problems,* James M. Henslin, ed. Upper Saddle River, N.J.: Prentice Hall, 2005:135.

Jacobs, David, Zhenchao Qian, Jason T. Carmichael, and Stephanie L. Kent. "Who Survives on Death Row? An Individual and Contextual Analysis." *American Sociological Review, 72,* August 2007:610–632.

Jones, Allen. "Let Nonviolent Prisoners Out." *Los Angeles Times,* June 12, 2008.

Karamouzis, Stamos T., and Dee Wood Harper. "An Artificial Intelligence System Suggests Arbitrariness of Death Penalty." *International Journal of Law and Information Technology, 16,* 1:2007.

Kontos, Louis, David Brotherton, and Luis Barrios, eds. *Gangs and Society: Alternative Perspectives.* New York: Columbia University Press, 2003.

Kubrin, Charis E., and Ronald Weitzer. "Retaliatory Homicide: Concentrated Disadvantage and Neighborhood Culture." *Social Problems, 50,* 2, May 2003:157–180.

Lombroso, Cesare. *Crime: Its Causes and Remedies,* H. P. Horton, trans. Boston: Little, Brown, 1911.

Lyall, Sarah. "Here's the Pub, Church and Field for Public Sex." *New York Times,* October 7, 2010.

Madigan, Nick. "Judge Questions Long Sentence in Drug Case." *New York Times,* November 17, 2004.

Mayer, John D. *Personality: A Systems Approach.* Boston: Allyn and Bacon, 2007.

McCarthy, Bill. "The Attitudes and Actions of Others: Tutelage and Sutherland's Theory of Differential Association." *British Journal of Criminology 36,* 1, 2011:135–147.

McCormick, John. "The Sorry Side of Sears." *Newsweek,* February 22, 1999b:36–39.

McShane, Marilyn, and Frank P. Williams, III., eds. *Criminological Theory.* Upper Saddle River, N.J.: Prentice Hall, 2007.

Merton, Robert K. "The Social-Cultural Environment and *Anomie.*" In *New Perspectives for Research on Juvenile Delinquency,* Helen L. Witmer and Ruth Kotinsky, eds. Washington, D.C.: U.S. Department of Health, Education, and Welfare, 1956:24–50.

Merton, Robert K. *Social Theory and Social Structure.* Glencoe, Ill.: Free Press, 1949. Enlarged ed., 1968.

Miller, Walter B. "Lower Class Culture as a Generating Milieu of Gang Delinquency." *Journal of Social Issues, 14,* 3, 1958:5–19.

O'Brien, Timothy L. "Fed Assesses Citigroup Unit $70 Million in Loan Abuse." *New York Times,* May 28, 2004.

Oppel, Richard A., Jr. "Steady Decline in Major Crimes Baffles Experts." *New York Times,* May 23, 2011.

Partington, Donald H. "The Incidence of the Death Penalty for Rape in Virginia." *Washington and Lee Law Review, 22,* 1965:43–75.

Ramirez, Mary Kreiner. "Prioritizing Justice: Combating Corporate Crime from Task Force to Top Priority." Washburn University School of Law, August 19, 2009.

Read, Madlen. "Citi Pays $18M for Questioned Credit Card Practice." Associated Press, August 26, 2008.

Reckless, Walter C. *The Crime Problem,* 5th ed. New York: Appleton, 1973.

Reiman, Jeffrey. *The Rich Get Richer and the Poor Get Prison: Ideology, Class, and Criminal Justice,* 9th ed. Boston: Allyn and Bacon, 2010.

Reuters. "Fake Tiger Woods Gets 200-Years-to-Life in Prison." April 28, 2001.

Rosenfeld, Richard. "Crime Decline in Context." *Contexts, 1,* 1, Spring 2002:25–34.

Sánchez-Jankowski, Martín. *Islands in the Street: Gangs and American Urban Society.* Berkeley: University of California Press, 1991.

Sánchez-Jankowski, Martín. "Gangs and Social Change." *Theoretical Criminology, 7,* 2, 2003:191–216.

Saranow, Jennifer. "The Snoop Next Door." *Wall Street Journal,* January 12, 2007.

Simon, Stephanie. "Naked Pumpkin Run." *Wall Street Journal,* October 31, 2009.

Sourcebook of Criminal Justice Statistics. Washington, D.C.: U.S. Government Printing Office, published annually.

Spitzer, Steven. "Toward a Marxian Theory of Deviance." *Social Problems, 22,* June 1975:608–619.

Statistical Abstract of the United States. Washington, D.C.: U.S. Census Bureau, published annually.

Sullivan, Andrew. "What's So Bad about Hate?" *New York Times Magazine,* September 26, 1999.

Sutherland, Edwin H. *Criminology.* Philadelphia: Lippincott, 1924.

Sutherland, Edwin H. *Principles of Criminology,* 4th ed. Philadelphia: Lippincott, 1947.

Sutherland, Edwin H. *White Collar Crime.* New York: Dryden Press, 1949.

Sykes, Gresham M., and David Matza. "Techniques of Neutralization." In *Down to Earth Sociology: Introductory Readings,* 5th ed., James M. Henslin, ed. New York: Free Press, 1988:225–231. Originally published 1957.

Szasz, Thomas S. *The Myth of Mental Illness,* rev. ed. New York: Harper & Row, 1986.

Szasz, Thomas S. "Mental Illness Is Still a Myth." In *Deviant Behavior 96/97,* Lawrence M. Salinger, ed. Guilford, Conn.: Dushkin, 1996:200–205.

Szasz, Thomas S. *Cruel Compassion: Psychiatric Control of Society's Unwanted.* Syracuse, N.Y.: Syracuse University Press, 1998.

UPI. "Experts: Cleveland Killer a Sexual Sadist." November 9, 2009.

Vigil, Tammy. "Boulder Police: No Full Frontal Nudity." Fox 31, Denver Colorado, June 11, 2009.

Walsh, Anthony, and Kevin M. Beaver. "Biosocial Criminology." In *Handbook on Crime and Deviance,* M. D. Krohn et al., eds. Dordrecht, New York: Springer, 2009:79–101.

Warren, Jennifer, Adam Gelb, Jake Horowitz, and Jessica Riordan. "One in 100: Behind Bars in America 2008." Washington, D.C.: Pew Charitable Trust, February 2008.

Watson, J. Mark. "Outlaw Motorcyclists." In *Society: Readings to Accompany Sociology: A Down-to-Earth Approach, Core Concepts,* James M. Henslin ed. Boston: Allyn and Bacon, 2006:105–114. Originally published 1980 in *Deviant Behavior, 2,* 1.

White, Joseph B., Stephen Power, and Timothy Aeppel. "Death Count Linked to Failures of Firestone Tires Rises to 203." *Wall Street Journal,* June 19, 2001:A4.

Wilson, James Q., and Richard J. Herrnstein. *Crime and Human Nature.* New York: Simon & Schuster, 1985.

Social Stratification

From Chapter 7 of *Sociology: A Down-to-Earth Approach, Core Concepts*, Fifth Edition. James M. Henslin.
Copyright © 2012 by Pearson Education, Inc. All rights reserved.

Social Stratification

Chad

Ah, New Orleans, that fabled city on the Mississippi Delta. Images from its rich past floated through my head—pirates, treasure, intrigue. Memories from a pleasant vacation stirred my thoughts—the exotic French Quarter with its enticing aroma of Creole food and sounds of earthy jazz drifting through the air.

The shelter for the homeless, however, forced me back to an unwelcome reality. The shelter was like those I had visited in the North, West, and East—only dirtier. The dirt, in fact, was the worst that I had encountered during my research. On top of that, this shelter was the only one to demand payment in exchange for sleeping in one of its filthy beds.

The men looked the same—disheveled and haggard, wearing that unmistakable expression of sorrow and despair. Except for the accent, you wouldn't know what region you were in. Poverty wears the same tired face wherever you are, I realized. The accent may differ, but the look remains the same.

I had grown used to the sights and smells of abject poverty. Those no longer surprised me. But after my fitful sleep with the homeless that night, I saw something that did. Just a block or so from

> **"I was startled by a sight so out of step with the misery and despair that I stopped and stared."**

the shelter, I was startled by a sight so out of step with the misery and despair I had just experienced that I stopped and stared.

I felt indignation swell within me. Confronting me were life-size, full-color photos mounted on the transparent Plexiglas shelter of a bus stop. Staring back at me were images of finely dressed men and women, proudly strutting about as they modeled elegant suits, dresses, diamonds, and furs.

A wave of disgust swept over me. "Something is cockeyed in this society," I thought, as my mind refused to stop juxtaposing these images of extravagance with the suffering I had just witnessed.

social stratification the division of large numbers of people into layers according to their relative property, power, and prestige; applies to both nations and to people within a nation, society, or other group

slavery a form of social stratification in which some people own other people

The disjunction that I felt in New Orleans was triggered by the ads, but it was not the first time that I had experienced this sensation. Whenever my research abruptly transported me from the world of the homeless to one of another social class, I experienced a sense of disjointed unreality. Each social class has its own way of thinking and behaving, and because these fundamental orientations to the world contrast so sharply, the classes do not mix well.

How extensive is the gap between the rich and the poor in the United States? What differences do wealth and poverty make for people's lives? In this chapter, we will answer such questions, but before we do, let's look at a broader context that will help us understand the situation in the United States.

An Overview of Social Stratification

Some of the world's nations are wealthy, others poor, and some in between. This layering of nations, as well as of groups of people within a nation, is called **social stratification.** This term refers to a system in which groups of people are divided into layers according to their relative property, power, and prestige. This ranking of large groups of people into a hierarchy according to their relative privileges is one of the most significant topics we discuss in this book, for it affects our life chances—from our access to material possessions to the age at which we die.

Every society stratifies its members. Some societies have greater inequality than others, but social stratification is universal. In addition, in every society of the world, gender is a basis for stratifying people. On the basis of their gender, people are either allowed or denied access to the good things offered by their society.

Let's consider three systems of social stratification: slavery, caste, and class.

Slavery

Slavery, whose essential characteristic is that *some individuals own other people,* has been common throughout world history. The Old Testament even lays out rules for how owners should treat their slaves. So does the Koran. The Romans also had slaves, as did the Africans and Greeks. In classical Greece and Rome, slaves did the work, freeing citizens to engage in politics and the arts. Slavery was most widespread in agricultural societies and least common among nomads, especially hunters and gatherers (Landtman 1938/1968). As we examine the major causes and conditions of slavery, you will see how remarkably slavery has varied around the world.

Causes of Slavery. Contrary to common assumption, slavery was usually based not on racism but on one of three other factors. The first was *debt*. In some societies, creditors would enslave people who could not pay their debts. The second was *crime*. Instead of being killed, a murderer or thief might be enslaved by the victim's family as compensation for their loss. The third was *war*. When one group of people conquered another, they often enslaved some of the vanquished. Historian Gerda Lerner (1986) notes that women were the first people enslaved through warfare. When tribal men raided another group, they killed the men, raped the women, and then brought the women back as slaves. The women were valued for sexual purposes, for reproduction, and for their labor.

Roughly twenty-five hundred years ago, when Greece was but a collection of city-states, slavery was common. A city that became powerful and conquered another city would enslave some of the vanquished. Both slaves and slaveholders were Greek. Similarly, when Rome became the supreme power of the Mediterranean area about two thousand years ago, following the custom of the time, the Romans enslaved some of the Greeks they had conquered. More educated than their conquerors, some of these slaves served as tutors in Roman homes. Slavery, then, was a sign of debt, of crime, or of defeat in battle. It was not a sign that the slave was viewed as inherently inferior.

© The Granger Collection, New York/The Granger Collection

Under slavery, humans, like horses, could be sold, leased, borrowed, even raffled off.

What three factors was slavery based on?

Conditions of Slavery. The conditions of slavery have also varied widely around the world. *In some places, slavery was temporary.* Slaves of the Israelites were set free in the year of jubilee, which occurred every fifty years. Roman slaves ordinarily had the right to buy themselves out of slavery. They knew what their purchase price was, and some were able to meet this price by striking a bargain with their owner and selling their services to others. In most instances, however, slavery was a lifelong condition. Some criminals, for example, became slaves when they were given life sentences as oarsmen on Roman warships. There they served until death, which often came quickly to those in this exhausting service.

Slavery was not necessarily inheritable. In most places, the children of slaves were slaves themselves, but in ancient Mexico, the children of slaves were free. In some places, the child of a slave who served a rich family might even be adopted by that family, becoming an heir who bore the family name along with the other sons or daughters of the household (Landtman 1938/1968:271).

Slaves were not necessarily powerless and poor. In almost all instances, slaves owned no property and had no power. Among some groups, however, slaves could accumulate property and even rise to high positions in the community. Occasionally, a slave might even become wealthy, loan money to the master, and, while still a slave, own slaves himself or herself (Landtman 1938/1968). This, however, was rare.

Bonded Labor in the New World. A gray area between slavery and contract labor is **bonded labor,** also called **indentured service.** People who wanted to start a new life in the American colonies but could not pay their passage across the ocean would arrange for a ship captain to transport them on credit. When they arrived, wealthy colonists would pay the captain for their voyage, and these penniless people would become the colonists' servants for a set number of years. During that period, the servants were required by law to serve their masters. If they ran away, they became outlaws who were hunted down and forcibly returned. At the end of their period of indenture, they became full citizens, able to live where they chose and free to sell their labor (Main 1965; Elkins 1968).

Slavery in the New World. When there were not enough indentured servants to meet the growing need for labor in the American colonies, some colonists tried to enslave Native Americans. This attempt failed miserably, in part because when Indians escaped, they knew how to survive in the wilderness and were able to make their way back to their tribe. The colonists then turned to Africans, who were being brought to North and South America by the Dutch, English, Portuguese, and Spanish.

Because slavery has a broad range of causes, some analysts conclude that racism didn't lead to slavery, but, rather, that slavery led to racism. Finding it profitable to make people slaves for life, U.S. slave owners developed an **ideology,** beliefs that justify social arrangements. Ideology leads to a perception of the world that makes current social arrangements seem necessary and fair. The colonists developed the view that their slaves were inferior. Some even said that they were not fully human. In short, the colonists wove elaborate justifications for slavery, built on the presumed superiority of their own group.

To make slavery even more profitable, slave states passed laws that made slavery *inheritable;* that is, the babies born to slaves became the property of the slave owners (Stampp 1956). These children could be sold, bartered, or traded. To strengthen their control, slave states passed laws making it illegal for slaves to hold meetings or to be away from the master's premises without carrying a pass (Lerner 1972). Sociologist W. E. B. Du Bois (1935/1992:12) noted that "gradually the entire white South became an armed camp to keep Negroes in slavery and to kill the black rebel."

The Civil War did not end legal discrimination. For example, until 1954 many states operated separate school systems for blacks and whites. Until the 1950s, in order to keep the races from "mixing," it was illegal in Mississippi for a white and an African American to sit together on the same seat of a car!

bonded labor (indentured service) a contractual system in which someone sells his or her body (services) for a specified period of time in an arrangement very close to slavery, except that it is entered into voluntarily

ideology beliefs about the way things ought to be that justify social arrangements

I interviewed this 8-year-old girl in India. Mahashury is a *bonded laborer* who was exchanged by her parents for a 2,000 rupee loan (about $14). To repay the loan, Mahashury must do construction work for one year. She will receive one meal a day and one set of clothing for the year. Because this centuries-old practice is now illegal, the master bribes Indian officials, who inform him when they are going to inspect the construction site. He then hides his bonded laborers. I was able to interview and photograph Mahashury because her master was absent the day I visited the construction site.

James M. Henslin

How did slavery in the United States differ from slavery in some other parts of the world? What was bonded labor?

TABLE 1	India's Caste System
Caste	**Occupation**
Brahman	Priests and teachers
Kshatriya	Rulers and soldiers
Vaishya	Merchants and traders
Shudra	Peasants and laborers
Dalit (untouchables)	The outcastes; degrading or polluting labor

caste system a form of social stratification in which people's statuses are lifelong conditions determined by birth

endogamy the practice of marrying within one's own group

In a *caste system*, status is determined by birth and is lifelong. At birth, these women received not only membership in a lower caste but also, because of their gender, a predetermined position in that caste. When I photographed these women, they were carrying sand to the second floor of a house being constructed in Andhra Pradesh, India.

James M. Henslin

There was no outright ban on blacks and whites being in the same car, however, so whites could employ African American chauffeurs.

Slavery Today. Slavery has again reared its ugly head in several parts of the world (Appiah and Bunzl 2007). The Ivory Coast, Mauritania, Niger, and Sudan have a long history of slavery, and not until the 1980s was slavery made illegal in Mauritania and Sudan (Ayittey 1998). It took until 2003 for slavery to be banned in Niger (Polgreen 2008).

The enslavement of children for work and sex is a problem in Africa, Asia, and South America (*Trafficking in Persons Report 2010*). A unique form of child slavery in some Mideast countries is buying little boys around the age of 5 or 6 to race camels. Their screams of terror are thought to make the animals run faster. In Qatar and the United Arab Emirates, which recently banned this practice, robots are supposed to replace the children (de Pastino 2005; Nelson 2009).

Caste

The second system of social stratification is caste. In a **caste system,** birth determines status, which is lifelong. Someone who is born into a low-status group will always have low status, no matter how much that person may accomplish in life. In sociological terms, a caste system is built on ascribed status. Achieved status cannot change an individual's place in this system.

Societies with this form of stratification try to make certain that the boundaries between castes remain firm. They practice **endogamy,** marriage within their own group, and prohibit marriage between castes. Elaborate rules about *ritual pollution*—inferior castes as sources of contamination—keep contact between castes to a minimum.

India's Religious Castes. India provides the best example of a caste system. Based not on race but on religion, India's caste system has existed for almost three thousand years (Chandra 1993a; Jaffrelot 2006). Table 1 lists India's four main castes. These four castes are subdivided into about three thousand subcastes, or *jati*. Each *jati* specializes in a particular occupation. For example, one subcaste washes clothes, another sharpens knives, and yet another repairs shoes.

The lowest group listed in Table 1, the Dalit, are also called India's "untouchables." If a Dalit touches someone of a higher caste, that person becomes unclean. Even the shadow of an untouchable can contaminate. Early morning and late afternoons are especially risky, for the long shadows of these periods pose a danger to everyone higher up the caste system. Consequently, Dalits are not allowed in some villages during these times. Anyone who becomes contaminated must follow *ablution*, or washing rituals, to restore purity.

Is there slavery today? What is caste?

Topham/The Image Works

Although the Indian government abolished the caste system in 1949, centuries-old practices cannot be eliminated so easily, and the caste system remains part of everyday life in India (Beckett 2007). The ceremonies people follow at births, marriages, and deaths, for example, are dictated by caste (Chandra 1993a). The upper castes dread the upward mobility of the untouchables, sometimes resisting it even with murder and ritual suicide (Crossette 1996; Trofimov 2007). From personal observations in India, I can add that in some villages Dalit children are not allowed in the government schools. If they try to enroll, they are beaten.

A U.S. Racial Caste System. Before leaving the subject of caste, we should note that when slavery ended in the United States, it was replaced by a *racial caste system*. From the moment of birth, everyone was marked for life (Berger 1963/2012). In this system, *all* whites, no matter how poor or uneducated, considered themselves of higher status than *all* African Americans. As in India and South Africa, the upper caste, fearing pollution from the lower caste, prohibited intermarriage and insisted on separate schools, hotels, restaurants, and even toilets and drinking fountains in public facilities. In another similarity, when any white met any African American on a sidewalk in the South, the African American had to move aside—which the untouchables of India still must do when they meet someone of a higher caste (Deliege 2001).

In early industrialization, children worked alongside adults. They worked 12 hours a day Monday to Friday and 15 hours on Saturday, often in dangerous, filthy conditions. In this 1909 protest in New York City, two girls are wearing banners with the slogan "ABOLISH CHILD SLAVERY" in English and Yiddish.

Social Class

As we have seen, stratification systems based on slavery and caste are rigid. The lines drawn between people are firm, and there is little or no movement from one group to another. A **class system,** in contrast, is much more open, for it is based primarily on money or material possessions, which can be acquired. This system, too, is in place at birth, when children are ascribed the status of their parents, but, in this system, unlike the others, individuals can change their social class by what they achieve (or fail to achieve). In addition, no laws specify people's occupations on the basis of birth or prohibit marriage between the classes.

A major characteristic of the class system, then, is its relatively fluid boundaries. A class system allows **social mobility,** movement up or down the class ladder. The potential for improving one's life—or for falling down the class ladder—is a major force that drives people to go far in school and to work hard. In the extreme, the family background that a child inherits at birth may present such obstacles that he or she has little chance of climbing very far—or it may provide such privileges that it makes it almost impossible to fall down the class ladder.

Global Stratification and the Status of Females

In *every* society of the world, gender is a basis for social stratification. In no society is gender the sole basis for stratifying people, but gender cuts across *all* systems of social stratification—whether slavery, caste, or class (Huber 1990). In all these systems, on the basis of their gender, people are sorted into categories and given different access to the good things available in their society.

class system a form of social stratification based primarily on the possession of money or material possessions

social mobility movement up or down the social class ladder

What does "a U.S. racial caste system" mean? How is gender a part of social stratification?

FIGURE 1 The Distribution of the Earth's Wealth

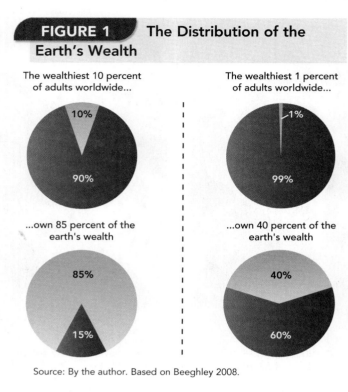

The wealthiest 10 percent of adults worldwide...

10%

90%

...own 85 percent of the earth's wealth

85%

15%

The wealthiest 1 percent of adults worldwide...

1%

99%

...own 40 percent of the earth's wealth

40%

60%

Source: By the author. Based on Beeghley 2008.

✳ Explore
Living Data
on **mysoclab.com**

Apparently these distinctions always favor males. It is remarkable, for example, that in *every* society of the world men's earnings are higher than women's. Men's dominance is even more evident when we consider female circumcision. That most of the world's illiterate are females also drives home women's relative position in society. Of the several hundred million adults who cannot read, about two-thirds are women (UNESCO 2011). Because gender is such a significant factor in what happens to us in life, we shall focus on it more closely.

The New Global Superclass

The growing interconnections among the world's wealthiest people have produced a *global superclass,* one in which wealth and power are more concentrated than ever before. There are only about 6,000 members of this superclass—*the richest 1,000 of this superclass have more wealth than the 2½ billion poorest people on this planet* (Rothkopf 2008:37). Almost all of them are white, and except as wives and daughters, few women are an active part of the superclass. Look at Figure 1. There is nothing in history to compare with this concentration of wealth.

Global Stratification: Three Worlds

As was noted at the beginning of this chapter, just as the people within a nation are stratified by property, power, and prestige, so are the world's nations. Until recently, a simple model was used to depict global stratification: *First World* referred to the industrialized capitalist nations, *Second World* to the communist (or socialist) countries, and *Third World* to any nation that did not fit into the first two categories. The breakup of the Soviet Union in 1989 made these terms outdated. In addition, although *first, second,* and *third* did not mean "best," "better," and "worst," they implied it. An alternative classification that some now use—developed, developing, and undeveloped nations—has the same drawback. By calling ourselves "developed," it sounds as though we are mature and the "undeveloped" nations are somehow retarded.

To resolve this problem, I use more neutral, descriptive terms: *Most Industrialized, Industrializing,* and *Least Industrialized* nations. We can measure industrialization with no judgment implied as to whether a nation's industrialization represents "development," ranks it "first," or is even desirable at all. The intention is to depict on a global level the three primary dimensions of social stratification: property, power, and prestige. The Most Industrialized Nations have much greater property (wealth), power (they usually get their way in international relations), and prestige (they are looked up to as world leaders).

The Most Industrialized Nations

The Most Industrialized Nations are the United States and Canada in North America; Great Britain, France, Germany, Switzerland, and the other industrialized countries of western Europe; Japan in Asia; and Australia and New Zealand in the area of the world known as Oceania. Although there are variations in their economic systems, these nations are capitalistic. As Table 2 shows, despite having only 16 percent of the world's people, they possess 31 percent of the Earth's land. Their wealth is so enormous that even their poor live better

TABLE 2 Distribution of the World's Land and Population

	Land	Population
Most Industrialized Nations	31%	16%
Industrializing Nations	20%	16%
Least Industrialized Nations	49%	68%

Sources: By the author. Computed from Kurian 1990, 1991, 1992.

What is the global superclass? Can you name some of the Most Industrialized Nations?

and longer lives than do the average citizens of the Least Industrialized Nations. From the Social Map on the next two pages, you can see the relative wealth and poverty of the world's nations.

The Industrializing Nations

The Industrializing Nations include most of the nations of the former Soviet Union and its satellites in eastern Europe. It also includes the poorer European countries, several South and Central American countries, and a few from Asia and Africa. As Table 2 shows, these nations account for 20 percent of the Earth's land and 16 percent of its people.

The dividing points between the three "worlds" are soft, making it difficult to know how to classify some nations. This is especially the case with the Industrializing Nations. Exactly how much industrialization must a nation have to be in this category? Although soft, these categories do pinpoint essential differences among nations. Most people who live in the Industrializing Nations have much lower incomes and standards of living than do those who live in the Most Industrialized Nations. The majority, however, are better off than those who live in the Least Industrialized Nations. For example, on such measures as access to electricity, indoor plumbing, automobiles, telephones, and even food, most citizens of the Industrializing Nations rank lower than those in the Most Industrialized Nations, but higher than those in the Least Industrialized Nations.

The benefits of industrialization are uneven. Large numbers of people in the Industrializing Nations remain illiterate and desperately poor. Conditions can be gruesome, as we explore in the following Thinking Critically section.

The contrast between poverty and wealth is a characteristic of all contemporary societies. This photo was taken in New York City.

Watch
Slum Features
on **mysoclab.com**

THINKING CRITICALLY
Open Season: Children as Prey

What is childhood like in the Industrializing Nations? The answer depends on who your parents are. If you are the son or daughter of rich parents, childhood can be pleasant—a world filled with luxuries and even servants. If you are born into poverty, but live in a rural area where there is plenty to eat, life can still be good—although there may be no books or television and little education. If you live in a slum, however, life can be horrible—worse even than in the slums of the Most Industrialized Nations (Barbassa 2010). Let's take a glance at a notorious slum in Brazil.

Not enough food—this you can take for granted—along with wife abuse, broken homes, alcoholism, drug abuse, and a lot of crime. From your knowledge of slums in the Most Industrialized Nations, you would expect these things. What you may not expect, however, are the brutal conditions in which Brazilian slum (*favela*) children live.

Sociologist Martha Huggins (Huggins et al. 2002) reports that poverty is so deep that children and adults swarm through garbage dumps to try to find enough decaying food to keep them alive. You might also be surprised to discover that the owners of some of these dumps hire armed guards to keep the poor out—so that they can sell the garbage for pig food. And you might be shocked to learn that some shop owners have hired hit men, auctioning designated victims to the *lowest* bidder!

Life is cheap in the poor nations—but death squads for children? To understand this, we must first note that Brazil has a long history of violence. Brazil also has a high rate of poverty, with only a tiny middle class, and is controlled by a small group of families who, under a veneer of democracy, make the country's major decisions. Hordes of homeless children, with no schools or jobs, roam the streets. To survive, they wash windshields, shine shoes, beg, and steal (Huggins and Rodrigues 2004).

The "respectable" classes see these children as nothing but trouble. They hurt business, for customers feel intimidated when they see begging children—especially

What are some of the differences between the Most Industrialized and the Industrializing Nations?

FIGURE 2 Global Stratification: Income[1] of the World's Nations

The Most Industrialized Nations

	Nation	Income per Person
1	Luxembourg	$77,600
2	Norway	$59,300
3	Singapore	$50,300
4	United States	$46,400
5	Hong Kong	$42,700
6	Switzerland	$41,600
7	Iceland	$39,800
8	Austria	$39,400
9	Netherlands	$39,000
10	Canada	$38,400
11	Sweden	$36,800
12	Australia	$38,500
13	Belgium	$36,600
14	Denmark	$36,200
15	United Kingdom	$35,400
16	Finland	$34,900
17	Germany	$34,200
18	France	$32,800
19	Japan	$32,600
20	Italy	$30,200
21	Taiwan	$30,200
22	Israel	$28,400
23	Slovenia	$28,200
24	New Zealand	$27,700
25	Korea, South	$27,700
26	Czech Republic	$25,100

The Industrializing Nations

	Nation	Income per Person
27	Ireland	$42,200
28	Spain	$33,700
29	Greece	$32,100
30	Portugal	$21,700
31	Slovakia	$21,100
32	Greenland	$20,000
33	Estonia	$18,800
34	Hungary	$18,800
35	Poland	$17,800
36	Croatia	$17,600
37	Russia	$15,200
38	Lithuania	$15,000
39	Malaysia	$14,700
40	Chile	$14,700
41	Libya	$14,600
42	Latvia	$14,500
43	Argentina	$13,800
44	Gabon	$13,700
45	Venezuela	$13,200
46	Mexico	$13,200
47	Bulgaria	$12,600
48	Mauritius	$12,400
49	Romania	$11,500
50	Costa Rica	$11,300
51	Turkey	$11,200
52	Brazil	$10,200
53	South Africa	$10,000
54	Cuba	$9,700
55	China	$6,500

The Least Industrialized Nations

	Nation	Income per Person		Nation	Income per Person
56	Uruguay	$12,600	72	Tunisia	$8,000
57	Botswana[2]	$12,100	73	Ecuador	$7,300
58	Panama	$11,900	74	Algeria	$7,100
59	Belarus	$11,600	75	Turkmenistan	$6,700
60	Lebanon	$11,500	76	Ukraine	$6,400
61	Kazakhstan	$11,400	77	Namibia	$6,400
62	Azerbaijan	$9,900	78	Bosnia	$6,300
63	Colombia	$9,200	79	Albania	$6,200
64	Macedonia	$9,000	80	Bhutan	$6,200
65	Suriname	$8,800	81	El Salvador	$6,000
66	Angola	$8,800	82	Egypt	$6,000
67	Peru	$8,600	83	Armenia	$5,900
68	Jamaica	$8,300	84	Jordan	$5,300
69	Belize	$8,200	85	Guatemala	$5,200
70	Dominican Republic	$8,200	86	Syria	$4,700
71	Thailand	$8,100	87	Bolivia	$4,600
			88	Morocco	$4,600

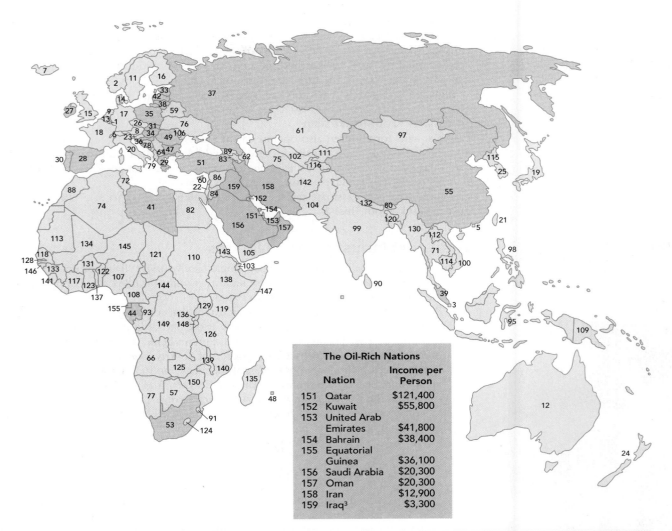

The Oil-Rich Nations	
Nation	Income per Person
151 Qatar	$121,400
152 Kuwait	$55,800
153 United Arab Emirates	$41,800
154 Bahrain	$38,400
155 Equatorial Guinea	$36,100
156 Saudi Arabia	$20,300
157 Oman	$20,300
158 Iran	$12,900
159 Iraq[3]	$3,300

The Least Industrialized Nations

Nation	Income per Person	Nation	Income per Person	Nation	Income per Person	Nation	Income per Person
89 Georgia	$4,500	106 Moldova	$2,400	122 Benin	$1,500	138 Ethiopia	$900
90 Sri Lanka	$4,500	107 Nigeria	$2,400	123 Ghana	$1,500	139 Malawi	$900
91 Swaziland	$4,400	108 Cameroon	$2,300	124 Lesotho	$1,500	140 Mozambique	$900
92 Honduras	$4,200	109 Papua-New Guinea	$2,300	125 Zambia	$1,500	141 Sierra Leone	$900
93 Congo	$4,200	110 Sudan	$2,300	126 Tanzania	$1,400	142 Afghanistan	$800
94 Paraguay	$4,100	111 Krygyzstan	$2,100	127 Haiti	$1,300	143 Eritrea	$700
95 Indonesia	$4,000	112 Laos	$2,100	128 Gambia	$1,300	144 Central African Republic	$700
96 Guyana	$3,900	113 Mauritania	$2,100	129 Uganda	$1,300	145 Niger	$700
97 Mongolia	$3,400	114 Cambodia	$1,900	130 Burma (Myanmar)	$1,200	146 Guinea-Bissau	$600
98 Philippines	$3,300	115 Korea, North	$1,800	131 Burkina Faso	$1,200	147 Somalia	$600
99 India	$3,100	116 Tajikistan	$1,800	132 Nepal	$1,200	148 Burundi	$300
100 Vietnam	$2,900	117 Cote d'Ivoire	$1,700	133 Guinea	$1,100	149 Congo, Dem. Rep.	$300
101 Nicaragua	$2,800	118 Senegal	$1,700	134 Mali	$1,100	150 Zimbabwe	$200
102 Uzbekistan	$2,800	119 Kenya	$1,600	135 Madagascar	$1,000		
103 Djibouti	$2,800	120 Bangladesh	$1,600	136 Rwanda	$1,000		
104 Pakistan	$2,600	121 Chad	$1,500	137 Togo	$900		
105 Yemen	$2,500						

[1]Income is a country's purchasing power parity based on a country's Gross Domestic Product, where the value of a country's goods and services are valued at prices prevailing in the United States. Totals vary from year to year and should be considered as approximations.
[2]Botswana's income is based largely on its diamond mines.
[3]Iraq's oil wealth has been disrupted by war.
Source: By the author. Based on *CIA World Factbook* 2010.

colonialism the process by which one nation takes over another nation, usually for the purpose of exploiting its labor and natural resources

teenaged males—clustered in front of stores. Some shoplift. Others break into the stores. With no effective social institutions to care for these children, one solution is to kill them. As Huggins notes, murder sends a clear message—especially if it is accompanied by ritual torture: gouging out the eyes, ripping open the chest, cutting off the genitals, raping the girls, and burning the victim's body.

Not all life is bad in the Industrializing Nations, but this is about as bad as it gets.

For Your Consideration

Death squads for children also operate in the slums of the Philippines ("Death Squads . . ." 2008). Do you think there is anything the Most Industrialized Nations can do about this situation? Or is it, though unfortunate, just an "internal" affair that is up to the particular nation to handle as it wishes?

The police also assassinate rapists and drug dealers ("Death to . . ." 2009). What do you think about this? ■

The Least Industrialized Nations

In the Least Industrialized Nations, most people barely survive, living on small farms or in villages, usually in large families. These nations account for 68 percent of the world's people but only 49 percent of the earth's land.

Poverty plagues these nations to such an extent that some families actually *live* in city dumps. This is hard to believe, but look at the photos in the following "Through the Author's Lens" feature, which I took in Phnom Penh, the capital of Cambodia. Although wealthy nations have their pockets of poverty, *most* people in the Least Industrialized Nations are poor. *Most* of them have no running water, indoor plumbing, or access to trained teachers or doctors. And it is in these nations that most of the world's population growth is occurring, placing even greater burdens on their limited resources and causing them to fall farther behind each year.

How Did the World's Nations Become Stratified?

How did the globe become stratified into such distinct worlds? The commonsense answer is that the poorer nations have fewer resources than the richer nations. As with many commonsense answers, however, this one, too, falls short. Many of the Industrializing and Least Industrialized Nations are rich in natural resources, while one Most Industrialized Nation, Japan, has few. Three theories explain how global stratification came about.

Colonialism

The first theory, **colonialism,** stresses that the earliest countries to industrialize got the jump on the rest of the world. Beginning in Great Britain about 1750, industrialization spread throughout western Europe. Plowing some of their profits into powerful armaments and fast ships, these countries invaded weaker nations, making colonies out of them (Harrison 1993). After subduing them, the more powerful countries left behind a controlling force in order to exploit these weaker nations' labor and natural resources. At one point, there was even a free-for-all among the industrialized European countries as they rushed to divide up an entire continent, slicing Africa into pieces. Even tiny Belgium got into the act and acquired the Congo, which was *seventy-five* times larger than itself.

Homeless people sleeping on the streets is a common sight in India's cities. I took this photo in Chennai (formerly Madras).

James M. Henslin

How does colonialism explain how the world's nations became stratified?

The purpose of colonialism was to establish *economic colonies*—to exploit a nation's people and resources for the benefit of the "mother" country. The more powerful European countries would plant their national flags in a colony and send their representatives to run the government, but the United States usually chose to plant corporate flags in a colony and let these corporations dominate the territory's government. Central and South America are prime examples. There were exceptions, such as the conquest of the Philippines, which President McKinley said was motivated by the desire "to educate the Filipinos, and uplift and civilize and Christianize them" (Krugman 2002).

Colonialism, then, shaped many of the Least Industrialized Nations. In some instances, the Most Industrialized Nations were so powerful that when dividing their spoils, they drew lines across a map, creating new states without regard for tribal or cultural considerations (Kifner 1999). Britain and France did just this as they divided up North Africa and parts of the Middle East—which is why the national boundaries of Libya, Saudi Arabia, Kuwait, and other countries are so straight. This legacy of European conquests is a background factor in much of today's racial–ethnic and tribal violence: Groups with no history of national identity were incorporated into the same political boundaries.

World System Theory

The second explanation of how global stratification came about was proposed by Immanuel Wallerstein (1974, 1979, 1990). According to **world system theory,** industrialization led to four groups of nations. The first consists of the *core nations,* the countries that industrialized first (Britain, France, Holland, and later Germany), which grew rich and powerful. The second group is the *semiperiphery.* The economies of these nations, located around the Mediterranean, stagnated because they grew dependent on trade with the core nations. The third group, the *periphery,* or fringe nations, developed even less. These are the eastern European countries, which sold cash crops to the core nations. The fourth group of nations includes most of Africa and Asia. Called the *external area,* these nations were left out of the development of capitalism altogether. The current expansion of capitalism has changed the relationships among these groups. Most notably, many formerly peripheral nations in Europe and Asia are now capitalist countries.

The **globalization of capitalism**—the adoption of capitalism around the world—has created extensive ties among the world's nations. Production and trade are now so interconnected that events around the globe affect us all. Sometimes this is immediate, as when a civil war disrupts the flow of oil, or—perish the thought—as would be the case if terrorists managed to get their hands on nuclear or biological weapons. At other times, the effects are like a slow ripple, as when a government adopts some policy that gradually impedes its ability to compete in world markets. All of today's societies, then, no matter where they are located, are part of a *world system*.

The interconnections are most evident among nations that do extensive trading with one another. The following Thinking Critically section explores implications of Mexico's *maquiladoras*.

THINKING CRITICALLY
When Globalization Comes Home: *Maquiladoras* South of the Border

Two hundred thousand Mexicans rush to Juarez each year, fleeing the hopelessness of the rural areas in pursuit of a better life. They have no running water or plumbing, but they didn't have any in the country either, and here they have the possibility of a job, a weekly check to buy food for the kids.

The pay is $100 for a 48-hour work week, about $2 an hour (Harris 2008).

This may not sound like much, but it is more than twice the minimum daily wage in Mexico.

Assembly-for-export plants, known as *maquiladoras,* dot the Mexican border (Wise and Cypher 2007). The North American Free Trade Agreement (NAFTA) allows U.S. companies to export materials to Mexico without paying tax and to then import the

world system theory how economic and political connections developed and now tie the world's countries together

globalization of capitalism capitalism becoming the globe's dominant economic system

Read
The Uses of Global Poverty: How Economic Inequality Benefits the West by Diane Stukulis Eglitis
on **mysoclab.com**

How does world system theory explain how the world's nations became stratified?

The Dump People: Working and Living and Playing in the City Dump of Phnom Penh, Cambodia

I went to Cambodia to inspect orphanages, to see how well the children are being cared for. While in Phnom Penh, Cambodia's capital, I was told about people who live in the city dump. *Live* there? I could hardly believe my ears. I knew that people made their living by picking scraps from the city dump, but I didn't know they actually lived among the garbage. This I had to see for myself.

I did. And there I found a highly developed social organization—an intricate support system. Because words are inadequate to depict the abject poverty of the Least Industrialized Nations, these photos can provide more insight into these people's lives than anything I could say.

After the garbage arrives by truck, people stream around it, struggling to be the first to discover something of value. To sift through the trash, the workers use metal picks, like the one this child is holding. Note that children work alongside the adults.

The children who live in the dump also play there. These children are riding bicycles on a "road," a packed, leveled area of garbage that leads to their huts. The huge stacks in the background are piled trash. Note the ubiquitous Nike.

This is a typical sight—family and friends working together. The trash, which is constantly burning, contains harmful chemicals. Why do people work under such conditions? Because they have few options. It is either this or starve.

© James M. Henslin, all photos

One of my many surprises was to find food stands in the dump. Although this one primarily offers drinks and snacks, others serve more substantial food. One even has chairs for its customers.

The people live at the edge of the dump, in homemade huts (visible in the background). This woman, who was on her way home after a day's work, put down her sack of salvaged items to let me take her picture.

CAMBODIA
★ Phnom Penh

I was surprised to learn that ice is delivered to the dump. This woman is using a hand grinder to crush ice for drinks for her customers. The customers, of course, are other people who also live in the dump.

At the day's end, the workers wash at the community pump. This hand pump serves all their water needs—drinking, washing, and cooking. There is no indoor plumbing. The weeds in the background serve that purpose. Can you imagine drinking water that comes from below this garbage dump?

Not too many visitors to Phnom Penh tell a cab driver to take them to the city dump. The cabbie looked a bit perplexed, but he did as I asked. Two cabs are shown here because my friends insisted on accompanying me.

I know they were curious themselves, but my friends had also discovered that the destinations I want to visit are usually not in the tourist guides, and they wanted to protect me.

© James M. Henslin, all photos

A photo taken inside a *maquiladora* in Matamoros, Mexico. The steering wheels are for U.S. automakers.

finished products into the United States, again without tax. It's a sweet deal: few taxes and $17 a day for workers starved for jobs.

That these workers live in shacks with no running water or sewage disposal is not the employers' concern.

Nor is the pollution. The stinking air doesn't stay on the Mexican side of the border. Neither does the garbage. Heavy rains wash torrents of untreated sewage and industrial wastes into the Rio Grande (M. Lacey 2007).

There is also the loss of jobs for U.S. workers. Six of the fifteen poorest cities in the United States are located along the sewage-infested Rio Grande. NAFTA didn't bring poverty to these cities. They were poor before this treaty, but residents resent the jobs they've seen move across the border (Thompson 2001).

What if the *maquiladora* workers organize and demand better pay? Farther south, even cheaper labor beckons. Guatemala and Honduras will gladly take the *maquiladoras*. Mexico has already lost many of its *maquiladora* jobs to places where people even more desperate will work for even less (Brown 2008). China, too, is competing for them (Utar and Ruiz 2010).

Many Mexican politicians would say that this presentation is one-sided. "Sure there are problems," they would say, "but that is always how it is when a country industrializes. Don't you realize that the *maquiladoras* bring jobs to people who have no work? They

The home of a *maquiladora* worker.

also bring roads, telephone lines, and electricity to undeveloped areas." "In fact," said Vicente Fox, when he was the president of Mexico, "workers at the *maquiladoras* make more than the average salary in Mexico—and that's what we call fair wages" (Fraser 2001).

During our economic crisis, the low wages of many *maquiladora* workers were cut in half (Muñoz Martinez 2010).

For Your Consideration

Let's apply our three theoretical perspectives.

Conflict theorists say that capitalists try to weaken the bargaining power of workers by exploiting divisions among them. In what is known as the *split labor market*, capitalists pit one group of workers against another to lower the cost of labor. How do you think that *maquiladoras* fit this conflict perspective?

When functionalists analyze a situation, they identify its functions and dysfunctions. What functions and dysfunctions of *maquiladoras* do you see?

Do *maquiladoras* represent exploitation or opportunity? As symbolic interactionists point out, reality is a perspective based on our experiences in social locations. What multiple realities do you see here? ■

Culture of Poverty

The third explanation of global stratification is quite unlike the other two. Economist John Kenneth Galbraith (1979) claimed that the cultures of the Least Industrialized Nations hold them back. Building on the ideas of anthropologist Oscar Lewis (1966a, 1966b), Galbraith argued that some nations are crippled by a **culture of poverty,** a way of life that perpetuates poverty from one generation to the next. He explained it this way: Most of the world's poor people are farmers who live on little plots of land. They barely produce enough food to survive. To experiment with new farming techniques is to court disaster, for failure would lead to hunger and death.

Their religion also encourages them to accept their situation, for it teaches fatalism: the belief that an individual's position in life is God's will. For example, in India, the Dalit are taught that they must have done very bad things in a previous life to suffer so. They are supposed to submit to their situation—and in the next life maybe they'll come back in a more desirable state.

culture of poverty the assumption that the values and behaviors of the poor make them fundamentally different from other people, that these factors are largely responsible for their poverty, and that parents perpetuate poverty across generations by passing these characteristics to their children

Evaluating the Theories

Most sociologists prefer colonialism and world system theory. To them, an explanation based on a culture of poverty places blame on the victim—the poor nations themselves. It points to their internal characteristics rather than to international political arrangements that benefit the Most Industrialized Nations at the expense of the Least Industrialized. But even taken together, these theories yield only part of the picture. None of these theories, for example, would have led anyone to expect that after World War II, Japan would become an economic powerhouse: Its dominant religion stressed fatalism, two of its major cities had been destroyed by atomic bombs, and it had been stripped of its colonies.

Each theory, then, yields but a partial explanation, and the grand theorist who will put the many pieces of this puzzle together has yet to appear.

Why Is Social Stratification Universal?

Why are all societies stratified? We shall first consider the explanation proposed by functionalists, which has aroused much controversy in sociology, and then explanations proposed by conflict theorists.

The Functionalist View: Motivating Qualified People

Functionalists take the position that the patterns of behavior characterizing a society exist because they are functional for that society. Because social inequality is universal, inequality must help societies survive. But how?

Davis and Moore's Explanation.   Two functionalists, Kingsley Davis and Wilbert Moore (1945, 1953), wrestled with this question. They concluded that stratification of society is inevitable because:

1. For society to function, its positions must be filled.
2. Some positions are more important than others.
3. The more important positions must be filled by the more qualified people.
4. To motivate the more qualified people to fill these positions, they must offer greater rewards.

To flesh out this functionalist argument, consider college presidents and military generals. The position of college president is more important than that of student because the president's decisions affect a large number of people, including many students. College presidents are also accountable for their performance to boards of trustees. It is the same with generals. Their decisions affect many people and sometimes even determine life and death. Generals are accountable to superior generals and to the country's leaders.

How does culture of poverty explain global stratification? Why do functionalists say that social stratification is inevitable?

Why do people accept demanding, high-pressure positions? Why don't they just take easier jobs? The answer, said Davis and Moore, is that these positions offer greater rewards—more property, power, and prestige. To get highly qualified people to compete with one another, some positions offer a salary of $2 million a year, country club membership, a private jet and pilot, and a chauffeured limousine. For less demanding positions, a $30,000 salary without fringe benefits is enough to get hundreds of people to compete. If a job requires rigorous training, it, too, must offer more salary and benefits. If you can get the same pay with a high school diploma, why suffer through the many tests and term papers that college requires?

Tumin's Critique of Davis and Moore.   Davis and Moore were not attempting to justify social inequality, just to explain *why* social stratification is universal. Nevertheless, their view makes many sociologists uncomfortable, for they see it as coming close to justifying the inequalities in society. Its bottom line seems to be: The people who contribute more to society are paid more, while those who contribute less are paid less.

Melvin Tumin (1953) was the first sociologist to point out what he saw as major flaws in the functionalist position. Here are three of his arguments.

First, how do we know that the positions that offer the higher rewards are more important? A heart surgeon, for example, saves lives and earns much more than a garbage collector, but this doesn't mean that garbage collectors are less important to society. By helping to prevent contagious diseases, garbage collectors save more lives than heart surgeons do. We need independent methods of measuring importance, and we don't have them.

Second, if stratification worked as Davis and Moore described it, society would be a meritocracy; that is, positions would be awarded on the basis of merit. But is this what we have? The best predictor of who goes to college, for example, is not ability but income: The more a family earns, the more likely their children are to go to college (Carnevale and Rose 2003; Belley and Lochner 2007). In this example, you see not merit, but money—a form of the inequality that is built into society. In short, people's positions in society are based on many factors other than merit.

Third, if social stratification is so functional, it ought to benefit almost everyone. Yet social stratification is *dysfunctional* for many. Think of the people who could have made valuable contributions to society had they not been born in slums, dropped out of school, and taken menial jobs to help support their families. Then there are the many who, born female, are assigned "women's work," ensuring that they do not maximize their mental abilities.

In Sum: Functionalists argue that some positions are more important to society than others. Offering higher rewards for these positions motivates more talented people to take them. For example, to get highly talented people to become surgeons—to undergo years of rigorous training and then cope with life-and-death situations, as well as malpractice suits—that position must provide a high payoff.

We will now turn to the conflict perspective on social class. Before you read further, you might want to look at Table 3, which compares the functionalist and conflict views on how society's resources are divided.

TABLE 3 Views of Stratification: The Distribution of Society's Resources	Who Receives the Most Resources?	Who Receives the Least Resources?
The Functionalist View	Those who perform the more important functions	Those who perform the less important functions
The Conflict View	Those who occupy the more powerful positions	Those who occupy the less powerful positions

Source: By the author.

The Conflict Perspective: Class Conflict and Scarce Resources

Conflict theorists don't just criticize details of the functionalist argument. Rather, they go for the throat and attack its basic premise. Conflict, not function, they stress, is the reason that we have social stratification. Let's look at the major arguments.

What are the criticisms of the functionalist explanation for why social stratification is universal?

Marx's Argument. If he were alive to hear the functionalist argument, Karl Marx would be enraged. From his point of view, the people in power are not there because of superior traits, as the functionalists would have us believe. This view is an ideology that members of the elite use to justify their being at the top—and to seduce the oppressed into believing that their welfare depends on keeping quiet and following authorities. What is human history, Marx asked, except the chronicle of class struggle? All of human history is an account of small groups of people in power using society's resources to benefit themselves and to oppress those beneath them—and of oppressed groups trying to overcome that domination.

Marx predicted that the workers would revolt. Capitalist ideology blinds them, but one day class consciousness will rip off that blindfold and expose the truth. When workers realize their common oppression, they will rebel. The struggle to control the means of production may be covert at first, taking such forms as work slowdowns and industrial sabotage. Ultimately, however, resistance will break out into the open. But the revolution will not be easy, for the bourgeoisie control the police, the military, and even the educational system, where they implant false class consciousness in the minds of the workers' children.

Current Applications of Conflict Theory. Just as Marx focused on overarching historic events—the accumulation of capital and power and the struggle between workers and capitalists—so do some of today's conflict sociologists. In analyzing global stratification and global capitalism, they look at power relations among nations, how national elites control workers, and how power shifts as capital is shuffled among nations (Jessop 2010).

Other conflict sociologists, in contrast, examine conflict wherever it is found, not just as it relates to capitalists and workers. They examine how groups *within the same class* compete with one another for a larger slice of the pie (Collins 1999; King et al. 2010). Even within the same industry, for example, union will fight against union for higher salaries, shorter hours, and more power. A special focus is conflict between racial–ethnic groups as they compete for education, housing, and even prestige—whatever benefits society has to offer. Another focus is relations between women and men, which conflict theorists say are best understood as a conflict over power—over who controls society's resources. Unlike functionalists, conflict theorists say that just beneath the surface of what may appear to be a tranquil society lies conflict that is barely held in check.

In Sum: Conflict theorists stress that in every society groups struggle with one another to gain a larger share of their society's resources. Whenever a group gains power, it uses that power to extract what it can from the groups beneath it. This elite group also uses the social institutions to keep itself in power.

Strains in the Global System

Global stratification is difficult to maintain, for every system contains unresolved issues, contradictions that can be covered up for a while, but that inevitably rear up. Some are just little dogs nipping at the heels of the world's elites. These issues can be resolved with a few tanks or bombs—or, better, with a scowl and the threat to bomb some small nation into submission.

At times, though, huge currents of history threaten to sweep a system of stratification aside—and with it, the elite who depend on that system for their positions of privilege. Such events are rare, but when they come they can bring cataclysmic disruptions. These historical shifts demand change, sometimes even the rearrangement of global power. We are now living through such a time. Russia and China's reluctant embrace of capitalism—and the more eager embrace by the eastern European nations—have been greeted with huge cracks in a creaking global banking system. Caught unaware, the global powers have desperately pumped trillions of dollars into

How do conflict theorists explain why social stratification is universal?

means of production the tools, factories, land, and investment capital used to produce wealth

bourgeoisie Marx's term for capitalists, those who own the means of production

proletariat Marx's term for the exploited class, the mass of workers who do not own the means of production

class consciousness Marx's term for awareness of a common identity based on one's position in the means of production

their economic/political systems. As curious as we are about the outcome and as much as our lives are affected, we don't know the end point of this current strain in the global system. We must await the outcome of the power elites' attempts to patch up the system that supports their global domination. Inevitably, this process will lead to a realignment of power and property.

What Determines Social Class?

Because social class is the social stratification system of the United States, let's look at social class in greater detail. Let's begin by looking at a disagreement that arose in the early days of sociology between Marx and Weber.

Karl Marx: The Means of Production

As agricultural society gave way to an industrial one, masses of peasants were displaced from their traditional lands and occupations. Fleeing to cities, they competed for the few available jobs. Paid only a pittance for their labor, they wore rags, went hungry, and slept under bridges or in shacks. In contrast, the factory owners built mansions, hired servants, and lived in the lap of luxury. Seeing this great disparity between owners and workers, Karl Marx (1818–1883) concluded that social class depends on a single factor: people's relationship to the **means of production**—the tools, factories, land, and investment capital used to produce wealth (Marx 1844/1964; Marx and Engels 1848/1967).

To see social class, people often focus on the superficial distinctions that people make among themselves—their clothing, speech, manners, education, and income. Such things, said Marx, camouflage the only dividing line that counts. There are just two classes of people: the **bourgeoisie** (*capitalists*), those who own the means of production, and the **proletariat** (*workers*), those who work for the owners. In short, people's relationship to the means of production determines their social class.

Marx did recognize other groups: farmers and peasants; a *lumpenproletariat* (people living on the margin of society, such as beggars, vagrants, and criminals); and a middle group of self-employed professionals. Marx did not consider these groups social classes, however, for they lacked **class consciousness**—a shared identity based on their position in the means of production. In other words, they did not perceive themselves as exploited workers whose plight could be resolved by collective action. Marx thought of these groups as insignificant in the future he foresaw—a workers' revolution that would overthrow capitalism.

Jacob Riis/Bettmann/Corbis

Bettmann/Corbis

Taken at the end of the 1800s, these photos illustrate the contrasting worlds of *social classes* produced by early capitalism. The sleeping boys shown in this classic 1890 photo by Jacob Riis sold newspapers in London. They did not go to school, and they had no home. The children on the right, Cornelius and Gladys Vanderbilt, are shown in front of their parents' estate. They went to school and did not work. You can see how the social locations illustrated in these photos would have produced different orientations to life and, therefore, politics, ideas about marriage, values, and so on—the stuff of which life is made.

According to Marx, what is social class?

The capitalists will grow even wealthier, Marx said, and the hostilities will increase. When workers come to realize that capitalists are the source of their oppression, they will unite and throw off the chains of their oppressors. In a bloody revolution, they will seize the means of production and usher in a classless society. When this happens, no longer will the few grow rich at the expense of the many. What holds back the workers' unity and their revolution is **false class consciousness,** workers mistakenly thinking of themselves as capitalists. Workers with a few dollars in the bank often see themselves as investors, or as capitalists who are about to launch successful businesses.

The only distinction worth mentioning, then, is whether a person is an owner or a worker. This decides everything else, Marx stressed, for property determines people's lifestyles, establishes their relationships with one another, and even shapes their ideas.

Max Weber: Property, Power, and Prestige

Max Weber (1864–1920) was an outspoken critic of Marx. He agreed that property is important, but said that it was only part of the picture. *Social class,* he said, has three components: property, power, and prestige (Gerth and Mills 1958; Weber 1922/1978). Some call these the three P's of social class. (Although Weber used the terms *class, power,* and *status,* some sociologists find *property, power,* and *prestige* to be clearer terms. To make them even clearer, you may wish to substitute *wealth* for *property.*)

Property (or wealth), said Weber, is certainly significant in determining a person's standing in society. On that point he agreed with Marx. But, added Weber, ownership is not the only significant aspect of property. For example, some powerful people, such as managers of corporations, *control* the means of production even though they do not *own* them. If managers can control the means of production for their own benefit—awarding themselves huge bonuses and magnificent perks—lack of ownership makes no practical difference in their generous use of the property for their own benefit.

Power, the second element of social class, is the ability to control others, even over their objections. Weber agreed with Marx that property is a major source of power, but he added that it is not the only source. For example, prestige can be turned into power. Two well-known examples are actors Arnold Schwarzenegger, who became governor of California, and Ronald Reagan, who was elected governor of California and then president of the United States.

Prestige, the third element in Weber's analysis, is often derived from property and power, for people tend to admire the wealthy and powerful. Prestige, however, can be based on other factors. Olympic gold medalists, for example, might not own property or be powerful, yet they have high prestige. Some are even able to exchange their prestige for property—such as those paid a small fortune for endorsing a certain brand of sportswear or for claiming to start their day with "the breakfast of champions." In other words, property and prestige are not one-way streets: Although property can bring prestige, prestige can also bring property. Figure 3 shows how property, power, and prestige are interrelated.

In Sum: For Marx, the only distinction that counted was property, more specifically people's relationship to the means of production. Whether we are owners or workers decides everything else, for this determines our lifestyle and shapes our orientation to life. Weber, in contrast, argued that social class has three components—a combination of property, power, and prestige.

With this background, let's turn our focus to social class in the United States.

Social Class in the United States

If you ask most Americans about their country's social class system, you are likely to get a blank look. If you press the matter, you will probably get an answer like this: "There are the poor and the rich—and then there are you and I, neither poor nor rich." This is just about as far as most Americans' consciousness of social class goes. Let's try to flesh out this idea.

false class consciousness
Marx's term to refer to workers identifying with the interests of capitalists

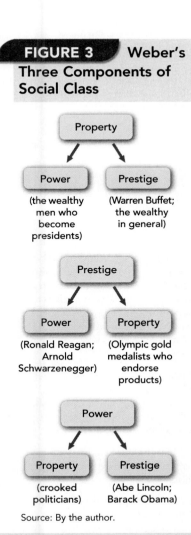

FIGURE 3 Weber's Three Components of Social Class

Property → Power (the wealthy men who become presidents) / Prestige (Warren Buffet; the wealthy in general)

Prestige → Power (Ronald Reagan; Arnold Schwarzenegger) / Property (Olympic gold medalists who endorse products)

Power → Property (crooked politicians) / Prestige (Abe Lincoln; Barack Obama)

Source: By the author.

According to Weber, what is social class?

Sociologists have no clear-cut, agreed-on definition of social class (Crompton 2010). Few agree with Marx that there are only two social classes, those who own the means of production and those who do not. This, they feel, lumps too many people together. Teenage "order takers" at McDonald's who work for $15,000 a year are lumped together with company executives who make $500,000 a year—because they both are workers at McDonald's, not owners. Most sociologists use the components Weber identified and define **social class** as a large group of people who rank closely to one another in property, power, and prestige. They look at how these three elements separate people into contrasting lifestyles, give them different chances in life, and provide them with distinct ways of looking at themselves and the world.

How do sociologists measure these three components of social class?

Property

Property comes in many forms, such as buildings, land, animals, machinery, cars, stocks, bonds, businesses, furniture, jewelry, and bank accounts. When you add up the value of someone's property and subtract that person's debts, you have what sociologists call **wealth**. This term can be misleading, as some of us have little wealth—especially most college students. Nevertheless, even if your net total comes to only $10, then that is your wealth. (Obviously, wealth as a sociological term does not mean wealthy.)

Distinguishing between Wealth and Income. Wealth and income are sometimes confused, but they are not the same. Where *wealth* is a person's net worth, **income** is a flow of money. Income has many sources: The most common is wages or a business, but other sources are rent, interest, or royalties, even alimony, an allowance, or gambling. Some people have much wealth and little income. For example, a farmer may own a lot of land (a form of wealth), but bad weather and low prices for crops can cause the income to dry up. Others have much income and little wealth. An executive with a $250,000 annual income may be debt-ridden. Below the surface prosperity—the exotic vacations, country club membership, private schools for the children, sports cars, and elegant home—the credit cards may be maxed out, the sports cars in danger of being repossessed, and the mortgage payments "past due." Typically, however, wealth and income go together.

Distribution of Property. Who owns the property in the United States? One answer, of course, is "everyone." Although this statement has some merit, it overlooks how the nation's property is divided among "everyone."

Overall, Americans are worth a hefty sum, about $48 trillion (*Statistical Abstract* 2011:Table 722). This includes all real estate, stocks, bonds, and business assets in the entire country. This wealth is highly concentrated. From Figure 4, you can see that most wealth, 70 percent, is owned by only *10 percent* of the nation's families. As you can also see from this figure, 1 percent of Americans own one-third of all U.S. assets.

Distribution of Income. How is income distributed in the United States? Economist Paul Samuelson (Samuelson and Nordhaus 2005) put it this way: "If we made an income pyramid out of a child's blocks, with each layer portraying $500 of income, the peak would be far higher than Mount Everest, but most people would be within a few feet of the ground."

As Figure 5 shows, if each block were 1½ inches tall, the typical American would be just *10 feet off the ground*, for the average per capita income in the United States is about $39,000 per year. (This average income includes every American, even children.) The typical family climbs a little higher, for most families have more than one worker, and together they average about $62,000 a year. Compared with the few families who are on the mountain's peak, the average U.S. family would find itself only 16 feet off the ground.

Prestige can sometimes be converted into property or power: Shaun White, the winner of two Olympic gold medals for snowboarding, gained endorsements worth millions. His corporate sponsors include Red Bull, Target, and Hewlett-Packard. He stars in his own video games.

social class according to Weber, a large group of people who rank close to one another in property, power, and prestige; according to Marx, one of two groups: capitalists who own the means of production or workers who sell their labor

property material possessions: animals, bank accounts, bonds, buildings, businesses, cars, cash, commodities, copyrights, furniture, jewelry, land, and stocks

wealth the total value of everything someone owns, minus the debts

income money received, usually from a job, business, or assets

How do most sociologists define social class? What is the difference between wealth and income?

FIGURE 4 — Distribution of the Property of Americans

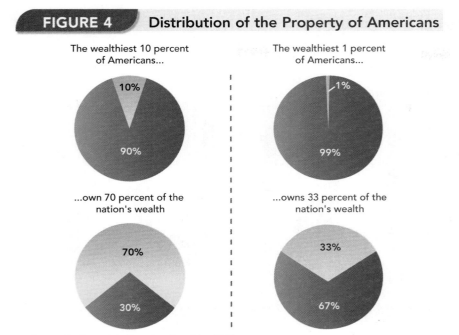

The wealthiest 10 percent of Americans...

10%

90%

...own 70 percent of the nation's wealth

70%

30%

The wealthiest 1 percent of Americans...

1%

99%

...owns 33 percent of the nation's wealth

33%

67%

Source: By the author. Based on Beeghley 2008.

FIGURE 5

Distribution of the Income of Americans

Some U.S. families have incomes that exceed the height of Mt. Everest, 29,028 feet

Average U.S. family income $62,000 or 16 feet

Average U.S. individual income $39,000 or 10 feet

If a 1½-inch child's block equals $500 of income, the average individual's annual income of $39,000 would represent a height of 10 feet, and the average family's annual income of $62,000 would represent a height of 16 feet. The income of some families, in contrast, would represent a height greater than that of Mt. Everest.

Source: By the author. Based on *Statistical Abstract of the United States* 2011:Tables 680, 696.

That some Americans enjoy the peaks of Mount Everest while most—despite their efforts—don't even make it to a tree top at the bottom presents a striking image of income inequality in the United States. Another picture emerges if we divide the entire U.S. population into five equal groups. As Figure 6 shows, the top fifth of the population receives *half* (50.0 percent) of all the income in the entire country. In contrast, the bottom fifth receives only 3.4 percent of the nation's income.

Two other features of Figure 6 are outstanding. First, notice how little change there has been in the distribution of income through the years. Second, look at how income inequality decreased from 1935 to 1970. *Since 1970, the richest 20 percent of U.S. families have grown richer, while the poorest 20 percent have grown poorer.* Despite numerous government antipoverty programs, the poorest 20 percent of Americans receive *less* of the nation's income today than they did decades ago. The richest 20 percent, in contrast, are receiving more, almost as much as they did in 1935.

The chief executive officers (CEOs) of the nation's largest corporations are especially affluent. The *Wall Street Journal* surveyed the 350 largest U.S. companies to find out what they paid their CEOs (Lublin 2011). Their median compensation (including salaries, bonuses, and stock options) came to $9,300,000 a year. (Median means that half received more than this amount, and half less.)

The CEOs' income is *200 times* higher than the average pay of U.S. workers (*Statistical Abstract* 2011:Table 680). This does *not* include their income from interest, dividends, or rents. Nor does it include the value of company-paid limousines and chauffeurs, airplanes and pilots, and private boxes at the symphony and sporting events. To really see the disparity, consider this:

> *Let's suppose that you started working the year Jesus was born and that you worked full time every year from then until now. Let's also assume that you earned today's average pay of $39,000 every year for all those years. You would still have to work another 150 years to earn the amount received by the highest-paid executive listed in Table 4.*

Imagine how you could live with an income like this. And that is precisely the point. Beyond these cold numbers lies a dynamic reality that profoundly affects people's lives.

How is income distributed in the United States?

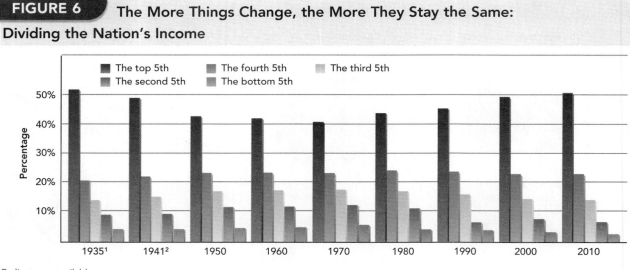

FIGURE 6 — The More Things Change, the More They Stay the Same: Dividing the Nation's Income

Legend: The top 5th · The fourth 5th · The third 5th · The second 5th · The bottom 5th

[1]Earliest year available.
[2]No data for 1940.
Source: By the author. Based on DeNavas-Walt et al. 2010:Table 3; *Statistical Abstract of the United States* 1960:Table 417; 1970:Table 489; 2011:Table 693.

power the ability to carry out your will, even over the resistance of others

A mere one-half percent of Americans owns over a quarter of the entire nation's wealth. Very few minorities are numbered among this 0.5 percent. An exception is Oprah Winfrey, who has had an ultra-successful career in entertainment and investing. Worth $2.7 billion, she is the 215th richest person in the United States. Winfrey has given millions of dollars to help minority children.

REUTERS/Mario Anzuoni/Landov

The difference in wealth between those at the top and those at the bottom of the U.S. class structure means that people experience vastly different lifestyles. For example:

A colleague of mine who was teaching at an exclusive Eastern university piqued his students' curiosity when he lectured on poverty in Latin America. That weekend, one of the students borrowed his parents' corporate jet and pilot, and in class on Monday, he and his friends related their personal observations on poverty in Latin America.

Few of us could ever say, "Mom and Dad, I've got to do a report for my soc class, so I need to borrow the jet—and the pilot—to run down to South America for the weekend." What a lifestyle! Contrast this with Americans at the low end of the income ladder who lack the funds to travel even to a neighboring town for the weekend. For parents in poverty, choices may revolve around whether to spend the little they have at the laundromat or on milk for the baby. The elderly might have to choose between purchasing the medicines they need or buying food. In short, divisions of wealth represent not "mere" numbers, but choices that make vital differences in people's lives. Let's explore this topic in the Down-to-Earth Sociology box.

Power

Let's look at the second component of social class: power.

Like many people, you may have said to yourself, "Sure, I can vote, but the big decisions are always made despite what I might think. Certainly *I* don't make the decision to send soldiers to Afghanistan or Iraq. *I* don't launch missiles into Yemen or Pakistan. *I* don't decide to raise taxes, lower interest rates, or spend billions of dollars to bail out Wall Street's fools and felons."

And then another part of you may say, "But I do participate in these decisions through my representatives in Congress, and by voting for president." True enough—as far as it goes. The trouble is, it just doesn't go far enough. Such views of being a participant in the nation's "big" decisions are a playback of the ideology we learn at an early age—an ideology that Marx said is

Can you summarize the trends in income distribution in the United States?

promoted by the elites to both legitimate and perpetuate their power. Sociologists Daniel Hellinger and Dennis Judd (1991) call this the "democratic facade" that conceals the real source of power in the United States.

The Power Elite. In Chapter 1, I mentioned that in the 1950s sociologist C. Wright Mills (1956) pointed out that **power**—the ability to get your way despite resistance—was concentrated in the hands of a few. He

TABLE 4	The Five Highest-Paid CEOs	
Executive	**Company**	**Compensation**
Philippe Dauman	Viacom	$84,300,000
Lawrence Ellison	Oracle	$68,600,000
Leslie Moonves	CBS	$53,900,000
Martin Franklin	Jarden	$45,200,000
Michael White	DirectTV	$32,600,000

Note: Compensation includes salary, bonuses, and stock options.

Source: Lublin 2011.
Table adapted from "The Top Ten Highest Paid CEOs" by WSJ Staff, from THE WALL STREET JOURNAL, April 1, 2010.; Excerpt from Gilbert, Dennis, and Joseph A. Kahl. *The American Class Structure: A New Synthesis.* 4th ed. Belmont, Calif.: Wadsworth Publishing, 1998.

Down-to-Earth **Sociology**

How the Super-Rich Live

It's good to see how other people live. It gives us a different perspective on life. Let's take a glimpse at the life of John Castle (his real name). After earning a degree in physics at MIT and an MBA at Harvard, John went into banking and securities, where he made more than $100 million (Lublin 1999).

Wanting to be connected to someone famous, John bought President John F. Kennedy's "Winter White House," an ocean-front estate in Palm Beach, Florida. John spent $11 million to remodel the 13,000-square-foot house so that it would be more to his liking. Among those changes: adding bathrooms number 14 and 15. He likes to show off John F. Kennedy's bed and also the dresser that has the drawer labeled "black underwear," carefully hand-lettered by Rose Kennedy.

At his beachfront estate, John gives what he calls "refined feasts" to the glitterati ("On History . . ." 1999). If he gets tired of such activities—or weary of swimming in the Olympic-size pool where JFK swam the weekend before his assassination—John entertains himself by riding one of his thoroughbred horses at his nearby 10-acre ranch. If this fails to ease his boredom, he can relax aboard his custom-built 42-foot Hinckley yacht.

The yacht is a real source of diversion. John once boarded it for an around-the-world trip. He didn't stay on board, though—just joined the cruise from time to time. A captain and crew kept the vessel on course, and whenever John felt like it he would fly in and stay a few days. Then he would fly back to the States to direct his business. He did this about a dozen times, flying perhaps 150,000 miles. An interesting way to go around the world.

How much does a custom-built Hinckley yacht cost? John can't tell you. As he says, "I don't want to know what anything costs. When you've got enough money, price doesn't make a difference. That's part of the freedom of being rich."

To paraphrase F. Scott Firzgerald, the super-rich are not like you or I. Shown here in weightlessness training is Charles Simonyi, who paid $25 million for a rocket ride to the International Space Station.
MAXIM MARMUR/AFP/Getty Images via Newscom

Right. And for John, being rich also means paying $1,000,000 to charter a private jet to fly Spot, his Appaloosa horse, back and forth to the vet. John didn't want Spot to have to endure a long trailer ride. Oh, and of course, there was the cost of Spot's medical treatment, another $500,000.

Other wealthy people spend extravagantly, too. Lee Tachman threw a four-day party for three friends. They had massages, ate well, took rides in a helicopter, a fighter jet, Ferraris, and Lamborghinis, and did a little paintballing—all for the bargain price of $50,000. At the 1 Oak Lounge in New York City, some customers pay $35,000 for a bottle of champagne (Haughney and Konigsberg 2008). Of course, it is a large bottle.

Parties are fun, but what if you want privacy? You can buy that, too. Wayne Huizenga, the founder of Blockbuster, who sold a half ownership in the Miami Dolphins for $550 million ("Builder Stephen . . ." 2008), bought a 2,000-acre country club, complete with an 18-hole golf course, a 55,000-square-foot-clubhouse, and 68 slips for visiting vessels. The club is so exclusive that its only members are Wayne and his wife (Fabrikant 2005).

Charles Simonyi has even outdone having your own country club. He bought a $25 million ticket for a rocket ride to the International Space Station. Simonyi liked the experience so much that he bought a second ticket (Leo 2008). No frequent flyer miles included. But as fast as prices are increasing, $50 million isn't worth what it used to be anyway.

For Your Consideration

→ What effects has social class had on your life? (Go beyond possessions to values, orientations, and outlooks on life.) How do you think you would see the world differently if you were John Castle, Lee Tachman, Charles Simonyi, or Mrs. Wayne Huizenga?

How does income lead to lifestyle? How do the super-rich live?

power elite C. Wright Mills' term for the top people in U.S. corporations, military, and politics who make the nation's major decisions

prestige respect or regard

status consistency ranking high or low on all three dimensions of social class

status inconsistency ranking high on some dimensions of social class and low on others; also called *status discrepancy*

met heavy criticism, for his analysis contradicted the dominant ideology of equality. This ideology is still dominant, and many don't like Mills' term **power elite,** which he coined to refer to those who make the big decisions in U.S. society.

Mills and others have stressed how wealth and power coalesce in a group of people who look at the world in the same way—and view themselves as a special elite. They belong to the same private clubs, vacation at the same exclusive resorts, and even hire the same bands for their daughters' debutante balls (Domhoff 1999a, 2006, 2010). This elite wields extraordinary power in U.S. society, so much so that *most* U.S. presidents have come from this group—millionaire white men from families with "old money" (Baltzell and Schneiderman 1988).

Continuing in the tradition of Mills, sociologist William Domhoff (1990, 2010) argues that this group is so powerful that the U.S. government makes no major decision without its approval. He analyzed how this group works behind the scenes with elected officials to determine both foreign and domestic policy—from setting Social Security taxes to imposing tariffs on imported goods. Although Mills' and Domhoff's conclusions are controversial—and alarming—they certainly follow logically from the principle that wealth brings power, and extreme wealth brings extreme power.

Prestige

The third component of social class is occupational prestige.

Occupations and Prestige. What are you thinking about doing after college? Chances are, you don't have the option of lolling under palm trees at the beach. Almost all of us have to choose an occupation and go to work. Look at Table 5 on the next page to see how the career you are considering stacks up in terms of **prestige** (respect or regard). Because we are moving toward a global society, this table also shows how the rankings given by Americans compare with those of the residents of sixty other countries.

Why do people give more prestige to some jobs than to others? Look again at Table 5, you will notice that the jobs at the top share four features:

1. They pay more.
2. They require more education.
3. They require more abstract thought.
4. They offer more independence (less supervision).

Now look at the bottom of the list. You can see that people give less prestige to jobs with the opposite characteristics: jobs that pay little, require less education, involve more physical labor, and are closely supervised. In short, the professions and the white-collar jobs are at the top of the list, the blue-collar jobs at the bottom.

ADAM DAVY/
PA Photos/Landov

One of the more interesting aspects of these rankings is how consistent they are across countries and over time. For example, people in every country rank college professors higher than nurses, nurses higher than social workers, and social workers higher than janitors. Similarly, the occupations that were ranked high twenty-five years ago still rank high today—and likely will rank high in the years to come.

Status Inconsistency

Ordinarily, we have similar ranks on all three dimensions of social class—property, power, and prestige. As you know, the homeless men in our opening vignette rank very low on these three dimensions, making them **status consistent.** Some

Shown here are sisters Venus and Serena Williams after winning gold medals at the Beijing Olympics. To determine the social class of athletes as highly successful as the Williams sisters presents a sociological puzzle. With their high prestige and growing wealth, what do you think their social class is? Why?

Is there a power elite in the United States? Why do you think occupational prestige is a component of social class?

people, however, have a mixture of high and low ranks. This condition, called **status inconsistency,** leads to some interesting situations.

Sociologist Gerhard Lenski (1954, 1966) analyzed how people try to maximize their **status,** their position in a social group. People who rank high on one dimension of social class but lower on others want people to judge them on the basis of their highest status. Those others, however, are trying to maximize their own positions, so they are likely to respond according to people's lowest ranking.

A classic study of status inconsistency was done by sociologist Ray Gold (1952). After apartment-house janitors unionized in Chicago, they made more money than some of the tenants whose garbage they carried out. Residents became upset when they saw janitors driving more expensive cars than they did. Some attempted to "put the janitor in his place" by making "snotty" remarks to him. For their part, the janitors took delight in knowing "dirty" secrets about the tenants, gleaned from their garbage.

People who are status inconsistent, then, are likely to confront one frustrating situation after another (Heames et al. 2006). They claim the higher status, but are handed the lower one. This situation, said Lenski (1954), tends to make people more politically radical. An example is college professors. Their prestige is very high, as you can see in Table 5, but their incomes are relatively low. Hardly anyone in U.S. society is more educated, and yet college professors don't even come close to the top of the income pyramid. In line with Lenski's prediction, the politics of most college professors are left of center. This hypothesis may also hold true among academic departments; that is, the higher a department's average pay, the more conservative are the members' politics. Teachers in departments of business and medicine, for example, are among the most highly paid in the university—and they also are the most politically conservative.

Instant wealth, the topic of the Down-to-Earth Sociology box on the next page, provides an interesting case of status inconsistency.

A Model of Social Class

Sociologists Joseph Kahl and Dennis Gilbert (Gilbert and Kahl 1998; Gilbert 2003) developed a six-tier model to portray the class structure of the United States and other capitalist countries. Think of this model, illustrated in Figure 7 as a ladder. Our discussion starts with the highest rung and moves downward. In line with Weber, on each lower rung you find less property (wealth), less power, and less prestige. Note that in this model education is also a primary measure of class.

TABLE 5	Occupational Prestige: How the United States Compares with Sixty Countries	
Occupation	United States	Average of Sixty Countries
Physician	86	78
Supreme Court judge	85	82
College president	81	86
Astronaut	80	80
Lawyer	75	73
College professor	74	78
Airline pilot	73	66
Architect	73	72
Biologist	73	69
Dentist	72	70
Civil engineer	69	70
Clergy	69	60
Psychologist	69	66
Pharmacist	68	64
High school teacher	66	64
Registered nurse	66	54
Professional athlete	65	48
Electrical engineer	64	65
Author	63	62
Banker	63	67
Veterinarian	62	61
Police officer	61	40
Sociologist	61	67
Journalist	60	55
Classical musician	59	56
Actor or actress	58	52
Chiropractor	57	62
Athletic coach	53	50
Social worker	52	56
Electrician	51	44
Undertaker	49	34
Jazz musician	48	38
Real estate agent	48	49
Mail carrier	47	33
Secretary	46	53
Plumber	45	34
Carpenter	43	37
Farmer	40	47
Barber	36	30
Store sales clerk	36	34
Truck driver	30	33
Cab driver	28	28
Garbage collector	28	13
Waiter or waitress	28	23
Bartender	25	23
Lives on public aid	25	16
Bill collector	24	27
Factory worker	24	29
Janitor	22	21
Shoe shiner	17	12
Street sweeper	11	13

Note. For five occupations not located in the 1994 source, the 1991 ratings were used: Supreme Court judge, astronaut, athletic coach, lives on public aid, and street sweeper.

Sources: Treiman 1977: Appendices A and D; Nakao and Treas 1990, 1994:Appendix D.

What is status inconsistency? How is status inconsistency related to political views?

The Big Win: Life after the Lottery

"If I just win the lottery, life will be good. These problems I've got, they'll be gone. I can just see myself now."

So goes the dream. And many Americans shell out mega-bucks every week, with the glimmering hope that "Maybe this week, I'll hit it big."

Most are lucky to win $20, or perhaps just another scratch-off ticket.

But there are those who hit it big. What happens to these winners? Are their lives all wine, roses, and chocolate afterward?

We don't have any systematic studies of the big winners, so I can't tell you what life is like for the average winner. But several themes are apparent from reporters' interviews.

The most common consequence of hitting it big is that life becomes topsy-turvy (Bernstein 2007). All of us are rooted somewhere. We have connections with others that provide the basis for our orientations to life and how we feel about the world. Sudden wealth can rip these moorings apart, and the resulting *status inconsistency* can lead to a condition sociologists call *anomie*.

First comes the shock. As Mary Sanderson, a telephone operator in Dover, New Hampshire, who won $66 million, said, "I was afraid to believe it was real, and afraid to believe it wasn't." Mary says that she never slept worse than her first night as a multimillionaire. "I spent the whole time crying—and throwing up" (Tresniowski 1999).

Reporters and TV crews appear on your doorstep. "What are you going to do with all that money?" they demand. You haven't the slightest idea, but in a daze you mumble something.

Then come the calls. Some are welcome. Your Mom and Dad call to congratulate you. But long-forgotten friends and distant relatives suddenly remember how close they really are to you—and strangely enough, they all have emergencies that your money can solve. You even get calls from strangers who have ailing mothers, terminally ill kids, sick dogs . . .

You have to unplug the phone and get an unlisted number.

You might be flooded with marriage proposals. You certainly didn't become more attractive or sexy overnight—or did you? Maybe money makes people sexy.

You can no longer trust people. You don't know what their real motives are. Before, no one could be after your money

because you didn't have any. You may even fear kidnappers. Before, this wasn't a problem—unless some kidnapper wanted the ransom of a seven-year-old car.

The normal becomes abnormal. Even picking out a wedding gift is a problem. If you give the usual toaster, everyone will think you're stingy. But should you write a check for $25,000? If you do, you'll be invited to every wedding in town—and everyone will expect the same.

Here is what happened to some lottery winners:

When Michael Klinebiel of Rahway, New Jersey, won $2 million, his mother, Phyllis, said that half of it was hers, that she and her son had pooled $20 a month for years to play the lottery. He said they had done this—but he had bought the winning ticket on his own. Phyllis sued her son ("Sticky Ticket" 1998).

When Mack Metcalf, a forklift operator in Corbin, Kentucky, hit the jackpot for $34 million, he fulfilled a dream: He built and moved into a replica of George Washington's Mount Vernon home. Then his life fell apart—his former wife sued him, his current wife divorced him, and his new girlfriend got $500,000 while he was drunk. Within three years of his "good" fortune, Metcalf had drunk himself to death (Dao 2005).

When Abraham Shakespeare, a dead-broke truck driver's assistant won $31 million in the Florida lottery, he bought a million dollar home in a gated community. He lent money to friends to start businesses, even paid for funerals. This evidently wasn't enough. His body was found buried in the yard of a "friend" (Lush 2010; McShane 2010).)

Chris Shaw of Jefferson City, Missouri, shown here, won $256 million. He said he would pay the $1,000 he owes on his truck, take his kids to Disneyworld, and get his teeth fixed. How do you think status inconsistency will affect his life?
AP Images/Orlin Wagner

Winners who avoid *anomie* seem to be people who don't make sudden changes in their lifestyle or their behavior. They hold onto their old friends and routines—the anchors in life that give them identity and a sense of belonging. Some even keep their old jobs—not for the money, of course, but because the job anchors them to an identity with which they are familiar and comfortable.

Sudden wealth, in other words, poses a threat that has to be guarded against.

And I can just hear you say, "I'll take the risk!"

For Your Consideration

→ How do you think your life would change if you won $10 million?

How does status inconsistency explain why instant wealth is upsetting?

| FIGURE 7 | The U.S. Social Class Ladder |

Social Class	Education	Occupation	Income	Percentage of Population
Capitalist	Prestigious university	Investors and heirs, a few top executives	$1,000,000+	1%
Upper Middle	College or university, often with postgraduate study	Professionals and upper managers	$125,000+	15%
Lower Middle	High school or college; often apprenticeship	Semiprofessionals and lower managers, craftspeople, foremen	About $60,000	34%
Working	High school	Factory workers, clerical workers, low-paid retail sales, and craftspeople	About $36,000	30%
Working Poor	High school and some high school	Laborers, service workers, low-paid salespeople	About $19,000	15%
Underclass	Some high school	Unemployed and part-time, on welfare	Under $12,000	5%

Source: By the author. Based on Gilbert and Kahl 1998 and Gilbert 2008; income estimates are modified from Duff 1995.

The Capitalist Class

Sitting on the top rung of the class ladder is a powerful elite that consists of just 1 percent of the U.S. population. As you saw in Figure 4, this capitalist class is so wealthy that it owns one-third of all the nation's assets. *This tiny 1 percent is worth more than the entire bottom 90 percent of the country* (Beeghley 2008).

Power and influence cling to this small elite. They have direct access to top politicians, and their decisions open or close job opportunities for millions of people. They even help to shape the views of the nation: They own our major media and entertainment outlets—newspapers, magazines, radio and television stations, and sports franchises. They also control the boards of directors of our most influential colleges and universities. The super-rich perpetuate themselves in privilege by passing on their assets and social networks to their children.

The capitalist class can be divided into "old" and "new" money. The longer that wealth has been in a family, the more it adds to the family's prestige. The children of "old" money seldom mingle with "common" folk. Instead, they attend exclusive private schools where they learn views of life that support their privileged position. They don't work for wages; instead, many study business or become lawyers so that they can manage the family fortune. These old-money capitalists (also called "blue-bloods") wield vast power as they use their extensive political connections to protect their economic empires (Sklair 2001; Domhoff 1990, 2006, 2010).

⬛▯ Read
Media Magic: Making Class Invisible
by Gregory Mantsios
on **mysoclab.com**

What is the capitalist class? What are its two divisions?

With a fortune of $56 billion, Bill Gates, a cofounder of Microsoft Corporation, is the second wealthiest person in the world. His 40,000-square-foot home (sometimes called a "technopalace") in Seattle, Washington, was appraised at $110 million.

© John Van Hasselt/Corbis

At the lower end of the capitalist class are the *nouveau riche*, those who have "new money." Although they have made fortunes in business, the stock market, inventions, entertainment, or sports, they are outsiders to the upper class. They have not attended the "right" schools, and they don't share the social networks that come with old money. Not blue-bloods, they aren't trusted to have the right orientations to life. Even their "taste" in clothing and status symbols is suspect (Fabrikant 2005). Donald Trump, whose money is "new," is not listed in the *Social Register,* the "White Pages" of the blue-bloods that lists the most prestigious and wealthy one-tenth of 1 percent of the U.S. population. Trump says he "doesn't care," but he reveals his true feelings by adding that his heirs will be in it (Kaufman 1996). He is probably right, for the children of the new-moneyed can ascend into the top part of the capitalist class—if they go to the right schools *and* marry old money.

Many in the capitalist class are philanthropic. They establish foundations and give huge sums to "causes." Their motives vary. Some feel guilty because they have so much while others have so little. Others seek prestige, acclaim, or fame. Still others feel a responsibility—even a sense of fate or purpose—to use their money for doing good. Bill Gates, who has given more money to the poor and to medical research than has anyone in history, seems to fall into this latter category.

The Upper Middle Class

Of all the classes, the upper middle class is the one most shaped by education. Almost all members of this class have at least a bachelor's degree, and many have postgraduate degrees in business, management, law, or medicine. These people manage the corporations owned by the capitalist class, run their own businesses, or pursue professions. As Gilbert and Kahl (1998) say,

> [These positions] may not grant prestige equivalent to a title of nobility in the Germany of Max Weber, but they certainly represent the sign of having "made it" in contemporary America. . . . Their income is sufficient to purchase houses and cars and travel that become public symbols for all to see and for advertisers to portray with words and pictures that connote success, glamour, and high style.

Consequently, parents and teachers push children to prepare for upper-middle-class jobs. About 15 percent of the population belong to this class.

Sociologists use income, education, and occupational prestige to measure social class. For most people, this works well, but not for everyone, especially entertainers. To what social class do DiCaprio, James, Lopez, and Gaga belong? Leonardo DiCaprio makes about $78 million a year, Lebron James $43 million, Jennifer Lopez $10 million, and Lady Gaga $90 million.

HANS DERYK/
Reuters/Landov

Elizabeth Goodenough/
Everett Collection

MARTIN BUREAU/AFP/
Getty Images/Newscom

Lia Toby/WENN.com/
Newscom

What is the upper middle class?

The Lower Middle Class

About 34 percent of the population belong to the lower middle class. Members of this class have jobs in which they follow orders given by members of the upper middle class. With their technical and lower-level management positions, they can afford a mainstream lifestyle, although they struggle to maintain it. Many anticipate being able to move up the social class ladder. Feelings of insecurity are common, however, with the threat of inflation, recession, and job insecurity bringing a nagging sense that they might fall down the class ladder (Kefalas 2007).

The distinctions between the lower middle class and the working class on the next rung below are more blurred than those between other classes. In general, however, members of the lower middle class work at jobs that have slightly more prestige, and their incomes are generally higher.

The Working Class

About 30 percent of the U.S. population belong to this class of relatively unskilled blue-collar and white-collar workers. Compared with the lower middle class, they have less education and lower incomes. Their jobs are also less secure and more routine, with closer supervision. One of their greatest fears is that of being laid off during a recession. With only a high school diploma, the average member of the working class has little hope of climbing up the class ladder. Job changes usually bring "more of the same," so most concentrate on getting ahead by achieving seniority on the job rather than by changing their type of work. They tend to think of themselves as having "real jobs" and regard the "suits" above them as paper pushers who have no practical experience (Morris and Grimes 2005).

The Working Poor

Members of this class, about 15 percent of the population, work at unskilled, low-paying, temporary and seasonal jobs, such as sharecropping, migrant farm work, housecleaning, and day labor. Most are high school dropouts. Many are functionally illiterate, finding it difficult to read even the want ads. They are not likely to vote (Beeghley 2008), for they believe that no matter what party is elected to office, their situation won't change.

Although they work full time, millions of the working poor depend on food stamps and donations from local food pantries to survive on their meager incomes (O'Hare 1996b). How can they work full time and still be poor? Suppose that you are married and have a baby 3 months old and another child 4 years old. Your spouse stays home to care for them, so earning the income is up to you. But as a high-school dropout, all you can get is a minimum wage job. At $7.25 an hour, you earn $290 for 40 hours. In a year, this comes to $15,080—before deductions. Your nagging fear—and recurring nightmare—is of ending up "on the streets."

The Underclass

On the lowest rung, and with next to no chance of climbing anywhere, is the **underclass.** Concentrated in the inner city, this group has little or no connection with the job market. Those who are employed—and some are—do menial, low-paying, temporary work. Welfare, if it is available, along with food stamps and food pantries, is their main support. Most members of other classes consider these people the "ne'er-do-wells" of society. Life is the toughest in this class, and it is filled with despair. About 5 percent of the population fall into this class.

The homeless men described in the opening vignette of this chapter, and the women and children like them, are part of the underclass. These are the people whom most Americans wish would just go away. Their presence on our city streets bothers passersby from the more privileged social classes—which includes just about everyone. "What are those obnoxious, dirty, foul-smelling people doing here, cluttering up my city?" appears to be a common response. Some people react with sympathy and a desire to do something. But what? Almost all of us just shrug our shoulders and look the other way, despairing of a solution and somewhat intimidated by their presence.

underclass a group of people for whom poverty persists year after year and across generations

Can you distinguish between the lower middle class, the working class, the working poor, and the underclass?

The homeless are the "fallout" of our postindustrial economy. In another era, they would have had plenty of work. They would have tended horses, worked on farms, dug ditches, shoveled coal, and run the factory looms. Some would have explored and settled the West. The prospect of gold would have lured others to California, Alaska, and Australia. Today, however, with no frontiers to settle, factory jobs scarce, and farms that are becoming technological marvels, we have little need for unskilled labor.

Consequences of Social Class

The man was a C student throughout school. As a businessman, he ran Arbusto, an oil company, into the ground. An alcoholic until age forty, he was arrested for drunk driving. With this background, how did he become president of the United States?

Accompanying these personal factors was the power of social class. George W. Bush was born the grandson of a wealthy senator and the son of a businessman who himself became president of the United States after serving as a member of the House of Representatives, director of the CIA, and head of the Republican party. For high school, he went to an elite private prep school, Andover; for his bachelor's degree to Yale; and for his MBA to Harvard. He was given $1 million to start his own business. When that business (Arbusto) failed, Bush fell softly, landing on the boards of several corporations. Taken care of even further, he was made the managing director of a professional baseball team, the Texas Rangers, and allowed to buy a share of the team for $600,000—which he sold for $15 million.

When it was time for him to get into politics, Bush's connections financed his run for governor of Texas and then for the presidency.

Does social class matter? And how! Think of each social class as a broad subculture with distinct approaches to life, so significant that it affects our health, family life, education, religion, politics, and even our experiences with crime and the criminal justice system. Let's look at how social class affects our lives.

Physical Health

If you want to get a sense of how social class affects health, take a ride on Washington's Metro system. Start in the blighted Southeast section of downtown D.C. For every mile you travel to where the wealthy live in Montgomery County in Maryland, life expectancy rises about a year and a half. By the time you get off, you will find a twenty-year gap between the poor blacks where you started your trip and the rich whites where you ended it. (Cohen 2004)

The principle is simple: As you go up the social-class ladder, health increases. As you go down the ladder, health decreases (Hout 2008). Age makes no difference. Infants born to the poor are more likely to die before their first birthday, and a larger percentage of poor people in their old age—whether 75 or 95—die each year than do the elderly who are wealthy.

How can social class have such dramatic effects on health? A fundamental reason is that health care in the United States is not a citizen's right but a commodity for sale. This gives us a two-tier system of medicine: superior care for those who can afford the cost and inferior care for those who cannot (Budrys 2003). Unlike the middle and upper classes, few poor people have a personal physician, and they often spend hours waiting in crowded public health clinics. When the poor

With tough economic times, a lot of people have lost their jobs—and their homes. If this happens, how can you survive? Maybe a smile and a sense of humor to tap the kindness of strangers. I took this photo outside Boston's Fenway Park.

James M. Henslin

How is physical health related to social class?

are hospitalized, they are likely to find themselves in understaffed and underfunded public hospitals, treated by rotating interns who do not know them and cannot follow up on their progress.

A second reason is lifestyles, which are shaped by social class. People in the lower classes are more likely to smoke, eat a lot of fats, become overweight, abuse drugs and alcohol, get little exercise, and practice unsafe sex (Chin et al. 2000; Dolnick 2010). This, to understate the matter, does not improve people's health.

There is a third reason, too. Life is hard on the poor. The persistent stresses they face cause their bodies to wear out faster (Geronimus 2010). The rich find life better. They have fewer problems and more resources to deal with the ones they have. This gives them a sense of control over their lives, a source of both physical and mental health.

Mental Health

Sociological studies from as far back as the 1930s have found that the mental health of the lower classes is worse than that of the higher classes (Faris and Dunham 1939; Srole et al. 1978; Pratt et al. 2007; Peltham 2009). Greater mental problems are part of the higher stress that accompanies poverty. Compared with middle- and upper-class Americans, the poor have less job security and lower wages. They are more likely to divorce, to be the victims of crime, and to have more physical illnesses. Couple these conditions with bill collectors and the threat of eviction, and you can see how such severe blows would undermine people's emotional well-being.

People higher up the social class ladder experience stress in daily life, of course, but their stress is generally less, and their coping resources are greater. Not only can they afford vacations, psychiatrists, and counselors, but *their class position also gives them greater control over their lives, a key to good mental health.* Consider these factors as you read the following Thinking Critically section.

THINKING CRITICALLY
Mental Illness and Inequality in Health Care

Standing among the police, I watched as the elderly nude man, looking confused, struggled to put on his clothing. The man had ripped the wires out of the homeless shelter's main electrical box and then led the police on a merry chase as he ran from room to room.

I asked an officer where they were going to take the man, and he replied, "To Malcolm Bliss" (the state mental hospital). When I commented, "I guess he'll be in there for a quite a while," he replied, "Probably just a day or two. We picked him up last week—he was crawling under cars stopped at a traffic light—and they let him out in two days."

The police explained that a person must be a danger to others or to oneself to be admitted as a long-term patient. Visualizing this old man crawling under cars in traffic or possibly electrocuting himself by ripping out electrical wires with his bare hands, I marveled at the definition of "danger" that the hospital psychiatrists must be using.

Stripped of its veil, the two-tier system of medical care is readily visible. The poor—such as this confused naked man—find it difficult to get into mental hospitals. If they are admitted, they are sent to the dreaded state hospitals. In contrast, private hospitals serve the wealthy and those who have good insurance. The rich are likely to be treated with "talk therapy" (forms of psychotherapy), the poor with "drug therapy" (tranquilizers to make them docile, sometimes known as "medicinal straitjackets").

For Your Consideration

How can we improve the treatment of the mentally ill poor? Take into consideration that the public does not want higher taxes. What about the broader, more fundamental issue: that of inequality in health care? Should medical care be a commodity that is sold to those who can afford it? Or do all citizens possess some fundamental right that should guarantee them high-quality health care. ◼

How is mental health related to social class?

Family Life

Social class also makes a significant difference in family life. Let's consider the influence of social class in our choice of spouse and our chances of getting divorced.

Choice of Husband or Wife.   Members of the capitalist class place strong emphasis on family tradition. They stress the family's history, even a sense of purpose or destiny in life (Baltzell 1979; Aldrich 1989). Children of this class learn that their choice of husband or wife affects not just them, but the entire family, that it will have an impact on the "family line." These background expectations shrink the field of "eligible" marriage partners, making it narrower than it is for the children of any other social class. As a result, parents in this class play a strong role in their children's mate selection.

Divorce.   The more difficult life of the lower social classes, especially the many tensions that come from insecure jobs and inadequate incomes, leads to higher marital friction and a greater likelihood of divorce. Consequently, children of the poor are more likely to grow up in broken homes.

Education

As we saw in Figure 7, education increases as one goes up the social class ladder. It is not just the amount of education that changes, but also the type of education. Children of the capitalist class bypass public schools. They attend exclusive private schools where they are trained to take a commanding role in society. Prep schools such as Andover, Groton, and Phillips Exeter Academy teach upper-class values and prepare their students for prestigious universities (Beeghley 2008; Stevens 2009).

Keenly aware that private schools can be a key to upward social mobility, some upper-middle-class parents make every effort to get their children into the prestigious preschools that feed into these exclusive prep schools. Although some preschools cost $23,000 a year, they have waiting lists (Rohwedder 2007). Not able to afford this kind of tuition, some parents hire tutors to train their 4-year olds in test-taking skills so they can get into public kindergartens for gifted students. They even hire experts to teach these preschoolers to look adults in the eye while they are being interviewed for these limited positions (Banjo 2010). You can see how such parental involvement and resources make it more likely that children from the more privileged classes go to college—and graduate.

Jennifer Lopez and her husband Marc Anthony, who just flew to Puerto Rico in their private jet. To the right is a middle-aged couple who live in an old motor home parked in Santa Barbara, one of the wealthiest communities in California.

AP Images/Andres Leighton

David Bacon/The Image Works

How does social class make a difference in family life? In education?

Religion

One area of social life that we might think would not be affected by social class is religion. ("People are either religious, or they are not. What does social class have to do with it?") Social class, however, is a significant sorter of people in all areas of social life, and religion is no exception to this principle. The classes tend to cluster in different denominations. Episcopalians, for example, are more likely to attract the middle and upper classes, while Baptists and the Assemblies of God draw heavily from the lower classes (Smith and Faris 2005). Patterns of worship also follow class lines: The lower classes are attracted to more expressive worship services and louder music, while the middle and upper classes prefer more "subdued" worship.

Politics

As I have stressed, people perceive events from their own corner in life. Political views are no exception to this principle of symbolic interaction, and the rich and the poor walk different political paths. The higher that people are on the social class ladder, the more likely they are to vote for Republicans (Hout 2008). In contrast, most members of the working class believe that the government should intervene in the economy to provide jobs and to make citizens financially secure. They are more likely to vote for Democrats. Although the working class is more liberal on *economic* issues (policies that increase government spending), its members are more conservative on *social* issues (such as opposing abortion and the Equal Rights Amendment) (Houtman 1995; Hout 2008). People toward the bottom of the class structure are also less likely to be politically active—to campaign for candidates or even to vote (Gilbert 2003; Beeghley 2008).

Crime and Criminal Justice

If justice is supposed to be blind, it certainly is not when it comes to your chances of being arrested (Henslin 2012). The white-collar crimes of the more privileged classes are more likely to be dealt with outside the criminal justice system, while the police and courts deal with the street crimes of the lower classes. One consequence of this class standard is that members of the lower classes are more likely to be in prison, on probation, or on parole. In addition, since those who commit street crimes tend to do so in or near their own neighborhoods, the lower classes are more likely to be robbed, burglarized, or murdered.

Social Mobility

No aspect of life, then—from marriage to politics—goes untouched by social class. Because life is so much more satisfying in the more privileged classes, people strive to climb the social class ladder. What affects their chances?

Three Types of Social Mobility

There are three basic types of social mobility: intergenerational, structural, and exchange. **Intergenerational mobility** refers to a change that occurs between generations—when grown-up children end up on a different rung of the social class ladder from the one occupied by their parents. If the child of someone who sells used cars graduates from college and buys a Toyota dealership, that person experiences **upward social mobility.** Conversely, if a child of the dealership's owner parties too much, drops out

intergenerational mobility
the change that family members make in social class from one generation to the next

upward social mobility
movement up the social class ladder

This young woman is being "introduced" to society at a debutante ball in Laredo, Texas. Like you, she has learned from her parents, peers, and education, a view of where she belongs in life. How do you think her view is different from yours?

© Bob Daemmrich/The Image Works

What difference does social class make in religion? In politics? In crime and criminal justice?

downward social mobility movement down the social class ladder

structural mobility movement up or down the social class ladder that is due more to changes in the structure of society than to the actions of individuals

of college, and ends up selling cars, he or she experiences **downward social mobility.** As discussed in the Cultural Diversity box below, social mobility comes at a cost.

We like to think that individual efforts are the reason people move up the class ladder—and their faults the reason they move down. In these examples, we can identify hard work, sacrifice, and ambition on the one hand, versus indolence and substance abuse on the other. Although individual factors such as these do underlie social mobility, sociologists consider **structural mobility** to be the crucial factor. This second basic type of mobility refers to changes in society that cause large numbers of people to move up or down the class ladder.

Cultural Diversity in the United States

Social Class and the Upward Social Mobility of African Americans

The overview of social class presented in this chapter doesn't apply equally to all the groups that make up U.S. society. Consider geography: What constitutes the upper class of a town of 5,000 people will differ from that of a city of a million. With fewer extremes of wealth and occupation, in small towns family background and local reputation are more significant.

So it is with racial–ethnic groups. All racial–ethnic groups are marked by social class, but what constitutes a particular social class can differ from one group to another—as well as from one historical period to another. Consider social class among African Americans (Cole and Omari 2003).

The earliest class divisions can be traced to slavery—to slaves who worked in the fields and those who worked in the "big house." Those who worked in the plantation home were exposed more to the customs, manners, and forms of speech of wealthy whites. Their more privileged position—which brought with it better food and clothing, as well as lighter work—was often based on skin color. Mulattos, lighter-skinned slaves, were often chosen for this more desirable work. One result was the development of a "mulatto elite," a segment of the slave population that, proud of its distinctiveness, distanced itself from the other slaves. At this time, there also were free blacks. Not only were they able to own property but some even owned black slaves.

After the War Between the States (as the Civil War is known in the South), these two groups, the mulatto elite and the free blacks, formed an upper class. Proud of their earlier status, they distanced themselves from other blacks. From these groups came most of the black professionals. After World War II, the black middle class expanded as African Americans entered a wider range of occupations. Today, more than half of all African American adults work at white-collar jobs, about 22 percent at the professional or managerial level (Beeghley 2008).

Corbis/SuperStock Royalty Free

An unwelcome cost greets many African Americans who move up the social class ladder: an uncomfortable distancing from their roots, a separation from significant others—parents, siblings, and childhood friends (hooks 2000; Lacy 2007). The upwardly mobile enter a world unknown to those left behind, one that demands not only different appearance and speech, but also different values, aspirations, and ways of viewing the world. These are severe challenges to the self and often rupture relationships with those left behind.

An additional cost is a subtle racism that lurks beneath the surface of some work settings, poisoning what could be easy, mutually respectful interaction. To be aware that white co-workers perceive you as different—as a stranger, an intruder, or "the other"—engenders frustration, dissatisfaction, and cynicism. To cope, many nourish their racial identity and stress the "high value of black culture and being black" (Lacy and Harris 2008). Some move to neighborhoods of upper-middle-class African Americans, where they can live among like-minded people who have similar experiences (Lacy 2007).

For Your Consideration

→ In the box on upward social mobility, we discussed how Latinos face a similar situation. Why do you think this is? What connections do you see among upward mobility, frustration, and racial–ethnic identity? How do you think that the upward mobility of whites is different? Why?

Can you give a brief history of the social mobility of African Americans?

To understand *structural mobility*, think about how changes in society (its *structure*) drive some people down the social class ladder and lift others up. When computers were invented, for example, new types of jobs appeared overnight. Huge numbers of people attended workshops and took crash courses, switching from blue-collar to white-collar work. In contrast, others were thrown out of work as technology bypassed their jobs. Individual effort was certainly involved—for some seized the opportunity while others did not—but the underlying cause was a huge social change that transformed the *structure* of work. This happens during depressions, too, when opportunities disappear, forcing millions of people downward on the class ladder. In this instance, too, their changed status is due less to individual behavior than to *structural* changes in society.

The third type of social mobility, **exchange mobility,** occurs when large numbers of people move up and down the social class ladder, but, on balance, the proportions of the social classes remain about the same. Suppose that a million or so working-class people are trained in some new technology, and they move up the class ladder. Suppose also that because of a surge in imports, about a million skilled workers have to take lower-status jobs. Although millions of people change their social class, there is, in effect, an *exchange* among them. The net result more or less balances out, and the class system remains basically untouched.

exchange mobility about the same number of people moving up and down the social class ladder, such that, on balance, the social class system shows little change

Women in Studies of Social Mobility

About half of sons pass their fathers on the social class ladder, about one-third stay at the same level, and about one-sixth fall down the ladder (Blau and Duncan 1967; Featherman 1979).

"Only sons!" said feminists in response to these classic studies on social mobility. "Do you think it is good science to ignore daughters? And why do you assign women the class of their husbands? Do you think that wives have no social class position of their own?" (Davis and Robinson 1988). The male sociologists brushed off these objections, replying that there were too few women in the labor force to make a difference.

These sociologists simply hadn't caught up with the times. The gradual but steady increase of women working for pay had caught them unprepared. Although sociologists now include women in their research on social mobility, how to determine the social class of married women is still in its infancy (Beller 2009).

Upwardly mobile women report how important their parents were in their success, how they encouraged them to achieve when they were just children. For upwardly mobile African American women, strong mothers are especially significant (Robinson and Nelson 2010). In their study of women from working-class backgrounds who became managers and professionals, sociologists Elizabeth Higginbotham and Lynn Weber (1992) found this recurring theme: parents encouraging their girls to postpone marriage and get an education. To these understandings from the micro approach, we need to add the macro level. Had there not been a *structural* change in society, the millions of new positions that women occupy would not exist.

The term *structural mobility* refers to changes in society that push large numbers of people either up or down the social class ladder. A remarkable example was the stock market crash of 1929 when thousands of people suddenly lost their wealth. People who once "had it made" found themselves standing on street corners selling apples or, as depicted here, selling their possessions at fire-sale prices. The crash of 2008 brought similar problems to untold numbers of people.

Bettmann/Corbis

Poverty

Many Americans find that the "limitless possibilities" of the American dream are quite elusive. As illustrated in Figure 7, the working poor and underclass together form about one-fifth of the U.S. population. This translates into a huge number, about 60 million people. Who are these people?

What are three types of social mobility? How do women fit into social mobility?

Watch
American Outrage
on **mysoclab.com**

Drawing the Poverty Line

To determine who is poor, the U.S. government draws a **poverty line.** This measure was set in the 1960s, when poor people were thought to spend about one-third of their incomes on food. On the basis of this assumption, each year the government computes a low-cost food budget and multiplies it by 3. Families whose incomes are less than this amount are classified as poor; those whose incomes are higher—even by a dollar—are considered "not poor."

This official measure of poverty is grossly inadequate. Poor people actually spend only about 20 percent of their incomes on food, so to determine a poverty line, we ought to multiply their food budget by 5 instead of 3 (Uchitelle 2001). Another problem is that mothers who work outside the home and have to pay for child care are treated the same as mothers who don't have this expense. The poverty line is also the same for everyone across the nation, even though the cost of living is much higher in New York than in Alabama. On the other hand, much of the income of the poor goes uncounted: food stamps, rent assistance, subsidized child care, and the earned income tax credit (DeNavas-Walt et al. 2010).

High rates of rural poverty have been a part of the United States from its origin to the present. This 1937 photo shows a 32-year old woman in California who had seven children and no food.

Library of Congress Image # USF34-T01-009095-C

What is the poverty line? Why is this measure of poverty inadequate?

That a change in the poverty line would instantly make millions of people poor—or take away their poverty—would be laughable, if it weren't so serious. Although this line is arbitrary, because it is the official measure of poverty, we'll use it to see who in the United States is poor. Before we do this, though, compare your ideas of the poor with the stereotypes explored in the Down-to-Earth Sociology box below.

Suburbanization of Poverty.   Until recently, poverty has been more common in rural areas than in the city or suburbs, but we have just had a major change. Extensive migration from the cities to suburbs combined with the collapse of the housing market has brought poverty to the suburbs. It has hit so hard that *most* of the nation's poor now live in the suburbs (Kneebone and Garr 2010).

Race–Ethnicity.   One of the strongest factors in poverty is race–ethnicity. As Figure 8 shows, only 11 percent of whites are poor, followed closely by Asian Americans at 12 percent. In contrast, 23 percent of Latinos live in poverty, while the total jumps even higher, to 25 percent for African Americans and Native Americans. Because whites are, by far, the largest group in the United States, their lower rate of poverty translates into larger numbers. As a result, there are more poor whites than poor people of any other racial–ethnic group. As part 2 of Figure 8 shows, half (49 percent) of all the poor are whites.

Children of Poverty

Children are more likely to live in poverty than are adults or the elderly. This holds true regardless of race–ethnicity, but from Figure 8 on the next page, you can see how much greater poverty is among Latino, African American, and Native American children. That millions of U.S. children are reared in poverty is shocking when one considers the wealth of this country and the supposed concern for the well-being of children. This tragic aspect of poverty is the topic of the following Thinking Critically section.

—Explore
Living Data
on mysoclab.com

Down-to-Earth **Sociology**

Some Facts about Poverty: What Do You Know?

Can you tell which of these statements are true?

Poverty is unusual. *False.* Over a four-year period, *one-third* (32 percent) of all Americans experience poverty for at least two months (DeNavas-Walt et al. 2010), and about *half* of the population will experience poverty at some time before they reach age 65 (Cellini at al. 2008).

People with less education are more likely to be poor. *True.* Most definitely

Most poor people are poor because they do not want to work. *False.* About 40 percent of the poor are under age 18, and another 10 percent are age 65 or older. About 30 percent of the working-age poor work at least half the year (O'Hare 1996a, 1996b).

Most of the poor are trapped in a cycle of poverty. *We have to go true and false on this one.* Most poverty lasts less than a year (Lichter and Crowley 2002), but just over half of those who escape poverty will return to poverty within five years (Ratcliffe and McKernan 2010).

Most children who are born in poverty are poor as adults. *False* (Ratcliffe and McKernan 2010).

Most African Americans are poor. *False.* This one was easy. We just reviewed some statistics in the box on upward mobility.

Most of the poor are African Americans. *False.* There are more poor whites than any other group.

Most of the poor are single mothers and their children. *False.* About 38 percent of the poor match this stereotype, but 34 percent of the poor live in married-couple families, 22 percent live alone or with nonrelatives, and 6 percent live in other settings (O'Hare 1996a, 1996b).

Most of the poor live on welfare. *False.* Only about 25 percent of the income of poor adults comes from welfare. About half comes from wages and pensions, and about 22 percent from Social Security (O'Hare 1996a, 1996b).

Sources: O'Hare 1996a, 1996b, with other sources as indicated.

For Your Consideration

➤ What stereotypes of the poor do you (or people you know) hold? How would you test these stereotypes?

How is poverty related to race–ethnicity?

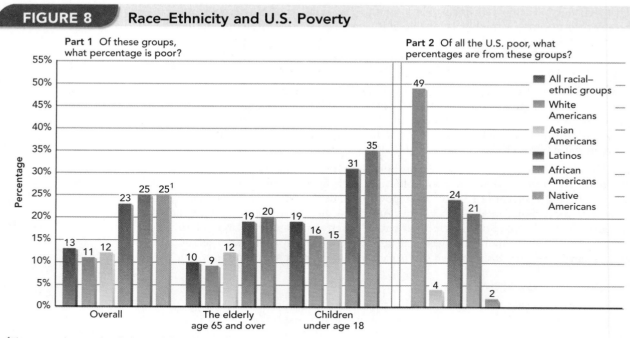

FIGURE 8 Race–Ethnicity and U.S. Poverty

Part 1 Of these groups, what percentage is poor?

Part 2 Of all the U.S. poor, what percentages are from these groups?

Legend:
- All racial–ethnic groups
- White Americans
- Asian Americans
- Latinos
- African Americans
- Native Americans

[1]The source does not break this total down by age.

Note: Only these groups are listed in the source. The poverty line is $22,025 for a family of four.

Source: By the author. Based on *Statistical Abstract of the United States* 2011:Tables 709, 712.

Beyond the awareness of most Americans are the rural poor such as this family in Maine. With low education and few good jobs available, life is hardscrabble. What do you think the future holds for these children?

Jean-Yves Rabeuf/The Image Works

Do births to single women cause poverty?

THINKING CRITICALLY
The Nation's Shame: Children in Poverty

One of the most startling statistics in sociology is shown in Figure 8. Look at the rate of childhood poverty: For Asian Americans, 1 of 8 children is poor; for whites, 1 of 7; for Latinos, 1 of 3 or 4; and for African Americans, an astounding 1 of 3. These percentages translate into incredible numbers—approximately *14 million* children.

Why do so many U.S. children live in poverty? A major reason is the large number of births to women who are not married, about 1.5 million a year. Look at how sharply this number has increased: In 1960, 1 of 20 U.S. children was born to a single woman. Today that total is about *eight times higher*, and single women now account for 2 of 5 (40 percent) of all U.S. births (*Statistical Abstract* 2011:Table 86).

But births to single women don't actually cause poverty. Consider the obvious: Children born to wealthy single women aren't reared in poverty, are they? Then consider this: In some industrialized countries, the birth rate of single women is higher than ours, but *our rate of child poverty is higher than all industrialized nations* (Garfinkel et al. 2010). The poverty rate is lower in these countries because the government provides extensive support for rearing these children—from providing day care to health checkups. As the cause of the poverty of children born to single women, then, why can't we point to the lack of government support for children?

Apart from the matter of government policy, births to single women follow patterns that have a negative impact on their children's welfare. The less education a single woman has, the more likely she is to bear children. As you can see from Figure 9, births to single women drop with each gain in education. As you know, people with lower education earn less, so this means that the single women who can least afford children are those most likely to give birth. Poverty brings these children huge obstacles to building a satisfying life. They are more likely to die in infancy, to go hungry, to be malnourished, to develop more slowly, and to have more health problems. They also are more likely to drop out of school, to commit street crimes, and to have children while still in their teens—thus perpetuating a cycle of poverty.

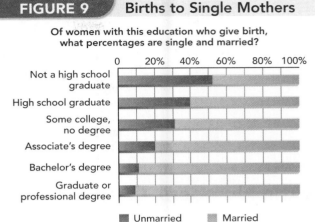

FIGURE 9 Births to Single Mothers

Of women with this education who give birth, what percentages are single and married?

■ Unmarried ■ Married

Note: Based on a national sample of all U.S. births in the preceding twelve months.

Source: Dye 2005.

For Your Consideration

With education so important to getting high-paying jobs, in light of Figure 9 what programs would you suggest for helping women attain more education? What programs would you suggest for reducing child poverty? Be specific and practical. ■

Horatio Alger myth the belief that due to limitless possibilities anyone can get ahead if he or she tries hard enough

Where Is Horatio Alger?
The Social Functions of a Myth

In the late 1800s, Horatio Alger was one of the country's most popular authors. The rags-to-riches exploits of his fictional boy heroes and their amazing successes in overcoming severe odds motivated thousands of boys of that period. Although Alger's characters have disappeared from U.S. literature, they remain alive and well in the psyche of Americans. From real-life examples of people from humble origin who climbed the social class ladder, Americans know that anyone who really tries can get ahead. In fact, they believe that most Americans, including minorities and the working poor, have an average or better-than-average chance of getting ahead—obviously a statistical impossibility (Kluegel and Smith 1986).

The accuracy of the **Horatio Alger myth** is less important than the belief that limitless possibilities exist for everyone. Functionalists would stress that this belief is functional for society. On the one hand, it encourages people to compete for higher positions, or, as the song says, "to reach for the highest star." On the other hand, it places blame for failure squarely on the individual. If you don't make it—in the face of ample opportunities

A society's dominant ideologies are reinforced throughout the society, including its literature. Horatio Alger provided inspirational heroes for thousands of boys. The central theme of these many novels, immensely popular in their time, was rags to riches. Through rugged determination and self-sacrifice, a boy could overcome seemingly insurmountable obstacles to reach the pinnacle of success. (Girls did not strive for financial success, but were dependent on fathers and husbands.)

How does the Horatio Alger myth help shape our views of poverty and success? Help to stabilize society?

to get ahead—the fault must be your own. The Horatio Alger myth helps to stabilize society: Since the fault is viewed as the individual's, not society's, current social arrangements can be regarded as satisfactory. This reduces pressures to change the system.

As both Marx and Weber pointed out, social class penetrates our consciousness, shaping our ideas of life and our "proper" place in society. When the rich look at the world around them, they sense superiority and anticipate control over their own destiny. When the poor look around them, they are more likely to sense defeat and to anticipate that unpredictable forces will batter their lives. Both rich and poor know the dominant ideology, that their particular niche in life is due to their own efforts, that the reasons for success—or failure—lie solely with the self. Like fish that don't notice the water, people tend not to perceive the effects of social class on their own lives.

By the Numbers: Changes Over Time

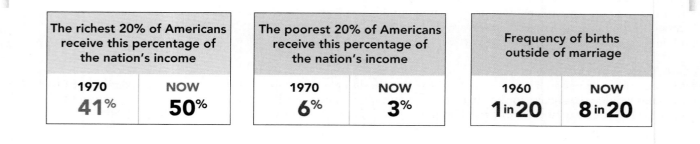

The richest 20% of Americans receive this percentage of the nation's income		The poorest 20% of Americans receive this percentage of the nation's income		Frequency of births outside of marriage	
1970	NOW	1970	NOW	1960	NOW
41%	**50%**	**6%**	**3%**	**1 in 20**	**8 in 20**

Summary and Review

An Overview of Social Stratification

What is social stratification?

Social stratification refers to a hierarchy of relative privilege based on property, power, and prestige. Every society stratifies its members, and in every society men as a group are placed above women as a group.

What are three major systems of social stratification?

Major systems of stratification are slavery, caste, and class. The essential characteristic of **slavery** is that some people own other people. In a **caste system,** status is determined by birth and is lifelong. A **class system** is much more open, for it is based primarily on money or material possessions. Gender cuts across all forms of social stratification.

How Did the World's Nations Become Stratified?

The main theories that account for global stratification are **colonialism, world system theory,** and the **culture of poverty.**

Why Is Social Stratification Universal?

To explain why stratification is universal, functionalists Kingsley Davis and Wilbert Moore argued that to attract the most capable people to fill its important positions, society must offer them greater rewards. Melvin Tumin said that if this view were correct, society would be a **meritocracy,** with all positions awarded on the basis of merit. Conflict theorists argue that stratification came about because resources are limited, and an elite emerges as groups struggle for them.

What Determines Social Class?

Karl Marx argued that a single factor determines **social class**: If you own the means of production, you belong to the **bourgeoisie** (capitalists); if you do not, you are one of the **proletariat** (workers). Max Weber argued that three elements determine social class: **property, power,** and **prestige.**

Social Class in the United States

Has income inequality declined in the United States?

On the contrary, income inequality has increased since the Great Depression of the 1930s.

How does occupational prestige differ around the world?

How people rank occupational prestige is similar from country to country. Globally, the occupations that bring greater prestige are those that pay more, require more education and abstract thought, and offer greater independence.

What is meant by the term status inconsistency?

Status is social ranking. Most people are **status consistent;** that is, they rank high or low on all three dimensions of social class. People who rank higher on some dimensions than on others are status inconsistent. The frustrations of **status inconsistency** tend to produce political radicalism.

A Model of Social Class

What six-class model portrays the social classes?

Kahl and Gilbert developed a six-class model based on Weber. At the top is the capitalist class. In descending order are the upper middle class, the lower middle class, the working class, the working poor, and the **underclass.**

Consequences of Social Class

How does social class affect people's lives?

Social class leaves no aspect of life untouched. It affects our chances of living and dying, of getting sick, of receiving good health care, of getting divorced, and of getting an education. It also influences our politics, religion, and contact with the criminal justice system.

Social Mobility

What are three types of social mobility?

The term **intergenerational mobility** refers to changes in social class from one generation to the next. **Structural mobility** refers to changes in society that lead large numbers of people to change their social class. **Exchange mobility** refers to balancing shifts of large groups moving from one class to another, with the net result that the relative proportions of the population in the classes remain about the same.

Poverty

Who are the poor?

The **poverty line** is arbitrary. Racial–ethnic minorities (except Asian Americans), children, and women-headed households are more likely than others to be poor. The poverty rate of the elderly is less than that of the general population.

How is the Horatio Alger myth functional for society?

The **Horatio Alger myth**—the belief that anyone can get ahead if only he or she tries hard enough—encourages people to strive to advance in society. It also deflects blame for failure from society to the individual.

Thinking Critically about this Chapter

1. How do slavery, caste, and class systems of social stratification differ?

2. The belief that the United States is the land of opportunity draws millions of legal and illegal immigrants to the United States. How do the materials in this chapter support or undermine this belief?

3. How has social class influenced your values, aspirations, and ideas about life?

4. What social mobility has your own family experienced? In what ways has this affected your life?

References

Aldrich, Nelson W., Jr. *Old Money: The Mythology of America's Upper Class*. New York: Vintage Books, 1989.

Appiah, Kwame Anthony, and Martin Bunzl, eds. *Buying Freedom: The Ethics and Economics of Slave Redemption*. Princeton, N.J.: Princeton University Press, 2007.

Ayittey, George B. N. "Black Africans Are Enraged at Arabs." *Wall Street Journal*, interactive edition, September 4, 1998.

Baltzell, E. Digby. *Puritan Boston and Quaker Philadelphia*. New York: Free Press, 1979.

Baltzell, E. Digby, and Howard G. Schneiderman. "Social Class in the Oval Office." *Society, 25*, September/October 1988:42–49.

Banjo, Shelly. "Prepping for the Playdate Test." *Wall Street Journal*, August 19, 2010.

Barbassa, Juliana. "Rio Cops Use Armor to Raid Slum Where Gang Based." Associated Press, November 25, 2010.

Beckett, Paul. "Caste Away." *Wall Street Journal*, June 23, 2007.

Beeghley, Leonard. *The Structure of Social Stratification in the United States*, 5th ed. Boston: Allyn & Bacon, 2008.

Beller, Emily. "Bringing Intergenerational Social Mobility Research into the Twenty-First Century: Why Mothers Matter." *American Sociological Review, 74*, August 2009:507–528.

Belley, Philippe, and Lance Lochner. "The Changing Role of Family Income and Ability in Determining Educational Achievement." National Bureau of Economic Research, Working Paper 13527, October 2007.

Berger, Peter. "Invitation to Sociology." In *Down to Earth Sociology: Introductory Readings*, 15th ed., James M. Henslin, ed. New York: FreePress, 2012. Originally published 1963.

Bernstein, David. "The $18-Million Dollar Headache." *Chicago Magazine*, April 2007.

Blau, Peter M., and Otis Dudley Duncan. *The American Occupational Structure*. New York: John Wiley, 1967.

Brown, Alan S. "Mexico Redux." *Mechanical Engineering*, January 2008.

Budrys, Grace. *Unequal Health: How Inequality Contributes to Health or Illness*. Lantham, Md: Rowmans and Littlefield, 2003.

"Builder Stephen Ross Buys Half of Dolphins from Huizenga." *International Herald Tribune*, February 22, 2008.

Carnevale, Anthony P., and Stephen J. Rose. "Socioeconomic Status, Race/Ethnicity, and Selective College Admissions." New York: The Century Foundation, March 2003.

Cellini, Stephanie R., Signe-Mary McKernan, and Caroline Ratcliffe. "The Dynamics of Poverty in the United States: A Review of Data, Methods, and Findings." *Journal of Policy Analysis and Management, 27*, 2008:577–605.

Chandra, Vibha P. "Fragmented Identities: The Social Construction of Ethnicity, 1885–1947." Unpublished paper, 1993a.

Chin, Nancy P., Alicia Monroe, and Kevin Fiscella. "Social Determinants of (Un)Healthy Behaviors." *Education for Health: Change in Learning and Practice, 13, 3*, November 2000:317–328.

CIA (Central Intelligence Agency). *The World Factbook*. Washington, D.C: U.S. Government Printing Office, 2010. Published annually.

Cohen, Patricia. "Forget Lonely. Life Is Healthy at the Top." *New York Times*, May 15, 2004.

Cole, Elizabeth R., and Safiya R. Omari. "Race, Class and the Dilemmas of Upward Mobility for African Americans." *Journal of Social Issues, 59, 4*, 2003:785–802.

Collins, Randall. "Socially Unrecognized Cumulation." *American Sociologist, 30, 2*, Summer 1999:41–61.

Crompton, Rosemary. "Class and Employment." *Work, Employment and Society, 24*, 2010:9–26.

Crossette, Barbara. "Caste May Be India's Moral Achilles' Heel." *New York Times*, October 20, 1996.

Dao, James. "Instant Millions Can't Halt Winners' Grim Side." *New York Times*, December 5, 2005.

Davis, Kingsley, and Wilbert E. Moore. "Some Principles of Stratification." *American Sociological Review, 10*, 1945:242–249.

Davis, Kingsley, and Wilbert E. Moore. "Reply to Tumin." *American Sociological Review, 18*, 1953:394–396.

Davis, Nancy J., and Robert V. Robinson. "Class Identification of Men and Women in the 1970s and 1980s." *American Sociological Review, 53*, February 1988:103–112.

"Death Squads Roam Davao—UN Monitors." *Manila Times*, February 13, 2008.

"Death to Undesirables: Brazil's Murder Capital." *The Independent*, May 15, 2009.

Deliege, Robert. *The Untouchables of India*. New York: Berg Publishers, 2001.

DeNavas-Walt, Carmen, Bernadette D. Proctor, and Jessica C. Smith. "Income, Poverty, and Health Insurance Coverage in the United States: 2009." *Current Population Reports P60-238*, Washington, D.C.: U.S. Census Bureau, September 2010.

de Pastino, Blake. "Photo in the News: Robot Jockeys Race Camels in Qatar." *National Geographic*, July 15, 2005.

Dolnick, Sam. "The Obesity-Hunger Paradox." *New York Times*, March 12, 2010.

Domhoff, G. William. *The Power Elite and the State: How Policy Is Made in America*. Hawthorne, N.Y.: Aldine de Gruyter, 1990.

Domhoff, G. William. "The Bohemian Grove and Other Retreats." In *Down to Earth Sociology: Introductory Readings*, 10th ed., James M. Henslin, ed. New York: Free Press, 1999a:391–403.

Domhoff, G. William. *Who Rules America? Power, Politics, and Social Change*, 5th ed. New York: McGraw-Hill, 2006.

Domhoff, G. William. "Wealth, Income, and Power." Website: Who Rules America, September 2010. http://sociology.ucsc.edu/whorulesamerica/

Du Bois, W. E. B. *Black Reconstruction in America: An Essay toward a History of the Part Which Black Folk Played in the Attempt to Reconstruct Democracy in America, 1860–1880*. New York: Atheneum, 1992. Originally published 1935.

Duff, Christina. "Superrich's Share of After-Tax Income Stopped Rising in Early '90s, Data Show." *Wall Street Journal*, November 22, 1995:A2.

Dye, Jane Lawler. "Fertility of American Women, June 2004." U.S. Census Bureau. *Current Population Reports*, December 2005.

Elkins, Stanley M. *Slavery: A Problem in American Institutional and Intellectual Life*, 2nd ed. Chicago: University of Chicago Press, 1968.

Fabrikant, Geraldine. "Old Nantucket Warily Meets the New." *New York Times*, June 5, 2005.

Faris, Robert E. L., and Warren Dunham. *Mental Disorders in Urban Areas*. Chicago: University of Chicago Press, 1939.

Featherman, David L. "Opportunities Are Expanding." *Society, 13*, 1979:4–11.

Fraser, Graham. "Fox Denies Free Trade Exploiting the Poor in Mexico." *Toronto Star,* April 20, 2001.

Galbraith, John Kenneth. *The Nature of Mass Poverty.* Cambridge, Mass.: Harvard University Press, 1979.

Garfinkel, Irwin, Lee Rainwater, and Timothy Smeeding. *Wealth and Welfare States: Is America a Laggard or a Leader?* New York: Oxford University Press, 2010.

Geronimus, Arline T., Margaret T. Hicken, Jay A. Pearson, Sarah J. Seashols, Kelly L. Brown, and Tracy Dawson Cruz. "Do US Black Women Experience Stress-Related Accelerated Biological Aging?" *Human Nature, 21,* 2010:19–38.

Gerth, H. H., and C. Wright Mills. *From Max Weber: Essays in Sociology.* New York: Galaxy, 1958.

Gilbert, Dennis L. *The American Class Structure in an Age of Growing Inequality,* 6th ed. Belmont, Calif.: Wadsworth Publishing, 2003.

Gilbert, Dennis L. *The American Class Structure in an Age of Growing Inequality,* 7th ed. Los Angeles: Pine Forge Press, 2008.

Gilbert, Dennis, and Joseph A. Kahl. *The American Class Structure: A New Synthesis,* 4th ed. Belmont, Calif.: Wadsworth Publishing, 1998.

Gold, Ray. "Janitors versus Tenants: A Status-Income Dilemma." *American Journal of Sociology, 58,* 1952:486–493.

Harris, Craig. "Fallout from Ariz. Employer Sanctions Law." *Arizona Republic,* September 15, 2008.

Harrison, Paul. *Inside the Third World: The Anatomy of Poverty,* 3rd ed. London: Penguin Books, 1993.

Haughney, Christine, and Eric Konigsberg. "Despite Tough Times, Ultrarich Keep Spending." *New York Times,* April 14, 2008.

Heames, Joyce Thompson, Michael G. Harvey, and Darren Treadway. "Status Inconsistency: An Antecedent to Bullying Behavior in Groups." *International Journal of Human Resource Management, 17,* 2, February 2006: 348–361.

Hellinger, Daniel, and Dennis R. Judd. *The Democratic Facade.* Pacific Grove, Calif.: Brooks/Cole, 1991.

Henslin, James M. *Social Problems: A Down-to-Earth Approach,* 10th ed. Boston: Allyn and Bacon, 2012.

Higginbotham, Elizabeth, and Lynn Weber. "Moving with Kin and Community: Upward Social Mobility for Black and White Women." *Gender and Society, 6,* 3, September 1992:416–440.

hooks, bell. *Where We Stand: Class Matters.* New York: Routledge, 2000.

Hout, Michael. "How Class Works: Objective and Subjective Aspects of Class Since the 1970s." In *Social Class: How Does It Work?* Annette Lareau and Dalton Conley, eds. New York: Russell Sage, 2008:52–64.

Houtman, Dick. "What Exactly Is a 'Social Class'?: On the Economic Liberalism and Cultural Conservatism of the 'Working Class.'" Paper presented at the annual meetings of the American Sociological Association, 1995.

Huber, Joan. "Micro-Macro Links in Gender Stratification." *American Sociological Review, 55,* February 1990:1–10.

Huggins, Martha K., and Sandra Rodrigues. "Kids Working on Paulista Avenue." *Childhood, 11,* 2004:495–514.

Huggins, Martha K., Mika Haritos-Fatouros, and Philip G. Zimbardo. *Violence Workers: Police Torturers and Murderers Reconstruct Brazilian Atrocities.* Berkeley: University of California Press, 2002.

Jaffrelot, Christophe. "The Impact of Affirmative Action in India: More Political than Socioeconomic." *India Review, 5,* 2, April 2006:173–189.

Jessop, Bob. "The Return of the National State in the Current Crisis of the World Market." *Capital and Class, 34,* 1, 2010:38–43.

Kaufman, Joanne. "Married Maidens and Dilatory Domiciles." *Wall Street Journal,* May 7, 1996:A16.

Kefalas, Maria. "Looking for the Lower Middle Class." *City and Community, 6,* 1, March 2007:63–68.

Kifner, John. "Building Modernity on Desert Mirages." *New York Times,* February 7, 1999.

King, Eden B., Jennifer L. Knight, and Michelle R. Hebl. "The Influence of Economic Conditions on Aspects of Stigmatization." *Journal of Social Issues, 66,* 3, September 2010:446–460.

Kluegel, James R., and Eliot R. Smith. *Beliefs about Inequality: America's Views of What Is and What Ought to Be.* Hawthorne, N.Y.: Aldine de Gruyter, 1986.

Kneebone, Elizabeth, and Emily Garr. "The Suburbanization of Poverty: Trends in Metropolitan America, 2000 to 2008." Washington, D.C.: Brookings, January 2010.

Krugman, Paul. "White Man's Burden." *New York Times,* September 24, 2002.

Kurian, George Thomas. *Encyclopedia of the First World,* Vols. 1, 2. New York: Facts on File, 1990.

Kurian, George Thomas. *Encyclopedia of the Second World.* New York: Facts on File, 1991.

Kurian, George Thomas. *Encyclopedia of the Third World,* Vols. 1, 2, 3. New York: Facts on File, 1992.

Lacey, Marc. "Tijuana Journal: Cities Mesh across Blurry Border, Despite Physical Barrier." *New York Times,* March 5, 2007.

Lacy, Karyn R. *Blue-Chip Black: Class and Status in the New Black Middle Class.* Berkeley: University of California Press, 2007.

Lacy, Karyn R., and Angel L. Harris. "Breaking the Class Monolith: Understanding Class Differences in Black Adolescents' Attachment to Racial Identity." In *Social Class: How Does It Work?* Annette Lareau and Dalton Conley, eds. New York: Russell Sage, 2008:152–178.

Landtman, Gunnar. *The Origin of the Inequality of the Social Classes.* New York: Greenwood Press, 1968. Originally published 1938.

Lenski, Gerhard. "Status Crystallization: A Nonvertical Dimension of Social Status." *American Sociological Review, 19,* 1954:405–413.

Lenski, Gerhard. *Power and Privilege: A Theory of Social Stratification.* New York: McGraw-Hill, 1966.

Leo, Jen. "Google's Space Explorer Sergey Brin." *Los Angeles Times,* June 12, 2008.

Lerner, Gerda. *Black Women in White America: A Documentary History.* New York: Pantheon Books, 1972.

Lerner, Gerda. *The Creation of Patriarchy.* New York: Oxford, 1986.

Lewis, Oscar. "The Culture of Poverty." *Scientific American, 115,* October 1966a:19–25.

Lewis, Oscar. *La Vida.* New York: Random House, 1966b.

Lichter, Daniel T., and Martha L. Crowley. "Poverty in America: Beyond Welfare Reform." *Population Bulletin, 57,* 2, June 2002:1–36.

Lublin, Joann S. "Living Well." *Wall Street Journal,* April 8, 1999.

Lublin, Joann S. "CEO Pay in 2010 Jumped 11%." *Wall Street Journal,* May 9, 2011.

Lush, Tamara. "Friend Charged with Hiding Fla. Lotto Winner Death." Associated Press, February 3, 2010.

Main, Jackson Turner. *The Social Structure of Revolutionary America.* Princeton, N.J.: Princeton University Press, 1965.

Marx, Karl. "Contribution to the Critique of Hegel's Philosophy of Right." In *Karl Marx: Early Writings,* T. B. Bottomore, ed. New York: McGraw-Hill, 1964:45. Originally published 1844.

Marx, Karl, and Friedrich Engels. *Communist Manifesto.* New York: Pantheon, 1967. Originally published 1848.

McShane, Larry. "Abraham Shakespeare, $31M Florida Lottery Winner, Found Dead 9 Months after Disappearing." *Daily News,* January 30, 2010.

Mills, C. Wright. *The Power Elite.* New York: Oxford University Press, 1956.

Morris, Joan M., and Michael D. Grimes. "Moving Up from the Working Class." In *Down to Earth Sociology: Introductory Readings,* 13th ed., James M. Henslin, ed. New York: Free Press, 2005:365–376.

Muñoz Martinez, Hepzibah. "The Double Burden on Maquila Workers: Violence and Crisis in Northern Mexico." El Colegio de la Frontera Norte, Matamoros, June 15, 2010.

Nakao, Keiko, and Judith Treas. "Occupational Prestige in the United States Revisited: Twenty-Five Years of Stability and Change." Paper presented at the annual meetings of the American Sociological Association, 1990. (As cited in Kerbo, Harold R. *Social Stratification and Inequality: Class Conflict in Historical and Comparative Perspective,* 2nd ed. New York: McGraw-Hill, 1991:181.)

Nakao, Keiko, and Judith Treas. "Updating Occupational Prestige and Socioeconomic Scores: How the New Measures Measure Up." *Sociological Methodology, 24,* 1994:1–72.

Nelson, Dean. "Former Camel Jockeys Compensated by UAE." *Telegraph,* May 5, 2009.

O'Hare, William P. "A New Look at Poverty in America." *Population Bulletin, 51,* 2, September 1996a:1–47.

O'Hare, William P. "U.S. Poverty Myths Explored: Many Poor WorkYear-Round, Few Still Poor after Five Years." *Population Today: News, Numbers, and Analysis, 24,* 10, October 1996b:1–2.

"On History and Heritage: John K. Castle." *Penn Law Journal,* Fall 1999.

Peltham, Brett W. "About One in Six Americans Report History of Depression." Gallup Poll. October 20, 2009.

Polgreen, Lydia. "Court Rules Niger Failed by Allowing Girl's Slavery." *New York Times,* October 27, 2008.

Pratt, Laura A., Achintya N. Dey, and Allan J. Cohen. "Characteristics of Adults with Serious Psychological Distress as Measured by the K6 Scale: United States, 2001–04." *Vital and Health Statistics, 382,* March 30 2007: 1–18.

Ratcliffe, Caroline, and Signe-Mary McKernan. "Childhood Poverty Persistence: Facts and Consequences." The Urban Institute, Brief 14, June 2010:1–10.

Robinson, Gail, and Barbara Mullins Nelson. "Pursuing Upward Mobility: African American Professional Women Reflect on Their Journey." *Journal of Black Studies, 40,* 6, 2010:1168–1188.

Rohwedder, Cecilie. "London Parents Scramble for Edge in Preschool Wars." *Wall Street Journal,* February 12, 2007.

Rothkopf, David. *Superclass: The Global Power Elite and the World They Are Making.* New York: Farrar, Straus and Giroux, 2008.

Samuelson, Paul Anthony, and William D. Nordhaus. *Economics,* 18th ed. New York: McGraw Hill, 2005.

Sklair, Leslie. *Globalization: Capitalism and Its Alternatives,* 3rd ed. New York: Oxford University Press, 2001.

Smith, Christian, and Robert Faris. "Socioeconomic Inequality in the American Religious System: An Update and Assessment." *Journal for the Scientific Study of Religion, 44,* 1, 2005: 95–104.

Srole, Leo, et al. *Mental Health in the Metropolis: The Midtown Manhattan Study.* Albany, N.Y.: New York University Press, 1978.

Stampp, Kenneth M. *The Peculiar Institution: Slavery in the Ante-Bellum South.* New York: Vintage Books, 1956.

Statistical Abstract of the United States. Washington, D.C.: U.S. Census Bureau, published annually.

Stevens, Mitchell. *Creating a Class: College Admissions and the Education of Elites.* Cambridge, Mass.: Harvard University Press, 2009.

"Sticky Ticket: A New Jersey Mother Sues Her Son over a Lottery Jackpot She Claims Belongs to Them Both." *People Weekly,* February 9, 1998:68.

Thompson, Ginger. "Chasing Mexico's Dream into Squalor." *New York Times,* February 11, 2001.

Trafficking in Persons Report. Washington, D.C.: U.S. Department of State, June 14, 2010.

Treiman, Donald J. *Occupational Prestige in Comparative Perspective.* New York: Academic Press, 1977.

Tresniowski, Alex. "Payday or Mayday?" *People Weekly,* May 17, 1999:128–131.

Trofimov, Yaroslav. "Brutal Attack in India Shows How Caste System Lives On." *New York Times,* December 27, 2007.

Tumin, Melvin M. "Some Principles of Social Stratification: A Critical Analysis." *American Sociological Review, 18,* August 1953:394.

Uchitelle, Louis. "How to Define Poverty? Let Us Count the Ways." New York Times, May 28, 2001.

UNESCO. "UNESCO Launches Global Partnership for Girls and Women's Education." June 2011.

Utar, Hale, and Luis Bernardo Torres Ruiz. "International Competition and Industrial Evolution: Evidence from the Impact of Chinese Competition on Mexican Maquiladoras." University of Colorado at Boulder and Banco de Mexico, July 2010.

"The Wall Street Journal Survey of CEO Compensation." *Wall Street Journal,* November 14, 2010.

Wallerstein, Immanuel. *The Modern World System: Capitalist Agriculture and the Origins of the European World-Economy in the Sixteenth Century.* New York: Academic Press, 1974.

Wallerstein, Immanuel. *The Capitalist World-Economy.* New York: Cambridge University Press, 1979.

Wallerstein, Immanuel. "Culture as the Ideological Battleground of the Modern World-System." In *Global Culture: Nationalism, Globalization, and Modernity,* Mike Featherstone, ed. London: Sage, 1990:31–55.

Weber, Max. *Economy and Society,* G. Roth and C. Wittich, eds. Berkeley: University of California Press, 1978. Originally published 1922.

Wise, Raul Delgado, and James M. Cypher. "The Strategic Role of Mexican Labor under NAFTA: Critical Perspectives on Current Economic Integration." *Annals of the American Academy of Political and Social Science, 610,* March 2007:120–142.

Wright, Erik Olin. *Class.* London: Verso, 1985.

Sex and Gender

From Chapter 8 of *Sociology: A Down-to-Earth Approach, Core Concepts*, Fifth Edition. James M. Henslin.

Sex and Gender

In Tunis, the capital of Tunisia, on Africa's northern coast, I met some U.S. college students and spent a couple of days with them. They wanted to see the city's red light district, but I wondered whether it would be worth the trip. I already had seen other red light districts, including the unusual one in Amsterdam where a bronze statue of a female prostitute lets you know you've entered the area; the state licenses the women and men, requiring that they have medical checkups (certificates must be posted); and the prostitutes add sales tax to the receipts they give customers. The prostitutes sit behind lighted picture windows while customers stroll along the narrow canal side streets and do "window shopping" from the outside. Tucked among the brothels are day care centers, bakeries, and clothing stores. Amsterdam itself is an unusual place—in cafes, you can smoke marijuana but not tobacco.

I decided to go with them. We ended up on a wharf that extended into the Mediterranean. Each side was lined with a row of one-room wooden shacks, crowded one against the next. In front of each open door stood a young woman. Peering from outside into the dark interiors, I could see that each door led to a tiny room with a well-worn bed.

> The prostitutes sit behind lighted picture windows while customers stroll along the narrow canal side streets and do "window shopping" from the outside.

The wharf was crowded with men who were eyeing the women. Many of the men wore sailor uniforms from countries that I couldn't identify.

As I looked more closely, I could see that some of the women had runny sores on their legs. Incredibly, with such visible evidence of their disease, customers still sought them out.

With a sick feeling in my stomach and the desire to vomit, I kept a good distance between the beckoning women and myself. One tour of the two-block area was more than sufficient.

Somewhere nearby, out of sight, I knew that there were men whose wealth derived from exploiting these women who were condemned to live short lives punctuated by fear and misery.

Afghanistan

gender stratification males' and females' unequal access to property, power, and prestige

sex biological characteristics that distinguish females and males, consisting of primary and secondary sex characteristics

gender the behaviors and attitudes that a society considers proper for its males and females; masculinity or femininity

In this chapter, we examine **gender stratification**—males' and females' unequal access to property, power, and prestige. Gender is especially significant because it is a *master status;* that is, it cuts across *all* aspects of social life. No matter what we attain in life, we carry the label *male* or *female*. These labels convey images and expectations about how we should act. Gender not only guides our behavior but also is a basis for making people unequal.

In this chapter's fascinating journey, we shall look at inequality between the sexes both around the world and in the United States. We explore whether it is biology or culture that makes us the way we are and review sexual harassment, unequal pay, and violence against women. This excursion will provide a good context for understanding the power differences between men and women that lead to situations such as the one described in our opening vignette. It should also give you insight into your own experiences with gender.

Issues of Sex and Gender

When we consider how females and males differ, the first thing that usually comes to mind is **sex,** the *biological characteristics* that distinguish males and females. *Primary sex characteristics* consist of a vagina or a penis and other organs related to reproduction. *Secondary sex characteristics* are the physical distinctions between males and females that are not directly connected with reproduction. These characteristics become clearly evident at puberty when males develop larger muscles, lower voices, more body hair, and greater height, while females develop breasts and form more fatty tissue and broader hips.

▶ **Read**

Night to His Day: The Social Construction of Gender by Judith Lorber on **mysoclab.com**

Gender, in contrast, is a *social,* not a biological characteristic. **Gender** consists of whatever behaviors and attitudes a group considers proper for its males and females. Sex refers to male or female, and *gender* refers to masculinity or femininity. In short, you inherit your sex, but you learn your gender as you learn the behaviors and attitudes your culture asserts are appropriate for your sex.

Because ideas of "proper" behavior for males and females differ from one society to another, so does gender. The photo montage on the next page illustrates some of these wide-ranging expectations.

The sociological significance of gender is that it is a device by which society controls its members. Gender sorts us, on the basis of sex, into different life experiences. It opens and closes doors to property, power, and prestige. Like social class, gender is a structural feature of society.

Before examining inequalities of gender, let's consider why the behaviors of men and women differ.

Differences in how we display gender often lie below our awareness. How males and females use social space is an example. In this unposed photo from Grand Central Station in New York City, you can see how males tend to sprawl out, females to enclose themselves. Why do you think this difference exists? Biology? Socialization? Both?

Gender Differences in Behavior: Biology or Culture?

Why are most males more aggressive than most females? Why do women enter "nurturing" occupations, such as teaching young children and nursing, in far greater numbers than men? To answer such questions, many people respond with some variation of "They're just born that way."

Is this the correct answer? Certainly biology plays a significant role in our lives. Each of us begins as a fertilized egg. The egg, or ovum, is contributed by our mother, the sperm that fertilizes the egg by our father. At the very instant the egg is fertilized, our sex is determined. Each of us receives twenty-three chromosomes from the ovum and twenty-three from the sperm. The egg has an X chromosome. If the sperm that fertilizes the egg also has an X chromosome, the result is a girl (XX). If the sperm has a Y chromosome, the result is a boy (XY).

MONIKA GRAFF/UPI/Landov

How do sex and gender differ?

Standards of Gender

Each human group determines its ideas of "maleness" and "femaleness." As you can see from these photos of four women and four men, standards of gender are arbitrary and vary from one culture to another. Yet, in its ethnocentrism, each group thinks that its preferences reflect what gender "really" is. As indicated here, around the world men and women try to make themselves appealing by aspiring to their group's standards of gender.

Mexico: Monica Rodriguez/Lifesize/Getty Images Royalty Free

Jordan: © Danita Delimont/Alamy

Kenya: © Jake Warga/Corbis

Kenya

Ethiopia

Ethiopia: © Robert Harding Picture Library/SuperStock

Brazil

Brazil: ©Reuters/Corbis

New Guinea

India

Tibet

New Guinea: Pacific Stock/SuperStock

India: AP Images/Ajit Solanki

Tibet: © Marco Simoni/Robert Harding World Imagery/Corbis

How does gender depend on culture?

The Dominant Position in Sociology

That's the biology. Now, the sociological question is, Does this biological difference control our behavior? Does it, for example, make females more nurturing and submissive and males more aggressive and domineering? Here is the quick sociological answer: The dominant sociological position is that *social* factors, not biology, are the reasons people do what they do.

Let's apply this position to gender. If biology were the principal factor in human behavior, all around the world we would find women behaving in one way and men in another. Men and women would be just like male spiders and female spiders, whose genes tell them what to do. In fact, however, ideas of gender vary greatly from one culture to another—and, as a result, so do male–female behaviors.

Despite this, to see why the door to biology is opening just slightly in sociology, let's consider a medical accident and a study of Vietnam veterans.

Opening the Door to Biology
A Medical Accident.

In 1963, 7-month-old identical twin boys were taken to a doctor for a routine circumcision. The physician, not the most capable person in the world, was using a heated needle. He turned the electric current too high and accidentally burned off the penis of one of the boys.

You can imagine the parents' disbelief—and then their horror—as the truth sank in. What could they do? After months of soul-searching and tearful consultations with experts, the parents decided that their son should have a sex-change operation (Money and Ehrhardt 1972). When he was 22 months old, surgeons castrated the boy, using the skin to construct a vagina. The parents then gave the child a new name, Brenda, dressed him in frilly clothing, let his hair grow long, and began to treat him as a girl. Later, physicians gave Brenda female steroids to promote female puberty (Colapinto 2001).

At first, the results were promising. When the twins were 4 years old, the mother said (remember that the children are biologically identical):

One thing that really amazes me is that she is so feminine. I've never seen a little girl so neat and tidy. . . . She likes for me to wipe her face. She doesn't like to be dirty, and yet my son is quite different. I can't wash his face for anything. . . . She is very proud of herself, when she puts on a new dress, or I set her hair. . . . She seems to be daintier. (Money and Ehrhardt 1972)

If the matter were this clear-cut, we could use this case to conclude that gender is determined entirely by nurture. Seldom are things in life so simple, however, and a twist occurs in this story.

Despite this promising start and her parents' coaching, Brenda did not adapt well to femininity. She preferred to mimic her father shaving, rather than her mother putting on makeup. She rejected dolls, favoring guns and her brother's toys. She liked rough-and-tumble games and insisted on urinating standing up. Classmates teased her and called her a "cavewoman" because she walked like a boy. At age 14, she was expelled from school for beating up a girl who teased her. Despite estrogen treatment, she was not attracted to boys. At age 14, when despair over her inner turmoil brought her to the brink of suicide, her father, in tears, told Brenda about the accident and her sex change.

"All of a sudden everything clicked. For the first time, things made sense, and I understood who and what I was," the twin said of this revelation. David (his new name) was given testosterone shots and, later, had surgery to partially reconstruct a penis. At age 25, David married a woman and adopted her children (Diamond and Sigmundson 1997; Colapinto 2001). There is an unfortunate end to this story, however. In 2004, David committed suicide.

Thomas Dallal/SIPA Press

David Reimer, whose story is recounted here.

Why is the door to biology slowly opening in sociology?

Excerpts from Money, John, and Anke A. Ehrhardt. *Man and Woman, Boy and Girl.* Baltimore: Johns Hopkins University Press, 1972.

The Vietnam Veterans Study. Time after time, researchers have found that boys and men who have higher levels of testosterone tend to be more aggressive. In one study, researchers compared the testosterone levels of college men in a "rowdy" fraternity with those of men in a fraternity that had a reputation for academic achievement. Men in the "rowdy" fraternity had higher levels of testosterone (Dabbs et al. 1996). In another study, researchers found that prisoners who had committed sex crimes and other crimes of violence had higher levels of testosterone than those who had committed property crimes (Dabbs et al. 1995). The samples were small, however, leaving the nagging uncertainty that these findings might be due to chance.

Then in 1985, the U.S. government began a health study of Vietnam veterans. To be certain that the study was representative, the researchers chose a random sample of 4,462 men. Among the data they collected was a measurement of testosterone. This sample supported the earlier studies. When the veterans with higher testosterone levels were boys, they were more likely to get in trouble with parents and teachers and to become delinquents. As adults, they were more likely to use hard drugs, to get into fights, to end up in lower-status jobs, and to have more sexual partners. Those who married were more likely to have affairs, to hit their wives, and, it follows, to get divorced (Dabbs and Morris 1990; Booth and Dabbs 1993).

This makes it sound like biology is the basis for behavior. Fortunately for us sociologists, there is another side to this research, and here is where *social class,* the topic of our previous chapter, comes into play. The researchers compared high-testosterone men from higher and lower social classes. The men from lower social classes were more likely to get in trouble with the law, do poorly in school, and mistreat their wives (Dabbs and Morris 1990). You can see, then, that *social* factors such as socialization, subcultures, life goals, and self-definitions were significant in these men's behavior.

In Sum: Sociologists acknowledge that biological factors are involved in some human behavior other than reproduction and childbearing (Udry 2000). Alice Rossi, a feminist sociologist and former president of the American Sociological Association, suggested that women are better prepared biologically for "mothering" than are men. Rossi (1977, 1984) said that women are more sensitive to the infant's soft skin and to their nonverbal communications.

Perhaps Rossi expressed it best when she said that the issue is not either biology or society. Instead, whatever biological predispositions nature provides are overlaid with culture. A task of sociologists is to discover how social factors modify biology, especially as sociologist Janet Chafetz (1990:30) said, to determine how "different" becomes translated into "unequal."

The sociological perspective—that of social factors in human behavior—dominates this book, and in the Thinking Critically section that follows, you will explore how gender is changing.

Sociologists study the social factors that underlie human behavior, the experiences that mold us, funneling us into different directions in life. The research on Vietnam veterans discussed in the text indicates how the sociological door is opening slowly to also consider biological factors in human behavior. This March 31, 1967, photo shows soldiers of the 1st Cavalry Division carrying a buddy who had just been shot.

© Bettmann/CORBIS

THINKING CRITICALLY
Making the Social Explicit: Emerging Masculinities and Femininities

Muscles rippling, a large male athlete strode into a class of 400 wearing a dress. The class broke into cheers, applauding his daring to break gender rules. The next week, a slightly-built, effeminate male student came into the same class wearing a dress. The class treated him like an outcast. As students moved away from him, he was surrounded by empty chairs (Anderson 2009:43).

People who are highly successful in meeting cultural stereotypes of gender are given more leeway to temporarily transgress gender boundaries. The two men wearing

From research on Vietnam veterans: How do social factors of human behavior override biological ones?

dresses illustrate this principle at work. The students knew that the hyper-masculine athlete was "just fooling around" or "making a point." But the effeminate man? No one was certain about him. His dress could have reflected "real" breaking of gender boundaries.

The Traditional Model of Gender. As you know, to show masculinity in U.S. society is to exhibit strength and dominance. Expected of males are large muscles, endurance and stamina, victory in competitive events, and achievement despite huge obstacles. And for men, all of life has been cast as a form of competition in which they are pitted against one another. Above all, masculinity means this—to avoid anything that might be considered feminine or girlish.

A good part of being masculine, then, is to show that you are *not* one of "them." In requiring distance from things considered feminine, the dominant masculine model has forced boys and men to mask emotion and compassion and to avoid the appearance of weakness, fear, or vulnerability.

On the feminine side, the dominant model has allowed women to show—and probably to feel—more emotions, to express greater compassion, and to feel and show fears and weaknesses. This feminine model has also dictated that women meet the flip side of masculine dominance—making the real woman submissive to the strong man.

▶ Watch
Boys Will Be Men
on **mysoclab.com**

It is often acceptable, even humorous, when it is obvious that gender rules are being broken to make a point. There also seems to be greater toleration for women breaking gender rules. Shown here are Anne Hathaway and James Franco at an Academy Awards presentation.

New Models of Gender. The times are changing, and new models are gradually replacing the traditional ones. In the new model of softer masculinity, slowly developing, men can be masculine *and* still show tenderness, ask for help, diaper babies, form emotional bonds with women and men, and even tenderly touch both women and men. The emerging model of femininity allows these same behaviors and emotions, which women already had under their old model, but the new one also encourages them to be more dominant. Cultural approval is given to women for competing in business and the professions—and *winning* in what had been a men's arena.

Actually, many models of femininity and masculinity are developing, which is why I use the plural form in the title of this box. As the new masculinities incorporate behaviors previously considered off limits or taboo, we can also expect a decrease of homophobia (dislike and fear of homosexuals). Homophobia seems to be based on the need to maintain gender boundaries, the need to mark a sharp distance from anyone who threatens the dominant model of masculinity. As cultural attitudes shift, no longer will there be this urgent need to show that "I'm not gay." As this model softens, then, so will attitudes toward homosexuals.

Sources: Based on Anderson 2009; Henslin 2012a.

For Your Consideration
Do you agree that the dominant form of masculinity and femininity is changing, that we are developing multiple femininities and masculinities? What have you experienced to indicate that this is a correct or incorrect observation? How about the author's statement that homophobia will decrease? ■

How is gender changing?

Gender Inequality in Global Perspective

patriarchy men-as-a-group
dominating women-as-a-group;
authority is vested in males

Around the world, gender is *the* primary division between people. Every society sorts men and women into separate groups and gives them different access to property, power, and prestige. These divisions *always* favor men-as-a-group. After reviewing the historical record, historian and feminist Gerda Lerner (1986) concluded that "there is not a single society known where women-as-a-group have decision-making power over men (as a group)." Consequently, sociologists classify females as a *minority group*. Because females outnumber males, you may find this strange. The term *minority group* applies, however, because it refers to people who are discriminated against on the basis of physical or cultural characteristics, regardless of their numbers (Hacker 1951). Women around the world struggle against gender discrimination. For an extreme case, see the Mass Media in Social Life box on the next page.

How Did Females Become a Minority Group?

Have females always been a minority group? Some analysts speculate that in hunting and gathering societies, women and men were social equals (Leacock 1981; Hendrix 1994) and that horticultural societies also had less gender discrimination than is common today (Collins et al. 1993). In these societies, women may have contributed about 60 percent of the group's total food. Yet, around the world, gender is the basis for discrimination.

How, then, did it happen that women became a minority group? Let's consider two theories that have been proposed to explain the origin of **patriarchy**—men dominating society.

Men's work? Women's work? Customs in other societies can blow away stereotypes. As is common throughout India, these women are working on road construction.

Human Reproduction. The *first* theory—the major one—points to human reproduction (Lerner 1986; Friedl 1990). In early human history, life was short. Because people died young, if the group were to survive, women had to give birth to many children. This brought severe consequences for women. To survive, an infant needed a nursing mother. If there were no woman to nurse the child, it died. With a child at her breast or in her uterus, or one carried on her hip or on her back, women were not able to move as quickly as men. Nor

Why do sociologists call women a minority group?

251

Women in Iran: The Times Are Changing, Ever So Slowly

A woman's testimony in court is worth half that of a man's testimony.

A woman may inherit from her parents only half what her brother inherits.

A woman who has sex with a man who is not her husband can be stoned to death.

A woman who refuses to cover her hair in public can receive 80 lashes with a whip.

Not exactly equality.

As you would expect, Iranian women don't like it. Until now, though, there was little that they could do. Controlled by their fathers until they marry and afterward by their husbands, women for the most part didn't know that life could be different.

Now the mass media along with a new literacy are spearheading change in gender relations. Iranian women are logging onto the Internet, and they are reading books. Satellite television is also beaming new information across geographic lines, bringing pictures of other ways of life, of an unfamiliar equality and mutual respect between women and men.

Thanks to the mass media, their eyes are being opened to the fact that not all the women in the world live under the thumbs of men. From this awareness is coming the realization that they don't have to live like this either, that there really is a potential for new relationships.

This awareness and the glimmer of hope that another way of life can be theirs have stimulated a women's movement.

A sign of fundamental change is Iranian women protesting in public. Can the genie be put back in the bottle? Unlikely.

REUTERS/via Your View/Landov

The movement is small—and protest remains dangerous. Some women have been fined, and for others it is worse. Alieh Eghamdoust, for example, is serving a three-year jail sentence for participating in a women's demonstration. Other protestors find brutality at home, from their husbands, fathers, or brothers.

Despite the danger, women are continuing to protest. They are even pressing for new rights in the Iranian courts. They are demanding divorce from abusive husbands—and some are getting it.

Not much has changed yet. A man can still divorce his wife whenever he wants, while a woman who wants to divorce a husband must go through a lengthy procedure and never can be sure she will be granted the divorce. A husband also gets automatic custody of any children over the age of 7.

But as women continue their struggle, change will come. One sign of hope: Fewer women are being stoned to death.

This, at least, is a beginning.

Sources: Based on Fathi 2009; Semple 2009.

For Your Consideration

→ What do you think gender relations will be like in Iran ten years from now? Why?

→ If the women's movement in Iran becomes popular and effective, do you think that relationships between men and women will be about the same as in the United States? Why or why not?

could they be away from camp for as long as the men could. Around the world, then, women assumed the tasks that were associated with the home and child care, while men hunted the large animals and did other tasks that required both greater speed and longer absences from the base camp (Huber 1990).

This led to men becoming dominant. When the men left the camp to hunt animals, they made contact with other tribes. They traded with them, gaining new possessions—and they also quarreled and waged war with them. It was also the men who made and controlled the instruments of power and death, the weapons that were used for hunting and warfare. The men heaped prestige upon themselves as they returned to the camp triumphantly, leading captured prisoners and displaying their new possessions or the large animals they had killed to feed the women and children.

Contrast this with the women. Their activities were routine, dull, and taken-for-granted. The women kept the fire going, took care of the children, and did the cooking. There was nothing triumphant about what they did—and they were not perceived as risking their lives for the group. The women were "simply there," awaiting the return of their men, ready to acclaim their accomplishments.

What is the main theory, based on reproduction, of how females became a minority group?

Men, then, took control of society. Their sources of power were their weapons, items of trade, and the knowledge they gained from their contact with other groups. Women did not have access to these sources of power, which the men enshrouded in secrecy. The women became second-class citizens, subject to whatever the men decided.

Hand-to-Hand Combat. The *second* theory is short and simple, built around warfare and body strength. Anthropologist Marvin Harris (1977) pointed out that tribal groups did a lot of fighting with one another. Their warfare was personal and bloody. Unlike today, their battles were hand-to-hand, with groups fighting fiercely, trying to kill one another with clubs, stones, spears, and arrows. And when these weapons failed, they hit and strangled one another.

It is obvious, said Harris, that women were at a disadvantage in hand-to-hand combat. Because most men are stronger than most women, men became the warriors. And the women? The men needed strong motivation to risk their lives in combat, rather than just running into the bush when an enemy attacked. The women became the reward that enticed men to risk their lives in battle. The bravest men were given more wives from the women at home—and the choice of the women they captured when they defeated an enemy. The women, in effect, became prisoners for sex and labor.

Which One? Is either theory correct—the one built around human reproduction or the one built around warfare? The answer lies buried in human history, and there is no way to test these theories. Male dominance could be the result of some entirely different cause. Gerda Lerner (1986) suggests that patriarchy could have even had different origins in different places.

Continuing Dominance. We don't know the origins of patriarchy, then, but whatever its origins, a circular system of thought evolved. Men came to think of themselves as inherently superior. And the evidence for their superiority? Their domination of society. (You can see how circular this reasoning is: Men dominate society because they are superior, and they know they are superior because they dominate society.) The men enshrouded many of their activities with secrecy and constructed rules and rituals to avoid "contamination" by females, whom they viewed as inferior by this time. Even today, patriarchy is always accompanied by cultural supports designed to justify male dominance. A common support is to designate certain activities as "not appropriate" for women, such as playing football, driving race cars, mining coal, or being a soldier or astronaut.

Tribal societies eventually developed into larger groups, and the hunting and hand-to-hand combat ceased to be routine. Did the men then celebrate the end of their risky hunting and fighting and welcome the women as equals? You know the answer. Men enjoyed their power and privileges, and they didn't want to give them up. They held onto them. Male dominance in contemporary societies, then, is a continuation of a millennia-old pattern whose origin is lost in history.

Sex Typing of Work

Anthropologist George Murdock (1937) analyzed data that researchers had reported on 324 societies around the world. He found that in all of them, activities are *sex typed*. In other words, every society associates certain activities with one sex or the other. He also found that activities considered "female" in one society may be considered "male" in another. In some groups, for example, taking care of cattle is women's work, while other groups assign this task to men.

A theory of how *patriarchy* originated centers on childbirth. Because only women give birth, they assumed tasks associated with home and child care, while men hunted and performed other survival tasks that required greater strength, speed, and absence from home. Following in the steps of her female ancestors, this woman in Yangshou, China, while she works, takes care of her grandchild.

PETER PARKS/AFP/GETTY IMAGES/Newscom

What is the theory, based on hand-to-hand combat, of how women became a minority group?

AP Images/Elaine Thompson

Anthropologist George Murdock surveyed 324 traditional societies worldwide. In all of them, some work was considered "men's work," while other tasks were considered "women's work." He found that hunting is almost universally considered "men's work." These Makah men in the state of Washington are preparing to hunt whales in their 32-foot canoe.

There was one exception, metalworking, which was considered men's work in all of the societies that Murdock examined. Making weapons, pursuing sea mammals, and hunting came close to being exclusively male activities, but there were a few exceptions. Although Murdock discovered no specific work that was universally assigned only to women, he did find that making clothing, cooking, carrying water, and grinding grain were almost always female tasks. In a few societies, however, such activities were regarded as men's work.

From Murdock's cross-cultural survey, we can conclude that nothing about biology requires men and women to be assigned different work. Anatomy does not have to equal destiny when it comes to occupations, for as we have seen, pursuits that are considered feminine in one society may be deemed masculine in another, and vice versa. The photo essay on pages 290–291 showing women at work in India underscores this point.

Gender and the Prestige of Work

You might ask whether this division of labor really illustrates social inequality. Or does it perhaps simply represent each group's arbitrary ways of dividing up labor, not gender discrimination?

This could be the case, except for this finding: *Universally, greater prestige is given to male activities—regardless of what those activities are* (Linton 1936; Rosaldo 1974). If taking care of goats is men's work, then the care of goats is considered important and carries high prestige, but if it is women's work, it is considered less important and given less prestige. Let's take an example closer to home. When delivering babies was "women's work" done by midwives, it was given low prestige. But when men took over this task, they became "baby doctors" with high prestige (Ehrenreich and English 1973; Rothman 1994). In short, *it is not the work that provides the prestige, but the sex with which the work is associated.*

Other Areas of Global Discrimination

Let's briefly consider four additional aspects of global gender discrimination. Later, when we focus on the United States, we shall examine these topics in greater detail.

The Global Gap in Education. Almost 1 billion adults around the world cannot read; two-thirds are women (UNESCO 2008; *CIA World Factbook* 2010). Illiteracy is especially common in Africa and the Middle East, although certainly not limited to those areas. In North America, only about half of the women in Haiti can read and write. The United Nations has made it a priority to increase literacy and monitors each country's progress. The statistics the United Nations uses, though, underestimate the problem. Some people are counted as literate if they can write their names (Falkenberg 2008).

The Global Gap in Politics. In 2008, Rwanda became the first country in the world to elect more women (56 percent) than men to its national legislature (Pflanz 2008). It is typical for women to be highly underrepresented in politics, however, and on average, women make up just 19 percent of the world's national legislative bodies ("Women in National Parliaments" 2010). At 17 percent, the United States is slightly below the average.

The Global Gap in Pay. In every nation, women earn less than men. As we shall see later, in the United States, full-time working women average only 70 percent of what men make. In some countries, women make much less than this.

Global Violence Against Women. One global human rights issue involves the customs and patterns of violence against women. Historical examples include foot binding in China,

How is prestige related to work? How is gender inequality related to education? To politics? To pay?

254

witch burning in Europe, and *suttee* (burning the living widow with the body of her dead husband) in India. Today we have rape, wife beating, female infanticide, and the kidnapping of women to be brides. There is also forced prostitution, which was probably the case in our opening vignette. Another notorious example is female circumcision, the topic of the following Cultural Diversity box.

Cultural Diversity around the World

Female Circumcision

"Lie down there," the excisor suddenly said to me [when I was 12], pointing to a mat on the ground. No sooner had I laid down than I felt my frail, thin legs grasped by heavy hands and pulled wide apart. . . . Two women on each side of me pinned me to the ground . . . I underwent the ablation of the labia minor and then of the clitoris. The operation seemed to go on forever. I was in the throes of agony, torn apart both physically and psychologically. It was the rule that girls of my age did not weep in this situation. I broke the rule. I cried and screamed with pain . . . !

Afterwards they forced me, not only to walk back to join the other girls who had already been excised, but to dance with them. I was doing my best, but then I fainted. . . . It was a month before I was completely healed. When I was better, everyone mocked me, as I hadn't been brave, they said. (Walker and Parmar 1993:107–108)

Worldwide, between 100 million and 140 million females have been circumcised, mostly in Muslim Africa and in some parts of Malaysia and Indonesia (World Health Organization 2008). In Egypt, 97 percent of the women have been circumcised, the same as in Indonesia (Douglas 2005; Slackman 2007). In some cultures, the surgery occurs seven to ten days after birth, but in others it is not performed until girls reach adolescence. Among most groups, it takes place between the ages of 4 and 8. Because the surgery is usually done without anesthesia, the pain is so excruciating that adults hold the girl down. In urban areas, physicians sometimes perform the operation; in rural areas, a neighborhood woman usually does it.

In some cultures, only the girl's clitoris is cut off; in others, more is removed. In Sudan, the Nubia cut away most of the girl's genitalia, then sew together the remaining outer edges. They bind the girl's legs from her ankles to her waist for several weeks while scar tissue closes up the vagina. They leave a small opening the diameter of a pencil for the passage of urine and menstrual fluids. When a woman marries, the opening is cut wider to permit sexual intercourse. Before a woman gives birth, the opening is enlarged further. After birth, the vagina is again sutured shut; this cycle of surgically closing and opening begins anew with each birth.

REUTERS/James Akena /Landov
An excisor (cutter) in Uganda holding the razor blades she is about to use to circumcise teenage girls.

What are the reasons for circumcising girls? Some groups believe that it reduces female sexual desire, making it more likely that a woman will be a virgin at marriage and, afterward, remain faithful to her husband. Others think that women can't bear children if they aren't circumcised.

The surgery has strong support among many women. Some mothers and grandmothers even insist that the custom continue. Their concern is that their daughters marry well, and in some of these societies uncircumcised women are considered impure and are not allowed to marry.

Feminists respond that female circumcision is a form of ritual torture to control female sexuality. They point out that men dominate the societies that practice it.

Change is on its way: A social movement to ban female circumcision has developed, and the World Health Organization has declared that female circumcision is a human rights issue. Fifteen African countries have now banned the circumcision of females. Without sanctions, though, these laws accomplish little. In Egypt, which prohibited female circumcision in 1996, almost all girls continue to be circumcised (Corbett 2008).

Sources: As cited, and Lightfoot-Klein 1989; Merwine 1993; Chalkley 1997; Collymore 2000; Tuhus-Dubrow 2007; UNIFEM 2008.

For Your Consideration

➤ Do you think it is legitimate for the members of one culture to interfere with the customs of another culture? If so, under what circumstances? What makes us right and them wrong? What if some African nation said that the common U.S. custom of circumcising males is wrong?

Finally, how would you respond to this Somali woman who said, "The Somali woman doesn't need an alien woman telling her how to treat her private parts."

How is female circumcision part of gender inequality?

Work and Gender: Women at Work in India

Traveling through India was both a pleasant and an eye-opening experience. The country is incredibly diverse, the people friendly, and the land culturally rich. For this photo essay, wherever I went—whether city, village, or country-side—I took photos of women at work.

From these photos, you can see that Indian women work in a wide variety of occupations. Some of their jobs match traditional Western expectations, and some diverge sharply from our gender stereotypes. Although women in India remain subservient to men—with the women's movement hardly able to break the cultural surface—women's occupations are hardly limited to the home. I was surprised at some of the hard, heavy labor that Indian women do.

The villages of India have no indoor plumbing. Instead, each village has a well with a hand pump, and it is the women's job to fetch the water. This is backbreaking work, for, after pumping the water, the women wrestle the heavy buckets onto their heads and carry them home. This was one of the few occupations I saw that was limited to women.

I visited quarries in different parts of India, where I found men, women, and children hard at work in the tropical sun. This woman works 8 ½ hours a day, six days a week. She earns 40 rupees a day (about ninety cents). Men make 60 rupees a day (about $1.35). Like many quarry workers, this woman is a bonded laborer. She must give half of her wages to her master.

Indian women are highly visible in public places. A storekeeper is as likely to be a woman as a man. This woman is selling glasses of water at a beach on the Bay of Bengal. The structure on which her glasses rest is built of sand.

Women also take care of livestock. It looks as though this woman dressed up and posed for her photo, but this is what she was wearing and doing when I saw her in the field and stopped to talk to her. While the sheep are feeding, her job is primarily to "be" there, to make certain the sheep don't wander off or that no one steals them.

© Jim Henslin

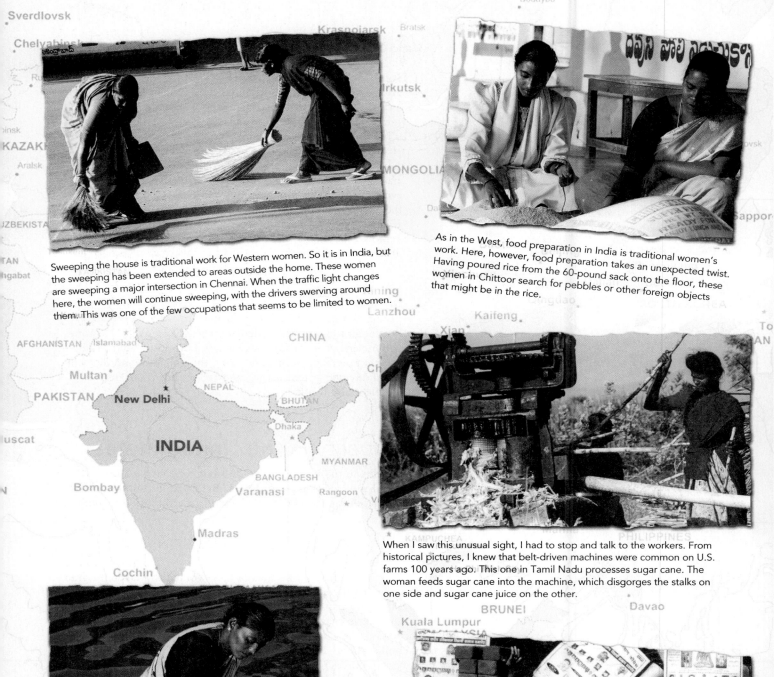

Sweeping the house is traditional work for Western women. So it is in India, but the sweeping has been extended to areas outside the home. These women are sweeping a major intersection in Chennai. When the traffic light changes here, the women will continue sweeping, with the drivers swerving around them. This was one of the few occupations that seems to be limited to women.

As in the West, food preparation in India is traditional women's work. Here, however, food preparation takes an unexpected twist. Having poured rice from the 60-pound sack onto the floor, these women in Chittoor search for pebbles or other foreign objects that might be in the rice.

James M. Henslin

When I saw this unusual sight, I had to stop and talk to the workers. From historical pictures, I knew that belt-driven machines were common on U.S. farms 100 years ago. This one in Tamil Nadu processes sugar cane. The woman feeds sugar cane into the machine, which disgorges the stalks on one side and sugar cane juice on the other.

This woman belongs to the Dhobi subcaste, whose occupation is washing clothes. She stands waist deep at this same spot doing the same thing day after day. The banks of this canal in Hyderabad are lined with men and women of her caste, who are washing linens for hotels and clothing for more well-to-do families.

A common sight in India is women working on construction crews. As they work on buildings and on highways, they mix cement, unload trucks, carry rubble, and, following Indian culture, carry loads of bricks atop their heads. This photo was taken in Raipur, Chhattisgarh.

Foot binding was practiced in China until about 1900. Tiny feet were a status symbol. Making it difficult for a woman to walk, small feet indicated that a woman's husband did not need his wife's labor. To make the feet even smaller, sometimes the baby's feet were broken and wrapped tightly. Some baby's toes were cut off. This photo was taken in Hubel Province, China. The woman getting the pedicure is reportedly 105 years old.

"Honor killings" are another form of violence against women (Yardley 2010a). In some societies, such as India, Jordan, Kurdistan, and Pakistan, a woman who is thought to have brought disgrace on her family is killed by a male relative—usually a brother or her husband, but sometimes her father or uncles. What threat to a family's honor can be so severe that men kill their own daughters, wives, or sisters? The usual reason is sex outside of marriage. Virginity at marriage is so prized in these societies that even a woman who has been raped is in danger of becoming the victim of an honor killing (Zoepf 2007; Falkenberg 2008). Killing the girl or woman—even one's own sister or mother—removes the "stain" she has brought to the family and restores its honor in the community. Sharing this view, the police in these countries generally ignore honor killings, viewing them as private family matters.

In Sum: Gender inequality is not some accidental, hit-or-miss affair. Rather, each society's institutions work together to maintain the group's particular forms of inequality. Customs, often venerated throughout history, both justify and maintain these arrangements. In some cases, the prejudice and discrimination directed at females are so extreme they result in their enslavement and death.

Gender Inequality in the United States

As we review gender inequality in the United States, let's begin by taking a brief look at how change in this vital area of social life came about. Before we do so, though, you might enjoy the historical snapshot presented in the Down-to-Earth Sociology box on the next page.

Fighting Back: The Rise of Feminism

In the nation's early history, the second-class status of U.S. women was taken for granted. A husband and wife were legally one person—him (Chafetz and Dworkin 1986). Women could not vote, buy property in their own names, make legal contracts, or serve on juries. How could things have changed so much in the last hundred years that these examples sound like fiction?

A central lesson of conflict theory is that power yields privilege. Like a magnet, power draws society's best resources to the elite. Because men tenaciously held onto their privileges and used social institutions to maintain their dominance, basic rights for women came only through prolonged and bitter struggle.

Feminism—the view that biology is not destiny and that stratification by gender is wrong and should be resisted—met with strong opposition, both by men who had privilege to lose and by women who accepted their status as morally correct. In 1894, for example, Jeannette Gilder said that women should not have the right to vote: "Politics is too public, too wearing, and too unfitted to the nature of women" (Crossen 2003).

Feminists, then known as suffragists, struggled against such views. In 1916, they founded the National Woman's Party, and in 1917 they began to picket the White House. After picketing for six months, the women were arrested. Hundreds were sent to prison, including Lucy Burns, a leader of the National Woman's Party. The extent to which these women had threatened male privilege is demonstrated by how they were treated in prison.

feminism the philosophy that men and women should be politically, economically, and socially equal; organized activities on behalf of this principle

How is gender inequality related to violence? Who were the suffragists?

Down-to-Earth **Sociology**

Women and Smoking: Let's Count the Reasons

(A humorous, but serious, look at historical changes in gender)

Why Women Shouldn't Smoke

1. Smoking ruins a woman's reputation and turns her into a tramp.

   "A man may take out a woman who smokes for a good time, but he won't marry her, and if he does, he won't stay married."

   Editorial in *The Washington Post*, 1914

2. Women who smoke drive young men wild, break up families, and even make men kill.

   "Young fellows go into our restaurants to find women folks sucking cigarettes. What happens? The young fellows lose all respect for the women, and the next thing you know the young fellows, vampired by these smoking women, desert their homes, their wives and children, rob their employers and even commit murder so that they can get money to lavish on these smoking women."

   A New York City alderman

3. It just doesn't look good (but it can be elegant).

   "To smoke in public is always bad taste in a woman. In private she may be pardoned if she does it with sufficient elegance."

   Alexandre Duval, a Parisian restaurateur, 1921

4. Smoking is so un-motherlike.

   It *"coarsens"* women and *"detracts from the ideal of fine motherhood."*

   The executive board of the Cleveland Boy Scouts, 1928

5. Smoking is a horrible evil that ruins women's sleep; plus it is bad for their skin.

   "The cigarette habit indulged by women tends to cause nervousness and insomnia and ruins the complexion. This is one of the most evil influences in American life today."

   Hugh S. Cumming, surgeon general of the U.S., 1920

6. Women just aren't as good as men at smoking.

   "Women really don't know how to smoke. One woman smoking one cigarette at a dinner table will stir up more smoke than a whole tableful of men smoking cigars. They don't seem to know what to do with the smoke. Neither do they know how to hold their cigarettes properly. They make a mess of the whole performance."

   The manager of a Manhattan hotel

Why Women Should Smoke

1. It helps avoid those bad body parts.

   "You can't hide fat, clumsy ankles. When tempted to overindulge, reach for a Lucky."

   The American Tobacco Company, 1930s

Bettmann/Corbis

An ad from 1929

(And with cancer, you'll lose even more weight!)

Challenging Gender

Opposition to women smoking was so strong that the police in New York City warned women not to light up—even in their own cars. Women's colleges also got into the act. Smith College students who were seen smoking, even off campus, were given a demerit. This was serious— three demerits and a woman would be kicked out of college.

Why do you think there was such strong opposition to women smoking in the early 1900s? There was no similar opposition to men smoking. Men were free to smoke wherever they wanted—in hotels and restaurants, in the street and at work, and in bars, which at that time were off limits to women.

Smoking brought such negative reactions because it was part of how women were breaking out of their traditional roles, a gender change that threatened the privileged position of men. To make this connection more explicit, listen to what Joseph Bailey, U.S. Senator from Texas, said in 1918: "If it were a question between their smoking and their voting, and they would promise to stay at home and smoke, I would say let them smoke."

Despite the strong opposition, more and more women began to smoke. As they continued to challenge the privileges of men in this and other areas of social life, they ushered in the gender relations that we have today.

For Your Consideration

→ Today if a woman in Iran drives a car, she is arrested. How is this a parallel to men's reaction to U.S. women smoking in the early 1930s?

In the early 1900s, men were offended by women smoking. Why?

Sex and Gender

Two men brought in Dorothy Day [the editor of a periodical that promoted women's rights], twisting her arms above her head. Suddenly they lifted her and brought her body down twice over the back of an iron bench. . . . They had been there a few minutes when Mrs. Lewis, all doubled over like a sack of flour, was thrown in. Her head struck the iron bed and she fell to the floor senseless. As for Lucy Burns, they handcuffed her wrists and fastened the handcuffs over [her] head to the cell door. (Cowley 1969)

This *first wave* of the women's movement had a radical branch that wanted to reform all the institutions of society and a conservative branch whose concern was to win the vote for women (Freedman 2001). The conservative branch dominated, and after winning the right to vote in 1920, the movement basically dissolved.

The *second wave* began in the 1960s. Sociologist Janet Chafetz (1990) points out that up to this time most women thought of work as a temporary activity intended to fill the time between completing school and getting married. For an example of how children's books reinforced such thinking, see Figure 1. As more women took jobs and began to regard them as careers, however, they compared their working conditions with those of men. This shift in their reference group changed the way women viewed their conditions at work. The result was a second wave of protest against gender inequalities. The goals of this second wave (which continues today) are broad, ranging from raising women's pay to changing policies on violence against women.

A *third wave* of feminism has emerged. It has many divisions, but three main aspects are apparent. The first is a greater focus on the problems of women in the Least Industrialized Nations (Spivak 2000; Hamid 2006). Some are fighting battles against conditions long since overcome by women in the Most Industrialized Nations. The second is a criticism of the values that dominate work and society. Some feminists argue that competition, toughness, calloused emotions, and independence represent "male"

The "first wave" of the U.S. women's movement met enormous opposition. The women in this 1920 photo had just been released after serving two months in jail for picketing the White House. Lucy Burns, mentioned on this page, is the second woman on the left. Alice Paul, who was placed in solitary confinement and is a subject of this 1920 protest, is featured in the photo circle of early female sociologists.

© Hulton-Deutsch Collection/Corbis

Can you contrast the three waves of feminism?

Excerpt from PIONEERS OF WOMEN'S LIBERATION by Joyce Crowley. Copyright © 1969 by Pathfinder Press. Reprinted with permission.

| FIGURE 1 | Teaching Gender |

Mother and Sally

Mother can sew.
Jane can sew.

"I will help," said Dick.
"I will help you with the pigs."

Father

The "Dick and Jane" readers were the top selling readers in the United States in the 1940s and 1950s. In addition to reading, they taught "gender messages." What gender message do you see here?

Housework is "women's work," a lesson girls should learn early in life.

Besides learning words like "pigs" (relevant at that historical period), boys and girls also learned that rough outside work was for men.

What does this page teach children other than how to read the word "Father"? (Look to the left to see what Jane and Mother are doing.)

Source: From *Dick and Jane: Fun with Our Family*, Illustrations © copyright 1951, 1979, and *Dick and Jane: We Play Outside*, copyright © 1965, Pearson Education, Inc., published by Scott, Foresman and Company. Used with permission.

qualities and need to be replaced with cooperation, connection, openness, and interdependence (England 2000). A third aspect is an emphasis on women's sexual pleasure (Crawford 2009).

Sharp disagreements among feminists have emerged regarding male–female relationships. Some, for example, defend their use of "erotic capital," women's sexual attractiveness and seductiveness, to get ahead at work. Others deplore this as a denial of ability and betrayal of equality (Hakim 2010).

Although U.S. women enjoy fundamental rights today, gender inequality continues to play a central role in social life. Let's first consider everyday life, the most pervasive form of gender inequality.

Gender Inequality in Everyday Life

Gender discrimination is common in everyday life. Let's look at the devaluation of femininity, which is often invisible, assumed as a background factor of social interaction.

Devaluation of Things Feminine. In general, a higher value is placed on things considered masculine, for masculinity symbolizes strength and success. Femininity, in contrast, is often perceived in terms of weakness and lack of accomplishment. People are often unaware that they make these relative evaluations, but if you listen carefully you can hear them pop up in their speech. Let's take a quick historical glance at one of these indicators. It might even be one that you have used:

Sociologist Samuel Stouffer headed a research team that produced The American Soldier *(1949), a classic study of World War II combat soldiers. To motivate their men, officers used feminine terms as insults. If a man showed less-than-expected courage or endurance, an officer might say, "Whatsa matter, Bud—got lace on your drawers?" ["Drawers" was a term for shorts or underpants.] A generation later, as officers trained soldiers to fight in Vietnam, they still used accusations of femininity to motivate their men. Drill sergeants would mock their troops by saying, "Can't hack it, little girls?" (Eisenhart 1975). The*

How does gender inequality show up in everyday life?

practice continues. Male soldiers who show hesitation during maneuvers are mocked by others, who call them girls. (Miller 1997/2007)

It is the same in sports. Anthropologist Douglas Foley (1990/2006), who studied high school football in Texas, reports that coaches insult boys who don't play well by shouting that they are "wearing skirts." In her research, sociologist Donna Eder (1995) heard junior high boys call one another "girl" when they didn't hit hard enough in football. In basketball, boys of this age also call one another a "woman" when they miss a basket (Stockard and Johnson 1980). If professional hockey players are not rough enough on the ice, their teammates call them "girls" (Gallmeier 1988:227).

In the ghetto, too, boys are under pressure to prove their manhood, and a boy who won't react violently to an insult is said to be "wearing a skirt" (N. Jones 2010).

These insults roll so easily off the tongues of men that it is easy to lose sight of their significance, that they represent a devaluation of females. Why do these insults show a devaluation of femininity? Sociologists Stockard and Johnson (1980:12) hit the nail on the head when they pointed out, "There is no comparable phenomenon among women, for young girls do not insult each other by calling each other 'man.'"

Gender Inequality in Health Care

Medical researchers were perplexed. Reports were coming in from all over the country: Women were twice as likely as men to die after coronary bypass surgery. Researchers at Cedars-Sinai Medical Center in Los Angeles checked their own records. They found that of 2,300 coronary bypass patients, 4.6 percent of the women died as a result of the surgery, compared with 2.6 percent of the men.

These findings presented a sociological puzzle. To solve it, researchers first turned to biology (Bishop 1990). In coronary bypass surgery, a blood vessel is taken from one part of the body and stitched to an artery on the surface of the heart. Perhaps the surgery was more difficult to do on women because of their smaller arteries. To find out, researchers measured the amount of time that surgeons kept patients on the heart-lung machine while they operated. They were surprised to learn that women spent *less* time on the machine than men. This indicated that the surgery was not more difficult to perform on women.

As women accomplish more in areas traditionally dominated by men, it is likely that the definition of femininity will change and the devaluation of femininity decrease.

As the researchers probed, a surprising answer unfolded: unintended sexual discrimination. When women complained of chest pains, their doctors took them only *one tenth as seriously* as when men made the same complaints. How do we know this? Doctors were *ten* times more likely to give men exercise stress tests and radioactive heart scans. They also sent men to surgery on the basis of abnormal stress tests, but they waited until women showed clear-cut symptoms of heart disease before sending them to surgery. Patients with more advanced heart disease are more likely to die during and after heart surgery.

Although these findings have been publicized among physicians, the problem continues (Jneid et al. 2008). Perhaps as more women become physicians, the situation will change, since female doctors are more sensitive to women's health problems. For example, they are more likely to order Pap smears and mammograms (Lurie et al. 1993). In addition, as more women join the faculties of medical schools, we can expect women's health problems to receive more attention in the training of physicians. Even this might not do it, however, as no one knows how stereotyping of the sexes produces this deadly discrimination, and women, too, hold our cultural stereotypes.

In contrast to unintentional sexism in heart surgery, there is a type of surgery that is a blatant form of discrimination against women. This is the focus of the Down-to-Earth Sociology box on the next page.

Gender Inequality in Education

The Past. Catching a glimpse of the past can give us a context for interpreting and appreciating the present. In many instances, as we saw in the box on women

© MIKE STONE/Reuters/Corbis

How is gender inequality in health care a life-or-death matter?

Excerpt from Miller, Laura L. "Women in the Military." In *Down to Earth Sociology: Introductory Readings*, 14th ed., James M. Henslin, ed. New York: Free Press, 2007. Originally published 1997.

Down-to-Earth Sociology

Cold-Hearted Surgeons and Their Women Victims

While doing participant observation in a hospital, sociologist Sue Fisher (1986) was surprised to hear surgeons recommend total hysterectomy (removal of both the uterus and the ovaries) *when no cancer was present*. When she asked why, the male doctors explained that the uterus and ovaries are "potentially disease producing." They also said that these organs are unnecessary after the childbearing years, so why not remove them? Doctors who reviewed hysterectomies confirmed this gender-biased practice. In three out of four cases, hysterectomies are, in their term, inappropriate (Broder et al. 2000).

Greed is a powerful motivator in many areas of social life, and it rears its ugly head in surgical sexism. Surgeons make money when they do hysterectomies, and the more of them that they do, the more money they make. Since women, to understate the matter, are reluctant to part with these organs, surgeons find that they have to "sell" this operation. As you read how one resident explained the "hard sell" to sociologist Diana Scully (1994), you might think of a used car salesperson:

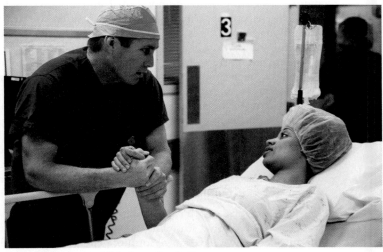

RubberBall Productions/Getty Image Royalty Free

> You have to look for your surgical procedures; you have to go after patients. Because no one is crazy enough to come and say, "Hey, here I am. I want you to operate on me." You have to sometimes convince the patient that she is really sick—if she is, of course [laughs], and that she is better off with a surgical procedure.

Used-car salespeople would love to have the powerful sales weapon that these surgeons have at their disposal: To "convince" a woman to have this surgery, the doctor puts on a serious face and tells her that the examination has turned up *fibroids* in her uterus—and they *might* turn into *cancer*. This statement is often sufficient to get the woman to buy the surgery. She starts to picture herself lying at death's door, her sorrowful family gathered at her death bed. Then the used car salesperson—I mean, the surgeon—moves in to clinch the sale. Keeping a serious face and emitting an "I-know-how-you-feel" look, the surgeon starts to make arrangements for the surgery. What the surgeon withholds is the rest of the truth—that a lot of women have fibroids, that fibroids usually do *not* turn into cancer, and that the patient has several alternatives to surgery.

In case it is difficult for someone to see how this is sexist, let's change the context just a little. Let's suppose that the income of some female surgeons depends on selling a specialized operation. To sell it, they systematically suggest to older men the benefits of castration—since "those organs are no longer necessary, and might cause disease."

For Your Consideration

➔ Hysterectomies are now so common that one of three U.S. women eventually has her uterus surgically removed (Whiteman et al. 2008). Why do you think that surgeons are so quick to operate? How can women find alternatives to surgery?

and smoking, change has been so extensive that the past can seem like it is from a different planet. So it is with education. Until 1832, women were not even allowed to attend college with men. When women were admitted to colleges attended by men—first at Oberlin College in Ohio—they had to wash the male students' clothing, clean their rooms, and serve them their meals (Flexner 1971/1999).

Female organs were a special focus of concern for the men who controlled education. They said that these organs dominated women's minds, making them less qualified than men for higher education. These men viewed menstruation as a special obstacle to women's success in education. It made women so feeble that they could hardly continue

How does gender inequality show up in surgery?

with their schooling, much less anything else in life. Here is how Dr. Edward Clarke, of Harvard University, put it:

> *A girl upon whom Nature, for a limited period and for a definite purpose, imposes so great a physiological task, will not have as much power left for the tasks of school, as the boy of whom Nature requires less at the corresponding epoch. (Andersen 1988)*

Because women are so much weaker than men, Clarke urged them to study only one-third as much as young men. And, of course, in their weakened state, they were advised to not study at all during menstruation.

The Change. Like out-of-fashion clothing, these ideas were discarded, and women entered college in growing numbers. As Figure 2 shows, by 1900 one-third of college students were women. The change has been so extensive that 57 percent of today's college students are women. This overall average differs with racial–ethnic groups, as you can see from Figure 3 on the next page. African Americans have the fewest men relative to women, and Asian Americans the most. As another indication of how extensive the change is, women now earn 57 percent of all bachelor's degrees and 60 percent of all master's degrees (*Statistical Abstract* 2011:Table 295). As discussed in the Down-to-Earth Sociology, could it be time to apply affirmative action for men?

Figure 4 on the next page illustrates another major change—how women have increased their share of professional degrees. The greatest change is in dentistry: In 1970, across the entire United States, only 34 women earned degrees in dentistry. Today, about 2,000 women become dentists each year. As you can also see, almost as many women as men now graduate from U.S. medical and law schools. It is likely that women will soon outnumber men in earning these professional degrees.

Gender Tracking. With such extensive changes, it would seem that gender equality has been achieved, or at least almost so, and in some instances—as with the changed sex ratio in college—we have a new form of gender inequality. If we look closer, however, we find something beneath the surface. Underlying these degrees is *gender tracking;* that is, college degrees tend to follow gender, which reinforces male–female distinctions.

✳ Explore
Living Data
on **mysoclab.com**

FIGURE 2   **Changes in College Enrollment, by Sex**

What percentages of U.S. college students are female and male?

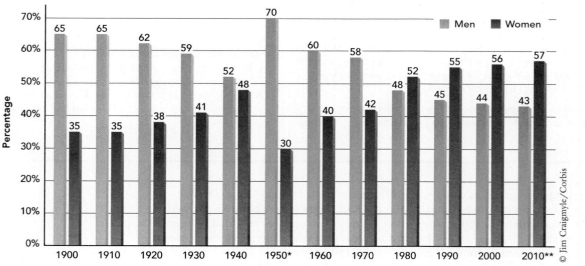

* This sharp drop in female enrollment occurred when large numbers of male soldiers returned from World War II and attended college under the new GI Bill of Rights.

** Projection by U.S. Department of Education 2008.

Source: By the author. Based on *Statistical Abstract of the United States* 1938:Table 114; 1959:Table 158; 1991:Table 261; 2011:Table 273.

How did gender inequality show up in education in the 1800s?

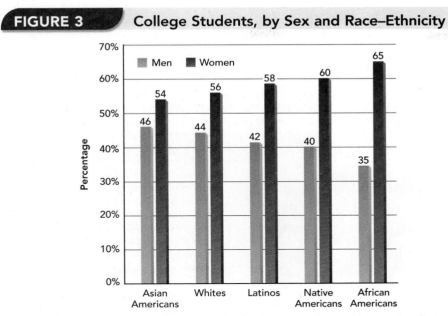

FIGURE 3 **College Students, by Sex and Race–Ethnicity**

Note: This figure can be confusing. To read it, ask: What percentage of a particular group in college are men or women? (For example, what percentage of Asian American college students are men or women?)

Source: By the author. Based on *Statistical Abstract of the United States* 2011:Table 275.

Here are two extremes: Men earn 95 percent of the associate degrees in the "masculine" field of construction trades, while women are awarded 96 percent of the associate degrees in the "feminine" field of "family and consumer sciences" (*Statistical Abstract* 2011:Table 297). Because gender socialization gives men and women different orientations to life, they enter college with gender-linked aspirations. Socialization—not some presumed innate characteristic—channels men and women into different educational paths.

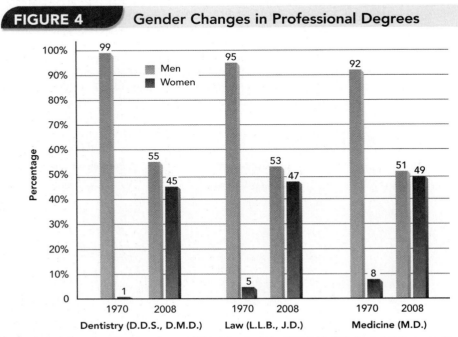

FIGURE 4 **Gender Changes in Professional Degrees**

Source: By the author. Based on *Digest of Education Statistics* 2007:Table 269; *Statistical Abstract of the United States* 2011:Table 300.

How does gender inequality show up in education today?

Down-to-Earth Sociology

Affirmative Action for Men?

The idea that we might need affirmative action *for men* was first proposed by psychologist Judith Kleinfeld (2002a). Many met this suggestion with laughter. After all, men dominate societies around the world, and they have done so for millennia. The discussion in this chapter has shown that as men exercised that dominance, they also suppressed and harmed women. To think that men would ever need affirmative action seems laughable at best.

In contrast to this reaction, let's pause, step back and try to see whether the idea has some merit. Look again at Figures 2 and 3. Do you see that women have not only caught up with men, but that they also have passed them by? Do you see that this applies to all racial–ethnic groups? That this is not a temporary situation, like lead cars changing place at the Indy 500, is apparent from the statistics the government publishes each year. For decades, women have steadily added to their proportion of college student enrollment and the degrees they earn.

This accomplishment is laudable, but what about the men? Why have they fallen behind? With college enrollment open

With fewer men than women in college, is it time to consider affirmative action for men?

equally to both men and women, why don't enrollment and degree totals now match the relative proportions of women and men in the population (51 percent and 49 percent)? Although no one yet knows the reasons for this—and there are a lot of suggestions being thrown about—some have begun to consider this a problem in need of a solution. In a first, Clark University in Massachusetts has begun a support program for men to help them adjust to their minority status (Gibbs 2008). I assume that other colleges will follow, as these totals have serious implications for the future of society—just as they did when fewer women were enrolled in college.

For Your Consideration

→ Do you think that women's and men's current college enrollments and degree totals represent something other than an interesting historical change? Why do you think that men have fallen behind? Do you think anything should be done about this imbalance? If so, what? Behind the scenes, so as not to get anyone upset, some colleges have begun to reject more highly qualified women to get closer to a male–female balance (Kingsbury 2007). What do you think about this?

Graduate School and Beyond. If we follow students into graduate school, we see that with each passing year the proportion of women drops. Table 1 below gives us a snapshot of doctoral programs in the sciences. Note how aspirations (enrollment) and accomplishments (doctorates earned) are sex linked. In five of these doctoral programs, men outnumber women, and in three, women outnumber men. In *all* of them, however, women are less likely to complete the doctorate.

	TABLE 1	Doctorates in Science, By Sex					
	Students Enrolled		**Docs Conferred**		**Completion Ratio**	
Field	**Women**	**Men**	**Women**	**Men**	**Women**	**Men**
Mathematics	36%	64%	31%	69%	−16	+8
Agriculture	49%	51%	42%	58%	−14	+13
Biological	56%	44%	49%	51%	−13	+16
Physical	32%	68%	28%	72%	−13	+6
Computer Sciences	25%	75%	22%	78%	−12	+2
Social Sciences	53%	47%	49%	51%	−8	+9
Psychology	75%	25%	71%	29%	−5	+16
Engineering	23%	77%	22%	79%	−4	+3

*The formula for the completion ratio is X minus Y divided by Y × 100, where X is the doctorates conferred and Y is the proportion enrolled in a program.
Source: By the author. Based on *Statistical Abstract of the United States* 2011:Tables 804, 808.

Why do some think that we might need affirmative action for men in education? Can they really be serious?

Following those who earn doctoral degrees to their teaching careers at colleges and universities, we find gender stratification in rank and pay. Throughout the United States, women are less likely to become full professors, the highest-paying and most prestigious rank. In both private and public colleges, professors' average pay is more than twice that of instructors (*Statistical Abstract* 2011:Table 291). Even when women do become full professors, their average pay is less than that of men who are full professors (AAUP 2010:Table 5).

Gender Inequality in the Workplace

To examine the work setting is to make visible basic relations between men and women. Let's begin with one of the most remarkable areas of gender inequality at work, the pay gap.

The Pay Gap

After college, you might like to take a few years off, travel around Europe, sail the oceans, or maybe sit on a beach in some South American paradise and drink piña coladas. But chances are, you are going to go to work instead. Since you have to work, how would you like to make an extra $740,000 on your job? If this sounds appealing, read on. I'm going to reveal how you can make an extra $1,540 a month between the ages of 25 and 65.

Historical Background. First, let's get a broad background to help us understand today's situation. One of the chief characteristics of the U.S. workforce is the steady growth in the numbers of women who work for wages outside the home. Figure 5 shows that in 1890 about one of every five paid workers was a woman. By 1940, this ratio had grown to one of four; by 1960 to one of three; and today it is almost one of two. As shown in this figure, during the next few years we can expect that the ratio will remain 53 percent men and 47 percent women.

Geographical Factors. Women who work for wages are not distributed evenly throughout the United States. From the Social Map on the next page, you can see that where a woman lives makes a difference in how likely she is to work outside the home.

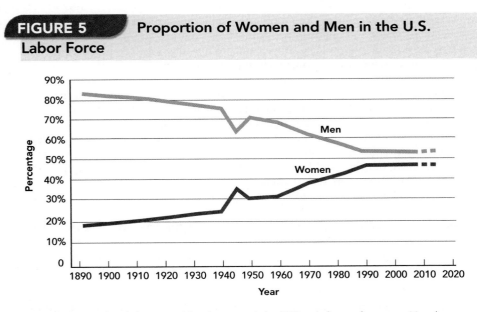

FIGURE 5 **Proportion of Women and Men in the U.S. Labor Force**

Note: Pre-1940 totals include women 14 and over; totals for 1940 and after are for women 16 and over. Broken lines are the author's projections.

Sources: By the author. Based on Women's Bureau of the United States 1969:10; *Manpower Report to the President*, 1971:203, 205; Mills and Palumbo 1980:6, 45; *Statistical Abstract of the United States* 2011:Table 585.

How has the proportion of women and men in the U.S. workforce changed over time?

FIGURE 6 Women in the Workforce

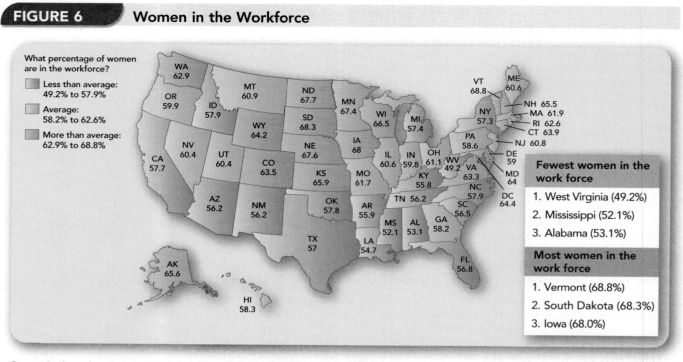

What percentage of women are in the workforce?

- Less than average: 49.2% to 57.9%
- Average: 58.2% to 62.6%
- More than average: 62.9% to 68.8%

WA 62.9
OR 59.9
ID 57.9
MT 60.9
ND 67.7
MN 67.4
WY 64.2
SD 68.3
NV 60.4
UT 60.4
CO 63.5
NE 67.6
IA 68
WI 66.5
MI 57.4
CA 57.7
KS 65.9
MO 61.7
IL 60.6
IN 59.8
OH 61.1
WV 49.2
AZ 56.2
NM 56.2
OK 57.8
AR 55.9
KY 55.8
VA 63.3
MD 64
TN 56.2
NC 57.9
SC 56.5
MS 52.1
AL 53.1
GA 58.2
TX 57
LA 54.7
FL 56.8
AK 65.6
HI 58.3
VT 68.8
ME 60.6
NH 65.5
MA 61.9
RI 62.6
CT 63.9
NY 57.3
NJ 60.8
PA 58.6
DE 59
DC 64.4

Fewest women in the work force
1. West Virginia (49.2%)
2. Mississippi (52.1%)
3. Alabama (53.1%)

Most women in the work force
1. Vermont (68.8%)
2. South Dakota (68.3%)
3. Iowa (68.0%)

Source: By the author. Based on *Statistical Abstract of the United States* 2011:Table 593.

Why is there such a clustering among the states? The geographical patterns that you see on this map reflect regional subcultural differences about which we currently have little understanding.

The "Testosterone Bonus." Now, back to how you can make an extra $740,000 at work—and maybe even more. You might be wondering if this is hard to do. Actually, it is simple for some and impossible for others. As Figure 7 on the next page shows, all you have to do is be born a male. If we compare full-time workers, based on current differences in earnings, this is how much more money the *average male* can expect to earn over the course of his career. Now if you want to boost that annual difference to $33,900 for a whopping career total of $1,356,000, be both a male and a college graduate. Hardly any single factor pinpoints gender discrimination better than these totals. As you can see from Figure 7, the pay gap shows up at *all* levels of education.

For college students, the gender gap in pay begins with the first job after graduation. You might know of a particular woman who was offered a higher salary than most men in her class, but she would be an exception. On average, men enjoy a "testosterone bonus," and employers start them out at higher salaries than women (Harris et al. 2005; Carter 2010). Depending on your sex, then, you will either benefit from the pay gap or be victimized by it.

The pay gap is so great that U.S. women who work full time average *only 70 percent* of what men are paid. As you can see from Figure 8, the pay gap used to be even worse. A gender gap in pay occurs not only in the United States but also in *all* industrialized nations.

Reasons for the Gender Pay Gap. What logic can underlie the gender pay gap? As we just saw, college degrees are gender linked, so perhaps this gap is due to career choices. Maybe women are more likely to choose lower-paying jobs, such as teaching grade school, while men are more likely to go into better-paying fields, such as business and engineering. Actually, this is true, and researchers have found that about *half* of the gender pay gap is due to such factors. And the balance? It consists of a

What is the "testoserone bonus"? Why is there a gender pay gap?

FIGURE 7 The Gender Pay Gap, by Education[1]

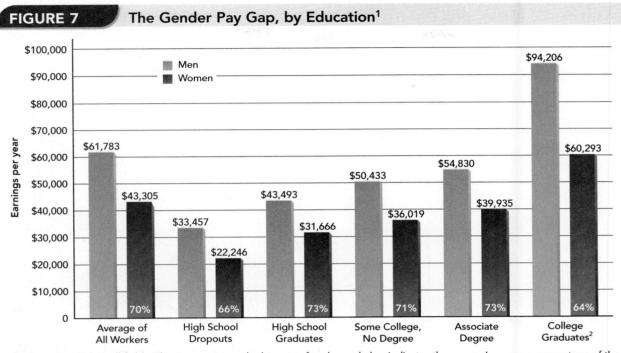

[1]Full-time workers in all fields. The percentage at the bottom of each purple bar indicates the women's average percentage of the men's income.
[2]Bachelor's and all higher degrees, including professional degrees.

Source: By the author. Based on *Statistical Abstract of the United States* 2011:Table 702.

combination of gender discrimination (Jacobs 2003; Roth 2003) and what is called the "child penalty"—women missing out on work experience and opportunities while they care for children (Hundley 2001; Chaker and Stout 2004).

The CEO Gap. As a final indication of the extent of the U.S. gender pay gap, consider this. Of the nation's top 500 corporations (the so-called Fortune 500), only 12 are headed by women (VenderMey 2011).

I examined the names of the CEOs of the 350 largest U.S. corporations, and I found that your best chance to reach the top is to be named (in this order) John, Robert, James, William, or Charles. Edward, Lawrence, and Richard are also advantageous names. Amber, Katherine, Leticia, and Maria apparently draw a severe penalty. Naming your baby girl John or Robert might seem a little severe, but it could help her reach the top. (I say this only slightly tongue-in-cheek. One of the few women to head a Fortune 500 company—before she was fired and given $21 million severance pay—had a man's first name: Carleton Fiorina of Hewlett-Packard. Carleton's first name is actually Cara, but knowing what she was facing in the highly competitive business world, she dropped this feminine name to go by her masculine middle name.)

Is the Glass Ceiling Cracking?

"First comes love, then comes marriage, then comes flex time and a baby carriage."
—Said by a supervisor at Novartis who refused to hire women (Carter 2010)

This supervisor's statement reflects blatant discrimination. Most gender discrimination in the workplace, however, seems to be unintentional, with much of it based on gender stereotypes.

Apart from cases of overt discrimination, then, what keeps women from breaking through the **glass ceiling,** the mostly invisible barrier that prevents women from reaching

glass ceiling the mostly invisible barrier that keeps women from advancing to the top levels at work

How does the gender pay gap differ by education?

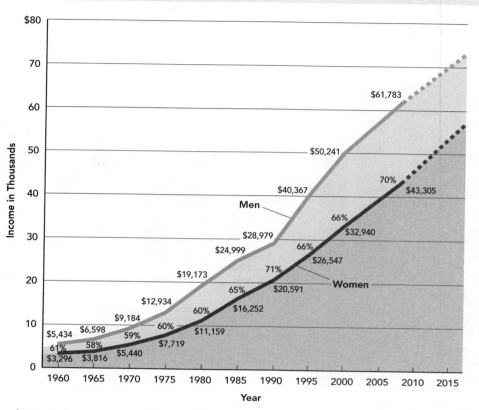

FIGURE 8 **The Gender Gap Over Time: What Percentage of Men's Income Do Women Earn?**

Source: By the author. Based on *Statistical Abstract of the United States* 1995:Table 739; 2002:Table 666; 2011:Table 702, and earlier years. Broken lines indicate the author's estimate.

AP Images/PRNewsFoto/PepsiCo

As the glass ceiling slowly cracks, women are gradually gaining entry into the top positions in society. Shown here is Indra Nooyi, the first woman to head PepsiCo.

the executive suite? The "pipelines" that lead to the top of a company are its marketing, sales, and production positions, those that directly affect the corporate bottom line (Hymowitz 2004; DeCrow 2005). Men, who dominate the executive suite, stereotype women as being good at "support" but less capable than men of leadership (Belkin 2007). They steer women into human resources or public relations. In these positions, successful projects are not appreciated in the same way as those that bring corporate profits—and bonuses for their managers.

Another reason for the strength of the glass ceiling is that women lack mentors—successful executives who take an interest in them and teach them the ropes. Lack of a mentor is no trivial matter, for mentors can provide opportunities to develop leadership skills that open the door to the executive suite (Hymowitz 2007; Yakaboski and Reinert 2011).

The Women Who Break Through. As you would expect, the women who have broken through the glass ceiling are highly motivated individuals with a fierce competitive spirit. They are willing to give up sleep, recreation, and family responsibilities for the sake of advancing their careers. What you might not have expected, but which makes sense when you consider the work environment, is that these women have also learned to play by "men's rules," developing a style that men expect and that makes them comfortable.

And the Future? Will the glass ceiling crack open? Some think so. They point out that women who began their careers twenty to thirty years ago are now running

Is the glass ceiling cracking? What keeps women from breaking through it?

major divisions within the largest companies, and from them, some will emerge as the new CEOs. Others reply that these optimists have been saying this same thing for years, that the glass ceiling continues to be so strong that most of these women have already reached their top positions (Carter 2010).

Sexual Harassment—and Worse

Sexual harassment—unwelcome sexual attention at work or at school, which may affect job or school performance or create a hostile environment—was not recognized as a problem until the 1970s. Before this, women considered unwanted sexual comments, touches, looks, and pressure to have sex as a personal matter, something between her and some "turned on" man, or an obnoxious one.

With the prodding of feminists, women began to perceive unwanted sexual advances at work and school as part of a *structural* problem. That is, they began to realize that the issue was more than a man here or there doing obnoxious things because he was attracted to a woman; rather, men were using their positions of authority to pressure women for sex. As women move into positions of authority, they, too, can become sexual harassers (Wayne et al. 2001). With most authority still vested in men, however, most of the sexual harassers are men.

Effects on Perception

As symbolic interactionists stress, labels affect the way we see things. Because we have the term *sexual harassment,* we perceive actions in a different light than people used to. We are now more apt to perceive a supervisor who makes sexual advances to a worker not as sexual attraction but as a misuse of authority. It is important to add that this is not just a "man thing." Unlike the 1970s, many women today are in positions of authority. In those positions they, too, sexually harass subordinates (Settles et al. 2011). With most authority still vested in men, however, most of the sexual harassers are men. Originally, sexual desire was an element of sexual harassment, but no longer. This changed when the U.S. Supreme Court considered the lawsuit of a homosexual who had been tormented by his supervisors and fellow workers. The Court ruled that sexual desire is not necessary—that sexual harassment laws also apply to homosexuals who are harassed by heterosexuals while on the job (Felsenthal 1998). By extension, the law applies to heterosexuals who are sexually harassed by homosexuals.

Gender and Violence

One of the consistent characteristics of violence in the United States—and the world—is its gender inequality. That is, females are more likely to be the victims of males, not the other way around. Let's briefly review this almost one-way street in gender violence as it applies to the United States.

Violence Against Women

We have already examined violence against women in other cultures; here we briefly review some primary features of gender violence.

Forcible Rape. The fear of rape is common among U.S. women, a fear that is far from groundless. The U.S. rate is 0.59 per 1,000 females (*Statistical Abstract* 2011:Table 310). If we exclude the very young and women over 50, those who are the least likely rape victims, the rate comes to about 1 per 1,000. This means that 1 of every 1,000 U.S. girls and women between the ages of 12 and 50 is raped *each year*. Despite this high number, women are safer now than they were ten and twenty years ago. The rape rate then was much higher than today.

Although any woman can be a victim of sexual assault—and victims include babies and elderly women—the typical victim is 16 to 19 years old. As you can see from Table 2, sexual assault peaks at those ages and then declines.

"Of course it isn't a case of sexual discrimination. We just don't think you're the right man for the job."

Although crassly put by the cartoonist, behind the glass ceiling lies this background assumption.

sexual harassment the abuse of one's position of authority to force unwanted sexual demands on someone

Why is sexual harassment a structural problem, not just a personal problem?

TABLE 2	Rape Victims
Age	Rate per 1,000 Females
12–15	1.9
16–19	3.3
20–24	2.3
25–34	1.3
35–49	0.8
50–64	0.3
65 and Older	0.09

Sources: By the author. A ten-year average, based on *Statistical Abstract of the United States*; 2002:Table 303; 2003:Table 295; 2004:Table 322; 2005:Table 306; 2006:Table 308; 2007:Table 311; 2008:Table 313; 2009:Table 305; 2010:Table 305; 2011:Table 312.

TABLE 3	Relationship of Victims and Rapists
Relationship	Percentage
Relative	7%
Known Well	33%
Casual Acquaintance	23%
Stranger	34%
Not Reported	2%

Sources: By the author. A ten-year average, based on *Statistical Abstract of the United States*; 2002:Table 296; 2003:Table 323; 2004–2005:Table 307; 2006:Table 311; 2007: Table 315; 2008:Table 316; 2009:Table 306; 2010:Table 306; 2011:Table 313.

Women's most common fear seems to be an attack by a stranger—a sudden, violent abduction and rape. However, contrary to the stereotypes that underlie these fears, most victims know their attackers. As you can see from Table 3, about one of three rapes is committed by strangers.

Males are also victims of rape, which is every bit as devastating for them as it is for female victims (Abdullah-Khan 2008). The rape of males in prison is a special problem, sometimes tolerated by prison guards, at times even encouraged as punishment for prisoners who have given them problems (Donaldson 1993; Lewin 2001).

Date (Acquaintance) Rape. What has shocked so many about date rape (also known as *acquaintance rape*) are studies showing how common it is (Littleton et al. 2008). Researchers who used a nationally representative sample of women enrolled in U.S. colleges and universities with 1,000 students or more found that 1.7 percent had been raped during the preceding six months. Another 1.1 percent had been victims of attempted rape (Fisher et al. 2000).

The most common drug used to facilitate date rape is alcohol, not GHB.

© Chris Rout/Alamy

Think about how huge these numbers are. With 11 million women enrolled in college, 2.8 percent (1.7 plus 1.1) means that over a quarter of a million college women were victims of rape or of attempted rape *in just the past six months.* (This conclusion assumes that the rate is the same in colleges with fewer than 1,000 students, which has not been verified.)

Most of the women told a friend what happened, but only *5 percent* reported the crime to the police (Fisher et al. 2003). The most common reason was thinking that the event "was not serious enough." The next reason given most often was uncertainty whether a crime had been committed. Many women were embarrassed and didn't want others, especially their families, to know what had happened. Others felt there was no proof ("It would be my word against his"), feared reprisal from the man, or mistrusted the police (Fisher et al. 2000).

Sometimes a rape victim feels partially responsible because she knows the person, was drinking with him, went to his place voluntarily, or invited him to her place. However, as a physician who treats victims of date rape said, "Would you feel responsible if someone hit you over the head with a shovel—just because you knew the person?" (Carpenito 1999).

Murder. All over the world, men are more likely than women to be killers. Figure 9 illustrates this gender pattern in U.S. murders. Note that although females make up about 51 percent of the U.S. population, they don't even come close to making up 51 percent of the nation's killers. As you can see from this figure, when women are murdered, about nine times out of ten the killer is a man.

What are the main findings on date rape? Age of victims? Relationship of victims to rapists?

Feminism and Gendered Violence. Feminist sociologists have been especially effective in bringing violence against women to the public's attention. Some use symbolic interactionism, pointing out that to associate strength and virility with violence—as is done in many cultures—is to promote violence. Others employ conflict theory. They argue that men are losing power, and that some men turn violently against women as a way to reassert their declining power and status (Reiser 1999; Meltzer 2002).

Solutions. There is no magic bullet for this problem of gendered violence, but to be effective, any solution must break the connection between violence and masculinity. This would require an educational program that encompasses schools, churches, homes, and the media. Given the gunslinging heroes of the Wild West and other American icons, as well as the violent messages that are so prevalent in the mass media, including video games, it is difficult to be optimistic that a change will come any time soon.

Our next topic, women in politics, however, gives us much more reason for optimism.

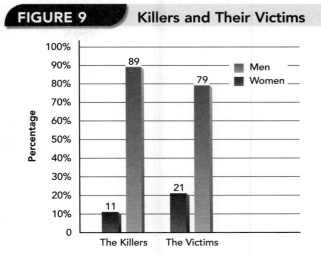

FIGURE 9   Killers and Their Victims

Source: By the author. Based on *Statistical Abstract of the United States* 2011:Tables 309, 320.

The Changing Face of Politics

Women could take over the United States! Think about it. There are eight million more women than men of voting age. But look at Table 4. Although women voters greatly outnumber men voters, men greatly outnumber women in political office. The remarkable gains women have made in recent elections can take our eye off the broader picture. Since 1789 almost 2,000 men have served in the U.S. Senate. And how many women? Only 38, including 17 current senators. Not until 1992 was the first African American woman (Carol Moseley-Braun) elected to the U.S. Senate.

TABLE 4   U.S. Women in Political Office

	Offices Held by Women (Percentage)	Offices Held By Women (Number)
National Office		
U.S. Senate	17%	17
U.S. House of Representatives	17%	73
State Office		
Governors	12%	6
Lt. Governors	18%	9
Attorneys General	8%	4
Secretaries of State	24%	12
Treasurers	20%	10
State Auditors	16%	8
State Legislators	24%	1,800

Source: Center for American Women and Politics 2010.

"Women in Elected Office" from the Center for American Women and Politics website. Copyright © 2010 by the Center for American Women and Politics. Reprinted with permission.

What would it take to sharply reduce gendered violence?

Hillary Clinton broke through the glass ceiling in politics when she was elected senator from New York: She also came close to being the Democratic nominee for president. She is shown here in her position as Secretary of State, meeting with Arab leaders in Morocco.

AP Images/Abdeljalil Bounhar

No Latina or Asian American woman has yet been elected to the Senate (National Women's Political Caucus 1998, 2011; *Statistical Abstract* 2011:Table 405).

We are in the midst of fundamental change. In 2002, Nancy Pelosi was the first woman to be elected by her colleagues as minority leader of the House of Representatives. Five years later, in 2007, they chose her as the first female Speaker of the House. These posts made her the most powerful woman ever in Congress. Another significant event occurred in 2008 when Hillary Clinton came within a hair's breadth of becoming the presidential nominee of the Democratic party. That same year, Sarah Palin was chosen as the Republican vice-presidential candidate. We can also note that more women are becoming corporate executives, and, as indicated in Figure 4, more women are also becoming lawyers. In these positions, women are traveling more and making statewide and national contacts. Along with other societal changes allowing women more freedom, such as the increasing view of child care as a responsibility of both mother and father, it is only a matter of time until a woman occupies the Oval Office.

Glimpsing the Future—with Hope

Women's fuller participation in the decision-making processes of our social institutions has shattered stereotypes that tended to limit females to "feminine" activities and push males into "masculine" ones. As structural barriers continue to fall and more activities are degendered, both males and females will have greater freedom to pursue activities that are more compatible with their abilities and desires as individuals.

As females and males develop a new consciousness both of their capacities and of their potential, relationships will change. Distinctions between the sexes will not disappear, but there is no reason for biological differences to be translated into social inequalities. If current trends continue, we may see a growing appreciation of sexual differences coupled with greater equality of opportunity—with the potential of transforming society (Gilman 1911/1971; Offen 1990). If this happens, as sociologist Alison Jaggar (1990) observed, gender equality can become less a goal than a background condition for living in society.

By the Numbers: Changes Over Time

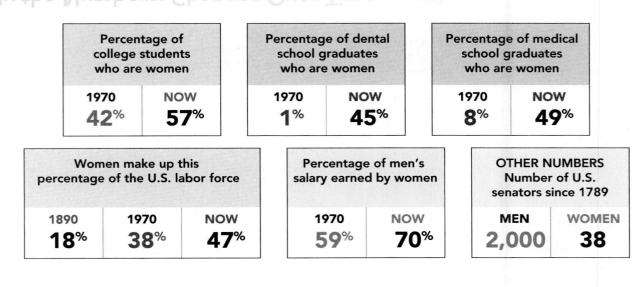

Percentage of college students who are women	
1970	**NOW**
42%	**57**%

Percentage of dental school graduates who are women	
1970	**NOW**
1%	**45**%

Percentage of medical school graduates who are women	
1970	**NOW**
8%	**49**%

Women make up this percentage of the U.S. labor force		
1890	**1970**	**NOW**
18%	**38**%	**47**%

Percentage of men's salary earned by women	
1970	**NOW**
59%	**70**%

OTHER NUMBERS Number of U.S. senators since 1789	
MEN	**WOMEN**
2,000	**38**

Summary and Review

Issues of Sex and Gender

What is gender stratification?

The term **gender stratification** refers to unequal access to property, power, and prestige on the basis of sex. Each society establishes a structure that, on the basis of sex and gender, opens and closes doors to its privileges.

How do sex and gender differ?

Sex refers to biological distinctions between males and females. It consists of both primary and secondary sex characteristics. **Gender,** in contrast, is what a society considers proper behaviors and attitudes for its male and female members. Sex physically distinguishes males from females; gender refers to what people call "masculine" and "feminine."

Why do the behaviors of males and females differ?

The "nature versus nurture" debate refers to whether differences in the behaviors of males and females are caused by inherited (biological) or learned (cultural) characteristics. Almost all sociologists take the side of nurture. In recent years, however, sociologists have begun to cautiously open the door to biology.

Gender Inequality in Global Perspective

Is gender stratification universal?

George Murdock surveyed information on tribal societies and found that all of them have sex-linked activities and give greater prestige to male activities. **Patriarchy,** or male dominance, appears to be universal. Besides work, male dominance is seen in education, politics, and everyday life.

How did females become a minority group?

The origin of discrimination against females is lost in history, but the primary theory of how females became a minority group in their own societies focuses on the physical limitations imposed by childbirth.

What forms does gender inequality take around the world?

Its many variations include inequalities in education, politics, and pay. It also includes domination in the form of violence, including female circumcision.

Gender Inequality in the United States

Is the feminist movement new?

In what is called the "first wave," feminists made political demands for change in the early 1900s—and were met with hostility, and even violence. The "second wave" began in the 1960s and continues today. An overlapping "third wave" is in process.

What forms does gender inequality take in everyday life, health care, and education?

In everyday life, a lower value is placed on things feminine. In health care, physicians don't take women's health complaints as seriously as those of men, and they exploit women's fears, performing unnecessary hysterectomies. In education, more women than men attend college, but many choose fields that are categorized as "feminine." More women than men also earn college degrees. However, women are less likely to complete the doctoral programs in science. Fundamental change is indicated by the growing numbers of women in law and medicine.

Gender Inequality in the Workplace

How does gender inequality show up in the workplace?

All occupations show a gender gap in pay. For college graduates, the lifetime pay gap runs well over a million dollars in favor of men. **Sexual harassment** also continues to be a reality of the workplace.

Gender and Violence

What is the relationship between gender and violence?

Overwhelmingly, the victims of rape and murder are females. Female circumcision and honor killing are special cases of violence against females. Conflict theorists point out that men use violence to maintain their power and privilege.

The Changing Face of Politics

What is the trend in gender inequality in politics?

A traditional division of gender roles—women as child care providers and homemakers, men as workers outside the home—used to keep women out of politics. Women continue to be underrepresented in politics, but the trend toward greater political equality is firmly in place.

Glimpsing the Future—with Hope

How might changes in gender roles and stereotypes affect our lives?

In the United States, women are increasingly involved in the decision-making processes of our social institutions. Men, too, are reexamining their traditional roles. New gender expectations may be developing, allowing both males and females to pursue more individual, less stereotypical interests.

Thinking Critically about this Chapter

1. What is your position on the "nature versus nurture" (biology or culture) debate? What materials in this chapter support your position?

2. Why do you think that the gender gap in pay exists all over the world?

3. What do you think can be done to reduce gender inequality?

References

All new references are printed in cyan.

AAUP (American Association of University Professors). "Report of the Committee on the Economic Status of the Profession." Washington, D.C.: Author, April 2010.

Abdullah-Kahn, Noreen. *Male Rape: The Emergence of a Social and Legal Issue.* New York: Palgrave Macmillan, 2008.

Andersen, Margaret L. *Thinking about Women: Sociological Perspectives on Sex and Gender.* New York: Macmillan, 1988.

Anderson, Elizabeth. "Recent Thinking about Sexual Harassment: A Review Essay." *Philosophy & Public Affairs, 34,* 3, 2006:284–312.

Anderson, Eric. *Inclusive Masculinity: The Changing Nature of Masculinities.* New York: Routledge, 2009.

Belkin, Lisa. "The Feminine Critique." *New York Times,* November 1, 2007.

Bishop, Jerry E. "Study Finds Doctors Tend to Postpone Heart Surgery for Women, Raising Risk." *Wall Street Journal,* April 16, 1990:B4.

Booth, Alan, and James M. Dabbs, Jr. "Testosterone and Men's Marriages." *Social Forces, 72,* 2, December 1993:463–477.

Broder, Michael S., David E. Kanouse, Brian S. Mittman, and Steven J. Bernstein. "The Appropriateness of Recommendations for Hysterectomy." *Obstetrics and Gynecology, 95,* 2, February 2000:199–205.

Carpenito, Lynda Juall. "The Myths of Acquaintance Rape." *Nursing Forum, 34,* 4, October–December 1999:3.

Carter, Nancy M. "Pipeline's Broken Promise." New York: Catalyst, 2010.

Center for American Women and Politics. "Fact Sheet: Women in Elective Office." May 2010.

Chafetz, Janet Saltzman. *Gender Equity: An Integrated Theory of Stability and Change.* Newbury Park, Calif.: Sage, 1990.

Chafetz, Janet Saltzman, and Anthony Gary Dworkin. *Female Revolt: Women's Movements in World and Historical Perspective.* Totowa, N.J.: Rowman & Allanheld, 1986.

Chaker, Anne Marie, and Hilary Stout. "After Years off, Women Struggle to Revive Careers." *Wall Street Journal,* May 6, 2004.

Chalkley, Kate. "Female Genital Mutilation: New Laws, Programs Try to End Practice." *Population Today, 25,* 10, October 1997:4–5.

CIA (Central Intelligence Agency). *The World Factbook.* Washington, D.C: U.S. Government Printing Office, 2010. Published annually.

Colapinto, John. *As Nature Made Him: The Boy Who Was Raised as a Girl.* New York: HarperCollins, 2001.

Collins, Randall, Janet Saltzman Chafetz, Rae Lesser Blumberg, Scott Coltrane, and Jonathan H. Turner. "Toward an Integrated Theory of Gender Stratification." *Sociological Perspectives, 36,* 3, 1993:185–216.

Collymore, Yvette. "Conveying Concerns: Women Report on Gender-Based Violence." Washington, D.C.: Population Reference Bureau, 2000.

Corbett, Sara. "A Cutting Tradition." *New York Times,* January 20, 2008.

Cowley, Joyce. *Pioneers of Women's Liberation.* New York: Merit, 1969.

Crawford, Bridget J. "The Third Wave's Break from Feminism." *International Law in Context,* 2009.

Crossen, Cynthia. "Deja Vu." *Wall Street Journal,* March 5, 2003.

Crossen, Cynthia. "When Worse Than a Woman Who Voted Was One Who Smoked." *Wall Street Journal,* January 7, 2008.

Dabbs, James M., Jr., and Robin Morris. "Testosterone, Social Class, and Antisocial Behavior in a Sample of 4,462 Men." *Psychological Science, 1,* 3, May 1990:209–211.

Dabbs, James M., Jr., Timothy S. Carr, Robert L. Frady, and Jasmin K. Riad. "Testosterone, Crime, and Misbehavior among 692 Male Prison Inmates." *Personality and Individual Differences, 18,* 1995:627–633.

Dabbs, James M., Jr., Marian F. Hargrove, and Colleen Heusel. "Testosterone Differences among College Fraternities: Well-Behaved vs. Rambunctious." *Personality and Individual Differences, 20,* 1996:157–161.

DeCrow, Karen. Foreword to *Why Men Earn More* by Warren Farrell. New York: AMACOM, 2005:xi–xii.

Diamond, Milton, and Keith Sigmundson. "Sex Reassignment at Birth: Long-term Review and Clinical Implications." *Archives of Pediatric and Adolescent Medicine, 151,* March 1997:298–304.

Digest of Education Statistics. Washington, D.C.: National Center for Education Statistics, 2007.

Donaldson, Stephen. "A Million Jockers, Punks, and Queens: Sex among American Male Prisoners and Its Implications for Concepts of Sexual Orientation." February 4, 1993. Online.

Douglas, Carol Anne, et al. "Kenya: FGM Increasingly Occurring in Hospitals." *Off Our Backs, 35,* January–February 2005:5.

Eder, Donna. *School Talk: Gender and Adolescent Culture.* New Brunswick, N.J.: Rutgers University Press, 1995.

Ehrenreich, Barbara, and Deidre English. *Witches, Midwives, and Nurses: A History of Women Healers.* Old Westbury, N.Y.: Feminist Press, 1973.

Eisenhart, R. Wayne. "You Can't Hack It, Little Girl: A Discussion of the Covert Psychological Agenda of Modern Combat Training." *Journal of Social Issues, 31,* Fall 1975:13–23.

England, Paula. "The Impact of Feminist Thought on Sociology." *Contemporary Sociology: A Journal of Reviews,* 2000:263–267.

Falkenberg, Katie. "Pakistani Women Victims of 'Honor.'" *Washington Times,* July 23, 2008.

Fathi, Nazila. "Starting at Home, Iran's Women Fight for Rights." *New York Times,* February 12, 2009.

Felsenthal, Edward. "Justices' Ruling Further Defines Sex Harassment." *Wall Street Journal,* March 5, 1998:B1, B2.

Fisher, Bonnie S., Francis T. Cullen, and Michael G. Turner. *The Sexual Victimization of College Women.* Washington, D.C.: U.S. Department of Justice, 2000.

Fisher, Bonnie S., Leah E. Daigle, Francis T. Cullen, and Michael G. Turner. "Reporting Sexual Victimization to the Police and Others: Results from a National-Level Study of College Women." *Criminal Justice and Behavior, 30,* 1, February 2003:6–38.

Fisher, Sue. *In the Patient's Best Interest: Women and the Politics of Medical Decisions.* New Brunswick, N.J.: Rutgers University Press, 1986.

Flexner, E. *Century of Struggle.* Cambridge, Mass.: Belknap, 1971. In Claire M. Renzetti and Daniel J. Curran, *Women, Men, and Society,* 4th ed. Boston: Allyn and Bacon, 1999.

Foley, Douglas E. "The Great American Football Ritual." In *Society: Readings to Accompany Sociology: A Down-to-Earth Approach, Core Concepts,* James M. Henslin, ed. Boston: Allyn and Bacon, 2006: 64–76. Originally published 1990.

Freedman, Jane. *Feminism.* Philadelphia: Open University Press, 2001.

Friedl, Ernestine. "Society and Sex Roles." In *Conformity and Conflict: Readings in Cultural Anthropology,* James P. Spradley and David W. McCurdy, eds. Glenview, Ill.: Scott, Foresman, 1990:229–238.

Gallmeier, Charles P. "Methodological Issues in Qualitative Sport Research: Participant Observation among Hockey Players." *Sociological Spectrum, 8,* 1988:213–235.

Gibbs, Nancy. "Affirmative Action for Boys." *Time,* April 3, 2008.

Gilman, Charlotte Perkins. *The Man-Made World or, Our Androcentric Culture.* New York: 1971. Originally published 1911.

Hacker, Helen Mayer. "Women as a Minority Group." *Social Forces, 30,* October 1951:60–69.

Hakim, Catherine. "Erotic Capital." *European Sociological Review,* 2010:499–518.

Hamid, Shadi. "Between Orientalism and Postmodernism: The Changing Nature of Western Feminist Thought towards the Middle East." *HAWWA, 4,* 1, 2006:76–92.

Harris, Kim, Dwight R. Sanders, Shaun Gress, and Nick Kuhns. "Starting Salaries for Agribusiness Graduates from an AASCARR Institution: The Case of Southern Illinois University." *Agribusiness, 21,* 1, 2005:65–80.

Harris, Marvin. "Why Men Dominate Women." *New York Times Magazine,* November 13, 1977:46, 115, 117–123.

Hendrix, Lewellyn. "What Is Sexual Inequality? On the Definition and Range of Variation." *Gender and Society, 28,* 3, August 1994:287–307.

Huber, Joan. "Micro-Macro Links in Gender Stratification." *American Sociological Review, 55,* February 1990:1–10.

Hundley, Greg. "Why Women Earn Less Than Men in Self-Employment." *Journal of Labor Research, 22,* 4, Fall 2001:817–827.

Hymowitz, Carol. "Through the Glass Ceiling." *Wall Street Journal,* November 8, 2004.

Hymowitz, Carol. "Raising Women to Be Leaders." *Wall Street Journal,* February 12, 2007.

Jacobs, Jerry A. "Detours on the Road to Equality: Women, Work and Higher Education." *Contexts,* Winter 2003:32–41.

Jaggar, Alison M. "Sexual Difference and Sexual Equality." In *Theoretical Perspectives on Sexual Difference,* Deborah L. Rhode, ed. New Haven, Conn.: Yale University Press, 1990:239–254.

Jneid, Hani, Gregg C. Fonarow, Christopher P. Cannon, et al. "Sex Differences in Medical Care and Early Death after Acute Myocardial Infarction." *Circulation,* December 8, 2008.

Jones, Nikki. *Between Good and Ghetto: African American Girls and Inner-City Violence.* New Brunswick, N.J. Rutgers University Press, 2010.

Kingsbury, Alex, "Many Colleges Reject Women at Higher Rates Than for Men." *U.S. News & World Report,* June 17, 2007.

Kleinfeld, Judith S. "Gender and Myth: Data about Student Performance." In *Through the Eyes of Social Science,* 6th ed., Frank J. Zulke and Jacqueline P. Kirley, eds. Prospect Heights, Ill.: Waveland Press, 2002a:380–393.

Leacock, Eleanor. *Myths of Male Dominance.* New York: Monthly Review Press, 1981.

Lerner, Gerda. *The Creation of Patriarchy.* New York: Oxford, 1986.

Lewin, Tamar. "Little Sympathy or Remedy for Inmates Who Are Raped." *New York Times,* April 15, 2001.

Lightfoot-Klein, A. "Rites of Purification and Their Effects: Some Psychological Aspects of Female Genital Circumcision and Infibulation (Pharaonic Circumcision) in an Afro-Arab Society (Sudan)." *Journal of Psychological Human Sexuality, 2,* 1989:61–78.

Linton, Ralph. *The Study of Man.* New York: Appleton-Century-Crofts, 1936.

Littleton, Heather, Carmen Radecki Breitkopf, and Abbey Berenson. "Women Beyond the Campus: Unacknowledged Rape among Low-Income Women." *Violence against Women, 14,* 3, March 2008:269–286.

Lurie, Nicole, Jonathan Slater, Paul McGovern, Jacqueline Ekstrum, Lois Quam, and Karen Margolis. "Preventive Care for Women: Does the Sex of the Physician Matter?" *New England Journal of Medicine, 329,* August 12, 1993:478–482.

Manpower Report to the President. Washington, D.C.: U.S. Department of Labor, Manpower Administration, April 1971.

Mattioli, Dana. "Ways Women Can Hold Their Own in a Male World." *Wall Street Journal,* November 25, 2008.

Meltzer, Scott A. "Gender, Work, and Intimate Violence: Men's Occupational Spillover and Compensatory Violence." *Journal of Marriage and the Family, 64,* 2, November 2002:820–832.

Merwine, Maynard H. "How Africa Understands Female Circumcision." *New York Times,* November 24, 1993.

Miller, Laura L. "Women in the Military." In *Down to Earth Sociology: Introductory Readings,* 14th ed., James M. Henslin, ed. New York: Free Press, 2007. Originally published 1997.

Mills, Karen M., and Thomas J. Palumbo. *A Statistical Portrait of Women in the United States: 1978.* U.S. Census Bureau, *Current Population Reports,* Series P-23, Number 100, 1980.

Money, John, and Anke A. Ehrhardt. *Man and Woman, Boy and Girl.* Baltimore: Johns Hopkins University Press, 1972.

Murdock, George Peter. "Comparative Data on the Division of Labor by Sex." *Social Forces, 15,* 4, May 1937:551–553.

National Women's Political Caucus. "Factsheet on Women's Political Progress." Washington, D.C., June 1998.

National Women's Political Caucus. "Women in Congress," 2011.

Offen, Karen. "Feminism and Sexual Difference in Historical Perspective." In *Theoretical Perspectives on Sexual Difference,* Deborah L. Rhode, ed. New Haven, Conn.: Yale University Press, 1990:13–20.

Pflanz, Mike. "Rwanda's Women Lead the Miraculous Recovery." *Telegraph,* October 17, 2008.

Reiser, Christa. *Reflections on Anger: Women and Men in a Changing Society.* Westport, Conn.: Praeger Publishers, 1999.

Rosaldo, Michelle Zimbalist. "Women, Culture and Society: A Theoretical Overview." In *Women, Culture, and Society,* Michelle Zimbalist Rosaldo and Louise Lamphere, eds. Stanford: Stanford University Press, 1974.

Rossi, Alice S. "A Biosocial Perspective on Parenting." *Daedalus, 106,* 1977:1–31.

Rossi, Alice S. "Gender and Parenthood." *American Sociological Review, 49,* 1984:1–18.

Roth, Louise Marie. "Selling Women Short: A Research Note on Gender Differences in Compensation on Wall Street." *Social Forces, 82,* 2, December 2003:783–802.

Rothman, Barbara Katz. "Midwives in Transition: The Structure of a Clinical Revolution." In *Dominant Issues in Medical Sociology,* 3rd ed., Howard D. Schwartz, ed. New York: McGraw-Hill, 1994:104–112.

Scully, Diana. "Negotiating to Do Surgery." In *Dominant Issues in Medical Sociology,* 3rd ed., Howard D. Schwartz, ed. New York: McGraw-Hill, 1994:146–152.

Semple, Kirk. "Idea of Afghan Women's Rights Starts Taking Hold." *New York Times,* March 2, 2009.

Settles, Isis H., Zaje A. T. Harrell, NiCole T. Buchanan, and Stevie C. Y. Yap. "Frightened or Bothered: Two Types of Sexual Harassment Appraisals." *Social Psychological and Personality Science,* March 29, 2011.

Slackman, Michael. "Voices Rise in Egypt to Shield Girls from an Old Tradition." *New York Times,* September 20, 2007.

Spivak, Gayatri Chakravorty. "Feminism 2000: One Step Beyond." *Feminist Review, 64,* Spring 2000:113.

Statistical Abstract of the United States. Washington, D.C.: U.S. Census Bureau, published annually.

Stockard, Jean, and Miriam M. Johnson. *Sex Roles: Sex Inequality and Sex Role Development.* Englewood Cliffs, N.J.: Prentice Hall, 1980.

Stouffer, Samuel A., Arthur A. Lumsdaine, Marion Harper Lumsdaine, Robin M. Williams, Jr., M. Brewster Smith, Irving L. Janis, Shirley A. Star, and Leonard S. Cottrell, Jr. *The American Soldier: Combat and Its Aftermath,* Vol. 2. New York: Wiley, 1949.

Tuhus-Dubrow, Rebecca. "Rites and Wrongs." *Boston Globe,* February 11, 2007.

Udry, J. Richard. "Biological Limits of Gender Construction." *American Sociological Review, 65,* June 2000:443–457.

UNESCO. "Gender Parity in Education: Not There Yet." March 2008.

UNIFEM. *Progress of the World's Women 2008/2009.* United Nations Development Fund for Women, 2008.

U.S. Department of Education, National Center for Education Statistics. "Projections of Education Statistics to 2017," September 2008:Table 10.

VanderMey, Anne. "Fortune 500 Women CEOs." *CNN Money,* May 5, 2011.

Walker, Alice, and Pratibha Parmar. *Warrior Marks: Female Genital Mutilation and the Sexual Blinding of Women.* New York: Harcourt Brace, 1993.

Wayne, Julie Holliday, Christine M. Riordan, and Kecia M. Thomas. "Is All Sexual Harassment Viewed the Same? Mock Juror Decisions in Same-and Cross-Gender Cases." *Journal of Applied Psychology, 86,* 2, April 2001:179–187.

Whiteman, Maura K., Susan D. Hillis, Denise J. Jamieson, Brian Morrow, Michelle N. Podgornik, Kate M. Brett, and Polly A. Marchbanks. "Inpatient Hysterectomy Surveillance in the United States, 2000–2004." *American Journal of Obstetrics and Gynecology,* January 2008:34e1–34e7.

"Women in National Parliaments." July 31, 2010.

Women's Bureau of the United States, Department of Labor. *Handbook on Women Workers.* Washington, D.C.: U.S. Government Printing Office, 1969.

World Health Organization. *Eliminating Female Genital Mutilation: An Interagency Statement.* United Nations, 2008.

Yakaboski, Tamara, and Leah Reinert. "Review of Women in Academic Leadership: Professional Strategies, Personal Choices." *Women in Higher Education, 4,* 1, 2011.

Yardley, Jim. "In India, Caste, Honor, and Killings Intertwine." *New York Times,* July 9, 2010a.

Zoepf, Katherine. "A Dishonorable Affair." *New York Times,* September 23, 2007.

Race and Ethnicity

From Chapter 9 of *Sociology: A Down-to-Earth Approach, Core Concepts*, Fifth Edition. James M. Henslin.

Race and Ethnicity

Imagine that you are an African American man living in Macon County, Alabama, during the Great Depression of the 1930s. Your home is a little country shack with a dirt floor. You have no electricity or running water. You never finished grade school, and you make a living, such as it is, by doing odd jobs. You haven't been feeling too good lately, but you can't afford a doctor.

Then you hear incredible news. You rub your eyes in disbelief. It is just like winning the lottery! If you join *Miss Rivers' Lodge* (and it is free to join), you will get free physical examinations at Tuskegee University *for life*. You will even get free rides to and from the clinic, hot meals on examination days, and a lifetime of free treatment for minor ailments.

You eagerly join *Miss Rivers' Lodge.*

After your first physical examination, the doctor gives you the bad news. "You've got bad blood," he says. "That's why you've been feeling bad. Miss Rivers will give you some medicine and schedule you for your next exam. I've got to warn you, though. If you go to another doctor, there's no more free exams or medicine."

You can't afford another doctor anyway. You are thankful for your treatment, take your medicine, and look forward to the next trip to the university.

> **"You have just become part of one of the most callous experiments of all time."**

What has really happened? You have just become part of what is surely slated to go down in history as one of the most callous experiments of all time, outside of the infamous World War II Nazi and Japanese experiments. With heartless disregard for human life, the U.S. Public Health Service told 399 African American men that they had joined a social club and burial society called *Miss Rivers' Lodge.* What the men were *not* told was that they had syphilis, that there was no real Miss Rivers' Lodge, that the doctors were just using this term so they could study what happened when syphilis went untreated. For forty years, the "Public Health Service" allowed these men to go without treatment for their syphilis—and kept testing them each year—to study the progress of the disease. The "public health" officials even had a control group of 201 men who were free of the disease (Jones 1993).

By the way, the men did receive a benefit from "Miss Rivers' Lodge," a free autopsy to determine the ravages of syphilis on their bodies.

New Mexico

Laying the Sociological Foundation

As unlikely as it seems, this is a true story. It really did happen. Seldom do race and ethnic relations degenerate to this point, but reports of troubled race relations surprise none of us. Today's newspapers and TV news shows regularly report on racial problems. Sociology can contribute greatly to our understanding of this aspect of social life—and this chapter may be an eye-opener for you. To begin, let's consider to what extent race itself is a myth.

Race: Myth and Reality

race a group whose inherited physical characteristics distinguish it from other groups

The Reality of Human Variety. With its population closing in on 7 billion, the world offers a fascinating variety of human shapes and colors. Skin colors come in all shades between black and white, heightened by reddish and yellowish hues. Eyes come in shades of blue, brown, and green. Lips are thick and thin. Hair is straight, curly, kinky, black, blonde, and red—and, of course, all shades of brown.

As humans spread throughout the world, their adaptations to diverse climates and other living conditions resulted in this profusion of colors, hair textures, and other physical variations. Genetic mutations added distinct characteristics to the peoples of the globe. In this sense, the concept of **race**—a group of people with inherited physical characteristics that distinguish it from another group—is a reality. Humans do, indeed, come in a variety of colors and shapes.

The Myth of Pure Races. Humans show such a mixture of physical characteristics that there are no "pure" races. Instead of falling into distinct types that are clearly separate from one another, human characteristics—skin color, hair texture, nose shape, head shape, eye color, and so on—flow endlessly together. The mapping of the human genome system shows that the so-called racial groups differ from one another only once in a thousand subunits of the genome (Angler 2000; Frank 2007). As you can see from the example of Tiger Woods, discussed in the Cultural Diversity box on the next page, these minute gradations make any attempt to draw lines of pure race purely arbitrary.

Humans show remarkable diversity. Shown here is just one example—He Pingping, from China, who at 2 feet 4 inches, is the world's shortest man, and Svetlana Pankratova, from Russia, who, according to the *Guinness Book of World Records,* is the woman with the longest legs. Race–ethnicity shows similar diversity.

PA Photos/Landov

The Myth of a Fixed Number of Races. Although large groupings of people can be classified by blood type and gene frequencies, even these classifications do not uncover "race." Rather, the term is so arbitrary that biologists and anthropologists cannot even agree on how many "races" there are (Smedley and Smedley 2005). Ashley Montagu (1964, 1999), a physical anthropologist, pointed out that some scientists have classified humans into only two "races," while others have found as many as two thousand. Montagu (1960) himself classified humans into forty "racial" groups. As the Down-to-Earth Sociology illustrates, even a plane ride can change someone's race.

The Myth of Racial Superiority. Regardless of what anthropologists, biologists, and sociologists say, however, people do divide one another into races, and we are stuck with this term. People also tend to see some races (mostly their own) as superior and others as inferior. As with language, however, no race is better than another. All races have their geniuses—and their idiots. Yet the myth of racial superiority abounds, a myth that is particularly dangerous. Adolf Hitler, for example, believed that the Aryans were a superior race, destined to establish an advanced culture and a new world order. This destiny required them to avoid the "racial contamination" that would come from breeding with inferior races. The Aryans, then, had the "cultural duty" to isolate or destroy races that threatened their racial purity and culture.

Put into practice, Hitler's views left an appalling legacy—the Nazi slaughter of those they deemed inferior: Jews, Slavs, gypsies, homosexuals, and people with mental and physical disabilities. Horrific images of gas ovens and emaciated bodies stacked like cordwood have haunted the world's nations. At Nuremberg, the Allies, flush with victory, put the top Nazis on trial, exposing their heinous deeds to a shocked world. Their public executions, everyone assumed, marked the end of such grisly acts.

Why is "race" a myth? What are the dangers of the myth of racial superiority?

Cultural Diversity in the United States

Tiger Woods: Mapping the Changing Ethnic Terrain

Tiger Woods, perhaps the top golfer of all time, calls himself *Cablinasian*. Woods invented this term as a boy to try to explain to himself just who he was—a combination of Caucasian, Black, Indian, and Asian (Leland and Beals 1997; Hall 2001). Woods wanted to embrace all sides of his family.

Like many of us, Tiger Woods' heritage is difficult to specify. Analysts who like to quantify ethnic heritage put Woods at one-quarter Thai, one-quarter Chinese, one-quarter white, an eighth Native American, and an eighth African American. From this chapter, you know how ridiculous such computations are, but the sociological question is why many people consider Tiger Woods an African American. The U.S. racial scene is indeed complex, but a good part of the reason is that Woods has dark skin and this is the label the media placed on him. "Everyone has to fit somewhere" seems to be our attitude. If they don't, we grow uncomfortable. And for Tiger Woods, the media chose African American.

The United States once had a firm "color line"—barriers between racial–ethnic groups that you didn't dare cross, especially in dating or marriage. This invisible barrier has broken down, and today such marriages are common (*Statistical Abstract* 2011:Table 60). Several college campuses have interracial student organizations. Harvard has two, one just for students who have one African American parent (Leland and Beals 1997).

As we enter unfamiliar ethnic terrain, our classifications are bursting at the seams. Consider how Kwame Anthony Appiah, of Harvard's Philosophy and Afro-American Studies Departments, described his situation:

> "My mother is English; my father is Ghanaian. My sisters are married to a Nigerian and a Norwegian. I have nephews who range from blond-haired kids to very black kids. They are all first cousins. Now according to the American scheme of things, they're all black—even the guy with blond hair who skis in Oslo." (Wright 1994)

I marvel at what racial experts the U.S. census takers once were. When they took the census, which is done every ten years, they looked at people and assigned them a race. At various points, the census contained these categories: mulatto, quadroon, octoroon, Negro, black, Mexican, white, Indian, Filipino, Japanese, Chinese, and Hindu. Quadroon (one-fourth black and three-fourths white) and octoroon (one-eighth black and seven-eighths white) proved too difficult to "measure," and these categories were used only in 1890. Mulatto appeared in

Tiger Woods as he answers questions at a news conference.
TORU HANAI/Reuters /Landov

the 1850 census, but disappeared in 1930. The Mexican government complained about Mexicans being treated as a race, and this category was used only in 1930. I don't know whose idea it was to make Hindu a race, but it lasted for three censuses, from 1920 to 1940 (Bean et al. 2004; Tafoya et al. 2005).

Continuing to reflect changing ideas about race–ethnicity, censuses have become flexible, and we now have many choices. In the 2010 census, we were first asked to declare whether we were or were not "Spanish/ Hispanic/Latino." After this, we were asked to check "one or more races" that we "consider ourselves to be." We could choose from White; Black, African American, or Negro; American Indian or Alaska Native; Asian Indian, Chinese, Filipino, Japanese, Korean, Vietnamese, Native Hawaiian, Guamanian or Chamorro, and Samoan. There were boxes for Other Asian and Other Pacific Islander, with examples that listed Hmong, Pakistani, and Fijian as races. If these didn't do it, we could check a box called "Some Other Race" and then write whatever we wanted.

Perhaps the census should list Cablinasian, after all. We could also have ANGEL for African-Norwegian-German-English-Latino Americans, DEVIL for those of Danish-English-Vietnamese-Italian-Lebanese descent, and STUDENT for Swedish-Turkish-Uruguayan-Danish-English-Norwegian-Tibetan Americans. As you read farther in this chapter, you will see why these terms make as much sense as the categories we currently use.

For Your Consideration

→ Just why do we count people by "race" anyway? Why not eliminate race from the U.S. census? (Race became a factor in 1790 during the first census. To determine the number of representatives from each state, slaves were counted as three-fifths of whites!) Why is race so important to some people? Perhaps you can use the materials in this chapter to answer these questions.

Based on this box, what is race?

The reason I selected these photos is to illustrate how seriously we must take all preaching of hatred and of racial supremacy, even though it seems to come from harmless or even humorous sources. The strange-looking person with his hands on his hips, who is wearing *lederhosen*, traditional clothing of Bavaria, Germany, is Adolf Hitler. He caused this horrific scene at the Landsberg concentration camp, which, as shown here, the U.S. military forced German civilians to view.

© Time Life Pictures/Getty Images

AP Images

Obviously, they didn't. In the summer of 1994 in Rwanda, Hutus slaughtered about 800,000 Tutsis—mostly with machetes (Gettleman and Kron 2010). In the same decade, Serbs in Bosnia massacred Muslims, giving us a new term, *ethnic cleansing*. As these events sadly attest, **genocide,** the attempt to destroy a group of people because of their presumed race or ethnicity, remains alive and well. Although more recent killings are not accompanied by swastikas and gas ovens, the perpetrators' goal is the same.

The Myth Continues. The *idea* of race, of course, is far from a myth. Firmly embedded in our culture, it is a powerful force in our everyday lives. That no race is superior and that even biologists cannot decide how people should be classified into races is not what counts. "I know what I see, and you can't tell me any different" seems to be the common attitude. Sociologists W. I. and D. S. Thomas (1928) observed, "If people define situations as real, they are real in their consequences." In other words, people act on perceptions and beliefs, not facts. As a result, we will always have people like Hitler and, as illustrated in our opening vignette, officials like those in the U.S. Public Health Service who thought that it was fine to experiment with people whom they deemed inferior. While few people hold such extreme views, most people appear to be ethnocentric enough to believe that their own race is—at least just a little—superior to others.

Ethnic Groups

In contrast to *race*, which people use to refer to supposed biological characteristics that distinguish one group of people from another, **ethnicity** and **ethnic** refer to cultural characteristics. Derived from the word *ethnos* (a Greek word meaning "people" or "nation"), *ethnicity* and *ethnic* refer to people who identify with one another on the basis of common ancestry and cultural heritage. Their sense of belonging may center on their nation or region of origin, distinctive foods, clothing, language, music, religion, or family names and relationships.

People often confuse the terms *race* and *ethnic group*. For example, many people, including many Jews, consider Jews a race. Jews, however, are more properly considered an ethnic group, for it is their cultural characteristics, especially their religion, that bind them together. Wherever Jews have lived in the world, they have intermarried. Consequently, Jews in China may have Chinese features, while some Swedish Jews are blue-eyed blonds. The confusion of race and ethnicity is illustrated in the photo a few pages ahead.

genocide the systematic annihilation or attempted annihilation of a people because of their presumed race or ethnicity

ethnicity (and ethnic) having distinctive cultural characteristics

What is the difference between ethnicity and race?

Can a Plane Ride Change Your Race?

Common sense and sociology often differ. This is especially so when it comes to race. According to common sense, our racial classifications represent biological differences between people. Sociologists, in contrast, stress that what we call races are *social* classifications, not biological categories.

Sociologists point out that *our "race" depends more on the society in which we live than on our biological characteristics.* For example, the racial categories common in the United States are only one of *numerous* ways by which people around the world classify physical appearances. Although various groups use different categories, each group assumes that its categories are natural, merely a response to visible biology.

To better understand this essential sociological point—that race is more social than it is biological—consider this: In the United States, children born to the same parents are all of the same race. "What could be more natural?" Americans assume. But in Brazil, children born to the same parents may be of different races—if their appearances differ. "What could be more natural?" assume Brazilians.

Consider how Americans usually classify a child born to a "black" mother and a "white" father. Why do they usually say that the child is "black"? Wouldn't it be equally as logical to classify the child as "white"? Similarly, if a child has one grandmother who is "black," but all her other ancestors are "white," the child is often considered "black." Yet she has much more "white blood" than "black blood." Why, then, is she considered "black"? Certainly not because of biology.

What "race" are these two Brazilians? Is the child's "race" different from her mother's "race"? The text explains why "race" is such an unreliable concept that it changes even with geography.
© Celia Mannings/Alamy

Such thinking is a legacy of slavery. In an attempt to preserve the "purity" of their "race" in the face of the many children whose fathers were white slave masters and whose mothers were black slaves, whites classified anyone with even a "drop of black blood" as black. They actually called this the "one-drop" rule.

Even a plane trip can change a person's race. In the city of Salvador in Brazil, people classify one another by color of skin and eyes, breadth of nose and lips, and color and curliness of hair. They use at least seven terms for what we call white and black. Consider again a U.S. child who has "white" and "black" parents. If she flies to Brazil, she is no longer "black"; she now belongs to one of their several "whiter" categories (Fish 1995).

If the girl makes such a flight, would her "race" actually change? Our common sense revolts at this, I know, but it actually would. We want to argue that because her biological characteristics remain unchanged, her race remains unchanged. This is because we think of race as biological, when *race is actually a label we use to describe perceived biological characteristics.* Simply put, the race we "are" depends on our social location—on who is doing the classifying.

"Racial" classifications are also fluid, not fixed. Even now, you can see change occurring in U.S. classifications. The category "multiracial," for example, indicates changing thought and perception.

For Your Consideration

→ How would you explain to "Joe and Suzie Six-Pack" that race is more a social classification than a biological one? Can you come up with any arguments to refute this statement? How do you think our racial–ethnic categories will change in the future?

Minority Groups and Dominant Groups

Sociologist Louis Wirth (1945) defined a **minority group** as people who are singled out for unequal treatment and who regard themselves as objects of collective discrimination. Worldwide, minorities share several conditions: Their physical or cultural traits are held in low esteem by the dominant group, which treats them unfairly, and they tend to marry within their own group (Wagley and Harris 1958). These conditions tend to create a sense of identity among minorities (a feeling of "we-ness"). In some instances, even a sense of common destiny emerges (Chandra 1993b).

Surprisingly, a minority group is not necessarily a *numerical* minority. For example, before India's independence in 1947, a handful of British colonial rulers dominated tens of millions of Indians. Similarly, when South Africa practiced apartheid, a smaller group of Afrikaners, primarily Dutch, discriminated against a much larger number of blacks. And all over the world, females are a

◉ Watch
Multiracial Identity
on **mysoclab.com**

minority group people who are singled out for unequal treatment and who regard themselves as objects of collective discrimination

How is it possible that a plane ride could change someone's race?

minority group. Accordingly, sociologists refer to those who do the discriminating not as the *majority,* but, rather, as the **dominant group,** for regardless of their numbers, this is the group that has the greater power and privilege.

Possessing political power and unified by shared physical and cultural traits, the dominant group uses its position to discriminate against those with different—and supposedly inferior—traits. The dominant group considers its privileged position to be the result of its own innate superiority.

Emergence of Minority Groups.   A group becomes a minority in one of two ways. The *first* is through the expansion of political boundaries. With the exception of females, tribal societies contain no minority groups. Everyone shares the same culture, including the same language, and belongs to the same group. When a group expands its political boundaries, however, it produces minority groups if it incorporates people with different customs, languages, values, or physical characteristics into the same political entity and discriminates against them. For example, in 1848, after defeating Mexico in war, the United States took over the Southwest. The Mexicans living there, who had been the dominant group prior to the war, were transformed into a minority group, a master status that has influenced their lives ever since. Referring to his ancestors, one Latino said, "We didn't move across the border—the border moved across us."

A *second* way in which a group becomes a minority is by migration. This can be voluntary, as with the millions of people who have chosen to move from Mexico to the United States, or involuntary, as with the millions of Africans who were brought in chains to the United States. (The way females became a minority group represents a third way, but, as discussed in the previous chapter, no one knows just how this occurred.)

How People Construct Their Racial–Ethnic Identity

Some of us have a greater sense of ethnicity than others, and we feel firm boundaries between "us" and "them." Others of us have assimilated so extensively into the mainstream culture that we are only vaguely aware of our ethnic origins. With interethnic marriage common, some do not even know the countries from which their families originated—nor do they care. If asked to identify themselves ethnically, they respond with something like "I'm Heinz 57—German and Irish, with a little Italian and French thrown in—and I think someone said something about being one-sixteenth Indian, too."

Why do some people feel an intense sense of ethnic identity, while others feel hardly any? Figure 1 portrays four factors, identified by sociologist Ashley Doane, that heighten or reduce our sense of ethnic identity. From this figure, you can see that the keys are relative size, power, appearance, and discrimination. If your group is relatively small, has little power, looks different from most people in society, and is an object of discrimination, you will have a heightened sense of ethnic identity. In contrast, if you belong to the dominant group that holds most of the power, look like most people in the society, and feel no discrimination, you are likely to experience a sense of "belonging"—and to wonder why ethnic identity is such a big deal.

We can use the term **ethnic work** to refer to the way people construct their ethnicity. For people who have a strong ethnic identity, this term refers to how they enhance and maintain their group's distinctions—from clothing, food, and language to religious practices and holidays. For people whose ethnic identity is not as firm, it refers to attempts to recover their ethnic heritage, such as trying to trace family lines or visiting the country or region of their family's origin. As illustrated by the photo essay a few pages ahead, many

dominant group the group with the most power, greatest privileges, and highest social status

ethnic work activities designed to discover, enhance, maintain, or transmit an ethnic or racial identity

This photo, taken in Ashkelon, Israel, illustrates the difficulty that assumptions about *race* and *ethnicity* posed for Israel. The Ethiopian Jews look so different from other Jews that it took several years for Israeli authorities to acknowledge their "true Jewishness" and allow them to immigrate.

Rafael Ben-Ari/Chameleons Eye via Newscom

What are minority and dominant groups? What is ethnic work?

Americans are engaged in ethnic work. This has confounded the experts, who thought that the United States would be a *melting pot,* with most of its groups blending into a sort of ethnic stew. Because so many Americans have become fascinated with their "roots," some analysts have suggested that "tossed salad" is a more appropriate term than "melting pot."

Prejudice and Discrimination

Because of their significance in social life, let's consider the origins and extent of prejudice and discrimination.

Learning Prejudice

Distinguishing Between Prejudice and Discrimination. Prejudice and discrimination are common throughout the world. In Mexico, Mexicans of Hispanic descent discriminate against Mexicans of Native American descent; in Israel, Ashkenazi Jews, primarily of European descent, discriminate against Sephardic Jews, from the Middle East; in China, the Han and the Uighurs discriminate against each other. In some places, the elderly discriminate against the young; in others, the young discriminate against the elderly. And all around the world, men discriminate against women.

Discrimination is an *action*—unfair treatment directed against someone. Discrimination can be based on many characteristics: age, sex, height, weight, skin color, clothing, speech, income, education, marital status, sexual orientation, disease, disability, religion, and politics. When the basis of discrimination is someone's perception of race, it is known as **racism.** Discrimination is often the result of an *attitude* called **prejudice**—a prejudging of some sort, usually in a negative way. There is also *positive prejudice,* which exaggerates the virtues of a group, as when people think that some group is superior to others. Most prejudice, however, is negative and involves prejudging a group as inferior.

Learning from Associating with Others. As with our other attitudes, we are not born with prejudice. Rather, we learn prejudice from the people around us. You probably know this, but here is a twist that sociologists have found. Michael Kimmel (2007), who interviewed neo-Nazi skinheads in Sweden, found that young men were

Figure 1   A Sense of Ethnicity

A Heightened Sense

A Low Sense

Part of the majority	Smaller numbers
Greater power	Lesser power
Similar to the "national identity"	Different from the "national identity"
No discrimination	Discrimination

Source: By the author. Based on Doane 1997.

discrimination an act of unfair treatment directed against an individual or a group

racism prejudice and discrimination on the basis of race

prejudice an attitude or prejudging, usually in a negative way

AP Photo/Bill Hudson

This photo, taken in Birmingham, Alabama, provides a glimpse into the intensity and bravery of the civil rights demonstrators of the 1960s.

How does prejudice differ from discrimination? What is the origin of prejudice?

289

Ethnic Work

Explorations in Cultural Identity

Ethnic work refers to the ways that people establish, maintain, and transmit their ethnic identity. As shown here, among the techniques people use to forge ties with their roots are dress, dance, and music.

Many African Americans are trying to get in closer contact with their roots. To do this, some use musical performances, as with this group in Philadelphia, Pennsylvania.

© E.A. Kennedy/The Image Works

Wearing traditional clothing and participating in a parade help to maintain the ethnic identity of these Americans who trace their origin to the Philippines.

©Lee Snider/The Image Works

RICK WILKING/Reuters/Landov

Many European Americans are also involved in ethnic work, attempting to maintain an identity more precise than "from Europe." These women of Czech ancestry are performing for a Czech community in a small town in Nebraska.

AP Photo/Lincoln Journal Star, Ken Blackbird

Many Native Americans have maintained continuous identity with their tribal roots. You can see the blending of cultures in this photo taken at the March Pow Wow in Denver, Colorado.

The Cinco de Mayo celebration is used to recall roots and renew ethnic identities. This one was held in Los Angeles, California.

© ROBERT GALBRAITH/Reuters/Corbis

attracted mostly by the group's tough masculinity, not its hatred of immigrants. Similarly, Kathleen Blee (2005), in conversations with female members of the KKK and Aryan Nations in the United States, discovered that they were attracted to the hate group because someone they liked belonged to it. They learned to be racists *after* they joined the group. In both the Blee and Kimmel studies, the members' racism was not the *cause* of their joining but, rather, joining was the cause of their racism.

Just as our associations can increase prejudice, so they can reduce prejudice, the topic of our Down-to-Earth Sociology box

The Far-Reaching Nature of Prejudice. It is amazing how much prejudice people can learn. In a classic article, psychologist Eugene Hartley (1946) asked people how they felt about several racial–ethnic groups. Besides Negroes, Jews, and so on, he included the Wallonians, Pireneans, and Danireans—names he had made up. Most people who expressed dislike for Jews and Negroes showed similar contempt for these three fictitious groups.

Hartley's study shows that prejudice does not depend on negative experiences with others. It also reveals that people who are prejudiced against one racial or ethnic group also tend to be prejudiced against other groups. People can be, and are, prejudiced against people they have never met—and even against groups that do not exist!

The neo-Nazis and the Ku Klux Klan base their existence on prejudice. These groups believe that race is real, that white is best, and that beneath society's surface is a murky river of mingling conspiracies (Ezekiel 1995). What would happen if a Jew attended their meetings? Would he or she survive? In the Down-to-Earth Sociology box, sociologist Raphael Ezekiel reveals some of the insights he gained during his remarkable study of these groups.

Internalizing Dominant Norms. People can even learn to be prejudiced against their own group. A national survey found that African Americans think that lighter-skinned African American women are more attractive than those with darker skin (Hill 2002). Participant observation in the ghetto also reveals a preference for lighter skin (Jones 2010). Sociologists call this *the internalization of the norms of the dominant group.*

To study the internalization of dominant norms, psychologists Mahzarin Banaji and Anthony Greenwald created the *Implicit Association Test.* In one version of this test, good and bad words are flashed on a screen along with photos of African Americans and whites. Most subjects are quicker to associate positive words (such as "love," "peace," and "baby") with whites and negative words (such as "cancer," "bomb," and "devil") with blacks. Here's the clincher: This is true for *both* whites and blacks (Dasgupta et al. 2000; Greenwald and Krieger 2006). Apparently, we all learn the *ethnic maps* of our culture and, along with them, their route to biased perception.

Individual and Institutional Discrimination

Sociologists stress that we should move beyond thinking in terms of **individual discrimination,** the negative treatment of one person by another. Although such behavior creates problems, it is primarily an issue between individuals. With their focus on the broader picture, sociologists encourage us to examine **institutional discrimination,** that is, to see how discrimination is woven into the fabric of society. Let's look at two examples.

Home Mortgages. Bank lending provides an excellent illustration of institutional discrimination. Earlier studies using national samples showed that bankers were more likely to reject the loan applications of minorities. When bankers defended themselves by saying that whites had better credit history, researchers retested their data. They found that even when applicants had identical credit, African Americans and Latinos were *60 percent* more likely to be rejected (Thomas 1991, 1992).

The subprime debacle that threw the stock market into a tailspin brought new revelations. Look at Figure 2. You can see that *minorities are still more likely to be turned down for a loan—whether their incomes are below or above the median income of their community.* Beyond this hard finding lies another just as devastating. In

individual discrimination person-to-person or face-to-face discrimination; the negative treatment of people by other individuals

institutional discrimination negative treatment of a minority group that is built into a society's institutions; also called *systemic discrimination*

What does "internalizing dominant norms" mean?

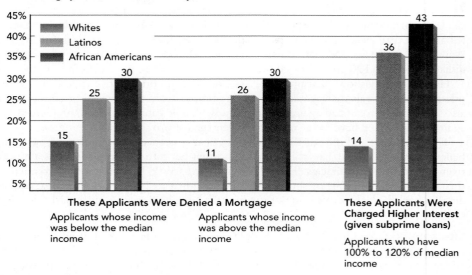

Figure 2   **Buying a House: Institutional Discrimination and Predatory Lending**

This figure, based on a national sample, illustrates *institutional discrimination*. Rejecting the loan applications of minorities and gouging them with higher interest rates are a nationwide practice, not the acts of a rogue banker here or there. Because the discrimination is part of the banking system, it is also called *systemic discrimination*.

These Applicants Were Denied a Mortgage

Applicants whose income was below the median income

Applicants whose income was above the median income

These Applicants Were Charged Higher Interest (given subprime loans)

Applicants who have 100% to 120% of median income

Source: By the author. Based on Kochbar and Gonzalez-Barrera 2009.

the credit crisis that caused so many to lose their homes, African Americans and Latinos were hit harder than whites. The last set of bars on Figure 2 shows a major reason for this: *Banks purposely targeted minorities to charge higher interest rates*. Over the lifetime of a loan, these higher monthly payments can come to an extra $100,000 to $200,000 (Powell and Roberts 2009).

Health Care. Losing your home is devastating. Losing your mother or baby is even worse. Look at Table 1. You can see that institutional discrimination can be a life-and-death matter. In childbirth, African American mothers are *three* times as likely to die as white mothers, while their babies are more than *twice* as likely to die during their first year of life. This is not a matter of biology, as though African American mothers and children are more fragile. It is a matter of *social* conditions, primarily nutrition and medical care.

It is important to understand that discrimination does not have to be deliberate. In some cases, no one is aware of it—neither those being discriminated against nor those doing the discriminating. Consider knee replacements and coronary bypass surgery. White patients

TABLE 1   **Race–Ethnicity and Mother/Child Deaths**

	Infant Deaths	Maternal Deaths
White Americans	5.6	9.5
African Americans	13.3	32.7

Note: The national database used for this table does not list these totals for other racial–ethnic groups. *White* refers to non-Hispanic whites. *Infant deaths* refers to the number of deaths per year of infants under 1 year old per 1,000 live births. *Maternal deaths* refers to the number of deaths per 100,000 women who give birth in a year.

Source: *Statistical Abstract of the United States* 2011:Table 113.

What is contact theory? Can you summarize insititutional discrimination in mortgages and health care?

Down-to-Earth Sociology

Living in the Dorm: Contact Theory

As you know from your friendships, friends influence one another as they talk about their experiences and share their ideas. Those experiences and ideas rub off on one another, influencing their views of the world.

It is no different for friends who are from different racial–ethnic groups. As they interact with one another, their understandings change and their perspectives broaden. Over time, if they cannot see the world through each other's eyes, they at least get a glimpse of what that world looks like.

If one of the goals of college is to increase students' understanding of the world and change their attitudes while helping to integrate racial–ethnic groups—and this is a big if—then why do some colleges have separate dorms for African American students, Jewish students, and so on? And when there aren't separate dorms, why do some colleges assign roommates so blacks will room with blacks and whites with whites?

The goal of such room assignments, of course, is to make minority students feel comfortable and help prevent them from feeling lost in a sea of white faces and suffering from *anomie*, feelings of not belonging.

These good intentions have an unanticipated result. As African American students interact in these "little corners" of the campus, their interracial friendships decrease. At the end of their freshman year in college, African American students have about 10 percent fewer interracial friends than when they began college. They are the only group to experience a decline in cross racial–ethnic friendships.

What happens if colleges assign students of different racial–ethnic groups to the same dorm rooms? These students end up with more interracial friendships than those who have roommates of their own race–ethnicity.

On the negative side, these mixed pairing arrangements are more likely to fail. About 17 percent end during the school year, compared to 10 percent of white–white pairings and 9 percent of black–black pairings. The dissatisfactions cut both ways, with blacks and whites requesting transfers at about the same rate.

But note that the vast majority of these interracial pairings last. They don't always blossom into friendships, of course, and like other roommate assignments, some roommates can barely tolerate one another. But contacts and cross-racial friendships do increase in most cases, changing understandings and perspectives. We need in-depth research to uncover who is changed in what ways.

To summarize the sociological research—mutual understandings increase, prejudice decreases, and relations improve when individuals of different racial–ethnic groups interact frequently and work toward mutual goals with equal status. The shorthand for these findings is *contact theory*.

Source: Based on Riley 2009.

Raphael Ezekiel

Contact theory indicates that prejudice decreases and relations improve when individuals of different racial–ethnic backgrounds who are of equal status interact frequently.

For Your Consideration

→ Do you think colleges should eliminate racially and ethnically themed dormitories? What is your opinion about colleges assigning students of different racial–ethnic groups to the same dorm rooms?

---

are more likely than either Latino or African American patients to receive these procedures (Skinner et al. 2003; Popescu 2007). Treatment after a heart attack follows a similar pattern: Whites are more likely than blacks to be given cardiac catheterization, a test to detect blockage of blood vessels. This study of 40,000 patients holds a surprise: Both black and white doctors are more likely to give this preventive care to whites (Stolberg 2001).

Researchers do not know why race–ethnicity is a factor in medical decisions. With both white and black doctors involved, we can be certain that physicians do not intend to discriminate. Apparently, the implicit bias that comes with the internalization of dominant norms becomes a subconscious motivation for giving or denying access to advanced medical procedures. Race seems to work like gender: Just as women's higher death rates in coronary bypass surgery can be traced to implicit attitudes about gender, so also race–ethnicity becomes a subconscious motivation for giving or denying access to advanced medical procedures.

Who do hate groups attract? What is their appeal?

Down-to-Earth Sociology

The Racist Mind

Sociologist Raphael Ezekiel wanted to get a close look at the racist mind. The best way to study racism from the inside is to do participant observation. But Ezekiel is a Jew. Could he study these groups by participant observation? To find out, Ezekiel told Ku Klux Klan and neo-Nazi leaders that he wanted to interview them and attend their meetings. He also told them that he was a Jew. Surprisingly, they agreed. Ezekiel published his path-breaking research in a book, *The Racist Mind* (1995). Here are some of the insights he gained during his fascinating sociological adventure:

> [The leader] builds on mass anxiety about economic insecurity and on popular tendencies to see an Establishment as the cause of economic threat; he hopes to teach people to identify that Establishment as the puppets of a conspiracy of Jews. [He has a] belief in exclusive categories. For the white racist leader, it is profoundly true . . . that the socially defined collections we call races represent fundamental categories. A man is black or a man is white; there are no in-betweens. Every human belongs to a racial category, and all the members of one category are radically different from all the members of other categories. Moreover, race represents the essence of the person. A truck is a truck, a car is a car, a cat is a cat, a dog is a dog, a black is a black, a white is a white. . . . These axioms have a rock-hard quality in the leaders' minds; the world is made up of racial groups. That is what exists for them.
>
> Two further beliefs play a major role in the minds of leaders. First, life is war. The world is made of distinct racial groups; life is about the war between these groups. Second, events have secret causes, are never what they seem superficially. . . . Any myth is plausible, as long as it involves intricate plotting. . . . It does not matter to him what others say. . . . He lives in his ideas and in the little world he has created where they are taken seriously. . . . Gold can be made from the tongues

Raphael Ezekiel

> of frogs; Yahweh's call can be heard in the flapping swastika banner. (pp. 66–67)

Who is attracted to the neo-Nazis and Ku Klux Klan? Here is what Ezekiel discovered:

> [There is a] ready pool of whites who will respond to the racist signal. . . . This population [is] always hungry for activity—or for the talk of activity—that promises dignity and meaning to lives that are working poorly in a highly competitive world. . . . Much as I don't want to believe it, [this] movement brings a sense of meaning— at least for a while—to some of the discontented. To struggle in a cause that transcends the individual lends meaning to life, no matter how ill-founded or narrowing the cause. For the young men in the neo-Nazi group . . . membership was an alternative to atomization and drift; within the group they worked for a cause and took direct risks in the company of comrades. . . .
>
> When interviewing the young neo-Nazis in Detroit, I often found myself driving with them past the closed factories, the idled plants of our shrinking manufacturing base. The fewer and fewer plants that remain can demand better educated and more highly skilled workers. These fatherless Nazi youths, these high-school dropouts, will find little place in the emerging economy . . . a permanently underemployed white underclass is taking its place alongside the permanent black underclass. The struggle over race merely diverts youth from confronting the real issues of their lives. Not many seats are left on the train, and the train is leaving the station. (pp. 32–33)

For Your Consideration

→ Use functionalism, conflict theory, and symbolic interaction to explain how the leaders and followers of these hate groups view the world. Use these same perspectives to explain why some people are attracted to the message of hate.

Theories of Prejudice

Social scientists have developed several theories to explain prejudice. Let's first look at psychological explanations, then at sociological ones.

Psychological Perspectives

Frustration and Scapegoats.

> *"Why are we having a depression? The Jews have taken over the banking system, and they want to suck every dollar out of us."*

How does implicit bias underlie unintentional discrimination?

This was a common sentiment in Germany in the 1930s during the depression that helped bring Hitler to power. People often unfairly blame their troubles on a **scapegoat**—often a racial–ethnic or religious minority. Why do they do this? Psychologist John Dollard (1939) suggested that prejudice is the result of frustration. People who are unable to strike out at the real source of their frustration (such as unemployment) look for someone to blame. This person or group becomes a target on which they vent their frustrations. Gender and age are also common targets of scapegoating.

Prejudice and frustration often are related. A team of psychologists led by Emory Cowen (1959) measured the prejudice of a group of students. They then gave the students two puzzles to solve, making sure the students did not have enough time to finish. After the students had worked furiously on the puzzles, the experimenters shook their heads in disgust and expressed disbelief that students couldn't complete such a simple task. They then retested the students. The results? Their scores on prejudice increased. The students had directed their frustrations outward, transferring them to people who had nothing to do with the contempt they had experienced.

The Authoritarian Personality.

"I don't like Swedes. They're too rigid. And I don't like the Italians. They're always talking with their hands. I don't like the Walloneans, either. They're always smiling at something. And I don't like librarians. And my job sucks. Hitler might have had his faults, but he put people to work during the Great Depression."

Have you ever wondered whether some people's personalities makes them more inclined to be prejudiced, and others more fair-minded? For psychologist Theodor Adorno, who had fled from the Nazis, this was no idle speculation. With the horrors he had observed still fresh in his mind, Adorno wondered whether there might be a certain type of person who is more likely to fall for the racist spewings of people like Hitler, Mussolini, and those in the Ku Klux Klan.

To find out, Adorno gave three tests to about two thousand people, ranging from college professors to prison inmates (Adorno et al. 1950). He measured their ethnocentrism, anti-Semitism (bias against Jews), and support for strong, authoritarian leaders. People who scored high on one test also scored high on the other two. For example, people who agreed with anti-Semitic statements also said that governments should be authoritarian and that foreign customs pose a threat to the "American" way.

Adorno concluded that highly prejudiced people have deep respect for authority and are submissive to authority figures. He termed this the **authoritarian personality.** These people believe that things are either right or wrong. Ambiguity disturbs them, especially in matters of religion or sex. They become anxious when they confront norms and values that are different from their own. To view people who differ from themselves as inferior assures them that their own positions are right.

Adorno's research stimulated more than a thousand research studies. In general, the researchers found that people who are older, less educated, less intelligent, and from a lower social class are more likely to be authoritarian. Critics say that this doesn't indicate a particular personality, just that the less educated are more prejudiced—which we already knew (Yinger 1965; Ray 1991). Nevertheless, researchers continue to study this concept (McFarland 2010).

Sociological Perspectives

Sociologists find psychological explanations inadequate. They stress that the key to understanding prejudice cannot be found by looking *inside* people, but, rather, by examining conditions *outside* them. For this reason, sociologists focus on how social environments influence prejudice. With this background, let's compare functionalist, conflict, and symbolic interactionist perspectives on prejudice.

Functionalism.

In a television documentary, journalist Bill Moyers interviewed Fritz Hippler, a Nazi who at age 29 was put in charge of the entire German film industry. When Hitler came to

scapegoat an individual or group unfairly blamed for someone else's troubles

authoritarian personality Theodor Adorno's term for people who are prejudiced and rank high on scales of conformity, intolerance, insecurity, respect for authority, and submissiveness to superiors

How can scapegoats, frustration, and prejudice be related? What is the theory of the authoritarian personality?

power, Hippler said, the Germans were no more anti-Semitic than the French. Hippler was told to increase anti-Semitism in Germany. Obediently, he produced movies that contained vivid scenes comparing Jews to rats—with their breeding threatening to infest the population.

Why was Hippler told to create hatred? Prejudice and discrimination were functional for the Nazis. Defeated in World War I and devastated by fines levied by the victors, Germany was on its knees. Runaway inflation was destroying its middle class. To help unite this fractured Germany, the Nazis created a scapegoat to blame for their troubles. In addition, the Jews owned businesses, bank accounts, fine art, and other property that the Nazis could confiscate. Jews also held key positions (as university professors, reporters, judges, and so on), which the Nazis could give as prizes to their followers. In the end, hatred also showed its dysfunctional face, as the Nazi officials hanged at Nuremberg discovered.

Prejudice becomes practically irresistible when state machinery is used to advance the cause of hatred. To produce prejudice, the Nazis harnessed government agencies, the schools, police, courts, and mass media. The results were devastating. Recall the identical twins featured in the Down-to-Earth Sociology box. Jack and Oskar had been separated as babies. Jack was brought up as a Jew in Trinidad, while Oskar was reared as a Catholic in Czechoslovakia. Under the Nazi regime, Oskar learned to hate Jews, unaware that he himself was a Jew.

That prejudice is functional and is shaped by the social environment was demonstrated by psychologists Muzafer and Carolyn Sherif (1953). In a boys' summer camp, the Sherifs assigned friends to different cabins and then had the cabin groups compete in sports. In just a few days, strong in-groups had formed. Even lifelong friends began to taunt one another, calling each other "crybaby" and "sissy."

The Sherif study teaches us several important lessons about social life. Note how it is possible to arrange the social environment to generate either positive or negative feelings about people, and how prejudice arises if we pit groups against one another in an "I win, you lose" situation. You can also see that prejudice is functional, how it creates in-group solidarity. And, of course, it is obvious how dysfunctional prejudice is, when you observe the way it destroys human relationships.

Conflict Theory.

"The Japanese have gone on strike? They're demanding a raise? And they even want a rest period? We'll show them who's boss. Hire those Koreans who've been trying to get work."

This did happen. When Japanese workers in Hawaii struck, owners of plantations hired Koreans (Jeong and You 2008). The division of workers along racial–ethnic and gender lines is known as a **split labor market** (Du Bois 1935/1992; Roediger 2002). Although today's exploitation of these divisions is more subtle, whites are aware that other racial–ethnic groups are ready to take their jobs, African Americans often perceive Latinos as competitors (Cose 2006), and men know that women are eager to get promoted. All of this helps to keep workers in line.

Conflict theorists, as you will recall, focus on how groups compete for scarce resources. Owners want to increase profits by holding costs down, while workers want better food, health care, housing, education, and leisure. Divided, workers are weak, but united, they gain strength. The *split labor market* is one way that owners divide workers so they can't take united action to demand higher wages and better working conditions.

Another tactic that owners use is the **reserve labor force.** This is simply another term for the unemployed. To expand production during economic booms, companies hire people who don't have jobs. When the economy contracts, they lay off unneeded workers. That there are desperate people looking for work is a lesson not lost on those who have jobs. They fear eviction and worry about having their cars and furniture repossessed. Many know they are just one or two paychecks away from ending up "on the streets."

Just like the boys in the Sherif experiment, African Americans, Latinos, whites, and others see themselves as able to make gains only at the expense of other groups. Sometimes this rivalry shows up along very fine racial–ethnic lines, such as that in Miami between Haitians

split labor market workers split along racial–ethnic, gender, age, or any other lines; this split is exploited by owners to weaken the bargaining power of workers

reserve labor force the unemployed; unemployed workers are thought of as being "in reserve"—capitalists take them "out of reserve" (put them back to work) during times of high production and then put them "back in reserve" (lay them off) when they are no longer needed

What are the functionalist and conflict views of prejudice?

and African Americans, who distrust each other as competitors. Divisions among workers deflect anger and hostility away from the power elite and direct these powerful emotions toward other racial and ethnic groups. Instead of recognizing their common class interests and working for their mutual welfare, workers learn to fear and distrust one another.

Symbolic Interactionism.

"I know her qualifications are OK, but yikes! She's ugly. I don't want to have to see her every day. Let's hire the one with the nice curves."

While conflict theorists focus on the role of the owner (or capitalist) class in exploiting racial and ethnic divisions, symbolic interactionists examine how labels affect perception and create prejudice.

How Labels Create Prejudice.   Symbolic interactionists stress that *the labels we learn affect the ways we perceive people.* Labels cause **selective perception;** that is, they lead us to see certain things while they blind us to others. If we apply a label to a group, we tend to perceive its members as all alike. We shake off evidence that doesn't fit (Simpson and Yinger 1972). Shorthand for emotionally charged stereotypes, some racial and ethnic labels are especially powerful. As you know, the term *nigger* is not neutral. Nor are *honky, cracker, spic, mick, kike, limey, kraut, dago, guinea,* or any of the other scornful words people use to belittle ethnic groups. As in the little vignette above, *ugly* can work in a similar way. Such words overpower us with emotions, blocking out rational thought about the people to whom they refer (Allport 1954).

Labels and Self-Fulfilling Stereotypes.   Some stereotypes not only justify prejudice and discrimination but also produce the behavior depicted in the stereotype. Let's consider Group X. According to stereotypes, the members of this group are lazy, so they don't deserve good jobs. ("They are lazy and wouldn't do the job well.") Denied the better jobs, most members of Group X do "dirty work," the jobs few people want. ("That's the right kind of work for that kind of people.") Since much "dirty work" is sporadic, members of Group X are often seen "on the streets." The sight of their idleness reinforces the original stereotype of laziness. The discrimination that created the "laziness" in the first place passes unnoticed.

To apply these three theoretical perspectives and catch a glimpse of how amazingly different things were in the past, read the Down-to-Earth Sociology box on the next page.

Global Patterns of Intergroup Relations

In their studies of racial–ethnic relations around the world, sociologists have found six basic ways that dominant groups treat minority groups. These patterns are shown in Figure 3. Let's look at each.

Genocide

When gold was discovered in northern California in 1849, the fabled "Forty-Niners" rushed in. In this region lived 150,000 Native Americans. To get rid of them, the white government put a bounty on their heads. It even reimbursed the whites for their bullets. The result was the slaughter of 120,000 Native American men, women, and children. (Schaefer 2004)

Could you ever participate in genocide? Don't be too quick in answering. Gaining an understanding of how ordinary people take part in genocide will be our primary goal in this section. In the events depicted in the little vignette above, those who did the killing were regular people—people like you and I. The killing was promoted by calling the Native Americans "savages," making them appear inferior, as somehow less than human. Killing them, then, didn't seem the same as killing whites in order to take their property.

selective perception seeing certain features of an object or situation, but remaining blind to others

What is the symbolic interactionist view of prejudice? Can you give an example of genocide in the United States?

Excerpt from MAJORITY AND MINORITY: THE DYNAMICS OF RACE AND ETHNICITY IN AMERICAN LIFE by Norman R. Yetman, 6th Ed. Copyright © 1999 by Norman R. Yetman. Reprinted with permission by Pearson Education, Inc. Upper Saddle River, NJ.

Down-to-Earth **Sociology**

The Man in the Zoo

The Bronx Zoo in New York City used to keep a 22-year-old pygmy in the Monkey House. The man—and the orangutan he lived with—became the most popular exhibit at the zoo. Thousands of visitors would arrive daily and head straight for the Monkey House. Eyewitnesses to what they thought was a lower form of human in the long chain of evolution, the visitors were fascinated by the pygmy, especially by his sharpened teeth.

To make the exhibit even more alluring, the zoo director had animal bones scattered in front of the man.

I know it sounds as though I must have made this up, but this is a true story. The World's Fair was going to be held in St. Louis in 1904, and the Department of Anthropology wanted to show villages from different cultures. They asked Samuel Verner, an explorer, if he could bring some pygmies to St. Louis to serve as live exhibits. Verner agreed, and on his next trip to Africa, in the Belgian Congo he came across Ota Benga (or Ota-benga), a pygmy who had been enslaved by another tribe. Benga, then about age 20, said he was willing to go to St. Louis. After Verner bought Benga's freedom for some cloth and salt, Benga recruited another half dozen pygmies to go with them.

After the World's Fair, Verner took the pygmies back to Africa. When Benga found out that a hostile tribe had wiped out his village and killed his family, he asked Verner if he could return with him to the United States. Verner agreed.

When they returned to New York, Verner ran into financial trouble and wrote some bad checks. No longer able to care for Benga, Verner left him with friends at the American Museum of Natural History. After a few weeks, they grew tired of Benga's antics and turned him over to the Bronx Zoo. The zoo officials put Benga on display in the Monkey House, with this sign:

The African Pygmy, 'Ota Benga.' Age 23 years. Height 4 feet 11 inches. Weight 103 pounds. Brought from the Kasai River, Congo Free State, South Central Africa by Dr. Samuel P. Verner. Exhibited each afternoon during September

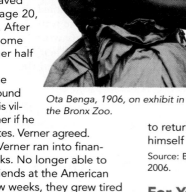

Ota Benga, 1906, on exhibit in the Bronx Zoo.

Exhibited with an orangutan, Benga became a sensation. An article in the *New York Times* said it was fortunate that Benga couldn't think very deeply, or else living with monkeys might bother him.

When the Colored Baptist Ministers' Conference protested that exhibiting Benga was degrading, zoo officials replied that they were "taking excellent care of the little fellow." They added that "he has one of the best rooms at the primate house." (I wonder what animal had the best room.)

Not surprisingly, this reply didn't satisfy the ministers. When they continued to protest, zoo officials decided to let Benga out of his cage. They put a white shirt on him and let him walk around the zoo. At night, Benga slept in the monkey house.

Benga's life became even more miserable. Zoo visitors would follow him, howling, jeering, laughing, and poking at him. One day, Benga found a knife in the feeding room of the Monkey House and flourished it at the visitors. Zoo officials took the knife away.

Benga then made a little bow and some arrows and began shooting at the obnoxious visitors. This ended the fun for the zoo officials. They decided that Benga had to leave.

After living in several orphanages for African American children, Benga ended up working as a laborer in a tobacco factory in Lynchburg, Virginia.

Always treated as a freak, Benga was desperately lonely. In 1916, at about the age of 32, in despair that he had no home or family to return to in Africa, Benga ended his misery by shooting himself in the heart.

Source: Based on Bradford and Blume 1992; Crossen 2006; Richman 2006.

For Your Consideration

→ 1. See what different views emerge as you apply the three theoretical perspectives (functionalism, symbolic interactionism, and conflict theory) to exhibiting Benga at the Bronx Zoo.
2. How does the concept of ethnocentrism apply to this event?
3. Explain how the concepts of prejudice and discrimination apply to what happened to Benga.

It is true that most Native Americans died not from bullets, but from the diseases the whites brought with them. Measles, smallpox, and the flu came from another continent, and the Native Americans had no immunity against them (Dobyns 1983; Schaefer 2004). But to accomplish the takeover of their resources, the settlers and soldiers destroyed the Native Americans' food supply (buffalos, crops). From all causes,

Can you explain how a human could have ever been a zoo exhibit?

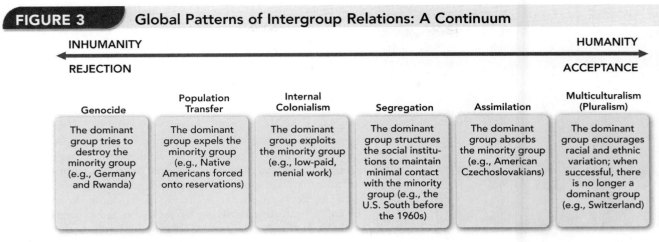

FIGURE 3   Global Patterns of Intergroup Relations: A Continuum

INHUMANITY   HUMANITY

REJECTION   ACCEPTANCE

Genocide	Population Transfer	Internal Colonialism	Segregation	Assimilation	Multiculturalism (Pluralism)
The dominant group tries to destroy the minority group (e.g., Germany and Rwanda)	The dominant group expels the minority group (e.g., Native Americans forced onto reservations)	The dominant group exploits the minority group (e.g., low-paid, menial work)	The dominant group structures the social institutions to maintain minimal contact with the minority group (e.g., the U.S. South before the 1960s)	The dominant group absorbs the minority group (e.g., American Czechoslovakians)	The dominant group encourages racial and ethnic variation; when successful, there is no longer a dominant group (e.g., Switzerland)

Source: By the author.

about *95 percent* of Native Americans died (Thornton 1987; Churchill 1997). Ordinary, "good" people were intent on destroying the "savages."

Now consider last century's two most notorious examples of genocide. In Germany during the 1930s and 1940s, Hitler and the Nazis attempted to destroy all Jews. In the 1990s, in Rwanda, the Hutus tried to destroy all Tutsis. One of the horrifying aspects of these two slaughters is that the killers did not crawl out from under a rock someplace. In some cases, it was even the victims' neighbors and friends who did the killing. *Their killing was facilitated by labels that marked the victims as enemies who deserved to die* (Huttenbach 1991; Browning 1993; Gross 2001).

In Sum: Labels are powerful; dehumanizing ones even more so. They help people to **compartmentalize**—to separate their acts of cruelty from their sense of being good and decent people. To regard members of some group as inferior opens the door to treating them inhumanely. In some cases, these labels help people to kill—and to still retain a good self-concept (Bernard et al. 1971). In short, *labeling the targeted group as inferior or even less than fully human facilitates genocide.*

Population Transfer

There are two types of **population transfer:** indirect and direct. *Indirect transfer* is achieved by making life so miserable for members of a minority that they leave "voluntarily." Under the bitter conditions of czarist Russia, for example, millions of Jews made this "choice." *Direct transfer* occurs when a dominant group expels a minority. Examples include the U.S. government relocating Native Americans to reservations and transferring Americans of Japanese descent to internment camps during World War II.

In the 1990s, a combination of genocide and population transfer occurred in Bosnia and Kosovo, parts of the former Yugoslavia. A hatred nurtured for centuries had been kept under wraps by Tito's iron-fisted rule from 1944 to 1980. After Tito's death, these suppressed, smoldering hostilities soared to the surface, and Yugoslavia split into warring factions. When the Serbs gained power, Muslims rebelled and began guerilla warfare. The Serbs vented their hatred by what they termed **ethnic cleansing:** They terrorized villages with killing and rape, forcing survivors to flee in fear.

Internal Colonialism

The term *colonialism* was used to refer to one way that the Most Industrialized Nations exploit the Least Industrialized Nations (p. 239). Conflict theorists use the term **internal colonialism** to describe how a country's dominant group exploits minority groups for its economic advantage. The dominant group manipulates the social

compartmentalize to separate acts from feelings or attitudes

population transfer the forced transfer of a minority group

ethnic cleansing a policy of eliminating a population; includes forcible expulsion and genocide

internal colonialism the policy of exploiting minority groups for economic gain

Can you give an example of population transfer in the United States?

institutions to suppress minorities and deny them full access to their society's benefits. Slavery, is an extreme example of internal colonialism, as was the South African system of *apartheid*. Although the dominant Afrikaners despised the minority, they found its presence necessary. As Simpson and Yinger (1972) put it, who else would do the hard work?

Segregation

Internal colonialism is often accompanied by **segregation**—the separation of racial or ethnic groups. Segregation allows the dominant group to maintain social distance from the minority and yet to exploit their labor as cooks, cleaners, chauffeurs, nannies, farm workers, and so on. In the U.S. South until the 1960s, by law African Americans and whites had to use separate public facilities such as hotels, schools, swimming pools, bathrooms, and even drinking fountains. In thirty-eight states, laws prohibited marriage between blacks and whites. Violators could be sent to prison (Mahoney and Kooistra 1995). The last law of this type was repealed in 1967 (Spickard 1989). In the villages of India, an ethnic group, the Dalits (untouchables), is forbidden to use the village pump. Dalit women must walk long distances to streams or pumps outside of the village to fetch their water (author's notes).

Amid fears that Japanese Americans were "enemies within" who would sabotage industrial and military installations on the West Coast, in the early days of World War II Japanese Americans were transferred to "relocation camps." To make sure they didn't get lost, the children were tagged like luggage.

Assimilation

Assimilation is the process by which a minority group is absorbed into the mainstream culture. There are two types. In *forced assimilation,* the dominant group refuses to allow the minority to practice its religion, to speak its language, or to follow its customs. Before the fall of the Soviet Union, for example, the dominant group, the Russians, required that Armenian children attend schools where they were taught in Russian. Armenians could celebrate only Russian holidays, not Armenian ones. *Permissible assimilation,* in contrast, allows the minority to adopt the dominant group's patterns in its own way and at its own speed.

Multiculturalism (Pluralism)

A policy of **multiculturalism,** also called **pluralism,** permits or even encourages racial–ethnic variation. The minority groups are able to maintain their separate identities, yet participate freely in the country's social institutions, from education to politics. Switzerland provides an outstanding example of multiculturalism. The Swiss population includes four ethnic groups: French, Italians, Germans, and Romansh. These groups have kept their own languages, and they live peacefully in political and economic unity. Multiculturalism has been so successful that none of these groups can properly be called a minority.

segregation the policy of keeping racial–ethnic groups apart

assimilation the process of being absorbed into the mainstream culture

multiculturalism a policy that permits or encourages ethnic differences; also called *pluralism*

pluralism the diffusion of power among many interest groups that prevents any single group from gaining control of the government

Racial–Ethnic Relations in the United States

Writing about race–ethnicity is like stepping onto a minefield: One never knows where to expect the next explosion. Serbian students have written to me, saying that I have been unfair to their group. So have American whites. Even basic terms are controversial. Some people classified as *African Americans* reject this term because they identify themselves as

Can you give examples of segregation, assimilation, and multiculturalism in the United States?

Bettmann/Corbis

blacks. Similarly, some Latinos prefer the term *Hispanic American*, but others reject it, saying that it ignores the Native American side of their heritage. Some would limit the term *Chicanos*—commonly used to refer to Americans from Mexico—to those who have a sense of ethnic oppression and unity; they say that it does not apply to those who have assimilated.

No term that I use here, then, will satisfy everyone. Racial–ethnic identity is fluid, constantly changing, and all terms carry a risk as they take on politically charged meanings. Nevertheless, as part of everyday life, we classify ourselves and one another as belonging to distinct racial–ethnic groups. As Figures 4 and 5 show, on the basis of these self-identities, whites make up 65 percent of the U.S. population, minorities (African Americans, Asian Americans, Latinos, and Native Americans) 34 percent. Between 1 and 2 percent claim membership in two or more racial–ethnic groups.

FIGURE 4 **Race–Ethnicity of the U.S. Population**

African Americans 13%
Asian Americans 4%
Native Americans 1%
Claim two or more races 2%
Latinos 15%
Whites 65%

Source: By the author. See Figure 5.

FIGURE 5 **U.S. Racial–Ethnic Groups**

Americans of European Descent[a]
199,491,000
65%

Group	Number	Percentage
German	50,272,000	16.5%
Irish[b]	36,278,000	11.9%
English/British	28,630,000	9.4%
Italian	17,749,000	5.8%
French[c]	11,526,000	3.8%
Polish	9,887,000	3.25%
Scottish[d]	9,365,000	3.1%
Dutch	4,929,000	1.6%
Norwegian	4,643,000	1.5%
Swedish	4,390,000	1.4%
Russian	3,130,000	1.0%
Welsh	1,980,000	0.6%
Czech	1,914,000	0.5%
Hungarian	1,539,000	0.5%
Danish	1,459,000	0.5%
Portuguese	1,419,000	0.5%
Greek	1,351,000	0.4%
Swiss	997,000	0.3%
Others	839,300	0.2%

Americans of African, Asian, North, Central, and South American, and Pacific Island Descent
104,743,000
34%

Group	Number	Percentage
Latino[e]	46,944,000	15.4%
African American	39,059,000	12.8%
Asian American[f]	13,549,000	4.5%
Native American[g]	3,083,000	1.0%
Arab	1,546,000	0.5%

Claim Two or More Race–Ethnicities 5,167,000 1.7%

Overall Total:
309,401,000

Percentage of Americans (0, 4%, 8%, 12%, 16%, 20%)

[a]This figure, which follows convention and lists Latinos as a separate category, brings into focus the problem of counting "racial–ethnic" groups. Because Latinos can be of any racial–ethnic group, I have reduced the total of the groups with which they self-identify by the number of Latinos who identify with those groups.
[b]Interestingly, this total is six times higher than all the Irish who live in Ireland.
[c]Includes French Canadian.
[d]Includes "Scottish-Irish."
[e]Most Latinos trace at least part of their ancestry to Europe.
[f]In descending order, the largest groups of Asian Americans are from China, the Philippines, India, Korea, Vietnam, and Japan. See Figure 9. Also includes those who identify themselves as Native Hawaiian or Pacific Islander.
[g]Includes Native Alaskans.

USA—the land of diversity.

PhotosToGo

Source: By the author. Based on *Statistical Abstract of the United States* 2010:Table 10; 2011:Table 52.

Why are racial–ethnic terms problematic? What are the major racial–ethnic groups in the United States?

As immigrants assimilate into a new culture, they learn and adapt new customs. These Muslim girls at an elementary school in Dearborn, Michigan, are in the process of assimilating into U.S. culture.

Jim West/PhotoEdit Inc.

WASP white anglo saxon protestant

white ethnics white immigrants to the United States whose cultures differ from WASP culture

Race and Ethnicity

As you can see from the Social Map on the next page, the distribution of dominant and minority groups among the states does not come close to the national average. This is because minority groups tend to be clustered in regions. The extreme distributions are represented by Maine and Vermont, each 5 percent minority, and by Hawaii, where minorities outnumber whites 75 percent to 25 percent. With this as background, let's review the major groups in the United States, going from the largest to the smallest.

European Americans

Benjamin Franklin said, "Why should the Palatine boors (Germans) be suffered to swarm into our settlements and by herding together establish their language and manners to the exclusion of ours? Why should Pennsylvania, founded by the English, become a colony of aliens, who will shortly be so numerous as to germanize us instead of our anglifying them?" (in Alba and Nee 2003:17)

At the founding of the United States, White Anglo Saxon Protestants (**WASPs**) held deep prejudices against other whites. There was practically no end to their disdainful stereotypes of **white ethnics**—immigrants from Europe whose language and other customs differed from theirs. The English despised the Irish, viewing them as dirty, lazy drunkards, but they also painted Poles, Jews, Italians, and others with similar disparaging brushstrokes. From the little vignette, you can see that they didn't like Germans either.

The political and cultural dominance of the WASPs placed intense pressure on immigrants to assimilate into the mainstream culture. The children of most immigrants embraced the new way of life and quickly came to think of themselves as Americans rather than as Germans, French, Hungarians, and so on. They dropped their distinctive customs, especially their languages, often viewing them as symbols of shame. This second generation of immigrants was sandwiched between two worlds: "the old country" of their parents and their new home. Their children, the third generation, had an easier adjustment, for they had fewer customs to discard. As white ethnics assimilated into this Anglo-American culture, the meaning of WASP expanded to include them.

And for those who weren't white? Perhaps the event that best illustrates the racial view of the nation's founders occurred when Congress passed the Naturalization Act of 1790, declaring that only white immigrants could apply for citizenship. Relationships between the various racial–ethnic groups since the founding of the nation has, at best, been a rocky one.

In Sum: Because Protestant English immigrants settled the colonies, they established the culture—from the dominant language to the dominant religion. Highly ethnocentric, they regarded as inferior the customs of other groups. Because white Europeans took power, they determined the national agenda to which other ethnic groups had to react and conform. Their institutional and cultural dominance still sets the stage for current ethnic relations, a topic that is explored in the Down-to-Earth Sociology box.

Latinos (Hispanics)

A Note on Terms. Before reviewing major characteristics of Latinos, it is important to stress that *Latino* and *Hispanic* refer not to a race but to ethnic groups. Latinos may identify themselves as black, white, or Native American. Some Latinos who have an African heritage refer to themselves as Afro-Latinos (Navarro 2003).

Numbers, Origins, and Locations. When birds still nested in the trees that would be used to build the *Mayflower*, Latinos had already established settlements in Florida and New Mexico (Bretos 1994). Today, Latinos are the largest minority group in the United States. As shown in Figure 7 on the next page, about 32 million people trace their origin to Mexico, 4 million to Puerto Rico, almost 2 million to Cuba, and about 8 million to Central and South America.

Although Latinos are officially tallied at 47 million, another 8 million Latinos are living here illegally. About 7 million are from Mexico, and the rest from Central and South America (*Statistical Abstract* 2011:Table 45). Most Latinos are citizens or legal

At the founding of the United States, what was the relationship of WASPs and white ethnics?

Excerpt from Alba, Richard, and Victor Nee. *Remaking the American Mainstream: Assimilation and Contemporary Immigration.* Cambridge, Mass.: Harvard University Press, 2003.

FIGURE 6 The Distribution of Dominant and Minority Groups

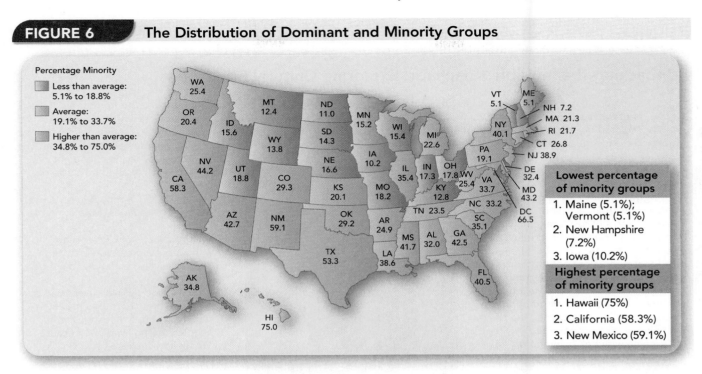

Source: By the author. Based on *Statistical Abstract of the United States* 2011:Table 19.

residents, but each year about 700,000 Latinos are arrested, most as they cross the border (*Statistical Abstract* 2011:Table 529). Before our economic crisis, when more jobs were available, the total was over one million a year. With this vast migration, about 20 million more Latinos live in the United States than Canadians (34 million) live in Canada. As Figure 8 shows, two-thirds live in just four states: California, Texas, Florida, and New York.

The massive unauthorized entry into the United States has aroused public concern. Arizona passed a law that gives its police the power to detain anyone suspected of being in the country illegally (Archibold 2010). This law aroused bitter opposition across the nation, as well as intense support for it. Another response was the planned construction of a wall along the 2,000 mile border between Mexico and the United States. After building just 53 miles of the wall at the horrendous cost of $1 billion, the wall was cancelled (Preston 2011). Civilian groups such as the Minutemen also patrol the border, but unofficially. To avoid conflict with the U.S. Border Patrol, the Minutemen do not carry guns. A second unofficial group, the Techno Patriots, patrols the border as well, using computers and thermal imaging cameras. When they confirm illegal crossings, they call the Border Patrol, whose agents make the arrests (Archibold and Preston 2008; Marino 2008).

Despite laws, walls, and patrols, as long as there is a need for unskilled labor and millions of people live in poverty, this flow of undocumented workers will continue. To gain insight into why, see the Cultural Diversity box.

FIGURE 7 Geographical Origins of U.S. Latinos

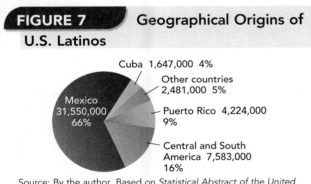

Cuba 1,647,000 4%

Other countries 2,481,000 5%

Mexico 31,550,000 66%

Puerto Rico 4,224,000 9%

Central and South America 7,583,000 16%

Source: By the author. Based on *Statistical Abstract of the United States* 2011:Table 37.

FIGURE 8 Where U.S. Latinos Live

New Mexico 2%
Colorado 2%
New Jersey 3%
Arizona 4%
Illinois 4%
New York 7%
Florida 8%

Other States 22%

California 28%

Texas 19%

Source: By the author. Based on *Statistical Abstract of the United States* 2011:Table 19.

How extensive is illegal immigration? What are some reactions to it?

Down-to-Earth Sociology

Unpacking the Invisible Knapsack: Exploring Cultural Privilege

Overt racism in the United States has dropped sharply, but doors still open and close on the basis of the color of our skins. Whites have a difficult time grasping the idea that good things come their way because they are white. They usually fail to perceive how "whiteness" operates in their own lives.

Peggy McIntosh, of Irish descent, began to wonder why she was so seldom aware of her race–ethnicity, while her African American friends were so conscious of theirs. She realized that people are not highly aware of things that they take for granted— and that "whiteness" is a "taken-for-granted" background assumption of U.S. society. To explore this, she drew up a list of taken-for-granted privileges that come with her "whiteness," what she calls her "invisible knapsack." Because she is white, McIntosh (1988) says:

1. When I go shopping, store detectives don't follow me.
2. If I don't do well as a leader, I can be sure people won't say that it is because of my race.

Adrianne Starnes/Landov

One of the cultural privileges of being white in the United States is less suspicion of wrongdoing.

3. When I watch television or look at the front page of the paper, I see people of my race presented positively.
4. When I study our national heritage, I see people of my color and am taught that they made our country great.
5. To protect my children, I do not have to teach them to be aware of racism.
6. I can talk with my mouth full and not have people put this down to my color.
7. I can speak at a public meeting without putting my race on trial.
8. I can achieve something and not be "a credit to my race."
9. If a traffic cop pulls me over, I can be sure that it isn't because I'm white.
10. I can be late to a meeting without people thinking I was late because "That's how they are."

For Your Consideration

→ Can you think of other "background privileges" that come to whites because of their skin color? (McIntosh's list contains forty-six items.) Why are whites seldom aware that they carry an "invisible knapsack"?

Spanish Language. The Spanish language distinguishes most Latinos from other U.S. ethnic groups. With 35 million people speaking Spanish at home, the United States has become one of the largest Spanish-speaking nations in the world (*Statistical Abstract* 2011:Table 53). Because about half of Latinos are unable to speak English, or can do so only with difficulty, many millions face a major obstacle to getting good jobs.

The growing use of Spanish has stoked controversy (Fund 2007). Perceiving the prevalence of Spanish as a threat, Senator S. I. Hayakawa of California initiated an "English-only" movement in 1981. The constitutional amendment that he sponsored never got off the ground, but thirty states have passed laws that declare English their official language.

Diversity. For Latinos, country of origin is highly significant. Those from Puerto Rico, for example, feel that they have little in common with people from Mexico, Venezuela, or El Salvador—just as earlier immigrants from Germany, Sweden, and England felt they had little in common with one another. A sign of these divisions is that many refer to themselves in terms of their country of origin, such as *puertorriqueños* or *cubanos*, rather than as Latino or Hispanic.

As with other ethnic groups, Latinos are separated by social class. The half-million Cubans who fled Castro's rise to power in 1959, for example, were mostly well-educated, well-to-do professionals or businesspeople. In contrast, the "boat people" who fled

---

What are some of the "cultural privileges" of being white in the United States?

Cultural Diversity in the United States

The Illegal Travel Guide

Manuel was a drinking buddy of Jose, a man I had met in Colima, Mexico. At 45, Manuel was friendly, outgoing, and enterprising.

Manuel, who had lived in the United States for seven years, spoke fluent English. Preferring to live in his hometown in Colima, where he palled around with his childhood friends, Manuel always seemed to have money and free time.

When Manuel invited me to go on a business trip with him, I accepted. I never could figure out what he did for a living or how he could afford a car, a luxury that none of his friends had. As we traveled from one remote village to another, Manuel would sell used clothing that he had heaped in the back of his older-model Ford station wagon.

At one stop, Manuel took me into a dirt-floored, thatched-roof hut. While chickens ran in and out, Manuel whispered to a slender man who was about 23 years old. The poverty was overwhelming. Juan, as his name turned out to be, had a partial grade school education. He also had a wife, four hungry children under the age of 5, and two pigs—his main food supply. Although eager to work, Juan had no job, for there was simply no work available in this remote village.

A "coyote" leads two people across the Rio Grande into Texas.
AP Images/German Garcia

As we were drinking a Coke, which seems to be the national beverage of Mexico's poor, Manuel explained to me that he was not only selling clothing—he was also lining up migrants to the United States. For a fee, he would take a man to the border and introduce him to a "wolf," who would help him cross into the promised land.

When I saw the hope in Juan's face, I knew nothing would stop him. He was borrowing every cent he could from every friend and relative to scrape the money together. Although he risked losing everything if apprehended and he would be facing unknown risks, Juan would make the trip, for wealth beckoned on the other side. He knew people who had been to the United States and spoke glowingly of its opportunities. Manuel, of course, the salesman he was, stoked the fires of hope.

Looking up from the children playing on the dirt floor with chickens pecking about them, I saw a man who loved his family. In order to make the desperate bid for a better life, he would suffer an enforced absence, as well as the uncertainties of a foreign culture whose language he did not know.

Juan opened his billfold, took something out, and slowly handed it to me. I looked at it curiously. I felt tears as I saw the tenderness with which he handled this piece of paper. It was his passport to the land of opportunity: a Social Security card made out in his name, sent by a friend who had already made the trip and who was waiting for Juan on the other side of the border.

It was then that I realized that the thousands of Manuels scurrying about Mexico and the millions of Juans they are transporting can never be stopped, for only the United States can fulfill their dreams of a better life.

For Your Consideration

→ The vast stream of immigrants illegally crossing the Mexican–U.S. border has become a national issue. What do you think is the best way to deal with this issue? Why? How does your social location affect your view?

later were mostly lower-class refugees, people with whom the earlier arrivals would not have associated in Cuba. The earlier arrivals, who are firmly established in Florida and who control many businesses and financial institutions, distance themselves from the more recent immigrants.

With 15.2 percent of the U.S. population, the potential political power of Latinos is remarkable. Several Latinos have been elected governors, and in 2010 Susana Martinez became the first Latina to govern a state (New Mexico). In the Senate, we might expect fifteen U.S. senators to be Latino. But there are only *four*. In addition, Latinos

Why is extensive illegal immigration from Mexico likely to continue?

For millions of people, the United States represents a land of opportunity and freedom from oppression. Shown here are Cubans who reached the United States by transforming their 1950s truck into a boat.

hold only 5 percent of the seats in the U.S. House of Representatives (*Statistical Abstract* 2011:Table 405). Among the reasons that keep the potential from becoming real we must count these divisions of national origin and social class.

As Latinos have become more visible in U.S. society and more vocal in their demands for equality, they have come face to face with African Americans who fear that Latino gains in employment and at the ballot box come at their expense (Hutchinson 2008). This rivalry even shows up in prison, where hostility between Latino and African American gangs sometimes escalates into violence (Thompson 2009). If Latinos and African Americans were to work together—since combined they make up more than one-fourth of the U.S. population—their unity would produce an unstoppable political force.

Comparative Conditions. To see how Latinos are doing on major indicators of well-being, look at Table 2 on the next page. As you can see, compared with white Americans and Asian Americans, Latinos have less income, higher unemployment, and more poverty. They are also less likely to own their homes. We get another view if we focus on education. In Table 3, you can see that Latinos are the most likely to drop out of high school and the least likely to graduate from college. In a postindustrial society that increasingly requires advanced skills, these totals indicate that huge numbers of Latinos will be left behind.

The umbrella term of *Latino* (or *Hispanic*) conceals as much as it reveals. To understand comparative conditions, we need to also look at people's country of origin, which remains highly significant not only for self-identity but also for determining life chances. As you can see from Table 2, Latinos who trace their roots to Cuba have less poverty and are more likely to own their homes. In contrast, those who trace their origin to Puerto Rico score lower on these indicators of well-being.

African Americans

It was 1955, in Montgomery, Alabama. As specified by law, whites took the front seats of the bus, and blacks went to the back. As the bus filled up, blacks had to give up their seats to whites.

When Rosa Parks, a 42-year-old African American woman and secretary of the Montgomery NAACP, was told that she would have to stand so that white folks could sit, she refused (Bray 1995). She stubbornly sat there while the bus driver raged and whites felt insulted. Her arrest touched off mass demonstrations, led 50,000 blacks to boycott the city's buses for a year, and thrust an otherwise unknown preacher into a historic role.

Reverend Martin Luther King, Jr., who had majored in sociology at Morehouse College in Atlanta, Georgia, took control. He organized car pools and preached nonviolence. Incensed at this radical organizer and at the stirrings in the normally compliant black community, segregationists also put their beliefs into practice—by bombing the homes of blacks and dynamiting their churches.

After slavery was abolished, the Southern states passed legislation (*Jim Crow* laws) to segregate blacks and whites. In 1896, the U.S. Supreme Court ruled in *Plessy v. Ferguson* that it was a reasonable use of state power to require "separate but equal" accommodations for blacks. Whites used this ruling to strip blacks of the political power they had gained after the Civil War. Declaring political primaries to be "white," they prohibited blacks from voting in them. Not until 1944 did the Supreme Court rule that political primaries weren't "white" and were open to all voters. White politicians then

How do Latinos rank on major indicators of well-being?

TABLE 2 — Race–Ethnicity and Comparative Well-Being

Racial–Ethnic Group	Income		Unemployment		Poverty		Home Ownership	
	Median Family Income	Compared to Whites	Percentage Unemployed	Compared to Whites	Percentage Below Poverty Line	Compared to Whites	Percentage Who Own Their Homes	Compared to Whites
Whites	$70,835	—	7.3%	—	9.3%	—	73%	—
Latinos	$43,437	39% lower	10.5%	31% higher	21.3%	129% higher	49%	33% lower
Cuba	NA[1]	NA	5.0%	32% higher	16.8%	81% higher	58%	21% lower
Central/South America	NA	NA	NA	NA	18.9%	103% higher	40%	45% lower
Mexico	NA	NA	8.4%	14% higher	24.8%	166% higher	49%	33% lower
Puerto Rico	NA	NA	8.6%	16% higher	25.2%	171% higher	38%	48% lower
African Americans	$41,874	41% lower	12.3%	41% higher	24.1%	159% higher	46%	37% lower
Asian Americans[2]	$80,101	13% higher	6.6%	10% lower	10.5%	13% higher	60%	14% lower
Native Americans	$43,190	39% lower	NA	NA	24.2%	160% higher	55%	25% lower

[1]Not Available
[2]Includes Pacific Islanders

Source: By the author. Based on *Statistical Abstract of the United States* 2011:Tables 36, 37, 626.

TABLE 3 — Race–Ethnicity and Education

Racial–Ethnic Group	Education Completed				Doctorates		
	Less Than High School	High School	Some College	College (BA or Higher)	Number Awarded*	Percentage of all U.S. Doctorates[1]	Percentage of U.S. Population
Whites	9.9%	29.3%	30.0%	19.3%	26,908	57.1	65.6
Latinos	39.2%	25.9%	21.8%	8.9%	2,267	3.6	15.4
African Americans	19.3%	31.4%	31.7%	11.5%	2,604	6.1	12.8
Asian Americans	14.9%	16.0%	19.5%	29.8%	2,734	5.7	4.5
Native Americans	24.3%	30.3%	32.5%	8.7%	127	0.4	1.0

*Numbers in thousands
[1]Percentage after the doctorates awarded to nonresidents are deducted from the total.

Source: By the author. Based on *Statistical Abstract of the United States* 2011:Tables 36, 37, 296, and Figure 5 of this text.

Can you compare the well-being of the largest racial–ethnic groups in the United States?

❋⌐Explore

Living Data

on **mysoclab.com**

rising expectations the sense that better conditions are soon to follow, which, if unfulfilled, increases frustration

passed laws that restricted voting only to people who could read—and they determined that most African Americans were illiterate. Not until 1954 did African Americans gain the legal right to attend the same public schools as whites, and, as recounted in the vignette, even later to sit where they wanted on a bus.

Rising Expectations and Civil Strife.   The barriers came down, but they came down slowly. In 1964, Congress passed the Civil Rights Act, making it illegal to discriminate on the basis of race. African Americans were finally allowed in "white" restaurants, hotels, theaters, and other public places. Then in 1965, Congress passed the Voting Rights Act, banning the fraudulent literacy tests that the Southern states had used to keep African Americans from voting.

African Americans then experienced what sociologists call **rising expectations.** They expected that these sweeping legal changes would usher in better conditions in life. However, the lives of the poor among them changed little, if at all. Frustrations built up, exploding in Watts in 1965, when people living in that ghetto of central Los Angeles took to the streets in the first of what were termed the *urban revolts*. When a white supremacist assassinated King on April 4, 1968, inner cities across the nation erupted in fiery violence. Under threat of the destruction of U.S. cities, Congress passed the sweeping Civil Rights Act of 1968.

Continued Gains.   Since then, African Americans have made remarkable gains in politics, education, and jobs. At 9 percent, the number of African Americans in the U.S. House of Representatives is *two to three times* what it was a generation ago (*Statistical Abstract* 1989:Table 423; 2011:Table 405). As college enrollments increased, the middle

Until the 1960s, the South's public facilities were segregated. Some were reserved for whites, others for blacks. This *apartheid* was broken by blacks and whites who worked together and risked their lives to bring about a fairer society. Shown here is a 1963 sit-in at a Woolworth's lunch counter in Jackson, Mississippi. Sugar, ketchup, and mustard are being poured over the heads of the demonstrators.

Fred Blackwell

What is the relationship of rising expectations and civil strife?

class expanded, and today 40 percent of all African American families make more than $50,000 a year. One in four earns more than $75,000, and one in eight over $100,000 (*Statistical Abstract* 2011:Table 695).

African Americans have become prominent in politics. Jesse Jackson (another sociology major) competed for the Democratic presidential nomination in 1984 and 1988. In 1989, L. Douglas Wilder was elected governor of Virginia, and in 2006 Deval Patrick became governor of Massachusetts. These accomplishments, of course, pale in comparison to the election of Barack Obama as president of the United States in 2008.

Current Losses. Despite these remarkable gains, African Americans continue to lag behind in politics, economics, and education. Only *one* U.S. senator is African American, many fewer than the twelve or thirteen we would expect based on the percentage of African Americans in the U.S. population. As Tables 2 and 3 show, African Americans average only 59 percent of white income, experience much more unemployment and poverty, and are less likely to own their homes or to have college educations. That two of five of African American families have incomes over $50,000 is only part of the story. Table 4 shows the other part—that almost one of every five or six African American families makes less than $15,000 a year.

The upward mobility of millions of African Americans into the middle class has created two worlds of African American experience—one educated and affluent, the other uneducated and poor. Concentrated among the poor are those with the least hope, the most despair, and the violence that so often dominates the evening news. Although homicide rates have dropped to their lowest point in thirty-five years, African Americans are *six* times more likely to be murdered than whites (*Statistical Abstract* 2011:Table 308).

Race or Social Class? A Sociological Debate. This division of African Americans into "haves" and "have-nots" has fueled a sociological controversy. Sociologist William Julius Wilson (1978, 2000, 2007) argues that social class has become more important than race in determining the life chances of African Americans. Before civil rights legislation, he says, the African American experience was dominated by race. Throughout the United States, African Americans were excluded from avenues of economic advancement: good schools and good jobs. When civil rights laws opened new opportunities, African Americans seized them. Just as legislation began to open doors to African Americans, however, manufacturing jobs dried up, and many blue-collar jobs were moved to the suburbs. As better-educated African Americans obtained white-collar jobs, they moved out of the inner city. Left behind were those with poor education and few skills.

Wilson stresses how significant these two worlds of African American experience are. The group that is stuck in the inner city lives in poverty, attends poor schools, and faces dead-end jobs or

AP Images/Charles Dharapak

In 2009, Barack Obama was sworn in as the 44th president of the United States. He is the first minority to achieve this political office.

TABLE 4	Race–Ethnicity and Income Extremes	
	Less than $15,000	**Over $100,000**
Asian Americans	7.3%	36.6%
Whites	6.6%	27.5%
African Americans	17.7%	13.4%
Latinos	14.6%	12.5%

Note: These are family incomes. Only these groups are listed in the source.
Source: By the author: Based on *Statistical Abstract of the United States* 2011:Table 695.

What are current gains and losses of African Americans? What is the debate on race or social class?

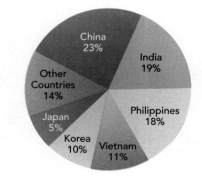

Sociologists disagree about the relative significance of race and social class in determining social and economic conditions of African Americans. William Julius Wilson, shown here, is an avid proponent of the social class side of this debate.

Ted Thai/Time Life Pictures/Getty Images

welfare. This group is filled with hopelessness and despair, combined with apathy or hostility. In contrast, those who have moved up the social class ladder live in comfortable homes in secure neighborhoods. Their jobs provide decent incomes, and they send their children to good schools. With middle-class experiences shaping their views on life, their aspirations and values have little in common with those of African Americans who remain poor. According to Wilson, then, social class—not race—is the more significant factor in the lives of African Americans.

Some sociologists reply that this analysis overlooks the discrimination that continues to underlie the African American experience. They note that African Americans who do the same work as whites average less pay (Willie 1991; Herring 2002) and even receive fewer tips (Lynn et al. 2008). This, they argue, points to racial discrimination, not to social class.

What is the answer to this debate? Wilson would reply that it is not an either-or question. My book is titled *The **Declining** Significance of Race,* he would say, not *The **Absence** of Race.* Certainly racism is still alive, he would add, but today social class is more central to the African American experience than is racial discrimination. He stresses that we need to provide jobs for the poor in the inner city—for work provides an anchor to a responsible life (Wilson 1996, 2007).

Racism as an Everyday Burden. Researchers sent out 5,000 résumés in response to help wanted ads in the Boston and Chicago Sunday papers. The résumés were identical, except some applicants had white-sounding names, such as Emily and Brandon, while others had black-sounding names, such as Lakisha and Jamal. Although the qualifications of these supposed job applicants were identical, the white-sounding names elicited *50 percent* more callbacks than the black-sounding names (Bertrand and Mullainathan 2002).

Certainly racism continues as a regular feature of society, often something that whites, not subjected to it, are only vaguely aware of. But for those on the receiving end, racism can be an everyday burden. Here is how an African American professor describes his experiences:

> [One problem with] being black in America is that you have to spend so much time thinking about stuff that most white people just don't even have to think about. I worry when I get pulled over by a cop. . . . I worry what some white cop is going to think when he walks over to our car, because he's holding on to a gun. And I'm very aware of how many black folks accidentally get shot by cops. I worry when I walk into a store, that someone's going to think I'm in there shoplifting. . . . And I get resentful that I have to think about things that a lot of people, even my very close white friends whose politics are similar to mine, simply don't have to worry about. (Feagin 1999:398)

Asian Americans

I have stressed in this chapter that our racial–ethnic categories are based more on social factors than on biological ones. This point is again obvious when we examine the category Asian American. As Figure 9 shows, those who are called Asian Americans came to the United States from many nations. *With no unifying culture or "race," why should people from so many backgrounds be clustered together and assigned a single label?* Think about it. What culture or race–ethnicity do Samoans and Vietnamese have in common? Or Laotians and Pakistanis? Or people from Guam and those from China? Those from Japan and those from India? Yet all these groups—and more—are lumped together and called Asian Americans. Apparently, the U.S. government is not satisfied until it is able to pigeonhole everyone into some racial–ethnic category.

Since *Asian American* is a standard term, however, let's look at the characteristics of the 14 million people who are lumped together and assigned this label.

FIGURE 9 Countries of Origin for Asian Americans

China 23%
India 19%
Other Countries 14%
Philippines 18%
Japan 5%
Korea 10%
Vietnam 11%

Source: By the author. Based on U.S. Census Bureau 2010.

How is racism an everyday burden for African Americans? Why is "Asian American" a diverse category?

A Background of Discrimination. Lured by gold strikes in the West and an urgent need for unskilled workers to build the railroads, 200,000 Chinese immigrated between 1850 and 1880. When the famous golden spike was driven at Promontory, Utah, in 1869 to mark the completion of the railroad to the West Coast, white workers prevented Chinese workers from being in the photo—even though Chinese made up 90 percent of Central Pacific Railroad's labor force (Hsu 1971).

After the railroad was complete, the Chinese competed with whites for other jobs. Anglos then formed vigilante groups to intimidate them. They also used the law. California's 1850 Foreign Miners Act required Chinese (and Latinos) to pay $20 a month in order to work—when wages were a dollar a day. The California Supreme Court ruled that Chinese could not testify against whites (Carlson and Colburn 1972). In 1882, Congress passed the Chinese Exclusion Act, suspending all Chinese immigration for ten years. Four years later, the Statue of Liberty was dedicated. The tired, the poor, and the huddled masses it was intended to welcome were obviously not Chinese.

When immigrants from Japan arrived, they encountered *spillover bigotry,* a stereotype that lumped Asians together, depicting them as sneaky, lazy, and untrustworthy. After Japan attacked Pearl Harbor in 1941, conditions grew worse for the 110,000 Japanese Americans who called the United States their home. U.S. authorities feared that Japan would invade the United States and that the Japanese Americans would fight on Japan's side. They also feared that Japanese Americans would sabotage military installations on the West Coast. Although no Japanese American had been involved in even a single act of sabotage, on February 19, 1942, President Franklin D. Roosevelt ordered that everyone who was *one-eighth Japanese or more* be confined in detention centers (called "internment camps"). These people were charged with no crime, and they had no trials. Japanese ancestry was sufficient cause for being imprisoned.

Dane Rex/Lightbox

Of the racial–ethnic groups in the United States, Asian Americans have the highest rate of intermarriage.

Diversity. As you can see from Tables 2 and 4, the income of Asian Americans has outstripped that of all groups, including whites. This has led to the stereotype that all Asian Americans are successful. Are they? Their poverty rate is actually higher than that of whites, as you can also see from Table 2. As with Latinos, country of origin is significant: Poverty is low for Chinese and Japanese Americans, but it clusters among Americans from Southeast Asia. Altogether, between 1 and 2 million Asian Americans live in poverty.

Reasons for Success. The high average incomes of Asian Americans can be traced to three major factors: family life, educational achievement, and assimilation into mainstream culture. Of all ethnic groups, including whites, Asian American children are the most likely to grow up with two parents and the least likely to be born to either a teenaged or single mother (*Statistical Abstract* 2011:Tables 69, 86). Common in these families is a stress on self-discipline, thrift, and hard work (Suzuki 1985; Bell 1991). This early socialization provides strong impetus for the other two factors.

The second factor is their unprecedented rate of college graduation. As Table 3 shows, 49 percent of Asian Americans complete college. To realize how stunning this is, compare their rate with those of the other groups shown on this table. Educational achievement, in turn, opens doors to economic success.

The most striking indication of the third factor, assimilation, is a high rate of intermarriage. Of Asian Americans who graduate from college, about 40 percent of the men and 60 percent of the women marry a non–Asian American (Qian and Lichter 2007). The intermarriage of Japanese Americans is so extensive that two of every three of their children have one parent who is not of Japanese descent (Schaefer 2004). The Chinese are close behind (Alba and Nee 2003).

Asian Americans are becoming more prominent in politics. With more than half of its citizens being Asian American, Hawaii has elected Asian American governors and sent several Asian American senators to Washington, including the two now serving there (Lee 1998; *Statistical Abstract* 2011:Table 405). The first Asian

What is the background of discrimination of Asian Americans? What are the reasons for their success?

American governor outside of Hawaii was Gary Locke, who served from 1997 to 2005 as governor of Washington, a state in which Asian Americans make up less than 6 percent of the population. In 2008 in Louisiana, Piyush Jindal became the first Indian American governor.

Native Americans

"I don't go so far as to think that the only good Indians are dead Indians, but I believe nine out of ten are—and I shouldn't inquire too closely in the case of the tenth. The most vicious cowboy has more moral principle than the average Indian."

—Teddy Roosevelt, 1886
(President of the United States 1901–1909)

Diversity of Groups. This quote from Teddy Roosevelt provides insight into the rampant racism of earlier generations. Yet, even today, thanks to countless grade B Westerns, some Americans view the original inhabitants of what became the United States as uncivilized savages, a single group of people subdivided into separate tribes. The European immigrants to the colonies, however, encountered diverse groups of people who spoke over 700 languages. Their variety of cultures ranged from nomadic hunters and gatherers to farmers who lived in wooden houses (Schaefer 2004). Each group had its own norms and values—and the usual ethnocentric pride in its own culture. Consider what happened in 1744 when the colonists of Virginia offered college scholarships for "savage lads." The Iroquois replied:

"Several of our young people were formerly brought up at the colleges of Northern Provinces. They were instructed in all your sciences. But when they came back to us, they were bad runners, ignorant of every means of living in the woods, unable to bear either cold or hunger, knew neither how to build a cabin, take a deer, or kill an enemy. . . . They were totally good for nothing."

They added, "If the English gentlemen would send a dozen or two of their children to Onondaga, the great Council would take care of their education, bring them up in really what was the best manner and make men of them." (Nash 1974; in McLemore 1994)

Native Americans, who numbered about 10 million, had no immunity to the diseases the Europeans brought with them. With deaths due to disease—and warfare, a much lesser cause—their population plummeted. The low point came in 1890, when the census reported only 250,000 Native Americans. If the census and the estimate of the original population are accurate, Native Americans had been reduced to about *one-fortieth* their original size. The population has never recovered, but Native Americans now number about 3 million (see Figure 5). Native Americans, who today speak 150 different languages, do not think of themselves as a single people who fit neatly within a single label (McLemore 1994).

From Treaties to Genocide and Population Transfer. At first, the Native Americans tried to accommodate the strangers, since there was plenty of land for both the few newcomers and themselves. Soon, however, the settlers began to raid Indian villages and pillage their food supplies (Horn 2006). As wave after wave of settlers arrived, Pontiac, an Ottawa chief, saw the future—and didn't like it. He convinced several tribes to unite in an effort to push the Europeans into the sea. He almost succeeded, but failed when the English were reinforced by fresh troops (McLemore 1994).

This depiction breaks stereotypes, but is historically accurate. Shown here is an Iroquois fort. Can you guess who the attackers are?

SuperStock

Why are the terms Native American and Indian diverse categories?

A pattern of deception evolved. The U.S. government would make treaties to buy some of a tribe's land, with the promise to honor forever the tribe's right to what it had not sold. European immigrants, who continued to pour into the United States, would then disregard these boundaries. The tribes would resist, with death tolls on both sides. The U.S. government would then intervene—not to enforce the treaty, but to force the tribe off its lands. In its relentless drive westward, the U.S. government embarked on a policy of genocide. It assigned the U.S. cavalry the task of "pacification," which translated into slaughtering Native Americans who "stood in the way" of this territorial expansion.

The acts of cruelty perpetrated by the Europeans against Native Americans appear endless, but two are especially notable. The first is the Trail of Tears. The U.S. government adopted a policy of population transfer (see Figure 3 on p. 329), which it called *Indian Removal*. The goal was to confine Native Americans to specified areas called *reservations*. In the winter of 1838–1839, the U.S. Army rounded up 15,000 Cherokees and forced them to walk a thousand miles from the Carolinas and Georgia to Oklahoma. Conditions were so brutal that about 4,000 of those who were forced to make this midwinter march died along the way. The second notable act of cruelty also marked the symbolic end of Native American resistance to the European expansion. In 1890 at Wounded Knee, South Dakota, the U.S. cavalry gunned down 300 men, women, and children of the Dakota Sioux tribe. After the massacre, the soldiers threw the bodies into a mass grave (Thornton 1987; Lind 1995; DiSilvestro 2006).

The Invisible Minority and Self-Determination. Native Americans can truly be called the invisible minority. Because about half live in rural areas and one-third in just three states—Oklahoma, California, and Arizona—most other Americans are hardly aware of a Native American presence in the United States. The isolation of about half of Native Americans on reservations further reduces their visibility (Schaefer 2004).

The systematic attempts of European Americans to destroy the Native Americans' way of life and their forced resettlement onto reservations continue to have deleterious effects. The rate of suicide among Native Americans is high, and their life expectancy is lower than that of the nation as a whole (Murray et al. 2006; Crosby et al. 2011). Table 3 shows that their educational attainment also lags behind most groups: Only 13 percent graduate from college.

Native Americans are experiencing major changes. In the 1800s, U.S. courts ruled that Native Americans did not own the land on which they had been settled and had no right to develop its resources. They made Native Americans wards of the state, and the Bureau of Indian Affairs treated them like children (Mohawk 1991; Schaefer 2004). Then, in the 1960s, Native Americans won a series of legal victories that gave them control over reservation lands. With this legal change, many Native American tribes have opened businesses—ranging from fish canneries to industrial parks that serve metropolitan areas. The Skywalk, opened by the Hualapai, which offers breathtaking views of the Grand Canyon, gives an idea of the varieties of businesses to come (Lacey 2011).

It is the casinos, though, that have attracted the most attention. In 1988, the federal government passed a law that allowed Native Americans to operate gambling establishments on reservations. Now over 200 tribes have casinos. *They bring in $26 billion a year, more than all the casinos in Las Vegas* (Pratt 2011; Statistical Abstract 2011:Table 1257). The Oneida tribe of New York, which has only 1,000 members, runs a casino that nets $232,000 a year for each man, woman, and child (Peterson 2003). This huge amount, however, pales in comparison with that of the Mashantucket Pequot tribe of Connecticut. With only 700 members, the tribe brings in more than $2 million a day just from slot machines (Rivlin 2007). Incredibly, one tribe has only *one* member: She has her own casino (Bartlett and Steele 2002).

Preferring to travel a different road entirely, some embrace the highly controversial idea of *separatism*. Because Native Americans were independent peoples when the Europeans arrived and they never willingly joined the United States, many tribes

Read
Race Specific Policies and the Truly Disadvantaged by William Julius Wilson on **mysoclab.com**

What major issues do Native Americans face?

maintain the right to remain separate from the U.S. government. The chief of the Onondaga tribe in New York, a member of the Iroquois Federation, summarized the issue this way:

> For the whole history of the Iroquois, we have maintained that we are a separate nation. We have never lost a war. Our government still operates. We have refused the U.S. government's reorganization plans for us. We have kept our language and our traditions, and when we fly to Geneva to UN meetings, we carry Hau de no sau nee passports. We made some treaties that lost some land, but that also confirmed our separate-nation status. That the U.S. denies all this doesn't make it any less the case. (Mander 1992)

pan-Indianism an attempt to develop an identity that goes beyond the tribe by emphasizing the common elements that run through Native American cultures

One of the most significant changes for Native Americans is **pan-Indianism.** This emphasis on common elements that run through their cultures is an attempt to develop an identity that goes beyond the tribe. Pan-Indianism ("We are all Indians") is a remarkable example of the plasticity of ethnicity. It embraces and substitutes for individual tribal identities the label "Indian"—originally imposed by Spanish and Italian sailors who thought they had reached the shores of India. As sociologist Irwin Deutscher (2002:61) put it, "The peoples who have accepted the larger definition of who they are, have, in fact, little else in common with each other than the stereotypes of the dominant group which labels them."

Native Americans say that it is they who must determine whether to establish a common identity and work together as in pan-Indianism or to stress separatism and identify solely with their own tribes. It is up to us, they say, whether we want to assimilate into the dominant culture or to stand apart from it; to move to cities or to remain on reservations; or to operate casinos or to engage only in traditional activities. "We are sovereign nations," they point out, "and we will not take orders from the victors of past wars."

Looking Toward the Future

Back in 1903, sociologist W. E. B. Du Bois said, "The problem of the twentieth century is the problem of the color line—the relation of the darker to the lighter races." Incredibly, over a hundred years later, the color line remains one of the most volatile topics facing the United States. From time to time, the color line takes on a different complexion, as with the war on terrorism and the corresponding discrimination directed against people of Middle Eastern descent.

In another hundred years, will yet another sociologist lament that the color of people's skins still affects human relationships? Given our past, it seems that although racial–ethnic walls will diminish, even crumble at some points, the color line is not likely to disappear. Let's close this chapter by looking at two issues we are currently grappling with, immigration and affirmative action.

The Immigration Debate

Throughout its history, the United States has both welcomed immigration and feared its consequences. The gates opened wide (numerically, if not in attitude) for waves of immigrants in the 1800s and early 1900s. During the past twenty years, a new wave of immigration has brought close to a million new residents to the United States each year. Today, more immigrants (38 million) live in the United States than at any other time in the country's history (*Statistical Abstract* 2007:Table 5; 2011:Table 40).

In contrast to earlier waves, in which immigrants came almost exclusively from western Europe, the current wave of immigrants is so diverse that it is changing the U.S. racial–ethnic mix. If current trends in immigration (and birth) persist, in about fifty years the "average" American will trace his or her ancestry to Africa, Asia, South America, the Pacific Islands, the Middle East—almost anywhere but white Europe. This change is discussed in the Cultural Diversity box on the next page.

MAINTAIN IMMIGRATION QUOTAS

ENOUGH IS ENOUGH

J. Harris

What is pan-Indianism? What is the immigration debate?

Cultural Diversity in the United States

Glimpsing the Future: The Shifting U.S. Racial–Ethnic Mix

During the next twenty-five years, the population of the United States is expected to grow by about 22 percent. To see what the U.S. population will look like at that time, can we simply add 22 percent to our current racial–ethnic mix? The answer is a resounding no. As you can see from Figure 10, some groups will grow much more than others, giving us a different-looking United States. Some of the changes in the U.S. racial–ethnic mix will be dramatic. In twenty-five years, one of every nineteen Americans is expected to have an Asian background, and in the most dramatic change, almost one of four is expected to be of Latino ancestry.

The basic causes of this fundamental shift are the racial–ethnic groups' different rates of immigration and birth. Both will change the groups' proportions of the U.S. population, but immigration is by far the more important. From Figure 10, you can see that the proportion of non-Hispanic whites is expected to shrink, that of Native Americans to remain the same, that of African Americans to increase slightly, and that of Latinos to increase sharply.

For Your Consideration

→ This shifting racial–ethnic mix is one of the most significant events occurring in the United States. To better understand its implications, apply the three theoretical perspectives.

Use the conflict perspective to identify the groups that are likely to be threatened by this change. Over what resources are struggles likely to develop? What impact do you think this changing mix might have on European Americans? On Latinos? On African Americans? On Asian Americans? On Native Americans? What changes in immigration laws (or their enforcement) can you anticipate?

To apply the symbolic interactionist perspective, consider how groups might perceive one another differently as their proportions of the population change. How do you think that these changed perceptions will affect people's behavior?

To apply the *functionalist perspective*, try to determine how each racial–ethnic group will benefit from this changing mix. How will other parts of society (such as businesses) benefit? What functions and dysfunctions can you anticipate for politics, economics, education, or religion?

FIGURE 10   Projections of the Racial–Ethnic Makeup of the U.S. Population

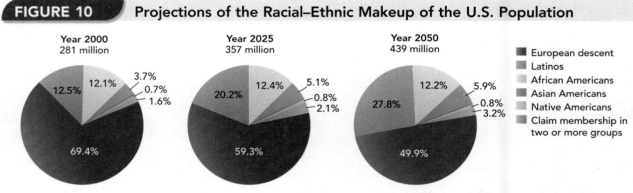

Year 2000
281 million

Year 2025
357 million

Year 2050
439 million

- European descent
- Latinos
- African Americans
- Asian Americans
- Native Americans
- Claim membership in two or more groups

Source: By the author. Based on U.S. Census Bureau 2009; *Statistical Abstract of the United States* 2011:Table 3. I modified the projections based on the new census category of membership in two or more groups and trends in interethnic marriage.

In some states, the future is arriving much sooner than this. In California, racial–ethnic minorities have become the majority. California has 21 million minorities and 15 million whites (*Statistical Abstract* 2011:Table 19). Californians who request new telephone service from Pacific Bell can speak to customer service representatives in Spanish, Korean, Vietnamese, Mandarin, Cantonese—or English.

What changes in the U.S. racial–ethnic mix are in process? Why?

As in the past, there is concern that "too many" immigrants will change the character of the United States. "Throughout the history of U.S. immigration," write sociologists Alejandro Portés and Rubén Rumbaut (1990), "a consistent thread has been the fear that the 'alien element' would somehow undermine the institutions of the country and would lead it down the path of disintegration and decay." A hundred years ago, the widespread fear was that the immigrants from southern Europe would bring communism with them. Today, some fear that Spanish-speaking immigrants threaten the primacy of the English language. In addition, the age-old fear that immigrants will take jobs away from native-born Americans remains strong. Finally, minority groups that struggled for political representation fear that newer groups will gain political power at their expense.

Affirmative Action

Affirmative action in our multicultural society lies at the center of a national debate about racial–ethnic relations. In this policy, initiated by President Kennedy in 1961, goals based on race (and sex) are used in hiring, promotion, and college admission. Sociologist Barbara Reskin (1998) examined the results of affirmative action. She concluded that although it is difficult to separate the results of affirmative action from economic booms and busts and the greater numbers of women in the workforce, affirmative action has had a modest impact.

The results may have been modest, but the reactions to this program have been anything but modest. Affirmative action has been at the center of controversy for almost two generations. Liberals, both white and minority, say that this program is the most direct way to level the playing field of economic opportunity. If whites are passed over, this is an unfortunate cost that we must pay if we are to make up for past discrimination. In contrast, conservatives, both white and minority, agree that opportunity should be open to all, but claim that putting race (or sex) ahead of an individual's training and ability to perform a job is reverse discrimination. Because of their race (or sex), qualified people who had nothing to do with past inequality are discriminated against. They add that affirmative action stigmatizes the people who benefit from it, because it suggests that they hold their jobs because of race (or sex), rather than merit.

This national debate crystallized with a series of controversial rulings. One of the most significant was *Proposition 209*, a 1996 amendment to the California state constitution. This amendment made it illegal to give preference to minorities and women in hiring, promotion, and college admissions. Despite appeals by a coalition of civil rights groups, the U.S. Supreme Court upheld this California law.

A second significant ruling was made by the U.S. Supreme Court in 2003. White students who had been denied admission to the University of Michigan claimed that they had been discriminated against because less qualified applicants had been admitted on the basis of their race. The Court ruled that universities can give minorities an edge in admissions,

The United States is the most racially–ethnically diverse society in the world. This can be our central strength, with our many groups working together to build a harmonious society, a stellar example for the world. Or it can be our Achilles heel, with us breaking into feuding groups, a Balkanized society that marks an ill-fitting end to a grand social experiment. Our reality will probably fall somewhere between these extremes.

Steve Chenn/Corbis

What is affirmative action? Why is it controversial?

but there must be a meaningful review of individual applicants. Mechanical systems, such as giving extra points because of race, are unconstitutional. This murky message satisfied no one, as no one knew what it really meant.

To remove ambiguity, opponents of affirmative action put amendments to several state constitutions on the ballot. The amendments, which make it illegal for public institutions to even consider race or sex in hiring, in awarding contracts, or in college admissions, failed in some states, such as Colorado, but became law in Michigan and Nebraska (Lewin 2007; Kaufman and Fields 2008).

With constitutional battles continuing, the issue of affirmative action in a multicultural society is likely to remain center stage for quite some time.

Toward a True Multicultural Society

The United States has the potential to become a society in which racial–ethnic groups not only coexist, but also respect one another—and thrive—as they work together for mutually beneficial goals. In a true multicultural society, the minority groups that make up the United States would participate fully in the nation's social institutions while maintaining their cultural integrity. Reaching this goal will require that we understand that "the biological differences that divide one race from another add up to a drop in the genetic ocean." For a long time, we have given racial categories an importance they never merited. Now we need to figure out how to reduce them to the irrelevance they deserve. In short, we need to make real the abstraction called equality that we profess to believe (Cose 2000).

By the Numbers: Changes Over Time

Percentage of Americans who claim membership in these groups:

European descent		
2000	NOW	2050
69%	65%	50%

Latino descent		
2000	NOW	2050
13%	15%	28%

African descent		
2000	NOW	2050
12%	13%	12%

Asian descent		
2000	NOW	2050
3.7%	4.4%	5.9%

Native American descent		
2000	NOW	2050
0.7%	1.0%	0.8%

What is needed to have a true multicultural society?

Summary and Review

Laying the Sociological Foundation

How is race both a reality and a myth?

In the sense that different groups inherit distinctive physical traits, race is a reality. There is no agreement regarding what constitutes a particular race, however, or even how many races there are. In the sense of one race being superior to another and of there being pure races, race is a myth. The *idea* of race is powerful, shaping basic relationships among people.

How do race and ethnicity differ?

Race refers to inherited biological characteristics; **ethnicity,** to cultural ones. Members of ethnic groups identify with one another on the basis of common ancestry and cultural heritage.

What are minority and dominant groups?

Minority groups are people who are singled out for unequal treatment by members of the **dominant group,** the group with more power and privilege. Minorities originate with migration or the expansion of political boundaries.

What heightens ethnic identity, and what is "ethnic work"?

A group's ethnic identity is heightened or reduced by its relative size, power, and physical characteristics, as well as the amount of discrimination it faces. **Ethnic work** is the process of constructing and maintaining an ethnic identity. For people without a firm ethnic identity, ethnic work is an attempt to recover their ethnic heritage. For those with strong ties to their culture of origin, ethnic work involves enhancing group distinctions.

Prejudice and Discrimination

Why are people prejudiced?

Prejudice is an attitude, and **discrimination** is an action. Like other attitudes, prejudice is learned in association with others. Prejudice is so extensive that people can show prejudice against groups that don't even exist. Minorities also internalize the dominant norms, and some show prejudice against their own group.

How do individual and institutional discrimination differ?

Individual discrimination is the negative treatment of one person by another, while **institutional discrimination** is negative treatment that is built into social institutions. Institutional discrimination can occur without the awareness of either those who do the discriminating or those who are discriminated against. Discrimination in health care is one example.

Theories of Prejudice

How do psychologists explain prejudice?

Psychological theories of prejudice stress the **authoritarian personality** and frustration displaced toward **scapegoats.**

How do sociologists explain prejudice?

Sociological theories focus on how different social environments increase or decrease prejudice. *Functionalists* stress the benefits and costs that come from discrimination. *Conflict theorists* look at how the groups in power exploit racial–ethnic divisions in order to control workers and maintain power. *Symbolic interactionists* stress how labels create **selective perception** and self-fulfilling prophecies.

Global Patterns of Intergroup Relations

What are the major patterns of minority and dominant group relations?

Beginning with the least humane, they are **genocide, population transfer, internal colonialism, segregation, assimilation,** and **multiculturalism (pluralism).**

Racial–Ethnic Relations in the United States

What are the major racial–ethnic groups in the United States?

From largest to smallest, the major groups are European Americans, Latinos, African Americans, Asian Americans, and Native Americans.

What are some issues in racial–ethnic relations and characteristics of minority groups?

Latinos are divided by social class and country of origin. African Americans are increasingly divided into middle and lower classes, with two sharply contrasting worlds of experience. On many measures, Asian Americans are better off than white Americans, but their well-being varies with country of origin. For Native Americans, the primary issues are poverty, nationhood, and settling treaty obligations. The overarching issue for minorities is overcoming discrimination.

Looking Toward the Future

What main issues dominate U.S. racial–ethnic relations?

The main issues are immigration, affirmative action, and how to develop a true multicultural society. The answers are significant for our future.

Thinking Critically about this Chapter

1. How many races do your friends or family think there are? Do they think that one race is superior to the others? What do you think their reaction would be to the sociological position that racial categories are primarily social?

2. A hundred years ago, sociologist W. E. B. Du Bois said, "The problem of the twentieth century is the problem of the color line—the relation of the darker to the lighter races." Why do you think that the color line remains one of the most volatile topics facing the nation?

3. If you were appointed head of the U.S. Civil Service Commission, what policies would you propose to reduce racial–ethnic strife in the United States? Be ready to explain the sociological principles that might give your proposals a higher chance of success.

References

All new references are printed in cyan.

Adorno, Theodor W., Else Frenkel-Brunswick, D. J. Levinson, and R. N. Sanford. *The Authoritarian Personality.* New York: Harper & Row, 1950.

Alba, Richard, and Victor Nee. *Remaking the American Mainstream: Assimilation and Contemporary Immigration.* Cambridge, Mass.: Harvard University Press, 2003.

Allport, Floyd. *Social Psychology.* Boston: Houghton Mifflin, 1954.

Angler, Natalie. "Do Races Differ? Not Really, DNA Shows." *New York Times,* August 22, 2000.

Archibold, Randal C. "Arizona Enacts Stringent Law on Immigration." *New York Times,* April 23, 2010.

Archibold, Randal C., and Julia Preston. "Homeland Security Stands by Its Fence." *New York Times,* May 21, 2008.

Bartlett, Donald L., and James B. Steele. "Wheel of Misfortune." *Time,* December 16, 2002:44–58.

Bean, Frank D., Jennifer Lee, Jeanne Batalova, and Mark Leach. "Immigration and Fading Color Lines in America." Washington, D.C.: Population Reference Bureau, 2004.

Bell, David A. "An American Success Story: The Triumph of Asian-Americans." In *Sociological Footprints: Introductory Readings in Sociology,* 5th ed., Leonard Cargan and Jeanne H. Ballantine, eds. Belmont, Calif.: Wadsworth, 1991:308–316.

Bernard, Viola W., Perry Ottenberg, and Fritz Redl. "Dehumanization: A Composite Psychological Defense in Relation to Modern War." In *The Triple Revolution Emerging: Social Problems in Depth,* Robert Perucci and Marc Pilisuk, eds. Boston: Little, Brown, 1971:17–34.

Bertrand, Marianne, and Sendhil Mullainathan. "Are Emily and Brendan More Employable than Lakish and Jamal? A Field Experiment on Labor Market Discrimination." Unpublished paper, November 18, 2002.

Blee, Kathleen M. "Inside Organized Racism." In *Life in Society: Readings to Accompany Sociology: A Down-to-Earth Approach,* 7th ed., James M. Henslin, ed. Boston: Allyn and Bacon, 2005:46–57.

Bradford, Phillips Verner, and Harvey Blume. *Ota Benga: The Pygmy in the Zoo.* New York: Delta, 1992.

Bray, Rosemary L. "Rosa Parks: A Legendary Moment, a Lifetime of Activism." *Ms., 6, 3,* November–December 1995:45–47.

Bretos, Miguel A. "Hispanics Face Institutional Exclusion." *Miami Herald,* May 22, 1994.

Browning, Christopher R. *Ordinary Men: Reserve Police Battalion 101 and the Final Solution in Poland.* New York: HarperPerennial, 1993.

Carlson, Lewis H., and George A. Colburn. *In Their Place: White America Defines Her Minorities, 1850–1950.* New York: Wiley, 1972.

Centers for Disease Control and Prevention. "Native American Suicides per 100,000, Ages 0–19, IHS Areas, 1989–1998." June 13, 2007.

Chandra, Vibha P. "The Present Moment of the Past: The Metamorphosis." Unpublished paper, 1993b.

Churchill, Ward. *A Little Matter of Genocide: Holocaust and Denial in the Americas, 1492 to the Present.* San Francisco: City Lights Books, 1997.

Cose, Ellis. "What's White Anyway?" *Newsweek,* September 18, 2000:64–65.

Cose, Ellis. "Black versus Brown." *Newsweek,* July 3, 2006:44–45.

Cowen, Emory L., Judah Landes, and Donald E. Schaet. "The Effects of Mild Frustration on the Expression of Prejudiced Attitudes." *Journal of Abnormal and Social Psychology.* January 1959:33–38.

Crossen, Cynthia. "How Pygmy Ota Benga Ended Up in Bronx Zoo as Darwinism Dawned." *Wall Street Journal,* February 6, 2006.

Dasgupta, Nilanjana, Debbie E. McGhee, Anthony G. Greenwald, and Mahzarin R. Banaji. "Automatic Preference for White Americans:

Eliminating the Familiarity Explanation." *Journal of Experimental Social Psychology,* 36, 3, May 2000:316–328.

Deutscher, Irwin. *Accommodating Diversity: National Policies that Prevent Ethnic Conflict.* Lanham, Md.: Lexington Books, 2002.

DiSilvestro, Roger L. *In the Shadow of Wounded Knee: The Untold Final Chapter of the Indian Wars.* New York: Walker & Co., 2006.

Doane, Ashley W., Jr. "Dominant Group Ethnic Identity in the United States: The Role of 'Hidden' Ethnicity in Intergroup Relations." *The Sociological Quarterly,* 38, 3, Summer 1997:375–397.

Dobyns, Henry F. *Their Numbers Became Thinned: Native American Population Dynamics in Eastern North America.* Knoxville: University of Tennessee Press, 1983.

Dollard, John, et al. *Frustration and Aggression.* New Haven, Conn.: Yale University Press, 1939.

Du Bois, W. E. B. *The Souls of Black Folk: Essays and Sketches.* Chicago: McClurg, 1903.

Du Bois, W. E. B. *Black Reconstruction in America: An Essay toward a History of the Part Which Black Folk Played in the Attempt to Reconstruct Democracy in America, 1860–1880.* New York: Atheneum, 1992. Originally published 1935.

Ezekiel, Raphael S. *The Racist Mind: Portraits of American Neo-Nazis and Klansmen.* New York: Viking, 1995.

Feagin, Joe R. "The Continuing Significance of Race: Antiblack Discrimination in Public Places." In *Majority and Minority: The Dynamics of Race and Ethnicity in American Life,* 6th ed., Norman R. Yetman, ed. Boston: Allyn and Bacon, 1999:384–399.

Fish, Jefferson M. "Mixed Blood." *Psychology Today,* 28, 6, November–December 1995:55–58, 60, 61, 76, 80.

Frank, Reanne. "What to Make of It? The (Re)emergence of a Biological Conceptualization of Race in Health Disparities Research." *Social Science & Medicine,* 64, 2007:1977–1983.

Fund, John. "English-Only Showdown." *Wall Street Journal,* November 28, 2007.

Gettleman, Jeffrey, and Josh Kron, "U.N. Report on Congo Massacres Draws Anger." *New York Times,* October 1, 2010.

Greenwald, Anthony G., and Linda Hamilton Krieger. "Implicit Bias: Scientific Foundations." *California Law Review,* July 2006.

Gross, Jan T. *Neighbors.* New Haven: Yale University Press, 2001.

Hall, Ronald E. "The Tiger Woods Phenomenon: A Note on Biracial Identity." *The Social Science Journal,* 38, 2, April 2001:333–337.

Hartley, Eugene. *Problems in Prejudice.* New York: King's Crown Press, 1946.

Herring, Cedric. "Is Job Discrimination Dead?" *Contexts,* Summer 2002:13–18.

Hill, Mark E. "Skin Color and the Perception of Attractiveness among African Americans: Does Gender Make a Difference?" *Social Psychology Quarterly,* 65, 1, 2002:77–91.

Horn, James P. *Land As God Made It: Jamestown and the Birth of America.* New York: Basic Books, 2006.

Hsu, Francis L. K. *The Challenge of the American Dream: The Chinese in the United States.* Belmont, Calif.: Wadsworth, 1971.

Hutchinson, Earl Ofari. "The Latino Challenge to Black America." *Washington Post,* January 11, 2008.

Huttenbach, Henry R. "The Roman *Porajmos:* The Nazi Genocide of Europe's Gypsies." *Nationalities Papers,* 19, 3, Winter 1991:373–394.

Jeong, Yu-Jin, and Hyun-Kyung You. "Different Historical Trajectories and Family Diversity among Chinese, Japanese, and Koreans in the United States." *Journal of Family History,* 33, 3, July 2008:346–356.

Jones, James H. *Bad Blood: The Tuskegee Syphilis Experiment,* 2nd ed. New York: Free Press, 1993.

Jones, Jeffrey Owen, and Peter Meyer. *The Pledge: A History of the Pledge of Allegiance.* New York: St. Martin's Press, 2010.

Kaufman, Jonathan, and Gary Fields. "Election of Obama Recasts National Conversation on Race." *Wall Street Journal,* November 10, 2008.

Kimmel, Michael. "Racism as Adolescent Male Rite of Passage." *Journal of Contemporary Ethnography,* 36, 2, April 2007:202–218.

Kochbar, Rakesh, and Ana Gonzalez-Barrera. "Through Boom and Bust: Minorities, Immigrants and Homeownership." Washington, D.C.: Pew Hispanic Center, May 12, 2009.

Lacey, Marc. "Majestic Views, Ancient Culture, and a Profit Fight." *New York Times,* April 23, 2011.

Lee, Sharon M. "Asian Americans: Diverse and Growing." *Population Bulletin,* 53, 2, June 1998:1–39.

Leland, John, and Gregory Beals. "In Living Colors." *Newsweek,* May 5, 1997:58–60.

Lewin, Tamar. "Colleges Regroup after Voters Ban Race Preferences." *New York Times,* January 26, 2007.

Lind, Michael. *The Next American Nation: The New Nationalism and the Fourth American Revolution.* New York: Free Press, 1995.

Lynn, Michael, Michael Sturman, Christie Ganley, Elizabeth Adams, Mathew Douglas, and Jessica McNeil. "Consumer Racial Discrimination in Tipping: A Replication and Extension." *Journal of Applied Social Psychology,* 38, 4, 2008:1045–1060.

Mahoney, John S., Jr., and Paul G. Kooistra. "Policing the Races: Structural Factors Enforcing Racial Purity in Virginia (1630–1930)." Paper presented at the annual meetings of the American Sociological Association, 1995.

Mander, Jerry. *In the Absence of the Sacred: The Failure of Technology and the Survival of the Indian Nations.* San Francisco, Calif.: Sierra Club Books, 1992.

Marino, David. "Border Watch Group 'Techno Patriots' Still Growing." Tucson, Arizona: KVOA News 4, February 14, 2008.

McFarland, Sam. "Authoritarianism, Social Dominance, and Other Roots of Generalized Prejudice." *Political Psychology,* 31, 3, June 2010:453–477.

McIntosh, Peggy. "White Privilege and Male Privilege: A Personal Account of Coming to See Correspondences through Work in Women's Studies." Wellesley College Center for Research on Women, Working Paper 189, 1988.

McLemore, S. Dale. *Racial and Ethnic Relations in America.* Boston: Allyn and Bacon, 1994.

Mohawk, John C. "Indian Economic Development: An Evolving Concept of Sovereignty." *Buffalo Law Review,* 39, 2, Spring 1991:495–503.

Montagu, M. F. Ashley. *Introduction to Physical Anthropology,* 3rd ed. Springfield, Ill.: Thomas, 1960.

Montagu, M. F. Ashley. *The Concept of Race.* New York: Free Press, 1964.

Montagu, M. F. Ashley, ed. *Race and IQ: Expanded Edition.* New York: Oxford University Press, 1999.

Murray, Christopher J. L., Sandeep C. Kulkarni, Catherine Michard, Niels Tomijima, Maria T. Bulzaccheili, Terrell J. Landiorio, and Majid Ezzati. "Eight Americas: Investigating Mortality Disparities across Races, Counties, and Race-Counties in the United States." *PLoS Medicine,* 3, 9, September 2006:1513–1524.

Nash, Gary B. *Red, White, and Black.* Englewood Cliffs, N.J.: Prentice Hall, 1974.

Navarro, Mireya. "For New York's Black Latinos, a Growing Racial Awareness." *New York Times,* April 28, 2003.

Office of Immigration Statistics. "Annual Report: Immigration Enforcement Actions: 2007." Washington, D.C.: U.S. Department of Homeland Security, December 2008.

Peterson, Iver. "1993 Deal for Indian Casino Is Called a Model to Avoid." *New York Times,* June 30, 2003.

Popescu, Ioana, Mary S. Vaughan-Sarrazin, and Gary E. Rosenthal. "Differences in Mortality and Use of Revascularization in Black and White Patients With Acute MI Admitted to Hospitals With and Without Revascularization Services." *Journal of the American Medical Association, 297,* 22, June 13, 2007:2489–2495.

Portes, Alejandro, and Rubén G. Rumbaut. *Immigrant America.* Berkeley: University of California Press, 1990.

Powell, Michael, and Janet Roberts. "Minorities Hit Hardest by Foreclosures in New York." *New York Times,* May 15, 2009.

Pratt, Timothy. "Nevada's Gambling Revenue Rises After Two Year Slump." Reuters, February 10, 2011.

Preston, Julia. "Homeland Security Cancels 'Virtual Fence' after Billion Is Spent." *New York Times,* January 14, 2011.

Qian, Zhenchao, and Daniel T. Lichter. "Social Boundaries and Marital Assimilation: Interpreting Trends in Racial and Ethnic Intermarriage." *American Sociological Review, 72,* February 2007:68–94.

Ray, J. J. "Authoritarianism Is a Dodo: Comment on Scheepers, Felling and Peters." *European Sociological Review, 7,* 1, May 1991:73–75.

Reskin, Barbara F. *The Realities of Affirmative Action in Employment.* Washington, D.C.: American Sociological Association, 1998.

Richman, Joe. "From the Belgian Congo to the Bronx Zoo." National Public Radio, September 8, 2006.

Riley, Naomi Schaefer. "The Real Path to Racial Harmony." *Wall Street Journal,* August 14, 2009.

Rivlin, Gary. "Beyond the Reservation." *New York Times,* September 22, 2007.

Roediger, David R. *Colored White: Transcending the Racial Past.* Berkeley: University of California Press, 2002.

Schaefer, Richard T. *Racial and Ethnic Groups,* 9th ed. Upper Saddle River, N.J.: Prentice Hall, 2004.

Sherif, Muzafer, and Carolyn Sherif. *Groups in Harmony and Tension.* New York: Harper & Row, 1953.

Simpson, George Eaton, and J. Milton Yinger. *Racial and Cultural Minorities: An Analysis of Prejudice and Discrimination,* 4th ed. New York: Harper & Row, 1972.

Skinner, Jonathan, James N. Weinstein, Scott M. Sporer, and John E. Wennberg. "Racial, Ethnic, and Geographic Disparities in Rates of Knee Arthroplasty among Medicare Patients." *New England Journal of Medicine, 349,* 14, October 2, 2003:1350–1359.

Smedley, Audrey, and Brian D. Smedley. "Race as Biology Is Fiction, Racism as a Social Problem Is Real: Anthropological and Historical Perspectives on the Social Construction of Race." *American Psychologist, 60,* 1, January 2005:16–26.

Spickard, P. R. S. *Mixed Blood: Intermarriage and Ethnic Identity in Twentieth Century America.* Madison: University of Wisconsin Press, 1989.

Statistical Abstract of the United States. Washington, D.C.: U.S. Census Bureau, published annually.

Stolberg, Sheryl Gay. "Blacks Found on Short End of Heart Attack Procedure." *New York Times,* May 10, 2001.

Suzuki, Bob H. "Asian-American Families." In *Marriage and Family in a Changing Society,* 2nd ed., James M. Henslin, ed. New York: Free Press, 1985:104–119.

Tafoya, Sonya M., Hans Johnson, and Laura E. Hill. "Who Chooses to Choose Two?" Washington, D.C.: Population Reference Bureau, 2005.

Thomas, Paulette. "U.S. Examiners Will Scrutinize Banks with Poor Minority-Lending Histories." *Wall Street Journal,* October 22, 1991:A2.

Thomas, Paulette. "Boston Fed Finds Racial Discrimination in Mortgage Lending Is Still Widespread." *Wall Street Journal,* October 9, 1992:A3.

Thomas, W. I., and Dorothy Swaine Thomas. *The Child in America: Behavior Problems and Programs.* New York: Alfred A. Knopf, 1928.

Thompson, Don. "Officials: Gang Rivalry Led to Calif. Prison Riot." Associated Press, December 10, 2009.

Thompson, Ginger. "Where Education and Assimilation Collide." *New York Times,* March 14, 2009.

Thornton, Russell. *American Indian Holocaust and Survival: A Population History Since 1492.* Norman: University of Oklahoma Press, 1987.

U.S. Census Bureau, Population Division. "Percent of the Projected Population by Race and Hispanic Origin for the United States: 2010 to 2050." Constant Net International Migration Series (NP2009-T6-C):Table 6-C, December 16, 2009.

U.S. Census Bureau. "Annual Social and Economic Supplement to Current Population Survey." Washington, D.C.: U.S. Government Printing Office, 2010.

Wagley, Charles, and Marvin Harris. *Minorities in the New World.* New York: Columbia University Press, 1958.

Willie, Charles Vert. "Caste, Class, and Family Life Experiences." *Research in Race and Ethnic Relations, 6,* 1991:65–84.

Wilson, William Julius. *The Declining Significance of Race: Blacks and Changing American Institutions.* Chicago: University of Chicago Press, 1978.

Wilson, William Julius. *When Work Disappears: The World of the New Urban Poor.* Chicago: University of Chicago Press, 1996.

Wilson, William Julius. *The Bridge over the Racial Divide: Rising Inequality and Coalition Politics.* Berkeley: University of California Press, 2000.

Wilson, William Julius. "Jobless Poverty: A New Form of Social Dislocation in the Inner-City Ghetto." In *The Inequality Reader: Contemporary and Foundational Readings in Race, Class and Gender,* David B. Grusky and Szonja Szelenyi, eds. Boulder: Westview Press, 2007:142–152.

Wirth, Louis. "The Problem of Minority Groups." In *The Science of Man in the World Crisis,* Ralph Linton, ed. New York: Columbia University Press, 1945.

Wright, Lawrence. "One Drop of Blood." *The New Yorker,* July 25, 1994:46–50, 52–55.

Yinger, J. Milton. *Toward a Field Theory of Behavior: Personality and Social Structure.* New York: McGraw-Hill, 1965.

Marriage and Family

From Chapter 10 of *Sociology: A Down-to-Earth Approach, Core Concepts,* Fifth Edition. James M. Henslin.

Marriage and Family

I was living in a remote village in the state of Colima, Mexico. I had chosen this nondescript town a few kilometers from the ocean because it had no other Americans, and I wanted to immerse myself in the local culture.

The venture was successful. I became friends with my neighbors, who were curious about why a gringo was living in their midst. After all, there was nothing about their drab and dusty town to attract tourists. So why was this gringo there, this guy who looked so different from them and who had the unusual custom of jogging shirtless around the outskirts of town and among the coconut and banana trees? This was their burning question, while mine was "What is your life like?"

We satisfied one another. I explained to them what a sociologist is. Although they never grasped why I would want to know about *their* way of life, they accepted my explanation. And I was able to get my questions answered. I was invited into their homes—by the men. The women didn't talk to men outside the presence of their husbands, brothers, or other women. The women didn't even go out in public unless they were accompanied by someone. Another woman would do, just so they weren't alone. The women did the cooking, cleaning and child care. The men worked in the fields.

I was culturally startled one day at my neighbor's house. The man had retired from the fields, and he and his wife, as the custom was, were being supported by their sons who worked in the fields. When I saw the bathroom, with a homemade commode made of clay—these were poor people—I asked him about the used toilet paper thrown into a pile on the floor. He explained

It was his wife's job to pick up the used toilet paper.

that the sewer system couldn't handle toilet paper. He said that I should just throw mine onto the pile, adding that it was his wife's job to pick up the used toilet paper and throw it out.

I became used to the macho behavior of the men. This wasn't too unlike high-school behavior—a lot of boisterous man-to-man stuff—drinking, joking, and bragging about sexual conquests. The sex was vital for proving manhood. When the men took me to a whorehouse (to help explain their culture, they said), they couldn't understand why I wouldn't have sex with a prostitute. Didn't I find the women attractive? Yes, they were good looking. Weren't they sexy? Yes, very much so. Was I a real man? Yes. Then why not? My explanation about being married didn't faze them one bit. They were married, too—and a real man had to have sex with more women than just his wife.

Explanations of friendship with a wife and respect for her fell on deaf cultural ears.

Florida

Marriage and Family in Global Perspective

These men and I were inhabiting the same physical space, but our cultural space—which we carry in our heads and show in our behavior—was worlds apart. My experiences with working-class men in this remote part of Mexico helped me understand how marriage and family can vastly differ from one culture to another. To broaden this perspective for interpreting our own experience with this vital social institution, let's look at how customs differ around the world.

What Is a Family?

"What is a family, anyway?" *Family* should be easy to define, since it is so significant to humanity that it is universal. Although every human group organizes its members in families, the world's cultures display an incredible variety of family forms. The Western world regards a family as a husband, wife, and children, but in some groups men have more than one wife (**polygyny**) or women more than one husband (**polyandry**). How about the obvious? Can we define the family as the approved group into which children are born? If so, we would overlook the Banaro of New Guinea. In this group, a young woman must give birth *before* she can marry—and she *cannot* marry the father of her child (Murdock 1949).

What if we were to define the family as the unit in which parents are responsible for disciplining children and providing for their material needs? This, too, seems obvious, but it is not universal. Among the Trobriand Islanders, it is not the parents but the wife's eldest brother who is responsible for providing the children's discipline and their food (Malinowski 1927).

Such remarkable variety means that we have to settle for a broad definition. A **family** consists of people who consider themselves related by blood, marriage, or adoption. A **household,** in contrast, consists of people who occupy the same housing unit—a house, apartment, or other living quarters.

We can classify families as **nuclear** (husband, wife, and children) and extended (including people such as grandparents, aunts, uncles, and cousins in addition to the nuclear unit). Sociologists also refer to the **family of orientation** (the family in which an individual grows up) and the **family of procreation** (the family that is formed when a couple has its first child).

What Is Marriage?

We have the same problem in defining marriage. For just about every element you might regard as essential to marriage, some group has a different custom.

Consider the sex of the bride and groom. Until recently, opposite sex was taken-for-granted. Then in the 1980s and 1990s, several European countries legalized same-sex marriages. Canada and several U.S. states soon followed.

Same-sex marriages sound so new, but when Columbus landed in the Americas, some Native American tribes already had same-sex marriages. Through a ceremony called the *berdache*, a man or woman who wanted to be a member of the opposite sex was officially *declared* to have his or her sex changed. The "new" man or woman put on the clothing and performed the tasks associated with his or her new sex, and was allowed to marry.

Even sexual relationships don't universally characterize marriage. The Nayar of Malabar never allow a bride and groom to have sex. After a three-day celebration of the marriage, they send the groom packing—and never allow him to see his bride again (La Barre 1954). This can be a little puzzling to figure out, but it works like this: The groom is "borrowed" from another tribe for the ceremony. Although the Nayar bride can't have sex with her husband, after the wedding she can have approved lovers from her tribe. This system keeps family property intact—along matrilineal lines.

---

polygyny a form of marriage in which men have more than one wife

polyandry a form of marriage in which women have more than one husband

family two or more people who consider themselves related by blood, marriage, or adoption

household people who occupy the same housing unit

nuclear family a family consisting of a husband, wife, and child(ren)

Often one of the strongest family bonds is that of mother–daughter. The young artist, an eleventh grader, wrote: "This painting expresses the way I feel about my future with my child. I want my child to be happy and I want her to love me the same way I love her. In that way we will have a good relationship so that nobody will be able to take us apart. I wanted this picture to be alive; that is why I used a lot of bright colors."

Courtesy of the National Parenting Association (NPA), N.Y. copyright 1994 by the NPA

What is a family? What is marriage? Why are they so difficult to define?

At least one thing has to be universal in marriage: We can at least be sure that the bride and groom are alive. So you would think. But even for this there is an exception. On the Loess Plateau in China, if a son dies without a wife, his parents look for a dead woman to be his bride. After buying one—from the parents of a dead unmarried daughter—the dead man and woman are married and then buried together. Happy that their son will have intimacy in the afterlife, the parents throw a party to celebrate the marriage (Fremson 2006).

With such encompassing cultural variety, we can define **marriage** this way—a group's approved mating arrangements, usually marked by a ritual of some sort (the wedding) to indicate the couple's new public status.

Common Cultural Themes

Despite this diversity, several common themes run through marriage and family. As Table 1 illustrates, all societies use marriage and family to establish patterns of mate selection, descent, inheritance, and authority. Let's look at these patterns.

Mate Selection.   Each human group establishes norms to govern who marries whom. If a group has norms of **endogamy,** it specifies that its members must marry *within* their group. For example, some groups prohibit interracial marriage. In some societies, these norms are written into law, but in most cases they are informal. In the United States, most whites marry whites, and most African Americans marry African Americans—not because of any laws but because of informal norms. In contrast, norms of **exogamy** specify that people must marry *outside* their group. The best example of exogamy is the **incest taboo,** which prohibits sex and marriage among designated relatives.

As you can see from Table 1, how people find mates varies around the world, from fathers selecting them to the highly personal choices common in Western cultures. Changes in mate selection are the focus of the Sociology and the New Technology box on the next page.

Descent.   How are you related to your father's father or to your mother's mother? You would think that the answer to this question would be the same all over the world—but it isn't. Each society has a **system of descent,** the way people trace kinship over generations.

---

family of orientation the family in which a person grows up

family of procreation the family formed when a couple's first child is born

marriage a group's approved mating arrangements, usually marked by a ritual of some sort

endogamy the practice of marrying within one's own group

exogamy the practice of marrying outside of one's group

incest taboo the rule that prohibits sex and marriage among designated relatives

system of descent how kinship is traced over the generations

TABLE 1	Common Cultural Themes: Marriage in Traditional and Industrialized Societies	
Characteristic	**Traditional Societies**	**Industrial (and Postindustrial) Societies**
What is the structure of marriage?	*Extended* (marriage embeds spouses in a large kinship network of explicit obligations)	*Nuclear* (marriage brings fewer obligations toward the spouse's relatives)
What are the functions of marriage?	Encompassing (see the six functions listed)	More limited (many functions are fulfilled by other social institutions)
Who holds authority?	*Patriarchal* (authority is held by males)	Although some patriarchal features remain, authority is divided more equally
How many spouses at one time?	Most have one spouse (*monogamy*), while some have several (*polygamy*)	One spouse
Who selects the spouse?	Parents, usually the father, select the spouse	Individuals choose their own spouses
Where does the couple live?	Couples usually reside with the groom's family (*patrilocal residence*), less commonly with the bride's family (*matrilocal residence*)	Couples establish a new home (*neolocal residence*)
How is descent figured?	Usually figured from male ancestors (*patrilineal kinship*), less commonly from female ancestors (*matrilineal kinship*)	Figured from male and female ancestors equally (*bilineal kinship*)
How is inheritance figured?	Rigid system of rules; usually patrilineal, but can be matrilineal	Highly individualistic; usually bilineal

Source: By the author.

What common cultural themes run through marriage? How does marriage differ in traditional and industrialized societies?

Sociology and the New Technology

Online Dating: Risks and Rewards

I had just moved to Colorado, and I didn't know anyone. I decided to go on the matchmaking Web site. I filled out the profile, but I didn't have high expectations. I searched for someone who liked similar activities and had a similar taste in music.

I could weed through the profiles and eliminate the Wackos, the Desperates, and the Shady. I e-mailed three men. Pedro seemed interesting. We wrote back and forth for a while. It was a little scary when he asked to meet somewhere. It was out of my comfort zone—I had never seen him, and none of my friends knew him.

We met at a neighborhood bar, where a local band was playing. We talked for hours. I knew so much about him before we met.

Then we started dating normally.

(Interview by the author of Brenda, a woman in her late 20s.)

Brenda's last statement is especially significant. Although Internet dating has lost much of its stigma, a residue remains. You can see how Brenda expresses her feelings that Internet dating is not quite normal.

As Internet dating becomes more popular, it will lose all stigma. Dating sites offer thousands of potential companions, lovers, or spouses. For a low monthly fee, you can meet the person of your dreams—or so go the advertising, and the hopes.

The photos on these sites are fascinating. Some seem to be lovely people—warm, attractive, and vivacious. Others seem okay, although perhaps a bit needy. Then there are the desperate, begging for someone—anyone—to contact them: women who try for sexy poses, their exposed flesh suggesting the promise of a good time, and men who do their best to look like hulks, their muscular presence promising the same.

As Brenda pointed out, the Internet also has the Wackos and the Shady. How do you avoid getting mixed up with them? Just trust your intuition or gut—those vague feelings that things are okay or not? Maybe, but some women have followed their feelings only to meet grisly ends at the hands of serial killers.

Not to worry. Just get *Date Check*, an app for the iPhone that offers a "sleaze detector" to investigate potential dates

(Rosen 2010). You can learn the person's criminal history and current and previous addresses.

Of course, many serial killers don't have criminal records. But at least no one who has been convicted of rape and killing will pass the test.

Pedro, by the way, who Brenda met online, did pass the test. Brenda and Pedro are now enjoying their third year of marriage. They are also expecting their first child.

For Your Consideration

→ What is your opinion of online dating sites? Have you used one? Would you consider using one (if you were single and unattached)? Why or why not?

Snapshots

© Jason Love/www.CartoonStock.com

Tall, Dark, and Handsome chats with Buxom Blonde.

---

bilineal system (of descent) a system of reckoning descent that counts both the mother's and the father's side

patrilineal system (of descent) a system of reckoning descent that counts only the father's side

We use a **bilineal system,** for we think of ourselves as related to both our mother's and our father's sides of the family. As obvious as this seems to us, when we look around the world we find that ours is only one way that people reckon descent. Some groups use a **patrilineal system,** tracing descent only on the father's side—they don't think of children as being related to their mother's relatives. Others don't consider children to be related to their father's relatives and follow a **matrilineal system,** tracing descent only on the mother's side. The Naxi of China don't even have a word for father (Hong 1999).

How is the Internet changing dating for some? What are bilineal, patrilineal, and matrilineal systems?

Inheritance.   Marriage and family are also used to determine rights of inheritance. In a bilineal system, property is passed to both males and females, in a patrilineal system only to males, and in a matrilineal system (the rarest form) only to females. No system is natural. Rather, each matches a group's ideas of justice and logic.

Authority.   Some form of **patriarchy,** a social system in which men-as-a-group dominate women-as-a-group, runs through all societies. Contrary to what some think, there are no historical records of a true **matriarchy,** a society in which women-as-a-group dominate men-as-a-group. Although U.S. family patterns are becoming more **egalitarian,** or equal, some of today's customs still reflect their patriarchal origin. One of the most obvious is the U.S. naming pattern: Despite some changes, the typical bride still takes the groom's last name, and children usually receive the father's last name.

Marriage and Family in Theoretical Perspective

As we have seen, human groups around the world have many forms of mate selection, ways to view the parent's responsibility, and ways to trace descent. Although these patterns are arbitrary, each group perceives its own forms of marriage and family as natural. Now let's see what pictures emerge when we view marriage and family theoretically.

The Functionalist Perspective: Functions and Dysfunctions

When functionalists look at marriage and family, they examine how they are related to other parts of society, especially the ways that marriage and family contribute to the well-being of society.

Why the Family Is Universal.   Although the form of marriage and family varies from one group to another, the family is universal. The reason for this, say functionalists, is that the family fulfills six needs that are basic to the survival of every society. These needs, or functions, are (1) economic production, (2) socialization of children, (3) care of the sick and aged, (4) recreation, (5) sexual control, and (6) reproduction. To make certain that these functions are performed, every human group has adopted some form of the family.

Functions of the Incest Taboo.   Functionalists note that the incest taboo helps families to avoid *role confusion*. This, in turn, facilitates the socialization of children. For example, if father–daughter incest were allowed, how should a wife treat her daughter— as a daughter or as a second wife? Should the daughter consider her mother as a mother or as the first wife? Would her father be a father or a lover? And would the wife be the husband's main wife or the "mother of the other wife"? And if the daughter had a child by her father, what relationships would everyone have? Maternal incest would also lead to complications every bit as confusing as these.

The incest taboo also forces people to look outside the family for marriage partners. Anthropologists theorize that *exogamy* was especially functional in tribal societies, for it forged alliances between tribes that otherwise might have killed each other off. Today, exogamy still extends both the bride's and the groom's social networks by adding and building relationships with their spouse's family and friends.

Isolation and Emotional Overload.   As you know, functionalists also analyze dysfunctions. The relative isolation of today's nuclear family creates one of those dysfunctions. Because they are embedded in a larger kinship network, the members of extended families can count on many people for material and emotional support. In nuclear families, in contrast, the stresses that come with crises—the loss of a job, a death, or even family quarrels—are spread among fewer people. This places greater strain on each family member, creating *emotional overload*. In addition, the relative isolation of the nuclear family makes it vulnerable to a "dark side"—incest and other forms of abuse, matters that we examine later in this chapter.

matrilineal system (of descent) a system of reckoning descent that counts only the mother's side

patriarchy a group in which men-as-a-group dominate women-as-a-group; authority is vested in males

matriarchy a society in which women-as-a-group dominate men-as-a-group; authority is vested in females

egalitarian authority more or less equally divided between people or groups (in heterosexual marriage, for example, between husband and wife)

Why are marriage and family universal? What six functions do they perform?

FIGURE 1 — Who Makes the Decisions at Home?

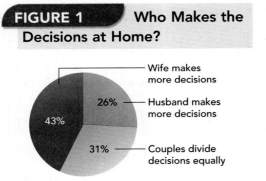

- 26% — Wife makes more decisions
- 43% — Husband makes more decisions
- 31% — Couples divide decisions equally

Note: Based on a nationally representative sample, with questions on who chooses weekend activities, buys things for the home, decides what to watch on television, and manages household finances.

Source: Morin and Cohn 2008.

"Women Call the Shots at Home; Public Mixed on Gender Roles in Jobs" by Pew Social Trends Staff from the Pew Research Center website. Copyright © 2008 by Social & Demographic Trends, a Pew Research Center project. Reprinted with permission. http://pewsocialtrends.org

James M. Henslin

In Hindu marriages, the roles of husband and wife are firmly established. Neither this woman, whom I photographed in Chittoor, India, nor her husband question whether she should carry the family wash to the village pump. Women here have done this task for millennia. As India industrializes, as happened in the West, who does the wash will be questioned—and may eventually become a source of strain in marriage.

The Conflict Perspective: Struggles between Husbands and Wives

Anyone who has been married or who has seen a marriage from the inside knows that—despite a couple's best intentions—conflict is a part of marriage. Conflict inevitably arises between two people who live intimately and who share most everything in life—from their goals and checkbooks to their bedroom and children. At some point, their desires and approaches to life clash, sometimes mildly, at other times quite harshly. Conflict among married people is so common that it is the grist of soap operas, movies, songs, and novels.

Power is the source of such conflict in marriage. Who has it? And who resents not having it? Throughout history, husbands have had more power, and wives have resented it. In the United States, as I'm sure you know, wives have gained more and more power in marriage. Do your think that one day wives will have more power than their husbands?

You probably are saying that such a day will never come. But maybe wives have already reached this point. From time to time, you've seen some surprising things in this book. Now look at Figure 1. Based on a national sample, this figure shows who makes decisions concerning the family's finances and purchases, what to do on the weekends, and even what to watch on television. As you can see, wives now have more control over the family purse and make more of these decisions than do their husbands. These findings are such a surprise that we await confirmation by future studies.

The Symbolic Interactionist Perspective: Gender, Housework, and Child Care

Changes in Traditional Gender Orientations. The opening vignette gave you a glimpse into extreme traditional gender roles. Apart from the specifics mentioned there, throughout the generations, housework and child care have been regarded as "women's work." As women put in more hours at paid work, men gradually did more housework and took more responsibility for the care of their children. Ever so slowly, cultural ideas shifted, with housework, care of children, and paid labor coming to be regarded as the responsibilities of both men and women. Let's examine this shift.

Who Does What? Figure 2 illustrates several significant changes that have taken place in U.S. families. The first is likely to surprise you. If you look closely at this figure, you will see that not only are husbands spending more time taking care of the children but so are wives. This is fascinating. How can *both* husbands and wives be spending more time in child care? This flies in the face of our mythical past, the *Leave-It-to-Beaver* images that color our perception of the present. We know that families are not leisurely lolling through their days as huge paychecks flow in, so if parents are spending more time with their children, just where is the time coming from?

Today's parents are squeezing out more hours for their children by spending less time on social activities and by participating less in organizations. But this accounts for only some of the time. To get the rest of the answer, look again at Figure 2. This time focus on the hours that husbands and wives spend doing housework. You can see that although men are doing more housework than they used to, women are spending less time on housework, so much less that the total hours that husbands and wives spend on housework have dropped from 38.9 to 29.1 hours a week. This leaves a lot more time to spend with the children.

Does this mean that today's parents aren't as fussy about housework as their parents were, and today's houses are dirtier and messier? This is one possibility. Or technology could be the explanation (Bianchi et al. 2006).

What are the conflict and symbolic interactionist perspectives on marriage and family?

FIGURE 2   In Two-Paycheck Marriages, How Do Husbands and Wives Divide Their Responsibilities?

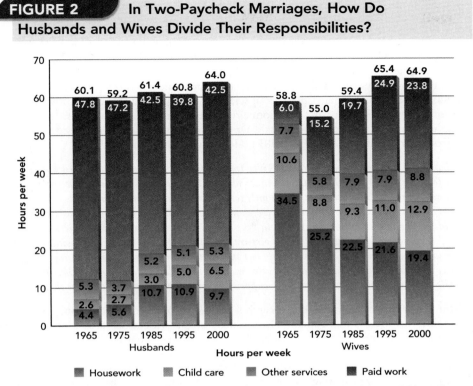

Source: By the author. Based on Bianchi et al. 2006. Housework hours are from Table 5.1, child care from Table 4.1, and work hours and total hours from Table 3.4. "Other services" is derived by subtracting the hours for housework, child care, and paid work from the total hours.

Our microwaves, dishwashers, washing machines, clothes dryers, and wrinkle-free clothing certainly save hours of drudgery. The "McDonaldization" that leads to so many "fast-food" meals, also reduces the time spent on food preparation and cleanup. Perhaps, then, home hygiene is about the same as before even though both parents spend more time with the children.

Finally, from Figure 2, you can see that husbands and wives spend their time differently. In what sociologists call a *gendered division of labor*, husbands still take the primary responsibility for earning the income and wives the primary responsibility for taking care of the house and children. You can also see that a shift is taking place in this traditional gender orientation: Wives are spending more time earning the family income, while husbands are spending more time on housework and child care. In light of these trends and with changing ideas of gender—of what is considered appropriate for husbands and wives—we can anticipate greater marital equality in the future.

The Family Life Cycle

We have seen how the forms of marriage and family vary widely, looked at marriage and family theoretically, and examined major changes in family relationships. Now let's discuss love, courtship, and the family life cycle.

Love and Courtship in Global Perspective

Have you ever been sick over love? Some people can't eat, and they are obsessed with thoughts of the one they love. When neuroscientists decided to study "love sickness," they found that it is real: Love feelings light up the same area of the brain that lights up when cocaine addicts are craving coke (Fisher et al. 2010).

What does a "gendered division of labor" mean? How has it changed in U.S. families?

romantic love feelings of erotic attraction accompanied by an idealization of the other

homogamy the tendency of people with similar characteristics to marry one another

Evidently, then, love can be an addiction. From your own experience, you probably know the power of **romantic love**—mutual sexual attraction and idealized feelings about one another. Although people in most cultures talk about similar experiences (Jankowiak and Fischer 1992), ideas of love can differ dramatically from one society to another. As the Cultural Diversity box on the next page explains, for example, Indians don't expect love to occur until *after* marriage.

Because love plays such a significant role in Western life—and often is regarded as the *only* proper basis for marriage—social scientists have probed this concept with the tools of the trade: experiments, questionnaires, interviews, and observations. In a fascinating experiment, psychologists Donald Dutton and Arthur Aron discovered that fear can produce romantic love (Rubin 1985). Here's what they did.

> *About 230 feet above the Capilano River in North Vancouver, British Columbia, a rickety footbridge sways in the wind. It makes you feel like you might fall into the rocky gorge below. A more solid footbridge crosses only ten feet above the shallow stream.*
>
> *The experimenters had an attractive woman approach men who were crossing these bridges. She told them she was studying "the effects of exposure to scenic attractions on creative expression." She showed them a picture, and they wrote down their associations. The sexual imagery in their stories showed that the men on the unsteady, frightening bridge were more sexually aroused than were the men on the solid bridge. More of these men also called the young woman afterward—supposedly to get information about the study.*

You may have noticed that this research was really about sexual attraction, not love. The point, however, is that romantic love usually begins with sexual attraction. Finding ourselves sexually attracted to someone, we spend time with that person. If we discover mutual interests, we may label our feelings "love." Apparently, then, *romantic love has two components*. The first is emotional, a feeling of sexual attraction. The second is cognitive, a label that we attach to our feelings. If we attach this label, we describe ourselves as being "in love."

Marriage

Ask Americans why they married, and they will say that they were "in love." Contrary to folklore, whatever love is, it certainly is not blind. That is, love does not hit us willy-nilly, as if Cupid had shot darts blindly into a crowd. If it did, marital patterns would be unpredictable. When we look at who marries whom, however, we can see the social channels that love follows.

The Social Channels of Love and Marriage.   The most highly predictable social channels are age, education, social class, and race–ethnicity. For example, a Latina with a college degree whose parents are both physicians is likely to fall in love with and marry a Latino slightly older than herself who has graduated from college. Similarly, a girl who drops out of high school and whose parents are on welfare is likely to fall in love with and marry a man who comes from a background similar to hers.

Sociologists use the term **homogamy** to refer to the tendency of people who have similar characteristics to marry one another. Homogamy occurs largely as a result of *propinquity*, or spatial nearness. This is a sociological way of saying that we tend to "fall in love" with and marry someone who lives near us or someone we meet at school, church, work, or a neighborhood bar. The people with whom we associate are far from a random sample of the population, for social filters produce neighborhoods, schools, and places of worship that follow racial–ethnic and social class lines.

As with all social patterns, there are exceptions. Although 93 percent of married Americans choose someone of their same racial–ethnic background, 7 percent do not. Seven percent doesn't sound like much, but with 60 million married couples in the United States, this comes to over 4 million couples (*Statistical Abstract* 2011:Table 60).

One of the more dramatic changes in U.S. marriage is the increase in marriages between African Americans and whites. Today it is difficult to realize how norm-shattering such marriages used to be, but they were once illegal in 40 states (Staples 2008).

What are the two components of romantic love? What is meant by the "social channels" of love and marriage?

Excerpt from Rubin, Zick. "The Love Research." In *Marriage and Family in a Changing Society*, 2nd ed., James M. Henslin, ed. New York: Free Press, 1985.

Cultural Diversity around the World

East Is East and West Is West:
Love and Arranged Marriage in India

After Arun Bharat Ram returned to India with a degree from the University of Michigan, his mother announced that she wanted to find him a wife. Arun would be a good catch anywhere: 27 years old, educated, intelligent, handsome—and, not incidentally, heir to a huge fortune.

Arun's mother already had someone in mind. Manju came from a middle-class family and was a college graduate. Arun and Manju met in a coffee shop at a luxury hotel—along with both sets of parents. He found her pretty and quiet. He liked that. She was impressed that he didn't boast about his background.

After four more meetings, including one at which the two young people met by themselves, the parents asked their children whether they were willing to marry. Neither had any major objections.

The Prime Minister of India and fifteen hundred other guests came to the wedding.

"I didn't love him," Manju says. "But when we talked, we had a lot in common." She then adds, "But now I couldn't live without him. I've never thought of another man since I met him."

Despite India's many changes, parents still arrange about 90 percent of marriages. Unlike the past, however, today's couples have veto power over their parents' selection. Another innovation is that the prospective bride and groom are allowed to talk to each other before the wedding—unheard of a generation or two ago.

Why do Indians have arranged marriages? And why does this practice persist, even among the educated and upper classes? We can also ask why the United States has such an individualistic approach to marriage.

The answers to these questions take us to two sociological principles. First, *a group's marriage practices match its values.* Individual mate selection matches U.S. values of individuality and independence, while arranged marriages match the Indian value of children deferring to parental authority. To Indians, allowing unrestricted dating would mean entrusting important matters to inexperienced young people.

Second, *a group's marriage practices match its patterns of social stratification.* Arranged marriages in India affirm

James M. Henslin

This billboard in Chennai, India, caught my attention. As the text indicates, even though India is industrializing, most of its people still follow traditional customs. This billboard is a sign of changing times.

caste lines by channeling marriage within the same caste. Unchaperoned dating would encourage premarital sex, which, in turn, would break down family lines. Virginity at marriage, in contrast, assures the upper castes that they know who fathered the children. Consequently, Indians socialize their children to think that parents have superior wisdom in these matters. In the United States, where family lines are less important and caste is an alien concept, the practice of young people choosing their own dating partners mirrors the relative openness of our social class system.

These different backgrounds have produced contrasting ideas of love. Americans idealize love as something mysterious, a passion that suddenly seizes an individual. Indians view love as a peaceful feeling that develops when a man and a woman are united in intimacy and share life's interests and goals. For Americans, love just "happens," while for Indians the right conditions create love. Marriage is one of those right conditions.

The end result is this startling difference: *For Americans, love produces marriage—while for Indians, marriage produces love.*

Sources: Based on Gupta 1979; Bumiller 1992; Sprecher and Chandak 1992; Dugger 1998; Gautham 2002; Easley 2003; Berger 1963/2012; Swati and Ey 2008.

For Your Consideration

→ What advantages do you see to the Indian approach to love and marriage? Could the Indian system work in the United States? Why or why not? Do you think that love can be created? Or does love suddenly "seize" people? What do you think love is anyway?

Can you contrast love in India and the United States? How do ideas of love match each culture?

FIGURE 3 — Marriages between Whites and African Americans: The Race–Ethnicity of the Husbands and Wives

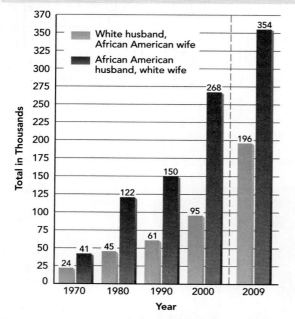

Source: By the author. *Based on Statistical Abstract of the United States 1990:Table 53; 2011:Table 60.*

In Mississippi, the penalty for interracial marriage was *life in prison* (Crossen 2004b). Despite the risks, a few couples crossed the "color line," but it took the social upheaval of the 1960s to break this barrier permanently. In 1967, the U.S. Supreme Court struck down the state laws that prohibited such marriages.

Figure 3 shows this change. Look at the race–ethnicity of the husbands and wives in these marriages, and you will see that here, too, Cupid's arrows don't hit random targets. Why do you think this particular pattern exists? Why do you think it is changing?

Childbirth

Ideal Family Size. The number of children that Americans consider ideal has changed over the years. As you can see from Figure 4, preferences have moved to having fewer children. The research shows an interesting religious divide, not between Protestants and Roman Catholics, who give the same answers, but by church attendance. Those who attend services more often prefer larger families than those who attend less often. The last couple of polls reveal something unexpected: Younger Americans (ages 18 to 34) prefer larger families than do those who are older than 34.

If they had their way, some couples would specify not just the number of children but also their characteristics, the topic of the Sociology and the New Technology box on the next page.

Marital Satisfaction. Sociologists have found that after the birth of a child marital satisfaction usually decreases (Claxton and Perry-Jenkins 2008; Senior 2010). To understand why, recall that a dyad (two persons) provides greater intimacy than a triad (after adding a third person,

✳ Explore
Living Data
on **mysoclab.com**

FIGURE 4 — The Number of Children Americans Think Are Ideal

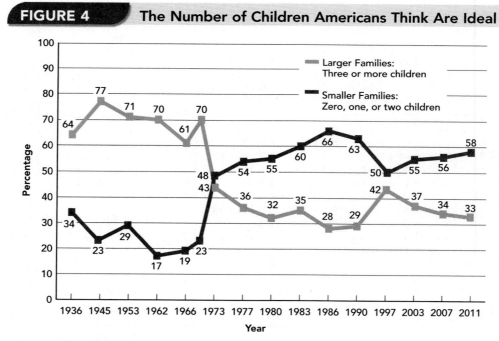

Source: Gallup Poll 2011.

How has the ideal U.S. family size changed over time? What new pattern (breaking at age 34) has emerged?

What Color Eyes? How Tall? Designer Babies on the Way

You aren't very athletic, but you want your daughter to be a basketball champ? You're short, but you want to make sure that your son is tall? You want your child to be musical?

Welcome to the world of Designer Baby Clinics, where you can put in your order. Not like fast food, of course, for it will still take the usual nine months. But you will get what you ordered.

Or at least this is the promise. A few technical details must still be worked out, but these hurdles are falling rapidly.

The allure of designer babies is apparent. To pick superior qualities for your child—this is sort of like being able to pick a superior college. To be able to do so much good for your child!

But with this allure come moral dilemmas. Let's suppose that a couple wants a green-eyed blond girl. As Figure 5 shows, the technicians will fertilize several eggs, test the embryos, and plant the one(s) with the desired characteristics in a uterus. And the ones that are not used? They will be flushed down the drain. Some people find this objectionable.

Others are concerned that selecting certain characteristics represents a bias against people who have different characteristics. To order a tall designer baby, for example, is this a bias against short people?

If this isn't quite clear, perhaps this will help. If there is a preference for boys, a lot of female embryos will be discarded.

There is also the issue of a super race. If we can produce people who are superior physically and intellectually, should we?

Or here is another issue. Two deaf parents want their child to share their subculture, not to be a part of the hearing world, which they fear will drive a wedge between them and their child (Naik 2009). Would it be moral or immoral to produce a deaf child?

Oh, the moral dilemmas our technologies bring!

For Your Consideration
➔ What are your answers to the questions raised in this box? On what do you base your answers?

FIGURE 5   On the Way to Designer Babies

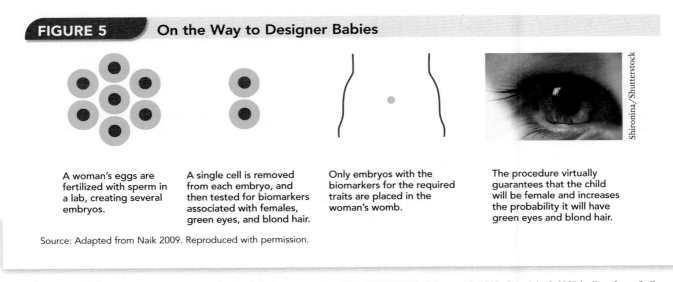

A woman's eggs are fertilized with sperm in a lab, creating several embryos.

A single cell is removed from each embryo, and then tested for biomarkers associated with females, green eyes, and blond hair.

Only embryos with the biomarkers for the required traits are placed in the woman's womb.

The procedure virtually guarantees that the child will be female and increases the probability it will have green eyes and blond hair.

Shironina/Shutterstock

Source: Adapted from Naik 2009. Reproduced with permission.

---

interaction must be shared). In addition, the birth of a child unbalances the life that the couple has worked out. To move from the abstract to the concrete, think about the implications for marriage of coping with a fragile newborn's 24-hour-a-day needs of being fed, soothed, and diapered—while the parents have less sleep and greater expenses.

Marital happiness increases when the last child reaches age 6, when the child starts school and is away from home a lot. This happiness is short-lived, though, and takes a nosedive when the child reaches age 12 or 13. You can figure this one out—the devil years of adolescence. But those years don't last forever (although many parents think they will), and happiness increases again when the last child gets through the troubled, rebellious years (Senior 2010).

Why does marital satisfaction tend to drop after the birth of the first child? What is the pattern of satisfaction after that?

"Your attitude is sucking all the fulfillment out of motherhood."

One of the most demanding, exasperating—and also fulfilling—roles in life is that of parent. To really appreciate this cartoon, perhaps one has to have experienced this part of the life course.

Read

Women and Men in the Caregiving Role by Rhonda J. V. Montgomery and Mary McGlinn Datwyler on **mysoclab.com**

Husbands and wives have children because of biological urges and because of the satisfactions they expect. New parents bubble over with joy, saying things like "There's no feeling to compare with holding your own child in your arms. Those little hands, those tiny feet, those big eyes, that little nose, that sweet face . . ." and they gush on and on.

There really is no equivalent to parents. It is *their* child, and no one else takes such delight in the baby's first steps, its first word, and so on. Let's turn, then, to child rearing.

Child Rearing

As you saw in Figure 2, today's parents—both mothers and fathers—are spending more time with their children than parents did in the 1970s and 1980s. Despite this trend, with mothers and fathers spending so many hours away from home at work, we must ask: Who's minding the kids while the parents are at work?

Married Couples and Single Mothers. Figure 6 compares the child care arrangements of single and married mothers. As you can see, their overall arrangements are similar. A main difference, though, is that when married women are at work the child is more likely to be under the father's care or in day care. For single mothers, grandparents and other relatives are more likely to fill in for the absent father.

Day Care. From Figure 6, you can see that about one of six or seven children is in day care. The broad conclusions of research on day care were reported. Apparently only a minority of U.S. day care centers offer high-quality care as measured by whether they provide stimulating learning activities, emotional warmth, and attentiveness to children's needs (Bergmann 1995; Blau 2000; Belsky 2009). A primary reason for this dismal situation is the low salaries paid to day care workers, who average only about $17,000 a year ("Career Guide. . ." 2011).

It is difficult for parents to judge the quality of day care, since they don't know what takes place when they are not there. If you ever look for day care, two factors best predict that children will receive quality care: staff who have taken courses in early childhood development and a low ratio of children per staff member (Blau 2000; Belsky et al. 2007). If you have nagging fears that your children might be neglected or even abused, choose a center that streams live Web cam images on the Internet. While at work, you can "visit" each room of the day care center via cyberspace and monitor your toddler's activities and care.

Nannies. For upper-middle-class parents, nannies have become a popular alternative to day care centers. Parents love the one-on-one care. They also like the convenience of in-home care, which eliminates the need to transport the child to an unfamiliar environment, reduces the chances that the child will catch illnesses, and eliminates the hardship of parents having to take time off from work when their child becomes ill. A recurring problem, however, is tensions between the parents and the nanny: jealousy that the nanny might see the first step, hear the first word, or—worse yet—be called "mommy." There are also tensions over different discipline styles and feelings of guilt or envy as the child cries when the nanny leaves but not when the mother goes to work.

Social Class. Do you think that social class makes a difference in how people rear their children? If you answered "yes," you are right. But what difference? And why? Sociologists have found that working-class parents tend to think of children as wildflowers that develop naturally, while in the middle-class mind children are like garden flowers that need a lot of nurturing if they are to bloom (Lareau 2002). These contrasting views

What patterns of child rearing has research on working class and middle class families revealed?

make a world of difference in how people rear their children. Working-class parents are more likely to set limits for their children and then let them choose their own activities, while middle-class parents are more likely to try to push their children into activities that they think will develop their thinking and social skills.

Sociologist Melvin Kohn (1963, 1977; Kohn and Schooler 1969) also found that the type of work that parents do has an impact on how they rear their children. Because members of the working class are closely supervised on their jobs, where they are expected to follow explicit rules, their concern is less with their children's motivation and more with their outward conformity. These parents are more apt to use physical punishment—which brings about outward conformity without regard for internal attitude. Middle-class workers, in contrast, are expected to take more initiative on the job. Consequently, middle-class parents have more concern that their children develop curiosity and self-expression. They are also more likely to withdraw privileges or affection than to use physical punishment.

Family Transitions

The later stages of family life bring their own pleasures to be savored and problems to be solved. Let's look at two transitions—children staying home longer and adults adjusting to widowhood.

"Adultolescents" and the Not-So-Empty Nest. Adolescents, especially the young men, used to leave home after finishing high school. (My high school graduation present was a suitcase.) When the last child left home at about age 17 to 19, the husband and wife were left with what was called an *empty nest.* Today's nest is not as empty as it used to be. With prolonged education and the higher cost of establishing a household, U.S. children are leaving home later. Many stay home during college, while others who strike out on their own find the cost or responsibility too great and return home. Much to their own disappointment, some even leave and return to the parents' home several times. As a result, 18 percent of all U.S. 25- to 29-year-olds are living with their parents. About 15 percent of this still-at-home group have children (U.S. Census Bureau 2010:Table A2).

This major historical change in how people become adults is playing out before our eyes. With the path to adulthood changing abruptly, its contours—its roadmap—are still being worked out. Although "adultolescents" enjoy the protection of home, they have to work out issues about turf, authority, and responsibilities—items that both the children and parents thought were long ago resolved.

Widowhood. As you know, women are more likely than men to become widowed. There are two reasons for this: On average, women live longer than men, and they usually marry men older than they are. For either women or men, the death of a spouse tears at the self, clawing at identities that had merged through the years. With the one who had become an essential part of the self gone, the survivor, as in adolescence, once again confronts the perplexing question "Who am I?"

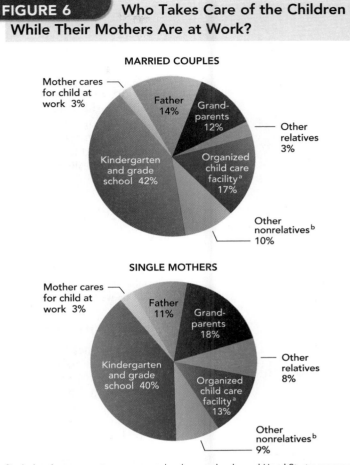

| FIGURE 6 | Who Takes Care of the Children While Their Mothers Are at Work? |

MARRIED COUPLES

Mother cares for child at work 3%
Father 14%
Grandparents 12%
Other relatives 3%
Kindergarten and grade school 42%
Organized child care facility[a] 17%
Other nonrelatives[b] 10%

SINGLE MOTHERS

Mother cares for child at work 3%
Father 11%
Grandparents 18%
Other relatives 8%
Kindergarten and grade school 40%
Organized child care facility[a] 13%
Other nonrelatives[b] 9%

[a]Includes day care centers, nursery schools, preschools, and Head Start programs.
[b]Includes in-home babysitters and other nonrelatives providing care in either the child's or the provider's home.

Source: *America's Children in Brief 2010*:Table FAM3A.

What are "adultolescents"? What problems do they and their parents face? What identity crisis does widowhood bring?

The death of a spouse produces what is called the *widowhood effect:* The impact of the death is so strong that surviving spouses tend to die earlier than expected. The "widowhood effect" is not even across the board, however, and those who have gone through anticipatory grief suffer fewer health consequences (Elwert and Christakis 2008). Apparently learning that their spouse was going to die gave them time to make preparations that smoothed the transition—from arranging finances to preparing themselves psychologically for being alone. You can see how saying goodbye and cultivating treasured last memories would help people adjust to the impending death of an intimate companion. Sudden death, in contrast, rips the loved one away, offering no chance for this predeath healing.

Diversity in U.S. Families

As we review some of the vast diversity of U.S. families, it is important to note that we are not comparing any of them to *the* American family. There is no such thing. Rather, family life varies widely throughout the United States. We have already seen in several contexts how significant social class is in our lives. Its significance will continue to be evident as we examine diversity in U.S. families.

African American Families

Note that the heading reads African American *families,* not *the* African American family. There is no such thing as *the* African American family any more than there is *the* white family or *the* Latino family. The primary distinction is not between African Americans and other groups, but between social classes (Willie and Reddick 2003). Because African Americans who are members of the upper class follow the class interests such as preservation of privilege and family fortune. They are especially concerned about the family background of those whom their children marry (Gatewood 1990). To them, marriage is viewed as a merger of family lines. Children of this class marry later than children of other classes.

Middle-class African American families focus on achievement and respectability. Both husband and wife are likely to work outside the home. A central concern is that their children go to college, get good jobs, and marry well—that is, marry people like themselves, respectable and hardworking, who want to get ahead in school and pursue a successful career.

African American families in poverty face all the problems that cluster around poverty (Wilson 2007; Bryant et al. 2010). Because the men are likely to be unemployed with few marketable skills, it is difficult for them to fulfill the cultural roles of husband and father. Consequently, these families are likely to be headed by a woman and to have a high rate of births to single women. Divorce and desertion are also more common than among other classes. Sharing scarce resources and "stretching kinship" are primary survival mechanisms. People who have helped out in hard times are considered brothers, sisters, or cousins to whom one owes obligations as though they were blood relatives; and men who are not the biological fathers of their children are given fatherhood status (Stack 1974; Hall 2008). Sociologists use the term *fictive kin* to refer to this stretching of kinship.

From Figure 7 you can see that, compared with other groups, African American families are the least likely to be headed by married couples and the most likely to be headed by

There is no such thing as *the* African American family, any more than there is *the* Native American, Asian American, Latino, or Irish American family. Rather, each racial–ethnic group has different types of families, with the primary determinant being social class.
Bill Bachmann/PhotoEdit Inc.

How do middle-class African American families and those in poverty differ?

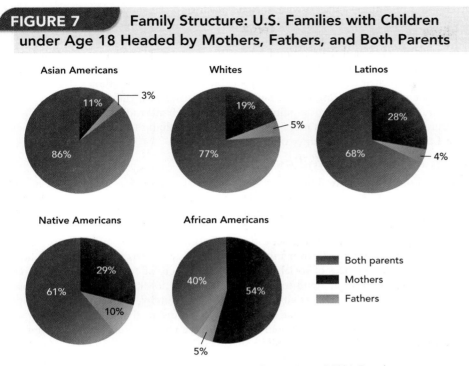

FIGURE 7 — Family Structure: U.S. Families with Children under Age 18 Headed by Mothers, Fathers, and Both Parents

Asian Americans
3%
11%
86%

Whites
19%
5%
77%

Latinos
28%
68%
4%

Native Americans
29%
61%
10%

African Americans
40%
54%
5%

■ Both parents
■ Mothers
■ Fathers

Sources: By the author. For Native Americans, "American Community . . ." 2004. For other groups, *Statistical Abstract of the United States* 2011:Table 69.

As with other groups, there is no such thing as *the* Latino family. Some Latino families speak little or no English, while others have assimilated into U.S. culture to such an extent that they no longer speak Spanish.

Bill Varie/Somos Images/Corbis

women. Because African American women tend to go farther in school than African American men, they face a *marriage squeeze*. That is, their pool of eligible partners with characteristics that match theirs has shrunk, and they are more likely than women in other racial–ethnic groups to marry men who are less educated than themselves (Eshleman 2000; Harford 2008).

Latino Families

As Figure 7 shows, the proportion of Latino families headed by married couples and women falls in between that of whites and Native Americans. The effects of social class on families, which I just sketched, also apply to Latinos. In addition, families differ by country of origin. Families from Mexico, for example, are more likely to be headed by a married couple than are families from Puerto Rico (*Statistical Abstract* 2011:Table 37). The longer that Latinos have lived in the United States, the more their families resemble those of middle-class Americans (Saenz 2004).

With such wide variety, experts disagree on what is distinctive about Latino families. Some researchers have found that Latino husbands/fathers play a stronger role than husbands/fathers in white and African American families (Vega 1990; Torres et al. 2002). Others point to the Spanish language, the Roman Catholic religion, and a strong family orientation coupled with a disapproval of divorce, but there are Latino families who are Protestants, don't speak Spanish, and so on. Still others emphasize loyalty to the extended family, with an obligation to support relatives in times of need (Cauce and Domenech-Rodriguez 2002), but this, too, is hardly unique to Latino families.

What is distinctive about Latino families?

machismo an emphasis on male strength and dominance

Descriptions of Latino families used to include **machismo**—an emphasis on male strength, sexual vigor, and dominance, like that recounted in the chapter's opening vignette—but *machismo* decreases with each generation in the United States and is certainly not limited to Latinos (Hurtado et al. 1992; Wood 2001; Torres et al. 2002). Compared to their husbands, Latina wives/mothers tend to be more family centered and display more warmth and affection for their children, but this is probably true of all racial–ethnic groups.

With such diversity among Latino families, you can see how difficult it is to draw generalizations. The sociological point that runs through all studies of Latino families, however, is this: Social class is more important in determining family life than is either being Latino or a family's country of origin.

Asian American Families

As you can see from Figure 7 on the previous page, Asian American children are more likely than children in other racial–ethnic groups to grow up with both parents. This significant difference is a foundation for the higher educational and income attainments of Asian Americans.

I also emphasized how Asian Americans, like Latinos, are not a single group. That Asian Americans emigrated from many different countries means that their family life reflects not only differences of social class but also a variety of cultures. Families whose origin is Japan, for example, tend to retain Confucian values that provide a framework for family life: humanism, collectivity, self-discipline, hierarchy, respect for the elderly, moderation, and obligation (Suzuki 1985). Obligation means that each member of a family owes respect to other family members and has a responsibility never to bring shame to the family. Conversely, a child's success brings honor to the family (Zamiska 2004). To control their children, these parents are more likely to use shame and guilt than physical punishment.

The cultural differences among Asian Americans are so extensive that many are not even familiar with Confucianism. In addition to the vast differences stemming from country of origin, Asian American family life also differs by length of residence in the United States. The more recent the immigration, the more that family life reflects the culture of origin, for like immigrants everywhere, recent immigrants continue their old patterns. The family life of Asian Americans who have been here for generations, in contrast, reflects few if any of the patterns of the country of origin. Trying to maneuver the gulf between the old and new cultures—bewildering worlds of incompatible expectations—creates such conflict that the children of Asian American immigrants have more mental problems than the children of those who have been here for generations (Meyers 2006; Ying and Han 2008).

Native American Families

Perhaps the most significant issue that Native American families face is whether to follow traditional values or to assimilate into the dominant culture (Frosch 2008). This primary distinction creates vast differences among families. The traditionals speak native languages and emphasize distinctive Native American values and beliefs. Those who have assimilated into the broader culture do not.

Figure 7 depicts the structure of Native American families. You can see that it is closest to that of Latinos. In general, Native American parents are permissive with their children and avoid physical punishment. Elders play a much more active role in their children's families than they do in most U.S. families: Elders, especially grandparents, not only provide child care but also teach and discipline children. Like others, Native American families differ by social class.

In Sum: From this brief review, you can see that race–ethnicity signifies little for understanding family life. Rather, social class and culture hold the keys. The more resources a family has, the more it assumes the characteristics of a middle-class nuclear family. Compared with the poor, middle-class families have fewer children and fewer unmarried mothers. They also place greater emphasis on educational achievement and deferred gratification.

What have researchers found about Asian American and Native American families?

One-Parent Families

An indication of how extensively U.S. families are changing is the increase in one-parent families. From Figure 8 on the next page, you can see that the percentage of U.S. children who live with two parents (not necessarily their biological parents) has dropped sharply. The concerns—even alarm—that are expressed about one-parent families may have more to do with their poverty than with children being reared by one parent. Because women head most one-parent families, these families tend to be poor. Although most divorced women earn less than their former husbands, four of five (81 percent) children of divorce live with their mothers (U.S. Census Bureau 2010:Table C3).

To understand the typical one-parent family, then, we need to view it through the lens of poverty, for this is its primary source of strain. The results are serious, not just for these parents and their children but also for society. Children from one-parent families are more likely to have behavioral problems in school, to drop out of school, to get arrested, to have physical and emotional health problems, and to get divorced (McLanahan and Sandefur 1994; Menaghan et al. 1997; McLanahan and Schwartz 2002; Amato and Cheadle 2005; Wen 2008). If female, they are more likely to have sex at a younger age and to bear children while still unmarried teenagers.

To search for *the* Native American family would be fruitless. There are rural, urban, single-parent, extended, nuclear, rich, poor, traditional, and assimilated Native American families, to name just a few. Shown here is a family from the Commanche tribe in New Mexico.

What are some research findings on one-parent families?

FIGURE 8 — The Decline of Two-Parent Families

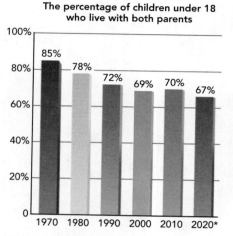

The percentage of children under 18 who live with both parents

*Author's estimate. 2010 is based on slight increases since 2000.

Source: By the author. Based on *Statistical Abstract of the United States* 1995:Table 79; 2011:Table 69.

FIGURE 9 — What Percentage of U.S. Married Women Never Give Birth?

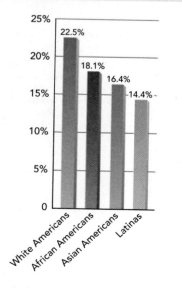

Source: By the author. Based on women ages 40–44 in Dye 2008.

As you know, whether a child has one or two parents makes a vital difference in that child's life, but recent research has brought a surprise. It does not matter if those parents are a man and a woman or a woman and a woman. Two women or two men who rear children together apparently do as well as a husband and wife (Farr et al. 2010).

Families without Children

While most married women give birth, about one of five do not (Dye 2008). This is *double* what it was twenty years ago. As you can see from Figure 9, childlessness varies by racial–ethnic group, with whites and Latinas representing the extremes. Some couples are infertile, but most childless couples have made a *choice* to not have children—and they prefer the term *childfree* rather than *childless*. Some decide before marriage that they will never have children, often to attain a sense of freedom—to pursue a career, to travel, and to have less stress (Letherby 2002; Koropeckyj-Cox 2007). In many cases, the couple simply postponed the time they planned to have their first child until either it was too late to have children or it seemed too uncomfortable to add a child to their lifestyle.

With trends firmly in place—more education and careers for women, advances in contraception, legal abortion, the high cost of rearing children, and an emphasis on possessing more material things—the proportion of women who never bear children is likely to increase. Consider this statement in a newsletter:

> We are DINKS (Dual Incomes, No Kids). We are happily married. I am 43; my wife is 42. We have been married for almost twenty years . . . . Our investment strategy has a lot to do with our personal philosophy: "You can have kids—or you can have everything else!"

Blended Families

The **blended family,** one whose members were once part of other families, is an increasingly significant type of family in the United States. Two divorced people who marry and each bring their children into a new family unit form a blended family. With divorce common, millions of children spend some of their childhood in blended families. I've never seen a better explanation of how blended families complicate family relationships than this description written by one of my freshman students:

> I live with my dad. I should say that I live with my dad, my brother (whose mother and father are also my mother and father), my half sister (whose father is my dad, but whose mother is my father's last wife), and two stepbrothers and stepsisters (children of my father's current wife). My father's wife (my current stepmother, not to be confused with his second wife who, I guess, is no longer my stepmother) is pregnant, and soon we all will have a new brother or sister. Or will it be a half brother or half sister?
>
> If you can't figure this out, I don't blame you. I have trouble myself. It gets very complicated around Christmas. Should we all stay together? Split up and go to several other homes? Who do we buy gifts for, anyway?

Gay and Lesbian Families

Although a handful of U.S. states allow people of the same sex to marry, 41 states have laws that prohibit same-sex marriages (Dematteis 2011). Walking a fine conceptual tightrope, some states recognize "registered domestic partnerships," giving legal status to same-sex unions but avoiding the term *marriage*. In this legal swamp, most gay and lesbian couples lack both legal marriage and the legal protection of "registered partnerships."

Why can we expect the percentage of U.S. women who never give birth to increase? What are blended families?

What are same-sex relationships like? Like everything else in life, these couples cannot be painted with a single brush stroke. As it does for opposite-sex couples, social class significantly shapes orientations to life. Sociologists Philip Blumstein and Pepper Schwartz (1985), who interviewed same-sex couples, found their main struggles to be housework, money, careers, problems with relatives, and sexual adjustment. If these sound familiar, they should be, as they are the same problems that heterosexual couples face. Same-sex couples are more likely to break up, and one argument for legalizing gay marriages is that this will make these relationships more stable. Where same-sex marriages are legal, like opposite-sex marriages, to break them requires a legal divorce.

Adoption by Gay and Lesbian Couples. Adoption by gay and lesbian couples has been a hot-button issue across the United States. A primary fear of heterosexuals is that children reared by homosexuals will somehow be forced into becoming homosexuals (Lewin 2009). With this concern in mind and following their professional curiosity, sociologists and psychologists have compared the children adopted by heterosexual and gay and lesbian couples. The results are consistent: The children reared by homosexual parents have about the same adjustment as children reared by heterosexual parents. In addition, their children are not more likely to have a gay or lesbian sexual orientation (Farr et al. 2010; Tasker 2010).

Why do gay and lesbian couples want to adopt children? To explore this question, anthropologist Ellen Lewin (2009) interviewed homosexual couples in San Francisco and Chicago who had adopted children. The reasons they gave are about the same as you would expect of heterosexual couples: to establish a family, love of children, wanting to give parentless children a home, to feel more adult, and to give meaning to one's life.

BRIAN BAER/MCT/Landov

Being fought in U.S. courts is whether or not marriage should be limited to heterosexual couples. Passions on both sides are deep, as illustrated by the two sides of the issue shown here.

Trends in U.S. Families

As is apparent from our discussion, marriage and family life in the United States are undergoing fundamental change. Let's examine some of the major trends.

The Changing Timetable of Family Life: Marriage and Childbirth

Figure 10 on the next page illustrates a profound change in U.S. marriage. As you can see, the average age of first-time brides and grooms declined from 1890 to about 1950. In 1890, the typical first-time bride was 22, but by 1950, she had just left her teens. For about twenty years, there was little change. Then in 1970, the average age took a sharp turn upwards, and *today's average first-time bride and groom are older than at any other time in U.S. history.*

Since postponing marriage is today's norm, it may surprise you to learn that *most* U.S. women used to be married before they turned 24. To see this remarkable change, look at Figure 11 on the next page. This change is so engrained in our culture that the percentage of women and men between 20 and 24 who are married is now just a *third or less* of what it was in 1970. Just as couples are postponing marriage, so they are putting off having children. Today's average U.S. woman now has her first child at age 25, the highest age in U.S. history (Mathews and Hamilton 2009).

Why have these changes occurred? As you know, it certainly is not because of a decline in the sex drive. This is still humming along. It is, rather, a fundamental change in **cohabitation,** adults living together in a sexual relationship without being married. Americans have postponed the age at which they first marry, but they have *not* postponed the age at which they first set up housekeeping with someone of the opposite sex. Let's look at this trend.

⊙ Watch
Motherhood Manifesto
on **mysoclab.com**

blended family a family whose members were once part of other families

cohabitation unmarried couples living together in a sexual relationship

How is the timetable of family life changing?

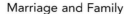

FIGURE 10 When Do Americans Marry? The Changing Age at First Marriage

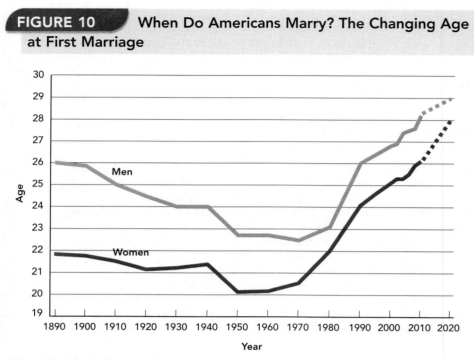

Note: This is the median age at first marriage. The broken lines indicate the author's estimate.
Source: By the author. Based on U.S. Census Bureau 2010.

FIGURE 11 Americans Ages 20–24 Who Are Married

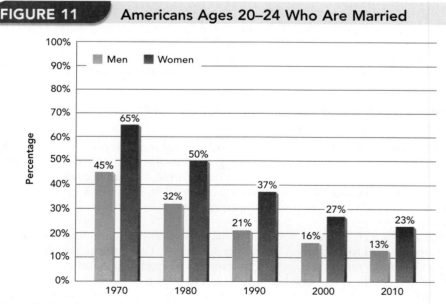

Source: By the author. Based on *Statistical Abstract of the United States* 1993:Table 60; 2002:Table 48; 2011:Table 57.

Cohabitation

What you see on Figure 12 on the next page is remarkable, for hardly ever in sociology do we have a total that rises this steeply and consistently. With cohabitation now about *twelve times* more common than it was in the 1970s, this figure represents a fundamental shift in attitudes and behavior. From a furtive activity, cohabitation has moved

What are the historical trends in age at first marriage? In being single for Americans ages 20–24?

into the mainstream: Today, *most* couples who marry have cohabited (Popenoe 2008), and about 40 percent of U.S. children will spend some time in a cohabiting family (Scommegna 2002).

Commitment is the essential difference between cohabitation and marriage. In marriage, the assumption is permanence; in cohabitation, couples agree to remain together for "as long as it works out." For marriage, individuals make public vows that legally bind them as a couple; for cohabitation, they simply move in together. Marriage requires a judge to authorize its termination, but if a cohabiting relationship sours, the couple separates, telling friends and family that "it didn't work out." In the Down-to-Earth Sociology box on the next page, let's explore what cohabitation means to the people who are living this experience.

Does Cohabitation Make Marriage Stronger? If couples set up housekeeping before they marry, are they less likely to divorce than couples who did not live together before marriage? It would seem that cohabitation would make marriage stronger. Cohabiting couples have the chance to work out so many real-life problems before marriage—and they marry only after sharing these experiences. To find out, sociologists compared divorce rates. It turns out that couples who cohabit before marriage are *more* likely to divorce (Osborne et al. 2007; Lichter and Qian 2008).

This goes directly against what we might expect. How do sociologists explain it? Some suggest that it is because cohabiting relationships are so easy to end (Dush et al. 2003). Because of this, people are less picky about choosing someone to live with ("It's probably a temporary thing") than choosing someone to marry ("This is really serious"). After couples cohabit, however, many experience a "push" toward marriage—from having common possessions, pets, and children to the subtle and not-so-subtle hints of family and friends. As a result, many end up marrying someone they would not otherwise have chosen as a spouse.

The "Sandwich Generation" and Elder Care

The "sandwich generation" refers to people who find themselves sandwiched between and responsible for two other generations, their children and their own aging parents. Typically between the ages of 40 and 55, these people find themselves pulled in two different directions. Many feel overwhelmed as these competing responsibilities collide. Some are plagued with guilt and anger because they can be in only one place at a time and have little time to pursue personal interests.

Concerns about elder care have gained the attention of the corporate world, and half of the 1,000 largest U.S. companies offer elder care assistance to their employees (Hewitt Associates 2004). This assistance includes seminars, referral services, and flexible work schedules to help employees meet their responsibilities

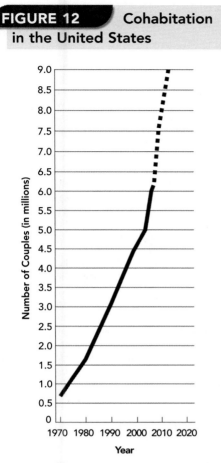

FIGURE 12 **Cohabitation in the United States**

Number of Couples (in millions)

Year

Note: Broken line indicates author's estimate

Source: By the author. Based on U.S. Census Bureau 2007 and *Statistical Abstract of the United States* 1995:Table 60; 2011:Table 63.

For reasons discussed in the text, large numbers of children are being reared by their grandparents. The grandparents are able to be positive role models, but this changes their retirement plans, their life orientations, and places physical and emotional strain on them.

Artiga Photo/Corbis

Why is the divorce rate higher among those who cohabited before marriage? What is the "sandwich generation"?

Down-to-Earth Sociology

"You Want Us to Live Together? What Do You Mean by That?"

What has led to the surge of cohabitation in the United States that you see in Figure 12? The primary reason is changed ideas of sexual morality. It is difficult for today's college students to grasp the sexual morals that prevailed before the 1960s. Prior to the sexual revolution of that period, almost everyone considered sex before marriage to be immoral. Premarital sex existed, to be sure, but it took place furtively and often with guilt. To live together before marriage was called "shacking up," and the couple was said to be "living in sin." A double standard also prevailed: It was the woman's responsibility to say no to sex before marriage, so she was considered to be the especially sinful one in cohabitation.

With premarital sex socially acceptable, and loads of sexual partners around, why rush into marriage? For those inclined to "settle down" somewhat, cohabitation offers a fairly safe alternative. It provides both sexual and emotional satisfactions within an ongoing relationship that does not require the long-term commitment of marriage.

Cohabitation also provides protection from divorce. Marriage sometimes seems so fragile and risky, as if it isn't going to last no matter how hard you try to make it work. Cohabitation removes this threat by offering an intimate relationship in which divorce is impossible. You can break up, but you can't get divorced.

And cohabitation is cheaper. You can set up housekeeping without the cost of a wedding—those expensive announcements, booking the church, the reception, the honeymoon. You don't even have to fork over for a license.

From the outside, all cohabitation may look the same, but not to the people who are living together. As you can see from Table 2, about 10 percent of couples consider themselves married, but for some reason, they don't want a marriage certificate. Some object to marriage on philosophical grounds ("What difference does a piece of paper make?"), while others are still legally married to someone else. Almost half of cohabitants (46 percent) view living together as a step on the path to marriage. For them, cohabitation is more than "going steady" but less than engagement. Another 15 percent of couples are simply "giving it a try." They want to see what marriage to one another might be like. For the least committed, about 29 percent, cohabitation is a form of dating. It provides a dependable source of sex and emotional support.

Look at the right side of the table, and you will see how important these different levels of commitment are. A half dozen years after the couples began to live together, those who view cohabitation as a substitute for marriage are the least likely to marry and the most likely to continue to cohabit. For couples who see cohabitation as a step toward marriage, the outcome is just the opposite: They are the most likely to marry and the least likely to still be cohabiting. Couples who are the most likely to break up are those who "tried" cohabitation and those for whom cohabitation was a form of dating.

For Your Consideration

→ Why does the meaning of cohabitation make a difference in whether couples marry? Can you classify cohabiting couples you know into these four types? Do you think there are other types? If so, what?

TABLE 2	What Cohabitation Means: Does It Make a Difference?				
			Relationship after Five to Seven Years		
				Of Those Still Together	
What Cohabitation Means	**Percent of Couples**	**Split Up**	**Still Together**	**Married**	**Cohabitating**
Substitute for Marriage	10%	35%	65%	37%	63%
Step Toward Marriage	46%	31%	69%	73%	27%
Trial Marriage	15%	51%	49%	66%	34%
Coresidential Dating	29%	46%	54%	61%	39%

Source: Recomputed from Bianchi and Casper 2000.

What different meanings does cohabitation have? What differences do those meanings make for getting married?

without missing so much work. Why are companies responding more positively to the issue of elder care than to child care? Most CEOs are older men whose wives stayed home to take care of their children, so they don't understand the stresses of balancing work and child care. In contrast, nearly all have aging parents, and many have faced the turmoil of trying to cope with both their parents' needs and those of work and their own family.

With people living longer, this issue is likely to become increasingly urgent.

Divorce and Remarriage

The topic of family life would not be complete without considering divorce. Let's first try to determine how much divorce there is.

Ways of Measuring Divorce

You probably have heard that the U.S. divorce rate is 50 percent, a figure that is popular with reporters. The statistic is true in the sense that each year almost half as many divorces are granted as there are marriages performed. The totals are 2.2 million marriages and about 1.1 million divorces (*Statistical Abstract* 2011:Table 129).

What is wrong, then, with saying that the divorce rate is about 50 percent? Think about it for a moment. Why should we compare the number of divorces and marriages that take place during the same year? The couples who divorced do not—with rare exceptions—come from the group that married that year. The one number has *nothing* to do with the other, so in no way do these two statistics reveal the divorce rate.

What figures should we compare, then? Couples who divorce come from the entire group of married people in the country. Since the United States has 60,000,000 married couples, and a little over 1 million of them get divorced in a year, the divorce rate for any given year is less than 2 percent. A couple's chances of still being married at the end of a year are over 98 percent—not bad odds—and certainly much better odds than the mass media would have us believe. As the Social Map on the next page shows, the "odds"—if we want to call them that—depend on where you live.

Over time, of course, each year's small percentage adds up. A third way of measuring divorce, then, is to ask, "Of all U.S. adults, what percentage are divorced?" Figure 14 on the next page answers this question. You can see how divorce has increased over the years and how race–ethnicity makes a difference for the likelihood that couples will divorce. If you look closely, you can also see that since 1990 the increase in divorce has slowed down.

Figure 14 shows us the percentage of Americans who are currently divorced, but we get yet another answer if we ask the question, "What percentage of Americans has ever been divorced?" This percentage increases with each age group, peaking when people reach their 50s ("Marital History . . ." 2004). Overall, about 43 to 46 percent of marriages end in divorce (Amato 2010), so a divorce rate of 50 percent is actually fairly accurate.

National statistics are fine, but you probably want to know if sociologists have found anything that will tell you about *your* chances of divorce. This is the topic of the Down-to-Earth Sociology box.

Children of Divorce

Children whose parents divorce are more likely than children reared by both parents to experience emotional problems, both during childhood and after they grow up (Amato and Sobolewski 2001; Weitoft et al. 2003). They are also more likely to become juvenile delinquents (Wallerstein et al. 2001) and less likely to complete high school, to attend college, or to graduate from college (McLanahan and Schwartz 2002). Finally, the children of divorce are themselves more likely to divorce, perpetuating a marriage–divorce cycle (Cui and Fincham 2010).

Is the greater maladjustment of the children of divorce a serious problem? This question initiated a lively debate between two researchers, both psychologists. Judith Wallerstein

" I NOW PRONOUNCE YOU SECOND HUSBAND AND FOURTH WIFE."

© Sidney Harris, ScienceCartoonPlus.com

This fanciful depiction of marital trends may not be too far off the mark.

How is it possible to get measurements of divorce that range from 2% to 50%?

FIGURE 13 The "Where" of U.S. Divorce

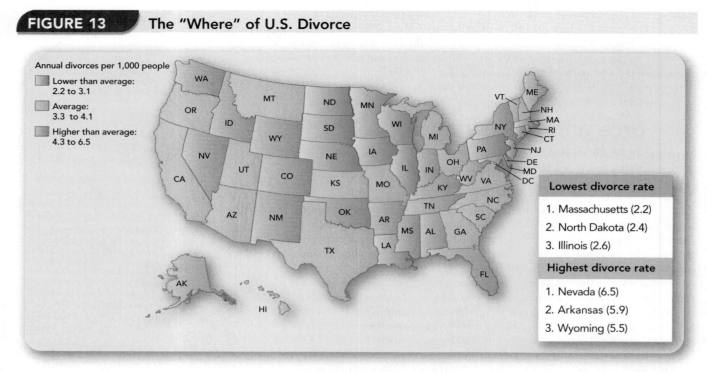

Note: Data for California, Georgia, Hawaii, Indiana, Louisiana, and Minnesota, based on the earlier editions in the source, have been decreased by the average decrease in U.S. divorce.

Source: By the author. Based on *Statistical Abstract of the United States* 1995:Table 149; 2002:Table 111; 2010:Table 126.

FIGURE 14 The Increase in Divorce

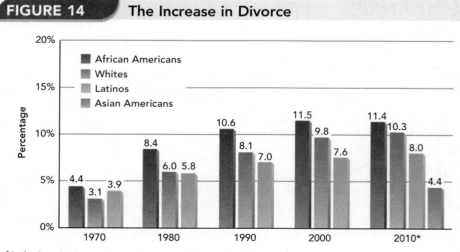

*Author's estimate

Note: This figure shows the percentage who are divorced and have not remarried, not the percentage who have ever divorced. Only these racial–ethnic groups are listed in the source. The source only recently added data on Asian Americans.

Source: By the author. Based on *Statistical Abstract of the United States* 1995:Table 58; 2011:Table 56.

What patterns of divorce do you see in Figure 13? In Figure 14?

Down-to-Earth Sociology

"What Are *Your* Chances of Getting Divorced?"

It is probably true that over a lifetime about half of all marriages fail (Whitehead and Popenoe 2004). If you have that 50 percent figure dancing in your head while you are getting married, you might as well make sure that you have an escape hatch open even while you're saying "I do."

Not every group carries the same risk of divorce. For some, the risk is much higher; for others, much lower. Let's look at some factors that reduce people's risk. As Table 3 shows, sociologists have worked out percentages that you might find useful. As you can see, people who go to college, participate in a religion, wait until marriage before having children, and earn higher incomes have a much better chance that their marriages will last. You can also see that having parents who did not divorce is significant. If you reverse these factors, you will see how the likelihood of divorce increases for people who have a baby before they marry, who marry in their teens, and so on. It is important to note, however, that these factors reduce the risk of divorce for *groups* of people, not for any particular individual.

Other factors increase the risk for divorce, but sociologists have not computed percentages for them. Here is one that might strike you as strange: Divorce is higher among couples whose firstborn child is a girl (Ananat and Michaels 2007; Dahl and Moretti 2008). The reason is probably that men prefer sons, and if the firstborn is a boy, the father is more likely to stick around (Gallup Poll 2011). A second factor is more obvious: The more co-workers you have who are of the opposite sex, the more likely you are to get divorced (McKinnish 2007). (I'm sure you can figure out why.) Another factor is marrying someone of a different race–ethnicity, which leads to more incompatible backgrounds. As we already discussed, cohabiting with the one you marry or with someone else prior to marriage raises the risk. Another factor that no one knows the reason for is working with people who are recently divorced (Aberg 2003). It could be that divorced people are more likely to "hit on" their fellow workers—and human nature being what it is. . . .

HO/AFP/Getty Images via Newscom

Divorces are often messy. To settle the question of who gets the house, a couple in Cambodia sawed their house in half.

TABLE 3	**What Reduces the Risk of Divorce?**
Factors That Reduce People's Chances of Divorce	**How Much Does This Decrease the Risk of Divorce?**
Some college (vs. high-school dropout)	–13%
Affiliated with a religion (vs. none)	–14%
Parents not divorced	–14%
Age 25 or over at marriage (vs. under 18)	–24%
Having a baby 7 months or longer after marriage (vs. before marriage)	–24%
Annual income over $25,000 (vs. under $25,000)	–30%

Note: These percentages apply to the first ten years of marriage.

Source: Whitehead and Popenoe 2004.

For Your Consideration

→ Why do you think that people who go to college have a lower risk of divorce? How would you explain the other factors shown in Table 3 or discussed in this box?

Why can't you figure your own chances of divorce by starting with some percentage (say 14 percent less likelihood of divorce if your parents are not divorced, another 13 percent for going to college, and so on)? To better understand this, you might want to read the section on the misuse of statistics.

What are your chances of getting divorced?

Courtesy of the National Parenting Association (NPA), N.Y.

It is difficult to capture the anguish of the children of divorce, but when I read these lines by the fourth-grader who drew these two pictures, my heart was touched:

Me alone in the park . . .

All alone in the park.

My Dad and Mom are divorced

that's why I'm all alone.

This is me in the picture with my son.

We are taking a walk in the park.

I will never be like my father.

I will never divorce my wife and kid.

claims that divorce scars children, making them depressed and leaving them with insecurities that follow them into adulthood (Wallerstein et al. 2001). Mavis Hetherington replies that 75 to 80 percent of children of divorce function as well as children who are reared by both of their parents (Hetherington and Kelly 2003).

Without meaning to weigh in on either side of this debate, it doesn't seem to be a simple case of the glass being half empty or half full. If 75 to 80 percent of children of divorce don't suffer long-term harm, this leaves one-fourth to one-fifth who do. Any way you look at it, one-fourth or one-fifth of a million children each year is a lot of kids who are having a lot of problems.

What helps children adjust to divorce? The children who feel close to both parents make the best adjustment, and those who don't feel close to either parent make the worst adjustment (Richardson and McCabe 2001). Other studies show that children adjust well if they experience little conflict, feel loved, live with a parent who is making a good adjustment, and have consistent routines. It also helps if their family has adequate money to meet its needs. Children also adjust better if a second adult can be counted on for support (Hayashi and Strickland 1998). Urie Bronfenbrenner (1992) says this person is like the third leg of a stool, giving stability to the smaller family unit. Any adult can be the third leg, he says—a relative, friend, or even a former mother-in-law—but the most powerful stabilizing third leg is the father, the ex-husband.

When the children of divorce grow up and marry, they are more likely to divorce than are adults who grew up in intact families. Have researchers found any factors that increase the chances that the children of divorce will have successful marriages? Actually, they have. They are more likely to have a lasting marriage if they marry someone whose parents did not divorce. These marriages have more trust and less conflict. If both husband and wife come from broken families, however, it is not good news. Those marriages tend to have less trust and more conflict, leading to a higher chance of divorce (Wolfinger 2003).

Grandchildren of Divorce

Paul Amato and Jacob Cheadle (2005), the first sociologists to study the grandchildren of couples who had divorced, found that the effects of divorce continue across generations. Using a national sample, they compared grandchildren—those whose grandparents had divorced with those whose grandparents had not divorced. Their findings are astounding.

What helps children adjust to divorce? How do consequences of divorce span generations?

The grandchildren of divorce have weaker ties to their parents, don't go as far in school, and don't get along as well with their spouses. As these researchers put it, when parents divorce, the consequences ripple through the lives of children who are not yet born.

Fathers' Contact with Children after Divorce

With most children living with their mothers after divorce, how often do fathers see their children? As you can see from Table 4, researchers have found four main patterns. The most common pattern is for fathers to see their children frequently after the divorce, and to keep doing so. But as you can see, a similar number of fathers have little contact with their children both right after the divorce and during the following years. Which fathers are more likely to see and talk often to their children? It is men who were married to the mothers of the children, especially those who are older, more educated, and have higher incomes. In contrast, men who were cohabiting with the mothers, as well as younger, less educated men with lower incomes, tend to have less contact with their children.

TABLE 4	Fathers' Contact with Their Children after Divorce		
Frequent[1]	Minimal[2]	Decrease[3]	Increase[4]
38%	32%	23%	8%

[1]Maintains contact once a week or more through the years

[2]Little contact after the divorce, maybe 2 to 6 times a year

[3]Has frequent contact after the divorce but decreases it through the years

[4]Has little contact after the divorce but increases it through the years. Sometimes called the "divorce activated" father.

Source: By the author: Based on Cheadle et al. 2010.

The Ex-Spouses

Anger, depression, and anxiety are common feelings at divorce. But so is relief. Women are more likely than men to feel that divorce is giving them a "new chance" in life. A few couples manage to remain friends through it all—but they are the exception. The spouse who initiates the divorce usually gets over it sooner (Kelly 1992; Wang and Amato 2000) and remarries sooner (Sweeney 2002).

Divorce does not necessarily mean the end of a couple's relationship. Many divorced couples maintain contact because of their children. For others, the "continuities," as sociologists call them, represent lingering attachments (Vaughan 1985; Masheter 1991; author's file 2005). The former husband may help his former wife paint a room or move furniture; she may invite him over for a meal or to watch television. They might even go to dinner or to see a movie together. Some couples even continue to make love after their divorce.

Then there are those who separate but never get around to getting divorced, the topic of our Down-to-Earth Sociology box on the next page.

Remarriage

Remarriage is now so common that one-fourth (24 percent) of married couples are on their second (or more) marriage (Elliott and Lewis 2010). As you can see in Figure 15, divorced people are as likely to marry other divorced people as someone who has not been married before. How do remarriages work out? The divorce rate of remarried people *without* children is the same as that of first marriages. Those who bring children into a new marriage, however, initiate more complicated, stressful relationships and are more likely to divorce again (MacDonald and DeMaris 1995). A lack of clear norms may also undermine these marriages (Coleman et al. 2000). As sociologist Andrew Cherlin (1989) noted, we lack satisfactory names for stepmothers, stepfathers, stepbrothers, stepsisters, stepaunts, stepuncles, stepcousins, and stepgrandparents. Not only are these awkward terms to use, but they also represent ill-defined relationships.

Two Sides of Family Life

Let's first look at situations in which marriage and family have gone seriously wrong and then try to answer the question of what makes marriage work.

The Dark Side of Family Life: Battering, Child Abuse, Marital Rape, and Incest

The dark side of family life involves events that people would rather keep in the dark. We shall look at spouse battering, child abuse, rape, and incest.

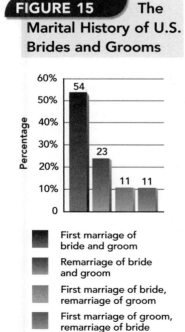

FIGURE 15 The Marital History of U.S. Brides and Grooms

- First marriage of bride and groom
- Remarriage of bride and groom
- First marriage of bride, remarriage of groom
- First marriage of groom, remarriage of bride

Source: By the author. Based on *Statistical Abstract of the United States* 2000:Table 145. Table dropped in later editions.

What patterns show up: In divorced fathers' with their children? Of ex-spouses? In how remarriages work out?

Down-to-Earth Sociology

Un-Divorce: Paths to Perpetual Separation

Unhappily married, John Frost took a new job in another state. Did his wife follow him? Did they get divorced? Neither. They continue to live in different states—and continue to remain married. They both like it this way.

Why would a couple separate but not get divorced? And why would they like being separated?

Couples separate for the same reason that people get divorced—they can't get along and they want to leave an unhappy marriage. But what keeps them from untying the knot?

John Frost, in the extract above, says that he and his wife see no reason to divorce. They get along better separated than they did while married, and to bring in lawyers would create bitterness between them. "Besides, I like my wife," John says. "I just can't live with her."

Perpetual separation can bring other benefits. One wife says that she likes it that she still gets invitations addressed to "Mr. and Mrs." Her fantasy marriage brings her some sort of emotional satisfaction.

For some, there is the practical matter of health insurance. The medical condition of a spouse can make it hard, expensive, or impossible to get insurance if the couple divorce. Un-divorce allows the working spouse to keep the sick spouse on the company insurance so he or she can continue to receive medical treatment.

Another practical matter is finances. With houses not selling and jobs scarce, some couples can't afford to divorce and move on to a new life. They continue to live together, but in a separate sort of way. A common solution is for one of them to move into the basement. (Apparently, it is usually the husband who moves downstairs.)

Craig Fritz/Twin Lens

Because of financial problems, this couple in Albuquerque, New Mexico, has postponed divorce for three years. They continue to live in the same house–and share the same dog.

Un-divorce can also avoid emotional costs. By not getting divorced, the couple is still legally married, their perpetual separation avoiding the pain that divorce would bring them.

There is also plain, simple inertia—like paying taxes or writing a term paper, just not getting around to an unpleasant task. The couple postpones divorce for years until un-divorce becomes their way of life. Others have religious reasons to avoid the divorce court.

Un-divorce can take creative paths. To prevent their kids from being shuffled from one place to another, one couple agreed to un-divorce. They rented an apartment and then took turns, one staying home with the kids and the other moving to the apartment.

Some un-divorces can be quite successful.

For 27 years, Warren Buffet, the financial guru, was separated from his wife, Susan. During this time, he lived with Astrid. The three grew so close that until Susan's death they sent out holiday cards together, signed "Warren, Susan, and Astrid."

As you would expect, of course, many un-divorces fail. Someone has a boyfriend or girlfriend who doesn't approve of un-divorce and insists that the partner get divorced. Then the whole thing falls apart.

Sources: Based on Levitz 2009; Paul 2010.

For Your Consideration

→ If you were married and no matter how hard the two of you tried, you simply did not get along, under what conditions would you consider un-divorce?

Spouse Battering. To study spouse abuse, some sociologists have studied just a few victims in depth, while others have interviewed nationally representative samples of U.S. couples. Although not all sociologists agree (Dobash et al. 1992, 1993; Pagelow 1992), Murray Straus (1992) concludes that husbands and wives are about equally likely to attack one another. If gender equality exists here, however, it certainly vanishes when it comes to the effects of violence—85 percent of the injured are women (Rennison 2003). A good part of the reason, of course, is that most husbands are bigger and stronger than their wives, putting women at a physical disadvantage in this literal battle of the sexes. The Down-to-Earth Sociology box on the next page discusses why some women remain with their abusive husbands.

The abuse of women is related to the sexist structure of society, and to socialization. Because they grew up with norms that encourage aggression and violence, some men

What paths lead to "un-divorce"? Does the husband or wife usually attack first?

Down-to-Earth Sociology

"Why Doesn't She Just Leave?" The Dilemma of Abused Women

"Why would she ever put up with violence?" is a question on everyone's mind. From the outside, it looks so easy. Just pack up and leave. "I know I wouldn't put up with anything like that."

Yet this is not what usually happens. Women tend to stay with their men after they are abused. Some stay only a short while, to be sure, but others remain in abusive situations for years. Why?

Sociologist Ann Goetting (2001) asked this question, too. To learn the answer, she interviewed women who had made the break. She wanted to find out what it was that set them apart. How were they able to leave, when so many women couldn't seem to?

1. *They had a positive self-image.* Simply put, they believed that they deserved better.
2. *They broke with old ideas.* They did not believe that a wife had to stay with her husband no matter what.
3. *They found adequate finances.* For some, this was easy. But others had to save for years, putting away just a dollar or two a week.
4. *They had supportive family and friends.* A support network served as a source of encouragement to help them rescue themselves.

If you take the opposite of these four characteristics, you can understand why some women put up with abuse: They don't think they deserve anything better, they believe it is their duty to stay, they don't think they can make it financially, and they lack a supportive network. These four factors are not of equal importance to all

Lannis Waters/The Palm Beach Post

Spouse abuse is one of the most common forms of violence. Shown here are police pulling a woman from her bathroom window, where she had fled from her husband, who was threatening to shoot her.

women, of course. For some, the lack of finances is the most important, while for others, it is their low self-concept or the lack of a supportive network.

There are two additional factors: The woman must define her husband's acts as abuse that warrants her leaving, and she must decide that he is not going to change. If she defines her husband's acts as normal, or perhaps as deserved in some way, she does not have a motive to leave. If she defines his acts as temporary, thinking that her husband will change, she is likely to stick around to try to change him.

Sociologist Kathleen Ferraro (2010) says that when she was a graduate student her husband "monitored my movements, eating, clothing, friends, money, make-up, and language. If I challenged his commands, he slapped or kicked me or pushed me down." Ferraro was able to leave only after she defined her husband's acts as intolerable abuse—rather than an unappealing situation that she had to put up with. She also decided that her husband was not going to change. Fellow students formed the supportive network that Ferraro needed to act on her new definition. Her graduate mentor even provided a safe place unknown to her husband after she left him.

For Your Consideration

→ On the basis of these findings, what would you say to a woman whose husband is abusing her? How about a man whose wife is abusing him? What other parts of this puzzle can you think of—such as the role of love?

feel that it is their right to control women. When frustrated in a relationship—or even by events outside it—some men become violent. The basic sociological question is how to socialize males to handle frustration and disagreements without resorting to violence (Rieker et al. 1997). We do not yet have this answer.

Child Abuse.

I answered an ad about a lakeside house in a middle-class neighborhood that was for sale by owner. As the woman showed me through her immaculate house, I was surprised to see a plywood box in the youngest child's bedroom. About 3 feet high, 3 feet wide, and 6 feet long, the box was perforated with holes and had a little door with a padlock. Curious, I asked what it was. The woman replied matter-of-factly that her son had a behavior problem, and this was where they locked him for "time out." She added that other times they would tie him to a float, attach a line to the dock, and put him in the lake.

Why don't abused wives "just leave"?

I left as soon as I could. With thoughts of a terrorized child filling my head, I called the state child abuse hotline.

As you can tell, what I saw upset me. Most of us are bothered by child abuse—helpless children being victimized by their parents and other adults who are supposed to love, protect, and nurture them. The most gruesome of these cases make the evening news: The 4-year-old girl who was beaten and raped by her mother's boyfriend, passed into a coma, and three days later passed out of this life; the 6- to 10-year-old children whose stepfather videotaped them engaging in sex acts. Unlike these cases, which made headlines in my area, most child abuse is never brought to our attention: the children who live in filth, who are neglected—left alone for hours or even days at a time—or who are beaten with extension cords—cases like the little boy I learned about when I went house hunting.

Child abuse is extensive. Each year, U.S. authorities receive about 2 million reports of children being abused or neglected. About 800,000 of these cases are substantiated (*Statistical Abstract* 2011:Table 340). The excuses that parents make are incredible. Of those I have read, the most fantastic is what a mother said to a Manhattan judge: "I slipped in a moment of anger, and my hands accidentally wrapped around my daughter's windpipe" (LeDuff 2003).

Marital or Intimacy Rape.   Marital rape seems to be more common than is usually supposed, but we have no national totals. Sociologist Diana Russell (1990) used a sampling technique that allows generalization, but only to San Francisco. Fourteen percent of married women told her that their husbands had raped them. In interviews with a representative sample of Boston women, 10 percent reported that their husbands had used physical force to compel them to have sex (Finkelhor and Yllo 1985, 1989). Compared with victims of rape by strangers or acquaintances, victims of marital rape are less likely to report the rape (Mahoney 1999).

With the huge numbers of couples who are cohabiting, we need a term that includes sexual assault in these relationships. Perhaps, then, we should use the term *intimacy rape*. And intimacy rape is not limited to men who sexually assault women. Sociologist Lori Girshick (2002) interviewed lesbians who had been sexually assaulted by their female partners. Girshick points out that if the pronoun "he" were substituted for "she" in her interviews, a reader would believe that the events were being told by women who had been raped by their husbands. Just as in heterosexual rape, these victims, too, suffered from shock, depression, and self-blame.

Incest.   Sexual relations between certain relatives (for example, between brothers and sisters or between parents and children) constitute **incest**. Incest is most likely to occur in families that are socially isolated (Smith 1992). Sociologist Diana Russell (n.d.) found that incest victims who experience the greatest trauma are those who were victimized the most often, whose assaults occurred over longer periods of time, and whose incest was "more intrusive"—for example, sexual intercourse as opposed to sexual touching.

Who are the offenders? The most common incest is apparently between brothers and sisters, with the sex initiated by the brother (Canavan et al. 1992; Carlson et al. 2006). With no random samples, however, we don't know for sure. Russell found that uncles are the most common offenders, followed by first cousins, stepfathers, brothers, and, finally, other relatives ranging from brothers-in-law to stepgrandfathers. All studies indicate that incest between mothers and their children is rare, more so than between fathers and their children.

The Bright Side of Family Life: Successful Marriages

Successful Marriages.   After examining divorce and family abuse, one could easily conclude that marriages seldom work out. This would be far from the truth, however, for about three of every five married Americans report that they are "very happy" with their marriages (Whitehead and Popenoe 2004). (Keep in mind that each year divorce eliminates about a million unhappy marriages.) To find out what makes marriage successful, sociologists Jeanette and Robert Lauer (1992) interviewed 351 couples who had been married fifteen

incest sexual relations between specified relatives, such as brothers and sisters or parents and children

Does marital rape exist? Why call it "intimacy rape"? What incest victims have the most difficult adjustment?

years or longer. Fifty-one of these marriages were unhappy, but the couples stayed together for religious reasons, because of family tradition, or "for the sake of the children."

Of the others, the 300 happy couples, all

1. Think of their spouses as best friends
2. Like their spouses as people
3. Think of marriage as a long-term commitment
4. Believe that marriage is sacred
5. Agree with their spouses on aims and goals
6. Believe that their spouses have grown more interesting over the years
7. Strongly want the relationship to succeed
8. Laugh together

Sociologist Nicholas Stinnett (1992) used interviews and questionnaires to study 660 families from all regions of the United States and parts of South America. He found that happy families

1. Spend a lot of time together
2. Are quick to express appreciation
3. Are committed to promoting one another's welfare
4. Do a lot of talking and listening to one another
5. Are religious
6. Deal with crises in a positive manner

Here are three more important factors: Marriages are happier when the partners get along with their in-laws (Bryant et al. 2001), find leisure activities that they both enjoy (Crawford et al. 2002), and agree on how to spend money (Bernard 2008).

Symbolic Interactionism and the Misuse of Statistics

Many students are concerned that divorce statistics mean they won't have a successful marriage. Because sociology is not just about abstract ideas, but is really about our lives, it is important to stress that you are an individual, not a statistic. That is, if the divorce rate were 33 percent or 50 percent, this would *not* mean that if you marry, your chances of getting divorced are 33 percent or 50 percent. This is a misuse of statistics—and a common one at that. Divorce statistics represent all marriages and have absolutely *nothing* to do with any individual marriage. Our own chances depend on our own situations—especially the way we approach marriage.

To make this point clearer, let's apply symbolic interactionism. From a symbolic interactionist perspective, we create our own worlds. That is, because our experiences don't come with built-in meanings, we interpret our experiences and act accordingly. As we do so, we can create a self-fulfilling prophecy. For example, if we think that our marriage might fail, we are more likely to run when things become difficult. If we think that our marriage is going to work out, we are more likely to stick around and to do things to make the marriage successful. The folk saying "There are no guarantees in life" is certainly true, but it does help to have a vision that a good marriage is possible and that it is worth the effort to achieve.

The Future of Marriage and Family

What can we expect of marriage and family in the future? We can first note that marriage is so functional that it exists in every society. Despite its many problems, then, marriage is in no danger of becoming a relic of the past, and the vast majority of Americans will continue to find marriage vital to their welfare.

Certain trends are firmly in place. Cohabitation, births to single women, and the age at first marriage will increase. As more married women join the workforce, wives will continue to gain marital power. As the number of elderly increase, more couples will find themselves sandwiched between caring for their parents and rearing their own children.

What makes marriages successful? Why is it wrong to apply sociological statistics to yourself?

Our culture will continue to be haunted by distorted images of marriage and family: the bleak ones portrayed in the mass media and the rosy ones perpetuated by cultural myths. Sociological research can help correct these distortions and allow us to see how our own family experiences fit into the patterns of our culture. Sociological research can also help to answer the big question: How do we formulate social policies that will support and enhance the quality of family life?

By the Numbers: Changes Over Time

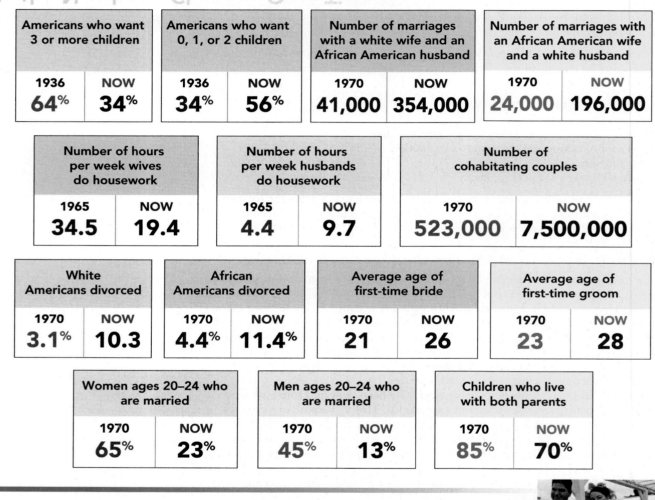

Americans who want 3 or more children		Americans who want 0, 1, or 2 children		Number of marriages with a white wife and an African American husband		Number of marriages with an African American wife and a white husband	
1936	NOW	1936	NOW	1970	NOW	1970	NOW
64%	34%	34%	56%	41,000	354,000	24,000	196,000

Number of hours per week wives do housework		Number of hours per week husbands do housework		Number of cohabitating couples	
1965	NOW	1965	NOW	1970	NOW
34.5	19.4	4.4	9.7	523,000	7,500,000

White Americans divorced		African Americans divorced		Average age of first-time bride		Average age of first-time groom	
1970	NOW	1970	NOW	1970	NOW	1970	NOW
3.1%	10.3	4.4%	11.4%	21	26	23	28

Women ages 20–24 who are married		Men ages 20–24 who are married		Children who live with both parents	
1970	NOW	1970	NOW	1970	NOW
65%	23%	45%	13%	85%	70%

Summary and Review

Marriage and Family in Global Perspective

What is a family—and what themes are universal?

Family is difficult to define because there are exceptions to every element that one might consider essential. Consequently, **family** is defined broadly—as people who consider themselves related by blood, marriage, or adoption. Universally, **marriage** and family are mechanisms for governing mate selection, reckoning descent, and establishing inheritance and authority.

What can we expect of marriage and family in the future?

Marriage and Family in Theoretical Perspective

What is a functionalist perspective on marriage and family?

Functionalists examine the functions and dysfunctions of family life. Examples include the **incest taboo** and how weakened family functions increase divorce.

What is a conflict perspective on marriage and family?

Conflict theorists focus on inequality in marriage, especially unequal and changing power between husbands and wives.

What is a symbolic interactionist perspective on marriage and family?

Symbolic interactionists examine the contrasting experiences and perspectives of men and women in marriage. They stress that only by grasping the perspectives of wives and husbands can we understand their behavior.

The Family Life Cycle

What are the major elements of the family life cycle?

The major elements are love and courtship, marriage, childbirth, child rearing, and the family in later life. Most mate selection follows patterns of age, social class, and race–ethnicity. Child-rearing patterns vary by social class.

Diversity in U.S. Families

How significant is race–ethnicity in family life?

The primary distinction is social class, not race–ethnicity. Families of the same social class are likely to be similar, regardless of their race–ethnicity.

What other diversity do we see in U.S. families?

Also discussed are one-parent, childless, **blended,** and gay and lesbian families. Each has its unique characteristics, but social class is important in determining their primary characteristics. Poverty is especially significant for single-parent families, most of which are headed by women.

Trends in U.S. Families

What major changes characterize U.S. families?

Three major changes are postponement of first marriage, an increase in **cohabitation,** and having the first child at a later age. With more people living longer, many middle-aged couples find themselves sandwiched between rearing their children and taking care of their aging parents.

Divorce and Remarriage

What is the current divorce rate?

Depending on what numbers you choose to compare, you can produce rates between 2 percent and 50 percent.

How do children and their parents adjust to divorce?

Divorce is difficult for children, whose adjustment problems often continue into adulthood. Consequences of divorce are passed on to grandchildren. Fathers who have frequent contact with their children after a divorce are likely to maintain it.

Two Sides of Family Life

What are the two sides of family life?

The dark side is abuse—spouse battering, child abuse, marital rape, and **incest,** all a misuse of family power. The bright side is that most people find marriage and family to be rewarding.

The Future of Marriage and Family

What is the likely future of marriage and family?

We can expect cohabitation, births to unmarried women, and age at first marriage to increase. The growing numbers of women in the workforce are likely to continue to shift the balance of marital power.

Thinking Critically about this Chapter

1. Functionalists stress that the family is universal because it provides basic functions for individuals and society. What functions does your family provide? *Hint:* In addition to the section "The Functionalist Perspective," also consider the section "Common Cultural Themes."

2. Explain why social class is more important than race–ethnicity in determining a family's characteristics.

3. Apply this chapter's contents to your own experience with marriage and family. What social factors affect your family life? In what ways is your family life different from that of your grandparents when they were your age?

References

All new references are printed in cyan.

Aberg, Yvonne. *Social Interactions: Studies of Contextual Effects and Endogenous Processes.* Doctoral dissertation, Department of Sociology, Stockholm University, 2003.

Amato, Paul. "Research on Divorce: Continuing Trends and New Developments." *Journal of Marriage and Family, 72,* 3, June 2010: 650–666.

Amato, Paul R., and Jacob Cheadle. "The Long Reach of Divorce: Divorce and Child Well-Being across Three Generations." *Journal of Marriage and Family, 67,* February 2005:191–206.

Amato, Paul R., and Juliana M. Sobolewski. "The Effects of Divorce and Marital Discord on Adult Children's Psychological Well-Being." *American Sociological Review, 66,* 6, December 2001:900–921.

"American Community Survey 2003." Washington, D.C.: U.S. Census Bureau, 2004.

America's Children in Brief: Key National Indicators of Well-Being, 2010. www.childstats.gov, July 2010.

Ananat, Elizabeth O., and Guy Michaels. "The Effect of Marital Breakup on the Income Distribution of Women with Children." Centre for Economic Performance, CEP Discussion Paper dp0787, April 2007.

Belsky, Jay. "Classroom Composition, Childcare History and Social Development: Are Childcare Effects Disappearing or Spreading?" *Social Development, 18,* 1, February 2009a:230–238.

Belsky, Jay. "Effects of Child Care on Child Development: Give Parents Real Choice." Unpublished paper, March 2009b.

Belsky, Jay, Deborah Lowe Vandell, Margaret Burchinall, K. Alison Clarke-Stewart, Kathleen McCartney, and Margaret Tresch Owen. "Are There Long-Term Effects of Early Child Care?" *Child Development, 78,* 2, March/April 2007:681–701.

Berger, Peter L. *Invitation to Sociology: A Humanistic Perspective.* New York: Doubleday, 1963.

Bergmann, Barbara R. "The Future of Child Care." Paper presented at the annual meetings of the American Sociological Association, 1995.

Bernard, Tara Siegel. "The Key to Wedded Bliss? Money Matters." *New York Times,* September 10, 2008.

Bianchi, Suzanne M., and Lynne M. Casper. "American Families." *Population Bulletin, 55,* 4, December 2000:1–42.

Bianchi, Suzanne M., John P. Robinson, and Melissa A. Milkie. *Changing Rhythms of American Family Life.* New York: Russell Sage Foundation, 2006.

Blau, David M. "The Production of Quality in Child-Care Centers: Another Look." *Applied Developmental Science, 4,* 3, 2000:136–148.

Blumstein, Philip, and Pepper Schwartz. *American Couples: Money, Work, Sex.* New York: Pocket Books, 1985.

Bronfenbrenner, Urie. "Principles for the Healthy Growth and Development of Children." In *Marriage and Family in a Changing Society,* 4th ed., James M. Henslin, ed. New York: Free Press, 1992:243–249.

Bryant, Chalandra M., Rand D. Conger, and Jennifer M. Meehan. "The Influence of In-Laws on Changes in Marital Success." *Journal of Marriage and the Family, 63,* 3, August 2001:614–626.

Bryant, Chalandra M., K.A.S. Wickrama, John Boland, et al. "Race Matters, Even in Marriage: Identifying Factors Linked to Marital Outcomes for African Americans." *Journal of Family Theory and Review, 2,* 3, September 2010:157–174.

Bumiller, Elisabeth. "First Comes Marriage—Then, Maybe, Love." In *Marriage and Family in a Changing Society,* 4th ed., James M. Henslin, ed. New York: Free Press, 1992:120–125.

Canavan, Margaret M., Walter J. Meyer, III, and Deborah C. Higgs. "The Female Experience of Sibling Incest." *Journal of Marital and Family Therapy, 18,* 2, 1992:129–142.

"Career Guide to Industries: 2010–11 Edition." Washington, D.C.: Bureau of Labor Statistics 2011.

Carlson, Bonnie E., Katherine Maciol, and Joanne Schneider. "Sibling Incest: Reports from Forty-One Survivors." *Journal of Child Sexual Abuse, 15,* 4, 2006:19–34.

Cauce, Ana Mari, and Melanie Domenech-Rodriguez. "Latino Families: Myths and Realities." In *Latino Children and Families in the United States: Current Research and Future Directions,* Josefina M. Contreras, Kathryn A. Kerns, and Angela M. Neal-Barnett, eds. Westport, Conn.: Praeger, 2002:3–25.

Cherlin, J. Andrew. "Remarriage as an Incomplete Institution." In *Marriage and Family in a Changing Society,* 3rd ed., James M. Henslin, ed. New York: Free Press, 1989:492–501.

Claxton, Amy, and Maureen Perry-Jenkins. "No Fun Anymore: Leisure and Marital Quality across the Transition to Parenthood." *Journal of Marriage and Family, 70,* February 2008:28–43.

Coleman, Marilyn, Lawrence Ganong, and Mark Fine. "Reinvestigating Remarriage: Another Decade of Progress." *Journal of Marriage and the Family, 62,* 4, November 2000:1288–1307.

Crawford, Duane W., Renate M. Houts, Ted L. Huston, and Laura J. George. "Compatibility, Leisure, and Satisfaction in Marital Relationships." *Journal of Marriage and Family, 64,* May 2002:433–449.

Crossen, Cynthia. "Déjà Vu." *New York Times,* February 25, 2004a.

Cui, Ming, and Frank D. Fincham. "The Differential Effects of Parental Divorce and Marital Conflict on Young Adult Romantic Relationships." *Personal Relationships, 17,* 3, September 2010:331–343.

Dahl, Gordon B., and Enrico Moretti. "The Demand for Sons." *Review of Economic Studies, 75,* 2008:1085–1120.

Dematteis, Lou. "Same-Sex Marriages, Civil Unions, and Domestic Partnerships." *New York Times,* July 11, 2011.

Dobash, Russell P., R. Emerson Dobash, Margo Wilson, and Martin Daly. "The Myth of Sexual Symmetry in Marital Violence." *Social Problems, 39,* 1, February 1992:71–91.

Dobash, Russell P., R. Emerson Dobash, Margo Wilson, and Martin Daly. "Marital Violence Is Not Symmetrical: A Response to Campbell." *SSSP Newsletter, 24,* 3, Fall 1993:26–30.

Dugger, Celia W. "Wedding Vows Bind Old World and New." *New York Times,* July 20, 1998.

Dush, Claire M. Kamp, Catherine L. Cohan, and Paul R. Amato. "The Relationship between Cohabitation and Marital Quality and Stability: Change across Cohorts?" *Journal of Marriage and Family, 65,* 3, August 2003:539–549.

Dye, Jane Lawler. "Fertility of American Women: 2006." Washington, D.C.: U.S. Census Bureau, August 2008.

Easley, Hema. "Indian Families Continue to Have Arranged Marriages." *The Journal News,* June 9, 2003.

Elliott, Diana B., and Jamie M. Lewis. "Embracing the Institution of Marriage: The Characteristics of Remarried Americans." Paper presented at the annual meetings of Population Association of America, April 17, 2010.

Elwert, Felix, and Nicholas A. Christakis. "The Effect of Widowhood on Mortality by the Causes of Death of Both Spouses." *American Journal of Public Health, 98,* 11, November 2008:2092–2098.

Eshleman, J. Ross. *The Family,* 9th ed. Boston: Allyn and Bacon, 2000.

Farr, Rachel H., Stephen L. Forssell, and Charlotte J. Patterson. "Parenting and Child Development in Adoptive Families: Does Parental

Sexual Orientation Matter?" *Applied Developmental Science, 14,* 3, 2010:164–178.

Ferraro, Kathleen J. "Intimate Partner Violence." In *Social Problems,* 7th ed., by James M. Henslin. Upper Saddle River, N.J.: Prentice Hall, 2010:373.

Finkelhor, David, and Kersti Yllo. *License to Rape: Sexual Abuse of Wives.* New York: Henry Holt, 1985.

Finkelhor, David, and Kersti Yllo. "Marital Rape: The Myth versus the Reality." In *Marriage and Family in a Changing Society,* 3rd ed., James M. Henslin, ed. New York: Free Press, 1989:382–391.

Fisher, Helen E., Lucy L. Brown, Arthur Aron, Greg Strong, and Deborah Masek. "Reward, Addiction, and Emotion Regulation Systems Associated with Rejection in Love." *Journal of Neurophysiology, 104,* 2010:51–60.

Fremson, Ruth. "Dead Bachelors in Remote China Still Find Wives." *New York Times,* October 5, 2006.

Frosch, Dan. "Its Native Tongue Facing Extinction, Arapaho Tribe Teaches the Young." *New York Times,* October 17, 2008.

Gallup Poll. "America's Preference for Smaller Families Edge Higher." Princeton, N.J. The Gallup Organization, June 30, 2011.

Gallup Poll. "Prefer Boys to Girls Just as They Did in 1941." Princeton, N.J.: The Gallup Organization, June 23, 2011.

Gatewood, Willard B. *Aristocrats of Color: The Black Elite, 1880–1920.* Bloomington, Ind.: Indiana University Press, 1990.

Gautham, S. "Coming Next: The Monsoon Divorce." *New Statesman, 131,* 4574, February 18, 2002:32–33.

Girshick, Lori B. *Woman-to-Woman Sexual Violence: Does She Call It Rape?* Boston: Northeastern University Press, 2002.

Goetting, Ann. *Getting Out: Life Stories of Women Who Left Abusive Men.* New York: Columbia University Press, 2001.

Gupta, Giri Raj. "Love, Arranged Marriage, and the Indian Social Structure." In *Cross-Cultural Perspectives of Mate Selection and Marriage,* George Kurian, ed. Westport, Conn.: Greenwood Press, 1979.

Hall, J. Camille. "The Impact of Kin and Fictive Kin Relationships on the Mental Health of Black Adult Children of Alcoholics." *Health and Social Work, 33,* 4, November 2008:259–266.

Harford, Tim. "Why Divorce Is Good for Women." The Undercover Economist, *Slate,* January 16, 2008.

Hayashi, Gina M., and Bonnie R. Strickland. "Long-Term Effects of Parental Divorce on Love Relationships: Divorce as Attachment Disruption." *Journal of Social and Personal Relationships, 15,* 1, February 1998:23–38.

Hetherington, Mavis, and John Kelly. *For Better or for Worse: Divorce Reconsidered.* New York: W. W. Norton, 2003.

Hewitt Associates. *Worklife Benefits Provided by Major U.S. Employers, 2003–2004.* Lincolnshire, Ill.: Hewitt Associates, 2004.

Hong, Lawrence. "Marriage in China." In *Til Death Do Us Part: A Multicultural Anthology on Marriage,* Sandra Lee Browning and R. Robin Miller, eds. Stamford, Conn.: JAI Press, 1999.

Hurtado, Aída, David E. Hayes-Bautista, R. Burciaga Valdez, and Anthony C. R. Hernández. *Redefining California: Latino Social Engagement in a Multicultural Society.* Los Angeles: UCLA Chicano Studies Research Center, 1992.

Jankowiak, William R., and Edward F. Fischer. "A Cross-Cultural Perspective on Romantic Love." *Journal of Ethnology, 31,* 2, April 1992:149–155.

Kelly, Joan B. "How Adults React to Divorce." In *Marriage and Family in a Changing Society,* 4th ed., James M. Henslin, ed. New York: Free Press, 1992:410–423.

Kohn, Melvin L. "Social Class and Parent–Child Relationships: An Interpretation." *American Journal of Sociology, 68,* 1963:471–480.

Kohn, Melvin L. *Class and Conformity: A Study in Values,* 2nd ed. Homewood, Ill.: Dorsey Press, 1977.

Kohn, Melvin L., and Carmi Schooler. "Class, Occupation, and Orientation." *American Sociological Review, 34,* 1969:659–678.

Koropeckyj-Cox, Tanya. "Attitudes about Childlessness in the United States." *Journal of Family Issues, 28,* 8, August 2007:1054–1082.

La Barre, Weston. *The Human Animal.* Chicago: University of Chicago Press, 1954.

Lareau, Annette. "Invisible Inequality: Social Class and Childrearing in Black Families and White Families." *American Sociological Review, 67,* October 2002:747–776.

Lauer, Jeanette, and Robert Lauer. "Marriages Made to Last." In *Marriage and Family in a Changing Society,* 4th ed., James M. Henslin, ed. New York: Free Press, 1992:481–486.

LeDuff, Charlie. "Handling the Meltdowns of the Nuclear Family." *New York Times,* May 28, 2003.

Letherby, Gayle. "Childless and Bereft? Stereotypes and Realities in Relation to 'Voluntary' and 'Involuntary' Childlessness and Womanhood." *Sociological Inquiry, 72,* 1, Winter 2002:7–20.

Levitz, Jennifer. "Divorced but Still Living Together." *Wall Street Journal,* July 13, 2009.

Lewin, Ellen. *Gay Fatherhood: Narratives of Family and Citizenship in America.* Chicago: University of Chicago Press, 2009.

Lichter, Daniel T., and Zhenchao Qian. "Serial Cohabitation and the Marital Life Course." *Journal of Marriage and Family, 70,* November 2008:861–878.

MacDonald, William L., and Alfred DeMaris. "Remarriage, Stepchildren, and Marital Conflict: Challenges to the Incomplete Institutionalization Hypothesis." *Journal of Marriage and the Family, 57,* May 1995:387–398.

Mahoney, Patricia. "High Rape Chronicity and Low Rates of Help-Seeking among Wife Rape Survivors in a Nonclinical Sample: Implications for Research and Practice." *Violence against Women, 5,* 9, September 1999:993–1016.

Malinowski, Bronislaw. *Sex and Repression in Savage Society.* Cleveland, Ohio: World, 1927.

"Marital History for People 15 Years Old and Over by Age, Sex, Race and Ethnicity: 2001." Annual Demographic Survey, Bureau of Labor Statistics and U.S. Census Bureau, 2004.

Masheter, Carol. "Postdivorce Relationships between Ex-Spouses: The Role of Attachment and Interpersonal Conflict." *Journal of Marriage and the Family, 53,* February 1991:103–110.

Mathews, T. J., and Brady E. Hamilton. "Delayed Childbearing: More Women Are Having Their First Child Later in Life." *NCHS Data Brief,* 21, Hyattsville, Md.: National Center for Health Statistics, August 2009:1–7.

McKinnish, Terra G. "Sexually Integrated Workplaces and Divorce: Another Form of On-the-Job Search." *Journal of Human Resources, 42,* 2, 2007:331–352.

McLanahan, Sara, and Gary Sandefur. *Growing Up with a Single Parent: What Hurts, What Helps.* Cambridge, Mass.: Harvard University Press, 1994.

McLanahan, Sara, and Dona Schwartz. "Life without Father: What Happens to the Children?" *Contexts, 1,* 1, Spring 2002:35–44.

Menaghan, Elizabeth G., Lori Kowaleski-Jones, and Frank L. Mott. "The Intergenerational Costs of Parental Social Stressors: Academic and Social Difficulties in Early Adolescence for Children of Young Mothers." *Journal of Health and Social Behavior, 38,* March 1997:72–86.

Meyers, Laurie. "Asian-American Mental Health." *APA Online,* February 2006.

Morin, Rich, and D'Vera Cohn. "Women Call the Shots at Home; Public Mixed on Gender Roles in Jobs." Pew Research Center Publications: September 25, 2008.

Murdock, George Peter. *Social Structure*. New York: Macmillan, 1949.

Naik, Gautam. "A Baby, Please. Blond, Freckles—Hold the Colic." *Wall Street Journal*, February 12, 2009.

Osborne, Cynthia, Wendy D. Manning, and Pamela J. Smock. "Married and Cohabiting Parents' Relationship Stability: A Focus on Race and Ethnicity." *Marriage and Family, 69*, December 2007:1345–1366.

Pagelow, Mildred Daley. "Adult Victims of Domestic Violence: Battered Women." *Journal of Interpersonal Violence, 7*, 1, March 1992:87–120.

Paul, Pamela. "The Un-Divorced." *New York Times*, July 30, 2010.

Popenoe, David. "Cohabitation, Marriage and Child Wellbeing: A Cross-National Sample." Rutgers: The National Marriage Project, 2008.

Rennison, Callie Marie. "Intimate Partner Violence, 1993–2001." Washington, D.C.: Bureau of Justice Statistics, February 2003.

Richardson, Stacey, and Marita P. McCabe. "Parental Divorce during Adolescence and Adjustment in Early Adulthood." *Adolescence, 36*, Fall 2001:467–489.

Rieker, Patricia P., Chloe E. Bird, Susan Bell, Jenny Ruducha, Rima E. Rudd, and S. M. Miller. "Violence and Women's Health: Toward a Society and Health Perspective." Unpublished paper, 1997.

Rosen, Jeffrey. "The Web Means the End of Forgetting." *New York Times*, July 19, 2010.

Rubin, Zick. "The Love Research." In *Marriage and Family in a Changing Society*, 2nd ed., James M. Henslin, ed. New York: Free Press, 1985.

Russell, Diana E. H. "Preliminary Report on Some Findings Relating to the Trauma and Long-Term Effects of Intrafamily Childhood Sexual Abuse." Unpublished paper, no date.

Russell, Diana E. H. *Rape in Marriage*. Bloomington: Indiana University Press, 1990.

Saenz, Rogelio. "Latinos and the Changing Face of America." Washington, D.C.: Population Reference Bureau, 2004:1–28.

Scommegna, Paola. "Increased Cohabitation Changing Children's Family Settings." *Population Today, 30*, 7, October 2002:3, 6.

Senior, Jennifer. "All Joy and No Fun." *New York*, July 4, 2010.

Smith, Beverly A. "An Incest Case in an Early 20th-Century Rural Community." *Deviant Behavior, 13*, 1992:127–153.

Sprecher, Susan, and Rachita Chandak. "Attitudes about Arranged Marriages and Dating among Men and Women from India." *Free Inquiry in Creative Sociology, 20*, 1, May 1992:59–69.

Stack, Carol B. *All Our Kin: Strategies for Survival in a Black Community*. New York: Harper, 1974.

Staples, Brent. "Loving v. Virginia and the Secret History of Race." *New York Times*, May 14, 2008.

Statistical Abstract of the United States. Washington, D.C.: U.S. Census Bureau, published annually.

Stinnett, Nicholas. "Strong Families." In *Marriage and Family in a Changing Society*, 4th ed., James M. Henslin, ed. New York: Free Press, 1992:496–507.

Straus, Murray A. "Explaining Family Violence." In *Marriage and Family in a Changing Society*, 4th ed., James M. Henslin, ed. New York: Free Press, 1992:344–356.

Suzuki, Bob H. "Asian-American Families." In *Marriage and Family in a Changing Society*, 2nd ed., James M. Henslin, ed. New York: Free Press, 1985:104–119.

Swati, Pandey. "Do You Take This Stranger?" *Los Angeles Times*, June 26, 2008.

Sweeney, Megan M. "Remarriage and the Nature of Divorce: Does It Matter Which Spouse Chose to Leave?" *Journal of Family Issues, 23*, 3, April 2002:410–440.

Tasker, Fiona. "Same-Sex Parenting and Child Development: Reviewing the Contribution of Parental Gender." *Journal of Marriage and Family, 72*, 1, February 2010:35–40.

Torres, Jose B., V. Scott H. Solberg, and Aaron H. Carlstrom. "The Myth of Sameness among Latino Men and Their Machismo." *American Journal of Orthopsychiatry, 72*, 2, 2002:163–181.

U.S. Census Bureau. "50 Million Children Lived with Married Parents in 2007." Washington, D.C.: U.S. Government Printing Office, 2007.

U.S. Census Bureau. "Annual Social and Economic Supplement to Current Population Survey." Washington, D.C.: U.S. Government Printing Office, 2010

Vaughan, Diane. "Uncoupling: The Social Construction of Divorce." In *Marriage and Family in a Changing Society*, 2nd ed., James M. Henslin, ed. New York: Free Press, 1985:429–439.

Vega, William A. "Hispanic Families in the 1980s: A Decade of Research." *Journal of Marriage and the Family, 52*, November 1990:1015–1024.

Wallerstein, Judith S., Sandra Blakeslee, and Julia M. Lewis. *The Unexpected Legacy of Divorce: A 25-Year Landmark Study*. Concord, N.H.: Hyperion Press, 2001.

Wang, Hongyu, and Paul R. Amato. "Predictors of Divorce Adjustment: Stressors, Resources, and Definitions." *Journal of Marriage and the Family, 62*, 3, August 2000:655–668.

Weitoft, Gunilla Ringback, Anders Hjern, Bengt Haglund, and Mans Rosen. "Mortality, Severe Morbidity, and Injury in Children Living with Single Parents in Sweden: A Population-Based Study." *Lancet, 361*, January 25, 2003:289–295.

Wen, Ming. "Family Structure and Children's Health and Behavior." *Journal of Family Issues, 29*, 11, November 2008:1492–1519.

Whitehead, Barbara Dafoe, and David Popenoe. "The Marrying Kind: Which Men Marry and Why." Rutgers University: The State of Our Unions: The Social Health of Marriage in America, 2004.

Willie, Charles Vert, and Richard J. Reddick. *A New Look at Black Families*, 5th ed. Walnut Creek, Calif.: AltaMira Press, 2003.

Wilson, William Julius. "Jobless Poverty: A New Form of Social Dislocation in the Inner-City Ghetto." In *The Inequality Reader: Contemporary and Foundational Readings in Race, Class and Gender*, David B. Grusky and Szonja Szelenyi, eds. Boulder: Westview Press, 2007:142–152.

Wolfinger, Nicholas H. "Family Structure Homogamy: The Effects of Parental Divorce on Partner Selection and Marital Stability." *Social Science Research, 32*, 2003:80–97.

Wood, Daniel B., "Latinos Redefine What It Means to Be Manly." *Christian Science Monitor, 93*, 161, July 16, 2001.

Ying, Yu-Wen, and Meekyung Han. "Parental Contributions to Southeast Asian American Adolescents' Well-Being." *Youth and Society, 40*, 2, December 2008:289–306.

Zamiska, Nicholas. "Pressed to Do Well on Admissions Tests, Students Take Drugs." *Wall Street Journal*, November 8, 2004.

Epilogue: Why Major in Sociology?

From Epilogue of *Sociology: A Down-to-Earth Approach, Core Concepts*, Fifth Edition. James M. Henslin.

Epilogue: Why Major in Sociology?

As you explored social life in this text, I hope that you found yourself thinking along with me. If so, you should have gained a greater understanding of why people think, feel, and act as they do—as well as insights into why *you* view life the way you do. Developing your sociological imagination was my intention in writing this text. I have sincerely wanted to make sociology come alive for you.

Majoring in Sociology

If you feel a passion for peering beneath the surface—for seeking out the social influences in people's lives, and for seeing these influences in your own life—this is the best reason to major in sociology. As you take more courses in sociology, you will continue this enlightening process of social discovery. Your sociological perspective will grow, and you will become increasingly aware of how social factors underlie human behavior.

In addition to people who have a strong desire to continue this fascinating process of social discovery, there is a second type of person whom I also urge to major in sociology. Let's suppose that you have a strong, almost unbridled sense of wanting to explore many aspects of life. Let's also assume that because you have so many interests, you can't make up your mind about what you want to do with your life. You can think of so many things you'd like to try, but for each one there are other possibilities that you find equally as compelling. Let me share what one student who read this text wrote me:

> I'd love to say what my current major is—if only I truly knew. I know that the major you choose to study in college isn't necessarily the field of work you'll be going into. I've heard enough stories of grads who get jobs in fields that are not even related to their majors to believe it to a certain extent. My only problem is that I'm not even sure what it is I want to study, or what I truly want to be in the future for that matter.
>
> The variety of choices I have left open for myself are very wide, which creates a big problem, because I know I have to narrow it down to just one, which isn't something easy at all for me. It's like I want to be the best and do the best (medical doctor), yet I also wanna do other things (such as being a paramedic, or a cop, or firefighter, or a pilot), but I also realize I've only got one life to live. So the big question is: What's it gonna be?

This note reminded me of myself. In my reply, I said:

> You sound so much like myself when I was in college. In my senior year, I was plagued with uncertainty about what would be the right course for my life. I went to a counselor and took a vocational aptitude test. I still remember the day when I went in for the test results. I expected my future to be laid out for me, and I hung on every word. But then I heard the counselor say, "Your tests show that mortician should be one of your vocational choices."
>
> Mortician! I almost fell off my chair. That choice was so far removed from anything that I wanted that I immediately gave up on such tests.
>
> I like your list of possibilities: physician, cop, firefighter, and paramedic. In addition to these, mine included cowboy, hobo, and beach bum. One day, I was at the dry cleaners (end of my sophomore year in college), and the guy standing next to me was a cop. We talked about his job, and when I left the dry cleaners, I immediately went to the police station to get an application. I found out that I had to be 21, and I was just 20. I went back to college.
>
> I'm very happy with my choice. As a sociologist, I am able to follow my interests. I was able to become a hobo (or at least a traveler and able to experience different cultural settings). As far as being a cop, I developed and taught a course in the sociology of law.
>
> One of the many things I always wanted to be was an author. I almost skipped graduate school to move to Greenwich Village and become a novelist. The problem was that I was too timid, too scared of the unknown—and I had no support at all—to give it a try. My ultimate choice of sociologist has allowed me to fulfill this early dream.

It is sociology's breadth that is so satisfying to those of us who can't seem to find the limit to our interests, who can't pin ourselves down to just one thing in life. Sociology covers *all* of social life. Anything and everything that people do is part of sociology. For those of us who feel such broad, and perhaps changing interests, sociology is a perfect major.

But what if you already have a major picked out, yet you really like thinking sociologically? You can *minor* in sociology. Take sociology courses that continue to pique your sociological imagination. Then after college, continue to stimulate your sociological interests through your reading, including novels. This ongoing development of your sociological imagination will serve you well as you go through life.

But What Can You Do with a Sociology Major?

I can just hear someone say: "That's fine for you, since you became a sociologist. I don't want to go to graduate school, though. I just want to get my bachelor's degree and get out of college and get on with life. So, how can a bachelor's in sociology help me?"

This is a fair question. Just what can you do with a bachelor's degree in sociology?

A few years ago, in my sociology department we began to develop a concentration in applied sociology. At that time, since this would be a bachelor's degree, I explored this very question. I was surprised at the answer: The short answer is: *Almost anything!*

Most employers don't care what you major in. (Exceptions are some highly specialized fields such as nursing, computers, and engineering.) *Most* employers just want to make certain that you have completed college, and for most of them one degree is the same as another. *College provides the base on which the employer builds.*

Because you have your bachelor's degree—no matter what it is in—employers assume that you are a responsible person. This credential implies that you have proven yourself: You were able to stick with a four-year course, you showed up for classes, listened to lectures, took notes, passed tests, and carried out whatever assignments you were given. On top of this base of presumed responsibility, employers add the specifics necessary for you to perform their particular work, whether that be in sales or service, in insurance, banking, retailing, marketing, product development, or whatever.

If you major in sociology, you don't have to look for a job as a sociologist. If you ever decide to go on for an advanced degree, that's fine. But such plans are not necessary. The bachelor's in sociology can be your passport to most types of work in society.

Final Note

I want to conclude by stressing the reason to major in sociology that goes far beyond how you are going to make a living. It is the sociological perspective itself, the way of thinking and understanding that sociology provides. Wherever your path in life may lead, the sociological perspective will accompany you.

You are going to live in a fast-paced, rapidly changing society that, with all its conflicting crosscurrents, is going to be in turmoil. The sociological perspective will cast a different light on life's events, allowing you to perceive them in more insightful ways. As you watch television, attend a concert, converse with a friend, listen to a boss or co-worker—you will be more aware of the social contexts that underlie such behavior. The sociological perspective that you develop as you major in sociology will equip you to view what happens in life differently from someone who does not have your sociological background. Even events in the news will look different to you.

The final question that I want to leave you with, then, is, "If you enjoy sociology, why not major in it?"

With my best wishes for your success in life,

Jim Henslin

Glossary

achieved statuses positions that are earned, accomplished, or involve at least some effort or activity on the individual's part

agents of socialization people or groups that affect our self-concept, attitudes, behaviors, or other orientations toward life

aggregate individuals who temporarily share the same physical space but who do not see themselves as belonging together

agricultural revolution the second social revolution, based on the invention of the plow, which led to agricultural societies

agricultural society a society based on large-scale agriculture

anticipatory socialization the process of learning in advance an anticipated future role or status

apartheid the separation of racial–ethnic groups as was practiced in South Africa

applied sociology the use of sociology to solve problems—from the micro level of classroom interaction and family relationships to the macro level of crime and pollution

ascribed status a position an individual either inherits at birth or receives involuntarily later in life

assimilation the process of being absorbed into the mainstream culture

authoritarian leader an individual who leads by giving orders

authoritarian personality Theodor Adorno's term for people who are prejudiced and rank high on scales of conformity, intolerance, insecurity, respect for authority, and submissiveness to superiors

back stages places where people rest from their performances, discuss their presentations, and plan future performances

background assumption a deeply embedded, common understanding of how the world operates and of how people ought to act

basic or pure sociology sociological research for the purpose of making discoveries about life in human groups, not for making changes in those groups

bilineal system (of descent) a system of reckoning descent that counts both the mother's and the father's side

biotech society a society whose economy increasingly centers on modified genetics to produce food, medicine, and materials

blended family a family whose members were once part of other families

body language the ways in which people use their bodies to give messages to others

bonded labor (indentured service) a contractual system in which someone sells his or her body (services) for a specified period of time in an arrangement very close to slavery, except that it is entered into voluntarily

bourgeoisie Marx's term for capitalists, those who own the means of production

capital punishment the death penalty

case study an intensive analysis of a single event, situation, or individual

caste system a form of social stratification in which people's statuses are lifelong and are determined by birth

category people, objects, and events that have similar characteristics and are classified together

class conflict Marx's term for the struggle between capitalists and workers

class consciousness Marx's term for awareness of a common identity based on one's position in the means of production

class system a form of social stratification based primarily on the possession of money or material possessions

clique a cluster of people within a larger group who choose to interact with one another

closed-ended questions questions that are followed by a list of possible answers to be selected by the respondent

coalition the alignment of some members of a group against others

cohabitation unmarried couples living together in a sexual relationship

colonialism the process by which one nation takes over another nation, usually for the purpose of exploiting its labor and natural resources

compartmentalize to separate acts from feelings or attitudes

conflict theory a theoretical framework in which society is viewed as composed of groups that are competing for scarce resources

control group the subjects in an experiment who are not exposed to the independent variable

control theory the idea that two control systems—inner controls and outer controls—work against our tendencies to deviate

core values the values that are central to a group, those around which it builds a common identity

corporate crime crimes committed by executives in order to benefit their corporation

counterculture a group whose values, beliefs, norms, and related behaviors place its members in opposition to the broader culture

crime the violation of norms written into law

criminal justice system the system of police, courts, and prisons set up to deal with people who are accused of having committed a crime

cultural diffusion the spread of cultural traits from one group to another; includes both material and nonmaterial cultural traits

cultural goals the objectives held out as legitimate or desirable for the members of a society to achieve

cultural lag Ogburn's term for human behavior lagging behind technological innovations

cultural leveling the process by which cultures become similar to one another; refers especially to the process by which Western culture is being exported and diffused into other nations

cultural relativism not judging a culture but trying to understand it on its own terms

cultural universal a value, norm, or other cultural trait that is found in every group

culture the language, beliefs, values, norms, behaviors, and even material objects that characterize a group and are passed from one generation to the next

culture of poverty the assumption that the values and behaviors of the poor make them fundamentally different from other people, that these factors are largely responsible for their poverty, and that parents perpetuate poverty across generations by passing these characteristics to their children

culture shock the disorientation that people experience when they come in contact with a fundamentally different culture and can no longer depend on their taken-for-granted assumptions about life

degradation ceremony a term coined by Harold Garfinkel to refer to a ritual whose goal is to remake someone's self by stripping away that individual's self-identity and stamping a new identity in its place

democratic leader an individual who leads by trying to reach a consensus

dependent variable a factor in an experiment that is changed by an independent variable

deviance the violation of norms (or rules or expectations)

differential association Edwin Sutherland's term to indicate that people who associate with some groups learn an "excess of definitions" of deviance, increasing the likelihood that they will become deviant

discrimination an act of unfair treatment directed against an individual or a group

division of labor the splitting of a group's or a society's tasks into specialties

documents in its narrow sense, written sources that provide data; in its extended sense, archival material of any sort, including photographs, movies, CDs, DVDs, and so on

domestication revolution the first social revolution, based on the domestication of plants and animals, which led to pastoral and horticultural societies

dominant group the group with the most power, greatest privileges, and highest social status

downward social mobility movement down the social class ladder

dramaturgy an approach, pioneered by Erving Goffman, in which social life is analyzed in terms of drama or the stage; also called dramaturgical analysis

dyad the smallest possible group, consisting of two persons

egalitarian authority more or less equally divided between individuals or groups (in heterosexual marriage, for example, between husband and wife)

ego Freud's term for a balancing force between the id and the demands of society

endogamy the practice of marrying within one's own group

ethnic cleansing a policy of eliminating a population; includes forcible expulsion and genocide

ethnic work activities designed to discover, enhance, or maintain ethnic or racial identity

ethnicity (and ethnic) having distinctive cultural characteristics

ethnocentrism the use of one's own culture as a yardstick for judging the ways of other individuals or groups, generally leading to a negative evaluation of their values, norms, and behaviors

ethnomethodology the study of how people use background assumptions to make sense out of life

exchange mobility about the same number of people moving up and down the social class ladder, such that, on balance, the social class system shows little change

exogamy the practice of marrying outside of one's group

experiment the use of control and experimental groups and dependent and independent variables to test causation

experimental group the group of subjects in an experiment who are exposed to the independent variable

expressive leader an individual who increases harmony and minimizes conflict in a group; also known as a *socioemotional leader*

face-saving behavior techniques used to salvage a performance (interaction) that is going sour

false class consciousness Marx's term to refer to workers identifying with the interests of capitalists

family two or more people who consider themselves related by blood, marriage, or adoption

family of orientation the family in which a person grows up

family of procreation the family formed when a couple's first child is born

feminism the philosophy that men and women should be politically, economically, and socially equal; organized activities on behalf of this principle

feral children children assumed to have been raised by animals, in the wilderness, isolated from humans

folkways norms that are not strictly enforced

front stage places where people give performances

functional analysis a theoretical framework in which society is viewed as composed of various parts, each with a function that, when fulfilled, contributes to society's equilibrium; also known as *functionalism* and *structural functionalism*

Gemeinschaft a type of society in which life is intimate; a community in which everyone knows everyone else and people share a sense of togetherness

gender the behaviors and attitudes that a society considers proper for its males and females; masculinity or femininity

gender socialization learning society's "gender map," the paths in life set out for us because we are male or female

gender stratification males' and females' unequal access to property, power, and prestige

generalized other the norms, values, attitudes, and expectations of people "in general"; the child's ability to take the role of the generalized other is a significant step in the development of a self

genetic predisposition inborn tendencies (for example, a tendency to commit deviant acts)

genocide the systematic annihilation or attempted annihilation of a people because of their presumed race or ethnicity

Gesellschaft a type of society that is dominated by impersonal relationships, individual accomplishments, and self-interest

gestures the ways in which people use their bodies to communicate with one another

glass ceiling the mostly invisible barrier that keeps women from advancing to the top levels at work

globalization the growing interconnections among nations due to the expansion of capitalism

globalization of capitalism capitalism (investing to make profits within a rational system) becoming the globe's dominant economic system

group people who have something in common and who believe that what they have in common is significant; also called a social group

group dynamics the ways in which individuals affect groups and the ways in which groups influence individuals

groupthink a narrowing of thought by a group of people, leading to the perception that there is only one correct answer and that to even suggest alternatives is a sign of disloyalty

hate crime a crime that is punished more severely because it is motivated by hatred (dislike, hostility, animosity) of someone's race–ethnicity, religion, sexual orientation, disability, or national origin

homogamy the tendency of people with similar characteristics to marry one another

Horatio Alger myth the belief that due to limitless possibilities anyone can get ahead if he or she tries hard enough

horticultural society a society based on cultivating plants by the use of hand tools

household people who occupy the same housing unit

hunting and gathering society a human group that depends on hunting and gathering for its survival

hypothesis a statement of how variables are expected to be related to one another, often according to predictions from a theory

id Freud's term for our inborn basic drives

ideal culture a people's ideal values and norms; the goals held out for them

ideology beliefs about the way things ought to be that justify social arrangements

illegitimate opportunity structure opportunities for crimes that are woven into the texture of life

impression management people's efforts to control the impressions that others receive of them

in-groups groups toward which one feels loyalty

incest sexual relations between specified relatives, such as brothers and sisters or parents and children

incest taboo the rule that prohibits sex and marriage among designated relatives

income money received, usually from a job, business, or assets

independent variable a factor that causes a change in another variable, called the dependent variable

individual discrimination person-to-person or face-to-face discrimination; the negative treatment of people by others

Industrial Revolution the third social revolution, occurring when machines powered by fuels replaced most animal and human power

industrial society a society based on the harnessing of machines powered by fuels

institutional discrimination negative treatment of a minority group that is built into a society's institutions; also called *systemic discrimination*

institutionalized means approved ways of reaching cultural goals

instrumental leader an individual who tries to keep the group moving toward its goals; also known as a *task-oriented leader*

intergenerational mobility the change that family members make in social class from one generation to the next

internal colonialism the policy of exploiting minority groups for economic gain

labeling theory the view that the labels people are given affect their own and others' perceptions of them, thus channeling their behavior into either deviance or conformity

laissez-faire leader an individual who leads by being highly permissive

language a system of symbols that can be combined in an infinite number of ways and can represent not only objects but also abstract thought

latent functions unintended beneficial consequences of people's actions

leader someone who influences other people

leadership styles ways in which people express their leadership

life course the stages of our life as we go from birth to death

looking-glass self a term coined by Charles Horton Cooley to refer to the process by which our self develops through internalizing others' reactions to us

machismo an emphasis on male strength and dominance

macro-level analysis an examination of large-scale patterns of society

macrosociology analysis of social life that focuses on broad features of society, such as social class and the relationships of groups to one another; usually used by functionalists and conflict theorists

manifest functions the intended beneficial consequences of people's actions

marriage a group's approved mating arrangements, usually marked by a ritual of some sort

mass media forms of communication, such as radio, newspapers, and television that are directed to mass audiences

master status a status that cuts across the other statuses that an individual occupies

material culture the material objects that distinguish a group of people, such as their art, buildings, weapons, utensils, machines, hairstyles, clothing, and jewelry

matriarchy a society in which women-as-a-group dominate men-as-a-group; authority is vested in females

matrilineal system (of descent) a system of reckoning descent that counts only the mother's side

means of production the tools, factories, land, and investment capital used to produce wealth

mechanical solidarity Durkheim's term for the unity (a shared consciousness) that people feel as a result of performing the same or similar tasks

medicalization the transformation of a human condition into a matter to be treated by physicians

medicalization of deviance to make deviance a medical matter, a symptom of some underlying illness that needs to be treated by physicians

micro-level analysis an examination of small-scale patterns of society; such as how the members of a group interact

microsociology analysis of social life that focuses on social interaction; typically used by symbolic interactionists

minority group people who are singled out for unequal treatment and who regard themselves as objects of collective discrimination

mores norms that are strictly enforced because they are thought essential to core values or the well-being of the group

multiculturalism a policy that permits or encourages ethnic differences; also called *pluralism*

negative sanction an expression of disapproval for breaking a norm, ranging from a mild, informal reaction such as a frown to a formal reaction such as a prize or a prison sentence

new technology the emerging technologies of an era that have a significant impact on social life

nonmaterial culture a group's ways of thinking (including its beliefs, values, and other assumptions about the world) and doing (its common patterns of behavior, including language and other forms of interaction); also called *symbolic culture*

nonverbal interaction communication without words through gestures, use of space, silence, and so on

norms expectations of "right" behavior

nuclear family a family consisting of a husband, wife, and child(ren)

open-ended questions questions that respondents answer in their own words

operational definition the way in which a researcher measures a variable

organic solidarity Durkheim's term for the interdependence that results from the division of labor; as part of the same unit, we all depend on others to fulfill their jobs

out-groups groups toward which one feels antagonism

pan-Indianism an attempt to develop an identity that goes beyond the tribe by emphasizing the common elements that run through Native American cultures

participant observation or fieldwork research in which the researcher participates in a research setting while observing what is happening in that setting

pastoral society a society based on the pasturing of animals

patriarchy a group in which men-as-a-group dominate women-as-a-group; authority is vested in males

patrilineal system (of descent) a system of reckoning descent that counts only the father's side

peer group a group of individuals, often of roughly the same age, who are linked by common interests and orientations

personality disorders the view that a personality disturbance of some sort causes an individual to violate social norms

pluralism the diffusion of power among many interest groups that prevents any single group from gaining control of the government

pluralistic society a society made up of many different groups

police discretion the practice of the police, in the normal course of their duties, to either arrest or ticket someone for an offense or to overlook the matter

polyandry a form of marriage in which women have more than one husband

polygyny a form of marriage in which men have more than one wife

population people; in research, a target group to be studied

population transfer the forced movement of a minority group

positive sanction a reward or positive reaction for following norms, ranging from a smile to a material reward

positivism the application of the scientific approach to the social world

postindustrial (information) society a society based on information, services, and high technology, rather than on raw materials and manufacturing

poverty line the official measure of poverty; calculated to include incomes that are less than three times a low-cost food budget

power the ability to carry out one's will, even over the resistance of others

power elite C. Wright Mills' term for the top people in U.S. corporations, military, and politics who make the nation's major decisions

prejudice an attitude or prejudging, usually in a negative way

prestige respect or regard

primary group a small group characterized by intimate, long-term, face-to-face association and cooperation

proletariat Marx's term for the exploited class, the mass of workers who do not own the means of production

property material possessions: animals, bank accounts, bonds, buildings, businesses, cars, cash, commodities, copyrights, furniture, jewelry, land, and stocks

public sociology applying sociology for the public good; especially the use of the sociological perspective (how things are related to one another) to guide politicians and policy makers

race a group whose inherited physical characteristics distinguish it from other groups

racism prejudice and discrimination on the basis of race

random sample a sample in which everyone in the target population has the same chance of being included in the study

rapport (ruh-POUR) a feeling of trust between researchers and the people they are studying

real culture the norms and values that people actually follow; as opposed to ideal culture

recidivism rate the percentage of released convicts who are rearrested

reference group a group whose standards we refer to as we evaluate ourselves

reliability the extent to which research produces consistent or dependable results

research method (or research design) one of seven procedures that sociologists use to collect data: surveys, participant observation, case studies, secondary analysis, analysis of documents, experiments, and unobtrusive measures

reserve labor force the unemployed; unemployed workers are thought of as being "in reserve"—capitalists take them "out of reserve" (put them back to work) during times of high production and then put them "back in reserve" (lay them off) when they are no longer needed

resocialization the process of learning new norms, values, attitudes, and behaviors

respondents people who respond to a survey, either in interviews or by self-administered questionnaires

rising expectations the sense that better conditions are soon to follow, which, if unfulfilled, increases frustration

role the behaviors, obligations, and privileges attached to a status

role conflict conflicts that someone feels between statuses because the expectations attached to one status are incompatible with the expectations of another status

role performance the ways in which someone performs a role; showing a particular "style" or "personality"

role strain conflicts that someone feels within a status

romantic love feelings of erotic attraction accompanied by an idealization of the other

sample the individuals intended to represent the population to be studied

sanctions either expressions of approval given to people for upholding norms or expressions of disapproval for violating them

Sapir-Whorf hypothesis Edward Sapir and Benjamin Whorf's hypothesis that language creates ways of thinking and perceiving

scapegoat an individual or group unfairly blamed for someone else's troubles

scientific method the use of objective, systematic observations to test theories

secondary analysis the analysis of data that have been collected by other researchers

secondary group compared with a primary group, a larger, relatively temporary, more anonymous, formal, and impersonal group based on some interest or activity

segregation the policy of keeping racial–ethnic groups apart

selective perception seeing certain features of an object or situation, but remaining blind to others

self the unique human capacity of being able to see ourselves "from the outside"; the views we internalize of how others see us

serial murder the killing of several victims in three or more separate events

sex biological characteristics that distinguish females and males, consisting of primary and secondary sex characteristics

sexual harassment the abuse of one's position of authority to force unwanted sexual demands on someone

shaman the healing specialist of a tribe who attempts to control the spirits thought to cause a disease or injury; commonly called a witch doctor

sign-vehicle   the term used by Goffman to refer to how people use social setting, appearance, and manner to communicate information about the self

significant other   an individual who significantly influences someone else

slavery   a form of social stratification in which some people own other people

small group   a group small enough for everyone to interact directly with all the other members

social class   according to Weber, a large group of people who rank close to one another in property, power, and prestige; according to Marx, one of two groups: capitalists who own the means of production or workers who sell their labor

social construction of reality   the use of background assumptions and life experiences to define what is real

social control   a group's formal and informal means of enforcing its norms

social environment   the entire human environment, including interaction with others

social institution   the organized, usual, or standard ways by which society meets its basic needs

social integration   the degree to which members of a group or a society feel united by shared values and other social bonds; also known as *social cohesion*

social interaction   one person's actions influencing someone else; usually refers to what people do when they are in one another's presence, but also includes communications at a distance

social location   the group memberships that people have because of their location in history and society

social mobility   movement up or down the social class ladder

social network   the social ties radiating outward from the self that link people together

social order   a group's usual and customary social arrangements, on which its members depend and on which they base their lives

social stratification   the division of large numbers of people into layers according to their relative property, power, and prestige; applies to both nations and to people within a nation, society, or other group

social structure   the framework of society that surrounds us; consists of the ways that people and groups are related to one another; this framework gives direction to and sets limits on our behavior

society   people who share a culture and a territory

sociobiology   a framework of thought that views human behavior as the result of natural selection and considers biological factors to be a fundamental cause of human behavior

sociological perspective   understanding human behavior by placing it within its broader social contexts

sociology   the scientific study of society and human behavior

split labor market   workers split along racial–ethnic, gender, age, or any other lines; this split is exploited by owners to weaken the bargaining power of workers

status consistency   ranking high or low on all three dimensions of social class

status inconsistency   ranking high on some dimensions of social class and low on others; also called *status discrepancy*

status   the position that someone occupies in a social group

status set   all the statuses or positions that an individual occupies

stereotype   assumptions of what people are like, whether true or false

stigma   "blemishes" that discredit a person's claim to a "normal" identity

strain theory   Robert Merton's term for the strain engendered when a society socializes large numbers of people to desire a cultural goal (such as success), but withholds from some the approved means of reaching that goal; one adaptation to the strain is crime, the choice of an innovative means (one outside the approved system) to attain the cultural goal

stratified random sample   a sample from selected subgroups of the target population in which everyone in those subgroups has an equal chance of being included in the research

street crime   crimes such as mugging, rape, and burglary

structural mobility   movement up or down the social class ladder that is due more to changes in the structure of society than to the actions of individuals

subculture   the values and related behaviors of a group that distinguish its members from the larger culture; a world within a world

superego   Freud's term for the conscience; the internalized norms and values of our social groups

survey   the collection of data by having people answer a series of questions

symbol   something to which people attach meaning and then use to communicate with others

symbolic culture   another term for nonmaterial culture

symbolic interactionism   a theoretical perspective in which society is viewed as composed of symbols that people use to establish meaning, develop their views of the world, and communicate with one another

system of descent   how kinship is traced over the generations

taboo   a norm so strong that it often brings revulsion if violated

taking the role of the other   putting yourself in someone else's shoes; understanding how someone else feels and thinks, so you anticipate how that person will act

teamwork   the collaboration of two or more people to manage impressions jointly

techniques of neutralization   ways of thinking or rationalizing that help people deflect (or neutralize) society's norms

technology   in its narrow sense, tools; its broader sense includes the skills or procedures necessary to make and use those tools

theory   a general statement about how some parts of the world fit together and how they work; an explanation of how two or more facts are related to one another

Thomas theorem   William I. and Dorothy S. Thomas' classic formulation of the definition of the situation: "If people define situations as real, they are real in their consequences"

total institution   a place that is almost totally controlled by those who run it, in which people are cut off from the rest of society and the society is mostly cut off from them

transitional adulthood   a term that refers to a period following high school when young adults have not yet taken on the responsibilities ordinarily associated with adulthood; also called *adultolescence*

transitional older years   an emerging stage of the life course between retirement and when people are considered old; approximately age 65 to 75

triad   a group of three people

underclass   a group of people for whom poverty persists year after year and across generations

unobtrusive measures   ways of observing people so they do not know they are being studied unstructured interviews interviews that use open-ended questions

upward social mobility   movement up the social class ladder

validity   the extent to which an operational definition measures what it is intended to measure

value cluster   values that together form a larger whole

value contradiction   values that contradict one another; to follow the one means to come into conflict with the other

values   the standards by which people define what is desirable or undesirable, good or bad, beautiful or ugly

variable   a factor thought to be significant for human behavior, which can vary (or change) from one case to another

WASP   white anglo saxon protestant

wealth   the total value of everything someone owns, minus the debts

white ethnics   white immigrants to the United States whose cultures differ from WASP culture

white-collar crime   Edwin Sutherland's term for crimes committed by people of respectable and high social status in the course of their occupations; for example, bribery of public officials, securities violations, embezzlement, false advertising, and price fixing

world system theory   how economic and political connections developed and now tie the world's countries together

ndex

Page references followed by "f" indicate illustrated figures or photographs; followed by "t" indicates a table.

9

9/11, 158

A

A factor, 20, 285
Aborigines, 138
Aborigines, of Australia, 138
abortion
    rates, 186
    statistics, 186-187
Abstract thinking, 76-77
Abuse, 20-22, 195, 205, 271, 329, 367
Abuse/violence
    by women, 258-260, 354
Abuse/violence, health issues related to
    depression, 98, 190, 239, 294-295, 351
    substance abuse, 232
    suicide, 37, 248, 313
Academic achievement, 89, 249
Acceptance, 54-55, 190, 299
acculturation, 54
Achieved status, 202
Acquaintance rape, 272
Acting out, 83
actor, 173
Acute myocardial infarction, 278
Addams, Jane, 11-12
Adler, Patricia, 31
Adler, Peter, 31, 89
Adolescence, 93, 335
Adoption
    closed, 365
    in China, 327
    open, 208, 367
Adult Children of Alcoholics, 359
Adultery, 167
Adulthood, 93-94, 138, 337, 368
Advertising, 83, 118, 178, 328, 368
advertising agencies, 118
Affair, 143, 167, 208, 258
Affection, 15, 171, 337
Afghanistan, 99, 207, 245
Africa, 42, 126, 138, 202, 254, 287, 365
African Americans (, 292
    churches, 273, 306
    in sports, 130, 296
    slavery and, 201
Afrikaners, 287
Affirmative action, 241, 264, 314
Age
    divorce and, 94
    health and, 99
agency, 44, 182, 240, 277
Age-related physiological changes
    in men, 271
    in women, 66
Aggravated assault, 180
Aggregate, 365
Aggression, 119, 320, 352
Aging
    global, 65, 356
    study of, 66, 99, 242
    successful, 98
Aging families
    theories, 208
Aging society
    gender gap in, 276-277
    personality and, 99, 160, 277, 318
    single, 15, 55, 92, 106, 150-151, 178, 216, 251,
        310-311, 328, 365
    stereotypes and, 359

agribusiness, 278
Agricultural revolution, 139-140, 365
Agricultural societies, 94, 131, 139-140, 200, 365
AIDS, 13, 99, 166
Aka, 137
Alaska, 228, 285
Albania, 82, 206
Alcohol
    abuse, 29-31, 229, 271
    effects, 90-91, 228, 271
    socialization, 91-92, 171
Alcohol abuse, 30
Alcoholics, 90, 359
Alcoholics Anonymous, 90
Alcoholics Anonymous (AA), 90
Alcoholism, 205
Algeria, 206
Alimony, 218
Amato, Paul R., 350
America, 37, 63, 132, 139, 195, 202, 254, 303, 349
American Association of Retired
    Persons, 150, 202, 365
American Association of University Professors, 277
American Civil Liberties Union, 12
American dream, 194, 233, 320
American Indian families
    children of, 15, 88, 179, 201, 302, 338
American Medical Association, 321
American non-European families, early
    family life of, 340
American Revolution, 58, 320
American Sociological Association, 13, 97, 145,
        241-242, 249, 320-321, 358
American women, 233, 273, 291, 339
Amish, 114-115, 148
Amsterdam, 245
Anarchy, 6
ancestry, 286
and Spanish, 201
Anderson, Elijah, 104
Anger, 47, 79, 125, 137, 279, 297, 345
Angola, 206
Animals, 13, 45-46, 70-71, 138-139, 202, 252, 367
Anime, 84
anomie, 144, 176-177, 224, 293
Anthropology, 46, 98, 165, 278, 298
Anticipatory grief, 338
Anticipatory socialization, 89-90, 365
anti-Semitism, 295-296
Antisocial behavior, 194, 277
Applied sociology, 12-13, 148, 363, 365
Appreciation, 274, 355
approach, 1, 39, 67, 101, 135, 163, 197, 243, 281,
        323, 361, 365
Arapaho tribe, 359
Architecture, 116, 140
Argentina, 206
Arguments, 214, 287
Armaments, 208
Armed forces, 50
Armenians, 300
arranged marriage, 359
Arranged marriages, 333
ART
    technology, 64
Aryan Nations, 291
Aryans, 284
Asch experiment, 155-156
Asch, Solomon, cards, 155
Ascribed status, 107, 202, 365
Asia, 202, 314
Asian American groups, 301
Asian American singles, 301
Asian American women (, 301
Asian Americans (, 236, 307
Asian/Pacific Islanders
    health of, 349

Assimilation, 299-300, 365
Associated Press, 66, 132, 195, 240-241, 321
Assumptions, 4-5, 42-43, 88, 114, 168, 288, 368
Atlanta University, 10
Attachment, 98, 241, 359-360
Attitude
    positive, 174, 289
Attraction, 15, 271, 332, 367
Authoritarian leaders, 154, 295
Authoritarian personality, 295, 365
authority, 18, 107, 155-156, 174, 251, 295, 327, 365
Avatars, 143
Awareness, 29, 42, 80, 109, 150, 190, 216, 246, 318,
    365

B

Baby boomers, 59
Back stages, 121, 365
Background assumptions, 124-126, 168, 366
Balance, 15, 77, 132, 175, 233, 266, 357, 366
Balance of power, 19
Bangladesh, 207
Banking, 142, 215, 292, 363
Banks, 110, 257, 292
Baptists, 231
Barack, Obama, 217, 309
Barbie dolls, 55, 81
Bargaining, 212, 296, 368
base, 168, 291, 335, 363, 368
Baseball, 75, 228
Basketball, 262, 335
Battered women, 360
Batterers, 30
Beauty, 45, 118
behavior, 4, 42, 69-70, 104-105, 138, 166-167, 213,
    246, 291, 344, 362-363, 366
Belarus, 206
Belgium, 206
beliefs, 42, 85, 104-105, 144, 171, 201, 286, 340, 365
Belsky, Jay, 99
berdache, 326
Berger, Peter, 4
bias, 26, 155, 186-189, 293-295, 335
Bible, 17, 110-111
Bicyclists, 21-22
Bikers, 173-174
Billboards, 31
Biotech society, 139, 365
Birth, 4-5, 70-71, 107, 151-152, 169, 202-203, 251,
    292, 326, 365-366
Birth control, 33
Black, 28, 52, 82, 115, 161, 188, 232, 284-285,
    359-361
Black America, 320
black community, 306, 360
Black families, 99, 359
Black middle class, 232
Black women, 241
Blacks, 188, 201-202, 287
Blame, 15, 213, 296, 342
Blended families, 342
Blended family, 342-343, 365
Blue, 11, 41, 81, 150, 222, 284
blue-collar jobs, 222, 309
Blue-collar workers, 86
Blumer, Herbert, 141
Boards of directors, 225
body image, 123
Body language, 114, 153, 365
Body weight, 132
Bolivia, 206
Bonded laborers, 201
Bonding, 73
booms, 296
Boot camp, 90-91
Border Patrol, 303
borders, 5